A TEXTBOOK OF PERSONNEL MANAGEMENT

George Thomason was born and brought up in the Lake District. He was educated at Sheffield and Toronto Universities and obtained his doctorate at University College, Cardiff, where he is now Montague Burton Professor of Industrial Relations.

He is a vice-president of the Council of Social Service for Wales and a member of the Advisory Conciliation and Arbitration Service's panel of single arbitrators.

For a time in the 1960s he was employed as Assistant to the Managing Director of Flex Fasteners Ltd and Porth Textiles Ltd.

He is married, with two children. A Companion of the Institute of Personnel Management, he is the author of three previous IPM titles: *Job Evaluation, Experiments in Participation* and *Improving the Quality of Organization.*

A Textbook of
Personnel Management

Third edition

George F Thomason

Institute of Personnel Management
Central House, Upper Woburn Place, London WC1H 0HX

For my daughter
Sian Elizabeth

ISBN 0 85292 167 5 Hardback
ISBN 0 85292 168 3 Paperback

Photoset, printed and bound in Great Britain by
REDWOOD BURN LIMITED
Trowbridge & Esher

Contents

Tables

Figures

Abbreviations used

ACAS	Advisory, Conciliation and Arbitration Service
All E R	All England Law Reports
APEX	Association of Professional, Executive, Clerical and Computer Staffs
ASLEF	Associated Society of Locomotive Engineers and Firemen
ASTMS	Association of Scientific, Technical and Managerial Staffs
AUEW	Amalgamated Union of Engineering Workers
BIM	British Institute of Management
BISAKTA	British Iron, Steel and Kindred Trades' Association
CAC	Central Arbitration Committee (formerly the Industrial Court and the Industrial Arbitration Board (1972–4))
CAWU	Clerical and Administrative Workers' Union, now APEX
CBI	Confederation of British Industry
CIR	Commission on Industrial Relations
C of E Act	Contracts of Employment Act
COHSE	Confederation of Health Service Employees
COIT	Central Office of Industrial Tribunals
DE	Department of Employment
DHSS	Department of Health and Social Security
D & HA	Docks and Harbours Act
EEPTU	Electrical, Electronics, Telecommunication and Plumbing Trade Union (formerly ETU: Electrical Trades Union)
EP Act	Employment Protection Act
EPEA	Electrical Power Engineers' Association
EEF	Engineering Employers' Federation
GMWU	General and Municipal Workers Union
H & SWA	Health and Safety at Work etc Act

ICR	Industrial Court Reports
IPM	Institute of Personnel Management
IRLR	Industrial Relations Law Reports
IR Act	Industrial Relations Act 1971
IT	Industrial Tribunal
ITR	Industrial Tribunal Reports
NALGO	National and Local Government Officers' Association
NATSOPA	National Society of Operative Printers and Assistants
NGA	National Graphical Association
NIRC	National Industrial Relations Court, 1972–4
NUBE	National Union of Bank Employees
NUPE	National Union of Public Employees
NUR	National Union of Railwaymen
RP Act	Redundancy Payments Act
SOGAT	Society of Graphical and Allied Trades
TASS	Technical and Supervisory Staffs Section of the AUEW
TGWU	Transport and General Workers Union
TUC	Trades Union Congress
TULR Act	Trade Union and Labour Relations Act, 1974; 1976
USDAW	Union of Shop, Distributive and Allied Workers

Preface to the third edition

The first edition of this textbook was written at a time when industry was trying to come to grips with the repeal and partial replacement of the 1971 Industrial Relations Act. Since then a new generation of legislation has been produced and personnel managers have had to develop an understanding of it as it applied in their work. At the same time, we have had the rise and fall of inflation and the development of a number of very different variants on the incomes policy theme. Coping with these variations has also occupied personnel managers greatly in this period. Whilst it would be a rash seer who would predict an era of stability in personnel management and industrial relations, it is distinctly possible that most of the foundations in law and central government policy are now laid for a reasonable period. There is more 'harmonization' with European practice to come and that will mean more change, and there remains the need to develop productivity in British industry. But it is now possible to develop a rather longer term perspective on objectives and practices in these fields.

For this reason, I have taken the opportunity in this third edition to review a good deal of the material in the first and second editions, and to place the revision within a new structure. To a greater extent than before, the structure reflects the proposals for divisions in the new Institute of Personnel Management examinations syllabus. Essentially, there are now four main parts to the book: chapters 1 to 3 deal with the area of employment and placement (in the older phrase) or 'employee resourcing' (in the newer jargon); chapters 4 to 6 cover the areas of employee motivation, performance and development and the specific contributions which the personnel practitioner can make there: chapters 7 to 9 examine the problems of authority in modern organizations and the methods and techniques of intervention in organizations with an emphasis on 'development'; and chapters 10 to 12 consider the aspects of industrial relations which are most directly associated with the particular undertaking, with particular attention given to the development of new local constitutions and processes. Although there are clear links and relationships between these parts, they can be read with understanding regardless of the order in which they are read. In each part I have tried to discuss the relevant principles, objectives and constraints, and methods and techniques in order. The whole is surrounded by an introductory historical chapter and a concluding chapter which projects into the future.

As before, I have tried to keep in the forefront of my mind, the needs of the student who wished to have an introduction to the subject in the round, and some kind of guide to the study of it. In a book of this length it is not, of course, possible to deal with every aspect of a complex field of practice and study. Therefore at the end of each chapter there are some suggestions for further reading, usually of material which goes into greater depth of treatment of the specialized aspects treated in the chapter. A bibliography, providing the full references, is given at the end of the book.

Anyone who writes a book of this nature always owes a debt to many people—colleagues in work, colleagues in the profession and students—whose contributions cannot be acknowledged in textual reference. I have been particularly fortunate in having the help of such colleagues at various times as Michael Fogarty, Peter Anthony, Ian Smith, David Dunkerley, Anne Crichton, Dave Simpson, John Bridge, Tom Keenoy, Kevin Wilson and Andrew Rix. Over the years many students on our diploma and masters degree programmes in personnel management in Cardiff have provided stimulation in tutorial and seminar discussions. Colleagues in the Institute, and particularly those in the Cardiff and Newport Branch, have also contributed a great deal to my understanding of the subject. My debt to them I cheerfully acknowledge, although I alone have the responsibility for what appears in the book itself. But the book would not have appeared at all without the patience and skill of Mrs B Clargo who, with the help of her two secretarial colleagues in the Department, Mrs M Price and Miss M Pugh, transformed the script into a connected and readable typescript for the printer.

Department of Industrial Relations and   *George F Thomason*
Management Studies,   *April 1978*
University College,
Cardiff

Introduction

Management of personnel and personnel management

In his famous play about robots, Karel Capek makes one of his characters assert that if an engineer had designed the human being, he would have made him (or her) less complicatedly and more efficient. The idea of starting something from scratch, or with a clean slate, in order to develop something for a limited and defined purpose is one with great appeal to mankind. If we have to think about how to get to a different point in the future, we often regret that we have to start from where we are now because if we could choose the starting point we could also give ourselves, we think, a better one from which to start on the journey. Reality is never like that, of course, and we always have to start from where we happen to be and make the best of it.

One exception to this general rule is that where one is writing a book: then it is possible to determine where one is going to start. I am going to start by suggesting that work in modern society is organized in such a way that, despite the complications of the reality around us, we can think of it as concerned with three things: first, with physical things, raw materials, plant and equipment, buildings and so on, which we often subsume under the heading of 'technology' and think of as something of concern to engineers and technical people; secondly, with human beings, managers, workers, and all manner and variety of them in the job and occupational settings, which we tend to refer to generically as 'personnel'; and thirdly, with money, finance, valued resources or, more simply, but more generally, as stocks and flows of value expressed in some tangible way, but which is thought to be the prime concern of financiers and accountants and those of similar ilk. If we look at the way the German board of directors (the Vorstand) is conceived, for example, we find it structured to embrace a technical director, a labour (or personnel) director, and a

3

finance director—and this may be worth considering because Germany may have had more opportunity than some others to start with a clean slate, because of its late start (Veblen, 1909) and because of the two major discontinuities in its development in 1918 and 1945.

Having started in this way, I am then enabled to say that this book will be primarily about the second of these areas, that of 'personnel' and its organization and management in modern industry and service undertakings. However, two other important things must be said. First, that the three fundamental concerns of modern work institutions are not separate and discrete but interrelated and interdependent, so that the technical side can in no sense operate in isolation from the other two nor can either of the others. Secondly, that all three of them have, in their turn, spawned many subsidiary specializations, which are in themselves important to the support of the modern enterprise, and which have to be fitted into the total process and picture. These interdependencies and further divisions make the reality much more complex than my first statement suggests, but I hold to it as a starting point because it enables us to *start* with one clear image even though, by the time we come to the end of the end of the analysis and argument, that image will have been qualified and fragmented to accommodate more of the reality.

We may start by sullying this initial image by following out some of the implications of these qualifications. First, we need to recognize that everyone who is engaged in modern work organizations, regardless of which particular concern he may be associated with, is concerned with personnel to some extent: if he manages finance, he must still work through people; if he is engaged on direct production tasks he at least works with people. Any person in a managerial or supervisory position within the organization is therefore in a position where he cannot escape the 'management of personnel' no matter what basic function or particular specialism he is involved in. This idea is developed in Woodward's attempt to overcome some of the 'confusions' which she found in her study over the concept of management 'function'. For mathematicians and sociologists, the term has its own connotations, but in management circles it is commonly employed to indicate something of the nature of specialization in contribution or activity. Woodward herself seeks to resolve some of the divergence in meaning attached to the term in management by distinguishing task functions from *element* functions. Task functions are related to the sequence of activities between inception and completion of a technical production process, and its financial lubrication. In a manufacturing enterprise it would be possible to distinguish financing the process from developing the product, its manufacture, and its marketing or distribution to customers, together with various 'sub-functions' within each of these main functions. Element functions on the other hand recognize that the 'generality' of managing may be divided up into specialist roles even though *any* manager will still (if he is to retain the title) be required to concern himself with them. Importantly, the management of 'personnel' is a function which qualifies as 'an element function' in so far as none can avoid it and still retain the title of manager (Woodward, 1965, Ch 7).

Because 'the personnel function' in organizations can be described as an element function, it is possible to regard it as no more than an integral part of any management function or task. A former head of the American Management Association expressed this idea somewhat pithily with his remark that "if management means getting results through people, then management is nothing more than personnel administration." (Appley, quoted in Odiorne, 1963.) A manager does not have to have the title of personnel manager (ie he does not have to be a 'specialist' in the IPM's word) to become concerned with personnel management (or personnel administration in the American version). This is recognized, therefore, in the Institute of Personnel Management's Golden Jubilee definition of personnel management which stated that:

> Personnel management is a responsibility of all those who manage people, as well as being a description of the work of those who are employed as specialists. It is that part of management which is concerned with people at work and with their relationships within an enterprise.

From this it follows that it is perfectly proper to write a book on the subject of personnel management to inform and guide managers in the performance of this 'element' function. Strauss and Sayles, for example, state that their book on *Personnel* (1967) "is addressed to the student of business who wants to equip himself to deal effectively with the human problems of the business organization" (p vi) and begin the book proper with the statement: "Personnel administration is the management of people. It is accomplished primarily through direct supervision and the development of official policies" (p 1). Pigors and Myers (1973) begin with the unequivocal statement that "the central theme of this book is the personnel responsibility of line management" (p 3). It ought however to be said that the American view (and both sets of authors quoted in this paragraph are Americans) of personnel management *is* different from the British at least in emphasis, partly because of the values of the American business sub-culture and partly because the manner in which American business has had to respond to worker organization has produced a different 'personnel' power structure from that found in Britain (we return to this point below, pp 15–23).

Whatever may be the reason for the difference in emphasis, such a difference does exist but mainly in terms of the extent to which 'personnel management' has been given legitimacy and status as a specialism in British industry. (This has been less the case in public service undertakings (civil service, local government service, health service) in Britain where the 'establishment function' (itself closer in conception to the American definition of the 'employment function' (Bloomfield and Willits, 1916) has until recently maintained itself as the only real example of personnel management). As the IPM's statement indicates clearly, there is a conception of personnel management as a 'specialism' although the hint that it is primarily associated with industry and commerce is contained in the concluding sentence of the same statement that it "applies not only to industry and commerce but to all fields of employment" (IPM, 1963).

That personnel management as a specialized field, distinct from the element function conception, is well recognized in the British context is suggested by Cuming, (1975) when he comments on the first part of the IPM's Jubilee statement.

"The first paragraph applies directly to small businesses or to those larger organizations, particularly in the public sector, where specialist personnel departments have not yet been established" (p 2). By implication, the 'normal' position would be an organization in which there would be a specialist personnel department, exercising "an advisory function, seeking to give practical help to line managers, but in no way detracting from their ultimate responsibility for controlling their subordinates" (*ibid*).

An older text on personnel management, that by Northcott (1955, third edn) makes this emphasis even more explicit where he outlines the "three essential relationships between the general structure of management and this specialized form of it" which had by then emerged from discussion and practice:

1 "Personnel management is an extension of general management" stressing management's "second responsibility" of "prompting and stimulating every employee to make his fullest contribution to the purpose of the business"
2 "It is an advisory service, . . . and a staff activity" carrying "no obvious authority except that which arises from its terms of reference and the knowledge and skill of the adviser"
3 "It becomes organized as a function, that is, a body of duties brought together as the responsibilities of one person and carried out wherever they occur in the establishment" and has caused

6

"trouble" with minor executives who feel that the combination of the duties into one office must mean that they have given up authority and prestige (p 12).

If the personnel function is indeed an element function to be discharged by any and every manager and if, for whatever reason, there is an attempt to remove this function from the direct and autonomous concern of the line manager, then it might be hypothesized that such 'trouble' would indeed result. The traditional view has been that the coalescence of personnel functional activities in specialist hands provides general and overall benefit. As Northcott's statement continues: "By this arrangement line management's skill and capacity are strengthened without any loss of its prestige or power and all the administrative and executive ranks become responsible for human relations in proportion to their spheres of authority and influence" (*ibid*, p 19).

The culmination of this line of argument is the position in which "the personnel function is the management of human resources" (Price in Brech, 1975, p 555) "concerned with the optimum deployment and development of people within an organization in order that the objectives of the organization may be met and effectively adapted to changing circumstances" (Department of Employment, 1972, quoted by Price, 1975, p 555).

In Price's view, personnel management in Britain has developed through three stages of identifying activities proper to a specialist function, developing a concern with aspects of personnel planning and creating a general change-agent role in relation to the organization. It had most recently moved to the stage in which "the relationship between the 'line and staff' concept of the personnel role [is] becoming less rigid and the recognition that the whole personnel function is changing to one that is seen as being concerned with the management of the human resources of that organization" (Price, 1975, pp 555–6). Since 'line management' has usually been defined with reference to the technical (development, production and marketing 'task') functions of enterprise, this conclusion implies that the 'personnel' function is now to be set over and against the technical one, rather in the manner in which it is conceived in the German Vorstand.

This perspective is convergent with the American conception of personnel management, resting upon a view of the enterprise or organization as a 'system' in which the personnel manager plays a 'system-agency' role. In their definition, for example, the Miners provide a definition of personnel management which is almost identical with that given by Price: "Personnel management may be defined as the process of developing, applying, and evaluating poli-cies, procedures, methods and programs relating to the individual in the organization. . . . Essentially, the personnel function is con-cerned with the management of *human* resources of an organization, in contrast to the material or financial resources" (Miner and Miner, 1977, p 4).

The identification of a function does not necessarily imply that it must be a specialist one but the options clearly exist. Megginson, for example, in developing his 'behavioural approach' to personnel administration acknowledges that managers can be their own 'per-sonnel' managers, but argues that a whole range of factors—trade union power, extension of government involvement in enterprise, increasing complexity of organizations and the development of the behavioural sciences, amongst others, have tended to push the 'func-tion' into a specialist position in contradistinction from the technical (Megginson, 1972).

More recently, Mant has criticized this tendency to separate and elevate the personnel function within work organizations in the Anglo-Saxon world, largely on the ground that it took authority and standing away from the technical generalists, capable of making pro-ductive things happen. "In time—and uniquely within Europe—personnel became the highest paid specialist field in British industry, higher even than sales, design and production. It was almost as if you hired an American to do the hatchet work and an Englishman to heal the wounds. This at a time when the status and pay of British engin-eers was declining steadily" (Mant, The Myth of the Manager, *Sunday Times*, 6 November 1977). This of course is a chicken and egg problem: Mant gives less weight to the counter-argument that be-cause the technical people refused to give attention to the personnel questions, they created the seeds of their own isolation.

If personnel management is to be regarded as synonymous with the management of people at work, the 'domain' may be regarded as co-extensive with the working population. This population, indi-cated in Table 1, on the basis of Census data for 1961 and 1971, ought strictly to be reduced by the number of those who are not actu-ally, or not within the usual cultural definition of the term, 'workers'. If in other words 'domain' is to be understood as identifying the population who are subject to some kind of managerial influence, we ought to drop out of account the 'entrepreneurs', the 'self-employed' and the 'managers' themselves in so far as they are not also managed. An approximation to the appropriate figure is provided by the data in table 2, which distinguishes the first two of these categories in the first two main classes distinguished, and the managers in the third. Together these account for something just over three million people out of the 23 million people included in the table, leaving about 20 million people as probably falling within the managerial domain. In so far as 'personnel management' is defined in its generalist sense, therefore, here is the target population.

Where the definition employed is the narrower one, developed by reference to specialization of the function, the domain is likely to be appreciably smaller, curtailed by reason of the 'type of industry', the size of establishment *and* the factors already identified in the previous paragraph.

Table 1

Economically active and inactive populations in
Great Britain, 1961 and 1971

Economic category	Males aged 15 yrs & over		Females aged 15 yrs & over	
	1961	1971	1961	1971
Total aged 15 yrs and over	16,992,300	19,560,100	18,705,940	21,487,840
Economically active	14,649,080	15,916,865	7,045,390	9,186,050
In employment	14,244,250	15,057,925	6,878,080	8,738,620
Out of employment	404,830	858,940	167,310	447,430
Sick	187,610	192,000	71,910	103,705
Other reason	217,220	666,940	95,400	343,725
Economically inactive	2,343,220	3,643,235	11,660,550	12,301,795
Retired	1,645,950	2,302,230	586,390	
Students in education	487,670	954,005	409,250	830,925
Permanently sick	35,750	282,920	15,150	221,250
Others	173,850	104,085	10,649,760	11,249,620

Source: Office of Population Censuses and Surveys: Economic Activity, Part I 1971 Census (HMSO, 1973)

From the studies which have been made of the location of specialist personnel practitioners, there is a strong suggestion that they are mainly to be found in certain broad categories of industry (defined by the Standard Industrial Classification) and to the generally larger-sized undertakings within them. Thus Anthony and Crichton have suggested that there are "few personnel specialists employed in normative organizations: most are found in utilitarian settings" (1969, p 157). The distinction being made is one between extractive, manufacturing and construction industries on the one hand, and service industries on the other. It is *not* one between private and public enterprise (even though the latter embraces a great deal of service), because private enterprise 'service' organizations do exist which do rely upon normative commitment and eschew employment of personnel specialists. The distinction is not perfectly made in these terms but it is broadly indicative of the personnel manager's *range* in terms of industrial types.

If we take this distinction and seek to enumerate the population concerned, on the basis of Department of Employment data for 1976 (table 3) we find that the 22.1 million employees in employment in Great Britain in June 1976 were divided roughly into 9.1 millions in production industries and 13.0 millions in the remaining service industries. Since 1973, the position has changed quite markedly as personnel managers are introduced into the reorganized local government and health services and, following the Fulton

Table 2

Main employment categories in Great Britain, 1971

Employment category	Males	Females
TOTAL IN EMPLOYMENT	14,407,960	8,268,760
Self-employed without employees	894,860	224,470
Self-employed with employees	576,940	146,790
Managers	1,384,580	286,770
large establishments	582,950	99,490
small establishments	801,630	187,280
Foremen and supervisors	780,100	208,550
manual	565,300	64,390
non manual	214,800	144,160
Apprentices, articled clerks and formal trainees	636,390	141,820
Professional employees	600,500	71,480
Other employees	10,133,580	7,509,320
Family workers (included above)	24,600	111,860

Source: Office of Population Censuses and Surveys: Economic Activity, Parts II, III, and IV, 1971 Census (10 per cent sample) (HMSO)

Report, into the public service, often in replacement of the older 'establishment officer', thus bringing in another 1.6 millions. Nevertheless, one would still expect to find a preponderance of personnel specialists in the production industries and the public services and relatively few elsewhere in the service industries other than communications (1.5 millions).

It is therefore not surprising that many authors still straightforwardly relate what they have to say on the subject to industry and commerce. Sayles and Strauss (1967) address themselves to 'the student of business'; others confine themselves to 'managed' organizations (and until recently 'management' tended to be associated mainly with business and commercial organizations). It was in industry and commerce that the 'twinges of conscience' to which Heller (1973) refers as the trigger for specialist personnel activities, occurred. The trade unions (at least in the form of Trades Union Congress affiliates) were mainly associated with this same field. There is therefore little doubt that personnel management has firm roots in this sector and even more particularly in the 'index of production' industries.

Table 3

Employees in employment in Great Britain at June 1976

Industry (Standard Industrial Classification 1968)	Males Full-time	Part-time*	Females Full-time	Part-time*	THOUSANDS TOTAL Males and females
All manufacturing industries	4,955.9	77.8	1,578.8	486.0	7,098.6
Agriculture, forestry, fishing[2]	253.4	29.3	57.4	41.5	381.6
Mining and quarrying	330.6	0.5	10.9	3.5	345.6
Construction	1,155.3	12.0	64.7	37.2	1,269.2
Gas, electricity and water	274.7	0.8	52.8	14.6	342.8
Total: index of production industries	6,716.5	91.1	1,707.2	541.3	9,056.1
Transport and communication	1,173.2	24.8	199.3	55.2	1,452.6
Distributive trades	1,038.4	144.7	733.0	753.2	.2,669.3
Insurance, banking, finance and business services	502.6	31.6	393.6	159.6	1,087.4
Professional and scientific services	986.8	154.6	1,273.3	1,144.4	3,559.1
Miscellaneous services[1]	776.4	181.3	557.9	736.6	2,252.2
Public administration and defence[3]	946.6	40.8	442.1	151.2	1,580.7
Total: all industries and services	12,398.0	699.0	5,366.0	3,585.0	22,048.0

* Part-time workers are defined as those normally employed for not more than 30 hours per week (excluding main meal breaks and overtime), but for agriculture see footnote [2]

[1] Excludes private domestic service

[2] The estimates for agriculture are taken from the June censuses of agriculture and exclude a small number of employees of agricultural machinery contractors. It should also be noted that the figures for full-time male and female workers include seasonal and temporary workers and that the definition of part-time is that used in the agricultural censuses

[3] Excluding members of HM Forces (296,860 males and 11,520 females in 1971)

The reason for the recent spread into non-manufacturing tells us something of the rationale for personnel practice. In the central government enterprises, it was introduced after and almost as a direct consequence of the Fulton Committee's report (1968); in local government and the national health service, it is after the implementation of proposals to reorganize the services to meet the needs for scale and economy (1974); in education (admittedly still only half-heartedly) perhaps as a consequence of governmental attempts to exert more cost control over the service during the 1960s and 1970s. In each case, the decision to introduce personnel management was almost a deliberate copying act, the concept being borrowed as an appropriate one from the world of commerce and industry.

If it began in the reputedly harsh conditions in the business organizations, was it the pressure for cost-reduction and efficiency in that context which brought it about? If so, what concerning the other types of organization—mutual benefit, service and commonweal (Blau and Scott, 1963)—made it unnecessary or undesirable to institute personnel management in such enterprises then, and what has made it necessary or desirable now? Size alone could not be the explanatory variable for which we are seeking, nor could it really have been technological complexity, since government departments were no less large and hospitals no less complex than those organizations in which personnel management did spring up. Perhaps it is the increasing pressure for efficiency and cost reduction in education, health, local government and even central government organizations which is associated with this new-found growth of the occupation.

The conditions in these services in the post-war world could not be regarded as being harsh in the sense in which industrial conditions were at, say, the turn of the century—in spite of statements about nurses, auxiliaries, teachers and dustmen's pay and conditions put forward in dispute conditions in the 1960s and 1970s by the worker associations involved. They may well have had a grievance, and in any case harshness is relative and defined by the culture, but they were not such as to motivate the 'welfare workers' to move into this context. Rather, personnel management was 'built-in' by the designers as a necessary part of the organizational system in the interests of 'control' in now more centralized arrangements. For these reorganizations in education, health, central government and local government services have usually followed upon the publication of specific reports (eg Fulton, 1968; Seebohm, 1968; Radcliffe-Maud, 1969; Bains, 1972; and Ogden, 1973) in which the case for both increase in scale (by merger) and increase in efficiency (through application of managerial, as distinct from administrative, methods) is argued.

12

Casual observation of the position in the production industries suggests that the specialist personel function is rarely found in small enterprises, although it may be discharged by managers who are not specialists or, increasingly often, by specialist personnel management agencies operating in such a way as to serve a group of small employers. Such local surveys as have been made tend to confirm that specialists are confined to the larger enterprises: Collins and Crichton (1966) found, for example, that in South Wales, of 101 organizations *not* employing personnel specialists (out of 254 replying to the questionnaire) 70 per cent employed less than 500 people. On this evidence, the smaller enterprises less frequently employ personnel managers but the dividing line of size is by no means clear-cut: the most common guestimate employed is that most enterprises of above 200 or 250 employees will have the services of personnel management available within the organization.

The best estimate of the number of such enterprises existing in the United Kingdom is probably that given in table 2 of the Bullock Committee Report (1977, p 5; see also para 3, pp 4 and 6). Confined to the private sector of the economy and painted with a broad brush, this suggests that there might be 1,199 enterprises employing over 1,000 people in the UK and at least another 895 employing between 201 and 1,000 (the latter figure being considered less reliable than the first). It could be expected that all of the first category and most of the second would employ personnel specialists in some rank or other, and that such exceptions as might exist would be more likely to be found in the non-manufacturing industry categories. (This table and para 3 of the Bullock Committee Report explaining methods of calculation are given on pp 14 & 15.)

In summary, therefore, it might be suggested that the specialist personnel practitioner, whether officer or manager, is more likely to be found in larger undertakings in the private sector and in public industrial and service undertakings; he or she is less likely to be found in service industries in the private sector although by no means absent from, say, transport or financial undertakings. This then indicates the domain of the personnel specialist, as distinct from the ordinary manager or supervisor who has more generalized responsibilities for 'personnel' (cf Bain, 1970).

But if this indicates where the personnel specialist is likely to be found, it does not tell us what he is likely to be doing, and what may be the *range* of his influence within the undertakings in which he is located. The definition of his range (cf Cartwright, 1975) is provided by the delimitation of what he is expected to do or decide, and therefore of his 'role' in relation to both undertaking and the 'personnel' who constitute his or her *raison d'être*. These expectations have changed

Table 4

United Kingdom enterprises with over 200 employees in the United Kingdom
Analysis by industry and number of employees

Standard Industrial Classification order	Sector	No of UK employees							TOTAL
		201–500	501–1,000	1,001–2,000	2,001–5,000	5,001–10,000	Over 10,000	Total over 2,000	
		Number of enterprises (of which controlled from overseas)							
I–III	Food, drink and tobacco	21 (3)	30 (7)	28 (4)	20 (4)	9 (3)	22 (1)	51 (8)	130 (22)
IV–V	Petroleum products etc and chemicals etc	34 (18)	31 (19)	24 (11)	21 (9)	8 (3)	7 (1)	36 (13)	125 (61)
VI–XII	Metal manufacturing, engineering, shipbuilding, vehicles	55 (17)	140 (30)	138 (31)	125 (34)	45 (9)	48 (10)	218 (53)	551 (131)
XIII–XV	Textiles and clothing	11 (1)	44 (4)	44 (2)	37 (3)	8 (—)	10 (—)	55 (3)	154 (10)
XVI–XIX	Other manufacturing	32 (5)	78 (5)	62 (8)	57 (7)	35 (1)	17 (3)	109 (11)	281 (29)
XX and XXII	Construction, transport and communications	32 (2)	44 (3)	55 (2)	40 (1)	16 (—)	11 (—)	67 (1)	198 (8)
XXIII	Wholesale and retail distribution	43 (10)	65 (4)	55 (7)	59 (5)	17 (1)	22 (3)	98 (9)	261 (30)
XXIV	Insurance, banking, finance and business services	124 (19)	73 (6)	37 (1)	32 (1)	18 (—)	11 (—)	61 (1)	295 (27)
XXVI	Miscellaneous services	17 (6)	21 (6)	18 (4)	22 (1)	12 (—)	9 (—)	43 (1)	99 (17)
	TOTAL	369 (81)	526 (84)	461 (70)	413 (65)	168 (17)	157 (18)	738 (100)	2,094 (335)

Note: See text (paragraph 3) for definitions and methodology.
Source: Department of Industry: quoted from the Report of the Committee of Inquiry on Industrial Democracy (Chairman: Lord Bullock) (HMSO, 1977), p 5

14

significantly over this century and, in looking at these changes and the present position of the specialist personnel function in the rest of the chapter, the object will be to indicate something of its range.

Table 4 "shows the number of enterprises employing 200 or more people in the United Kingdom, broadly divided into nine economic sectors and into six size groups, by reference to the numbers of employees in the United Kingdom. The figures are taken from accounts published in 1973–74. Where the accounts of subsidiary companies are consolidated with those of their United Kingdom holding companies, those subsidiaries are not counted as separate enterprises, and the United Kingdom employees of all consolidated subsidiaries in the group are counted together. But where the accounts of partly-owned subsidiaries or associated companies are not consolidated with those of the group, those subsidiaries are counted as separate enterprises and their United Kingdom employees are not counted as employees of the group. For example, Imperial Metal Industries Ltd (although a quoted company) is consolidated in the accounts of its parent, Imperial Chemical Industries Ltd (ICI) and therefore does not count as a separate enterprise; but Carrington Viyella Ltd and Tioxide Group Ltd (although associated companies of ICI) are counted as separate enterprises, and their United Kingdom employees are counted separately. The number of enterprises controlled from overseas is given in brackets after each figure. The population in the table consisted originally of enterprises with net assets in 1968 of £2 million or more, or with gross income in 1968 of £200,000 or more. Enterprises whose separate existence ceased between 1968 and 1973–74 have been removed. Certain sectors (eg agriculture, banking and petroleum) and United Kingdom enterprises whose main interests were overseas were excluded from the original population. But the sectors known to include exterprises employing large numbers of people in the United Kingdom have been analysed individually, and such enterprises have been added to the population. Enterprises included in *The Times 1,000, 1975–76* and *The Top Private Companies 1974–75* have also been added, if not already present. The figures in the two left-hand columns of the table may therefore be understated, but it is unlikely that any enterprises employing 1,000 or more people in the United Kingdom have been excluded."

The evolution of the specialist function

The range of specialist personnel practice has evolved gradually since the turn of the century. There are currently, it might be said, two main views of the 'place' of specialist practice in the scheme of things organizational. The first of these places the personnel function as part of the 'supply' or 'procurement' process in work undertakings, the emphasis thus being upon the manning processes, the distinction being drawn with 'production', which it then serves. The second regards specialist personnel practice as primarily 'protectionist' in its orientation, concerned to develop attitudes and structures supportive of the work institution itself.

Historically, these conceptions are interwoven with three separate 'streams' of activity and orientation. The 'procurement' stream proper was and is focused chiefly upon the technical activities of manning or employee resourcing, and has an ideological orientation to 'efficiency' as efficiency is defined. The welfare stream, concerned with provision of welfare facilities and orientated chiefly to the individual worker has much in common, ideologically, with the negotiating-with-the-unions stream, concerned initially with curtailing and later with containing and constitutionalizing the external and usually collective challenges to the system. Although each has its set of activities and its value-orientations, there is a good deal of congruence between them, thus making it possible for them to coalesce into a single conception.

The origins of what is now called personnel management lie in the developments in industry during the three decades around the turn of the century. This was the period in which, in Britain, industrial rationalization involving significant increases in scale and in division of labour first made itself felt. This had direct and indirect consequences. First, workers were now gathered together in larger aggregates. This produced a consequential reduction in their direct contact with the employer (who now mediated his role through an increasing number of specialist managers). Some employers now felt that the long-established duty of care for the welfare of employees should be allocated to one such specialist who might be described as 'the conscience' of the employer. It also led to a connected development of alternative loyalties on the part of the herded workers, who increased their rate of development of separate autonomous associations which could look after their interests now that the employer was less visible and approachable. This led employers in turn to maintain or reassert their control. The first led to the introduction or appointment of welfare officers, essentially the case workers of the industrial organization, and the second to the appointment of labour officers in the role of holding these new associations at bay or in check by any means which might indeed include attention to welfare.

Secondly, the role prescriptions of workers of any and all categories were now more precisely drawn. Whilst this had its consequences for worker attitudes towards their jobs, it also placed a pressure upon the employer to set about the tasks of prescribing work roles more carefully than in the past, and of selecting personnel to carry them out. This pressure manifested itself, on the one hand, in

16

what came to be known as 'scientific management' in the hands of men like Taylor, Gantt and the Gilbreths, and on the other in the introduction of 'employment offices' into organizations to handle the recruitment side of the equation. But for both to function to the level of efficiency expected, it was necessary that the underlying principles in role definition and employee selection would be accepted and applied in the line management area (see below pp 165–86). It was probably this requirement which enabled the employment officers, in particular, to expand their role conceptions to embrace wider concerns with training and advice-giving in relation to the line managers and supervisors.

Thus it might be represented that the latter roles, of employment officer evolving into personnel officer, were from the first concerned with the technical problem of securing labour efficiency; the other roles of welfare officer and labour relations officer, whilst they came together with the first set, were more oriented towards a particular ideology of paternalism related not merely to efficiency as a general objective, but rather to efficiency on the terms of the established (and probably paternalistic) order of authority. The one might be said to have provided a basis for the role in utility and the other in value or ideology, although these are not polar distinctions.

The activities generally regarded as those of 'personnel management' do not necessarily imply the acceptance of an efficiency ideology. Certainly the 'title' adopted (of personnel *management*) does tend to imply this, and some characterizations of personnel management in the early days also associate the activities with efficiency and productivity objectives. But it is also possible to detect an ideology focused on more personalized human goals and conditions, and based on the belief that the practitioner's client was the person not the organization or enterprise. As this developed it may well have come to embrace the alternative efficiency-related ideology but the trace is still to be found at the present time. Thus what made the activities of the personnel practitioner socially *valued* was as much the concern with the lot of the worker in modern industry. The ideology may have been paternalistic, often associated with particular religious positions and this weighed as heavily as, and probably more heavily than, the interest in efficiency for some of them.

Cuming, for example, argues that the "origins of personnel management can be found wherever enlightened employers have tried over the years to improve the lot of their workers" (Cuming, 1975). Niven's historical account of the Institute of Personnel Management asserts, in this same vein, that it was "the plight of workers . . . which was to mould the form welfare work was to take" (Niven, 1967). At this early stage in the development of what later became personnel management, it was often difficult to avoid the conclusion that the work was 'charitable' in the Lady Bountiful sense: indeed many of the first practitioners were women, and Niven records that the first such woman appointed spent her first morning in the factory placing flowers in the workrooms.

A similar motivation might also be inferred in other later initiatives taken by employers to establish 'improved' work procedures (such as rest pauses, tea breaks and amenities) and improved communications procedures (such as joint consultative committees and suggestions schemes). The concern for employees' health and for their safety at work was also often one which developed from a general belief that the employer was in the status of the medieval lord and therefore ought as a duty to look after the general well-being of his 'subjects'. Many of these 'concerns' remain within the portfolio of the welfare officer or personnel manager—one of his tasks is still to attend the funerals of employees!—but it is perhaps important to recognize that the progressive evolution of these concerns has left the personnel officer capable of being described as Miller does, as "the custodian of the corporate conscience", (Miller, 1975) a kind of corporate chaplain whose antecedents were also born of a Christian, authoritarian paternalism.

With the development of greater knowledge and understanding of people at work, brought about by developments during and after the first world war, and given a major fillip by the publication of the Hawthorne studies in the later 1930s (Roethlisberger and Dickson, 1939), it became possible to 'sell' personnel management in terms of its contribution to efficiency. There had always been a strand of development, in the establishment of employment offices within companies, for example, which placed the emphasis here. It is not therefore suggested that this orientation developed only as a result of the incursions of psychologists and social psychologists into this traditional 'welfare' function; what is distinctly possible is that this 'knowledge' development provided a foundation on which the 'welfare' school of personnel practitioners could go forward in unison with these others, by placing an emphasis on their contribution to efficiency—as in the argument that 'good human relations pay'. The ideology now became double rooted, one still oriented towards people goals and the other developed in relation to organization objectives.

The secularization of this mission, in Britain at least, was a process which took place only after the second world war. At that time, the work of the social psychologists, particularly of the Hawthorne investigators in America, made its impact in our society. The Hawthorne studies themselves were fairly straightforward pieces of

academic research and yielded a number of important generalizations, particularly about the place of 'the group' or 'the informal
social structure' of work organizations, which had an important influence on the development of the academic discipline itself (see
Homans, 1951). In addition, and initially in the hands of Elton Mayo
(1933; 1945) but later of Stuart Chase (1950) the implications of these
research findings (together with those of some other war-time researchers) were developed into what amounted to a new ideology.

In essence, this new ideology emphasized in a way in which traditional industrial practice and classical management texts had not
done hitherto, the importance of people as people at work. The individual person was seen to have a primary anchorage in his own local
group—whether in work (Roethlisberger and Dickson, 1939) in the
community (Warner and Lunt, 1941; Katz and Lazarsfeld, 1955) or
even in the army (Stouffer *et al*, 1949)—which in turn was necessary
to the full development of himself or his personality; if, then, the way
in which work and work relationships were organized denied this
group space, the individual personality would be by so much de-
nuded *and* industry would itself be the loser; however, this same
point could be supported on more moral grounds, and it was argued
that industry just could not be allowed to continue to be so
'inhuman'—it offended the canons of orthodoxy in a democratic society. The basis of a new mission was thus established.

During the 1950s, therefore, we find this mission being pursued
throughout management, under the banners which proclaimed the
need for 'better human relations in industry'. The evangelism was
directed at management in general but inevitably those who occupied roles as personnel specialists found themselves cast in the extra
roles of change agents, catalysts or pace makers as part of the cru-
sade. Inevitably too the crusaders found that they could not succeed
simply by appealing to morality and much effort was therefore
devoted to hardening up the soft features of human relations, particularly by trying to show that better human relations meant bigger
profits, increased efficiency or a more contented labour force (and
therefore a more comfortable life for the managers) (see Urwick and
Brech, 1947). The movement made its impact on industry, and even
when the fire died out of it, a sufficiently large trace was left behind to
mark its passing.

The impact on the personnel managers themselves was even
greater. In the same period, universities began to provide specific
training programmes for them, and if the connection with social
work and social science was close, a distinction nevertheless
remained. But the close connection was there, partly because the
'welfare' function inside and outside industry was similar, and partly

(and more importantly in the longer run) because the major training need of the personnel manager was in the applied social sciences (at this time mainly psychology and social psychology). The welfare worker's charitable concern for his or her fellow men or women now had a theoretical or scientific base to it which could improve practice, and the educational system was willing to perform the function of certifying competence. A far cry from simply arranging the flowers in the workroom, but still in the same tradition.

Largely because of the historical evolution of the welfare officers' organizations into associations of personnel managers during the twentieth century, it is usual to regard these welfare exercises as the first manifestation of the separation of the personnel management function as a specialism. It is however possible that another type of exercise at about the same time in the evolution of the management process has as much claim to be recognized in paternity. This was the exercise of offering a barrier to the 'independent' organization of the workers, a process often identified as 'keeping the unions out'. Those who were employed in an agency role for this purpose appeared to be concerned with the same kind of welfare activity as that noted in the preceding paragraph. But where the early women welfare officers, often in the Quaker firms, were motivated by a type of charity, those who headed the union Indians off at the pass, were not to be described simply in these (charitable) terms: rather they must be regarded as animated in intentions by the ideological value of upholding the prerogative of management to manage without challenge, in order that benefit would accrue to the principals. This is different, at least in emphasis, from the animation of the welfare officer.

The later development from this second characterization was also somewhat different. The early resisters of trade union pressures were turned by the tide of union development into what became known as the firefighters. Their role became not merely one of dealing with worker/union troubles when they appeared (pure firefighting) but seeking to impose procedural constraints upon the workers' organizations in order that the 'difficulties' could be contained as far as possible. The genesis of the now highly valued 'voluntary system of collective bargaining' (see Flanders, 1965; *Donovan Commission Report*, 1968) is to be found in this rather than the welfare officer stable, and it was animated by very different ideas from those associated with the Quaker firms. The latter-day industrial relations officer may believe that workers and managements have a single frame of reference, but his activities would suggest that he does not hold this belief in relation to the unions and management and, in *that* context, the notion of a corporate conscience is seemingly not

20

very appropriate (Anthony and Crichton, 1969).

What is appropriate is the conception of this aspect of personnel management as concerned with (initially) privileges or prerogatives and (later) rights. It would be idle to pretend that there was not about this strand of development a paternalism comparable to that associated with the welfare function, or that the initial reaction to the new unionism of the 1880s onwards was not one which emphasized the defence of the existing prerogatives of the employer and his management. But as this relationship developed, it became more one between 'equals' (at least to the extent that the trade union established an 'independent' role for 'the workers' collectively). Progressively, the simple prerogative question gave way to negotiations over the rules of work and, although the basic question reared its head from time to time, each party came to recognize that the other had rights which, whilst they did not necessarily balance, nevertheless allowed the process of joint regulation to proceed with fairness or justice.

It was this 'system of voluntary collective bargaining' (Flanders, 1965) which both underpinned the personnel manager's role (as well as that of the union officers) and brought into the personnel management ambit a different stock of knowledge from that required by the other strand in the function. Because the personnel manager was concerned with negotiations as well as welfare and all that, the material which was being produced by the industrial relations students and later by the sociologists in their examination of social conflict and social change, was brought into the training programmes to supplement that supplied by the individual and social psychologists. This incorporation of conflict studies of one type or another might be said to represent a rationalizing of the approach to protecting prerogatives and preserving a paternalistic order, equivalent to the secularization of the welfare mission. It did not necessarily change the objective, but it at least promised to develop the capacity of the management to achieve it.

In its origins and as it has developed, this stream of personnel activity has a strong ideological affinity with the 'welfare' stream, both of them being protectionist. The latter approach, aimed at the individual, sought to improve the lot of the worker and this as a consequence, whether intended or not, might make him more accepting of the system in which he was caught up; the former, aimed at aggregates and collectivities, sought to preserve a system which promised benefits of wealth for all or to adjust that system in an ordered way in order to effect improvements, some of which at least were ones suggested by the representative and associated state bodies. If this began as a simple protecting role, it has since developed into an accommodating and adjusting role related to the organization as an entity, within which standards of fairness and equity have been redefined and developed. These two streams can then be covered by a single statement in the IPM's Jubilee definition:

"Personnel management aims to achieve both efficiency and justice, neither of which can be pursued successfully without the other. It seeks to bring together and develop into an effective organization the men and women who make up an enterprise, enabling each to make his own best contribution to its success both as an individual and as a member of a working group. It seeks to provide fair terms and conditions of employment, and satisfying work for those employed" (IPM, 1963).

This 'concern' with fairness and justice is first the modern expression of the dominant ideology of the welfare officer. It can be stated in a way which suggests its possible segmentation from the concern with efficiency. Thus Miller argues that the personnel management role is "different from other staff jobs in that it has to serve not only the employer, but also act in the interests of employees as individual human beings, and by extension, the interests of society" (Miller, 1975). Similarly, Spates finds a conception of the personnel management role which provides a place for the goals and aspirations of the workers, to an extent which is perhaps not to be found in other conceptions. For him, the function of personnel administration is concerned with "organizing and treating individuals at work so that they will get the greatest possible realization of their intrinsic abilities, thus attaining maximum efficiency for themselves and their group and thereby giving to the concern of which they are part its determining competitive advantage and its optimum results" (Spates, 1964).

The concern with fairness etc has acquired new connotations in the light of major developments in the form of new conventions in the bargaining process itself and in a spate of legislation which began to flow in the 1960s. Both conventionally and statutorily, new rules are being imposed on the employment game, and these are not only changing what the personnel manager must do in pursuing his role, but threaten to make the older ideologies of a paternalistic sort impossible to hold. Instead of having privileges at the grace and favour of the employer, perhaps upheld in power bargaining by the workers' associations, the worker has now either established by his collective power, or been granted through legislation, that these privileges are his by right.

The methods and procedures which were originally designed to secure order on the employer's terms are now established as a means of underpinning employees' rights, or of securing order on the *employees'* terms. Particularly with the appearance of the Industry and Employment Protection Acts in 1975, therefore, a number of commentators have been led to raise the question of what future exists for the personnel management function and role. Clearly, where that role is defined with reference to the need to establish control (Goodrich, 1921) in the employer interest, this question must arise when power shifts to the extent that recent legislation and the proposed legislation on participation indicate.

The attempt to preserve autonomy in this situation has led the personnel manager into embracing modern systems theories in which the role of helping the organizations as a whole to adjust to changes in the internal and external environments has been assumed to the personnel function. The personnel manager is often recognized as uniquely fitted by his professional experience, ethic and training to develop this aspect, whether expressed in terms of securing more efficient organization or in terms of creating procedures for the conversion of inefficient conflict into more efficient agreement. This is found in the advocacy of Miner and Miner for example, who suggest that personnel managers ought to be concerned with "strategies specifically tailored to changing demands from the outside world or to internal problems" (Miner and Miner, 1977, p 44).

The development of technique
In distinction from these two streams of development, there was a development of personnel practice on the basis of techniques concerned with 'procurement' or 'labour supply'. These were contributory to undertaking efficiency, and therefore to the efficiency ethic, so that it would be improper to suggest that they were 'value-free'; but there is a sense in which these techniques were developed by practitioners for themselves alone, or simply because they were marketable in industry which was increasing its scale and its impersonality. The sense of this is conveyed in Miner and Miner's description of personnel management as 'technique-bound', or in the statement that "the field has attracted many individuals who are strongly committed to particular techniques rather than to broad managerial problem-solving" (Miner and Miner, 1977, p 43). By clear implication, the personnel practitioner sold and deployed his skills in certain areas, but in doing so tended to respond to decisions about objectives and criteria of success taken higher in the undertaking and outside the ambit of personnel management as such.

What the practitioner was expected to apply his skills to was early on identified by Elbourne (1934) under six elemental headings:

1 Personal relationships, including mutual consultation and individual guidance, where required, on employees' problems

2 Organization relationships, including definition of responsibilities and duties, the notification of appointments, transfers etc, and organized mechanisms for joint consultation and the dissemination of information
3 Employment procedures, including labour supply and the determination of conditions and regulations of employment
4 Education and training—operative staff (both factory and administrative), supervisors and executives
5 Physical working conditions, including matters of health, convenience and safety
6 Social services and amenities, internal and external to the firm; physical, educational, social or recreational.

These remain broadly indicative of the areas of application of the practitioner's skills.

The skills themselves were generally those associated with interpersonal communication, and as applied to these areas, were regarded by Northcott, writing in 1955, as constituting "a body of related duties which fit in so well with each other that they can suitably and effectively be made the responsibility of one executive and can be thought of structurally as a department of a business" (Northcott, 1955, p 213). This immediately establishes a link between the practice of the personnel specialist and the efficiency of the undertaking, and an involvement at the level of executive control in the classical conception of management.

Thus 'control' is defined by Tannenbaum to mean "the use of formal authority to assure, to the extent possible, the attainment of the purposes of action by the methods or procedures which have been devised. The execution of this function involves the selection and training of individuals, the provision of incentives, and the exercise of supervision" (Tannenbaum, 1948).

In some texts, this association is still present. French, for example, talks of the "personnel system process" as involving (in language reminiscent of both Fayol and Tannenbaum) "the planning, co-ordinating and controlling of a network of organization-wide processes and facilitating systems, pertaining to the task of specialization, staffing, leadership, justice, determination, appraisal, compensation, collective bargaining, organizational training and development" (French, 1964, but see also French, 1974, ch 4 and especially p 53). Sayles and Strauss indicate a similar perspective in their statement that "personnel administration is accomplished primarily through direct supervision" (Strauss and Sayles, 1960, p 1). Megginson is even more conceptually akin to Tannenbaum in his statement that "the most significant aspect of personnel management is to be found through the direction and control of human resources of an organization in its daily operations" (Megginson, 1972).

The selection and incentive elements in the Tannenbaum definition are to be found in other texts. Thus Cuming, in common with a number of others, argues that the function is concerned with "obtaining and retaining employees . . . getting and keeping workers . . . and obtaining the best possible staff for any organization and having got them looking after them so that they will want to stay" (Cuming, 1968). Bakke also produces a similar conception wrapped around in social scientific terminology when he argues that 'personnel activities' are set in train to "perpetuate people and their qualities" and that control activities are designed *inter alia* to "reward and penalize or promise rewards or penalties for behaviour, or in the interest of making it conform to the type desired by the person or persons administering the rewards and penalties" and to "review, appraise and rate performance, performers and results according to standards established, assign people (as well as other resources) to positions on scales pertaining to a number of dimensions (such as prestige, importance, power, ability, acceptability etc)" (Bakke, 1950).

The acceptance of the perspective of personnel management as being concerned with the organization as basic referent, which is contained in a number of these quotations, as in the Price and Miner conceptions quoted earlier, ensures that the 'people' referent of some earlier perspectives acquires instrumental value, and that the personnel management activities now acquire meaning by reference to organizational goals. Thus Miner and Miner: "Another way to define personnel management is in terms of its goals, and in this sense the goals that personnel management seeks to achieve within the organization are the same as the goals of management in general. Although personnel managers carry out a unique set of activities having to do with the utilization of human resources, this work is done with a view to accomplishing exactly the same objective as is the work of other managers'" (Miner and Miner, 1977, p 4). Here, therefore, the objectives of personnel management become those of developing and recommending strategies and procedures that will contribute to the organization's productivity goals and of maintaining the organization as an ongoing unit in the face of internal and external pressures and stress (Miner and Miner, 1977, p 5).

The mainsprings of activity in this conception are therefore, as Price makes clear in his contribution to Brech (1975), those of planning and changing the organization as an instrument for achieving the efficiency, productivity or 'task' goals of the enterprise. Because these are activities of a higher order of decision than merely applying social skills to secure fit of methods to reality, the personnel manager now comes into his own as an administrator rather than merely as a 'practitioner' with a definable range of skills. He, like any other manager, must be concerned with objective setting for the 'personnel function' within the overall objectives of the enterprise, and with developing plans or strategies for the acquisition, development and deployment of human resources necessary to meet the needs of the undertaking. He thereby comes to be associated with 'administration' (in the Chamberlain conception of administration as concerned with determining methods of goal achievement) (1948), and with the middle level bands in Paterson's schema, and not merely with the 'executive', lower level, activities associated with his former collection of people-oriented skills.

With this association with methods of controlling manpower, motivation (or morale), and performance levels attainable, personnel management became highly marketable as a skill. Firms were led to hire such people to allow a fund of strategic *and* tactical advice to be placed on tap, but not at this stage necessarily on *top* (Lyons, 1971).

This marketable foundation of practice was, and to a considerable extent still is (although something may have been added to it as it has become concerned with policy-making) skill in what is usually described as the 'inter-personal area', essentially the skills of communication—whether to secure information or to persuade. This skill could and can be applied to a wide range of activities within organizations, all of which focus upon the 'people' referent:

(a) the manning or manpower development function where, although different forms and combinations of terms are used, various authors seem to recognize some role for the personnel department in securing enough of the right personnel to man the tasks required by the organization, this sometimes being seen as concerned primarily or exclusively with recruitment or sometimes with manpower development training

The communications skills are in evidence in descriptions of work roles, interviewing for selection or promotion, developing adequate records and reports for the planners, counselling and training etc.

(b) the 'motivational' function which reflects itself in activities to develop an adequate reward package for the labour force, including wage and salary determination and administration, and welfare activities which also have a 'reward' and 'incentive' element. With this aspect there may also be coupled activities which are concerned with the development of normative or disciplinary rules to govern conduct within the work system and, in consequence, activities which are concerned with discipline at the individual level

The communications skills involved here are essentially of the same order, involving securing market information, 'communicating' evaluations through the wage packet, training for employee development within the undertaking, and communicating normative and judicial rules and decisions.

(c) the function of developing an effective relationship with employee representatives (mainly in the shape of trade union officers but by no means confined thereto) and therefore of negotiation in its widest sense, probably on issues which fall within the other two areas of activity, but extending beyond this to include special areas like health and safety and the usual subjects of consultation in which attempts are made to communicate normative standards in relation to many of the areas of work life

These skills may, in some sense, be special, because of the association with power and conflict, but they remain in practice 'inter-personal skills', not unlike those involved in the other areas.

A 'people' referent, linked with inter-personal communications, or 'social' skills—the like of which most normal people must perforce develop in order to cope with life in any social context, may not by themselves form a solid enough foundation for a separate and specialist role. Any manager, it can be argued, needs both such a referent and skills in order to do his job: why then a specialist function? There are those who have expressed considerable doubt, even cynicism, about the possibility of putting this 'rag-bag' of activities together.

This hypothesis has been articulated in essentially the same fashion by Drucker (1961), Crichton (1968) and McFarland (1968). Drucker commented trenchantly that "personnel administration . . . is largely a collection of incidental techniques without much internal cohesion. Some wit once said maliciously that it puts together and calls personnel management "all those things that do not deal with work of people and that are not management. . . . As personnel administration conceives the job of managing worker and work, it is partly a file clerk's job, partly a social worker's job, partly firefighting to head off union trouble or to settle it . . . the things the personnel administrator is typically responsible for—safety and pension plans, the suggestion system, the employment office and union's grievances are necessary chores. . . . I doubt though that they should be put together in one department for they are a hodgepodge . . . They are neither one function by kinship of skills required to carry out the activities nor are they one function by being united together in the work process. . . .". Crichton (1968) talks of the 'ambivalence' about the personnel specialist and refers to the allocation process as one entailing "collecting together such odd jobs from management as they are prepared to give up". McFarland (1968) also refers to the personnel department as the chief executive's dumping ground for unwanted tasks.

This view is perhaps not surprising because the generality of early personnel work achieved its coherence largely by reference to 'people' (as the IPM Jubilee statement still asserts) and therefore to those skills which might be most closely associated with 'people'— the skills of communication and consolation which manifest themselves in many different ways and forms within a complex work organization. Interviewing, explaining, consulting, persuading, suggesting, and even instructing, are all inter-personal skills rooted in communication, and they all have their particular forms of organizational connotation in selection, induction, training, consultation, counselling, motivating and even paying of employees. Both the concern of the caring employer for the welfare of his employees, stemming from what Heller refers to as the "twinges of social conscience" (Heller, 1961; in McFarland, 1971, p 31) *and* that of the system for efficiency in its employees when bureaucratic impersonality had replaced the personal touch of the owner, could be expressed through these media.

The development of personnel management beyond this embrace of control techniques as applied to procurement and retention, however, relied to some extent upon the 'industrial relations' and 'procurement' streams of activity being brought together in a more general conception of role.

The role of the industrial relations specialist, in its earlier conceptions, was capable of being represented as that of protecting the enterprise from those consequences of trade union influence upon decisions which would, *inter alia*, reduce the 'freedom' of the employer to engage and deploy whatever labour he chose. Although essentially protectionist in conception, and although associated with a particular managerial ideology, it was nevertheless concerned to protect the efficiency 'ethic' as this was then defined. But to a considerable extent, the industrial relations officer role was less involved with technique and more with issues of will and judgement, often thought to be outside the scope of technique.

This was less the case with procurement activities in the labour market area, and here it was the change in the external circumstances which gave the nudge to practice. For as long as labour remained plentiful the personnel specialist had no strong foundation on which to develop from his "low level of prestige in industry and commerce" (Wellman, 1972, p 32; see also Lawrence, 1973, p 5). When that condition changed, partly as a result of the greater general influence of trade unionism on decision taking at various levels inside and outside work institutions, this industrial relations, protectionist role could become linked with a new conception of the administered wage effort bargain. The personnel manager now had a comparably 'protectionist' role based on the ability "to present information regarding the enterprise in its labour market" which allowed him to become "involved in high-level strategic decision-taking activities of the firm" in the manpower planning area (cf Wellman, 1972, p 32).

What is now expected of him is that, in the interchange between the organization and its environment on appropriate labour resources, the personnel manager shall provide (by recommendation and for wider approval within the organization) plans or strategies which will be calculated to ensure that it has the right kind of labour resources in the right quantities at the appropriate time to enable it to meet its production objectives, or alternatively that its production objectives can be tailored in the light of such conclusions to fit the manpower situation where it is inflexible and immutable from the organization's standpoint. Although, as Lawrence asserted in 1973, a good deal of manpower's planning occurs two levels below the head of the personnel department, the need for the undertaking to get its manpower interchange relationships right in a condition of full employment and more stringent control of labour movement by legislation and other governmental policies such as those concerned with incomes, helped to bring the top level of personnel management more closely into the corporate planning process.

The 'place' of the practitioner
If this diverse pattern of development is put together, it suggests that personnel practice, as a specialism, now has a range touching upon the whole question of determining the relative 'status' of persons in the employment relationship. On the one hand, the personnel practitioner is concerned to protect and maintain the 'employer' status, or the opportunity for the undertaking as a work enterprise to secure, retain and relinquish those human beings which it requires to perform its many tasks *and* the freedom of the 'employer' to continue to operate without undue restriction from external factors or forces. On the other, he is involved in setting the objectives and standards appertaining to the status or dignity or treatment of those human beings whilst in that employment. It is, as it were, generally regarded

29

as legitimate, for the personnel practitioner to attempt to influence all of these aspects of the work system.

It may then be asked how this 'range' of influence is itself protected and/or maintained and enhanced. There are, essentially, two different answers possible to this question, each indicating one of the two main routes that developing practice over the years has taken. One of them has been to develop a 'professional' approach to practice, by which is meant merely that the practitioners might autonomously choose objectives and strategies in relation to whomsoever they then chose to regard as their clients, without necessarily having to embrace the ideologies of organizations or 'systems' of efficiency. This aspiration to autonomy is clear in the Institute of Personnel Management's statement of its objectives:

1 to provide an association of professional standing for its members through which the widest possible exchange of knowledge and experience can take place
2 to develop a continuously evolving professional body of knowledge to assist its members to do their jobs more effectively in response to changing demands and conditions
3 to develop and maintain professional standards of competence
4 to encourage investigation and research in the field of personnel management and the subjects related to it
5 to present a national viewpoint on personnel management and to establish and develop links with other bodies, both national and international concerned with personnel.

(IPM, 1977, p 1)

Of these, the first three are of particular significance for determining the place of the personnel specialist in the undertaking. Together they suggest that the practitioner must be knowledgeable about and experienced in the 'people-concerns' of undertakings, and responsive to standards of competence in both advising and assisting the client-organizations in demonstrating those concerns. By implication the personnel specialist is seen to stand over against the employing organization, and not necessarily to be part of it, however much he or she may contribute to its objectives.

On the other hand, the employing organization displays an interest in using the skills of the personnel practitioner as a part of its own resources. This interest in acquiring personnel skills in the circumstances of changing environmental circumstances offers the practitioner a second route to a secured place in the scheme of things. The basic claim to skill in executive roles (for example, of interviewing for selection) might offer one place; a knowledge of the underlying theories and an ability to apply them to the achievement of worker cooperation and contribution, yet another; and a developed judgemental ability related to the determination of objectives and policies, a third. In the evolution of personnel practice, as it has been revealed briefly above, there has been an almost continuous progression through these three 'levels' of management decision and action within undertakings, culminating in the present position where the personnel director stands as the apex of a hierarchy of personnel work of a directive, administrative and executive kind (cf Chamberlain, 1948, ch 1).

At the first, executive level the personnel practitioner operates at a managerial decision level not very different from that of the supervisor, and does so largely by applying his basic inter-personal and communications skills within a framework of directives and administrative methods laid down for him. At the second, administrative level he develops and recommends procedures and methods for others in the organization to follow in carrying out their roles, using his knowledge of theory in so doing, and operating largely within an advisory 'staff' role. At the third, directorial level, his chief task is to contribute to the establishment of objectives, overall policies and standards which shall govern conduct, and the criteria which will be employed to evaluate success, and at this level, whilst the kinds of knowledge and skill applicable at lower levels are still relevant, the main abilities are likely to be more associated with 'judgement' (cf Vickers, 1965).

In this latest and broadest conception of personnel practice, therefore, there is a degree of protection for the whole gamut of personnel work by virtue of the power and position of the top level of the function. It now becomes comparable in terms of domain, even if different in its range, from the general management function in organizations. The function as a whole must now, in accordance with normal 'systems thinking' (cf Miner and Miner, 1977),

(a) know where it is going and integrate its objectives with those of others in the organization as a foundation for all other action
(b) derive the guide lines and the criteria for action from such objectives
(c) decide upon strategies and tactics for realizing these objectives, calling upon such range of specialist expertise as is appropriate
(d) have (or be given) structural and procedural access to those parts of the system which it must necessarily influence
(e) develop and secure sanction for its own measurement/assessment operations (which might require others to supply information) and
(f) constantly monitor the consequences of its own decisions as a

basis for up-dating of objectives or methods.

Whilst this does offer a protection, it also provides a foundation for tension between this 'managerial' and 'efficiency' orientation and the archetypal 'professional' orientation.

This seems to pose a dilemma for the profession, which it appears not yet to have resolved. The 'welfare approach', and a good deal of the early formal activity of personnel specialists, emphasized professionalism in what might be termed the 'archetypal' mould, namely one based on a direct inter-personal relationship with the client-as-person—in the present sense, with the emloyee. The 'labour management approach', on the other hand, and much of the more recent activity of personnel *managers*, has tended to concentrate on aggregates of employees (eg 'labour' or 'the workforce') and on the use of 'aggregated data' (eg payroll, manpower stocks and flows, hours lost in disputes) with the consequence that the 'professionalism' of the personnel manager becomes more that of the organizational profession. This distinction is to be found within the professional occupation, where one sub-group conceives itself to have a 'man-in-the-middle' role and function, and another seeks to emphasize its essentially 'managerial' approach and function (cf Lawrence, 1973, pp 45; Watson, 1977).

This difference is also to be discerned in the different views which are put forward concerning what is appropriate and relevant training for professional managers. The first orientation, to the individual employee as client, suggests that the basic disciplines ought to be psychological and social psychological (ie understanding the individual in interaction with his fellow) and the applied subjects, personnel management (which should have a strong 'social skills' and welfare orientation) training and development (with emphasis upon learning theories and individual growth) and law (oriented towards individual rights and the corollary of employer's duties in respect of treatment).

The second orientation, to the enterprise as client, suggests that the basic disciplines should comprise the 'policy sciences' (in the American phrase)—economics, sociology and political science (which deal mainly in aggregated data)—supported by the necessary 'tool subjects' of accounting, statistics, and operations research which facilitate the production of aggregated data, and by the applied subjects of 'personnel management policy' and industrial relations and, in order to key these into the environment, 'business and management systems' in general.

This choice is a very real and ever-present one in personnel management. The option elected by the individual is, of course, a matter for him or her, but the profession as a whole is likely to seek to effect a compromise in the form of a synthesis of the two—as indeed it may be seen to do in both the professional courses and the skills courses which the Institute of Personnel Management currently supports. These courses rest on the view that personnel management is concerned with both service to individual clients and service to organizational clients. But on the one hand an individual personnel manager is unlikely to possess a role which simultaneously serves both clients equally (either as he sees it himself or as the clients see it) and, on the other, his progression through the occupation might well take him from one role to the other (and thus require him to switch from one theoretical orientation to the other). A composite definition of the professional role, and a composited form of preparation to undertake it, is consequently very likely to create a tension within the occupational group itself.

The personnel management's professional quest must therefore be that of seeking a definition of the occupational role which will be acceptable to society (or to work organizations) and of establishing a supportive preparation for the assumption of that role. In this search for solutions, it must first, resolve the question of client-orientation in the role and, secondly, establish which foundations of theory (certified knowledge) are most pertinent to that role. In principle, there seems to be no reason why these questions must be answered in the singular (ie that there is only one role definition possible, or that there is only one form of professional training which is appropriate). But there is some reason to suggest that some answers are required if the occupational group is to substantiate its claim to a mandate from society to regulate the affairs of the occupational group.

The current conception of the personnel function
The current conception of personnel management reflects its diverse origins and lines of development and the different levels or breadths of decisions taken with organizations.

There is, on the one hand, the role of the specialist who ensures the supply of labour to the undertaking. This stems from the development of a specialist role at the time when large scale enterprise found it increasingly difficult to secure adequate labour from purely local labour markets on the basis of the old methods of personnel contact. From this the personnel specialist both developed skills in the 'employee resourcing' area and emphasized the development of the 'techniques' of the personnel practitioner. With the passage of time, and particularly during the tight labour markets of the period since the second world war, this kind of activity had to be gathered up in a more systematic fashion, and gave rise to the concept of 'manpower planning', in which personnel practitioners became more clearly identified with managerial as distinct from specialist practitioner activities.

On the other hand, the function of personnel management acquired two distinct ideological associations from the two kinds of custodian roles from which it also developed. The original welfare officer, as a kind of custodian of the corporate conscience, developed skills closely akin to those involved in employee resourcing, and gave them a meaning in individual welfare terms. The early negotiators, as custodians of the corporate identity, had also to acquire skills in the inter-personal, negotiating area, but also gave the function a meaning in terms of the corporate entity. In time these also came together to emphasize the general function of protecting the corporate undertaking as a concept, and also allowed the function's influence to be seen as relevant at the aggregated and disaggregated levels.

As all of these have come together in recent years, therefore, the personnel function has come to be regarded as distinct from the technical and financial functions (as identified above) and as having its own 'technology' (the logics of its relevant techniques) and its own 'ideologies' (generally bifurcated between the welfare of the individual employee and the welfare of the undertaking as a whole). For similar reasons, it is concerned both with professional practice, associated with the application of inter-personal skills, and with managerial activity, defined in terms of decision-taking on behalf of the aggregate. These cross-currents at one and the same time help account for the differences which are found in the conceptions of personnel management throughout economic enterprises, and provide the foundations for the discernable tensions within the profession itself.

The major distinctions and the major tensions can be identified by setting, in the form of a matrix, the answer to the question of 'for whose benefit?' the activity is undertaken (enterprise or individual) against the level of decision involved, corporate (policy) administrative (method) and executive (control).

Personnel management, like any other brand of management, is concerned with the functions of planning, organizing and controlling. Related to the personnel element of the system, these are discharged through policy formation (indicating objectives and standards to apply generally, and particularly on the manning of the enterprise and the climate which it will create for working); through design and development of organization appropriate to the work to be done and to the goals, aspirations and values of those who will be called upon to do it (manifesting itself in appropriate definitions of roles and relationships and of the cultural values which will animate both); and

34

Table 5
Personnel management activities

The textbook usually includes the following activities of personnel management	The enterprise usually requires action to provide the following	The individual usually demands action to create the following
1 Personnel policy formation (general)	A statement of objectives and standards to be followed by all acting in the name of the organization.	A perception of the organization's 'care' for its members, including a notion of justice and fairness.
1a Manpower policy and planning (dealing with the interface between enterprise and labour market)	A statement of how the enterprise projects itself into the future as an appropriately manned enterprise.	A perception of the organization's concern to maintain efficiency in manning consistent with security of those who have invested their working lives in it.
1b Policy and planning in respect of the work environment (welfare amenities, health and safety and services)	A costed statement of the conditions under which employment is offered in order to secure contributions required of employees at all levels.	A perception of the treatment offered by the employer to employees, including opportunities for personal development and growth.
2 Organization design (job analysis, communications, procedures, recognition)	An organization equipped with adequately defined roles and adequate communications channels to permit optimization of contribution.	An organization equipped with adequate structures and procedures to allow individual and sectional goals to be given due consideration.
2a Communications (disclosure, counselling and consultation)	A solution to the top-down and lateral communications problems of organizations.	A reasonable opportunity for all employees to be informed of problems, policies and projections.
2b Mutual influence (joint negotiating, disciplinary committees)	A bargaining structure which meets the demand consistently with time and money, costs of securing acceptance of policies etc.	An adequate opportunity to employees to exert their influence upon policies, practices, and projects.
3 Control of labour	Informed action on activities intended to secure appropriate labour: (i) recruitment and selection (ii) performance appraisal (iii) promotion etc (iv) training (v) reward package (vi) environmental climate	Fair and consistent actions intended to ensure the dignity of labour: (i) job opportunities (ii) recognition of worth (iii) development of person (iv) learning opportunity (v) fair rewards (vi) good treatment
4 Control of power	Definition of authority or discretion to decide, usually by tacit or open agreement manifest in: (i) job definitions (ii) rule books (iii) collective agreements	Acceptance of fair definitions of authority and discretion preferably by open discussion and joint agreement manifest in: (i) collective agreements (ii) union rule books (iii) joint decisions

through the control of the operation of the working arrangements to ensure adequate task performance and fair treatment to all concerned.

The work activities of the personnel officer are defined with reference to these, and it is possible to link the activity titles generally given in the textbooks to them. In addition, this work can be oriented in either or both of two directions, each being defined by the definition of the purpose for which it is undertaken. Thus a personnel policy may be conceived as responding to the enterprise's need to secure adequate contributions from employees (the 'effort' part of the bargain) or as responding to the human aspiration to be treated with 'dignity' whilst at work (the 'wage' part of the bargain—in the broadest sense of the term). Similarly, recruitment activity may be undertaken to secure employees who can make a required contribution at least cost to the enterprise, or aimed at providing individuals with full opportunities to make a contribution to society: whilst it can be argued that if either orientation is pursued 'properly' the other criteria will also be satisfied, such a happy outcome is by no means automatic in an imperfect world and the distinction remains worthy of recognition as a source of potential tension in the role.

This is a feature of the personnel management role which is particularly worthy of recognition in the light of changes made in social policy in Britain in the 1960s and 1970s. The opportunity which is provided by these twin orientations of the role to deprecate the manner in which the function is discharged, or to dismiss it as a hodgepodge of unrelated and unjustified activities, existed before these changes occurred. But the translation of welfare privileges into rights and the imposition of social as distinct from individual values at the aggregated level, by means of social policy borne by legislation in the 1960s and 1970s, throws the whole problem into new relief. On the one hand, the personnel officer now finds his activities prescribed by legislation, at one level, where he becomes the custodian of the means of discharging the employer's legal duties concerning personnel employed. (This process will be indicated in chapter 1 which seeks to show how the old 'welfare' concept has been underpinned by statutory conceptions of right and duty.) On the other, he now finds his skills deriving from his work with personnel aggregates being placed at a considerable premium as a result of the creation of new rights for labour in the aggregated sense. (These changes form part of the subject matter of chapters 2 and 5). Where therefore he might have liked to think of himself somewhat whimsically in the past as a 'man-in-the-middle' or as having a rather special and close relationship with the union officers, (Anthony, 1977) the discussion of the role of the 'labour director' in schemes

36

for employee participation, and the donation of new privileges to shop stewards in recent legislation, must raise questions about the place of the personnel officer in the scheme of things.

Nevertheless, thirdly, there is a focus to the role, and this occurs in the concern with 'people' in the system. However the role might have grown up, and in spite of the fact that it is sometimes concerned with individuals and sometimes with aggregates, it is concerned with the treatment or management of people in the enterprise, and not (to make the contrast) with the physical, inanimate elements of it. Making this broad general distinction between the management of the physical assets and the management of the human assets, allows the personnel officer to be aligned firmly and unequivocally with the second type of management to the virtual exclusion of the first. And what may be of more significance, the personnel officer is probably the only specialist in the enterprise who can be distinguished in this precise way: all his colleagues have some concern with the management of physical assets, but these are for the personnel manager little more than a component in the definition of the human *situation*.

It is perhaps for this reason that the personnel function as a specialist department of organization has survived (and indeed grown) in a soil which, if Drucker's 'trash-can' or Pigors' 'maid-of-all-work' strictures are to be accepted, could not be regarded as the most fertile. The personnel specialist's activities in relation to persons or aggregates vary widely; they make strange bed-fellows from the points of view of ends served and skills required; but they do acquire an integrity by reference to people. Further, it is this singularity of focus which justifies the separation of the function in spite of the fact that every other person in the enterprise must also be concerned with personnel, and which ensures its survival in a situation where the license of enterprise to 'use' people to realize its objectives is being subjected to new 'conditions'.

Further reading
(Suggestions for further reading follow each chapter. They are selected to provide the student with a small number of suggestions for further reading to deepen his or her appreciation of the main subject(s) discussed in the chapter. These and other works referred to in the chapter are also listed in the bibliography at the end of the book).

On the history of the development of personnel management in Britain, see M M Niven (1967); A Crichton (1968)

On different perspectives of the growth of personnel management, see C H Northcott (1955); R R Hopkins (1955); P D Anthony and A Crichton (1969); D E McFarland (ed) (1968)

General textbooks on personnel management include M W Cuming (1975); R Naylor and D Torrington (1974); D Torrington (1977); T P Lyons (1971)

American general texts most often used in Britain are L R Sayles and G Strauss (1967 seconded); P Pigors and C A Myers (1971); W French (1971); W French (1974); L C Megginson (1972); D S Beach (1975); J B Miner and M G Miner (1977).

(The distribution of chapter titles in these general texts is indicated in the table on the following page: it is based on chapter titles and does not therefore indicate content in detail nor does it include *all* the chapter heads in all of the books listed.)

Students in industrial undertakings will probably find the subject covered for their context in the books quoted above; more recently, a number of specialist books have appeared on personnel management in the public services and students in these fields in particular might find the following of relevance to their employment context:

Millard (1972) and Cuming (1971) on personnel management in the health services; Fowler (1975) on personnel management in the local government service; Armstrong (1971) on personnel management in central government organization; and Boella (1974) on personnel management in the hotel and catering industry.

On more specialist aspects of the function, students are referred to the ends of the various chapters.

Table 6

Textbook coverage of personnel management
(*Main topics covered in major textbooks, identified from titles of chapters, and indicated in the table by chapter number*)

Authors / Topic	Northcott 1955	Cuming 1968	Naylor & Torrington 1974	Strauss & Sayles 1966	Pigors & Myers 1973	Beach 1975	French 1974	Miner 1977
Objectives/ policy	2 & 3	2	1			3	9	1
Organization of function	1 & 10	20, 21				4	30	
Manpower planning			2					
Employment	12		3		15	11		
Recruitment	11	4, 5	3	19	15	9, 10	11–13	
Wage determination		12					19, 20	10,11,13
Termination			10		17	13		
Employee records	12				12			
Promotion		6		20	17	13	14	
Employee services	19		11	30		29		20
Welfare		18	11					
Health safety	18	19		29	22	28		17
Benefit planning			11					
Employee development	17		5, 6	22		15	17, 18	14
Interviewing/ counselling				10	10			12
Resource control								
Standard setting				26				
Appraisal		8	7	23	16	12	15	8, 9
Training	14	10, 11		21, 24	16	14	16	15
Discipline/rules				13	18	23		
Motivation/ incentives	4, 5	3		5, 27–8	6, 21	17		
Wage and salary administration	15, 16	12, 13	8	25	20	25, 26		16
Supervision				6–8, 15	7		7	18
Morale	17							
Industrial relations			16, 17			5		
Negotiations	8, 20	14, 15	18, 20		13	6, 24	22–26	19
Joint consultation	9		14					
Procedures			21–23					
Organizational development					3			6
Job analysis					14	8	10	7
Work groups	7			3		18–19		
Organizational analysis						7		
Communications		9, 16	13–15	9, 14		22		21
OD					5	16–21		
Environment	6	18	12				27–28	

Note: where the chapter title does not include the noun in the left hand column (or one very close to it) a chapter number is not included: the book may however treat the substance indicated in another chapter with a different name or in a more generally titled chapter.

1 The structure of the employment relationship

The structure of enterprise

Personnel managers are, as we have noted, chiefly to be found in the undertakings and organizations of our society which are established for some trading or service purposes. These undertakings are generally of a larger rather than a smaller size measured by the number of employees involved, and one definition of the personnel practitioner's role emphasizes his concerns with those employees on behalf of the 'undertaking'. The role is therefore very much a product of the 'fact' of employment and of the 'fact' of organizational scale. No matter what emphasis the personnel practitioner gives to his role, therefore, he must inevitably respond to the facts of there being 'employees' and of there being organization. In this present chapter, it is proposed to explore briefly the nature of the trading or 'work' organization, and the nature of the relationship which is established between organization and employee.

The starting point is the structure of enterprise in our society. Such enterprise is essentially concerned with 'trading': arrangements are made, by one or more individuals, to engage in trade—production, distribution and exchange of goods and some services—from which they hope to derive some benefit for themselves by way of profit or distributed dividend. Some other undertakings are established with rather different purposes, such as the supply of a needed service but without necessarily individual beneficiaries: public service undertakings are a case in point. The purpose, and the question of who benefits from the arrangement, may thus both vary (see Blau and Scott, 1963), and the relationship between the 'undertaking' and the individual employee may be affected by this in both formal and informal senses. Nevertheless the structures created primarily for the development of 'trading' activities tend to be dominant, the principles which apply to them tending to carry over into the others (which are not trading organizations).

Private enterprise organization

Private enterprise takes a number of distinct forms in our society. The main distinctions are between 'individual traders each trading on his own account', partnerships, private companies and public companies. These separate forms tend to be adopted to suit particular circumstances. But there is some possibility of interchange between the first two and the third types. The choice is sometimes made on the basis of how far the 'owners' are willing to disclose information about their business affairs in order to secure the legal benefits of the corporate form of trading with limitation of liability for debts. In principle, it would be possible for any of these forms of trading organization to be established without 'employees' being involved in them, but in practice the bigger the organization (as measured by money invested, for example) the more likely it will be that the enterprise will employ helpers, who are not 'traders', 'partners', or 'corporators' but employees.

The individual trader form of enterprise is usually small-scale: an individual may with little formality start trading in his own name and *may* hire employees to help him. As an individual trader he will, as a natural person, assume liability for any debts he may incur in the course of trading and the bigger his or her involvement becomes, the more likely it is that he will seek to secure some limitation of his 'personal' liability, by registering (with more formality) as a private company with limited liability. He or she can do this quite easily, although he or she will need to find a second shareholder (a spouse or a solicitor) who will agree to contribute, say, a pound share. This form of trading will require the filing of information, initially and annually, with the registrar of companies, where it will be available for inspection by others. This form of trading is found commonly in agriculture, distribution and some other trades in which individuals frequently 'set up in business' as self-employed persons.

The partnership is one stage removed from this. Two persons may decide to go into business together, trading on a joint account. If the number of persons so decided is not more than 20 (except in some types of business) they may opt for this form of trading, as do many of those who provide professional services (accountants, lawyers, medical practitioners). They can then cooperate with each other in trading, but possess most of the advantages of the individual trader. If they trade in their own names (as in the string of names often found on solicitors' door-plates) there are few formalities required, because the natural persons who have liability for debts are clearly identifiable by this device. When they do not trade in their own names, the name of the partnership must be registered, along with the names of the partners. The partners will normally have unlimited liability for the debts of the undertaking, but some of them may have limited liability under the terms of the Limited Partnership Act of 1907: the limited partner is therefore more in the position of a lender of money to the undertaking than is the full or general partner.

Neither the individual trader nor the partnership can exist in perpetuity—if only because natural persons die. When that occurs or even when a partner retires, the individual trader ceases to be a trader, and the partnership is terminated (although it may be recreated amongst the partners remaining as a separate venture). This difficulty of coping with the departure of the natural person has generally been held to be one of the disadvantages of these forms of trading. Apart from the cost to any remaining individuals of creating a new entity to take over from the old, there are disadvantages for any employees who might find themselves 'without an employer': this problem has been met in the Contracts of Employment and Redundancy Payments Acts, Acts which allow the calculation of continuous employment to ignore demise where the trade or partnership is continued by a 'successor'.

The lack of perpetuity in the arrangements for trading was one of the advantages sought and secured in the company or corporate form of enterprise. This also allowed larger aggregations of capital to be assembled for trade, and paved the way for a means of limiting the liability of those corporators who contributed (subscribed) capital to the joint venture. Such corporate arrangements are, essentially, partnerships without the same directness of ownership and control. Since 1844, companies have been permitted to come into existence simply as a result of complying with the requirements of the Companies Acts and registering under them: before that time, they required a petition to the Sovereign (or Privy Council) or a special Act of Parliament, both of which were costly and time-consuming processes which did not commend themselves to the burgeoning industry and commerce of last century (Levy, 1950).

Currently, companies formed by registration under the Companies Acts, may be either private or public companies. A private company, at present, is one which by its Articles (essentially the constitution which governs it) places restrictions on the rights of members to transfer their shares, forbids the issue of shares to the public and limits the number of its shareholders (not including employees and ex-employees) to no more than 50. The other category, the public company, is currently defined as one whose Articles do not so restrict it, so that it is really the 'residual' category of company. Where the private company needs only two shareholders in order to comply with the registration requirements, the public company must have a minimum of seven (although there is no maximum number). By implication, the public company is usually larger than the private one, but this is not a necessary condition or implication, if size is measured by subscribed capital, number of employees or market value of sales.

A company may opt, at formation, for limited or unlimited liability for its shareholders. In the first case, the liability of the shareholders for debts will be limited to the amount of the share, whilst in the second no such restriction is imposed, so that the shareholder has some of the characteristics of the individual trader or unlimited partner. (In some usually charitable professional or intellectual organizations registered under the Companies Acts, the limitation may be by guarantee—the subscribers agreeing to contribute a small sum if the organization has to be wound up, rather than to subscribe to shares). Where the shareholders' liability is limited, this fact has to be made known in the name of the company, by the addition of 'limited' (or Ltd) to the end of the name in which the company registers.

Because of the need for the United Kingdom to harmonize its companies legislation with that in the European Economic Community, these forms of company organization will change at the end of 1978. The main change will be the drawing of a new distinction between public and private companies (with limited liability) and the reflection of this in the style of the company's name. From that date, companies with a minimum subscribed capital (£50,000 has been suggested as the minimum for Britain) whose shares are publicly available and whose shareholders' liability is limited, will be required to carry a style of 'plc' or 'inc' (the style is not yet finally decided) whilst the new residual category of all the rest will carry the existing style of 'Ltd'. (This new, EEC-inspired distinction will have relevance to the proposals of the Fifth Draft Directive of the EEC on the subject of worker participation, which is currently under discussion but which, when adopted and implemented, will be intended to apply to the 'new' style of *public* company.)

At present, on present definitions, there are in Britain over half a million private companies and between 15,000 and 16,000 public companies. There are a very large number of individual traders and partners (about a million without employees and over half a million with employees). But the bulk of employment in private enterprise organizations is with the companies: according to Bullock, the top 1,000 companies (mainly public but including some of the larger private ones) provide employment for 7,160,000 employees (Bullock

Committee Report, 1977, p 7).

Industrial government and management
Private enterprise industrial and commercial government tends to rest upon certain principles and to possess a typical form. In some ways it is not dissimilar to the 'government' of the public sector undertakings although the parallels are by no means exact. It is also currently under debate, and later we shall have occasion to consider the proposals for changes in this pattern of government (see pp 435–42).

The basic principle followed—although it may be as often honoured in the breach as in the observance—is that in trading, the owner of the assets of the enterprise shall be the prime beneficiary of any benefit or advantage gained from trading. In the 'individual trader' and 'partnership' forms, the rights and the liabilities of the 'owners' are openly specified and upheld in law. The owners are identifiable as persons and they may hire others to assist them but they are either agents or servants and clearly to be distinguished from the owners, both as persons and in terms of their powers. In the company form of trading, the operation of the principle is somewhat less clear, both in law and in practice, and the form of government adopted is necessarily more complex, involving a number of quite distinct levels of decision, responsibility and function.

The notion of a company or corporation rests upon a kind of legal fiction, that it shall be regarded as having perpetual personality, separate and distinct from the persons who, in whatever capacity, are brought into association with it. Strictly, the shareholders who subscribe capital to the company are not the owners of the assets of the company, but their subscription gives them title to share in the profits of the trading venture and in the distribution of assets on its dissolution. Nor are the directors, as directors, the owners of the assets, even though they may own some of the shares and even though they may have been the original promoters of the venture: they have extensive powers to run the company's affairs and in this sense act as agents, as well as fiduciaries of the shareholders, but essentially they function as controllers of the assets without being their owners. Thus neither the shareholders (the 'members' of the company) nor the directors of it, whether individually or collectively in either case, are either the company or the owners of the company. In so far as the 'company' exists at all in a tangible form, it exists as a constitution (which is committed to paper and registered with the Registrar of Companies) known as the Memorandum and Articles of Association of the Company. This constitution says what the company is in business for, how its capital shall be subscribed for, and how it shall be

44

run in the interests of the corporators. The Articles of Association constitute the instrument of company government, by which the statutes (rights and obligations) of the shareholders in general meeting and the directors in board meeting or severally, are fixed, and provisions made for the actual day to day management of the affairs of the enterprise.

As a fictional person, the company must necessarily be related to the real persons or interests which are associated with it. The first such interest group are the shareholders. They are the members of the company, and under companies legislation, they have certain rights which may be exercised through the device of the general meeting (whether annual, extraordinary or special): they cannot, in other words, simply exercise their rights as individual shareholders and there are even some restrictions on the rights of 'a majority' of shareholders. The main power which they can (in general meeting) exercise is that of appointing and dismissing the directors—those who are charged with actually running the company—but they can also initiate actions in law and, by following a prescribed form of action, change the Articles of Association (possibly in ways which might curb the powers of the directors in the shareholders' interest). Such authority as the shareholders' meeting has, however, in the running of the company, rests upon their control over the form of the Articles of Association and the tenure of the directors. Legislation also prescribes their rights, *vis à vis* the directors, to certain kinds of information about the state of the enterprise and the manner in which it is being run, this being designed to inform the judgement of the shareholders in their deliberations and decisions (Companies Acts, 1948-67).

From the time when companies were formed only as Chartered or Statutory Companies, the need to give freedom to the directors to manage the company has been recognized. From 1844, companies legislation has sought to protect the interests of the shareholders and creditors by means of legal requirements to disclose true information and to report on stewardship, and by providing penalties for fraud or other breaches of the directors' fiduciary duties to 'the company'. But the law has served to allow considerable flexibility in the way in which the Articles of Association are drawn up and in the allocation under those Articles of the powers of directors *vis à vis* the shareholders as a body. Consequently, the directors' powers are usually, although not necessarily in every individual case, quite wide: it is common for directors to be allocated all powers which are not by the Companies Acts themselves and the Articles reserved to the shareholders in general meeting. Although therefore it is possible to argue, as does Sullivan (1977) that the shareholders' meeting is a significant part of the authority or governmental structure of the company, this may be so, *de jure*, only to the extent that the shareholders can appoint and dismiss the directors and alter the Articles. Where as a matter of fact as those who have explored the issue of the divorce of 'ownership' from 'control' in companies have argued (cf Berle and Means, 1930; Florence, 1954), the shareholders are so diverse a group as to make effective shareholder control virtually impossible, their power could be regarded as minimal compared with that of the board of directors.

The 'Governors'
In private enterprise organization, therefore, three categories of controller or agent can be discerned:

1 The agent, the person who is authorized to act on behalf of another person (who is referred to as his principal), usually to the extent of entering into contracts on his behalf. Such agent may be a servant, employee or an independent contractor, coincidentally with his being an agent, and there are similarities between the vicarious liability of both principal and employer for torts committed by the agent or the servant respectively, although there are differences in the statutory rules which apply to them

2 The executively-employed partner, or the partner who may be engaged in the day to day activity of the enterprise whilst yet being a contributor of capital and a bearer of the risks of the venture. Where he could be discerned to have joined in common with others in a venture to pursue profit and to have accepted unlimited liability for the enterprise along with the other partners, he would be regarded as a part of the employer concept, not an employee. On the other hand, one so executively engaged who had been promised a share of the profits of the venture as remuneration for his services, but who had not put up capital, pledged his credit or undertaken to bear the risks of the venture, would be treated as an employee, not as a partner

3 The directors and managers of a corporation or company, who might be regarded as having a slightly more ambiguous status than the agent or the partner in relation to the 'principal'. In the case of the agent (as in category (1) above) the principal is a 'person' who might be quite readily identified, at least in principle; in the case of the executive partner, (as in category (2) above) the equivalent of the 'principal' related to agency is to be found in 'the partnership' which again, because of the need to identify members thereof for legal purposes, comprises readily identifiable persons (who include himself as a principal); but in

the case of the company or corporation, there may be identifiable 'prime beneficiaries' (the shareholders) but the 'principal' is an *abstract* entity defined by the memorandum and articles of association which becomes associated with real persons only through the concept of a board of directors as a collectivity. The ambiguity arises, because these directors, not being partners with the liabilities of partners, are also often servants or employees of the fictional principal (by virtue of service contracts negotiated with fellow directors) in whose name they act as agents *and* trustees (in a special sense). Consequently, the general principles of the law of agency are slightly modified and extended in their application to the board of directors, which as an entity is a trusted agent of the corporation, but which as individuals is often composed of employees or servants.

The board of directors, as presently constituted, is the key organ of government and management in private enterprise undertakings. In Gower's words, "the general meeting is merely one of the company's two primary organs and most of the company's powers are not vested in it but through the board of directors. And . . . the directors exercise these powers either directly or through managers appointed by them" (1969, p 515). The board, either directly or through executive agents or servants appointed by it, thus normally runs or manages the company, on a 'day to day' basis, subject always to the power of the shareholders to dismiss them, and to alter the Articles in such a way that their powers might be curbed or restricted for the future if they are dissatisfied with their performance. In spite of this potential curb on their exercise of power, in the ordinary situation the directors are the key managing organ of the company: they are the logical successors of the entrepreneurial heroes of the laissez-faire industrial period.

The major role which the board performs on behalf of the company is that of contracting in the name of the company. Here, the relationship of the directors to the company is essentially one of agency, and as agents they can and do commit the company to obligations, even if these must be entered into 'in the interests of the company' usually interpreted by the Courts to mean in the interests of the shareholders. But in Gower's interpretation the board is seen to have the power to "substitute a managing director for themselves as one of the primary organs of the company" and in these circumstances "the managing director will have sole power to exercise those functions entrusted to him by the board, which may if the board thinks fit, include all its powers except such as the articles or the Companies Act require to be performed by the board itself" (Gower, 1969, p 141).

This power will commonly include the power to contract with others, and thus provides the foundation for the exercise of a managerial authority within the company.

Although the company will enter into a wide variety of contracts with others, in our present context the contract of most relevance is that in employment, which is entered into with 'employees'. The employee's contract of employment with a company is a contract with the abstract entity (or 'person') entered into through the agency of the directors or the managing director or the directors, according to the extent to which the powers to contract on behalf of the company may be delegated. The question of who is the employer in the context of a trading company is therefore one which can be answered in a number of different ways, according to the manner in which the Articles of Association confer powers. Importantly, 'ownership', most closely associated with the shareholder concept in the company, is not a necessary prerequisite of possession of power to contract with employees: the controllers in the form of directors and managers can and usually do have the power to contract in this way.

In legislation, some of which antedates the Companies Act of 1844, recognition is given to the authority of 'managers' (under various titles) to contract in employment. The 1831 Truck Act, one of the first pieces of general legislation to impose conditions upon the employment contract, establishes the simple principle that ownership was not a requirement of employer status. Section 25 states that "in the meaning and for the purposes of this Act . . . all masters, bailiffs, foremen, managers, clerks and other persons, engaged in the hiring, employment, or superintendence of the labour of any such artificers, shall be and be deemed to be 'employers'" and shall moreover be competent to contract as employers with such artificers. The same conception occurs in slightly extended form in the Hosiery Manufacture (Wages) Act, 1874, s 7 which states that "within the meaning and for the purposes of this Act, all masters, foremen, managers, clerks, contractors, sub-contractors, middlemen and other persons engaged in the hiring, employment, or superintendence of the labour of any such artificers shall be and be deemed to be 'employers'", and shall be competent to contract as stated above (Thompson and Rogers, 1956, 19th edn, pp 1021 and 1041).

These agents, as much as the fictional legal person created by the Companies Acts, are the successors to the mediaeval concept of 'Master', which is continued in law in relation to the contract of employment. In the last piece of legislation which employed this and the related term 'Servant' in its title, the 1867 Master and Servant Act repealed in 1875, the natural and the fictional persons are both identified in these terms. It is there stated that the word 'employer' shall include "any person, firm, corporation, or company who has entered into a contract of service with any servant, workman, artificer, labourer, apprentice or other person; *and* the steward, agent, bailiff, foreman, manager or factor of such person, firm, corporation or company." (S 2). Both the corporation and the agents of the corporation are thus made competent to contract in employment.

The public sector
In a mixed economy there are other forms of organization which are engaged in trade, and yet others in which work is done even if not 'for trade' in the usual sense of the term. These other forms are often referred to collectively as the public sector of the economy, and may be divided into two sub-categories, one concerned with 'trade' as in the nationalized industries, and the other concerned with public service, ranging from central and local government service, through the health and educational services to the armed and police services, in which trade as such is not a prime objective. In terms of the development of the employer concept there is more difference, generally speaking, between these two sub-categories than there is between private and public sector industrial concerns.

The nationalized industries show great similarity to the registered company, particularly in the legal personality and existence which companies acquire by complying with the requirements of the Companies Acts. In the public corporation, the legal personality is usually created specifically by a statute. Thus the National Coal Board, the 12 original Area Gas Boards and the original Central Electricity Authority were statutorily incorporated by the Acts which nationalized these three industries: it was not necessary for them, as it would be for a company, to comply with the requirements of the Companies Acts before they achieved the status of being incorporated bodies.

As these few examples indicate, the act of nationalizing an industry did not necessarily lead to the creation of a single incorporated entity to govern the industry. The gas industry was run first by a number of such bodies whilst the National Coal Board was established as a single entity from the start. In a number of cases, for example, gas, airways and steel, the original arrangements have subsequently been altered by statute to replicate (or more nearly so) the structure adopted for the coal industry; in electricity, changes have been made in both directions. Steel represents a different kind of hybrid, since it was nationalized (on both occasions, 1950 and 1968) in such a way that the pre-existing company structure was retained for a time, and in the first nationalization period, the direction of the former companies remained subject to the requirements of the Companies Acts.

In the cases mentioned so far (and in some others) the public corporations are *not* Crown bodies. As with the Transport Act of 1962 and the Television Act of 1964, the Act itself may declare that the corporation is not a Crown body. Where the creating Act is silent, the rule which the Courts have applied to resolve whether a public corporation enjoys the privileges of the Crown is one which measures the extent of the control exercised over the corporation by the responsible Minister. By this test, the corporations in coal, gas, electricity and transport industries are not Crown bodies but the National Health Service is. The importance of this distinction is that an Act of Parliament does not apply to Crown bodies unless the Act specifically says that it does. Thus Crown bodies are not bound by the Contracts of Employment Act nor by the Redundancy Payments Act, but they are bound by many of the provisions of the Employment Protection and Trade Union and Labour Relations Acts (although not by all) except for certain restricted kinds of employment.

Outside the nationalized industries and certain other Government-created bodies mentioned above, the main source of employment in the public sector is that of the public service. This embraces the Civil Service—which has its industrial and non-industrial sections—and Local Government Service, as well as other services like the National Health Service in which there is close and direct control by a Minister of the Crown. In the national services, the Minister may be regarded as the lynch-pin between 'the Crown' exercising its 'governmental' powers through Parliament and the Government of the day, and the employees. The nature of 'government' of such undertakings is not therefore to be equated with government of a registered company, although in some respects parallels can be drawn. Furthermore, employees are treated as Crown servants with, in principle, fewer rights than are ascribed to other employees in the private sector, and this is justified in terms of the necessity for 'democratic control' of the public service. Similar considerations also apply to local government employees, although generally they do have more 'rights' than their national counterparts, even if issues of participation and workers' control remain complicated by the 'democratic imperative'.

The government of undertakings in the public sector consequently reveals more variety than does the private, 'company' sector. At one end of the spectrum, the nationalized industries and similar undertakings, are run by a 'board' with essentially the same powers as the present board of directors in a registered company. In place of the shareholders' meeting, however, there stands Parliament whose powers are not exactly like those of the shareholders but are in many ways similar. At the other end, there are those who might be described as 'office-holders' rather than as servants of some undertaking: the clearest example is provided by the police service, where each 'officer' is essentially the holder of an office of 'constable' (from the Chief Constable to the constable on the beat). Although there may be arrangements for discipline within such undertakings, therefore, the individual office holder acts on the basis of his 'office' not by reason of delegated authority from superior board or person (cf Rideout, 1967, pp 12-13). In between these extremes, the major category of undertaking is the 'public service' (whether local or national) in which the acceptance of the principle of general democratic control of the service provided affects the manner in which the undertaking arranges its authority.

The public sector, as defined here, employed 7,314 million people in mid-1976; these were distributed between public corporations (1.951 m), central government (including HM Forces) (2.342 m) and local authorities (3.021 m) (*Economic Trends*, December 1977 and Department of Employment *Gazette*, February 1978, p 209).

Employees: the hired help
Trading ventures, regardless of their form, often require the help or services of others to enable them to realize their trading objectives. Some of that 'help' may be provided by those particular categories of employee at which we have just looked—the executive directors and the managers and agents. These may provide a rather special kind of help, which has to be distinguished from the assistance required of those who will engage in actual production, selling or developmental activities of the undertaking. This help is often referred to as 'the workers' or 'the employees'. The workers are the ones who do the 'ordinary' manual or mental work within undertakings, but the concept may well include those with the special relationship mentioned above and professional workers. The 'employee' on the other hand is one who is employed under a contract of employment and, whilst this may well include all those already mentioned, the legal definition of employee is important to the understanding of the relationship which exists between the 'employer' (or master) and a particular but broad class of worker (see Rideout, 1976, ch 1). The personnel manager in his role is generally involved with this particular class of individual.

The conditions under which the employee provides help to the trading venture (or the employer) is a matter which it is assumed will be established freely and voluntarily by the two parties themselves in the first place—by what the employer and employee agree in the establishment of 'the contract of employment' to do for each other. Since they are unlikely to agree to all the details of the rights and obligations which will subsist under that contract, the common law, legislation and collective agreements (negotiated by the employees' representatives and the employer) all, in various ways, stand ready to fill in some of these details. The status of the employee, and of 'the worker' is most generally defined by reference to common and statute law, and an understanding of the 'position' of the employee requires an appreciation of the manner in which the law perceives it.

The modern concept of employee has grown out of the older concept of servant, and in common law it is still usual to use this term for some purposes, even though it was last employed in legislation in 1867, in the Master and Servant Act which was repealed in 1875. As Fox (1974) has argued, the older mediaeval concept of servant to a master was carried over into the industrial revolution by the common law, and the employer was thereby enabled to require of the newly-freed employee similar duties of loyal and faithful service which the mediaeval master had been able to exact from the then unfree servant. The more clinical concept of 'employee', used to reflect something of the freedom of contract ushered in by the new era, was not introduced into legislation until 1875.

Since that date, 'master and servant' has generally been replaced by 'employer and workman' (for example, in Employers and Workmen Act, 1875, s 10 (continued in Statute Law (Repeals) Act, 1973, Sched 2 para 2), Trade Disputes Act 1906 (repealed by Industrial Relations Act, 1971, Sched 9), Industrial Courts Act, 1919, s 8, and (although it employs the concept of 'worker') Wages Councils Act 1959, s 24. In 1965 the further change to 'employer and employee' was made in the Redundancy Payments Act, s 25, and this has been continued in the Contracts of Employment Act 1972, s 11, the Industrial Relations Act, 1971, s 167 (now repealed), the Trade Union and Labour Relations Acts, 1974–6, and the Employment Protection Act, 1975, s 126. The more modern 'employer and employee' concepts may be both more clinical in their conception, and purport to indicate greater equality or independence than the earlier ones, but the definitions used and the tests still applied by judges often hark back to the earlier concepts and their meanings and connotations (cf Hepple and O'Higgins, 1976, ch 3; Gayler and Purvis, 1972, pp 22-33).

The term 'servant' derives from concepts developed in feudal times, and connotes that the 'servant' stems from the 'serf' who was regarded as *owing* service to a 'lord' (and master). The concept denotes a type of personalized dependency which certainly the more clinical 'employee' attempts to avoid. As Lord Goddard commented on the lingering historical connotation "a master was regarded as having a proprietary right in his servant" but this should now apply only to "menial" or domestic servants. (Jones (Bros Hunstanton) v Stevens (1955) 1 QB 275, p 252.) But it is still possible to detect in modern definitions some lingering connotations of this same kind. These remain, for example, in the term 'domestic servant' so often excluded explicitly from employment legislation, presumably on the grounds that such servants agree to provide a personal service to the employer or more usually his or her domestic ménage in return for consideration in cash and/or kind. Domestic servants, in this sense have been defined as those "whose main or general function is to be about their employer's persons, or establishments, residential or quasi-residential for the purpose of ministering to their employer's needs or wants, or to the needs or wants of those who are members of such establishments, or of those resorting to such establishments, including guests" (R v Louth Justices (1900) 2 IR 714).

Some at least of the connotations of service tend to linger in respect of employees generally. In the common law, 'service' is the concept which continues to be used in legal argument but, that practice apart, there are some occupational categories which are smitten with the brand of service to an extent which does not adhere to the generality.

One example is provided by employees on the railways, who retained the title of 'railway servants' long after the word had been dropped for others, because railway companies exacted "a more exacting form of service from their employees" (Sharp, 1951, p 238), who found the lingering association brought into a recent court decision. Thus *The Times* Law Report (18 May 1972) of the case of Secretary of State for Employment v ASLEF and others, was carried under a headline of The Railwayman's Duty of Faithful Service by virtue of the arguments advanced by the Solicitor General:

> Criticism has been made of the President of the Industrial Court's reference to the duty of every employee to behave fairly to his employer and to do a fair day's work. The duty of faithful service was part of an employee's general duty to his employer: (Friedman's *Modern Law of Employment* (p 446) and Pearce v Foster (1886) 17 QB 536). The duty of faithful service was the matching equivalent of the employer's duty to take reasonable care of his employee. Robb v Green (1895) 2 QB 315) showed the implied obligation of faithful service. Therefore . . . the admitted intention of the work-to-rule was to disrupt or to interfere with the provision of goods and services which was not a performance of

one's duty of faithful and diligent service. The concept of working to disrupt one's employer's business was incompatible with faithful service. . . .

Clearly, the argument could be, and to some extent was extended to any employee engaged under a contract of employment: but it may be wondered whether it would have been argued so strongly *in these terms* had the employees not been railway *servants* so recently (but see also, Rideout, 1976, pp 75-8).

A second example is provided by the 'civil servants' who, technically, serve the Crown as the apex of the executive and in this capacity have a clear historical link with older feudal conceptions of the dependency relationship. In principle, civil servants hold their offices (employment) at the Crown's pleasure and are dismissable at will, with or without notice (see Shenton v Smith (1895) AC 229; Gould v Stuart (1896) AC 575; Riordan v War Office (1961) 1 WLR 210; Reilly v The King (1934) AC 176, 179-80; Rodwell v Thomas (1944) KB 596). Those in Crown employment were for many years considered not to have a contract of employment but the more modern view is that they have. Nevertheless not all legislation applies to all employed by the Crown. The Contracts of Employment Act 1972 and the Redundancy Payments Act 1965 are amongst protective Acts which do not apply, either expressly or by necessary implication; but most of the rights granted to employees and workers under the Employment Protection Act 1975 and the right of appeal against 'unfair dismissal' under the Trade Union and Labour Relations Act 1974 do apply to those in Crown employment. But for these purposes those included under the heading of in Crown employment are the civil servants 'proper' and those in most of the creatures of Government, such as the Land Commission, but *not* usually employed in the commercial enterprises generally referred to as the nationalized industries. Even in this there are exceptions but there are some 'public servants', such as those who are in the employment of the Health Authorities, who are explicitly covered by some legislative protections and equally explicitly not covered by some others.

In each of these three categories, domestic and menial servants, 'railway servants' and public servants, the notion of dependency upon a master tends to be continued, almost in spite of the provisions of more recent legislation which is designed to reduce such dependency. There is however another side to this coin, which affects certain other limited categories of person who in the economic sense are employed, but who nevertheless do not work under a contract of service or of employment. These are the 'self-employed', persons who may contract to provide services (in the plural in this case) to another

54

but without either party intending that there shall as a result be set up a dependency relationship of the master and servant type. Thus Lord Denning in the case of Stevenson, Jordan and Harrison Limited v MacDonald and Evans (1952) 1 TLR 101: "A ship's master, a chauffeur and a reporter on the staff of a newspaper are all employed under a contract of service, but a ship's pilot, a taxi-man, and a newspaper contributor are employed under a contract for services." The important point of distinction is that the latter retain greater independence of the other party to the contract than do the former.

It may be that some such persons are 'obviously' employed under a contract for services but that others may or may not be—if the intentions of the parties can be read aright. The Courts have sought to develop appropriate tests to determine the issue in doubtful cases. The former test was whether a person was subject to the control of a master, in the sense that an employee "works under the control of another, not only as to *what* he must do, but also how and when he must do it" (Hepple and O'Higgins, 1976, p 134). This test is somewhat 'old fashioned' now that cultural values seem to be moving society in the direction of emancipation from the master-servant relationship, for reasons which are indicated by Hepple and O'Higgins: "The control test assumes that the employer is both a manager and a technical expert; in other words it reflects a stage of society in which the employer could be expected to be superior to the employee in skill and knowledge" (*ibid*).

The strict application of the control test to those in highly skilled or professional occupations led to considerable difficulties, and eventually to an extension of the test to embrace the question whether the person was 'part and parcel of an organization' or not. Kahn-Freund acknowledges that there has to be a 'master': "there can be no employment relationship without a power to command and a duty to obey" (1972, p 9), but suggests the crucial question was "Did the alleged servant form part of the alleged master's organization?" (1951, *Modern Law Review*, pp 505–6). This was later expressed by Lord Denning as: "Under a contract of service, a man is employed as part of the business, and his work is done as an integral part of the business; whereas under a contract for services, his work, although done for the business, is not integrated into it but is only accessory to it." (Stevenson, Jordan and Harrison Limited v MacDonald and Evans (1952) 1 TLR, 111).

More recently a more complex test has been applied (Ready Mixed Concrete Ltd v Minister of Pensions (1968) 2 QB 497). This test is to be applied in three stages, and to qualify as an employee or servant, the person must (a) agree to provide his own work and skill in the performance of some service for his employer or master; (b) be subject to the other's control in a sufficient degree to make that other the master; and (c) have a contract whose other provisions are consistent with its being treated as a contract of service.

Any person who carries out 'work' for another would meet the first test. But such workers may not intend and may not in fact put themselves under the control of another, and the remaining terms of the contract may be more akin to a commercial contract than to a contract of employment. The person may, for example, own his own tools and the equipment necessary to the performance of the work, and he may under his contract bear the risk of loss or the chance of profit on the work venture, and he may generally avoid some of the detailed control of how and when (or the manner) in which he carries out the work. In such cases, the exhibited degree of independence of the 'master' will tend to place him in the category of self-employed. Nevertheless, as Hepple and O'Higgins point out, the "form of the question will dictate the answer given" and if it were to be asked whether the contract was consistent with its being a contract for services, a different answer might well be found in any given case" (Hepple and O'Higgins, 1976, p 136). Even if the 'multiple' test is not yet adequate for the purpose to which it is applied, it remains clear that the lawyers are still seeking, in all these tests, to establish a basis for determining both the degree of dependency inherent in work contracts and the point along the implied continuum at which it can be said that 'independency starts here'.

Apart from the question of how much independence the individual has in relation to the other party to his contract, his rights will be vitally affected by whether he is an employee, strictly defined, or a workman (or worker) which is—usually more broadly defined. Thus, now, many rights and protections are afforded to *workers*, defined broadly in this way. This applies for example, to sex and racial discrimination protections. But some are confined to the more restricting category of *employees*, as in those contained in the Contracts of Employment and Redundancy Payments Acts and the rights in respect of unfair dismissal (although some specific categories of employee are excluded from these) (see pp 75 and 111).

Strictly, an employee is one who works under a contract of employment, but the law has sought to spell this out in greater detail for purposes of allocating rights on the individual contract itself. The Contracts of Employment Act 1972 defines an employee as "an individual who has entered into or works under (or where the employment has ceased, worked under) a contract with an employer, whether the contract be for manual labour, clerical work or otherwise, be express or implied, oral or in writing, and whether it be a contract of service or of apprenticeship." The Redundancy

Payments Act 1975 has a similar definition. But in both cases there are categories of employee who are excluded from the rights and benefits of the Acts. The Industrial Relations Act 1971· (repealed 1974) and the Trade Union and Labour Relations Act 1974 (which is followed in this respect by the Employment Protection Act 1975) also define 'employee' similarly, but with the express exclusion of the members of the police service or those with the powers of a constable.

The main distinction between this definition (of employee) and that of a workman or worker is that the self-employed person is now usually included in the latter. The purpose in this case is the allocation of rights which are more extensive than those contained in the individual contract. The early definition of 'workman' (in the Employers and Workmen Act 1875) included those engaged in manual labour and working under a contract with an employer "whether the contract be . . . express or implied, oral or in writing, and be a contract of service or *a contract personally to execute any work or labour*." It is the last clause which brings in the self-employed person, and this same clause is brought into the definition of workers in the Trade Union and Labour Relations Act 1974 (and in the Industrial Relation Act 1971 and the Employment Protection Act 1975). Although the police service is still excepted from the definition of worker, the modern statutory definition of the 'worker' is broad and expressly covers three categories of person, only the first of which is that of 'employee'.

'Worker' means an individual regarded in whichever (if any) of the following capacities is applicable to him, that is to say, as a person who works or normally works or seeks to work:
  (a) under a contract of employment, or
  (b) under any other contract (whether express or implied, and if express, whether oral or in writing) whereby he undertakes to do or perform personally any work or services for another party to the contract who is not a professional client of his; or
  (c) in employment under or for the purpose of a government department (otherwise than as a member of the naval, military or air forces of the Crown or of any women's service administered by the Defence Council) in so far as such employment does not fall within either of the preceding paragraphs, otherwise than in the police service. (TULR Act 1974, S 30).

For the first time in the Industrial Relations Act 1971, but continued in the Trade Union and Labour Relations Act 1974, the 'independent contractors' in the National Health Service—the general practitioners of medicine, dentistry, ophthalmy or pharmacy—who had previously been regarded as providing services under a rather different conception of the contract are included within the meaning of the word 'worker'. The effect of this is to acknowledge that there are some groups of persons in work who may be called and call themselves professional workers by virtue of their having individual clients but who nevertheless work under an employment contract with some enterprise or organization, whilst some others, in the same occupations or similar ones, may work under a contract *with* individual clients in relation to whom the worker stands in a less ambiguous professional relationship. "Parliament has expressly provided that one group of persons with 'professional clients' are to be regarded as 'workers' [those providing medical, pharmaceutical, dental and ophthalmic services under the National Health Service Act] but "expressly excludes those others who have a contract with comparable 'professional clients' (although neither term is defined in the Act, and both may therefore call for juridical interpretation to determine the boundary) (see Hepple and O'Higgins, 1976, p 128).

Only the armed and police services are thus excluded from the 'worker' category; all those who work under a contract with an employer, including those employed by the Crown, and whether 'of service' or 'for services' are included in this general definition, excepting only those services provided directly to professional clients. This is a development from the earlier position in which workmen (as in the Trade Disputes Act 1906) meant simply "all persons employed in trade or industry (whether or not in the employment of the employer with whom a trade dispute arises)". This led the Donovan Commission to recommend a broader definition, which has now been followed in legislation subsequent to its report in 1968: "The expression 'employee' means any person who has entered into or works under (or, in the case of a contract which has been terminated, worked under) a contract with an employer, whether the contract be by way of manual labour, clerical work or otherwise, be expressed or implied, oral or in writing, and whether it be a contract of service or of apprenticeship or a contract personally to execute any work or labour."

This extension of the concept of 'employee' in the legal definition of 'worker' is of some significance, not only in relation to establishing rights and duties but also in worker attitudes towards work (see, for example, below pp 213–17 or towards unionization (cf Bain, 1970; Bain, Coates and Ellis, 1973). As the classification used in Table 7 indicates, there may not be many 'self-employed' professionals, but there are a larger number of other workers who

58

Table 7
Socio-economic class, Great Britain, 1971

		Males	Females
1	*Employers and managers in central and local government, industry, commerce etc—large establishments* Persons who employ others or generally plan and supervise in non-agricultural enterprises employing 25 or more persons	596,970	101,390
2	*Employers and managers in industry, commerce etc—small establishments* As in 1 but in establishments employing fewer than 25 persons	1,231,450	315,510
3	*Professional workers—self-employed* Self-employed persons engaged in work normally requiring qualifications of university degree standard	139,720	11,220
4	*Professional workers—employees* Employees engaged in work normally requiring qualifications of university degree standard	659,670	76,310
5	*Intermediate non-manual workers* Employees not exercising general planning or supervisory powers, engaged in non-manual occupations ancillary to the professions but not normally requiring qualifications of university degree standard; persons engaged in artistic work and not employing others in it; and persons engaged in occupations otherwise included in group (6) who have an additional and formal supervisory function	886,360	1,011,090
6	*Junior non-manual workers* Employees, not exercising general planning or supervisory powers, engaged in clerical, sales and non-manual communications and security occupations, excluding those who have additional and formal supervisory functions	1,895,660	3,407,820
7	*Personal service workers* Employees engaged in service occupations caring for food, drink, clothing and other personal needs	159,620	1,141,730
8	*Foremen and supervisors—manual* Employees (other than managers) who formally and immediately supervise others engaged in manual occupations, whether or not themselves engaged in such occupations	563,550	55,320
9	*Skilled manual workers* Employees engaged in manual occupations which require considerable and specific skills	4,774,690	548,780
10	*Semi-skilled manual workers* Employees engaged in manual occupations which require slight but specific skills	2,033,160	1,144,550
11	*Unskilled manual workers* Other employees engaged in manual occupations	1,221,550	667,140
12	*Own account workers [other than professional]* Self-employed persons engaged in any trade, personal service or manual occupation not normally requiring training of university degree standard and having no employees other than family workers	709,860	175,590
13	*Farmers—employers and managers* Persons who own, rent or manage farms, market gardens or forests, employing people other than family workers in the work of the enterprise	145,660	11,090
14	*Farmers—own account* Persons who own or rent farms, market gardens or forests and having no employees other than family workers	131,280	20,780
15	*Agricultural workers* Employees engaged in tending crops, animals, game or forests, or operating agricultural or forestry machinery	242,440	58,610
16	*Members of the armed forces*	239,790	12,010
17	Indefinite	276,180	375,060

Source: as for table 2, above p 10

nevertheless regard themselves as 'professionals'—and more would regard themselves in this way who are not recognized by the Registrar General as falling into this category (cf Prandy, 1965). If the archetypal profession is made up of those who work with individual clients, there are an increasing number of professions which are 'organizational', as is the personnel management 'profession'. But it is the element of greater independency, carrying over from the classical conception of a profession, which helps account for, and to some extent justify, the differences in attitudes which are discernible between 'professionals' and non-professionals (see below, chapter 10).

A fortiori, this consideration also applies to those who have some kind of agency relationship in modern enterprise (see above, pp 46–9). An agent or a director, for example, may be an employee (by reason of a service contract with the board), and thus a servant within the language of the common law) but he is not to be equated simply with any other employee, nor indeed simply with any other 'worker'. There is a basis for differentiation which affects, first, the identity or solidarity possibilities of the directors themselves in relation to the other employees and, secondly, these same possibilities in relation to those managers who can, in some senses, be regarded as the 'hired help' of the directors in carrying out their 'managerial' roles. However much convergence there may be in attitudes towards 'unionization' as between managerial and shop floor workers, for example, the current differential definitions of 'status' must affect the final outcome of such a process. It must also contribute to continued differentiation in much the same fashion that professional and other workers tend to see their worlds as rather different.

The terms of the contract
The concepts of 'employer' and 'employee' thus subsume a structure of rights and duties which, together, establish the position or 'status' of each category. What constitute the rights and duties can only be understood by reference to what it is that the contractors themselves agree to in establishing the contract, *and* what is otherwise imported or imputed to the contract in addition to or in substitution for what is thus agreed. The concept that there is a contract at all allows the relationship to be thought of as a set of mutual promises, freely and voluntarily made by the parties. This is a useful device but, as Kahn-Freund has argued (1977, p 12), it should not be mistaken for a description of the actuality of contracting in employment.

If these promises are important to the parties, they may both wish to have them recognized in law and enforced against the other if he should default. For this to be possible the contracting process must satisfy five conditions.

First, the persons or the parties making the agreement must be competent (in the eyes of the law) to make such agreements. There are limitations on 'competence' associated with age, mental condition, health or dependency, and there are differences in conditions attached to competence according to whether the contractor is a person (acting in his own right) or a corporation (a body which is 'given' a legal personality for convenience).

Secondly, the parties must clearly intend that the agreement shall constitute a legally-binding contract and give rise to obligations which might be enforced through the Courts. Generally speaking social contracts are presumed not to be intended to create such obligations, whilst commercial and business contracts are presumed to be so intended.

Thirdly, the objects of the contract must themselves be legal, as the Courts will not lend themselves to the enforcement of a contract (even if it would qualify on other grounds) which has as its object the achievement of some result which would be illegal or which identifies as the means of meeting the contract terms actions which would be illegal.

Fourthly, there must be both offer and acceptance in the same terms between the parties. An employer's offer of employment at a particular rate of pay, must be accepted by the employee in the terms of the offer, although it may be accepted (or indeed offered) by conduct rather than in words. A man who is invited to turn up to work on a Monday morning, and who is given work when he does, would be deemed to have had an offer and to have accepted it by reason of conduct.

Fifthly, in the employment contract context, the agreement on the terms of the offer must be supported by consideration of an identifiable and recognizable sort (usually of course a wage). Consideration has been defined as consisting "either in some right, interest, profit or benefit accruing to one party, or some forebearance, detriment, loss or responsibility given, suffered, or undertaken by the other", or as requiring "that something of material value shall be given or some other detriment shall be sustained by the recipient of a promise in order to make that promise enforceable" (Mansfield Cooper and Wood, 1966 edn p 37).

Only if these requirements of the law are met, in the particular employment contract, can Courts or tribunals recognize or enforce the agreement. These requirements are thus 'prior' to the establishment of a contract of employment. When they are met, the employment contract may be regarded as subject to the four sets of influence upon its actual terms.

First, what the parties actually agree to 'explicitly' is one source of the 'contract terms'. But in employment relationships, what is agreed may be quite minimal—to work at a certain place for a wage—and a great deal more may be taken as agreed by the parties because of what is 'customarily' meant by such a simple reciprocal promise. Thus the question of what is 'really meant' and what is 'customary' may fall to be resolved at some stage in the relationship, if there is a difference of view about either. Historically, one of the roles of the trade union representative has been to try to influence the answers to these questions, and one of the roles of the common law has been to try to resolve these issues where they are brought before the Courts. In both cases, it should be noted, a body of doctrines or understandings about *how* the questions should be resolved, have grown up.

Secondly, therefore, the contract terms are subject to influence, especially where the actual promises are minimal or silent on specific aspects, by 'custom' in the trade or in the employer's undertaking and by the understandings and agreements which have been developed in those circumstances between the employer (and his 'agents') and the worker (and his 'representatives'). It is in the nature of employment, that the first reciprocal promise made by each party is likely to be both minimal and general, so that it is necessary as the relationship progresses through time for the details to be filled in to cope with the dynamic involved. The predilection of the worker over the past century or so has been to guide this process of filling in the details by 'collective bargaining'—the evolution of guiding principles and precedents through discussion between the agents and representatives.

Thirdly, in distinction from this 'internal' process of evolving rules about how the questions about contract terms are to be answered, the common law has ever stood ready to do the same thing on the basis of its doctrines and rules. Where the collective bargaining process is sanctioned by lockouts and strikes and similar forms of industrial action, the common law processes are sanctioned by the penalties available to the Courts. But the common law has developed in its own notions of what is 'normal' or 'standard' in the relationship of the employment contract, and it has established its own rules as to what is recognizable and enforceable in the way of a contract of employment. Both of these influence what the parties do and agree to in contracting—it has to if they intend that the bargain shall be enforceable—but it is often quite separate and distinct in its conceptions of what is right and wrong, or correct and incorrect conduct. This contains a potential for conflict between these two sets of influence upon the contract.

Fourthly, what the parties may agree individually or collectively (through agents and representatives) and what the common law may impute to the contract in accordance with its doctrines, are both subject to an overriding influence—that of specific legislation relating to both the processes or methods of contracting in employment, and the terms and conditions which may by any of these processes be agreed or deemed to have been agreed. This has always been so in the modern industrial period but, in the past two decades or so, legislation has burgeoned as an influence upon contracting processes and contract terms to an extent which markedly affects the old assumption that contracts were 'freely' and 'voluntarily' entered into by the parties. The important general consequence of this has been that, no matter what the parties may actually have agreed under certain headings in the contract, and no matter what, in accordance with the understandings and agreements of collective bargaining or with the doctrines of the common law, they may have been deemed to have agreed to, it is now to be presumed conclusively that they intended to agree to those terms (like minimum notice) which are stipulated in the legislation.

One way of looking at these various influences upon the employment contract is to see the first two as related to the worker's interest in preservng his only marketable asset (his labour power) in a way which will maximize his commercial advantage in hiring out to employers, and the last two as concerned to preserve some 'balance of advantage' as between the parties to the process of contracting. This notion of balance tends to be defined differently according to the cultural values which have applied in our society: by and large, the common law has developed its doctrines in response to a high value placed upon the enhancement of 'trade' from the middle ages onwards and tends therefore to define the balance of advantage in terms which favour trade over alternative objectives; but recent legislation has sought to shift the balance to favour the worker *as producer* rather than the worker *as consumer* whose interest the enhancement of trade might be expected to serve. In consequence, this shift has altered the status or rights and duties of the parties.

Rights and duties in employment
For as long as it remained or remains possible to read into the terms of a contract the connotations of 'service', the employer retains an advantage over the employee in that he can determine (ie control) what the worker shall do in that employment. The basic, common law duties of the employer to the employee under these circumstances, are those of remuneration for work done (service rendered), provision of opportunity to work in a limited number of circumstances (but by no means generally), taking reasonable care of the

63

employee whilst in the employer's employment, and where there is agency on the part of the employee to indemnify the servant for any loss sustained in service. These may be supported, supplemented or increased by duties imposed by statute (eg Health and Safety at Work Act, Employment Protection Act or Contracts of Employment Act) as indicated below, but they are also being modified by interpretation in the Courts. For example, the 'duty to provide work', which has until recently been regarded as a very minimal duty applicable to certain special forms of service (eg editors, media producers or artistes) appears to have been extended in some recent cases (cf FT Breach v Epsylon Industries Ltd (1976) IRLR, pp 180-3; Bosworth v Angus Jowett (1977) IRLR, p 374).

The employee's duties in employment are largely established by (a) the acceptance of an offer of employment for a wage or salary, and (b) what the common law then imputes to a contract of employment thus established. It is then assumed that the individual has agreed to serve the employer (using the older common law term 'service' in this context) in a defined capacity. He is seen to be contracting to make his services freely available to the employer who, in the interests of his business as he determines these, may make use of these services as and when he sees fit. In effect this gives rise to two categories of 'offer' on the part of the employee, one having to do with actual performance of the service to the employer, based on 'competence' to do the work, and the other to do with conduct within the framework of organization established by the employer to contain the work contribution of the several employees. In essence this means that he must obey any lawful orders given by the employer (whether directly or through agents, such as managers or supervisors) and he must obey those rules which have been devised as in the interests of the employer. This duty is general and, in spite of requirements of legislation on particulars of the contract of employment, no contract ever specifies precisely which services the employer will require to make use of or when he will do so.

An employee who applies for a specific job which calls for an equally specific type or level of skill thereby warrants that he has the type and level required, and the employer would be entitled to expect these to be applied. If this were not to be so, the employee would be open to dismissal. *Prima facie,* an employee who engaged in a go-slow, or who refused to work overtime after agreeing to work it as required, would be in breach but one who worked to rule would not be in the breach simply for doing so; the whole question here turning on the argument that to do so was designed to impede the employer's interests rather than further them. This could be extended to cover laziness or insobriety if these could be held to prevent the application of the skill and diligence sought. In carrying out the job, the employee also has a duty to take reasonable care of the employer's property, and in general to work in good faith or provide faithful service to his employer. He must not therefore put himself in a position where his own interest (say in a part-time job) conflicts with his duty to the employer (although in appropriate cases the contract may define this aspect) nor must he disclose confidential information to a third party who is not entitled to receive it (this having particular significance in respect of bank employees', lawyers', accountants' or doctors' knowledge of clients' affairs).

As Foulkes states the general position: "An employee must obey those orders and rules which are within the scope of the work he agreed to do, and to find out what he agreed to do we look at the terms of his contract and the accepted practices of his trade and of the organization he works for." (Foulkes, 1971, p 103.) If a rule appears to the employer to be necessary for the proper functioning of the business, it will be one which in the eye of the law he is entitled to enforce by the usual disciplinary processes. An employee does not have to obey an order which might expose him to threat of violence or to disease (unless he has specifically contracted to do so), nor does he have to accept an employer's instruction to give his services in some other place, or at a different period from the usual one (eg week-ends), unless he has either specifically contracted to do so, or unless custom and practice make it reasonably clear that such instructions are 'normal' for the job or the organization. The main test applied to determine whether failure or refusal to obey an order should justify dismissal (the main and ultimate remedy) was that applied in Laws v London Chronicle Ltd (1959) and is whether conduct on the part of the employee could be regarded as a deliberate disregard of the conditions of service in the particular circumstances surrounding them as to justify the employer in dismissing the employee.

This principle might also be said to apply in respect of other misconduct, not amounting to a refusal to obey an order. In this case (as indeed in the others mentioned) the question that has to be determined is whether the misconduct 'goes to the root of the contract' as if it does the misconduct (eg theft by a manager in a position of trust) might be held to justify instant dismissal whereas, if it does not, the misconduct (eg a *single* act of insolence or rudeness to a foreman) might be held not to do so. Certain categories of misconduct, such as theft or the threatening or offering of physical violence, raise questions of liability to third parties, so that although, for example, an employer does not necessarily have to exercise his right to dismiss an employee for theft of his property, the possibility of third party liability would make it sensible for him to do so if the theft was of another employee's property.

In toto, therefore, what the employee contracts to do is to submit himself to the authority (or control) of an employer in all matters which might be said to come within the scope of the work he offers to carry out. Because of the inherent difficulty of defining the contractual terms with precision, the employer has relatively unrestricted power, exercised through his orders and the rules applicable in the employer's organization, and the employee has comparatively few safeguards or protections except in so far as he himself, or someone (whether union or state) acting in his interests, can curb that power. The history of the employment contract is one of progressive restriction of the employer's prerogatives and privileges in these ways, although he remains possessed of such authority and power (see chapter 7) over the employee's competence and conduct as has not yet been restricted either by collective bargaining or legislation.

Both of these have provided the employee with new rights which are reciprocated by employer duties. Those established under collective agreements or common understandings between the employer and organized labour are both more varied (or less standardized) and subject to the trade union continuing able to mobilize adequate sanctions against the employer in the event of breach of the 'rule' establishing the right. But those established by legislation are relatively standardized (ie they apply to employees of a defined class regardless of other considerations) and are sanctioned by law.

The main employee rights in this category are:

1 a right not to be discriminated against in employer decisions in respect of engagement, treatment in employment or dismissal on the basis of sex, marital status (if the discrimination is against the married person) or ethnic origin

2 a right to be paid for work performed or service rendered, and if engaged in most manual occupations outside the public service, to be paid in coin of the realm, unless he explicitly agrees otherwise

3 a right to belong to a trade union if he so wishes (but not a right not to belong), and to engage in its activities (in some circumstances with time off for the purpose) if he so wishes, although not necessarily at *any* time

4 a right to work in some very special cases, limited in number, or to compensation for lay-off up to a certain limit

5 an embryonic right to adequate instruction and training for general purposes, but a more explicit right to instruction and training in safe methods of working

6 a right to expect the employer to exercise reasonable 'care' for the employee's health and safety at work

7 a right to basic information about the employment contract under which he works, about the enterprise for which he works, and about the reason why his contract of employment is terminated

8 a right to question decisions by the employer which touch on his employment and to appeal against such decisions either to an outside adjudication tribunal or to an internal body which serves a similar function

9 a right to either a minimum amount of notice as provided for in statute law or the amount of notice either expressed in his employment contract or reasonable for the occupation and industry

10 a right not to be unfairly or wrongfully dismissed from his employment which implies a right to require the employer not to

Table 8

Minimum periods of continuous employment to qualify for certain individual rights accorded by legislation

	Minimum period	Nature of the right	Source in law
1	No period	Not to be dismissed for trade union membership or activities	TULRA Sch 1 para 6
2	No period	Not to be dismissed for reasons of pregnancy	EPA S 34
3	No period	Not to have action short of dismissal taken against him/her for trade union membership or activities	EPA S 53
4	No period	To time off with pay for industrial relations activities or training therefor (officials)	EPA S 51
5	No period	To time off without pay to take part in trade union activities	EPA S 58
6	No period	To time off without pay to take part in public duties	EPA S 59
7	No period	To payments (established under new legislation) in the event of employer insolvency	EPA S 64
8	No period	To receive an itemized pay statement	EPA S 81
9	4 weeks	To guarantee payments for lay off	EPA S 22
10	4 weeks	To payments in event of medical suspension	EPA S 29
11	4 weeks	Not to be dismissed because of a medical suspension	EPA S 29(4)
12	4 weeks	To receive notice as prescribed by statute as a minimum	C of E S 1
13	within 13 weeks	To receive written statement of terms and conditions of employment. (If then changed, within four weeks)	C of E S 4
14	26 weeks	Not to be unfairly dismissed	TULRA Sch
15	26 weeks	To request and receive a written statement of reasons for any dismissal	EPA S 70
16	Two years after age of 18 yrs	To redundancy payment in event of dismissal by reason of redundancy	EPA S 8
17	Two years as above	To time off to look for work or to arrange retraining	EPA S 61
18	Two years measured back	To maternity pay (six weeks) in event of pregnancy	EPA S 36
19	From beginning of 11th week of confinement	To return to work after pregnancy	EPA S 48

determine his contract in a discriminatory fashion or in breach
of the contract terms themselves
11 a right, in certain industries (the Wages Council trades) to payment of wages at a rate which is laid down by regulation as a
statutory minimum (cf O'Higgins, 1976); see also p 83 below).*

Such rights constitute the other side of the coin of the employer's
duty to employees; it therefore follows that part of the personnel
manager's role will involve him in ensuring that the employer is not
in breach of his duty and does not deny to the individual employee
any such rights as may thus be established by statute. The magnitude
and implications of this should not be underestimated. The first may
be illustrated by quoting Selwyn's Law of Employment on the
matter:

> The changes which have taken place in the law of employment in
> the past 10 years or so . . . represent the emergence of a complete
> new philosophy in the relationship which exists between employer
> and employed, with new standards to achieve in personnel poli-
> cies. . . . The traditional prerogative rights of management are
> being constantly eroded, for the law now imposes requirements
> which follow from the new concepts of equal partnership in em-
> ployment matters. The old days of 'hire and fire' have been
> replaced by the doctrines of mutual respect and consideration, as
> the relationship of 'master and servant', servile in its implications,
> has altered beyond recognition. If some employers bemoan the
> changing scene it is because they have not yet taken cognizance of
> the new style of employment law which is applicable to the last
> quarter of the present century. Industrial dinosaurs die hard.
> (Selwyn's *Law of Employment,* Butterworth, 1976).

The implications are also likely to be diverse. From the individual's
standpoint, these changes give him 'job property rights' in some
respects similar to the 'property rights' of shareholders (see above
pp 44–45). The individual's stake in his job is now more firmly
acknowledged in law and enforced through his contract by virtue of
the rights to minimum notice, compensation for loss of job through
no fault of his own and to be dismissed only for good cause. It is also
supported by the greater freedom which he can expect, as a right, to
time off under certain circumstances, to demand information and to

---

* A more detailed identification of the duties thereby imposed upon the
  employer, is given in the appendix to this chapter: it discusses these duties
  as constraints upon the action of the employer in establishing, servicing
  and terminating the contract of employment in sequence in order to provide a broad checklist

question decisions taken by the employer.

From the corporate standpoint, this same kind of development is likely to reinforce the trend towards regarding employees as assets. This process has gone further ahead in the USA where the trade unions have been more assiduous in developing job property rights through the collective contracts, but the trend is also discernible in Britain, in spite of the absence of appropriate accounting conventions to apply to this area. As Bramham has put this "Treatment of manpower as a cost rather than an asset probably has its roots in the regard in which labour was held when accounting conventions were established. The prime concern of management at the time was the use of machinery and the proper exploitation of expensive investment. In comparison manpower was poorly regarded, the object being to replace it with an effective machine wherever possible. Manpower was a cost and capital was an asset and generated income." (Bramham, 1975). But if manpower is costly to replace by a machine, there may be more pressure to treat that manpower as an asset of the business and account it along with all other assets. This will tend to have important implications for manpower planning and development.

The treatment of employees as business assets has not yet gone far mainly because of the absence of appropriate accounting standards and conventions, but the idea that labour should be treated as a form of capital rather than merely as an expense is catching on (Hekiemian and Jones, 1967). The value of the human asset might be assessed in two quite different ways: either in terms of its cost, representing the investment in it to date by way of training, evaluation and recruitment; or in terms of its potential contribution, representing the expected benefit which it might yield in the future. The two are not necessarily correlated, certainly at the extremes of the range, even if in the middle the two may generally go together. Nevertheless it is the first of these which is currently exercising the minds of managers concerned with this problem: in the more constrained labour market faced by employers, the costs of securing manpower and of developing it to a state of proficiency requisite to the needs of the undertaking are leading management to think more seriously about the accounting aspects of manpower and accountants to think more purposively about the manner in which manpower accounting data might be presented as a guide to decision-taking (cf Giles and Robinson, 1972). This also has other wider implications: "If management believes manpower to be an income generator and not solely a cost, it will set about motivating employees and releasing the effort, aspirations and creativity that one suspects lie in all people" (Bramham, 1975).

Enforcement of rights and obligations

The enforcement of rights and obligations of the various categories of worker and employer varies according to the right/duty which it is sought to enforce, and to some extent according to its sources (ie whether deriving from the mutual promises, the common law doctrines, collective agreements, or legislation). There are four separately distinguishable 'judicial' processes involved in the enforcement process:

1 the judicial processes within the employment entity itself, based upon the idea that any administrative structure must carry within itself a mechanism for determining whether actions taken have been fair and equitable and in accordance with 'the rules'
2 the joint judicial processes associated with the arrangements for collective bargaining and involving particularly the grievance or complaints procedures, often now provided for in formal agreements between trade unions and management even if carrying over some of the main features of (1)
3 the judicial processes associated with the common law courts, chiefly in the present context, the County and the High Courts from which there is appeal to the Court of Appeal and ultimately to the House of Lords
4 the judicial processes associated with the relatively new 'industrial tribunals', from which appeal on points of law is to the Employment Appeal Tribunal, and ultimately to the Appeal Court and the House of Lords. These are to be distinguished from the processes associated with the Advisory, Conciliation and Arbitration Service (ACAS) and the Central Arbitration Committee (CAC) which are more concerned with matters of 'interests' rather than 'right' (see below, pp 418–22).

These do not quite amount to a Labour Court system of the continental type, but much of the legislation which allows action in the tribunals has responded to the desire to be 'good Europeans' and the analogy is worth drawing. Not only has the new legislation affected worker (and employer) statuses but it has virtually created a separate judicial system external to the employment relationship itself, with which a personnel practitioner needs to be familiar.

The first two of these might be regarded as a process of private law-making and law-enforcement. The initial position is that in which the employer establishes his own mechanism and procedures for resolving differences over rights and obligations existing within the framework of the works rules. Brown has commented on this aspect in the following terms, as a preface to discussing the establishment of a formal appeals procedure within the Glacier Metal Company: "Differences of opinion between people, and particularly between managers and subordinates, are inevitable in an Executive System. Means of ventilating these differences, and of seeking redress from a higher level of authority, come into being willy-nilly. If these means are allowed to grow haphazardly, they take on forms which are inefficient and damaging to the company. The chief danger of an unrecognized and, therefore, unformulated appeals mechanism is that it may informally institute by-passing of managerial levels. Decisions are then made without data on the full situation being available. The hearing of a grievance by a high-level manager, without the presence of the manager whose decision is being questioned, or of the intervening managers, undermines the whole managerial-subordinate relationship" (Brown, 1960, p 250).

This recognition led the Glacier Company to formalize its appeals procedure to allow individuals or representatives of groups to appeal against decisions of managers either acting without their authority in the exercise of their prescribed roles, or unfairly and inequitably in consequence of the exercise of the discretionary role (cf Brown, 1960, ch 18). It was also a part of this whole exercise to develop new and formalized policies ('the rules') within the company, in order that all concerned might have a clearer conception of just what the rules were and just what the limits to authority were. Similar exercises of re-examining and re-formulating the rules, and of establishing more formal appeals procedures have been instituted in many other companies for similar reasons, and also because of the consequences of legislation affecting the 'job property rights' of the worker (cf Butteriss, 1971; Thomason, 1971).

Such developments currently tend to be associated with the negotiation of new procedures with the recognized trade unions. Until recently, trade unions tended to accept the 'customary' procedures for handling complaints and grievances, which often bore a close resemblance to the judicial procedures established within the management system. The rights of the individual to be accompanied by a trade union officer would normally be acknowledged but the procedure which involved a 'joint' adjudication early in the sequence of steps was, and to some extent still is, unusual. To an extent this reflects the traditional trade unionist's unwillingness to 'participate' in what are seen as managerial decisions, the preference being for argument with that decision both before (to influence it) and after (to change it). In effect, therefore, many joint procedures were the managerial system procedures with a built-in right for the individual complainant to be accompanied or represented (by his trade union officer) and to have the matter processed within a specified time limit at each stage (see below, pp 470–75).

The third adjudication process is that wich occurs in the Civil Courts, whenever an individual feels that he has suffered from a breach of contract, failure on the part of the other to carry out a statutory duty, or from some tort committed by another. If employers and employees find themselves involved in court actions, these are likely to provide the most probable foundation for them. Actions founded on contract or tort up to £1,000 (the figure is likely to increase with inflation, of course) would normally be begun in the County Courts; actions on the same foundations involving a sum higher than this would normally be originated in the Queen's Bench Division of the High Court. Employees or employers are most likely to find themselves involved with one or other of these Courts of first instance in matters relating to employment (if, of course, with any Court at all). From either of these Courts, any appeal would be to the Court of Appeal (Civil Division), and thence to the House of Lords (cf Padfield, 1972, pp 188 *et seq*) (Criminal cases move through a different set of Courts, beginning with the Magistrates Court which has power to commit for trial to the Crown Court (which can also hear appeals from the lower Court); appeal from the Crown Court is to the Criminal Division of the Court of Appeal and thence to the House of Lords) (cf Howells and Barrett, 1975, pp 90–96).

The adjudication which might be associated with these civil Courts are those which relate to contract law—differences as to whether the other has kept his side of the bargain, and therefore questions of what the terms of the bargain were in so far as the common law rules can determine this, and tort, actions to secure compensation (damages) for an injury suffered at the hands of another or to prevent (by injunction) damage from being done or, in some cases, simply to secure a declaration of 'rights' from the court. The important distinction to be made, is broadly between the 'old' concepts of contract, developed in the common law (as discussed above) and the new 'rights' and 'duties' recently created by legislation since 1962. The former still fall to be adjudicated ('recognized and enforced') within the Civil Court system but the latter, for the most part, fall to be adjudicated within the industrial tribunal system (cf Greenhalgh, 1973).

The industrial tribunals are relatively new in Britain, having gradually evolved from the administrative tribunal established in the 1964 Industrial Training Act (S 12) to determine disputes about levy and grant provided for in that Act as a mechanism for increasing the amount of training conducted in Britain. This original jurisdiction was gradually extended, by the Redundancy Payments Act 1965, the

Docks and Harbours Act 1966, the Equal Pay Act 1970, the Contracts of Employment Act 1972, the Trade Union and Labour Relations Act 1974, the Employment Protection Act 1975, and the Health and Safety etc at Work Act 1974.

Taken together, these provide for the tribunals to determine the following questions:

1 over the adequacy or the accuracy of the information an employer is required to give to an employee on his contract terms (C of EA S 4) and on his pay (EPA S 84)
2 over rights to compensation and the amount of that compensation in the event of redundancy or loss of income on reorganization of an employing authority (RPA Ss 9, 42 & Sch 7)
3 over any claim in respect of the statutorily imputed contract term that women shall be given equal treatment with men in the same employment (EPayA S 2 & SDA S 63)
4 over whether any given work is to be regarded as dock work (D&HA S 51)
5 over any complaint that an individual has been unfairly dismissed or has not been given adequate or accurate information on reasons for dismissal (TULRA Sch 1 para 13)
6 over complaints relating to any of the payments (guarantee payments, S 27, entitlement under a protective award, S 103, remuneration on suspension from work on medical grounds, S 32, maternity pay, S 46, debts on insolvency of employer, S 66) to which the individual now has rights (EPA)
7 over whether an employer has given an employee time off to perform public duties or to look for work, or to carry out trade union duties etc (EPA S 60)
8 over a trade union's complaint that an employer has failed to follow the statutorily established redundancy procedure (EPA S 101)
9 over an appeal against an improvement or a prohibition notice served by an inspector as provided for in the Health and Safety at Work Act (H&SWA S 22)
10 over an employer's interference with an employee's rights to belong to a trade union and take part in its activities (EPA S 54).

(see Hepple and O'Higgins, 1976, pp 64–66).

Appeal on questions of law lies with the Employment Appeal Tribunal (Ss 87–8 and Sch 6, EPA) in respect of matters placed within the tribunals' jurisdiction by the Contracts of Employment, Redundancy Payments (except on compensation for the income consequences of reorganization), Trade Union and Labour Relations (in respect of unfair dismissal) and Employment Protection Acts. The questions posed by the Docks and Harbours Act, the Industrial Training Act, and the Health and Safety at Work Act, on the other hand, lead to the Queens' Bench Division of the High Court, where appeal is made. Appeal is important in connection with prediction of the likely decisions of the tribunals (as indeed is the case also in the Courts). A higher Court's decisions bind all lower Courts and, in theory at least (the matter is under debate) themselves; the decisions of the Employment Appeal Tribunal, on matters of law decided on appeal are therefore binding on the tribunals (see Hepple and O'Higgins, 1976, p 67, in their interpretation of the law (the *facts* could, in other words, lead to different judgements). The relative novelty or youth of the tribunals and the few appeals so far heard and decided therefore helps to account for the very real difficulties experienced in making forecasts about the likely outcome of tribunal cases.

Further reading
On the current general requirement of 'the law' in relation to contracts, see Hepple and O'Higgins (1976); an alternative is Rideout (1976)

A more historical perspective is provided by Wedderburn (1971).

On the principles involved in contract see Kahn-Freund (1977) and Fox (1974)

Textbooks such as Hepple and O'Higgins (1976) or McGlynn (1977), tend to summarize the position arrived at by the date of writing, but because of the newness of this field, they can go out of date very quickly on Court and tribunal interpretations. What might prove to be major and important decisions are often reported in non-law journals, as for example, by *Personnel Management* from time to time, but particular circumstances may require more detailed knowledge possessed only by legal practitioners or by managers who deliberately seek to keep up to date. It is therefore necessary for those in management confronted with the necessity of taking decisions in these matters to keep up to date with the main decisions taken by tribunals in their interpretation of what is requisite under statutory or delegated legislation. There are four main series of law reports in the employment field: Knight's Industrial Reports (now called Managerial Law), Industrial Tribunal Reports (HMSO), Industrial Court Reports (now called Industrial Cases Reports) and Industrial Relations Law Reports. Periodicals of relevance are *Industrial Law Journal, Industrial Relations Review and Report, Industrial Relations Legal Information Bulletin* and *Incomes Data Briefs.* The Department of Employment Gazette is the most useful source of statistical data on the use of and outcomes from cases before the industrial tribunals, information relevant to the assessment of the degrees of risk involved, either that such litigation will be employed or that penalties of certain types will be applied.

Appendix A: constraints on personnel decisions imposed by legislation

Introduction

A number of pieces of legislation, dating chiefly from 1963, have sought and served to change the status of the employee and/or the worker *vis à vis* the employer. In consequence, many areas of personnel policy are now constrained by law, and whatever may be considered good personnel policy in certain areas must develop from a foundation of legal right for the employee/worker and legal duty for the employer. In this appendix, the main legislative provisions which offer such constraints are identified and outlined. It is however necessary to refer to both the legislation itself and the cases decided by the industrial tribunals and the Employment Appeal Tribunal from time to time, or to obtain legal advice in relation to particular cases, before embarking upon a course of action. The purpose of this summary is to provide a guide to the territory, and to do so in a way which will allow later chapters to refer briefly to the constraints which it is necessary to bring into the discussion.

This discussion is organized under the main headings of recruitment of personnel, servicing on-going employment, and termination of employment. The legislation referred to includes:

Disabled Persons (Employment) Act 1944
The Contracts of Employment Act 1972
The Race Relations Act 1976
The Sex Discrimination Act 1975
The Employment Protection Act 1975
The Industrial Training Act 1964
Employment and Training Act 1973
The Payment of Wages Act 1960
The Equal Pay Act 1970

The Health and Safety at Work etc Act 1974
The Trade Union and Labour Relations Acts 1974-6
The Redundancy Payments Act 1965

Recruitment

In principle, an employer is free to choose whomsoever he wishes for employment, provided he does so on criteria of the person best fitted or suited for that employment. In two main categories of criteria there is a modification of this unrestricted right: in the first place choice on criteria of sex or marital status, under the provisions of the Sex Discrimination Act 1975, could be held to be unlawfully discriminatory; in the second place choice on criteria related to the race or ethnic origin of the person would, under the provisions of the Race Relations Act 1976, also be unlawfully discriminatory.

These two pieces of legislation seek to banish the use of sex, race or ethnic origin as criteria of choice of employees for employment, promotion, training or any other benefit or advantage in connection with work. Primarily, the employer is enjoined to avoid recruiting, selecting or employing persons in such a fashion that one sex or certain racial or ethnic groups are denied opportunity or treatment accorded to the other sex or to other racial or ethnic groups. In respect of the recruitment process, therefore, the employer must ensure that he avoids *direct* discrimination by advertising for one sex rather than another or for one ethnic group rather than another; by short-listing interviewing or testing one rather than the other; and/or by offering a job on terms which discriminate between these categories. He must also ensure that such discrimination is avoided as between married persons and single persons, except that he may specifically treat married persons *more* favourably than single ones (but not less favourably).

This kind of requirement is for the time being somewhat tempered by the possibility that the employer may still ask for qualifications for the job (provided that he can demonstrate their necessity) which are more likely to be possessed by men than by women. In the longer run, however, the other provisions of the Sex Discrimination and Race Relations Acts which are aimed at ensuring comparability of opportunity for education, training and qualification will tend to reduce this inherent disadvantage which may be suffered at the moment by women or by other groups. Certain occupations, very limited in number, are exempted from these provisions in the Sex Discrimination Act—mainly those where sex is required for authenticity (as in modelling or acting) or is desirable for reasons of public taste and decency (as with lavatory attendants) or where it would be unreasonable for the employer to provide facilities for both sexes in situations which have previously been single sex (as in the provision of sleeping or other accommodation on construction camps or lighthouses).

The employer must also bear in mind that, in situations in which the treatment actually accorded to persons may be non-discriminatory in itself, the consequences of the treatment may still be *indirectly* discriminatory. In connection with recruitment, for example, the proportions of the two sexes in a job or occupational category may be such as to discriminate against women, possibly because women are less likely to have the necessary qualifications or experience, and it will become progressively more important for the employer to be able to show that this result is not the result of discrimination. In both areas, race and sex, it will be necessary for the employer to develop positive employment policies, which, rather than accepting the world as it is, seek to effect changes which will demonstrate greater equality of both opportunity and treatment of the different sexes and the different races (cf Wainright, 1970).

Under the Contracts of Employment Act 1972 (as amended), it is necessary to issue to almost all new employees, within 13 weeks of starting, a summary of the terms and conditions of the appointment; in some cases, this will accompany the letter of appointment.

This duty is imposed on the employer for all new employees, except:

1 Where the employee is normally employed, or expected to be employed for less than 16 hours in one week (although if an employee started in this category and subsequently changed so that he began normally to work for 16 hours or more, the provision would apply from the date of the change) or less than eight hours and five years continuous service
2 Where the employee is hired for a task not expected to last for more than 12 weeks and does not in fact last for more than this period
3 Where he or she is a registered dock worker engaged on dock work
4 Where he or she is employed in the Merchant Navy or in the fishing fleets
5 Where the employee is a Crown servant
6 Where the employee normally works for his employer abroad and is employed abroad
7 Where the employee is husband or wife of the employer.

There are three ways in which the employer might discharge this duty:

(a) Where the terms of the employment contract are normally

expressed in written form, and the individual employee is either given a copy or has access to it in the course of his employment, this will meet the requirement provided that it contains the information detailed in (c) below.

(b) Where the particulars referred to in (c) below are contained in some document or documents which the individual employee has reasonable access to and reasonable opportunities to read in the course of his employment, the employer may refer the employee to this document(s) for any or all the particulars in (c) below.

(In both these cases, it will also be necessary to issue the note referred to below and to keep the documents up to date.)

(c) Otherwise, the employer is required to give the employee, within 13 weeks of his engagement, a written statement which will contain the following information (varied only by the 'reference' provision in (b) above):

1 The identity of the parties to the employment contract

2 The date on which the employment began (and, if it is a contract for a fixed term, the date on which it will end)

3 A statement as to whether "any employment with a previous employer counts as part of the employee's continuous period of employment with him, and if so, specifying the date on which the continuous period of employment began"

4 "The title of the job which the employee is employed to do" (a generic title might be employed instead of a specific one unless tribunals rule otherwise)

5 The terms of the contract as at a specified date not more than one week before the date on which the statement is given:
   (i)   the scale or rate of remuneration or the method of calculating remuneration
   (ii)   the intervals at which remuneration is paid (ie whether weekly, monthly or by some other period)
   (iii) any terms and conditions relating to hours of work (including any terms and conditions relating to normal working hours)
   (iv)   any terms and conditions relating to
          —entitlement to holidays, including public holidays, and holiday pay (the particulars given being sufficient to enable the employee's entitlement, including any entitlement to accrued holiday pay on termination of employment to be precisely calculated)
          —incapacity for work due to sickness or injury, including any provisions for sick pay
          —pensions and pension schemes (provided that these are

not provided for in or under another Act of Parliament) and including a statement in most cases as to whether a contracting out certificate is in force

(v) the length of notice which the employee is obliged to give and entitled to receive to determine his contract of employment. If the employment contract is for a fixed term, the date when the contract is due to expire must also be stated.

If there are no particulars to be entered under any of these headings or sub-headings, this fact is to be stated.

This must be accompanied by a note which:

1 Specifies "any disciplinary rules applicable to the employee", or refers to a document which is reasonably accessible to the employee and which specifies such rules
2 Indicates to whom (person or committee) an employee "can apply if he is dissatisfied with any disciplinary decision relating to him"—in other words, to whom he appeals—and what steps are open to him beyond the first level of appeal. (This need not embrace matters relating to health or safety at work)
3 Specifies the person (or position) to whom an employee can take a grievance relating to his employment to seek redress and the manner in which the application for redress shall be made
4 Either explains the steps consequent upon any such application or refers to a reasonably accessible document which explains those steps. (It is possible that there may not be any consequent steps within the organization, but compliance with the Code of Industrial Practice may require a grievance procedure to be negotiated).
(See Contracts of Employment Act 1972; Trade Union and Labour Relations Act 1974; Employment Protection Act 1975)

If after the date to which the statement relates there is a change in the terms to be included (under (c) above) or referred to (under (b) above) in the statement, the employer has the duty to inform the employee of the change by a written statement; if the written statement is not left with the employee it has to be preserved and the employer must ensure that the employee has reasonable access to it and can read it in the course of his employment. This duty must be discharged within one month of the change being introduced. It is met if the employer uses the method (b) above and indicates initially that any changes will be entered into the document within one month of being introduced. It is also met if the method (a) above is used and if written statements of variations in the contract are issued to the employee from time to time as they are made.

Originally, penalties were provided in the Contracts of Employment Act for failure to comply without reasonable excuse but these were removed in 1965. Failure to comply with these requirements in respect of information opens up the possibility of complaint by the individual to the industrial tribunal. The powers of the tribunal in the event of finding the complaint well founded are to state what the statement ought to have included, the conclusion as to what 'ought' to be the case being determined by reference to the express or implied terms of the individual's contract.

Servicing the employment

Whilst the individual is in the employment of the enterprise, the employer has certain duties to perform, but he is likely to accept much wider obligations to secure the desired level of contribution and the willing loyalty of the employee.

The duties imposed by legislation focus essentially on the payment and amount of wages, the latter concerning certain categories only, and on the health and safety of employees whilst in his employ or on the employer's premises. Beyond that, the employer will seek to provide the right levels of both monetary incentive and of personal development or advancement in order to secure contribution and loyalty. In addition he will also seek to establish procedures which will order the relationship between himself and the individual employee, particularly on works rules.

The payment of wages

The payment of wages to employees is governed by two main pieces of legislation. First, the Truck Act of 1831 remains in force and prevents the payment of the workmen in goods or in kind except under special circumstances, and prevents the deduction of amounts from the workmen's wages for bad workmanship, for instance. This meant that for large classes of workmen payment had to be made in coin of the realm. Secondly, the Payment of Wages Act 1960 made it possible to pay these classes of workmen by cheque, postal order or money order rather than in coin of the realm.

The employer is allowed to pay in one of these ways only if the employee concerned makes a request for such payment in writing. The request from the employee may stipulate that he wishes the whole of his wages or only part to be paid in this fashion. The request will lapse if the employer does not answer the request within two weeks of receiving it; it would not then be possible for the employee to be paid in one of these ways unless the employee provided a separate request for payment. Just as the employee is allowed to exercise his own discretion in this matter, so too the employer is not bound to make payments in the ways indicated simply because he has a request to do so from his employee. He may or may not do so but can stipulate that he will only do so at some date in the future (when he will have to notify the employee in writing) or he may give notice in writing to the employee that he refuses to accede to the request.

The employer must ensure that all cheques are made payable to the employee to whom the wages are due by name, or to his order: all payments into a bank account must be to the credit of the account specified in the written request. If either of these conditions is not fulfilled the employer is in breach of the Act. Similarly, the employer must not make any charge for wages paid in any one of the ways stipulated in the Act. Once both parties have agreed in writing to make payments in one of these ways, the arrangement will hold good until either party ends it by written notice. If notice is given it must amount to four weeks, although this period may be shortened at the mutual agreement of the two parties.

There are special provisions for paying wages to employees who are away from work through illness or personal injury, or through reasons connected with their work, who would otherwise be paid in cash. Provided the employee does not give notice to his employer that he does not want to be paid other than by cash, the employer is permitted under the Act to pay wages by postal order or money order (but not in any other ways allowed by the Act), even if he does not have the written request of the employed persons. Where the employer takes advantage of this permission under the Act, he must still meet the conditions about giving full particulars in the pay statement. Provision is also made in the Act for the individual employee, if he or she wishes, to authorize someone else (such as a trade union official, a lawyer, a bank manager, a relative or a friend) to act on the employee's behalf in either making or cancelling a request for payment of wages in one of the ways allowed by the Act.

Certain rights under the Truck Acts and the Payment of Wages Act of 1960 are generalized by the EP Act Ss 81-4. The employee must ge given a written itemized pay statement before, or at the time when he is paid. The items required are:

(a) The *gross* amount of wages or salary (not component bonuses or commissions, for example)
(b) The amounts of any *variable* deductions where pay varies (such as income tax, graduated pension and national insurance contributions)
(c) The amounts of any fixed deductions (eg trade union contributions), which duty may be discharged either by listing the fixed deductions on the pay statement or by issuing annually

a standing complete statement of fixed deductions showing amounts of each, the purpose of each, and the intervals at which deduction is made, and by giving written notice of amendments during the year if necessary

(d) The net amount of wages or salary payable (and if this net amount is paid in different ways, the amount and method of each part payment).

The main effect of this is to create the concept of an 'unnotified deduction' which an industrial tribunal can require the employer to repay (on substantiated complaint) up to a maximum of 13 weeks at the amount 'unnotified'.

Only in the Wages Councils and Statutory Joint Industrial Council trades and industries are there statutory minimum wages to be paid by the employer. But such statutory minima can also apply where the employer is a contractor to supply central or local government bodies with goods or services (under the Fair Wages Resolution) and where a trade union has secured an award from the CAC under the provisions of the Employment Protection Act governing the extension of terms and conditions of employment under S 98 and Schedule 11. A similar consequence for the employer can also arise under certain circumstances in connection with claims for recognition or information disclosure by an independent trade union to the CAC, under Ss 16 and 21 of the same Act.

Payment for lay-off and medical suspension
Although the duty to provide work is not normally laid upon the employer by the express or implied terms of the contract of employment, there are two circumstances in which the law (the Employment Protection Act, 1975, Ss 22–33) gives the employee a right to payment when he cannot work for a reason which is outside his control.

First, the Employment Protection Act gives to all employees with four weeks' continuous employment, a right against the employer to payment of up to five days' normal pay (up to a maximum of £6 per day) during any three month period (calculated from 1 February, 1 May etc) if and when they are laid off *for a whole day*.

The employee must meet certain requirements in the circumstances:

(a) he must have at least four weeks' continuous service when the lay-off occurs
(b) he must be laid off for all the working hours normally worked on a normal working day
(c) he must be laid off because of a temporary redundancy or other event which makes it impossible for the employer to provide him

with work, other than a trade dispute involving his employer or an associated employer
(d) he must not have refused an offer of alternative employment which was suitable for him to undertake in all the circumstances
(e) he must comply with all reasonable requirements imposed by the employer to ensure that he is available to work if work should become available.

Importantly, lack of supplies (eg raw materials or components) because of a dispute in another company's plant, or lack of fuel or power for reasons beyond the control of the employer, do not absolve the employer from duty to pay guarantee payments: the rationale is that if the fault does not lie with the employee or his fellow employees payment is due.

Where a collective agreement provides for payment for lay-off, it usually provides for a guaranteed *weekly* payment: now the employee is able to choose which scheme, contractual or statutory, is most beneficial to him, and the employer is not permitted to choose the cheapest of two parallel schemes. He can however attempt to arrange any lay-offs to minimize cost to himself.

Provision is made for *all* parties to a collective agreement or wages order to apply to the Secretary of State for exemption from this requirement of guarantee payments. There is a proviso that the collective agreement must meet the criteria relating to appeals against non-payment, and it is likely that the terms of collective agreement will have to be no less favourable to the employee than the statutory requirements before exemption will be granted.

An employee who feels he has not received the whole or part of his entitlement on this score will be able to present a complaint to an industrial tribunal within three months: the tribunal is empowered to order the employer to make the appropriate payment if the complaint is found well-founded. Whilst an employer probably needs to keep records of guarantee payments to groups of employees (eg departments affected) he probably does not need to keep separate records for each individual (assuming always that records of sickness, holidays, and so on are separately maintained).

This part of the Act is considered by the Government to be more costly to employers generally than all the other provisions of the Act together—by an estimated factor of four. The incidence of this cost will however vary appreciably from industry to industry, according to the lay-off policies and practices associated with them.

Secondly the same Act (S 29) gives the employee who is suspended from work on medical grounds—because of a requirement imposed under legislation or a Code of Practice—a right to payment by the employer whilst suspended for a period not exceeding 26 weeks. To qualify, the employee must have been employed for four weeks, must be fit (in health) to work, must not have unreasonably refused an offer of alternative work which is suitable, and must comply with any reasonable requirements of the employer designed to ensure that his services continue to be available. In the event of non-payment, the individual may complain to an industrial tribunal and, if the complaint is found to be substantiated, the tribunal may order the payment which it finds due to the individual. An employer who hires a replacement for the individual during the period of suspension may, if he informs that replacement that he or she is replacing someone on medical suspension and if he dismisses that replacement so that the suspended person may resume employment, so dismiss the replacement for good cause.

Discrimination in payments to different categories
Just as discrimination in hiring, promoting and firing between sexes and races has been outlawed, so too has discrimination in the fixing of amounts of payment for the same or essentially similar work. Whatever may be said in the individual contract or in the collective agreement, therefore, recent statutes require non-discrimination in the actual payment. From the end of December 1975 the Equal Pay Act and the Sex Discrimination Act have begun a process of ending discrimination between men and women in employment (and in certain other areas like education and training) and the two Acts must now be read together. In broad terms, the Equal Pay Act attempts to eliminate discrimination in pay and other terms and conditions of employment, whilst the Sex Discrimination Act tries to develop "a common strategy and philosophy, a parity of treatment, approach and attitude" not only in respect of contractual terms, but also in "the whole range of intangible non-contractual relationships which arise when interviews take place, advertising occurs, selection is finally determined in the case of applications for jobs, promotion and the rest" (House of Commons, Official Report Standing Committee 8, 1 May 1975).

Discrimination against both men and women is covered, and so too is discrimination against married persons in favour of single ones. The Sex Discrimination Act applies to all employees, of whatever age, in Great Britain, unless excepted by the Act (and there are few exceptions) and to all employers with six or more employees (including any in associated employers' establishments), partnerships of six or more, trade unions, employers' associations, educational, training and qualifying bodies, advertisers, employment agencies and labour contractors.

The main intention in the Sex Discrimination Act is that women generally, married women particularly and also married men, shall have comparable opportunities to work and in work as the other categories of employee. As time passes this will acquire more teeth as more women are admitted to training, re-training and qualifying courses, but for the moment the employer has some chance to continue the present pattern, where his establishment is fully manned (or womanned!), where it would be unreasonable to provide special facilities for women, and where he can show that a discriminatory qualification is necessary to the job.

As this Act applies to the servicing of employment, it focuses particularly upon the access women are permitted (and particularly married women) to training courses, promotion and transfer and benefits, facilities and services. In many cases it will be necessary to review practices and procedures relating to issues like travelling expenses, flexible hours, clothing allowances, opportunities to work overtime and even provision of hairdressing facilities, as well as the more obvious questions of selection for training and promotion.

The main intention of the Equal Pay Act is to improve the terms and conditions of employment of women at work by bringing them to parity with those of men. The Act aims to do this in one of two ways:

(a) by establishing the right of the individual woman to equal treatment when she is employed either on work of the same or a broadly similar nature to that of men or in jobs which, although different from those carried out by men, have nevertheless been given the same value as men's jobs under a job evaluation exercise

(b) by providing for the Central Arbitration Committee to remove discrimination in collective agreements, employers' pay structures and statutory wages orders where these contain any provisions applying specifically to men only or to women only, and which have been referred to it. It is provided that where the individual woman employee has a disagreement with her employer on her rights under the Act, she may refer the complaint to an industrial tribunal for a decision.

According to Section 1 (1), (4) and (5) of the Act, as an individual a woman has a right to equal treatment with men when she is employed on like work, which is defined as work which is the same or broadly similar in nature to that carried out by men; or in a job which has been given an equal value to men's jobs under a job evaluation scheme, even though the nature or content of the job itself may be different. This right is granted to women in particular but also to men. The Act also provides for making comparisons to determine whether this right has been infringed. The woman may draw comparisons with men or with men's jobs only where the men in question are employed by her employer or by an associated employer; even then the comparison would only be permitted if the terms and conditions of employment of the men in different locations or establishments of the same or associated employer were themselves common. If, for example, an employer had three separate factories and the men's terms and conditions in the three factories were all different, the woman who felt grieved about her terms and conditions of employment in comparison with those of men would only be able to draw comparisons with men in her own particular employing establishment and not across the three plants belonging to the one employer. It should be noted that for this purpose people are considered to be employed at an establishment, if they are employed either in the establishment or from the establishment (for example, travelling salesmen would be employed from an establishment in this sense. (S 1(6)(b)). A ship is also treated as an establishment for this purpose, but certain restrictions do apply to the provisions of the Act in relation to people employed on aircraft, hovercraft or ships registered in Great Britain but employed wholly outside the country.

The Act seeks to define what is meant by the same or broadly similar work. Work qualifies in this way only if the differences between the woman's work and the work of men occur sufficiently often or if the nature and extent of the differences are themselves appreciable. If the differences between the work carried out by men and women are of practical importance in relation to the terms and conditions of employment, under S 1(4) the work would not be regarded as broadly similar. Thus if there were only three jobs in a factory, and men and women were employed interchangeably on one job but men were employed on job Y at a higher rate of pay, there would be no possibility of the woman comparing her job with job Y because the difference between job X and job Y would have practical importance in relation to the terms and conditions of employment (that is the difference is recognized in higher pay).

Where job evaluation has been carried out and the terms and conditions of employment are based on the results of job evaluation, and a job carried out by women has been given an equal value with a job carried out by men, in those circumstances both the men and the women concerned must receive the same terms and conditions of employment (S 1(1)(b)). For example, where a job evaluation using a points evaluation method had been carried out before the Act came into effect, and the number of points allocated to a woman's job equalled the number of points given to a man's job, the woman would have a claim to the same terms and conditions of employment as the man doing a different job, but which had been evaluated with the same number of points. The Act also makes it possible for a woman to claim the same terms and conditions of employment as the man when a job evaluation has been carried out and has given a different value to the women's work; but where this has come about because the job evaluation was "made on a system setting different values for men and women on the same demand under any heading". This means that many traditional job evaluation exercises would not by themselves allow an employer to escape the implications of the Act in raising the pay and other conditions of employment of women, simply because the results of the job evaluation had produced different pay rates. Where it could be shown that the job evaluation itself was carried out with the intention of producing a different rate for men and women, the woman would have a claim for improved treatment. In Section 1(5) the Act requires the results of a job evaluation exercise carried out in this way to be adjusted so that, in so far as two jobs make the same demand of a worker, they would be evaluated equally. It should be made clear that the Act by itself makes no requirement for job evaluation to be done; these comments relate only to job evaluation which for other reasons has been carried out in the organization.

Where a woman feels that she has a case she may refer her complaint to an industrial tribunal, which is empowered to deal with it. If the tribunal finds the complaint well founded, it may award arrears of remuneration (for up to two years before the date on which she referred the claim to the tribunal) and may also award damages in respect of non-cash benefits up to the same limit. There is no claim of arrears before 29 December 1975. It is also open both to an employer to refer the case to a tribunal and also for the Secretary of State for Employment to do so where it appears that a woman has a claim to equal treatment but that it is not reasonable to expect her to take the steps to make the reference herself. It is also provided that, where an equal pay question comes up in another Court, where an industrial tribunal is competent to decide the issue the Court may refer the question to a tribunal.

It does not follow from this that no man may be paid more than a woman even when both are engaged on the same or broadly comparable work. Where this is so, it will be for the employer to show that the advantage enjoyed by the man (or the woman) is enjoyed because it is 'genuinely due to a material difference (other than the difference of sex)' between the woman's case and the man's. It is not, for example, uncommon to pay people differential rates because of length of service, level of output or for reasons connected with merit.

Provided that such differences in payment do not discriminate between one sex and the other but simply between one individual worker and another regardless of sex, the Act does not require that the payment levels be brought into line. It follows that, if a woman has longer service with the employer than a man engaged in broadly comparable work, the system must allow her to receive higher payment. The principle upheld in the legislation is that the system of payment must not distinguish between men and women as classes; any difference that does exist must be genuinely due to material difference between the individual man's case and the individual woman's case. The individual rights granted by the Equal Pay Act apply to all persons employed under a contract of service or of apprenticeship, or a contract personally to execute any work or labour. The main exception concerns employment wholly or mainly outside Great Britain and the Act does not extend to Northern Ireland, but it does apply to workers of all ages.

It is not a requirement that a woman shall have terms and conditions of employment exactly equal to a man's. Certain matters are excepted, particularly where the employment of women is governed by legislation regulating the employment of women as, for example, under the Factories Acts; the Act does not preclude the unequal treatment of women in the terms and conditions of employment they may enjoy on the birth or expected birth of a child. Equal treatment is not required on terms and conditions concerning retirement, marriage or death or to any provision made in connection with retirement, marriage or death. The Act therefore carries implications for the statement of further particulars of the Contract of Employment which the employer is required to issue to his employees within 13 weeks of their engagement; it also carries important implications for servicing the individual's employment during which he is employed (see Mepham 1974). Furthermore in the few cases which have so far been taken to appeal on the Equal Pay Act, it is clear that permitted variations will be defined in a narrow fashion rather than a broad one, and this might be predicted to apply to the interpretation made in the Sex Discrimination Act, partly at least because conformity with Common Market practice here may force stricter interpretations than might originally have been intended in domestic legislation (see Wallington, 1978).

Interruption of the contract of employment
The duty of the employee to make himself available for work when required by the employer is modified in the Employment Protection Act in two main ways, both of which allow the individual employee in defined circumstances to interrupt the continuity of the contract

without breaking it. Previously this was justifiable only on medical or trade dispute grounds, and/or with the prior permission of the employer. Now it is extended to cover, specifically, females who become pregnant whilst in employment, and a number of other categories of employee who are given a right to time off from work for certain categories of activity. The employer is likely in these circumstances to develop new codes, in consultation with the trade unions, to govern the administration of these new rights.

The most important of these, applying only to female employees, are the three rights on maternity pay, maternity leave and to avoid dismissal merely on the ground of pregnancy.

(a) Where a woman employee becomes pregnant and wishes to continue working, it is likely to prove difficult for the employer to dismiss her unless she is manifestly incapable of carrying on her job because of the pregnancy, or unless her continued employment would cause contravention of a duty or restriction imposed by or under any enactment. (Pregnant women are subject to a restriction of this sort in the Ionizing Radiations (Unsealed Radioactive Substances) Regulations, 1968, but broader restrictions may apply under the Health and Safety at Work Act).

Furthermore, if a suitable vacancy exists in the employment unit, the employer might be under a duty to offer such a vacancy to a pregnant employee or face a claim for unfair dismissal. The Act lays down criteria of suitability and, on the face of it, many vacancies might theoretically fall within this definition. This also applies where a pregnant woman is not permitted to return after maternity leave. She could similarly claim unfair dismissal.

The only real defence open to the employer here is that the job has become redundant in the interval—but this will patently not be so if he hires a permanent or temporary replacement for her. The question of a suitable vacancy is relevant here as in the case of a woman becoming pregnant but, in the case of a woman returning, the employer has a duty to seek a suitable vacancy, not only in his own enterprise, but in associated employers' enterprises as well. Even if a suitable vacancy does not exist, it may be preferable, in the face of a potential claim to an industrial tribunal, to offer the returning employee the least unsuitable vacancy and allow her to make the decision, rather than the employer doing so (see Rubenstein 1975).

(b) A pregnant employee acquires a right to six weeks' maternity pay (which the employer may recover from a new Maternity Fund to be financed by higher employer's National Insurance contributions) provided:

(i) that she has not resigned before the 11th week before the expected confinement (so that it will apply even if she is fairly dismissed before this date, and even if she is not actually at work immediately before the 11th week, provided that the contract of employment remains in existence)

(ii) that she has two years' continuous employment calculated back from the beginning of the 11th week before the expected date of confinement (with the same qualification as in brackets above)

(iii) that she notifies the employer orally (or in writing if requested to do so by the employer) at least three weeks before her absence begins (or as soon thereafter as is practicable if that is not reasonably practicable) that she will be absent because of pregnancy or confinement.

Pay is to be calculated at the rate of 90 per cent of a normal week's pay less the statutory maternity allowance (whether or not she is entitled to it), and may be paid as a lump sum at the 11th week mentioned or at the normal payment interval over the six weeks following (not at the end) and may well be taxed as normal pay.

(c) A woman has the new right to return to work for up to 29 weeks following a confinement, and qualifies for this maternity leave in the same way as for maternity pay. The woman must give the employer at least one week's notice of intention to return, but both employer and employee may postpone the date of recommencement for four weeks, the employer for four weeks for any reason, and the woman for four weeks for medical reasons. This in effect allows a basic 40 weeks of maternity leave which can be increased by postponement to 44 weeks.

The right is to return to the job "in which she was employed under the original contract of employment and on terms and conditions not less favourable than those which would have been applicable to her if she had not been so absent". But job is defined as meaning "the nature of the work which she is employed to do in accordance with her contract and the capacity and place in which she is so employed". If she was employed as a sales assistant she must return as a sales assistant, but not necessarily to the same department: if she was employed as a millinery sales assistant, however, she must return as a millinery sales assistant.

"Terms and conditions not less favourable than those which would have been applicable to her if she had not been so absent" means: "as regards seniority, pension rights and other similar rights, that the period or periods of employment prior to the employee's absence shall be regarded as continuous with her employment following that absence"—for these rights the period of absence does not count. But for purposes of statutory rights (redundancy, notice, unfair dismissal award entitlements) the period of absence does count (under Schedule 16). Two different standards of continuous service thus exist.

Two standards also exist in respect of these statutory rights to return to work after pregnancy, and any rights given by a collective agreement, but the Act requires (Schedule 3) that these rights may not be exercised seperately but rather must be composited. If a collective agreement gives an employee a right to return up to two years from confinement, even if not in the same grade as before, she may now elect to return in the period up to two years (ie to elect her contractual right in this respect) but also elect to return to work in her original job (ie to elect her statutory right in this respect), and this composite right may be enforced through the Industrial Tribunals.

The only other possible defence is that something has happened to the woman herself in the interval to make her employment undesirable, for example conviction of a felony. Such circumstances are likely to be exceptional and will be affected by the recommendations of the ACAS Code on disciplinary rules and procedures.

The general problem about maternity provisions in the Act is the uncertainty which it generates for the employer: will a pregnant woman exercise her right to return? Who knows? How then decide what to do about covering her job during her absence?

—Termination interviews between the pregnant woman and a manager to assess the likelihood of return may help. These can ensure that the woman knows what her rights are in the matter, what child-minding facilities might be available to her after 40 weeks, what the enterprise policy on absence is (in case she is forced to be absent to mind the child etc) and thus help both parties to come to a realistic assessment of the possibilities of return.
—By individual or collective negotiation of contracts it is possible for the employer to exert some influence on the scope he haa for offering vacancies to the returning employee: the wider the terms of the individual contract, the greater scope for offering vacancies on her return.
—Hiring of temporary replacements is the most likely device to be adopted where special skills are not at a premium. A replacement can be hired on a temporary basis, and the contract will state that he or she will be dismissed when the woman returns

from maternity leave—this being admitted as a 'substantial reason' for dismissal in the Act. If there were to be suitable vacancies for such a temporary employee the employer might still have to offer them or face a claim for unfair dismissal. This would, however, only apply where the temporary had accumulated 26 weeks' service: a fixed term contract of 25 weeks may well become a common device to overcome this difficulty.

—In many employment circumstances, the employer may simply treat maternity leave as any other kind of absence, and muddle along with other staff covering for the woman on maternity leave.

The right to time off, not related to pregnancy and confinement, applies generally to any employee for purposes of performing certain public duties or when he is under notice of dismissal and for the purpose of finding alternative employment and/or arranging training, to any employee who is a union member for purposes of taking part in certain trade union activities, and to union members who are lay officials or representatives for purposes of engaging in industrial relations activities or of undergoing training for them. Such periods of time off will not be taken as breaking the contract of employment but there are conditions which apply distinctly in each case:

(a) Shop stewards and other officials of a trade union recognized by the employer for collective bargaining purposes have a right to be permitted reasonable time off with pay during working hours to enable them to carry out their duties as officials which are concerned with industrial relations affecting their employer (or associated employer) and to enable them to undergo industrial relations training.

(b) Any union member (provided the union is recognized) has a right to reasonable time off to take part in union activities or to represent the union, but the Act imposed no obligation on the employer to pay for time off for taking part in trade union activities.

As it was enjoined to do by S 6 of the Employment Protection Act, the ACAS has produced a Code of Practice covering time off for lay officials and trade union members, which became operative on 1 April 1978, on which date the relevant sections of the Act (Ss 57 and 58) also came into force.

This code suggests that "members should be permitted to take time off during working hours for such purposes as voting in union elections" . . . and to attend union meetings at times to be agreed which would involve least disruption of production (eg at the end of a working shift). In any agreement drawn up to guide such activities,

93

provision might be made for time off for other activities where member participation might lead to the development of "sound union structure at the workplace and effective communication and collective representation" (Code, p 3). Lay officials of the union are recognized to be in a special position in relation to trade union activities, and the Code therefore suggests that they might need more time off for attendance at union policy-making meetings and conferences and at other meetings of external bodies where the official may represent the union. This aspect, it is also suggested, should be the subject of agreement to offer guidance on both the time to be allowed off and on the kinds of activities which might be accorded relevance.

Otherwise, the Code suggests that officials should be allowed time off with pay, for industrial relations purposes, to engage in:

(a) collective bargaining with any level of management
(b) meetings with members called to inform them of the outcomes of negotiations or consultations with management
(c) meetings with other lay officials or full-time union officers to discuss business of an industrial relations nature
(d) interviews with and on behalf of union members on grievance and disciplinary matters
(e) appearing on behalf of constituents before an outside body on industrial relations matters
(f) explanations to new employees of the role of the union in the workplace industrial relations structure (Code, p 2).

In addition, given that the official needs training to perform his duties more satisfactorily, he should, it is recommended, be allowed time off with pay for initial basic training, arranged as soon after appointment as possible, and for subsequent training in specialist aspects of industrial relations where his duties change or where the situation changes to create a new need. The courses of training should be relevant to the industrial relations functions performed, and should be approved by the Trades Union Congress or the official's own union, but each course will probably have to be considered for this purpose on its merits because of the variations in need which are likely to exist. It is further recommended that management and the representatives of recognized unions should draw up their own Codes to guide decisions and conduct, in particular to cover the problems likely to arise where the activities in which the official wishes to engage might be construed as both industrial relations and trade union activity.

(c) Any employee has a right to time off to perform any specified public duty, including membership of a statutory tribunal, the magisterial bench, a local authority or the governing body of an educational establishment. The employer is not obliged to pay the employee for this time off. No code is to be published on this matter, and so the Act establishes the criteria of what is reasonable: this takes into account the time necessary to carry out the public duty, the time the employee has already had off for union duties or activities, the circumstances of the employer's business and the consequences for that business of the employee taking such time off.

The rights to time off for these reasons do not depend on any period of continuous service, although those related to trade union duties and activities apply only where the trade union concerned is recognized; none of these rights apply where the individual is working for less than 16 hours per week.

(d) Any employee who has more than two years' continuous service and who is given notice of dismissal for reasons of redundancy is given a right to reasonable time off at his basic rate of pay (excluding voluntary overtime) to seek other employment or to make arrangements for training to fit himself for another job (but not to undergo actual training).

All four of these 'time off' provisions, and that relating to pregnancy and confinement, thus allow the individual to interrupt the continuity of his service for specific and defined reasons. Together, they alter the 'conditions' of service to which employees (generally or in defined sub-categories, like union officials) are assumed to be subject.

Discipline and grievance
The 'control' exercised by the employer, mainly through the control of conduct whilst at work, or through 'discipline' is also now subjected to certain constraints and conditions. The employer remains responsible for disciplinary rules and for their application, but the ACAS Code of Practice on Disciplinary Practices and Procedures (1977) recommends practices and procedures which restrict the discretion of the employer and require their conformity to principles of equity and natural justice. (see below, pp 470–75). Because the employer is required under the Contracts of Employment Act 1972 to give new employees a statement on the disciplinary and grievance procedures, it is necessary for the employer to have such procedures but there is, as yet, no legal enjoinder that they must be developed jointly with the trade unions, even if this is the clear intention in the Code of Practice. The principle behind the requirement as it stands currently is that the disciplinary rules, and the penalties which might be attached to breach of them, should be certain and known to those

covered and affected by them, and it is this which represents the main new constraint upon the employer's power to 'control'.

Health and safety at work
The duty of the employer for health and safety has been established in common law and statute for many years, but its precise form has changed remarkably frequently, culminating in a major change with the Health and Safety at Work Act 1974. Health and safety have also been closely associated with the welfare function of the personnel department, although the interventions might be regarded as rather piecemeal.

In the past, the role of the personnel officer in health matters has frequently been confined to such actions as were necessary to secure attendance at work. A major part of the record keeping which went on in the department concerned absentee statistics, which were broken down into sickness absences or non-sickness absences. From here, the personnel officer came to police absenteeism and, when sickness benefit schemes were introduced by the employer, these too came into the department's purview and the monitoring role continued.

The statutory obligation to provide facilities for first aid at work was also administered by the welfare officer. Later, when nurses were brought on to the payroll of larger employers, this too became associated with the personnel department so that, when medical services began to appear in factories, the personnel department found itself providing the administration of this service too, using the services of a part-time or full-time medical practitioner. Eventually, the personnel manager often found himself dealing with the whole medical service; the advent of occupational health programmes further extended his range of activity.

This was perhaps not too far removed from what might be regarded as the mainstream of development from the original welfare function. The welfare/personnel officer was the obvious person in an organization to take note of the work of the Industrial Fatigue (later Health) Research Board in this country and the early Hawthorne investigations in America. He was expected to have a knowledge of the causal relationships between lighting, ventilation, noise, rest pauses and shift working patterns and the performance of the individual. In earlier years, as indeed Northcott's book *Personnel Management* strongly attests, this was seen as a major part of the health and welfare role of the personnel manager. More recently, these theories have become somewhat less fashionable although no less significant than they might have been earlier, and attention has therefore wandered from this area to much more specific policing arrangements in relation to either performance versus non-performance whilst at work, or of absence in relation to attendance. Over this period the personnel manager has tended to assume the role of the functional specialist within the organization who ensures either or both of two things: either that the employer complies with the statutory requirements on health and safety; or the establishment of good health and safety policies, often in association with the medical officer, within the organization which faces complex problems, for example, in advanced chemical technologies.

When Northcott was writing his textbook he was able to explain the policy of the progressive employer at that time on accident prevention. In his view, the personnel manager was a functional representative of the management who would seek, with the help of the medical officer, to remove all avoidable risks, help management to create in the minds of foremen a sense of responsibility, and develop among employees both the safety habit and a knowledge of the procedures and practices by which safety might be ensured. He then went on to detail the duties which might follow for the personnel manager arising out of this general statement of principle. One effect of the new legislation is to impose upon the employer a responsibility which is, if anything, greater than that indicated by Northcott as applicable to the progressive employer. Whether or not the personnel manager will be specifically charged with the health and safety function within the organization in future may be questioned, because of the sheer complexity of the duty which this new Act imposes. The personnel manager may well retain overall responsibility for health and safety. But if so, it is likely that he will have to be much more knowledgeable about a much more complex statute and set of regulations and codes than before.

In the 1960s and early 1970s a number of developments (such as the thalidomide episode in 1963, Aberfan in 1966 and the Flixborough disaster in 1974) focused public attention on the problems of coping with the safety consequences of the new technologies, whether technologies of product or of process. In 1970 the Robens Committee was set up to look at this whole question and its report in 1972 sought to establish a completely new approach to legislation which was eventually embodied in the new Act.

The Robens Committee argued that the previous statutory system suffered from three fundamental defects: first there was too much law; secondly, much of it was so badly structured as to make it difficult for those required to comply with it to understand it; and thirdly, there were too many different enforcement agencies with inspectorates for a number of totally separate purposes specified in the legislation. The Committee therefore sought to reverse the traditional approach to the regulation of health and safety at work. This new approach was fully accepted by the new Act which set up as its objectives:

first securing the health, safety and welfare of persons at work

secondly, protecting persons other than persons at work against risks to health or safety arising out of or in connection with the activities of persons at work

thirdly, controlling the keeping and use of explosives or highly inflammable or dangerous substances and preventing people from acquiring, possessing or illegally using such substances

fourthly, controlling the emission of noxious or offensive substances from any area.

The general principle enunciated by the Robens Committee was that responsibility for preventing industrial hazards and sickness should be pinned squarely on those who create them. This meant that where industry was developing new products and new processes, it should assume and retain responsibility not only for the safety of those who were employed in its establishment but also for the safety of those who might advertently or inadvertently be brought into contact with them. The new legislation sought to replace the existing statutes, and regulations made under those statutes on particular hazards, by a new and more positive approach to the problem in which general duties would be imposed upon employers and specific regulations would be made within that framework of general duty. The new legislation was designed to place on the employer the onus of running his business with due regard to the health and safety of those he employed and those with whom the establishment might establish some possible contact (as in the case of Aberfan).

Attention to health and safety may have been given in the past not only because of specific statutory provisions but also because the employer felt a moral obligation to do so. With the new Act, what was previously *good* practice (as distinct from merely mandatory under the law) has been brought within the framework of statutory duty, for the breach of which there is provision for an unlimited fine and/or two years' prison sentence. Prosecution may be begun even if no accident has occurred, and actions may be begun against the employer, occupier, owner etc, on the one part, against the employee who acts so as to risk or cause injury to himself or others, and against "anyone" who interferes with or misuses "anything provided in the interests of health, safety and welfare". The Act also recognizes that there might be both criminal and civil liability. As Mitchell summarizes the situation (1975): "anyone who after 1 April 1975 does not take such steps as are reasonably practicable to ensure the health, safety and welfare at work of each employee may be sentenced to an unlimited fine and/or two years imprisonment" and, as he points out, the word welfare which occurs here is nowhere defined in the Act.

The particular questions which arise for the personnel department are whether the enterprise has adequate policies, practices and rules to meet the requirements of the new Act, what should be done to ensure that employees do not breach these rules and how to deal with such breaches if and when they do occur.

The statutory duty upon the employer is clear: he must provide any safety equipment or appliances that may be required, together with such plant, materials and appliances that the individual might need to carry out his work. The employer must also ensure that all machinery is properly guarded and that the employee is not exposed to any unnecessary risk in carrying out his work. If the employee fails to take precautions specified by the employer, the employer may well be held liable in whole or in part if the employee is injured or suffers damage to his health as a result, if the employer is unable to show that he has used all reasonable persuasion and propaganda "to induce the employee to use any equipment provided or to so conduct himself as to avoid exposure to hazard."

Under the Act, the employer's civil liability for the safety of his employees is converted into a criminal responsibility, so it is important that the employer does not render himself guilty of any "consent", "connivance" or "neglect" which causes a breach of the Act. It is therefore incumbent upon the employer to persuade employees to take proper care of themselves. Even if they prefer not to use guards or equipment because this might interfere with their bonus earnings, because they find the equipment uncomfortable or clumsy or simply because they are lazy, it remains necessary for the employer to take every care to ensure that they will conform to company policies and practices on health and safety.

To meet the requirements of the Health and Safety at Work Act, recent writers on the subject have sought to provide a management checklist to ensure that the employer has a defence in cases where the employee contributes to his own accident or disease. The Industrial Society Guide to the Health and Safety at Work Act (1974) provides one. In his fuller treatment, Mitchell (1974) provides a much lengthier checklist, in which he seeks to provide defences not only for alleged breaches under the Health and Safety at Work Act but also against complaints of wrongful or unfair dismissal which might arise from action by an employer to attempt to ensure that employees conform to safety policy and practice within the company.

The employer must now take certain actions in order to fulfil his duties under the new legislation and, equally importantly, consider how he might do this without falling foul of other duties, such as the duty not to dismiss unfairly.

1 He must explain the manner in which plant or equipment is inteded to be worked and seek by all reasonable steps to ensure that the employee knows both how to use it and what the potential hazards are and how to reduce them
2 He must take steps to ensure that employees understand the provisions of the Act, both in respect of employers' (and occupiers' etc) duties and of employees' duties, even to the extent of providing specific training. The main duty imposed upon the *employee* is that of cooperating with the employer in the provision and maintenance of a healthy and safe working environment. It is likely that disciplinary codes will in future have to accommodate both rules and penalties consistent with this duty
3 He must communicate to employees information on all health and safety matters and state what health and safety policies and practices apply, and the names or designations of all with special responsibilities for (as in the case of safety officers) or concerns with (as in the case of trade union representatives on safety committees) health and safety
4 He must make provision for safety representatives appointed by recognized independent trade unions and, where a request from two such safety representatives is made, he must also provide for a safety committee with whom he must consult on health and safety matters, and whose help he must solicit in ensuring that health and safety policies and regulations are implemented (although such a committee is not given a statutory duty in any of these respects)
5 He must ensure that any employee breaking any rule or departing from any policy or practice is informed of this and requested to desist; in the case of repeated breaches or departures, the employer will be able to treat the matter as a disciplinary issue, although how it should then be handled will depend upon the disciplinary procedures in operation (see above pp 470–72)
6 He must provide for the full recording of both policies and programmes on safety, *and* of activities such as training consultation etc undertaken to ensure that the statutory duty is discharged. Any detected breaches of rules or departures from policy and practice together with subsequent action taken concerning them, should also be recorded.

These are likely to constitute reasonable steps in following the provisions of the new legislation, but differences in technology and situ-

100

ation may mean that more or fewer than those mentioned will be required to avoid liability.

Informing and training
The thrust of a good deal of this new legislation which affects the continuing relationship of the parties to the employment contract is that the employee shall be *informed* of terms and conditions, and relevant procedures and practices, which apply to him or her in that relationship. Thus the employee is to be informed of the nature of his contract and the terms and conditions which it contains; he is to be told what procedures exist for handling the employer's complaints about his conduct or competence and the employee's complaints about the employer's treatment of him; he has to be informed of the manner in which his pay packet is composed; and he has to be instructed in the general disciplinary rules and the health and safety rules and in any methods of operation which are relevant thereto. In most of these cases, the requirements of the law are satisfied if the individual is given a statement or reasonable access to one.

Nevertheless, the question remains of what constitutes adequate communication in these areas—in some of which, particularly those of health and safety, communication is important in its own right and regardless of the prescriptions of law. Even in the straightforward cases, the personnel practitioners are likely to see it as necessary to ensure that practices, rules and procedures are not merely provided in a written statement, but explained in oral communication, possibly as part of the induction process for new employees. In the other cases, this may need to be developed as a deliberate training programme.

Nevertheless, although the need for or desirability of training is frequently alluded to in the legislation which has already been mentioned, only in the Health and Safety at Work Act is relevant training made to form part of the employer's duty to employees. For the rest, even in transfers associated with, for example, pregnancy or the avoidance of redundancy, training is not imposed as a duty, although the legislation and the various codes of practice leave no doubt as to its desirability and its association with 'good industrial relations'. Part of the reason for this 'withholding' attitude in the legislation is that the strategy for training in Britain has been founded upon the principle of encouraging 'voluntary' responses by the manipulation of rewards and penalties upon the employer for his training activity or lack of it. Whilst training has figured as a part of the process of restructuring of British personnel management and industrial relations since the 1960s, it has developed within a 'permissive' rather than a 'mandatory' framework of legislation.

It is not to be doubted that training in and for industry was much neglected before the enactment of the Industrial Training Act of 1964. A White Paper in 1962 went so far as to link the failures and inadequacies of training with the general economic problems faced by the country in the post-war period: "Ever since the war, industry in this country has been short of skilled labour. This has usually been so, even in those parts of the country where the general demand for labour has been relatively small. There is no doubt that shortages of skilled labour have been an important factor in holding the rate of economic expansion . . ."

But in general shortages of skilled labour were the rule; action to improve the situation was urgently needed and that meant more training. But: "At its best the standard of training in this country is high; unfortunately this is by no means universal. Much is barely adequate and some definitely unsatisfactory." (Department of Employment, 1962.) The object must therefore be to increase the volume of training and improve its standards generally to bring up the average to the level of the best.

This was attempted by the Industrial Training Act of 1964, which in itself might be said to have heralded a new era of Government intervention in such affairs. From the time of the first world war, the Minister of Labour had power to provide training courses for the unemployed and the disabled. The Employment and Training Act of 1948 extended these powers by making it possible for the Minister to provide training courses for either those in unskilled categories who were willing to take up a skilled trade, or men in employment who might be helped by training to achieve more regular employment. The last of these required a joint application for assistance from the employer and workmen concerned, but the other powers were exercised at the discretion of the Minister himself (cf Young, 1968, chapter 1).

The 1964 Act clearly built upon the 1948 Act, using some of the notions which it contained as a basis for extension. But it introduced the important new principle that all employers, regardless of whether they provided any training or not, had to contribute to a fund to be used for training purposes. By what was in effect a payroll tax, all employers were henceforth required to contribute to the cost of training whether or not they felt the need to undertake training in their establishments. Behind this Act, lay the belief that everyone was equally likely to require training or re-training and that the costs should be evenly distributed throughout industry.

In comparison with approaches adopted in latter legislation on other matters, this Act of 1964 did not create a duty to provide training at the level of the establishment. It was not an Act to compel employers to engage in training activities whether they wanted to or not. Rather, it sought to manipulate the incentive/disincentive system as this applied to training: employers were free to evade training involvement but they would now do so only after considering what it would in any event cost them in levy against what, with training schemes, they might secure by way of grant. The small employer might still regard a training scheme as not worth the candle and rely upon training given in large undertakings to supply his future needs for trained manpower: but he would now have some firm indication of the cost of this dependence and this would be a real cost figure passing through his books. This was a good part of the rationale of the Act; the marginal increase in training activity which has apparently occurred since 1964 may well reflect the entry of a number of such employers into the training arena in order to get their levy back.

The Industrial Training Act empowered the Minister of Labour (now Secretary of State for Employment) to establish industrial training boards for any activities of industry or commerce and require him to appoint a Central Training Council to advise him on the exercise of his functions under the Act. The functions of the industrial training boards under this Act were:

(a) to provide or secure the provision of sufficient training courses and other facilities for employees in their respective industries
(b) to make recommendations about the providers, length, nature, standard and content of training for different occupations and about the further education to be associated with the training
(c) to pay grants to employers providing training of an approved standard either on their premises or by giving time off for training on approved courses
(d) to impose a levy on employers in their industry in order to carry out these functions, this to be achieved through a levy order made by the Minister on the advice of the board.

In reality, few industrial training boards provided courses, and most reliance has been placed upon securing training courses either in employers' or educational/training establishments. Boards vary in the extent to which they have actively researched the need in their industry for future manpower and to which they have used their power to authorize research into methods of training. Conditions attached to grants have also varied from board to board and through time; but generally employers who are willing to allow their employees time off to attend courses on a day release or sandwich course basis have been able to secure grants, as have those who provide their own courses in their own training establishments. Levies are normally expressed as a percentage of payroll (including for this purpose the emoluments of directors) but varied appreciably in their size from 0.5 per cent to 3.8 per cent in the period up to the implementation of the Employment and Training Act 1973. The Minister is empowered to obtain information from employers so that the levy may be correctly assessed and to make grants or loans to the boards to assist them in their work.

The Training Act and the training boards stimulated both greater interest and activity in the training field. The Government itself concluded that "the general levy/grant schemes provided an essential shock treatment which led to a major change in the attitude of large sections of British industry to systematic training", although it went on to say that it saw no reason why this should remain a permanent feature of the arrangements for training. Not only were the boards enabled to bring together about 5,000 staff, most of whom were directly concerned with training, but many firms were led to recruit and appoint training officers for the first time: in the middle 1960s the shortage artificially induced by the Act resulted in a considerable premium being placed on training officers' salaries. This in turn led to the recognition of the need to give more specific attention to the general problem of training training officers (see Central Training Council, 1966, and CTC, 1968).

An alternative view is that the Industrial Training Act produced more trainers and trainees over this period, although the quality of the training they provided or received varied appreciably. Certainly some of the training boards have done a great deal to improve the quality of training in their industries, in particular the Engineering ITB (see EITB, 1968). There can be less doubt about the truth of the other general conclusions reached by the Government's consultative document: that the boards have played a main part in "creating a new climate of interest in training on the part of the management". What remains in doubt is whether this increased interest is being expressed, either in terms of training personnel or training programmes, in a sensible and effective way.

Beginning in February 1972 with the publication of the Government's 'plan for discussion' under the title of *Training for the Future*, the whole operation of this Act was subjected to review. The outcome was the 1973 Employment and Training Act, which *inter alia* created a new kind of organization to run the whole manpower services of the country. From 1 January 1974 the Manpower Services Commission, made up of representatives of employers, trade unions and educationists, took over the whole oversight of the employment and training services which had previously come under the Department of Employment. It was equipped with two executive organizations, the Employment Service Agency (ESA), previously established within the Department, to run the employment exchanges element of the service, together with the professional and executive recruitment (PER) and the vocational guidance services; and the Training Services Agency (TSA), also first established within the Department, and responsible for co-ordinating the work of the industrial training boards and for running the Training Opportunities Scheme (TOPS). Although this Act merely gave a new direction to activities already being developed within the Department of Employment, it also promised to set the whole employment and training service on a more responsive basis in relation to industry (see DE *Gazette*, August 1973).

As this Act related to training, it established the relationship between the Secretary of State, the Commission and the Industrial Training Boards, leaving the power to establish or abolish a board or to vary its scope with the Secretary of State, who would act on the recommendation of the Commission. The appointment of assessors to attend board meetings previously exercised by the Secretary of State was passed to the Commission, although other Secretaries of State would continue to appoint assessors as appropriate (see DE *Gazette*, December 1973).

Apart from this, the major provision of the Act was to provide for exemption of certain firms from the levy grant system. Exemption was to apply in general to small firms and in particular to firms which, in the board's opinion, trained workers adequately. In those cases the enterprise concerned would be freed from the need to pay levy and to secure part or the whole of this back in grant; but it could still use the advisory services of the board, which would now be separately funded for the purpose. As the boards had developed in the intervening period, much of their most valuable work had been concerned with determining training need and adequate standards of training provision. The new Act encouraged the boards to continue in this role, which would provide the major foundation for the future work of the industrial training boards.

The duty which the boards had previously had to raise a levy was translated by the Act into a power to do so, although the Commission was given power to direct an industrial training board to submit levy proposals for its industry. To meet the criticism previously heard about the size of the levy in some industries, the Act placed an upper limit of 1 per cent of payroll in normal circumstances, but allowed the Secretary of State to retain the power to make a levy order above this limit subject to the approval of Parliament. This was seen as ensuring that all firms and not merely small ones would be able to free themselves from the complications of the levy/grant system or from the complication of transferring large sums of money at one date in the calendar only to receive them back at another date (see DE *Gazette*, August and December 1973).

The effect of this change in the legislative provision was therefore to reduce some of the bureaucracy which had crept into the previous system; at the same time, it was hoped that the same level of commitment to training would be maintained as had developed under the training board system, and that the quality of advice which could be made available to enterprises about their training programmes and activity would be continued. This has enabled the training boards to continue to develop their more systematic approach to the determination of training need and training provision at the enterprise level (see, for example, Ward and Bird, 1968; and Steers, 1966).

In effect, this more systematic approach has accomplished two things:

it has brought the training process out of the realms of by guess and by God conceptions and into those of systems theories and models; instead of training activity being conceived in and justified by faith, it can and is now developed within a framework of planned activity, emphasizing objective-setting, determination of appropriate means, guided implementation and control activity within a framework of a system model (cf Shone and Paterson, 1963; Buckley, 1967);

it has made it possible to integrate training activity *per se* with larger scale planning models; for example, within the model of manpower planning at the level of the society or of the enterprise, or within the corporate planning models now more widely employed in business and service organizations (cf Falk and Clark, 1966; Patten, 1971). It does not (or at least not yet) provide the individual employee with any 'right' to a quantity of training, nor the employer with any 'duty' to provide it; but in some circumstances, where it is not provided, the employee might be able to argue some other substantive case the more effectively before a tribunal.

Termination of employment
The personnel department's concern with the termination of employment has had a history almost as long as the separate recognition of the function itself. In the very early days, the social worker's concern with the unemployed was only narrowly distinguished from the welfare worker's concern with the treatment of the employed. The firing of employees in the early years tended to remain the prerogative of line management, being a matter of economics not welfare. Only as the personnel function developed, and as

it took over functions previously discharged by the supervisor or foreman, did it come to have any part to play in guiding the decision to dismiss; even then it was largely by advice about consistent standards and practices rather than taking or vetting the decision itself. But the personnel department came to be the administrative element in this process, seeing to the documentation involved and keeping (and occasionally analysing) records of what was happening. By dint of costing what could be shown to be happening it proved possible, in the tighter labour market of the post-war economy, to show that indiscriminate firing and replacement was bad economy as well as inconsistent with the image of the good employer. Once this happened, the personnel officer could be said to be in business as an influencer of what happened in the termination of contracts.

More recently, legislation and government policy together have combined to make dismissal both more difficult and more costly to the employer. The personnel department thus falls heir to administering the termination of employment contracts in a situation which is heavily constrained by public policy. If that policy could also be said to have the aim of improving standards applied to dismissal, whilst at the same time helping to preserve some of the dignity of the dismissed individual, the welfare component of the personnel function could scarcely react in dismay: to an extent, it must represent support for policies which personnel departments have themselves been seeking to establish.

These policies relate to the establishment of what might be termed the equitable application of the private power of the employer to terminate the employment of the individual employee. Such equity has in the past been sought by means of giving due notice (where what is due has been established in the contract itself, or imposed by statute upon the contract where it did not provide such notice as public policy thought equitable) and by means of restricting the exercise of the employer's private power to determine the contract to certain grounds stipulated in the contract itself (whereby the employee might protect himself against dismissal for reasons not covered by the grounds provided for in the contract). The remedy open to the individual employee in these circumstances, where he was dismissed without due notice, or where he was dismissed on grounds not provided for in the contract, was an action for damages for wrongful dismissal.

However, over and above the remedies available for wrongful dismissal, there are now remedies available for unfair dismissal. To comprehend this important change, however, it is useful to consider in turn how recent legislation has restricted the employer's opportunity to influence the length of due notice and the opportunity to determine what is a sufficient cause of dismissal.

Legislative restrictions on 'due notice'
Recently, a number of Acts of Parliament have established minimum periods of notice which must be given by either party. The effect of the Contract of Employment Act 1972, as amended by the Employment Protection Act, has been to impute to any employment contract which contains periods of notice less than those set out in the Acts the stipulations as to minima contained in the Acts.

First, an employee who has been in continuous employment for four weeks or more with one employer (or an associated employer) is required to give not less than one week's notice of his intention to terminate his contract. His actual contract of employment may of course require him to give more notice.

Secondly, an employer is required to give anyone who has been in continuous employment with him (or an associated employer) for four weeks or more not less than one week's notice, (unless the individual is hired for a task which is not expected to last for more than 12 weeks and does not in fact do so), the week being counted (in this as in the previous case) from the day following the giving of the notice, subject to the stipulations of the contract of employment itself. This minimum applies to those employed for up to two years. Thereafter, the employee is entitled to one week's extra notice for each year of service up to a maximum of 12 weeks after 12 years' service.

Thirdly, these requirements now apply to employees working 16 hours per week or more; to employees working 16 hours per week or more but whose contracted hours are varied downwards to more than eight hours (until the reduced hours have been worked for 26 weeks or more); and to employees who work between eight and 16 hours per week after five years' (260 weeks) continuous employment.

Fourthly, where an employee is dismissed without notice or with inadequate notice, for purposes of calculating qualifying period of service and any unfair dismissal compensation, his service will be taken as running to the date on which the statutorily required notice would have expired. (This aims to stop employers dismissing employees before they qualify (at 26 weeks) to bring an unfair dismissal complaint.)

Fifthly, unfair dismissal complaints may be brought before a tribunal during the notice period. (This permits the tribunal to adjudicate before notice will expire in some cases, thus allowing an adjudication in well-founded complaints that notice be withdrawn, rather than that the employee be reinstated.)

Rights to waive notice and to accept payment in lieu of notice are not affected; the definition of continuous employment and methods of calculating it are contained in Schedule 1 of the 1972 Act, as amended.

The giving of due notice thus remains a necessary protection of the parties seeking to determine a contract of employment, but what constitutes due notice is defined as to its minimum by legislation for certain categories of employee identified above. The terms of an individual contract may still provide for longer periods of notice than those stipulated above, and these will remain enforceable (see Hill v C A Parsons & Co Ltd (1972) Ch 305; (1971) 3 All ER, 1345).

Apart from the generality of the above provisions, recent legislation has interfered with the question of notice in a number of special circumstances.

On redundancy, the Employment Protection Act provides that trade unions shall be informed of *any* redundancy at the 'earliest opportunity' and that consultation be initiated with the recognized independent trade unions at this time—on pain of a tribunal award of at least 28 days' pay to affected employees if this is not done.

Where an employer proposes to make 10 or more workers redundant he is required to consult representatives of recognized unions before implementing his proposals. (This applies regardless of whether the 10 or more work long or short hours, have long or short service (except the 12 weeks' category) or are members or non-members of the recognized union.) If consultation is not so initiated by the employer, the *trade union* may seek and secure a protective award from a tribunal. This requires the employer to pay the employees whom it was proposed to make redundant for a stipulated period at the discretion of the tribunal, and up to a maximum of 90 days' pay where the redundancy involved 100 or more employees within a 90 day period, 60 days' pay where the redundancies involved 10 or more employees in a 30 day period, and 28 days' pay in any other case.

An individual covered by a protective award is entitled to the appropriate pay, and can bring a claim before an industrial tribunal to recover it, but such an award to an individual and any contractual payments or pay in lieu of notice falling within the protected period will go towards discharging the employer's obligations under the protective award.

It is required that consultations begin at 'the earliest opportunity' with the recognized trade union, and time periods are laid down: 10 or more employees affected in one establishment must produce consultation at least 30 days before the first proposed redundancy, and the employer must therefore consider what to do about notice to individuals.

The safest procedure would be to give notice to individuals and invite consultation at the time (where the notice period is long enough to require this) because consultation will either confirm the redundancy and its date (in which case the notice will stand and long delays will be avoided) or it will reject or postpone the redundancy (in which case the employer can offer to withdraw the notice, and thus offer a reasonable defence to any subsequent claim).

A further constraint on the giving and receiving of notice in connection with redundancy occurs in the Employment Protection Act in the requirement that, when an employee is faced with redundancy and/or a revised contract of employment, he has a right to try any alternative employment offered for a fixed period of four weeks, without in anyway foregoing his or her rights to a redundancy payment if at the end of that four week trial period he decides that the new job is not for him. The offer of new work does not have to be in writing: when a job is changed, it will be deemed that the individual is dismissed (technically); but if the individual stays on the new job for a four week trial period, he will be deemed to have accepted the new job and the employer will be deemed to have accepted him in it.

The trial period is not a matter of choice or election: when an employee starts on a new or changed job, 'there shall be a trial period'. It will normally be of four weeks, but the parties can agree in writing that it will be longer and when it will end, if it is for the purpose of 'retraining the employee for employment' under his new contract. If the employee decides to terminate during the trial period, he will be held to have been dismissed from his previous job, not that he had resigned from the new job. If the employee does not make out on the new job, the employer may also cut his losses, determine the contract and make redundancy payment, but in this case the reason must be connected with the new job (and not, for example, gross misconduct).

Legislative restrictions on 'sufficient reason'
This brings us to the question of what might constitute a sufficient reason for determining a contract of employment. Giving notice is a useful protection against possible common law actions but sometimes, as with gross misconduct, it may not be absolutely necessary. The occasions on which the employer could dismiss with or without notice, for a reason which he considered sufficient were frequent in the past, although progressively subject to reduction by trade union actions and collective agreements. More significantly, until 1965, the law did not require an employer to have or to give a reason for dismissing an employee, even though, in terms of the contract's terms relating to reasons and due notice, it might assume the reason to have

been a proper one.

In the 1960s public policy changed, and implicitly recognized that the proper dismissal of an employee might nevertheless occasion him or her some loss of legitimate expectations and therefore ought to be compensated for. This principle was first applied to redundancy dismissal. The Redundancy Payments Act required the employer to provide additional compensation to the redundant employee for the loss of 'accrued property rights in the employment' since the reason for termination is not the fault of the employee. He is therefore entitled to notice, or to payment in lieu of notice; and although he may be fairly and correctly dismissed for this reason, the law now says that he should also receive a certain amount of monetary compensation over and above his notice to compensate him for such loss of seniority and similar rights and privileges as he might have acquired in his employment. This compensation is to be worked out on the basis of the time he has been in the employment and of his age, and at the maximum would amount to 30 weeks' pay (at weekly rates up to a maximum of £100) for 20 or more years' service over the age of 41 years.

In more recent years statutes have introduced the concept of unfair dismissal, by which it is intended to establish that the individual employee has a right to continue in his employment unless and until there is a good reason for its termination which does not depend upon an arbitrary exercise of private power by the employer. The law has intervened to require (a) that there should be an identifiable reason for termination, (b) that that reason should be sufficient to make it 'fair' (as defined), and (c) that it should be communicated to the employee at his request. In 1965 the Redundancy Payments Act established the presumption that every dismissed employee would be regarded as having been dismissed by reason of redundancy (and therefore entitled to redundancy compensation in addition to due notice unless the employer established that the reason was other than this). In 1971, the Industrial Relations Act established the concept of unfair dismissal and placed the onus of proof on the employer to show

1 That the main or only reason for dismissal was a fair one by virtue of its being:

   (a) related to the capability or qualifications of the employee for performing work of a kind which he was employed by the employer to do, or
   (b) related to the conduct of the employee, or
   (c) that the employee was redundant, or
   (d) that the employee could not continue in work without causing

either the employer or the employee to contravene a legal duty or restriction.

2 That he (the employer) had acted reasonably in treating that reason as sufficient to justify dismissal
3 That the decision to dismiss was taken on the substantial merits of the case and was equitable in its consequences.

This concept, and the right of the individual not to be unfairly dismissed, has been reinstated in the Trade Union and Labour Relations Acts 1974–76 and extended in the Employment Protection Act, 1975. In particular, an employee who has 26 weeks' continuous service with an employer may now demand a written statement of the reasons for his dismissal, and the employer is required to accede to the request within two weeks, on pain of having the tribunal award the employee a sum equivalent to two weeks' pay if it finds the complaint justified. This stipulation is designed to help the dismissed employee determine whether he has been fairly or unfairly dismissed, and whether he therefore has a complaint which could be put to the tribunal. Thus, in ten years, Statute law has changed the position from one in which the employer need never give reasons for dismissal to one in which written reasons must be supplied on request.

Essentially, what makes a dismissal unfair is the exercise of the employer's power to determine the contract in either an arbitrary or a discriminatory fashion. Given the existence of good reasons for terminating an individual's employment (listed above), the employer would still be open to an action for unfair dismissal before a tribunal if he showed discrimination in selecting employees for dismissal.

Where the main or only reason for dismissal relates to the employee's capability (assessed by reference to skill, aptitude, health or any other physical or mental quality) or qualifications (represented by degrees, diplomas or other academic, technical or professional qualifications and/or experience relevant to the position held) the dismissal might still be unfair if comparable employees were treated differently, or if it could be sustained that the assessment was unreasonable. In the first category, it will probably be necessary to ensure that, for example, two employees with similar health or absence records are not treated differently with respect to termination; in the second, that a decision to dismiss for incompetence is not taken suddenly after many years of successful performance of the job. The greater cost of dismissing unsatisfactory employees must therefore focus attention on the improvement of selection and appraisal procedures and will probably make the need to reduce the well-known tendency to leniency in most control arrangements in employment more urgent, if only to establish a foundation of consistency in treatment of employees.

Closely analagous to this, in some ways, is the situation when a woman in employment becomes pregnant. It will be fair to dismiss such a person if, before the effective termination date (ie the end of the twelfth week before the expected confinement) she is or must become incapable of performing the work she is employed to do; but it will become unfair if the employer fails to offer her the alternative of any suitable vacancy that may exist. Similarly, it will be fair not to offer re-engagement after maternity leave if in the meantime her job has become redundant (in which case she would qualify for redundancy compensation) but unfair if the employer did not offer re-engagement to perform suitable and appropriate work, at the same place and in a similar capacity and on similar terms and conditions, when a suitable vacancy existed in his or an associated employer's establishment. The link between this situation and the general one in the preceding paragraph is that pregnancy is not to be regarded as a sufficient cause of dismissal in itself, since no fault lies with the employee in relation to her contract terms.

Where the main or the only reason for dismissal is misconduct on the part of the employee, there are circumstances in which dismissal without notice is justifiable. But given the new requirement of the Employment Protection Act and the recommendation of the existing Code of Practice that disciplinary rules and penalties are communicated to employees, departure from these will probably provide grounds for an unfair dismissal complaint to the Tribunal. Action is therefore called for to ensure that the organization's disciplinary rules are adequate to sustain as fair, decisions to dismiss employees on the ground of misconduct. In any event, peremptory dismissal, possibly in the heat of the moment, is in future likely to be at a considerable discount.

Where the main reason for dismissal is redundancy, discrimination in selecting any individual employee for redundancy, where that redundancy "applied equally to one or more other employees in the same undertaking who held positions similar to that held by him and who have not been dismissed by the employer" and where the selection was made "in contravention of a customary arrangement or agreed procedure relating to redundancy" and there were no good reasons for departing from it, would also provide a presumption that the dismissal was still unfair, attracting a compensatory award over and above the basic award for loss of job property rights.

In some ways comparable to this concept of discrimination in selection for redundancy is the discrimination in offering re-engagement to employees dismissed in the course of a strike or a lock-out. This could also lead to a successful complaint that the dismissal was unfair, where dismissal by way of a lock-out or for taking part in a strike is itself fair. The question here turns on whether only some of the class of employees involved were dismissed, or alternatively only some of them were offered reinstatement or re-engagement at the end of the action. The reason for dismissal in the latter case is then substituted as the reason for non-re-engagement (TULRA Schedule 1, Ss (7) and (8)).

Where, in the exercise of private power to dismiss, the employer breaks these new rules of fairness, the aggrieved may not only seek redress through his trade union (which may pressure the employer to change his decision) but may also take a complaint to an industrial tribunal. That tribunal is empowered to grant various remedies if the complaint is found to be substantiated, and it is in these remedies that the curb on the employer's use of his power lies.

Where the main or only reason relates to contravention of a legal duty or restriction (which is predictably likely to arise most often in connection with duties on both employer and employee under the Health and Safety at Work Act) discrimination will again make a fair dismissal unfair. The main problems here will be either to ensure that *all* employees who refuse or fail to discharge the duty to cooperate with the employer in health and safety matters are treated in the same way, or to determine where the dividing line shall be drawn amongst degrees of cooperation/non-cooperation to justify dismissal on one side of the line or some lesser penalty on the other. The safest course here is likely to be to draw up an establishment code in cooperation with the safety representatives and apply it firmly, but equitably, through a joint committee.

The Trade Union and Labour Relations Acts 1974–6, (Schedule 1, para 6 (3)–(6) introduce a category of *inadmissible* reasons for dismissal, and reliance upon such a reason to justify dismissal would render it unfair. The inadmissible reasons are connected with an employee's acting, or proposing to act, on behalf of an independent trade union, either by becoming a member or by taking part in its activities (including a refusal to take any part in a trade union which is not independent).

Discrimination against individual employees for refusing to join or take part in a union which is not independent, for joining or acting within an independent trade union, provides a presumption of unfairness and, if the tribunal so found, would produce a special higher level of compensation award if the employer did not re-instate or re-employ. Selection of an employee for redundancy for such a reason would also render that decision unfair (Schedule 1, S 6 (7)).

Where a union membership agreement exists with the employer

which requires all employees of the class in question to belong to one or another independent trade union, dismissal of the employee for refusing to join, or continue in membership of one or other of these unions, will be regarded as fair unless the individual can establish genuine objection on ground of religious belief to being a member of any trade union whatsoever.

Dismissal of a person on ground of race or sex also comes into this category of dismissal for 'inadmissible reason' and the higher rate of compensation would similarly apply.

Although the right not to be dismissed for inadmissible reasons applies to everyone, the right not to be unfairly dismissed does not apply to certain categories of employee. It does not extend to:

1 An employee who is the husband/wife of the employer
2 Those who are registered dock workers engaged in dock work
3 Those engaged in the fishing fleets and who share in the profits or gross earnings of the vessel
4 Those who, under their contracts, normally work outside Britain, with certain exceptions in the case of merchant seamen
5 Those who have not, at the time of dismissal, been employed continuously for 26 weeks or more unless the reason is an inadmissible reason
6 Those who at the effective date of termination had reached normal retiring age for the class of employee, or at the age of 65 (men) or 60 (women), with the same qualification as in 5
7 Those working under fixed term contract in certain cases (TULRA Schedule 1, S 12 as amended by EPA Act Schedule 16).

The preferred remedy provided in the Employment Protection Act is one of (a) withdrawal of notice (if the complaint is heard during the notice period) or (b) reinstatement or (c) re-engagement. It is provided that a tribunal, on finding an unfair dismissal complaint well-founded, must ascertain whether the employee would prefer reinstatement or re-engagement as a remedy and, if so, then consider whether this remedy would be feasible as well as just and equitable in the circumstances. If it does so consider it, the tribunal may make an award in these terms.

This comes close to overturning by legislation a principle which has hitherto been followed by the Courts in actions for wrongful dismissal. Before the passage of the legislation referred to above, and indeed still, it is open to an individual employee to start an action in the ordinary Courts when he considers that his dismissal was in breach of his employment contract, and for that reason wrongful. The Court was in a position to award one of three remedies. The first, an injunction restraining the employer from taking the proposed action of dismissing the individual, would be likely to have limited applicability in the field of employment, but in any case suffers from the same defect as the third in the eyes of the Court. The second, an award of damages based largely on the principle of compensating the individual for what he had lost as a result of the employer's action if in breach of contract, would generally yield little in the way of money, since it would be bound by the period of notice for the most part multiplied by his salary or wage and frequently mitigated. Because the first and third remedies were seen to have defects in relation to employment, this was the most commonly applied remedy by the Courts.

The third remedy, an order of specific performance by which the Court could require the employer to remedy the breach itself and therefore reinstate the individual, has been little used in the present century. The Court's reluctance to order specific performance in relation to dismissal complaints rests on two foundations: first, that it would be difficult to supervise the enforcement of such an order; secondly, that it would mean ordering that two persons should maintain a personal relationship in circumstances where one or other might not wish this—in the words of Lord Justice Fry in the case of De Francesco v Barnham (1890), "I think the Courts are bound to be jealous, lest they should turn contracts of service into contracts of slavery". More recently this provided the reasoning behind the decision in Rex v National Arbitration Tribunal ex parte Crowther (1948), in which it was held, that the National Arbitration Tribunal had no jurisdiction to make an award directing the reinstatement of certain workers. This principle is also followed in cases which appear before the Central Arbitration Committee, although single arbitrators *have* awarded reinstatement.

It remains true that the spirit of this dictum is maintained even in the Employment Protection Act: reinstatement or re-engagement will still take place only if both parties concerned wish it. All that changes is that the cost to the employer of not agreeing is increased.

On finding a complaint well-founded, the tribunal is enjoined to explain to the complainant "what orders for reinstatement or re-engagement may be made . . . and in what circumstances they may be made" and to "ask him whether he wishes the tribunal to make such an order". If he expresses such a wish, the tribunal may then make such an order. The tribunal is required to consider reinstatement before considering re-engagement, if the employee wishes. It must also consider whether such an order would be practicable from the employer's point of view, and just from the employee's point of view even in circumstances where the individual caused or contributed to some extent to the dismissal.

116

An order for reinstatement requires the employer to treat the employee as if he had never been dismissed, and will include specifications of:

(a) any amount payable to the employee in arrears of pay (including bonuses) for the period between termination and reinstatement
(b) any rights and privileges, including seniority and pension rights, which must be restored to the employee
(c) the date by which the order must be complied with.

Furthermore, if the employee would have benefited from an improvement in his terms and conditions of employment had he not been dismissed, the order will require that he receive those benefits as if he had not been dismissed.

An order for re-engagement is an order that the employee be engaged by the employer, a successor employer or an associated employer, in employment comparable to that from which he was dismissed or in other suitable employment. The order will specify the identity of the employer, the nature of the employment, the remuneration for it, any amount payable by the employer in arrears of pay (including bonuses) for the period between date of termination and re-engagement, any rights and privileges which must be restored to the employee and the date by which the order must be complied with. Approximately the same considerations apply here as with the reinstatement orders, except that the latter must be considered first and that, in considering contributory fault, the tribunal must seek to provide re-engagement on terms "which so far as is reasonably practicable (are) as favourable" as those contained in any order for reinstatement.

In the case of both reinstatement and re-engagement orders, the tribunal is required, in considering both what is practicable and the amount of compensation which might be paid, to disregard the fact that the employer may have hired a permanent replacement of the employee dismissed, unless the employer shows that it was not practicable for him to have the work done without hiring such a replacement. When reinstatement or re-engagement is ordered, the calculation of arrears of pay will take into account any payments made by the employer (whether in lieu of notice or *ex gratia*) or by another employer in employment or social security benefit, together with any other such benefits as the tribunal think appropriate in the circumstances.

If such an order is not made, or if the terms of such orders are not fully complied with, the tribunal must make an award of compensation to be paid by the employer to the employee, based on its calculation of the loss sustained by the complainant as a consequence of the incomplete compliance. This also applies where the order for reinstatement or re-engagement is not complied with at all. In that case, the award of compensation will have three parts:

1 A basic award, which will be paid in any case of unfair dismissal or (fair) redundancy, regardless of whether the individual affected has suffered any 'loss' as a consequence of the dismissal or the redundancy. It is calculated on the basis of length of service and age (EPA, S 67, S 68, S 69), working backwards from the date of dismissal and counting only the 20 years most favourable to the employee, but subject to a minimum basic award of two weeks' pay. (A 'week's pay' is calculable according to the formula given in the Act and from 1 February 1978 is subject to a maximum of £100 per week.) An individual's entitlement, in the event of fair redundancy or as a basic award for unfair dismissal, is made up from:

> $1\frac{1}{2}$ weeks' pay for each full year of employment when the employee is aged 41 years and over
> 1 week's pay for each year between age 22 and 41
> $\frac{1}{2}$ week's pay for each year between 18 and 22

2 A compensatory award, applicable to unfair dismissals only, calculated in accordance with what the tribunal considers just and equitable in the circumstances, and taking into account any loss sustained by the individual and any question of mitigation (EPA, S 70). This is paid in addition to the basic award (or the redundancy payment) where unfairness is established, but is subject to deduction for contributory fault on the part of the dismissed individual. The compensatory award is subject to a maximum of £5,200 and is awarded by the tribunal on the basis of loss not, as in the case of the basic award, on the basis of the actual pay rate applicable to the individual. In appropriate circumstances, therefore, a tribunal might award nothing under this head, whilst in others the maximum figure might be awarded regardless of how this might relate to the particular individual's pay rate

3 Where there is failure to reinstate or re-engage after a tribunal has made such an order, a further award of up to £2,600 may be made; this in turn may be increased to £5,200 where the reason for unfair dismissal was racial or sexual discrimination or related to union membership or participation in union activities. As in the case of the basic award, these figures are related to 'a week's pay' and were last increased on 1 February 1978. This imposes a special penalty on the employer if he does not reinstate or re-engage against the judgement of the tribunal and the wishes of the dismissed employee. The intention of this third element is therefore to create

the presumption that the main remedy for unfair dismissal shall be re-employment; to this extent therefore the employer will need to develop procedures for preventing the situation arising and for coping with the reinstated employee.

2 Managing the employment function

Introduction

The employment 'function', that part of the enterprise or organization specifically charged with the planning, control and execution of the entity's interchange with the labour market, has traditionally formed a part of the 'personnel function'. In some cases, the 'labour office' through which all applicants for employment and all whose employment was being terminated passed, was the starting point for what later grew into a personnel department. In Britain, the 'welfare function' appears to have had greater priority, although the redistribution of labour effected by call-up to the forces and 'dilution' in industry during the first world war, gave the employment office and function a greater urgency (cf Niven, 1967; Renold, 1950). The development of employment offices in American industry occurred at roughly this same time, for "the more efficient handling of labour" (Nichols in Bloomfield and Willits, 1916, p 1) and although "the employment office [usually became] the personnel department because its work necessitates such close relationship with the working force" (Bloomfield and Willits, 1916, p vii) there is a suggestion of greater emphasis upon efficiency in hiring and firing (Kelly, 1918) than upon 'welfare' *per se*.

In 1955, Northcott gave appreciable weight to the employment function in his *Principles and Practice of Personnel Management*. He saw "the responsibilities of the employment department" as falling "mainly under two headings, the supply and placement of workers and the maintenance and study of records" (of such phenomena as absence and labour turnover) but admitted that as a consequence of this involvement, "some advice on employment policy is a responsibility" (Northcott, 1955, third edn p 226). By this date in Britain, this function had acquired a degree of coherence and systematization, the 'full employment' conditions of the post-world war two epoch having lent some urgency to this development. As in the American experience, so in the British, this function developed into a broader 'personnel function', but still quite commonly at present

120

members of personnel departments are involved in recruitment, selection, induction and initial training and in termination of employment processes, and still on this foundation offer advice to the undertaking of employment policy. But the 'function' may be said to have developed beyond executive tasks associated with these interchanges to encompass manpower planning and employment policy formation, embracing more 'sophisticated' methods and techniques than those once employed.

The present chapter discusses this general function. It is conceived on an assumption which will be relaxed later—that the employment function can be thought of in the impersonal terms which follow from the kinds of consideration reviewed in the preceding chapter. 'Employment' is thus concerned with the establishment or termination of an employment contract, and *can* be discussed in those terms. This neglects for the present that those who are caught up in the contract are people with a lot of thoughts and feelings, which will not be brought into the discussion until chapter 4 although eventually their influence on the employment function will have to be acknowledged. But since we cannot discuss everything at once and still present a coherent account of the personnel function, this restriction is imposed in the present chapter. Employment is treated in impersonal 'system' terms to establish what methods are applicable to the development of plans and strategies for the securing of appropriate amounts of labour, or manpower, to meet the requirements of the enterprise or organization.

In order to give a structure to the chapter, therefore, we adopt a model of the enterprise as a 'system' seen to be interchanging with its environment over a boundary (cf Miner and Miner, 1977, ch 3; Buckley, 1967; Kast and Rosenzweig, 1970). The interchanges involve not only manpower but also components, products, money and many other things, although here we shall be directly concerned only with the first of these. The enterprise is seen to have a need both to attract labour from the environment and to return labour to it and the size of the need will vary with a number of internal and external circumstances at which we must look. That need will find expression as a *demand* for labour, which must take into account the *supply* of labour which exists in the environment. The relationship between these two concepts forms the foundation of the interchange. In order to carry out an 'employment function' effectively, we argue, those charged with doing so require a knowledge of both internal demand and external supply, *and* a knowledge of how to interrelate these in the interests of the criteria established to define 'success' in this context. These criteria will usually be derived from the enterprise itself: the securing of the right number of the right people for employment

121

in the enterprise at the right time as determined by the production etc objectives which the enterprise has set for itself (cf Silverman, 1970). They do not have to be derived in this way but other criteria are likely in our society to be marginal in their effects upon manpower decisions, although impositions of some constraints by Government, trade unions and professional associations may still prove important in some cases (eg in redundancy plans or in policies of engagement of labour by sex or colour).

It would not be outside the ideological remit of the personnel manager to conceive manpower planning in terms of employee satisfaction but it is common to see it in terms of performance. Thus models of manpower planning are usually constructed against an objective which is concerned to realize efficiency or secure 'performance' from all those engaged. Such models, of whichever type, will follow the normal distribution of steps: objective-setting, criterion-determining, predictor-calculating, assessment-making and decision-taking, followed by an evaluation process which will start the sequence over again. Where the objective is conceived in performance terms, the criteria, predictors, assessments etc will all be set up in terms of this dependent variable but, where satisfaction is taken to indicate purpose, the criteria etc would be established in these other terms.

It may therefore be worth making a distinction between purposes—indicated by 'performance' and 'satisfaction' in the preceding paragraph—and objectives which might well be multiple in order to serve the 'purpose' more fully or adequately. If we make the assumption that we will in the rest of the chapter be concerned with 'performance' purposes, we might then recognize a number of relevant objectives, such as:

(a) the recruitment and retention of the amount of skill required to perform the work of the system
(b) the provision of sufficient flexibility in the manpower to permit system adaptability to changes in the internal or external environments
(c) the minimization of the costs of manpower planning itself consistent with these objectives and measuring costs in whatever terms are sanctioned by the norms of the system (eg 'social' costs might be included)
(d) the accomplishment of these objectives inside the framework of norms for any system of purposive activity (eg without resorting to slave or sweated labour conditions or infringing legal requirements).

As between these, priorities might well change as circumstances

122

Figure 1
Sources of labour to the undertaking

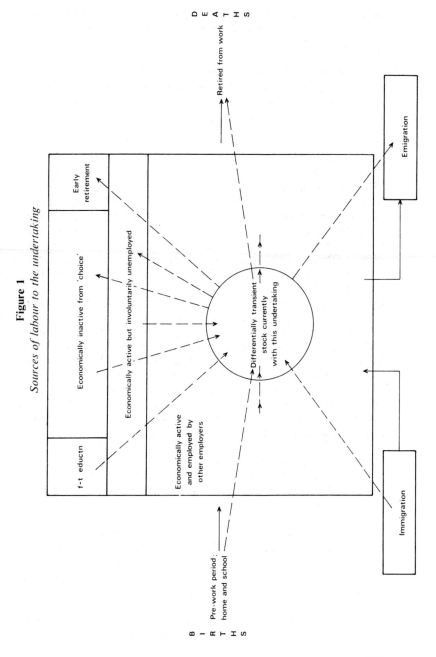

change, and therefore very different weights may be given to such objectives from time to time or from organization to organization. A high level of labour wastage which was proving costly, might well raise the priority of 'recruitment to reduce short stays' over the objective of securing the highest 'quality' of labour; poor work performance, for similar reasons might be expected to raise the importance of this objective relative to others. The establishment of objectives is therefore an important first step in developing any plan for manpower performance.

Manpower planning

'Manpower planning' may be defined as a process whereby courses of action are determined upon in advance, and continually up-dated, with the aim of ensuring that (a) the demands of an enterprise for labour (or manpower in any given sex-age-skill manifestation) are as accurately projected as possible and (b) that the supply of such labour to the enterprise is maintained in balance with those demands. This decision-process does not take place in a vacuum, and it must therefore be carried out in relation to the environments in which the enterprise moves and on the basis of past, present and projected future information about enterprise demand and supply positions. "Manpower planning", says Moss, "is the attempt to explain, predict and influence manpower changes in relation to the changing economic, technical and social situation of establishments" (Moss, 1974, p 9). Patten quotes LeBreton and Henning (1961) to establish the general features of any plan: "A plan of any type may be defined as a predetermined course of action. Every plan should have three characteristics: first, it should involve the future; second, it must involve action; and third, there should be an element of personal or organizational identification or causation, which means simply that the future course of action will be taken by the planner or someone designated by him within an organization or within society" (Patten, 1971, p 13). In other words, any plan includes object-setting, administrative decision and execution, thus linking predicted futures with calculated means and purposive action.

Bell provides a clear exposition of what is requisite in manpower planning which is consistent with these views. He treats it as "the systematic analysis of the company's resources, the construction of a forecast of its future manpower requirements from this base, with special concentration on the efficient use of manpower at both these stages, and the planning necessary to ensure that the manpower supply will match the forecast requirements." The manpower plan thus becomes the consequence of reconciling, within the constraints imposed upon decision by the company's circumstances, the outcomes from (a) the analysis of manpower resources, (b) the forecasts of future demands or requirements and (c) the forecasts of probable internal and external supply of manpower (Bell, 1974, pp 9–10).

The plan itself will then have to cover areas of action which are relevant to the matching of expected needs with expected supply from various (internal and external) sources. It must say something about the expected performance of labour in order to indicate what marginal additions or subtractions will be required at various points in time to meet the productivity requirements; it must provide for action to recruit, transfer, promote or discharge labour in accordance with this estimation and in conformity with other constraints of legality and cost; it must reflect an assessment of the part which training and development of the existing labour force or new recruits might make to the achievement of the equilibrium between requirement and offer; and it must be set against a set of personnel policies, outside the manpower planning area strictly defined, which will provide appropriate back-up for those actions which are more strictly to do with manpower planning. These elements are presented in diagrammatic form, based on Bell's own figures (1974, pp 10 & 12).

The steps in the process of developing a plan of this kind are outlined by Stainer, who identifies:

(a) development of the criteria which will be employed in making judgements about the data
(b) determination of what data are relevant to the decisions required
(c) collection and collation of this data in order that it may be transmitted to those who must decide
(d) allocation of persons to decision-taking roles, on the basis of assumed competence to interpret the data
(e) taking of decisions about manpower, either unilaterally or in negotiations
(f) controlled implementation of the decisions thus taken, this implying that the process of feeding back data will also be involved (cf Stainer, 1971, pp 3 & 4).

These statements are apposite to manpower planning at whatever level it may be required within the economy:

(a) the macro level which embraces demand and supply components at the national or supra-national level
(b) the intermediate level where the concern is with stocks and flows in respect of whole industries or geographical regions or regional labour markets
(c) the micro level where the problem is defined in terms of

balancing flows and stocks at the level of the corporation or undertaking.

At each of these levels, three components of estimation are required. These are (i) the level of demand representing the translation of employer need into effective demand upon the supplies available; (ii) the internal supply, representing the amount of the existing stock available to the entity in question which will remain available for and seeking continuing employment into the future; and (iii) the external supply composed of those not yet available to the entity for employment which may nevertheless be regarded as potentially available for the future (cf Bryant, 1972, pp 14–15).

Figure 2

Elements of manpower planning and in the employment plan

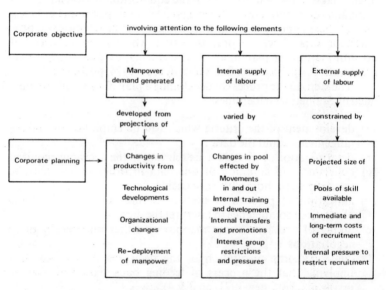

Based on: D J Bell: *Planning Corporate Manpower* (Longman, 1974), pp 10 and 12 (composited)

Forecasting

Manpower planning thus aims to ensure that an organization so reacts to its internal and external environments that it has now, and will continue to have in the future, the numbers and qualities of people who will be required to enable the undertaking to achieve its

126

output (whether of goods or of services) within whatever cultural constraints of efficiency may be imposed upon it. As with any other 'planning' process, therefore, it involves the forecasting of likely future situations with the object of identifying demand, and the determination of a series of actions which can be calculated to ensure that as far as possible those predicted needs will be met. No forecast of the future can be completely accurate but reasonable estimates of probability can be made on the basis of various hypotheses; therefore the value of the plan will always depend upon just how close such forecasts can be brought in relation to actual out-turns in the future. No theory about what degree or kind of change in independent variables is necessary in order to produce a particular effect can be absolutely perfect; and therefore no plan can be perfect in its consequences even if the forecasts are accurate. But on both counts systematic analysis is likely to prove more useful, in a complex set of environments, than mere hunch or guesswork. It is the complexity of the environments which leads us to systematic planning, not a fashionable supersession of 'hunch'.

Manpower planning, like any planning activity, rests upon forecasts and forecasts are frequently dismissed as being necessarily wrong. This, as Brech has argued (1975), is to mistake the nature and purpose of forecasting in management. "Forecasting is the use of a numerate and logical system, incorporating judgement values, to evaluate the probabilities of future occurrences or outcomes. It is not a scientific method of prophecy, which implies knowing the future with certainty. . . It identifies possible outcomes and assigns them their relative probabilities. The logical structure is based on the known relationships and past experience . . . and . . . incorporates an assessment of how people or events are likely to react as judged from that experience, after allowing for known or probable changes in the environment" (Brech, 1975, third edn p 28). In effect this process of systematically forecasting can help increase understanding of uncertainties and converts them into 'risks' of more calculable dimensions. Any plan based upon forecasting in this sense may well turn out to be wrong, but the forecasting process helps to indicate something of the likelihood of its being so or to inform the planner of the risk run by the plan.

It has to be recognized that the best information which is available to a decision-taker in making any kind of forecast is that which relates to the situation (to which the decision is to be related) as it has developed in the past. The basis of most forecasting, in other words, is extrapolation from the known (past) to the unknown (future). But as Bell, amongst others, continually asserts in his discussion of the various kinds of forecasting required in manpower planning, the data required may not exist (because it has not been recorded at all, or not recorded in a useable form, or not kept over a long enough period of past time), so that the choice of forecasting method may be "restricted by the availability of data" (Bell, 1974, p 19). It is this which makes the recording of data within the 'production system' as well as within the 'personnel system' of great importance from the standpoint of the manpower planner. Division of responsibilities between line management, management services departments and personnel departments, quite frequently renders 'bits' of separate data quite unsuitable for this (forecasting) purpose, and it is this which leads Bell to suggest that, even where adequate data does not exist at any one moment, a 'dummy run' forecast might be carried out if only to indicate what data are required and so to inform the minds of those concerned (Bell, 1974, p 19) and Bartholomew to argue that manpower planners must state what they need (Bartholomew, in Smith, 1970 see also p 132 below).

Where in the past the personnel management textbook concentrated on only two aspects of record keeping—the maintenance of fundamental personal information (like name, address, age, starting date, promotions, pay rate) and the collection of data which was thought to indicate something of the state of 'morale' in the enterprise (like time-keeping, absenteeism, labour turnover, discipline cases, dispute incidence), the greater involvement of personnel specialists in economic decisions about manpower has changed the pattern of data collection and the uses to which it is put (cf Stainer, 1971, ch 4). The data which was previously regarded as the province of production or wages departments is now necessary to manpower planning and employee resourcing processes and is therefore brought together more often. The predisposition of the personnel specialist to use his own data simply for purposes of divining the state of morale is complemented by its use for monitoring recruitment, selection and placement activities as well as for assessment of labour quality. In keeping with these changes, more systematic attention has been given to the record-keeping function (see Industrial Society, 1969; Butteriss, 1975).

The kinds of data required for manpower planning purposes fall into two broad categories, the performance data and the stock and flow data. It is the first type which is most often associated with line management and management services responsibilities, and the second which is traditionally more the concern of the personnel department or employment office.

The first data are described as 'workload data' and may be derived in two quite different ways. In the one case, what is needed is some 'indicator' such as the level of demand for, say, the product or the service which the manpower in question will be concerned with making or providing. This will not always be discoverable for particular categories of labour but, where it is and where it can be given a value, it can be used to forecast demand for manpower, if there is a direct relationship between the indicator and the demand. A single shoe-repairer might provide an illustration: if the demand for shoe repairs (or for fitted heels) could be expected to double over the next year, and if the number of repairs or heel fittings thus predicted to be demanded linked directly with the number of units of manpower required, then a prediction of a requirement of two repairers at the end of the year would be reasonably made. But of course the relationships are not always so direct and so discernible (see Rowntree and Stewart, in Smith, 1976, pp 39–40). Bell refers to this approach as 'direct' analysis calling for the application of statistical methods of ratios and regression analysis (Bell, 1974, p 22), with which it is necessary to link analysis of productivity changes which might be expected with changes in volume (Bell, 1976, pp 28–40).

The alternative is to use the more conventional work performance data of the kind which manufacturing industry tends to amass in plenty (whether it presents it or uses it for manpower planning purposes or not). Essentially, this requires the development of data which indicates the performance of a standard unit of manpower in any given category—the performance of a 'trained operator working at standard pace in standard conditions' at either incentive or non-incentive rates as the case may be. These data are also not always derivable or available, dependent upon the kind of work which is being done but, where they are, they offer a basis in past fact for future forecast. If the standard or average performance of a semi-skilled machinist is known (in these terms) as a result of work study or more simply of calculated averages, it becomes possible to base estimates of future manpower demand upon this as related to expectations of changes in product demand. Bell discusses these methods more fully in terms of the development of inductive methods (managerial estimates) and of standard relationships based on work study (Bell, 1974, pp 26–8).

The data more likely to be available from the personnel department are those which relate to the stocks and flows of manpower within the organization. For purposes of internal forecasting, the data most readily usable are those which mean simply plotting numbers (stocks) of staff (in categories) against past time, fitting curves thereto and extrapolating the curve into the future. To do so demands statistics of numbers over a sufficient period to permit these operations to be carried out and sufficient numbers in homogeneous categories to make the calculations worthwhile. Both of these will restrict the opportunity in many instances. These data need eventually to be married with the other categories of data mentioned above, and that may mean bringing together data from two very different departmental sources (Rowntree and Stewart, in Smith, 1976, pp 37–38).

Flow information of a sort is also available in the personnel department, although quite often the data are collected for quite other purposes than manpower planning and for this reason are often not useable. The four main sub-categories of flow data which are required for this purpose are summarized by Butler and Rowntree (in Smith, 1976, p 54) as follows:

1 "out-movement from the organization for whatever reason, termed *wastage* [or labour turnover in many undertakings]—this covers voluntary resignation, retirement, death etc
2 "in-movement from outside the organization to any grade, termed *recruitment*
3 "movement between jobs leading to a change of grade. When this flow is upward within the hierarchy it is termed *promotion*; a movement in the opposite direction is termed *demotion*
4 "movement from job to job within the same grade" which may be referred to as *transfer*.

The value of these data for manpower planning purposes depends upon the possibility that exists for relating them to other information usually associated with the personnel record—such as age, date of starting, length of service, salary and wage position and development etc. If the information is to be used to predict what may happen in the future, it is in other words insufficient to know what the 'rate' of labour turnover is, but necessary to know how this relates to these variables of age, length of service etc and therefore what are the potentialities for flow in the next 'x' years in the existing labour force (see Butler and Rowntree, in Smith, 1976, pp 54–77; and Bell, 1974, ch 4).

Differential availability and dispersed location of data are two related problems in this area. Another relates to the subjectivity of some information. Much of the basic information for forecasting purposes is "only available *subjectively* from the appropriate manager" (Bartholomew, Hopes and Smith, 1976, p 6) (italics added); and that "success in manpower planning depends heavily on the formation of good judgements about the likely variations of parameters [and this] involves eliciting the managers' perceptions in a form suitable for analysis" (*ibid*, p 16). A third problem arises from the assumed necessity to use statistical methodology in order to carry out any manpower planning activity at all. It is true that the conversion of uncertainty into calculated risk, where this is possible at all, "is an area where the statistician is presumed to be the expert" (*ibid,* p 6) but many useful exercises of manpower planning call for (and indeed can support no more than) a sensible calculation of future probabilities on quite limited data (cf Bell, 1974, p 19). In the more complex manning situation, the personnel manager will have some involvement in forecasting of internal demand, internal supply and external supply, and even if more specialist personnel are engaged on the actual statistical manipulation involved, he must have some appreciation of the processes involved.

Demand forecasting
Manpower demand forecasts start with "the formulation of the organization's overall objectives" for the period over which the forecast is to be made. This, as Lawrence points out, is likely to be a very short period because of the uncertainties involved in long term forecasting and the high costs therefore likely to be associated with it in relation to minor benefits (Lawrence, 1973, p 15). For a similar reason, many organizations "have little idea of what they want to be" (*ibid*) and therefore have no statement of forward objectives at all. Even where they do, "it is not always easy to interpret a corporate plan into a set of manpower requirements" (*ibid*) within a framework of economic, social, political and technological change of which little is under the control of the undertaking itself.

The statements of objectives, where they do exist, may be stated in ways which have very different implications for manpower demand forecasts. The objectives may be stated as a 17 per cent return on capital, as the achievement of a market share of, say, 45 per cent, or as the sales of a stated number of product-units. These three statements have an increasing amount of direct relevance to manpower demand forecasting: the 'labour content' of a product unit is known and can be fed into the forecast directly even if it is varied by a factor representing estimates of either technological change or the effects of learning curves upon labour performance; the number of units to be sold multiplied by the labour content is likely to give an estimate of demand in which a certain confidence might be reposed and the same might be said of the effect of stating objectives in terms of market share. The statement of objectives merely in terms of a return on capital might leave much more room for change of the product mix in the light of changes in sales or profitability of different lines, in which case the consequences in terms of labour content might be extremely difficult to predict with any confidence at all (Jones, Bell, Center and Coleman, 1967, pp 45–9).

These difficulties may help to account for the failure of corporations to come to terms with the need to link manpower planning with more general corporate planning (cf Smith, 1971, p 49). Lawrence, noting this tendency, and the prevalence of system models offered to guide the necessary interlinking (see figure 7 on p 20 of Lawrence, 1973) suggests that "typically the responsibility for manpower planning resides about two levels below the head of personnel (whence there are those who can achieve a great deal)" (ibid, p 21), but that it may still be sensible to develop the forecasts of the supply position (ie to deal with the tractable problems) and leave the plan "flexible and responsive to the needs of the organization" on the demand side (ibid).

As Smith has summarized the position, demand forecasting, "in the mechanistic sense is the prediction of the future based on observed regularities in the past; and practical forecasting must make due allowance also for foreseeable changes in policy, organization and technology which may break the established trends and relationships" (Smith, 1971, p 49). He also makes it clear that there is "no ready-made methodology for forecasting manpower demand which can be taken off the peg by any organization coming new to manpower planning" (Smith, 1971, p 48). The firm must develop its own methods of calculation and extrapolation, and correlation to suit its own circumstances, employing the relevant statistical techniques where they are available, usable and useful, but bearing in mind that managerial knowledge of future 'facts' and judgement of likely future relationships are likely to be as important as the techniques themselves in increasing understanding and prediction (ibid, p 48).

The two main categories of statistical technique available for this purpose are 'single cell techniques' useful in relation to relatively stable situations and therefore to the short-run forecast, and 'matrix techniques' which allow the exploration of more complex interrelationships between skills and industries (Bosworth and Evans, 1973). The first of these is particularly useful as a technique for extrapolating employment in a particular skill in a particular sector over a period and, with more sophisticated techniques, it can handle a long time series, which is more difficult to do in the matrix method. The single cell methods of making forecasts on the basis of a simple production gradient has some value: this says that manpower changes equal the product of (production × the gradient of change in production). To this can be added other factors such as technological change (cf Stainer, 1971, ch 6).

The matrix techniques are likely to be more useful to the undertaking seeking to make forecasts for a number of skills in a number of sectors or departments, where cells in the matrix can be considered to influence what may happen in other cells because of 'substitution' or 'productivity' effects (Leicester, 1968). What is 'predicted' by this method is the way in which the matrix might change as between two points in time, now and a date in the future. "A matrix is set up in which the columns might represent the different activities or departments of an organization, and the rows the skills that are required. If this matrix can be prepared for two points in time, estimates can be made of the value of the row multipliers (r) and the column multipliers (s) that are necessary to describe the transition of the matrix over time" (Lawrence, 1973, p 19; see also Bosworth and Evans, 1973).

Forecasting internal supply
In order to meet estimated future demands for manpower, the undertaking must needs rely upon two main supply pools, one internal and the other external, but with the one forming a part of the other. The internal pool comprises those already employed, diminished by those who leave or are dismissed for a variety of reasons and increased by those who may be developed by training and experience. The external pool comprises those people who form the population of the country working or likely to be seeking work, modified by recruitment by competing organizations, and by additions to stock from the educational system, retraining programmes and redundancies elsewhere.

This aspect of forecasting is both more developed and more reliable largely because the data necessary is, in principle, more readily accessible to the forecasters and extrapolation of developments on the supply side is the more readily assessable by the managers who live with it. Forecasts of supply from internal sources start with the basic demographic data on the existing labour force, age, sex, length of service, capability (eg in terms of skills possessed or experience gained), which ought to be available in any personnel department. Projection of this population into the future will inevitably mean dropping off those who can be predicted to retire or quit in the period, say over 10 years. The modification of the existing stock by projections of labour turnover may be done crudely, using gross data (eg a simple variation at 10 per cent turnover per annum), or in a more sophisticated way based on calculation of turnover rates for age, sex and skill cohorts, and taking into account the predicted effects of changes in dismissal practice (eg under the Employment Protection Act) or changes in transferability of pension rights etc (see, particularly, Young, 1961 and 1965; Jones, Bell Center, Coleman, 1967). No matter how sophisticated the method of forecasting, the resultant prediction will be no better than the assumptions fed in as to how changes are likely to make their presence felt in the future.

The long-standing involvement of the personnel people in gathering certain types of data on the labour force employed—the old 'employment function'—now acquires a new relevance and significance in the face of the need to make forecasts of the future. Statistics on labour turnover and on internal movement (by transfer, promotion etc) have usually been collected in detail and for many years where the employment function has been allowed to develop and these provide input data which can be extrapolated to inform predictions of how the existing labour force will diminish or change in the future.

Unfortunately, much of the data which is gathered and processed in personnel departments tends to be in a form which may allow very simplified predictions, but does not permit statistical analysis of the more complicated type. The basic distinction here is between the use of statistics in deterministic models and their use in stochastic models. The first model involves an abstraction from the complexities of the reality on the basis of averages—such as average age, average length of service or average rates of labour turnover etc. That it abstracts from the reality in this way is normal and natural, and necessary to the taking of decisions, because we cannot take decisions if we have to consider every individual event on its own. But the *kind* of abstraction, based on averages, does not permit the probability of a predicted outcome to be calculated and it is this—the calculation of probability—which is involved in stochastic models. These try to work out the probability or likelihood of some event or outcome coming about and, because of this, they are statistically more complex. But even the first kind of model can be linked across to allow probabilities to be calculated and, when that is done, when the uncertainty is reduced to statements about risk, these too become the more complicated as a consequence.

What these methods centre attention on are the dynamics of manpower populations and flows. In relation to internal supply forecasting, they demand analysis of the likelihood of people staying (being retained) in the undertaking (using labour turnover indexes of the British Institute of Management type, stability indexes for the whole or categories and the development of retention profiles) and of the probabilities of internal movements (from age or length of service categories to others, from grades to others, from salary levels to others, or any combination thereof) to give a prediction of structure on these dimensions at 'n' months or years into the future (according to the time horizon being used). It follows that in order to make these kinds of calculation the data required will have to be assembled in a usable form, and it is this which has not always been done in the past, because then either it was collected for other purposes or it was collected to inform a deterministic model rather than a stochastic one.

The point may be illustrated with reference to the old chestnut of personnel record keeping, labour turnover. This has usually been calculated in the form of a 'crude wastage rate', which may indicate how the undertaking is doing in comparison with other undertakings but does not of itself say much about what might happen to a cohort of new recruits taken on today in terms of stability or turnover (cf Lawrence, 1973, p 7). Some of the early work by the Tavistock Institute of Human Relations considered wastage in relation to length of service, on the hypothesis that leaving was a mathematical function of the length of service of the individual (Hill, 1951; Rice, 1951; Rice and Trist, 1952, Rice, *et al,* 1950). This and the work of the National Coal Board in the early 1960s suggested that the relationship of labour wastage and length of service was log-normal; in effect, a given cohort of recruits will demonstrate high wastage initially and will then 'settle down' to a steady and diminishing rate of quitting. The NCB studies also showed a high correlation between wastage rate and the distance that miners had to travel to work (Tomlinson, 1964). Such studies thus offer an explanation and a model of labour wastage over a period and can be employed to structure forecasts of future internal supply (Bell, 1974, pp 43–55).

These early 'life expectancy' or 'actuarial' studies gave rise to various methods of profiling—the simple drawing of 'pictures' of a future structure of the labour force on such dimensions as age, length of service or expected grade in which located (Bell (1974) illustrates some of these on pp 63 and 64, as does Lawrence (1973) on p 10). One such profile, based on such actuarial calculations might be introduced in the diagram on p 123 above in place of the simple circle which is employed to indicate the nature of the boundary between an undertaking and its environment: the arrows showing entrance would then all lead to the 'base' of the profile and those indicating termination would take off from the survival graph. What is thus being depicted is only one step on from what is attempted in the production of 'back-up' charts in management succession planning, where the emphasis is usually upon individuals rather than 'cohorts' of entrants and upon individual promotability and promotion rather than probabilities of movement between grades.

The developments from these early calculations during the 1950s and 1960s have sought to improve the predictions, where the data has been available, by the application of stochastic methods. Perhaps the most complicated and least easily understood approach,

135

from the non-statistician's standpoint, is the use of the linear programming model (Purkiss, in Wilson, 1969, pp 67–78; Morgan, in Smith, 1970, pp 317–25) designed to estimate costs of policy variants in respect of recruitment and termination. The other two main variants are described by Lawrence in the following terms: "The analytical models divide roughly into two sorts. The Markov or 'push' type assume that promotions are not dependent upon vacancies occurring, but instead are the result of management 'pushing' individuals along their career paths at fixed rates. These models are descriptive, technically comprehensible and computationally fairly simple. At the other extreme the renewal or 'pull' type models assume that all promotions are the result of vacancies occurring, as if employees are 'pulled' through the organization to fill gaps as they arise. Unfortunately, these models suffer from being computationally inconvenient and mathematically obscure to the non-technical person" (Lawrence, 1973, p 14; see also, Bell, 1970, pp 57–62; Bartholomew, 1967).

These difficulties led the attempt to develop Markov models based upon the observation that promotions are the result of both push and pull factors and giving a result which was both "more realistic in its assumptions and computationally attractive" (*ibid*). The model is made to represent any desired configuration of separate manpower groupings (grades, particular kinds of people within them, staff at different locations etc) and the required flows to and from the groupings, either between them, or to them from outside the system or from them to outside the system. The model is computerized and what is fed into the model is described by Lawrence (1973) as follows:

(a) current strength by grade and age
(b) wastage rates by grade and age
(c) age distributions of recruits into the system, specific for each recruitment grade
(d) grade-specific 'rules' for the selection of promotees. These are in terms of age bands from which specified proportions of total promotees from the grade, in a time period, are selected
(e) where there is more than one inward flow to a grade, the proportion of total vacancies in the grade to be filled by each
(f) where there is more than one outward flow from a grade (other than wastage, which the model treats as a first call on the strength), the order in which flows are to be treated
(g) the required future strength of each grade, usually expressed by a positive or negative growth factor.

(Lawrence, 1973, p 14)

136

Figure 3
Some stationary population models

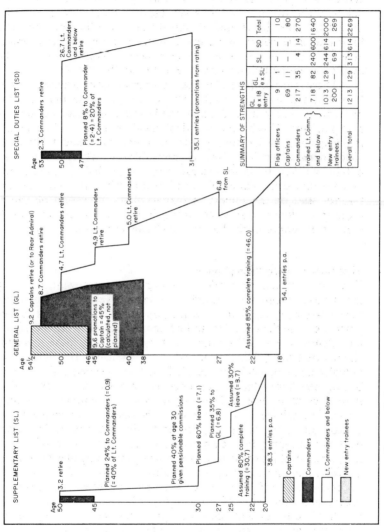

Source: J Lawrence, "Manpower and Personnel Models in Britain",
Personnel Review Vol 2, No 3, Summer, 1973, p 10

137

This data-input allows the computer to go through the process of filling vacancies created by wastage or promotion according to whether there is to be growth or contraction in the grouping concerned, and does this by external recruitment or promotion from below, taking into account the given age distribution for recruits, the promotion rules to be applied and the specified flow proportions. Shortfalls in recruitment are made up from those in other promotable age bands in proportion to their specified contributions to the total of promotees (Lawrence, 1973, p 14; Smith, 1976).

These more sophisticated exercises remain comparable in intention, although not form, to those which the personnel manager has often attempted in the past under the heading of manpower succession planning. This fits the one ideological orientation of personnel management, which emphasizes the inherent involvement with individual persons, but it tends to be applicable only where the category of labour concerned is not so large as to make individual predictions as to the future internal supply position impossible. In smaller undertakings, and on the subject of management succession planning, these 'individualistic' approaches may be all that is necessary and all that can be supported by the data which can be generated.

Management succession planning

The approach usually made to management succession planning may be used to illustrate the affinity of manpower planning of a sort to the case work method (see below, pp 238–42). The affinity arises partly because the vacancies to be filled in the future are individual and identifiable on a 'back-up' chart, and partly because it is considered that the qualities required in the manager are highly individualized and of a different nature from those needed in the manual or routine white collar worker. There is some reason to suppose that in some circumstances, at least, the approach to manpower planning may in future have to take on more of the caste of management succession planning than it has needed to do in the past. The more employing organizations come to regard recruitment to jobs in terms not merely of skills but in terms of securing matching of expectancies of individual and organization (Mumford, 1970, p 77), the more it becomes necessary to consider personal 'qualities' and position 'offers' in a framework of mutuality. For both of these reasons it is worth while to look at succession planning before examining the more general approach to manpower planning (cf Patten, 1971).

The problem of identifying possible 'successors' from within the undertaking (a measure of 'internal supply') is very often dealt with in association with procedures related to improving on the current job performance, to improving communication between the boss and subordinate and to providing data to allow testing of initial selection choices. 'Management appraisal' or 'management review' is a generic term which is used to apply, in various combinations, to these different problems and solutions but the effect is that, for all but the very top personnel, the approach to succession planning is wrapped around with other performance appraisal requirements. On its own, succession planning is usually stated to be concerned with the identification of more junior personnel with capacity and capability to move into more senior positions (usually with some development), in order that the organization has some appreciation at any one moment not only of what stock of trained manpower it has available for its current needs, but also what stock it has potentially to meet future exigencies, assuming that the future 'need' will replicate the current stock by number and skill (see above, pp 133–38).

Because of the association with performance review, some plans attempt to base assessments of future capacity and capability on current performance as predictors of that capability but in other cases a distinct set of criteria are postulated as relevant to the prediction of likely future promotion. In one company, whose plan was reported in the *Financial Times* some years ago, the aim was to identify 'managerial talents' in subordinate staff on the basis of their possession of (a) a sense of reality; (b) a power of analysis, (c) an ability to anticipate; (d) imagination, and (e) 'the helicopter quality'. Salaman and Bristow summarize the problem which arises when managers are invited to rate subordinates on a five point scale for such factors as diligence, application, job knowledge etc: "Such a system presents a number of difficulties. The characteristics listed might be so vague as to be almost meaningless; they might be irrelevant to some or all of the people who are to be assessed; or they might be more important for some jobs than others. Sometimes it is not clear to those who are doing the job rating exactly what is meant by the characteristics that they are dealing with and they might not agree on what would constitute evidence of such a characteristic; this can increase the difference between ratings and make it impossible to compare them. Sometimes raters are asked to add their ratings to make a grand total, even when it should be clear that some of the characteristics are far more crucial to job success than others" (1970, p 37). Nevertheless, in spite of known problems of this type, such attempts at appraisal are perpetrated.

Once made and reported to the centre, these judgements are transferred to a back-up table or a back-up chart (see p 142 below) in order to show (a) which persons(s) already engaged might stand as potential replacements for any listed manager, and (b) what is the

Division . . . .
Approved by . . . .
Date . . . .

Figure 4

Forward planning and replacement schedule (confidential)
Management record showing appraisals, anticipated position
vacancies and probable back-up men

PRESENT AND PROJECTED MANAGEMENT ORGANIZATION						PROBABLE BACK-UP MEN				
name	age	present and projected positions	performance appraisal summaries	recommended for	replacement estimated to take place	name		age	present position	estimated time required to qualify
						1				
						2				
						3				
						1				
						2				
						3				
						1				
						2				
						3				
						1				
						2				
						3				
						1				
						2				
						3				

likely prognosis for development and promotion of any of the charted personnel. Clearly, there are problems asssociated with the assessments themselves, where they are based upon 'dimensions of characteristics' of persons which psychologists would not claim to be able to measure and where, as is often the case, no or very little training is given to the assessors to enable them to establish norms and development motivation and ability to assess. It is probably in reflection, partially at least, of these problems that such back-up charts are often not employed when an actual vacancy occurs, the decision being taken at that point to throw the vacancy open to competition in the more normal fashion. This consideration led Browning (1963) to suggest that management succession planning was best done on a relatively informal basis without systematic annual trawling of superordinate's assessments of subordinates on this dimension.

A similar judgement is usually made about the generality of manpower in smaller undertakings where, by whatever methods, some judgement can be made of the likely availability of labour across the whole hierarchical spectrum. In these circumstances it is neither sensible from the point of view of the data base, nor economically profitable to engage in exercises which involve a set of sophisticated statistical techniques. Large organizations, and particular large tracts of the public service, may be able to develop these forecasting techniques with great advantage, but not the small undertaking. But there is no reason why the implications of these more sophisticated developments for the production of data should be ignored in the less complex situation of the smaller undertaking or labour category. A feasibility study might suggest that the more refined techniques were just not worth applying, but it might also suggest better methods of making judgements within the existing framework.

External supply forecasting
Such predictions must inevitably deal with only one part, and possibly even the smaller part in the longer term of the total supply picture. To a greater or lesser extent an organization (even one which is not foreseeing expansion) will be dependent upon what happens to the pool outside the enterprise. This pool consists at any one time of a pool of actual and potential workers: the actual workers are those 'in employment'; the potential comprises those not in employment, whether because of unemployment or because, like many women, they choose not to work in those circumstances. The pool will be diminished in size by demise and retirement from the active labour force, and increased by those entering the labour market from the

141

Figure 5

Organization chart showing management potential

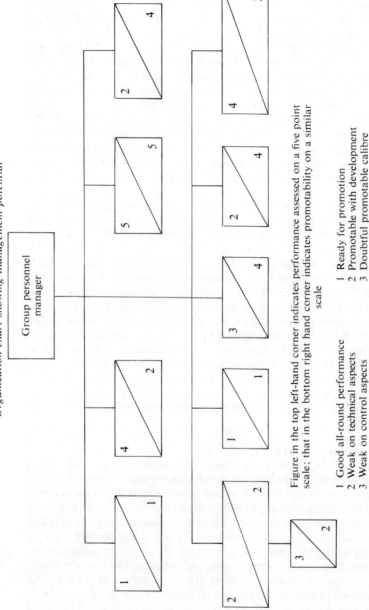

Figure in the top left-hand corner indicates performance assessed on a five point scale; that in the bottom right hand corner indicates promotability on a similar scale

1 Good all-round performance
2 Weak on technical aspects
3 Weak on control aspects
4 Weak on human relations
5 Weak on administration

1 Ready for promotion
2 Promotable with development
3 Doubtful promotable calibre
4 Impending retirement
5 Should be transferred

educational system or more simply from not working at all (again like the housewives). Clearly, the overall size of this pool will be affected by changes in the birth and death rates, by changes in school-leaving or retirement ages, and by changes in economic and social conditions (affecting the motivation of the 'non-working' groups to enter upon the labour market). At present, for example, there is some pressure to reduce the age of retirement and to increase the opportunities for young people to engage in further and higher education, both of which will, if implemented, affect the size of the available labour force, as will the post-war declining birth rate now affecting Britain.

Since the quantities in the wider external manpower pool are generally larger than those relating to internal demand and supply forecasting, it would be possible to make more probable forecastings of stocks and flows here, as indeed is achieved in national manpower forecasting although even here there is no determinancy. Nevertheless what may be expected to happen to the 'external pool' can usually be expressed with greater confidence than what may be expected for the internal one. The diagram of stocks and flows presented by the Edinburgh Group (at p 56) indicates the broad dimensions of this situation, although for the particular employer the addition of an 'output' to other employments might help to complete the picture (see Jones, Bell, Center and Coleman, 1967). That presented by Donald (1966) for the Health Service is comparable but introduces certain other features peculiar to that kind of service industry. Such models alone will not indicate for the particular enterprise what part of this stock will be available to it, in varying circumstances of future demand. This calculation must be made in relation to likely conditions of competition for the available labour supply, which in turn has two components: first, how much competition from other undertakings can be expected in the particular labour market, which might reflect no more than mere numbers demanded; and secondly, how much can be expected in varying conditions of 'offer' by the enterprise and its competitors (eg whether the enterprise can create an image of being a 'better employer' than others).

The outputs of public manpower planning are of relevance at the undertaking level, particularly in so far as what is projected for the manpower in the economy as a whole will provide both constraint and relevant data for intra-enterprise decisions. In terms of a planning 'model', what happens in the environment (represented by national manpower planning) must be fed into the local model. In the British context at present this raises problems.

Although "aggregate supply projections are the simplest and

most commonly made" (Patten, 1971, p 47) they are made at the level of the economy and "are limited almost exclusively to estimates of changes in the numbers of persons" (*ibid*), and more especially of persons by industry of employment and occupation, not skill. 'Skill' as a supply element is rarely projected at all, except in connection with specific formal training (eg the stocks and flows of scientists and engineers) in colleges and universities. In particular, the stock of skilled craftsmen, in engineering or electronics, is not and probably could not be calculated without a specific *ad hoc* study; consequently, in this major post-war shortage, the kind of projection which the undertaking's manpower planner would like to have is not available to him. Although there were high hopes of an improvement in manpower supply data, both in the 1960s (in association with the Industrial Training Act) and in the 1970s (with the establishment of the Manpower Services Commission and its specialized agencies for employment and training) these have not been realized by way of better information from public sources (cf Bell, 1974; and Dodge, 1977).

The problems associated with forecasting of external supply, are not so much associated with statistical techniques as with the availability of 'statistics' (data) and of knowledge of decided or possible developments within competitor undertakings. Particularly where manual and routine clerical labour is concerned, what the manpower planner is interested in is information about the local labour market (in the case of managerial and professional labour, the 'local' labour market may be more closely identified with the 'national' market). This may be important where the purpose of the plan is to forecast likely situations to be encountered in relocation of plant or office.

As Bell says, "the company manpower planner must make do with what information he can get" on this dimension (Bell, 1974, p 75). His own knowledge of what has happened and what might happen is unlikely to be supplemented by statistical data from official sources, except on a general national (and in a limited number of cases on an occupational) basis, where the very broad trends may be available to him from the Department of Employment *Gazettes*, the Monthly Abstract of Statistics, the particular Industry Training Board, and the special studies of some researchers. This is 'disappointing', says Bell (*ibid,* p 74), and his best advice is contained in the statement that "a good manager keeps very closely in touch with all the employers in his area" (*ibid,* p 73).

The outcome of such an exercise will be to indicate how much manpower the enterprise can reasonably expect to be able to take up from the labour markets for the different categories of skill and experience which it considers on the basis of its demand analysis it will require. The general conclusion is likely to be that in future, for a variety of reasons, there will be greater pressure upon the enterprise itself to secure its manpower requirements less by recruitment directly from the labour market and more by redeployment following training and re-training of the existing labour force. Although the educational system, the main contributor of labour to employment, is currently subject to considerable pressures to change, any advantage to manning which might be expected from this source is likely to be outweighed, from the present point of view, by further restrictions on the employer's licence to manipulate labour to and from the labour market.

Major influences on demand and supply variables

Any attempt to convert uncertainty into risk in the area of manpower planning, based on the application of forecasting techniques, does not by itself produce a plan. This merely provides some information on which such plans can be based, and that part of the exercise calls for the exercise of managerial judgement as the strategy to be adopted to ensure that, at the target date in the future, there will be a calculable chance of the undertaking having available to it the amount and quantity of labour which is likely to be required. But the manpower planner's concepts of demand and supply, as we have discussed them above, are not to be equated simply to these concepts as employed by economists. In fact, there are two other important issues which enter into the latter calculation, and therefore into the calculations of the manpower planners themselves, when the plans are being developed.

These questions concern the price and the cost of the labour. The supply of labour to the undertaking (netted from those offering themselves for employment and those terminating their employment) will be affected by the attractiveness of the wage (used as a shorthand expression for the 'total reward package') and also by the other facilities which the employment might offer to the individual. The supply forecasts must therefore be set against what might be considered to be the attractive or attracting wage. But in addition the supply position is to some extent, and at some cost, capable of being modified by many undertakings by the mechanism of training. This may be regarded as having three different influences. First, it could in itself function as a positive factor in the reward package as perceived by the individual. Secondly, it can be employed to retain labour which would otherwise be dismissed (eg as redundant) or quit (eg because of lack of perceived opportunity for development and advancement). Thirdly, it can be used to produce a supply of qualified labour where none such exists on the open labour market.

The attractive wage

One major element in planning manpower is the wage or salary offered to new starters to attract them to join the undertaking. This is not influenced by exactly the same factors as play upon the wage or salary necessary to retain personnel once they have joined it (March and Simon, 1958, ch 4). The starting wage offered has to overcome individual inertia—whether he/she is employed elsewhere or whether he is dependent upon transfer payments—whereas this same inertia will tend to act to the employer's advantage once employment has been taken up. Conscious decisions are called for on both scores in manpower planning, but they are increasingly 'conscious' decisions for many employing organizations since they cannot be assumed to face a freely competitive market in labour. The decision may not be within the unilaterally exercised discretion of the employer or manager but it remains a decision.

Manpower planning can be regarded as a consequence of the development of 'administered wages' and 'administered employment' in place of the free market system which may actually, but which was certainly assumed to, have preceded it. In a perfect market system, labour supply and demand were assumed to be brought into balance by the operation of the price mechanism, and 'manpower planning' was not undertaken as a separate exercise from that of determining whether to produce. With the growth of trade unions deliberately seeking to modify the unimpeded effects of market forces upon wage rates and employment, and a comparable growth of employer organization to meet this challenge (cf Ross, 1948), *that* set of market forces no longer enjoyed untrammelled influence. Manpower planning as a political decision-taking process aimed at adjusting supply, demand and price features within some other set of values, was substituted. On the money value dimension, this change had the effect of replacing the simple equation of labour cost equals labour price equals wage rate with a much more complex one of cost equals the aggregate of a large number of separate components of 'labour benefit' and thus allowed considerable possibility of combination of different cost-bearing benefits as the cost of labour. On the quantity of labour dimension, the change had the effect of replacing the simple 'man' unit of supply and demand and admitting many different facets of demand and supply to the bargaining table, such as units of effort or contribution.

In Britain, in recent years, the traditional method of determining the wage rate, by negotiation between employer and trade union representatives, has been thrown into disarray by full employment, technological change and inflation. The first two have exerted their influence mainly upon the power of the worker (and his trade union) and the second has additionally effected significant changes in the composition of jobs themselves; but the third has, arguably, had the major effect in so far as it has caused bargaining to take place in conditions of greater uncertainty in which there are few devices for reducing this to a more calculable risk. Whether the cause of the inflation itself is external to the economy, and whether it is properly describable as demand pull or cost push inflation, attempts to deal with the uncertainty are themselves often contributory to the inflation because of the 'margins' which the negotiators seek to provide for in their settlements—in the absence of governmental restrictions on levels and forms of settlements (cf Jackson, Turner and Wilkinson, 1972).

Two main methods of dealing with this problem are discernible: the pursuit of an uncertainty-reducing 'round' of bargaining, and the search for a method of administering the external relativities in pay fixing.

In the first, the pay fixing process is seen as beginning with a feeling on the part of workers of a sense of relative deprivation, either because their existing pay does not 'go as far as it did' or because they see some other more powerful group securing increases in pay whilst they stay still. This gives rise to claims which seek either a 'cost of living' addition to wages to make up for the inflation loss or restoration of relativity or comparability to put them back into their 'proper' place in the league table of pay. These feelings and the claims they give rise to are likely to be more powerful as stimulators of a new round of bargaining over pay than purely 'economic factors', such as those associated with productivity and mere ability to pay at the micro level or unemployment and balance of payments at the macro level.

From this point of initiation, bargaining in recent years has come increasingly to take the form of the development of 'rounds'. In the 1960s, the idea of a 'round' of wage demands and wage increases began to gain ground (even though disguised to some extent by the prevalence of local bargaining in some industries) and progressively groups which were not originally in the 'rounds' were brought in, so that by the middle 1970s very few categories were left out (one could, for example, argue that only the MPs themselves were caught outside the process when new policies appeared in 1975, although some other groups, like judges and university teachers, had only just made it and had not perhaps become very proficient in pursuing the rounds). During this period, too, except where government pay policies placed restrictions on the rounds, the tendency developed for the absolute level of increases to increase year by year, producing an escalator effect on inflation, and for the length of a round to shorten, with

147

a similar effect compounded. Nevertheless by 1975 the idea of an annual round of pay bargaining had established itself, and most groups of workers, from the lowest paid to the highest paid white collar workers had established their 'position' in the round, some coming in early and others late.

The importance of this concept of a 'round', viewed from the standpoint of planning wage rates for attraction and retention of labour at appropriate levels of efficiency, is that it lends itself to the practice of building in 'margins' to cover for the uncertainty expected to exist before the next round can be carried out. Where the situation is 'open,' particularly where it is not constrained by central pay policies of governments or labour market institutions (such as the 'social contract'), the negotiated rate is likely to contain explicit margins, in the form of automatic escalations made contingent upon inflationary changes or of re-opening provisions allowing renegotiation in similar circumstances. In the constrained situation the opportunity for negotiating such marginal protections may be denied, and the same objective is therefore sought via other kinds of provision: the negotiation of fringe benefits which have value to the worker and are a cost on the employer but which have tended not to be accounted as a part of the wage settlement. All these have the general effect of protecting the worker against inflation, to some extent, but they do not facilitate wage rate or wage cost forecasting by the employer.

Partly for this reason, employers have become keener to introduce systematic procedures for determining some elements of the wage and salary structures. These include attempts to 'abandon piecework' as a control device because it tends, in a condition of inflation to associate itself with inflation of wage costs; attempts to abandon or at least restrict overtime working for comparable reasons; and plans to introduce job evaluation schemes in order to allow the differential position to be stabilized even if the minimum hiring rate might still be left to escalate. All these help to increase the importance of plant or company wide negotiations at the expense of national or supra-plant bargaining, and thus focus more attention on the methods and techniques of wage and salary administration as within the purview and competence of the personnel department. From the employers' standpoint, the development of such control methods and their containment within locally controllable negotiating frameworks offer some hope that the uncertainties inherent in the situation of change might be reduced to more predictable risks.

One aim of a wage system, from the standpoint of the employer, has been (a) to attract labour from the market and to retain it at the lowest rate consistent with securing enough in quantity to satisfy his production needs, and (b) to ensure that such labour will make a sufficient contribution to the enterprise's tasks to allow it to survive in its product market(s) at the prices he can secure.

The aims of salary systems are comparable in that they "should *inter alia* influence suitable candidates in sufficient number to apply for and accept employment in the undertaking, facilitate the deployment of employees in such a way as will conduce to the maximum efficiency of the undertaking, influence such people as are suitable to the current and future needs of the undertaking (and only such people) to remain in its employment, and be adequately related to the attainment and continuance of high performance by individuals" (NBPI, Report No 132, 1969, pp 7–8). Salary policy, says Bowley (1972), "should help *inter alia* to attract staff of the right calibre, encourage staff to stay with the company (if it is in their own and the company's best interests) and facilitate movement of staff across departmental, divisional or sectional boundaries" (Bowley, 1972, p 6).

The personnel manager's involvement in realizing these objectives was in the past largely twofold. He had to assemble information (in discussion with fellow personnel managers or through local wage rate and salary surveys) on the rates being paid to classes (eg skilled, semi-skilled or unskilled) or categories (eg fitters and turners, machine operators or process workers) of labour in order either to determine what rates ought to be paid within his own establishment, or to fix the parameters for offer and settlement within a framework of negotiations with local trade union representatives on the structure of rates to apply in the company. He had also to engage in the actual bargaining processes themselves and, in so doing, had to secure acceptance not only of the particular rate of pay but also of the validity and applicability of certain underlying assumptions about what factors determined whether a rate was 'right' by comparison with other parts of the market considered relevant. Success in both depended ultimately upon a sufficient stability in the structures of rates and in the assumptions underlying them in the environment of the company.

Where in the past there may have been a known or easily ascertainable 'supply price' for broad categories of labour (like skilled men or labourers) the task of the personnel practitioner in establishing what might be the expected price to be paid 'on the market' was less difficult than now, when even broad skill categories tend to be more closely identified with specific undertakings and their job requirements, from which more volatile rate structures have developed.

Because of this development, the calculation of a blue-collar

149

labour market price may call for more systematized techniques, based upon the concept of a wage or salary survey, described by Elliott (1960) as "one of the most modern techniques at our disposal" which removed the "obstacle to anyone who is interested in knowing what is generally paid for a particular type of man".

The problem was seen then as essentially a technical one, that of getting the mix right. Thus Roy (1960), talking of surveys by professional institutions of the salaries of their own members, commented that they were suspect in that "one is never sure that the cross-section or the sample conforms to the sample of technical staff and scientific staff in one's own company". The real answer, he suggested, was to get companies to supply complete information on all their scientific staff in a scatter chart. "If you get several companies common to that field, as we do—and we have selected surveys covering 6,000 scientists—they are only suspect in that your cross-section of scientific staff compares with the cross-section of these other companies. However, I think surely that that comparison will be closer than a comparison with institutions where they depend on the person willingly giving the information to that institution".

More recently, Carvalho commented on what becomes a much more intractable problem when the rate of change increases: "External equity is not established logically if historical data are used to 'update' a compensation program. Any updated compensation program is out of date before it is used simply because it requires time to update the program". Time only becomes of the essence when either increased mobility deflects the direction of market forces, or an increased rate of wage settlement in inflationary conditions more quickly renders historical data obsolete. Since both these phenomena appear to be present in modern economics, they may help account for the pressure to find other methods of determining both general and differential levels of pay (Carvalho, 1971, pp 217–218).

The objectives of salary policy for the higher echelons of management are generally not different from those pursued at lower levels. Such differences as do exist reflect mainly the different shape of this labour market (which will tend to be national at least and probably international in scope) and the different nature of the bonus or incentive payments generally regarded as applicable at this level. Additionally, determination of the 'compensation' package for this class of labour has in the past needed to pay close attention to remuneration in relationship to the incidence of taxation (although fiscal drag has more recently focused attention on this kind of problem for other wages and salaries). Nevertheless, when all such calculations have been made, the object of the compensation package is to attract and retain the senior managers etc required and to elicit their continued contribution to the health of the enterprise as a whole.

The methods employed to realize the objective are also not different in principle. In form, surveys must give attention to a more diverse scatter of elements in the compensation programme, and quite often must spread over wider territory, for example, comparing executive compensation as a totality throughout Europe and/or North America. In this case too, comparison of like with like generally means controlling for the size of establishment or company, and distinguishing between public and private enterprise and, on the international level, making careful calculations as to the effects of taxation on the value of the compensation. Although such international comparisons are not confined to senior management compensation but also apply to various professional categories of employee, it is in the first area that the major problems of comparability lie, as compensation of scientists, engineers or doctors tends to be less ramified and related to more easily definable work roles.

In all three of these cases, wages, salaries and professional or executive compensation, what is sought is an indication of the right 'absolute' level of remuneration, and this is what essentially the survey (however shaped) is designed to provide. In all cases the data supplied in these ways will be historical data, and the need is for decisions about 'correct' future levels of remuneration. In general terms, two major problems arise for the personnel manager in the present context: (a) how far historical data offer a guide to future action, especially when—as may the case currently in Britain—society may be passing through a period of change in its cultural values as these relate particularly to remuneration of different classes of labour? (b) how far action is possible to bring remuneration into line with either intra-national or international rates of compensation, when national remuneration policies and taxation systems are designed to effect outcomes which are clearly in opposition to achieving such comparability?

In order to provide a more systematic foundation for making inter-organizational comparisons of pay, Lupton & Bowey (1972–1973, ch 2; and Bowey & Lupton, 1973) have offered a method of comparing the characteristics of different jobs and the reward composition of different jobs. "It is usual for employees to compare their earnings with those of persons doing similar work in other organizations. Much collective bargaining is based on claims for parity supported by such comparisons. If the employer resists the claim on the ground that the work is not in fact similar or cites other comparisons unfavourable to the employee, then the appeal must be to some procedure that both claimants can accept" (Lupton and Bowey, 1973, p 50). The authors argue that job evaluation arrangements do not prevent unfavourable comparisons with pay in other organizations being made, and that the methods of *internal* job ranking are not suitable for inter-organizational comparisons, so that a distinct procedure is necessary.

In their view, comparisons of jobs in different organizations need to be based upon a systematic assessment and comparison of the selected jobs on the basis of skill, responsibility, mental effort, physical effort and working conditions, each of which can be broken down into sub-factors in order to ensure that jobs which are as nearly as possible the same as the one in the home organization can be identified. Since the individuals concerned and their representatives at the bargaining table will recognize that these factors and sub-factors will have different importance as a factor in wages, these can then be weighted; Lupton and Bowey indicate possible weights which have been applied, but do not regard them as sacrosanct (*ibid,* p 53). A secondary weighting exercise is then carried out to ensure that widely different amounts of a particular and unimportant factor is not given overweight in the comparison and a method of conversion which reduces the scores on all factors in the comparison jobs to a plus or a minus by comparison with the zero score assigned to that factor in the bench-mark job in the home organization. (The scores are, however, all treated as positive (pluses) in order to avoid cancelling out.) The latter will thus end us up with a score of zero, and the comparison jobs chosen will have variable positive scores on each of the factors and in total from which a conclusion can be drawn as to which 'other job' is closest in terms of its demands on the incumbent to the home organization job. This makes it possible to "ensure that in comparing the pay of a benchmark job and a comparison job, one knows the extent to which one is comparing like with like" (Lupton and Bowey, 1973, p 64).

Comparing the 'closest' jobs in terms of pay means that the pay must be broken down into its component parts, in order to cope with the problem of variability of earnings from week to week. Average weekly earnings are divided into "the part that is guaranteed (eg base rate, job rate), the part that is regular, although not guaranteed (eg the pay for regular overtime) and thirdly, the part that is sporadic and unreliable (such as very high bonus earnings or irregular and unpredictable overtime)". To the first two, a figure for sporadic pay is then added, defined as the amount that can be relied upon for five weeks out of six, diminished by an amount equal to two-thirds of the deviation of sporadic pay: the formula: guaranteed earnings, plus regular overtime plus (sporadic pay minus two-thirds deviation of sporadic pay) then yields the 'compounded earnings'. This particular formula can be varied according to the desires of the calculator or the parties to negotiation of pay on the basis of comparisons.

In order to systematize the approach to inter-organizational comparison, Lupton and Bowey suggest a procedure within which four choices have to be made: of which jobs are to be compared, of what weights are to be used for factors, as to the limits to be set in 'secondary weighting', and of the rule to be used for comparing earnings (particularly in relation to the irregular elements). These decisions can be taken by the salary administrator to help discover what might keep the internal rates in line with those outside, or by the parties to negotiations, when they will form 'agreements' in the usual industrial relations sense of the term (Lupton & Bowey, 1973, p 71). The method can also be used either as it is or with modifications to take into account a different range of actors thought appropriate, to determine comparisons for white collar jobs in organizations, supplementing the salary surveys available which usually suffer from the same problem of determining what in the way of 'other jobs' is really comparable in terms of the demands which they make (Lupton and Bowey, 1973, p 122).

Training to increase labour supply
However attractive the reward package may be, it will not by itself attract a predicted supply of labour in the requisite skill categories from the open labour market, if that kind of labour does not exist as a mobile or potentially mobile group. The kind of problem envisaged here is exemplified by the fairly persistent shortage experienced by companies of skilled craftsmen in the post-war world: there are skilled craftsmen in employment but there are generally speaking not enough to meet the demand in most places and, whilst it can be argued that this ought to force the wage to rise and so restore the eroded differentials and increase the supply, this strategy is constrained by public policy (at least) and firms will therefore have to seek other means of increasing the supply.

Generically speaking, the main mechanism for this purpose is training. Training has generally been regarded as inadequately carried out for much of the post-war period, and the succession of developments from the enactment of the Industrial Training Act of 1964 to the creation of the Manpower Services Commission and its subordinate employment and training agencies in 1973, has been embarked upon in order to try to remedy this situation. This seeks to encourage undertakings to engage in more and better training. But there have also been developments of legislation increasing the cost to the employer of getting the manning wrong (eg Redundancy Payments and Employment Protection Acts) and these also 'encourage'

153

companies to consider alternative strategies to simple hiring and firing in order to get the equilibrium right. When these are coupled with the labour market situation itself—the skill shortages and the difficulties of measuring changes in the external supply position—training in its generic sense acquires a greater interest for undertakings.

It might be said that some kind of training takes place in any undertaking, whether it is the formal intention or not. Any individual brought into a work (social) situation which has novel features for him or her, must develop some perception of the expectations which surround the role, and in following out this imperative he or she will pick up information relevant to that role, whether anyone intends or orders it or not. Increasingly, for the reasons just mentioned, employers are now developing some policy and programme of training. This varies in its degree of formality according to many factors in the situation of which perhaps the most important is the size and technical complexity of the organization concerned, and the specificity of the skills required in the jobs available within it. At one extreme the training may mean no more than on-the-job instruction by a supervisor who attempts to show the individual how to carry out the particular job that he is hired to do. At the other extreme, organizations may establish elaborate policies and ramified programmes of training to cope with the whole spectrum of need for induction and technical training, training for personal development, and training for all aspects of supervision and management.

Whether an undertaking should engage in training, and if so in what kind of training for what purpose, may be determined against strategic and tactical criteria. Whether training is worthwhile is a question which can be answered differently according to the source of the criteria used: the assessment might be made in terms of the effects of training upon the individual or in terms of its consequences for the enterprise. In the first context, training consequences will link to the goals of the individual, whether these be immediate (as shown up in terms of greater job satisfaction, greater reward or greater job security) or distant (related, for example, to his expectations of career development and long term job security or equally long-term considerations of his self-concept). In the second, training consequences will be assessed against the immediate contributions to improved job performance or immediate enhancement of the qualities of manpower required by the organization, and against the longer term opportunities which the training provides to avoid costly dismissal/recruitment exercises to effect adjustments between demand and supply. In both cases, there are costs involved: to the

154

individual who must take the trouble to unlearn some routine and acquire others; or to the enterprise which must expend money on the training (and forego the individual's contribution whilst it is underway) and any benefits must therefore be calculated net of these.

It tends to follow from this that in a period of economic decline for the enterprise, the net benefit of training will tend to be small in the short run, since the main aim will then be retrenchment and the main constraint will be a shortage of revenue which will have the effect of making the relative cost high and of discounting the longer term future benefits. Consequently the enterprise will tend to cut its training activity in periods of recession. Nor does it follow that the individual's conclusions from his calculation will be vastly different from this. Whilst the individual is employed in the enterprise, the main aim must be to secure his job property rights, which tend to depend most closely on seniority in the job. In such circumstances, staying put and contributing at a level which is adjudged to be consistent with retention of employment, may prove to be a preferred strategy to undertaking training to improve some hypothetical future chances of employment or advancement. When the individual has no employment, this calculation may well produce a very different conclusion, as indeed it may do for those (such as apprentices and trainees) who are taking part in a deliberate exercise of preparing for a future employment rather than in an established employment.

Both of these criteria are relevant to the manpower planner, in so far as the individual-oriented criteria relate to the notion of an attractive reward package, and the enterprise-oriented criteria link with conclusions as to the likelihood of appropriately skilled and able personnel being available in the labour market at the time when the undertaking forecasts it will require them. For the moment we will concentrate on the second of these, returning to the first under the heading of personnel development, in chapter 6 below.

Whether training, as such, can contribute to the plan (in projection or in implementation) will depend upon its capacity to meet the needs revealed by the forecasts. Not all forecasts need training as a major element in the strategy, although the increased emphasis upon employment stability and job property rights do suggest that the achievement of labour force flexibility will in future depend more so than in the past upon training. Therefore training will reflect this need element together with the element of satisfaction achievable through training.

From this point of view, training may be regarded as capable in appropriate circumstances of alleviating three difficulties, those of general skill requirement, specific skill (or limited role prescription) requirement, and (in a slightly more general context than manpower planning) motivational deficiency.

In the first category, are those who enter the undertaking without skill (or skill of the needed kind) but are recruited for skilled work; the obvious example is the school leaver who enters upon an apprenticeship. Although undertakings might think it cheaper to recruit fully trained personnel, this cannot generally be done unless a public training service carries out this function; some organization somewhere must provide this 'basic' training that new entrants or job changers need in order to carry out their assigned roles. Where the 'external supply' pool is empty, it may therefore prove necessary to establish a formal programme of initial, skill training as a part of the overall strategy for manning the undertaking. Training for future craftsmen usually takes the form of apprentice training, through which the skills of the craft are in some fashion or another transmitted to the young person who has decided to embark upon a craftsman's career. The fact that another employer may subsequently reap the benefit of this training does not alter the fact that employers in general must make adequate provision for training if the system of free recruitment is to work at all adequately. Non-craftsmen also require training and here it is more likely that the training will more often be given on-the-job because possibilities for transference of skill are less than in the case of craftsmen. To develop the appropriate amount and type of skill, therefore, formal training programmes are likely to be required.

Secondly, training may be incorporated in the strategy to improve or implant the skills which the individual will need in order to work within the particular organization. In certain occupational categories, the skills might already be present in the newly hired employee. Here the training process complements and completes the selection process. In an ideal world the organization might seek to recruit into its ranks those employees who came with the precise skills and the precise expectations that the organization requires of them. Frequently this is not so and writers on organizations like Fayol and Urwick were therefore led to propose that the organization had a main responsibility to get the work patterns right, but should otherwise take what it could get in the way of people to carry out this work. It would tend to follow from this view that training would be necessary to ensure that new employees fully appreciated what skills they would be expected to develop in relation to their jobs, and what other expectations would surround their conduct within the organization.

Organizations will vary in the extent to which they can rely upon recruitment of this type. For example, the engineering or printing craftsman might reasonably be expected to have acquired the skills which would be required in his employment in any particular organization. On the other hand, the semi-skilled worker might enter the organization without ever having seen technology of that kind before, and might therefore be expected to have very little other than highly generalized skill to carry out semi-skilled work; it would therefore follow that in those circumstances the onus of training the individual to the level of skill required by the technology would fall upon the employer. In any case it could not be presumed that a new employee would know what the objectives, policies and standards of the organization were, so that even if the man arrived with a complete package of skills he would still need some element of induction training to ensure that he understood the context within which he would now be expected to work. In this sense of induction training in particular, therefore, one could refer to training as complementing the selection process.

Thirdly, training may also be used as a method of increasing the motivation of the employee either to work harder or to make a more effective contribution to the objectives of the employer. The argument here runs that if the individual understands what his work is all about in terms of the total set of activities which are carried out by the employer, then morale in the organization will be likely to be higher than otherwise and that because of the higher morale thus engendered the performance of people working within that organization will be increased. It must however be said that the attempts that have been made to uncover the relationship between morale and productivity have not been uni-directional in their conclusions; there is certainly no simple and direct relationship between morale and productivity as far as the evidence goes. Nevertheless, the belief is pervasive and most organizations would work on the assumption that training is one way by which the values as well as the aims of the organization can at least be explained to the employee in the hope at least that his performance will benefit from a knowledge of what these are.

The strategies and tactics of training will thus respond to these different objectives. Where, for example, a craftsman is hired into an organization as a craftsman, the training programme will necessarily emphasize the need for inducting the individual to the new organizational system. Where the new employee is hired to carry out semi-skilled work of which he has had no experience before, the training programme will have to cater not only for the induction of the employee but also the development of skills to an appropriate level and of an appropriate type. Since organizations are both different in the mix of skills that they require at any one time and in the extent to which they are affected by technological changes, it is unlikely that one-off training exercises will suffice to meet the problem faced by them. It is likely that different types of training programmes will be required for different categories or grades of labour so that the total training spectrum includes apprentice training, young-person training in semi-skilled work, induction of new employees, and up-dating training for both hired-in craftsmen and for existing employees. But it is very likely that, with major changes in work method or changes in the underlying technology of the organization, the organization will have to establish a training programme which is oriented not so much to young or new employees as to the development and modification of skills that have already been acquired at some earlier stage in the individual's career. The total training package is not therefore likely to appear as a simple single process of training.

It tends to follow that the organization will have to give thought to the question of 'who will train?'. On the one hand a certain amount of training may be left to the supervisor to carry out on the job and, although it may therefore be necessary to give the supervisor some instruction in *how* to train, the extent to which the training process must be formalized to meet this particular requirement is perhaps quite limited. However, organizations will have to be mindful of the likelihood that individual employees will, willy-nilly, acquire their training whether it is deliberately provided or not, and that therefore the individual might learn practices and the values associated with them from his informal work group, from his formal work group (including from supervision) or from the trade union of which he might well be a member, and these practices and values may be inimicable with those required by the organization. Recognition of this possibility is likely to lead organizations to accept the view that even this kind of training ought to be formalized at least to some extent, possibly by giving supervisors deliberate and formal instruction in how to train and induct employees.

Where however the organization relies upon a large labour force of largely semi-skilled labour and where therefore it cannot rely upon recruiting fully trained people from the labour market, it might well prove advantageous to consider developing not only a formal programme of training but a cadre of trainers to carry it out. In this case the trainers would be staff experts and would normally themselves have had at some stage some formal training in both how to devise training programmes and how to carry out the actual process of training in accordance with best principles derived from learning theory.

The major problem that now arises is simply a manifestation of a common problem which is to be found whenever staff experts are brought into the organization, namely the tension which might develop between the staff specialists and the line management or supervision. Here the problem as seen by line management will be the problem that trainers displace the goals of training by making the training process itself an end which does not necessarily accord with the ends of production or selling or with whatever the line manager may be directly concerned. The problem as seen by the training expert is more likely to emphasize the undoing of the results of training by inefficient activities on the part of supervision and management whose attempt to pursue production objectives will very often undercut the achievements of the training department through its training programmes. In this sense the tension is no more than the commonly experienced tension, which will usually be well understood by the personnel manager who will have a responsibility for developing the training function in most organizations.

Some implications
The development of the 'employment function' in recent years, under the influence of social and legislation changes, has been in the direction of increasing complexity of aims and methods. The aim of achieving an equilibrium in labour supply and demand was relatively easy in conditions of large-scale unemployment; it becomes more difficult to achieve in conditions of full employment which are also characterized by changing attitudes to work and changing conceptions of rights and obligations particularly on discharge of labour.

For this sort of reason, the methods which have been developed under the general heading of manpower planning (or manpower resourcing) become both more complicated and also more sophisticated. Methods of assessing the internal demand and potential internal supply make increasing use of statistical understanding even if not of very complicated statistical methods (in most cases). The planning process itself, in the sense of strategy development, is forced to embrace a variety of considerations, such as what might be effected by training and development or by restructuring the reward package as a whole, beyond those focused upon the simpler concepts of hiring and firing. As the above discussion has indicated, a place remains for manpower planning on the basis of predictions about individual units of manpower—particularly at the managerial level—but the future is more likely to require computer capacities to help solve the problems of achieving an equilibrium in this area (see Bell, 1974, ch 7; and Smith, 1976, ch 15).

Computers are well-known to be limited in the help they can provide to decision takers by the quality of the information fed into them. Decisions about manpower cannot be taken on the basis of 'partial' data (eg only on the basis of what the personnel office collects) and the use of computers puts more emphasis on the need for a common form of output and a common focus for input. Most long-standing textbooks of personnel management have devoted space to records and record keeping (eg Northcott, 1955), but have often not linked this to decision taking in a sufficiently comprehensive and adequate fashion. It was therefore often the introduction of the computer which brought together data associated with different departments (wages department, medical section, personnel department, production department) and which sharpened the actual recording process (cf Butteriss, 1975, pp 85–102; and Mumford, 1969; Bell, 1974, ch 8; Smith, 1976, ch 15).

This development has also forced a reconception of what constitutes information or data, usable in the manpower planning process. Managers, including personnel managers, are increasingly drawn away from a concern with information about individuals and towards information about categories. Individual information fed into a process of manpower planning tends to overwhelm the managerial process, even if it is also acceptable because it relates to 'real people'. Categorization of data on the other hand is more manageable, but may well prove less acceptable because it appears to be 'less real' (or abstract) and by this token 'less accurate'. Such perceptions are then likely to influence the willingness of managers to use the data, or to base judgements or predictions upon them. This pull towards greater numeracy in the planning process is essentially a draw towards an understanding and appreciation of the notion of 'probability', even if one does not have the statistical techniques to calculate it.

Whilst this pull is being exerted for these reasons, the legislation which has been enacted in recent years on the subject of individual rights in employment, has exerted its pressure towards the keeping of individual ('case') records, so that what has happened to any individual in employment can be ascertained readily in the event of a disagreement or challenge. The need for 'case-workers' or for treatment of individuals as individuals is therefore increased at the same time that the need for new developments of thought about aggregated data is being developed. The long-established case-worker versus manager distinction in the personnel profession is thus to some extent heightened by these developments and remains consequently to be resolved.

Further reading
Students may find it useful to read Bell (1974) on the general approach to manpower planning and forecasting, supplemented by Stainer (1971); more complex models and methods are to be found in Smith (1970) and (1976) and in Bartholomew (1976). (Bibliographies

are to be found in the Department of Employment Gazette, July 1976, pp 722–6; November 1976, pp 1231–4; October 1977, pp 1093–6).

Additional help on records and record-keeping may be obtained from Taverner, (1973); on the establishment of the wage on offer from Lupton and Bowey (1974); and on training in this context from Singer (1969); Bass and Vaughan (1968); Holding (1965).

3 Securing human resources

Processes and activities

By itself manpower planning is sterile, unless some action is taken in accordance with it, to take in needed labour and to discharge it, and to deploy and re-deploy it within the undertaking as occasion may require. We need therefore, at this point in the development of the general theme of the book, to look at those processes and activities which are necessarily set in train in the execution of a manpower plan. There are naturally many of these, but for convenience of treatment it is proposed in this chapter to restrict consideration to those which can be related directly to the setting up and maintenance of the contract of employment.

This is a somewhat mechanistic approach to the general question of developing such relationships, but it does permit the bringing together of a number of activities and a number of related technical skills which have long stood as part of the stock-in-trade of the personnel specialist.

The general view is that, in carrying out a manpower plan, it is necessary to undertake actions related to recruitment, selection, engagement, transfer, advancement, promotion, termination, re-instatement and re-engagement, all of which entail some element of definition of the rights and duties of the parties to the employment contract. It does not follow that all of these elemental stages must have equal weight or equal applicability in the particular case; indeed, re-instatement and re-engagement are abnormal processes but for completeness they are included here. Taken together, they do permit us to review in one logical sequence the processes which might be associated with the implementation of manpower plans.

They also associate themselves with a set of inter-personal skills of the kind which the personnel specialist has usually been considered to possess as his main marketable commodity. At any and all of the elemental stages in this process as outlined, communication, structured in terms of the individual employee and the representative or agent of the employing undertaking, must take place. The individual employee both seeks and gives information and the agent does likewise, and each may be regarded as having his own set of criteria by which to decode that information and to evaluate it, for his own purposes, which will normally be quite different. The obvious examples of this are the selection interview or test and the interview for promotion. In these instances, the parties must exchange some information so that a decision can be reached.

It will no doubt be true that in many undertakings formal arrangements for exchanging information do not exist for some of the other processes identified (for example, transfers or termination). But however informal these processes may be, some exchange of information is necessary and the effect of recent legislation upon them is likely to be that of greater formalization of these activities in the future, as individuals become more conscious of 'their rights' established in this way.

Application of traditional inter-personal skills in the employment context must therefore take place within a framework of constraint derived from the sources of 'the terms and conditions' which have been identified in chapter 1 above: the common law, the collective agreement, the legislation applicable, as well as from the requirements of the undertaking itself as expressed in the manpower plan. A knowledge of the 'law', the terms of union agreements and of the intentions of the planners is thus a prerequisite of successful executive activity at this level. All these constraints are woven together to influence the directions taken by the activities of the specialists charged with securing and terminating employees.

Legislation has not yet exerted great influence on this part of the process, as most of it has been directed towards changes in, and termination of, employment contracts rather than their establishment (see, pp 106–119). There are two important exceptions to this general rule, where the main direct impact is upon the recruitment/selection process itself. Previously the main exception to this was to be found in the widely ignored Disabled Persons (Employment) Act of 1944, which imposed a duty on employers of 20 or more to employ a percentage of registered disabled persons (for whose voluntary registration the Act also made provision. S 9(1)). The percentage currently applicable, by order and fixed after consultation, is three per cent, but it is believed that 60 per cent of private employers and a high proportion of public ones (the Crown is not bound by the Act but has agreed to observe its provisions) do not meet this quota figure *de jure*, even if many of them do so *de facto* by employing people who have not bothered to register as disabled. Failure to comply could lead to a fine or imprisonment or both, but only after review and report by

District Advisory Committees and consequential legal action in the name of the Minister.

The recent exceptions constrain the employer's freedom to choose such employees as he might think most suitable, first by certain provisions in legislation which are designed to prevent discrimination on grounds other than fitness to carry out the work. This legislation covering racial, ethnic or sex discrimination is likely to cause the employer, here as in other areas related to the treatment and opportunities offered to employees, to review the whole strategy and structure of his approach to choices of employees, and the employer and trade union to review some provisions in collective agreements which restrict the employer to hiring certain categories of person (eg members of particular trade unions), to ensure that they do not run counter to the requirements of legislation.

The restrictions introduced since 1965 upon the employer's freedom to dismiss labour makes it more urgent (and less costly) for the employer to select in relation to (a) predictable long-term need, (b) competence or at least trainability, and (c) character or at least disposition to behave in accordance with customary rules of conduct. This pressure arises from the requirements of legislation (currently the Trade Union and Labour Relations Act (as amended by the Employment Protection Act) and the Redundancy Payments Act) that the employer shall uphold the employee's right not to be unfairly dismissed, on pain of a tribunal award of reinstatement or re-engagement and/or a 'fine' upon the employer in the form of compensation of a variable amount to the employee affected, and his right not to be dismissed even in the event of redundancy without some compensation for loss of accrued property rights (seniority etc) in the job.

The costs of this to the employer are two: the cost of time spent on the unfair dismissal claim, and the cost of any award which might be made (not excluding the 'cost' of reinstating or re-engaging the claimant). To discover a figure for the first of these is almost impossible, although companies have spoken of figures of between £1,000 and £1,500 per 'case'. The number of 'cases' in any given year can be obtained from the DE *Gazette* which regularly reports this (see DE *Gazette*, October 1977, p 1078; and November 1977, p 1214). Thus in 1976, of a total of 33,701 cases completed, 8.7 per cent were withdrawn without benefit of conciliation and 13.2 per cent involved compensation awarded by the tribunal. The average compensation agreed in conciliation (based on mid-points in the frequency distribution) before the 'basic award' concept was introduced, was £236 and that awarded by the tribunals was £445. Reinstatement and re-engagement do not occur with high frequency in these data, but they are not without their significance.

Nevertheless, these provisions of legislation and the use being made of them by dismissed employees, must be taken into account as one of the constraints on activity to recruit labour into association with undertakings. The cost of a 'mistake' or a 'bad decision' is now raised.

1 Job analysis

The starting point of administrative action in manpower planning is the job itself and the information generated by it. The job itself is currently under the microscope in many organizations which have begun to question existing job structure and design (Carby, 1976). This and manpower planning both start with a process of job analysis (Roff and Watson, 1961) which generates the information necessary to the production of a job description of *what is* and to the development of a proposal of *what might be*. Not all organizations carry out job analysis or write job descriptions. Many rely upon generalized knowledge of the job or upon a method of recruitment by occupation, rather than job, and sometimes this can be sufficient to enable small organizations to get by. The more systematic approaches to this problem become necessary in complex and large-scale organizations which are forced by circumstances to give attention to either efficiency or human satisfaction, or both.

The job description ought to be based upon the work carried out in the organization, although it should not necessarily be assumed that what happens to exist in the way of necessary tasks at the moment must continue to do so. A job is usually defined as a collection of tasks which are put together, mainly on the basis of convenience, to enable one person to be fully occupied whilst at work; he may have a main task, but will probably also have a number of ancillary tasks as well. In fact, a job which is composed of only one task is likely to be a highly repetitive and routine one; the grouping of a number of tasks adds variety and interest. At the same time it should be noted that it is correspondingly easier to describe a single-task job; covering all the side-tasks in a job description is always more difficult and time-consuming.

Although the individual's occupation may be meaningful to him, the work tasks discharged must achieve a degree of integrity in relation to the product or the process which provides the focus for the enterprise as a whole. The process of job analysis requires a similar perspective. Roff and Watson have referred to this as a necessary understanding of the person's work in relation to everyone else's work in the organization. This, they argue, is necessary if the job analysis is to yield information which will be of use in job design,

165

selection, training, or job evaluation; without this understanding the outcome is a rather meagre description of a bundle of activities divorced from the context which gives it meaning. Even where job descriptions seek to take both of these into account, they do not necessarily do it well; to achieve worthwhile results, it is necessary to approach job analysis in a systematic way.

The first step in job analysis therefore is to ask those who know what is involved in a job to express it. This means everything covered by paragraph 3 on pp 170–73 below. Normally an enterprise goes only part of the way with this, and often does so only because it is normal, customary or fashionable. For example, it may have an organization chart, or it may have a flow diagram; it may have work study or synthetic data on performance standards; it may have some 'requirements' for new recruits expressed in terms of education or experience: it may have an appraisal system linked to salary review. All of these, and more, are involved in a manpower planning system, but if they are to be of any real value they must be related to and integrated with an overall plan. For job analysis it is necessary to get out and polish up the old lamps represented by the organization chart, or the job description which sets out duties, and responsibilities, or the standards data so that they can be linked to one another in a systematic fashion.

The organization chart (usually more explicit in relation to managerial jobs than to manual jobs) offers a first identification of the separate jobs and offices which currently exist within the organization. It usually identifies the job by title and the present incumbent by name and, by virtue of the lines drawn between the positions, it indicates lines of authority, responsibility, communication and possibly work flow.

In spite of this book's frequent statement that the organization chart ought to be supported by a statement of duties and responsibilities, this is not frequently done. When it is, the description is usually in the form of a general statement of the incumbent's main activities. It tends to supplement the more cryptic information given on the chart itself, rather than stand in its own right. When it does so stand, it is often produced in occupational rather than job/task terms, referring to the occupation of . . . fitter and turner, systems analyst, nurse etc, in which the occupational sub-cultural definition of the tasks is by implication all that is required for selection and, by extension, for planning purposes.

There is nothing inherently wrong with the production of a job description which is adequate for occupational purposes (and particularly so where recruitment—as in hospitals—is to a profession rather than to a service organization). However, the likelihood is that such a description will serve the organizational purposes inadequately. Most of the many reports on aspects of manpower for the hospital service are in fact couched in these terms: 'Cog-wheel on doctors'; 'Salmon on senior nurses'; 'Zuckerman on scientific and technical services'; 'Parish on building occupations'; Tyler on engineers'; and 'Lycett Green on administrative and clerical occupations'. Each of them might in fact be regarded as prevented by its terms of reference from looking at hospital manpower from a hospital standpoint.

Hospitals are not unique in this respect. Even outside professional organizations it is not all that usual to find an enterprise taking a total organizational view of its manpower. Questioning whether existing jobs are correctly divided or combined, whether descriptions of duties and responsibilities are sensible within the context of the whole, and whether present incumbents really match up to the criteria stated or implied, is not frequent. Consequently, the positive contribution which such data as exists might make is reduced by the likelihood that it is held in different parts of the enterprise and not brought together systematically. A personnel department may well hold data on the existing stock of manpower, for example, whilst the data on performance lie with a separate work study department.

However, particular attention should be paid to the source of criteria of job performance. The standards to be applied in the judgement of whether a particular performance is correct or adequate may be founded on very different sets of sub-cultural values: those of the task-system itself, the organization, the occupation, or the informal group surrounding the task. Such distinctions are acknowledged in the literature, even if infrequently utilized in practical manpower planning exercises. Criteria for judging any job incumbent might be established in terms of variations in contribution to:

(a) the trade, occupation or profession as a simple task-system
(b) the section, department or enterprise
(c) the organized occupational group (trade union, profession)
(d) the informal work group, linked to a set of tasks.

Such criteria do exist and are used, if not deliberately or systematically. It remains open to any system to make them articulate, although it is more likely that the systems which will do so are the enterprise and the profession rather than the other two.

This requires us to recognize that criterion data are available in many organizations although they are infrequently used in a specific fashion. At the manual worker level they are found in work study data which are frequently seen as supports for an incentive bonus scheme, rather than as a basis for selection or promotion; at the white collar level they may appear in similar form, and in the higher echelons they may appear as criteria established in relation to key results areas. If, at the one level, the material is often difficult to employ because of formal or informal controls over variations in performance, at the other it is as frequently obscured by the apparent heterogeneity of jobs which renders comparisons difficult. Possibly for these reasons the data are often not employed consciously in devising a manpower plan.

What this means is that the likelihood that the basic data which it ought to be possible to derive from the job description is at best only imperfectly collated. To some extent those who are made responsible for selection (whether for employment, rotation or promotion) will therefore work with partial or inadequate criteria; where, say, both personnel department and line managers are familiar with these processes to different extents, they may well be working to different or even opposing criteria. The point is not to determine whether the one or the other ought to carry out the function, but rather to suggest that whichever does so, alone or in combination, ought to be in possession of as many of the facts as possible. Job analysis offers one way of assembling these facts, but it does not automatically ensure that they will be built into a comprehensive and integrated plan.

2 The job description
The production of a job description might ideally follow the job analysis. This is increasingly common, but the resultant job description may be required to form a basis for a number of different subsequent activities:

(a) *recruitment*, in which case it should contain information which will make clear the qualities and qualifications needed in the person who will fill the job
(b) *training*, in which case it must contain the same information as (a) but with special attention to areas of likely difficulty or deficiency
(c) *manpower utilization*, in which case particular attention will have to be paid to the way in which tasks are combined in the job so that, for example, a re-division or re-combination could be worked out from the data provided
(d) *job evaluation*, in which case the description will need to contain information on whatever factors must or will be taken into account in devising a wage/salary structure on the basis of job content

168

(e) *productivity negotiation* for which it will be necessary to have indications in the job descriptions of standards of performance expected or required at a current rate for the job, so that variations can be readily traced.

Even so, it should not be assumed that a job description, however systematic its production, can indicate everything about a job. Every verbal description is an abstraction from a reality which is always more complicated than the abstract form of words which describes it. All that can be aspired to is a carefully carried out and controlled analysis and description of that which those involved or concerned would regard as the important elements of the job.

This means that the preparation of a job description will need to involve not only specialist job analysts, but also the man doing the job, his superior(s) and probably others like training officers who have a special insight into the work being carried on. No matter who is observed at work or consulted about it, the final result should represent a distillation of all the significant features. If the description is also to be used for evaluation it should be of a common form and constant length in order to minimize judgemental bias arising from variation on these points.

Since everything about a job cannot be included in the job description it is important to determine just what should be included. This decision can, of course, be based on hunch or can respond to fashion or custom. However, if it is to be more systematic, it is necessary to consider the criteria which will be adopted to assess for success or adequacy. In this area it is neither particularly easy to determine these criteria nor to construct a means of determining them. Refinement of job analysis tends to have this as a main objective.

Where selection processes are concerned, it is particularly important to know what one is selecting for. Normally it is for a particular job or a particular kind or level of performance in that job. This, by itself, implies that there will be some standard in mind when selecting, even if only one based on judgement of what a normal operator would produce in that job. The check-back on the worker in the job and on the supervisor's perception of the job, normally built into the job analysis, gives information for this but such conception of the normal is only one of many conceptions which may be employed.

Any individual might be assessed on any of the foundations (a-e) identified above. A management representative might well concentrate on (b) at the expense of the others; the man's colleagues might well employ different criteria.

To summarize any job description must include certain features:

1 *Identification of the job:* usually by stating the title of the job, the section or department in which it is found, and the level in the hierarchy at which it is placed (usually by identifying to whom the man doing it reports).

   Some jobs are easily identified by title: everyone knows what is done by a nurse, a fitter or a cook. Others are less easy to identify in this way, and the job titles saggar-maker's bottom knocker or river or even systems analyst are not particularly helpful unless the reader happens to be in the industry concerned. Therefore, job descriptions usually amplify.

2 *Description of the job:* usually setting out in brief the main tasks which go to make up the job and indicating how this job differs from other jobs which may, superficially, appear similar. An example is given by the position descriptions in the Salmon report under the general heading of 'role'.

   For this purpose, it is important to develop and use (as the Salmon report does) a standardized and defined terminology to describe the purposes, functions or tasks involved. In this way the same word does not appear in different descriptions meaning different things because of the local language normally used, and different words are not used to mean essentially the same thing for the same kind of reason.

3 *Description of job content:* usually stated in a more detailed and expanded form as the body of the job description. In drawing up this part it is important to have the objectives very much in mind. A job description required merely for recruitment might be less rigorous than one to be used in evaluation. Nevertheless, it is sensible when preparing job descriptions to assume that they may be needed for any of the purposes identified on the previous page, and to prepare accordingly. Marrying the requirements of these various objectives leads to the following specification for a description of job content. It should include:

(a) *What is done* This will include the person's activities, whether manual or mental (eg 'files', 'checks figures', 'plans activities for others', 'tends patients', diagnoses conditions' etc), and his main and subsidiary tasks. This ought to be a description of the job in its more 'mechanical' aspects such that an outsider can gain an understanding of what is involved for the job-holder.

(b) *How it is done* Here the attempt is made to indicate whether the individual does the job alone and unaided or whether he has tools, equipment or organization to help him. This part of the description will show what 'things' and 'people' are needed for the job. Sometimes the things will include office equipment, measuring instruments, manuals and procedures, or complex plant (like computers); sometimes the job will depend upon getting a team to work as an integrated whole; sometimes the job will require little more than physical strength or stamina plus some intelligence or a capacity for exercising individual judgement. Such features vary from job to job, and even from task to task. They may also vary over time, and some attempt should therefore be made to indicate such variations.

(c) *Why the person does it* The answers to this question focus on the context of the job in the work-flow sense. This part of the description will attempt to relate the one job to other jobs around or connected with it, and to link it to the overall objectives of the section, department or enterprise. This is an important element, particularly where the pattern of tasks is changing because of the possible introduction of new objectives or technologies. Without this attempt to give meaning to the job by linking it to its work context, the necessary foundation for monitoring manpower utilization or changing relative evaluations will be lacking. The data for this part of the description is often collected by the management services organization, but the job description is prepared independently by the personnel department who have less information than the former on work flow patterns; in consequence this part of the description may be deficient.

(d) *What standard of performance is regarded as normal?* This is often left out of manual worker descriptions, but frequently included in managerial descriptions (where it appears in the guise of 'key results expected'). At manual levels, this requirement can be met by using work study data; at managerial levels it can embrace data produced in applications of management by objectives methods. Whether or not such standards are included openly, they are always implied in any job description: there is always some standard of performance which is regarded as normal even if different occupational groups may have different conceptions of this. One part of the function of work study at the manual level and of activity analysis at a managerial/professional level is to make them explicit. Although there is often prejudice against the statement of applicable standards in job descriptions, their omission leaves the way open for personalized and idiosyncratic review.

(e) *In what conditions is the work done?* This covers physical working conditions of the job at the time it is described. Such a description is necessary to prepare for job evaluation, selection or subsequent monitoring. To describe these conditions is, of course, to imply a normal, and normal will vary from situation to situation. What are normal conditions in a foundry are not normal conditions in a hospital, and what is normal on a ward is not necessarily normal in the kitchen. Consequently, the working conditions specified in this section will depart from a conception of the normal and will identify specific abnormalities. The most common items include the following:

dirt	work done in confined spaces
heat or cold	wetness of working environ-
necessity for protective clothing	ment
monotony	dust, fumes, gas hazards
noise or vibration	exposure to infection or disease
exposure to weather	other disagreeable conditions
hazard or danger	(eg smells)

Not all of these will necessarily figure in any one job description.

4 *Special features*: This means the peculiar features of the job in question which, if point 3 (above) is carried out systematically ought to be covered already, but which might form the subject of a special section if only because they will probably have a particular influence upon the man specification. In this section a special note might be made, say, of the fact that a job requires operations using differential calculus, driving on a public highway or lengthy sessions with potentially difficult clients. Opportunity might also be taken here to indicate any special organizational features of the job—whether for example it is part of a promotion line or merely a dead-end job.

The criteria for different kinds of work also vary in the ease with which they can be established and accepted. The work of a clerk or a manual worker is often relatively easy to describe. This is because (a) it is relatively *stable* in its form and content, and (b) it is often concerned with a *rate* of output which can be measured fairly easily. With the development of more complex technologies, with consequent influences on job stability and manual control, this is likely to be less so in the future. There is still some variation in the performance of such workers on fairly stable jobs, in spite of trade union and informal group control of it, and this can be used to derive reliable criteria.

The work of a manager is usually more difficult to describe in spite of the work of the activity and job analysts, and its inherent complexity and fluidity are likely to perpetuate this problem. Criteria are less easy to determine. What makes for a good manager is less easy to describe than what makes for a good workman, because the inherent variety in the job itself masks the variations in performance even if we intuitively have some ideas on the existence of such variations. The development of criteria is therefore likely to prove more costly and difficult in consequence.

3 The person specification

The criteria having been derived from the job analysis, the next task is to translate these into a specification of the attributes of the person who might meet these job criteria. Different tasks may call for persons with 'individual' attributes which will 'precisely' fit that job, or for persons with general attributes which will broadly fit the job requirement: it by no means follows that for every job there is a single person who has the right combination of qualities and qualifications. There are, in other words, some jobs which in their generality call for a class or category of labour, and it becomes possible to specify the person required as simply one of a class—a skilled craftsman, a bookkeeper or a labourer. But there are also jobs which are much more individual in the person-attributes they appear to require, and for these it may be necessary to write the ideal man/woman specification which will match the job. Indeed, as more jobs become industry-specific and even enterprise-specific as a result of technological development, many of the old 'class' specifications may prove less adequate, and the pressure be on to develop personal specifications, of the sort indicated in the table on the following page, drawn from Plumbley, (1976).

But whichever kind of result is produced by this kind of analysis, it is to be predicted that in future management will be led to give more attention to specifying the criteria of the person required as a basis for developing more adequate predictors. Because staff will probably prove to be more costly and difficult to dismiss in the future, it will become more necessary than before to translate the job requirement into a specification of kind of person thought most likely to be able to do it competently. It follows that the aspects of the person which are called in question in work must match up to the aspects of the job which make demands upon the person and, as Rodger has suggested, "the requirements of an occupation (or job) must be described in the same terms as the attributes of the people who are being considered for it' (1952). The data on the job itself which have been discussed in the preceding section must now be stated in terms which will enable an individual or class of persons to be identified as willing and able to do the job which has thus been described. Such a description will then form the basis for selection of persons to fill jobs.

Table 9

The person specification

Physical make-up	Minimum height 5′ 4″
	Pleasant appearance
	Brisk, clear speech, free from impediments
Attainments	Essential to have evidence of application, concentration and capacity for detailed work
	Desirable to have some knowledge of technical drawing and of engineering terms
	Education should reflect academic or technical bias
	'O' levels or the equivalent are desirable
	Previous experience of record keeping in technical office or library is essential
	Experience of working with engineering drawings is desirable
General intelligence	Brisk reactions and an accurate memory are needed rather than ability to solve complex problems
Specialized aptitudes	Neat, quick and accurate at clerical work
Interests	Practical and social
Disposition	Self-reliant, helpful, friendly
Circumstances	Likely to stay for at least three years
Type of person	Traditionally this job has been done by a female but it could equally be done by a male. No restriction on race, colour or creed
Contra-indications	Obvious shyness.

Source: Philip Plumbley, *Recruitment and Selection*, (IPM, London, 1976) pp. 35–36

The question to which the person specification seeks to provide an answer is therefore what qualities and qualifications ought a person to have, if he is to do this particular job to the level of adequacy which is implicit in the criterion. These are minimum attributes, and not either average or maximum, and they could be determined in accordance with the values of the enterprise, the profession or any other sub-culture which might be associated with the job. They need in every case to be minimum, so that the size of the 'feedstock' for the job vacancy is made as large as possible.

Qualifications are usually more easily allocated than qualities. This is partly because qualifications have at least a superficial objectivity about them whereas qualities seem to be almost entirely subjective; moreover, qualifications seem to be more readily 'measurable' (eg as in examinations) where qualities appear to require complex psychological tests or equally complex interpersonal judgements. The effect of this is to distil the person specification down to the level of a statement of education, training and experience (the qualifications) required, and to supplement this with relatively vague statements about personal attributes. The criteria of the person are then

174

often more vaguely defined than the criteria of the work.

The distinctions in objectivity or precision may, be more apparent than real. If consideration is given to the qualifications associated with the job descriptions, for example, one might be forced to recognize that the requirement of a degree qualification might prove to be a rather blunt instrument of measurement in the face of the actual job of work to be done, and that on-the-job experience might in turn produce a very variable effect upon an individual in terms of qualification. In these senses a statement about apparently objective qualifications for a job may differ very little from statements to the effect that an individual must have a helpful, friendly and self-reliant disposition. The seeming precision of the one may be no less reliable than the seeming imprecision of the other.

Nevertheless, for most ordinary selection and promotion purposes, we might recognize that the *categories* of the variable, which might be expected to vary with performance on a job, can be identified quite readily. In the most general sense, these may be placed under three main headings:

(a) *Intellectual requirements* usually measured in terms of training and skill or experience. This part of the specification will deal with the previous experience of men usually chosen to do the job, and the subsequent training they will require in order to do the job in a satisfactory way. If the man has to acquire any manual or mental dexterity to do the job at the speed at which the job is usually performed this will be noted

(b) *Physical requirements* usually assessed by physical strength and health history. Sufficient information will be included under this heading to ensure that the reader can judge the muscular strength of the men to do the work, and also the amount of effort they will normally expend when working without the incentive of a bonus. If the people who do the job must possess particular sensory qualities this will also be mentioned

(c) *Personality requirements* some of which are subsumed under the heading (a) above, but others of which creep in without the benefit of careful definition. Examples are:

good memory	ability to reason
speed of reaction	even temperament
cooperativeness	perseverance
mechanical sense	initiative
disparate attention	ability to visualize
sense of responsibility	

Of these three categories, the first two are of a rather different order from the third. They seem on the face of it to lend themselves to fairly precise and objective measurement, even if the measures are themselves normatively defined. A person of any age, sex and size who has no very acute physical handicap nor a history of poor health can be assumed capable of coping with most run-of-the-mill jobs that are available; and therefore only rather special job requirements are likely to call for the category of physical requirements in question, such as need for particular levels of vision or manual dexterity. A person of a given level of terminal education who has no history of physical or mental illness can also be assumed to have a capacity which is indicated by the level of educational attainment, which may in many cases be attested by the possession of some scrap of paper; experience which is 'certified' by some testimonial or reference may also be taken as indicative of capacity (on the legal constraints on references, see Hepple and O'Higgins, 1976, pp 512–513).

Such certifications are usually capable of predicting only generalized competence in a particular field: they usually say nothing about the more particular capabilities of the individual in working with this group on these particular problems or tasks in this particular organization. It is for this reason that such organizations as have organization-specific requirements of labour have been willing to explore the possibilities of developing their own independent criteria and predictors, some of them quite complex. Where the number of criteria which can be distinguished, especially if the organizational and occupational sub-cultures are both allowed to determine them, is large and their predictability varies appreciably, it may be necessary in recruitment to develop person specifications of great complexity. Taylor presents a list of 17 criteria for scientists arranged in descending order of their predictability from a number of test scores, rank being accorded by the percentage of significant validity coefficients above zero (the figure is given in parentheses). Although a degree of bias is introduced into this list, because of the particular method developed in the research (those affected are marked with an asterisk) this does not invalidate the rank nor does it detract from the point to be made here that the criteria are extremely varied in themselves. Perusal of the following list will show that, as it were, there are many ways in which the success of the scientist might be evaluated.

Although this may render it difficult to develop an adequate criterion strategy for jobs of this general type and pose the question whether it is worth it, if the job possesses these complex and multiple criterion characteristics, the development of adequate predictors will depend upon their adequate development. What normally justifies this activity is the growth in the proportion of white collar occupations and therefore their relative cost compared with manual jobs.

176

Table 10
Criteria of the success of a research scientist

9	Likeableness as a research team member (44%)	17	Supervisory rating of creativity (29%)
5	Scientific and professional society membership (43%)	16*	Supervisory rating of drive-resourcefulness (25%)
13	Current organizational status (38%)	4*	Originality of written work (20%)
6*	Judged work output (35%)	10	Visibility (20%)
8*	Supervisory ratings on overall performance (35%)	11	Recognition for organizational contributions (17%)
15	Peer rankings on productivity (35%)	2	Recent publications (14%)
1*	Productivity in written work (32%)	14	Contrast monitoring load (11%)
7	Creative rating by laboratory chiefs (29%)	12*	Status seeking, 'organizational-man' tendencies (08%)
		3	Quality (without originality of research reports (02%)

Taylor, Smith, Ghiselin and Ellison, 1961

Given the criteria, it may be asked what about the individual will permit us to predict any of these criteria—assuming for the moment that we have tests or other devices which will permit measurement of the variables identified. In a second part of this exercise, Taylor presents data on which predictors were most useful (most highly correlated). The first of the criteria in the list above, likeableness as a member of the research team, was variously predictable from the test factors on the following page, and the second, professional society membership, from those on the succeeding page. Although the significance of any particular predictor from any of the tests used may be low, these illustrations may be used here to show how some of the criteria which one might want to predict in selection may possibly or probably associate with characteristics in the individual which are not 'obviously' linked.

4 Recruitment

Apart from the requirement that employers shall not discriminate between racial and national groups in their recruitment advertising, the employer remains relatively free from constraint in recruiting people, except where he has some agreement with the union(s) which may restrict this freedom (see below, pp 427–30).

The starting point is the staff requisition form, to be completed by the departmental head in whose department a vacancy occurs for transmission to the personnel department. This requisition should

Table 11 (a)
Criterion 9: likeableness as a member of the research team

Nr	Predictor	r	Nr	Predictor	r
81	MSL Writing skills	.46	142	BIB Intellectual thoroughness	.27
34	SR Discrimination of value	.41	28	SR Desire for discovery	.26
37	SR Creativity	.34	136	BIB Emotional restraint	.26
138	BIB Self-sufficiency	.34	141	BIB Liking to think	.25
31	SR Flexibility	.33	85	MSL Being well known	.24
145	BIB Modal response	—.33	86	MSL Quantity of reports	.24
24	SR Cognition	.31	91	Apparatus test: total	.24
36	SR Intuition	.31	135	BIB Professional self-confidence	.23
139	BIB Inner directedness	.31	100	MAT Parents-home	.22
27	SR Desire for principles	.30	42	PRI Tolerance of ambiguity	.21
101	MAT Narcism (comfort)	.30	64	Match problems: Nr correct	.20
78	MSL Reading skills	.30	95	MAT Self-sentiment	.20
59	PRI Artistic (vs. practical)	.28	22	SR Math ability	.19
74	Visual imagery: % marked correct	.28	48	PRI Gregariousness	.20
79	MSL Speaking skills	.27	87	MSL Theoretical contributions	.19

The initials in the above table, and in table 11 (b), refer to test instruments, as follows:

BIB = Biographical Information Blank
MAT = Motivational Analysis Test
MSL = Minimum Satisfactory Level
PRI = Personality Research Inventory
SR = Self Ratings

(see Taylor *et al.* 1961; and Blum and Naylor, 1968)

give sufficient information about the vacancy to permit the personnel department to advertise it and carry out an initial screening of applicants. Information required includes department, job title (reference to establishment in appropriate cases), date new man required to start work, wage/salary range appropriate, and identification of the appropriate job description and man specification, assuming these to exist. Depending on economic circumstances and legislative constraints on hiring and firing, such a request should be checked against establishment (where this concept is used) or against the data on stocks and flows of manpower.

The next step is preparing and inserting an advertisement of the vacancy. This may be prepared by the departmental head and given

Table 11 (b)

Criterion 5: society membership

Nr	Predictor	r	Nr	Predictor	r
37	MSL Theoretical contributions	.41	82	MSL Quantity of work output	.27
87	SR Creativity	.39	139	BIB Inner directedness	.27
81	MSL Writing skills	.37	91	Apparatus test: total	.26
36	SR Intuition	.36	31	SR Flexibility	.24
89	MSL Original work	.35	33	SR Independence	.24
145	BIB Modal response	.34	35	SR Cooperation	.24
29	SR Information ability	.33	53	PRI Belief in rights of groups	.23
86	MSL Quantity of reports	.33	141	BIB Liking to think	.22
28	SR Desire for discovery	.33	142	BIB Intellectual thoroughness	.21
27	SR Desire for principles	.31	21	SR Drive	.20
24	SR Cognition	.30	60	PRI Spiritual (vs. natural)	.21
140	BIB Dedication to work	.29	80	MSL Listening skills	.20
144	BIB Self-reported academic level	.28	22	SR Math ability	.19
32	SR Persistence	.27	25	SR Integrity	.20
34	SR Discrimination of value	.27	135	BIB Professional self-confidence	.19

to the personnel department or it may be prepared in the personnel department itself; but economies can be made by passing all advertisements through the personnel department, provided that it does evaluate its own advertising performance. The advertisement may be placed internally (usually by agreement with the unions), externally, or both, but ought in the latter case to be based upon some assessment of the effectiveness of advertising in a particular medium (Braithwaite and Pollock, 1974). When posted, a copy of the advertisement may be sent to the departmental head concerned to confirm that action has been taken and to indicate when future action will be required. The implicit centralization of this process reflects a prediction that such closer control will prove to be necessary both economically and politically.

Advertisements may draw enquiries from some of those who read them but enquiries may also come from individuals looking for certain types of job 'on spec'. The fortuitous appearance of an applicant when a vacancy exists could result in immediate processing and possible appointment if the criteria are met. In either case, the enquirer will have to complete an application form as a first step in the procedure of informing the organization about a potential recruit; he will be given further particulars (ideally in the form of a job description) as a first step in informing him about the job; whilst the first part of this procedure is often done, the second is not.

When the personnel department receives the application form, it can screen applications to eliminate those who are unsuitable, given the requirements stipulated in the job description and man specification. In theory, the advertisement ought to have discouraged such applicants but in fact many people are willing to chance their arm in applying for jobs for which they may know they are marginally unqualified or unsuitable. This screening will result in a list of candidates whose references may then be taken up. In addition, the personnel department will be supplied incidentally with data on the local labour market for that type and class of labour; such information can be logged and used in developing manpower and recruitment strategies.

Whether references are taken up at all, or whether they are collected in writing or by telephone will usually depend upon the kind of vacancy and upon the state of the labour market for that particular grade. When they are sought in writing, the employing organization has a choice of simply asking for a written reference, usually a letter, or of inviting the referee to supply assessments on a standardized form which identifies qualities and qualifications deemed important in the job. The first will usually produce a statement which may or may not tell the potential employer what he would like to know; the second is often ignored or misinterpreted by the referee as being too complex for speedy completion.

Where references are taken up before interview, this makes a second screening possible: if the references are comprehensive, this can certainly be done but many are rather curious eulogies of doubtful validity and unlikely to be very useful. Whether or not such a secondary screening takes place, it is usual to invite applicants for interview. This may in some cases form a part of the secondary screening, for example, when it is carried out by the personnel staff in order to draw up a short-list for interview by departmental heads.

The stage then comes when the candidate will be interviewed with a view to final selection or rejection. This may concern only a departmental head or be undertaken by a panel drawn from, say, the personnel department, departmental heads etc. It may be undertaken as a straight interview designed to supplement information already available on the application form and references, or it may be supplemented by tests where validated ones are available for the vacancy in question; it should be borne in mind that few are so validated (see Anastasi, 1961; Albright, Glennon and Smith 1963; Guion, 1965; Lawshe, 1948; Thorndike, 1949; Vernon, 1960; Wood, 1960). It may be structured or unstructured, ignoring or making use of interview methods and techniques which are now widely publicized (Anstey and Mercer, 1956; Fraser, 1966; Rodger, 1952; Sidney and Brown, 1961). The outcome will be a decision to appoint or to recommend appointment (where a higher vetting authority is given responsibility). It is normal for the departmental head to have final authority in the sense that none can be imposed upon him (although he may be denied the authority to appoint whom he prefers).

The personnel department can exercise its discretion in its role here, in the interests of improving practice. It has an essentially administrative or monitoring role in the whole sequence of recruiting and selecting for vacancies up to this point; in exercising it the department usually has the authority to ensure that establishments are not exceeded in requests for staff etc or that advertising is non-discriminatory as well as effective. Whether selection is done by interview or not or whether it involves the use of tests or not, the personnel department must not only possess the skills to carry out interviews or to administer tests, but must also seek to ensure that these are applied systematically by the other supervisors and/or managers who engage in recruiting: the personnel department's object is to achieve results which are at once efficient and fair, and which will also do least damage to the image of the employing organization in the minds of those who are put through the process.

In some industries and in many enterprises, this process is often badly botched, either because inadequate care is taken to establish the recruitment process, or because whim or fad leads to the employment of totally inappropriate methods. The increased cost of faulty recruitment (arising from the difficulty and cost of dismissing the mistakes) and the greater requirement for careful justification of the decisions taken (because of the possibility of complaints of unfair discrimination, for example) might between them help the personnel manager to ensure that more care is given to these activities in future.

Getting and giving information
The skills of the personnel practitioner in this area are associated with various aspects of communication. The selection process, assuming it conforms to the legislative and moral constraints, means the giving of information to the potential recruit—through advertisement of the job vacancy, through further particulars which might include the job description, through more general information which might be contained in an employee or staff handbook which describes the organization and sets out the rules to be observed and the benefits to be obtained from employment within it; such specific information may be given at the interview at the request of the candi-

date and now, through the 'particulars of the employment contract', has to be given to the recruited applicant where he is not given an actual contract (or access to one) with the same information in it. It also means gathering information from the applicant to enable the selectors to make correct decisions against the criteria established for the job in question, through the application form when completed, through references where these are used, through the application of interviewing skills, through examinations (eg proficiency tests and medical examinations) and through the application of tests in special circumstances and for particular purposes where such tests are valid and reliable. Taken together, these two objectives should be pursued in such a way that a candidate is left with the "feeling that he has had 'a fair crack of the whip' and the 'organization' with the feeling that it has secured the best candidate available in all the circumstances" (cf Cuming, 1968, p 66).

The personnel specialist normally has a responsibility in relation to this communication process which has two aspects: he must ensure that any part he plays in the process conforms to best practice in terms of method and skill; and he must ensure that others in the organization who are necessarily involved in the process also follow that practice. The discharge of both is facilitated by *proformae* and procedures which have been devised to guide the exercise, and this may be illustrated with reference to the central activity, the interview. A number of different 'guides' have been provided, the five-point and the seven-point plans being the best well-known (Fraser, 1966; Rodger, 1952).

The seven-point plan is a checklist of job requirements which have to be met in the person appointed to the job, and may be expressed as 'questions' and 'answers' which the interviewer might ask and hope to receive during the course of the interview:

1 *Physical make-up*
   Q   What does the job demand in the way of general health, strength, appearance, manner, voice?
   A   Has the candidate any defects of health or physique that may be of occupational importance? How agreeable are his appearance, bearing and speech?

2 *Attainments*
   Q   What does it demand by way of general education, specialized training, and previous experience?
   A   What type of education has he had, and how well has he done educationally? What occupational training and experience has he had already, and how well has he done in his previous jobs?

3 *General intelligence*

Q   What level is required to do the job (a) satisfactorily, (b) well?

A   How much intelligence can he display and does he ordinarily display? (This may be assessed by testing)

4 *Special aptitudes*

Q   Does the job involve any special dexterity—manual, verbal, musical, artistic etc?

A   Has he any marked mechanical aptitude? manual dexterity? verbal facility? artistic or musical ability? (Again, may be found by tests)

5 *Interests*

Q   How far does the job require a special interest in, for example, outdoor life, being with other people, artistic expression? Are any hobbies likely to be relevant?

A   To what extent are his interests intellectual? practical-constructional? physical-active? social? artistic?

6 *Disposition*

Q   Does the job call for any of the following qualities— leadership, acceptability to others, reliability, sense of responsibility, self-reliance?

A   How acceptable does he make himself to other people? Does he influence others? Is he steady and dependable? Is he self-reliant?

7 *Circumstances*

Q   How will the pay, prestige, status of job affect the worker's private life?

A   What are his domestic circumstances? How large a family? Does he own his house? Is he willing to travel? (Based on Cuming, 1968, pp 68–69).

The five-point plan is in principle similar although it uses different 'check' headings: impact on other people, qualifications, brains and abilities, motivation and adjustment. Although in the particular case the precise form of the answers to the questions about the job requirement will vary, the important suggestion in these plans is that some systematic plan should be used by interviewers. Such a plan will impose a discipline, and will help to reduce the likelihood of 'snap' judgements (which usually involve judging on stereotyping—the 'cloth cap' means . . . —or on a 'halo' effect—a good looking blonde is probably good at typing) and, if initially following a plan tends to stilt the interviewers' approach, practice with a plan of some kind will probably overcome this and still lead to improved performance all round.

The interview may in some cases be the only source of information available to the selectors, but in most it will supplement the biographical information given on the application form (see Plumbley, 1976, pp 132–133 for an example of an application form). Some of the 'information' sought in systematic interview can be obtained from this form (even if it still requires supplementation at interview). Plumbley suggests that "it can provide some provisional evidence and clues concerning the applicant's

biographical data and personal circumstances
career pattern and attainments
powers of self-expression
range and depth of interests
intelligence and special aptitudes
behavioural patterns and preferences." (Plumbley, 1976, p 134).

On the basis of the factual information given and these 'clues' which can be gleaned, it may be possible to do a preliminary sort into definitely unsuitable, possible and probable categories. Translation of the last or the last two categories into successful applications may depend, in the general case, upon interview, and in the specific case upon interview and further tests.

One category of these is to be regarded as a specialist examination in essentially the same category as the interview itself. This is the medical examination, long-used in some special types of work (teaching and medical care, for example, where there are potential hazards in the work itself) but now being increasingly used in general selection. A *proforma* covering the matters to be assessed in the examination is often provided, and appointment of otherwise successful candidates may be made conditional upon passing this examination. The completed medical examination form is then incorporated with the personal information contained in the employee's file.

The new Health and Safety at Work Act would seem to make it at least desirable for employers in future to ensure that anyone who is subjected not merely to hazard or to health risk but also to stress in the job, whether at a managerial level or on the shop floor, should be required to undergo compulsory medical examination. If, for example, an employee suffers a heart attack and medical evidence suggests that this attack could have been prevented or at least predicted if the patient had known about it in advance, and if further the stress of the job carried out by the employee were to be alleged to have been a prime cause of the development of the condition or of the heart attack itself, the employer might well be open to prosecution for having failed to take such steps as were 'reasonably practicable'

184

to safeguard the health of the individual concerned. But this policy on the part of the employer does not provide a complete answer to the problem that the employer might face.

If, for example, in the course of a compulsory medical examination an incipient heart condition is discovered, what does the employer do? He could take the diagnosis of the medical officer, relate it to the stress conditions of the job being carried out by the individual and draw the inference that the individual ought to be moved to a less stressful job. If the employer were to do this, the employee himself might not agree, more especially since the job offered would be likely to carry less income. The individual might therefore claim that the employer was engaging in the practice of 'constructive dismissal'; if the employee refused to take the new job offered, he might well appear before a tribunal seeking compensation for unfair dismissal. Again, the problem is only likely to be resolved when the matter has been tested by the Courts. The employer is unlikely to be able to predict what action he might safely take in all these circumstances. What does seem reasonably clear is that, where there is reason to suppose that the conditions in which the individual works are likely to affect his health and welfare, the employer should make provision for a periodical medical examination if he is to ensure a reasonable defence.

A problem also arises under this same heading concerning the employment of disabled persons. Many employers have to employ a proportion of registered disabled persons. The Health and Safety at Work Act makes no distinction between the disabled and the normal person in imposing duties on the employer. It may well prove that the disabled person is exposed to much greater risk in some sense than the normal person; the discharge of the employer's duty on what would be reasonable or reasonably practicable for normal persons might prove insufficient for the registered disabled. Again, a matter of welfare policy is therefore called in question by this particular provision of the Act.

Those who have written on the new Act have frequently offered employers a checklist which might help to provide them with an adequate defence if challenged and an example is provided by Mitchell (1974, pp 18–20).

Other tests which may be employed to supplement the interview and biographical information blank may be placed in two categories. First, those which indicate attainments or typical performance, and applicable where the applicant is required to have, and represents himself as having, certain attainments and competences. In some cases an external 'certification', whether of apprenticeship, educational attainment or proficiency in skill, may be accepted in lieu of the first of these and they may be supplemented by test of normal or typical performance (eg the dictation of a letter to a shorthand typist applying for a job). Where this is not so and yet it remains important to have a measure of attainment, it is possible to use attainment tests, although as Plumbley say "though laymen can devise attainment tests they are ill-advised to do so, unless they have a thorough understanding of the statistical concepts involved. For example, a battery of attainment tests for secretarial work will cover vocabulary, grammar, spelling, punctuation, arithmetic, etc. and within each aspect the items will be graded in order of difficulty, so that the battery will show the candidate's level of attainment and degree of accuracy" (Plumbley, 1976, p 163).

Secondly, three other categories of test which are also supplementary present different problems of administration because of their reliance upon psychological knowledge which may not always be perfectly present in the lay tester. These are intelligence tests, special aptitude tests, and personality tests, all of which are better not used unless the test results are vital to decision because of the job requirements, or unless there are trained testers available to administer and interpret them. In any event, consideration has to be given to the 'acceptability' of the tests to the applicant, since test results are often assigned a threat status by the testee, who, without careful handling, may then reject the resultant offer because of what is imputed to the firm's agents as the intention of applying such tests (see Plumbley, 1976, p 164).

Taken together, these give appreciable amounts of information about the candidate to the selectors, who can then use it in reaching a decision about whom to appoint. It should be emphasized, however, that the candidate should also have been offered an opportunity to elicit a comparable amount and range of information, by one means or another, so that whether a job is offered or not that candidate would be able to decide whether to accept it or not. It may well be that the individual 'just wants a job, any job'; even in that case of 'no choice' the information given in the selection process ought to be sufficient to permit him or her to appreciate what, even in this no choice situation, he or she is taking on.

Completion of the selection process
It could be represented that the selection process is never 'completed': like education it is a continuous process of re-selection on a mutual basis. The subsequent processes of transfer, promotion and demotion and termination could also be said to reflect and rely upon similar methods and techniques to those which have just been touched upon when discussing initial recruitment. But for the sake of

organizing material for this chapter, it may be suggested that the selection or recruitment process may be regarded as 'completed' by three further activities: the communication of the decisions taken, together with any consequential information relevant thereto; the induction of the new employee; and the provision of any training which may have been judged necessary to bring the attainment of the individual into conformity with the job requirements.

The recruitment process proper is completed by (a) informing the unsuccessful candidates that the post has been filled (and in a tight labour market possibly offering to hold the application on file pending further vacancies), and (b) issuing a letter of appointment to the successful candidate(s) or informing the candidate of his appointment on the spot. Under the Contracts of Employment Act 1972 (as amended), it is necessary to issue to almost all new employees within 13 weeks of starting work a summary of the terms and conditions of the appointment; in some cases, this will accompany the letter of appointment.

This required information for the new employee can only be the bare minimum. He or she is likely to require much more than this, if only because of the nature of the obligations which the employee assumes (or is deemed to assume) on taking up employment. Faithful service of the employer, in an agreed capacity and possibly based upon a warranted skill or competence will, *inter alia*, require the employee to obey those rules which are relevant to the employment and to apply his knowledge and skills in the way desired by the employer. It is therefore necessary for the new employee to acquire information and knowledge about the situation in which he now finds himself, and correspondingly necessary for the employer to make these available to him, usually through an induction and/or an induction training process and programme. By this means the new employee may be placed in the position where he can give the required service and do so in accordance with custom and practice or the rules appertaining to the undertaking. This will not be 'the end of the process' of familiarizing the individual with the requirements of the role, because as we have already noted above the requirements are likely to change with the exigencies of the business, but it is an important beginning of it.

Induction
Induction is conceived as a way of ensuring that the new employee, whether he/she is a young person or not, is adequately introduced to the job and the organization within which he/she will perform it. It is fairly obvious that the individual must somehow, and that fairly quickly, familiarize himself with the tasks he will be expected to per-

form. It may be less obvious that if he is to perform these tasks adequately he must have an adequate understanding of the organization within which those tasks occur and of the way in which he will be expected to perform them in conformity with custom and practice and with the required standards. A failure to provide the individual with information about his job (which the individual himself would regard as of primary importance) might help to account for the high rate of labour turnover in the early months of engagement of new employees.

Giving information about the organization, its objectives, policies and standards might be seen as more in the interests of the employer than the employee (who might well regard this information as of less immediate relevance to him as a new employee). There is however a sense in which the individual employee will at some stage seek this kind of information in order to form a judgement as to the desirability of continuing to work for that employer. Although the immediacy of this information may therefore be lower, it is both normal and sensible to regard the giving of this information as part of the induction process.

The mistake is often made by employing organizations of assuming that *this* information is as important to the employee as it might seem to be to the employer, and the information is frequently given too soon and without later reinforcement so that the effect of providing such information is usually dissipated. The legal requirements about further particulars of the contract and the giving of information to individual employees in written form will no doubt follow in due course. Since the individual cannot wait for 13 weeks for some of this information, it has to be built into an induction programme at this early stage.

The duties imposed upon the employer by the Contracts of Employment Act, the Trade Union and Labour Relations Acts, the Health and Safety at Work Act and the Employment Protection Act might be regarded as an attempt to distil best company practice in this particular respect into a set of duties which should be discharged by any employer, although in formalizing the duty in the legislation there is a mechanical consequence: the individual employee may be given further particulars of his contract within 13 weeks of his engagement. But the personnel manager must recognize that some at least of this kind of information is required by the employee at the beginning of his employment with the organization.

The way in which the induction programme is presented will probably call for the giving of information to the new employee on two different planes.

First, there is clearly a requirement for information about the

188

organization as a whole and this is likely to be carried out fairly informally in the small organization by someone fairly senior in the management team. In the larger organization a more formal programme might be arranged which would include a welcome to the organization by a member of corporate management who might spend some time talking about the development of the enterprise over the years, and who might support this with films about the firm's activities and by presenting visual data in the form of organization charts or charts showing sales or profitability or performance on other relevant dimensions. At this general level too it is likely that the induction programme would include a tour of the organization's buildings and departments so that the individual may have some feel for the general lay-out and activities which are carried on within that organization and this would provide a reasonable basis for informing new employees about the social and welfare facilities available. For example, the tour would include a visit to the pay office, which might provide an opportunity to tell the individual how he would be paid, and a tour of the sports and social facilities might provide a chance for someone to explain what facilities are available to the new employee on what conditions. Where the programme is as elaborate as this, there will be a tendency to put on the programme only when enough recruits have been assembled to warrant so much staff time.

The second plane of information referred to is that which focuses much more clearly on the actual job of work that the individual will have to do and the department or section within which he will be expected to do it. This information is probably best provided by the supervisor who has been trained to carry out the role. What is most often needed and provided is first a tour of the department, providing an opportunity to explain how each job within the department fits into the main flow of production or activity; secondly, the departmental rules about time-keeping, breaks for refreshment, health and safety rules, accident prevention, the issue of protective clothing, and any actions to be taken in the case of emergency, and explaining procedures on reporting sickness or other absence. It is also necessary here to tell the new worker what his rights are on union membership and activity and how he can process a grievance or put his views to management; this stage would ideally include some discussion of consultative arrangements in the organization and of suggestion schemes if they are run. If the organization recognizes trade unions, this would be an appropriate occasion on which to introduce the new employee to the shop representatives of the union and to anyone who has other representational functions within that particular section or department.

Certain matters still remain to be discussed with the individual employee by a member of the personnel department itself, such as information on the firm's policies and practices on helping individual employees with any private, financial or domestic problems, on the policies and practices on the development of the individual's qualifications and education, and, thirdly, information on remuneration policy and practice followed within the organization. At this stage information is usually given verbally. Legal requirements on giving further particulars of the contract in written form will doubtless be met later (see pp 78–81), but the individual needs some basic information immediately which must therefore be built into the induction programme at this early stage.

Monitoring selection
A further stage of the selection process is that of evaluating the selection processes and methods themselves.

The main problem of selection which any organization encounters is that which denies it the opportunity to check on the suitability of those who 'got away'. Unfortunately, this is often used as an excuse for not doing anything to check the validities and reliabilities of the methods which are employed in selection processes. To take this course is to miss the opportunities which the organization has for checking, using those who are selected and employed. Although these may be only a part-sample of the total feedstock, they are available for measurement operations, and productive of much more information than could be obtained in the selection process itself. If the appropriate assumption is made that they are a part-sample, and the better part of the sample if the selection processes are effective, data on them can be employed most effectively in checking on existing methods *and* existing objectives.

The success of selection can be evaluated, and it is not necessary that evaluation should proceed by way of 'sophisticated' techniques. Every piece of information can be evaluated against the performance of those selected. For example, age, length of experience, any test results and interviewer's opinion, can all be set against performance to indicate how successful they proved as predictors in selection. The determination of performance is difficult: supervisor's opinions or assessments of performance are frequently unreliable, and it is therefore better to use objective data (eg work results may be measured by bonus earnings—or length of stay with the company before voluntary departure).

Assessment of the success of selection procedures requires two sets of information to be set alongside one another. For example, the managers' opinions of a man at selection can be set against length of stay, these being plotted on a graph. If the selection procedure is a good (valid) one, the result of the plot will be a thin sausage-shape; the thinner it is, the better is the procedure. This requires that the manager scale his opinions, even if this is done only in terms of broad categories (eg very good, good, average, poor or very poor). Objective data may well lend itself to continuous plotting (eg length of stay in weeks). (See figure 6 below).

Figure 6

Prediction and experience

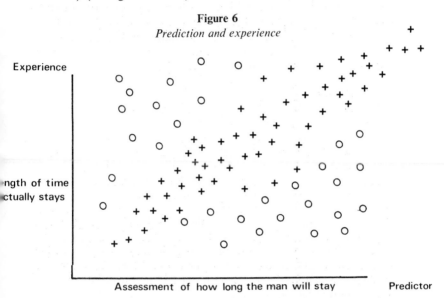

A quick and simple way of carrying out this evaluation is to divide both sets of data into two categories, such as the better half and the worse half, so that half the population is in each category. This information can then be placed in four boxes of the following table:

Those who were predicted at selection to be

		in the better half	in the worse half
Those whose actual job performance is in	the better half of the performers	a	b
	the worse half of the performers	c	d

If each box has an appropriately equal number in it, then the selection procedure is no more valid than chance would allow, or than could be obtained by tossing a penny to determine what category a person should fall into. A very good selection procedure would result in the population being divided more or less equally between boxes a and d.

This can be converted approximately into correlation by (i) working out an index: (a × d) divided by (b × c), and (ii) converting this index into the equivalent correlation from the table below:

Index	Equivalent correlation
35.0	0.9
15.5	0.8
8.9	0.7
5.8	0.6
4.0	0.5
2.9	0.4
2.2	0.3
1.7	0.2
1.3	0.1

The nearer the correlation to 1.0 the better the selection procedure.

This provides but one of many possible illustrations of the manner in which the personnel function is being wooed away from a possibly excessive interest in data as a basis for no more than morale considerations, and towards a use of data to monitor the personnel and manpower decision-processes.

Termination of contracts or deselection
It is to be expected that many employees who are secured in the manner indicated in this chapter will subsequently change their jobs within the enterprise. Sometimes this may result from voluntary transfer or promotion as the individual pursues a career within it, and sometimes because of the exigencies of the business which might reduce or eliminate the need for certain jobs or certain skills. Increasing restrictions on the employer's opportunity to discharge labour (see appendix to chapter 1 above) may lead to much more job changing within the undertaking than may have occurred in earlier years. During this process, both supervisors and personnel practitioners are likely to be involved in the tasks of selecting and preparing people for the new jobs, following procedures and methods not too dissimilar from those discussed above.

Time, and the implementation of manpower plans in a

changeable market, will also lead to terminations of the employment contract and the final 'de-selection' of the individual from the organization. Where the termination is voluntary on the part of the individual, he or she may cause no more than a small administrative action to effect the termination (giving of cards, tax statements and so on) and possibly, in a termination interview, to provide data which might be used in monitoring employment practice and policy within the undertaking. Where the 'voluntary leaving' is because of retirement, the personnel department may (as happens in an increasing number of undertakings) be drawn into a process of helping prepare the individual for the new status and condition. This may mean providing pre-retirement courses, frequently off the job, in which various experts (eg in health of the old, income and tax matters, or in welfare services and provision) may inform and advise or counsel the person retiring (and in some cases, even the spouse) about the likely problems they may encounter. Where death occurs in service, the personnel practitioners also often have to help the family to deal with the immediate and longer-term (eg pension or benefit) problems.

A number of terminations occur involuntarily from the employee's standpoint. Here, the activities imposed upon the personnel specialists are somewhat different. In the first place, there is likely to be a responsibility upon the personnel department to see that procedures exist to support any decision by the employer to discharge an employee: this means, in effect, ensuring that there are procedures for monitoring the performance of the individual employee in a fair and equitable fashion, for applying known disciplinary and safety (etc) rules in a manner which accords with the principles of natural justice, and for allowing any redundancy which may be declared to be dealt with in a non-discriminatory and open manner as is required by legislation and (often) union-management agreement. Secondly, it is often a responsibility of the personnel department to ensure that (in the interests of both the employer and the employee) these procedures are followed and that the principles of equity and natural justice are observed in doing so, in order both to avoid difficulties before tribunals or with the unions, and to help ensure that the individual(s) affected retains a reasonable amount of respect for the employer even when discharged. Where in spite of all the employer is taken before a tribunal about a dismissal, it will also often fall to the personnel specialist either to represent or support the representative of the employer in that context.

The personnel specialist will then find himself required to exercise a number of his basic skills in smoothing this de-selection process. He or she will need to design appropriate procedures, secure their adoption by others, police their operation, and become concerned in them in ways which will make use of his inter-personal and communication skills. He will, for example, quite often find himself counselling not only the affected employee(s) but the supervisors and managers who may be involved in the process. He will also have to ensure that the requirements of law are complied with. He will have to relate termination and de-selection to the manpower plan for the undertaking. The skills and knowledge called for in this part of the exercise will therefore be broadly similar to those of the recruitment processes, even if the context and procedures involved are somewhat different.

The broad import of the material in this chapter is that the personnel practitioner, in his executant role within the employment function, applies skills of analysis, judgement and communication to facilitate the development of a satisfactory or equilibrium relationship between the demands of the undertaking for labour and the supply of labour available. Those skills have to be addressed to both sides of the equation: there is a need for technical analysis of the work demands and of the offers represented by those who present themselves for vacancies, and there is a need to facilitate the exchange of information all along the line to enable the necessary judgements to be made. Up to this point in the discussion, the whole matter of effecting this manpower balance has been treated in its technical aspect and little attention has been paid to the basic humanity of the manpower involved: this forms the subject of the next chapter, in so far as it relates directly to the personnel practitioner's role and function.

Further reading
On the subject matter of this chapter students may find it useful to consult
Bramham (1975) on the practical aspects of manpower planning
Boydell (1970) on job analysis and Singer and Ramsden (1969) on skills analysis
Ray (1971) and Baithwaite and Pollock (1974) on advertising
Ungerson (1970) and Plumbley (1976) on recruitment and selection
Anstey and Mercer (1956) and Fraser (1971 and 1966) on selection and selection interviewing
Albright, Glennon and Smith (1963) and Miller (1975) on psychological testing
Marks (1974) on induction.

4 Individual goals and expectations in work

Behaviour and action

The personnel practitioner is, as we saw in the introduction, predisposed to express his or her concern as being with 'people at work'. When society refers to these people at work in general and formal terms, they become 'workers' or, in a more restricted meaning, 'employees', as we saw in chapter 1. These two different views find expression in two different perspectives adopted by personnel specialists themselves. One sees the objective of the personnel function as being the 'humanizing' of the work situation, that is as being a means of turning the more limited concept of 'employee' into the more human concept of a person. The other sees the objective as one of mediation between the employer and the 'employee' and is based upon the recognition of a basic inequality in that contractual relationship.

In the one perspective, the problem is that workers are expected to behave like 'cogs' in a machine, that is, as essentially unthinking parts or elements in the total productive system; since this denies these same workers their essential humanity, work must be humanized. But what does that 'humanization' process imply? Essentially, that workers being persons must be placed in a position where they *act* in a thinking fashion (rather than merely behave in the way in which atoms are thought to behave in the face of various stimuli). But in the other perspective, the role of the personnel specialist is founded upon the view that workers do act as thinking beings and that it is the likely conflict between this *action* and the action of others with different interests which requires mediation. The personnel specialist, in either of these perspectives, cannot therefore escape the problem of human will, as the element in the human situation which distinguishes the worker from the machine.

Both these perspectives are equally valid. The distinction is drawn here because in the present chapter we want to look at people more as people (or persons) and less as employees or workers in the sense in which the preceding chapters have employed these terms.

A first question which therefore has to be asked about workers (of whatever grade or status) is whether what they do (in work or at work) is a simple and predictable reaction to definable stimuli *or* a more complex and consciously-thought-out response to the situation as the person defines it. The answer to this question is unlikely to be straightforward. On the one hand, we would certainly not expect people to act like automata all the time, nor would we expect them to think out every one of their actions before committing it. Therefore we would neither expect workers to be capable of being labelled as reactors or as responders (in the above senses). On the other hand, we would expect people to do some things without thinking and to do others only as a result of some thought. Therefore, it becomes a part of the answer to the question to determine what it is that people respond to in a reflexive manner and what it is that they respond to only after thinking out the action. We are unlikely to be able to give general or categorical answers to these kinds of question, although we might expect to find some answers if we either observed behaviour or asked questions of the workers in whom we might be interested (cf Roethlisberger and Dickson, 1939; Goldthorpe, 1968).

If we were to observe or question enough workers, we might in the end feel that we have enough data to generalize about workers' behaviours or actions. (We might note also that to do this we do not have to be researchers; by our experience we make a large number of observations and secure a large number of answers to questions and, rightly or wrongly, we use these as a basis for generalization.) In particular, we might feel that we had enough data to enable us to say that we had found the 'key' to explain why workers do what they do; our generalization might then take the form that 'workers do what they do because they are ambitious . . . or goal-seeking . . . or seeking for personal equilibrium'. Each of these statements suggests that, at least to some extent, what the worker does he does as a result of some degree of thinking or rational analysis which precedes behaviour or action (cf Simon, 1954, p 1). But the generalization might take another form—'that workers do what they do simply because they have to eat but they are lazy and don't want to think out their action'. This is the kind of insight which McGregor used as the assumption of his Theory X approach to management (McGregor, 1960). But this kind of generalization suggests that workers *are* cogs in some machine (perhaps a biological one) and that they do simply react to the environment, without conscious thought. And of course different people have developed generalizations about workers on just these kinds of foundation and in forms of words not widely dissimilar from the ones used in this paragraph (cf Bowey, 1976, ch 1).

These kinds of perspective may be set up *prior* to the analysis of organizational behaviour or human action. Before we can talk sensibly about 'how people behave (that is, through what processes)' we have to adopt some 'model of man', because the model we adopt will seek to explain either passivity in behaviour or activity in response (or perhaps both if we choose a hybrid or synthetic model rather than one of the two polar types briefly identified above). Thus if we view man as inherently lazy our analysis will seek to explain laziness, whilst if we see man as inherently active it will seek to explain a quite different dynamic.

A good deal thus depends upon what view we take as to the nature of man. The literature of the social sciences is replete with views of man which constantly throw up opposing, either-or, perspectives. Porter, Lawler and Hackman (1975, ch 2) argue that man has been seen in the following alternative frameworks:

1 As emotionally controlled at an often-unconscious level or As rationally oriented and therefore as essentially calculating

2 Behaviouristically, by which all behaviour is to be explained in terms of environmental control or Phenomenologically, by which all action is to be explained as a consequence of conscious thought

3 As an economic animal or almost as a hedonistic one, consciously seeking material satisfaction and avoiding conditions like starvation or As a self-actualizing animal, in which personal growth and development provide stronger draws than mere money or materialism

4 As essentially passive or reflexive, responding only to that which cannot be avoided (as in the Theory X assumptions) or As essentially active and responsive, capable and willing to contribute to wider goals, provided the disposing condition is right (Theory Y).

These four categories emphasize different dimensions but through each of the two columns there runs a linking thread, one of passive or negative reaction to blind fate, and the other of active or positive response to a mutable environment. Each in turn demonstrates a consonance with perspectives of group and organizational behaviour, the one associated with 'system' perspectives in which the individual is seen as reacting, and the other with 'social action' perspectives in which the individual is seen as striving (at least) to respond.

There does not seem to be a simple answer to the question posed. What seems more likely is the proposition that some workers, some of the time, and in some spheres of action will simply react whilst some workers (maybe the same ones) some of the time and in some spheres of action will respond in a more calculated or conscious fashion. Which of these two possibilities applies in the particular case is likely to remain for local determination, although some degree of generalization is possible on the basis of observation or analysis.

A second question which then has to be asked is how this reaction or response is produced. The answers to this question are likely to take us into the realms not only of the environmental stimuli which may impinge upon the worker in question, but also of the 'motivation' of the worker (to use the concept most often applied to indicate broadly the processes which in the individual precede behaviour or action). Although a great deal of thinking has gone into answering this question, there is no simple generally acceptable answer or theory. At various times in the recent past, different theories have proved fashionable, each in turn being overtaken by another which ousted it from the pinnacle of popularity. Each has its adherents still, and whilst one would like to hope that each succeeding fashion represents an improvement upon or a refinement of what has gone before, that remains a hope rather than a demonstrable fact.

One of the main problems here is that whilst it is possible to see what a person does, it is not possible to 'see' how he arrives at his decision to do it. Consequently the explanation of how and why the action comes about represents an exercise in logical thinking, of the type: 'if such and such an output can be observed to occur in association with such and such an assumed stimulus, a rational explanation of how one gets from stimulus to response might take the following form . . .' This is in effect the foundation of much of need theory or motivation theory, represented in the work of Maslow (1943); Vroom, (1964); Lawler, (1971) and others. The logic leads to the setting up of assumed 'hierarchies' or continua of needs or goals and the postulation of sequential steps in the thought processes. These may be 'sensible' and 'persuasive' but they are often very difficult to test in reality, and consequently they have mainly heuristic value for the manager: he can try them and see for himself whether they 'work' or are useful. They are not and cannot ever be facts.

One conclusion possible here is that some of these quite sophisticated theories may be considered to have more relevance to the 'more sophisticated' responses that people might be observed to make to situations, and possibly less relevance to some of the simpler, reactive behaviours which may be observed in practice. In other words, where the worker does engage in conscious deliberation about his responses to a situation, the processes through which he goes may be incapable of explanation without some of the more complex theories; where however his behaviour is a simple reaction of an unthinking sort the explanation *may* be much simpler. Some workers may simply work for the money but others may, in a more complex way, work for a more cogent set of reasons which could only be fitted into a much more sophisticated theory. But what is important about this conclusion in the present context is that *any one worker*, who may sometimes react and sometimes respond, may be incapable of being understood without both levels of theory about his motivation being brought into play to explain what he is observed to do.

The identification of needs

If we were to see the human animal as a complex chemico-electro-mechanical system, we might well rest content to explain all behaviour in the concepts drawn from chemistry, electronics and mechanics. The view has recently been propounded that man's behaviour is to be explained in terms of genes and that much human conduct is just so much frill to basic *and pre-determined* drives which spring from the genetic urges (cf Dawkins, 1976). This kind of perspective is unlikely to prove very acceptable to thinking man, because of its extremeness of assertion. But other less extreme perspectives do have an appeal, some of them because they appear to permit a self-excusing explanation of human response. This is broadly the case with current theories of motivation based upon the concept of a human need or drive.

The foundation for this construction is therefore an assumption as to what is either (a) a normal condition or (b) a preferred position for the individual. It is assumed in many theories of motivation, for example, that an individual will engage in seeking or avoidance behaviours, in order to produce a situation in which he is in state of equilibrium or to avoid one in which he is in a state of tension. This assumption is fundamental to a good deal of thinking in science (including the social sciences) and although it is by no means universally accepted it is as useful as it is prevalent in allowing analysis to proceed. The assumption then allows the relationship between need and behaviour to be consisered as a 'motivational cycle'.

First, the individual is seen to have inner needs (or needs experienced internally) which may be characterized as states of internal tension, imbalance or disequilibrium, which the individual will be motivated to reduce or eliminate.

Secondly, a response of motivated behaviour which is likely to follow the development of a state of need on the part of the individual and which will be characterized by action which in the intention of the individual will be directed towards alleviating the inner tension.

Thirdly, a concept of goal or the object of the motivated behaviour which is defined as that which, once it has been obtained, might be expected to reduce the state of imbalance.

The first and last elements in this cycle are frequently considered together, often on the assumption that if the need can be asserted by argument the goal is then given. This seems to be the position taken by Maslow (1943), who attempts to explain why people act in the way they are observed to do. Nevertheless, there are others who have accepted the broad foundations of this theory, but have gone on to examine the nature of goals. This might be suggested to be the position of Herzberg (1958) who focuses his attention on what people 'want': it also underpins the many studies of 'what workers want from work' (cf Brown, 1953).

The second element concerns a very different kind of theoretical explanation becase it deals with mechanisms rather than with the two related 'end-states' indicated in the first and the third elements. The area has been explored mainly by Lewin (1951), Vroom (1964) and Lawler (1971). These explanations are founded upon the elements of decision (or choice) and action, and necessarily involve a more complex array of elements, including belief and preference systems in the individual, and in the external environment as perceived by the individual.

Maslow, for example, has developed a human needs theory which has secured wide acceptance amongst managers, largely through the work of McGregor (1960). A categorial theory, it first distinguishes five broad classes of need which might be associated with man, but generally speaking they leave little room for the accommodation of an active, thinking response to the environment. The five categories are:

1 *Physiological needs* These are seen as the basic needs of the human organism, such as food, water, air, sleep, sex etc. The individual is seen to have needs, in other words, simply at the level of the animal organism which may be distinguished from needs which arise because he is also a socialized individual

2 *Safety needs* The emphasis here is upon the need of the individual person for a generally ordered existence in a stable environment freed from threats to the safety of the person as a person and threats to the opportunities which exist within that existence to satisfy various needs which he might have

3 *Love needs* These are seen as needs to develop relationships of affection with other individuals and the need for the individual to have some recognized place as a member of a group or a number of groups. The latter is often translated as a need to secure acceptance by the individual's peers or associates and might be described as a

relatively low level example of the need for affection

4 *Esteem needs*   The main point at issue here is that the individual needs to be able to satisfy himself by developing a firm basis for self evaluation. The need for self respect, self esteem and for the esteem of others depends to some extent upon the environment being relatively stable, but it also switches the emphasis away from environmental factors and towards a basis in the individual for developing a proper or stable evaluation of the self

5 *Self actualization needs*   This conception of need moves the concept further forward and relates to the need for self fulfilment or the need to achieve full use of the individual's own capacity for doing things. The emphasis at this level is almost entirely upon realization of the human individuality or personality and although it depends upon a relatively stable and benign environment it is in itself nothing to do with that environment.

Consistently with a conception of inner need, this categorization identifies inner states in the sense that what supports the classification is how the individual feels about his relation to the environment. It is, however, founded on a concept of individual equilibrium, such that the individual need is identifiable by reference to a departure from a physiological or psychological equilibrium or balance, and prepares the way for saying what an individual might do if this assumed preferred 'steady-state' is disturbed. For this reason, it becomes difficult to conceive of an individual reacting positively to an undisturbed equilibrium and therefore of him deliberately upsetting the equilibrium in order to satisfy some other inner need, such as those for challenge or excitement or change. In Maslow's categorization, this can only or must mainly appear in connection with self-actualization.

The second major theoretical proposition advanced by Maslow is that these categories of need are hierarchically structured. The individual will be led to respond to these needs in a serial fashion, attempting to satisfy the physiological needs first, before moving to the attempted satisfaction of the safety needs etc. This theory is advanced in three propositions:

1 The behaviour of any person would be dominated by the most basic category of need remaining unfulfilled at any particular time
2 The individual would seek to satisfy his needs systematically, beginning with the lower order ones and rising to the higher ones
3 The more basic needs would therefore be capable of description as being more 'prepotent' and would take precedence over the higher ones.

When, therefore, self-actualization needs are placed in this position in a hierarchy, disequilibriating drives or behaviours find their place in the scheme only 'at the top of the hierarchy', suggesting that an individual is unlikely to respond to a need for, say, excitement until after he has satisfied all other, lower-order needs.

On *a priori* grounds, therefore, this theory might be questioned both because of its presumption of equilibrium in the individual as the normal state, and because of the related tendency to conceive of normal needs in terms of considerable passivity on the part of the human being. The testing of Maslow's theory has tended to cast doubt on the validity of the second of these, and the alternative process theories appear to offer a more satisfactory alternative to the first assumption.

The empirical testing of Maslow's hypotheses has tended to concentrate on the determination of whether the concept of a hierarchy of prepotency of need offers a useful means of explaining human behaviour. In a series of studies, Porter (1961–3) produced evidence to suggest that whilst there is something in the notion of a hierarchy, it may apply only to those who have some choice, by virtue of being able by their position to satisfy the lower order needs comfortably enough and thus focus on higher order ones. Concentrating his attention mainly amongst managers in organizations, he was able to show that basic needs were most likely to be satisfied and that higher order needs were least likely to be satisfied although the satisfaction tended to vary as one moved up the managerial hierarchy. This suggests that the organization as it is presently conceived might be better able to raise both interests in and satisfaction of higher order needs only at the highest level. At lower levels within the organization it could well be that the position of the individual has so far made the question of satisfying self-actualization needs a rather academic one and that, since the individual does not as frequently seek satisfaction of these needs at that level of organization, he does not in fact see the organization as providing him with satisfaction of them.

This kind of cross-sectional research gives some clues on the validity of the Maslow propositions. Since the findings suggest that there might be something in the hierarchy of needs perspective, they satisfy a necessary condition for supporting the theory. They do not however provide a sufficient condition. To meet this condition, it is necessary for the research to be longitudinal, or linked to passage of time, without necessarily being spread over time.

Hall and Nugaim (1968) asked the question as to how perceptions of need satisfaction were linked with perceptions of need intensity or importance at any one moment. On Maslow's theory, it would be predicted that a perception of high need satisfaction at one level (say love) would be associated with a perception of high need intensity or importance at the next higher level (ie esteem). What these researchers ought to have found, to support the Maslow propositions, was just this: what they did find was that need satisfaction and need intensity were positively associated. This suggests that where the need is seen to be satisfied it is also seen to be important, and this goes against the Maslow theory.

These and other researchers (eg Wabha and Bridwell, 1975) have therefore concluded that, whilst the notion of a hierarchy of needs may still be relevant to this discussion of need and motivation, the postulation of five levels, as by Maslow, is capable of being attacked as inoperable in practice, and may indeed be totally irrelevant. This has led to the development of alternative statements about the nature of the need hierarchy.

Alderfer (1972) has, for example, suggested a modification in which he recognizes only three categories of need. Identified as an ERG theory, the three categories identified are: *existence* (close to Maslow's lower order needs of a physiological and material nature), *relatedness* (close to the love and esteem levels in Maslow by virtue of their dependence on other persons) and *growth* (rather like the self-actualization in its emphasis on creativity and self-fulfilment). These he perceives to form a continuum rather than a hierarchy, thus permitting different personalities to 'fit' themselves at different points along it without presuming that the point of 'fit' must be better or worse than another's because it is 'higher'. His perspective also allows that some needs can be treated as persistent over time whilst others are more ephemeral and intermittent, and because any individual may be seeking to redress a number of different categories of need at any one time (according to his expectations of success in each or any) action which might appear inconsistent with long-run need satisfaction can be fitted into the view now taken of needs.

As Landy and Trumbo summarize the difference between these two theories, it amounts to this: "The difference between Alderfer and Maslow can be described in both *content* and *process* terms. They differ in content terms—for Maslow there are five needs; for Alderfer there are three. They also differ in process terms—for Maslow the process is one of fulfilment-progression; for Alderfer, both fulfilment-progression and frustration-regression are important dynamic elements" (Landy and Trumbo, 1976, p 300).

Some testing of this perspective in real work suggests that it might be more useful than the simple need hierarchy theory in explaining the behaviour of people at work. In the words of Landy and Trumbo, "In a sense, Alderfer's view of motivation is a more hopeful one for managers. It provides them with the possibility of constructively channelling the energy of their subordinates even when the individual's higher-level needs are blocked. This energy can be directed toward lower-level needs. The ERG variation is a very new one. A good deal of research will have to be done before it can be accepted as a reasonable view of how and why people expend energy in work settings."

In some distinction from both Maslow's and Alderfer's hierarchies, Herzberg (1966) has put forward a series of propositions which rest upon a two-level hierarchy. He sees all individuals as possessed of two categories of need only, the hygiene needs and the motivator needs. The first relate to the provision of a 'healthy', 'comfortable' or acceptable environment, whether for work or anything else, and are generally lower order needs in the Maslow hierarchy. In work these might include relative pay, security, fellow-worker relationships, authority relationships, general working conditions, rules and policies. The second are higher order, or growth, needs, and are assumed to be the needs which pertain significantly to the *human* animal: these are seen to be met in independence of action, responsibility in work, and recognition of performance out of the ordinary. These are more usefully discussed when linked with goals of motivated behaviour but it may be noted here that they do presuppose that the individual has certain innate characteristics which lead him to seek satisfaction at the 'purely animal' level (the hygiene area) and at the 'distinctly human' level, and that these relate to the inner need state as firmly as do Maslow's 'needs'.

Whatever the drives of the individual, it could be represented that the individual's motivation is to be explained in terms of what it is 'outside himself' that he wants, regardless of the 'reason' why he wants it. It might be represented, in other words, that observed behaviour may be explained teleologically by reference to what it is the individual establishes as his goals.

One interpretation of Herzberg's empirical study is that, whatever inner needs individuals may be regarded as responding to, they are able to articulate their perceptions and evaluations of work as a means of satisfying these in ways which suggest that there are 'environmental objects' to which they attach varying values. Whatever the 'kind' of person involved, and whatever his inner drive, there is a tendency to attach higher value to certain environmental objects and lower value to others. These in turn may be categorized into the two broad classes of motivators and hygiene factors, each with a different potential as a desired goal. Importantly, feeling good or bad, in themselves inner states, is shown to trigger in the mind of the individual perceptions of parts of the environment associated with these two inner states. Hence the notion that there is a 'goal' outside the person which will affect his feelings, but hence also the notion of the environment as a potent influence in structuring, for the individual, 'what it is that might be said to motivate him'.

Gellerman's discussion of 'the effects of work upon work' and 'the effects of behaviour upon behaviour' (1974) also involves this conception of goal-seeking behaviour as something channelled by the opportunities presented by the environment. "Most people, he suggests, are capable of a wide variety of behaviour, and their actual conduct in any given situation will depend on the way in which environment draws upon their available 'inventory' of possible responses. Further, the 'environment' has to be understood more broadly: it not only includes working conditions, compensation and supervision (the main concerns of the 'benevolent' phase of personnel management) but also the experiences generated by doing the job and the web of communications in which the job is embedded. Recognizing that behaviour is usually a response, rather than an inevitable acting out of some inner drive, managers have become increasingly concerned with the extent to which they can deliberately shape the environment in which the response is made" (p 41), and "Behavioural scientists have become increasingly fascinated with the effect of behaviour itself upon behaviour: that is with the extent to which actions are largely explicable as *re*-actions to what other people do" (p 53).

If the individual may be conceived in social and work situations to respond in this fashion to what is presented to him, he may also be conceived as making no response to that which is not presented to him or not available to him as a stimulus. This in essence is the view taken by Lewin (1951) in his attempts to explain why people behave in the ways they do, particularly at the level of consumption conduct. His researches focused on the question of why people ate the food they did eat, and why, when they had a choice of food, they would choose one food rather than another.

A motivated response to the environment
If the view of man as 'driven' to satisfy inner (and inescapable) needs is rejected, the remaining alternative is to see him as capable of thinking out a response to the opportunities which are presented to him by his environment. This may make him appear to be more rational or more calculating, but nevertheless as more human than in the alternative view (cf Hull, 1943). It is not, however, necessary to suppose that the human being must always act in this fashion. For some purposes in some areas of behaviour and in some conditions of the environment, he may well respond as a system driven from within by

pressures which he cannot escape, but for others he may equally well respond as a thinking being. This, indeed, tends to provide the rationale of the 'development' implicit in a move up the Maslow hierarchy of prepotency or along the continuum proposed by Aldefer. In relation to work activity and motivation, and in current conditions of relative affluence, it may be sensible to recognize the relevance of this alternative view of man as a being capable of change or growth as a consequence of his ability to make critical assessments of the opportunities provided by the environment.

Something of this assumption characterizes the theories of those who have conceived of motivation in terms of process rather than content. These drop the assumption that man is necessarily driven by his inner needs and that these are sufficient to explain motivated behaviour. In their place, the emphasis is placed upon trying to answer the question how the thinking individual proceeds in ordering his actions to suit himself. The transition from one kind of theory to the other is effected by Lewin, who saw the individual as a decision taker, but as one constrained in the decisions he takes by the decisions of others, whom he calls gatekeepers. These 'others' perform the special role of developing an individual's preferences by the expedient of repetitively presenting him with certain stimuli: the clearest example which he employs to illustrate this is the mother who repetitively serves the family members with certain dishes and repetitively avoids serving certain others. Since these dishes are likely to have a value to the hungry family members, the repetition might be expected to lock them into a particular scale of preferences, which will then tend to affect their subsequent behaviour (Lewin, 1953).

These ideas have been developed by Vroom, who seeks to answer the question of *how* the individual decides what is the most attractive course of action for him to take. He argues that attractiveness will represent the combined attractiveness of realizing a particular goal (as this may be varied by the likelihood of his doing so by adopting one course of action) and the attractiveness of not realizing (or only partially realizing) other outcomes because the one course of action is adopted (varied also by the individual's calculation of the probabilites involved in these).

Vroom argues that the attractiveness of that course of action to the individual will vary not only with the attractiveness of the first goal that is postulated, but also according to the effect that taking that course of action would have on realizing various other goals. A decision to go to work in the morning denies the individual the opportunity to work in the garden and the probability that he cannot work in the garden if he follows that course of action is one. But the decision to go to work might result in a certain level of income at the end of the week which would have some attractiveness to the individual and the probability of his receiving that income at the end of the week might be regarded as 0.9. This calculation could be worked out in a much greater detail but it illustrates the sort of notion that Vroom is seeking to put forward.

The second proposition advanced by Vroom is that the pressure (force) on a person to carry out a particular course of action will depend upon the combined attractiveness of the various outcomes when he has made this sort of calculation. Clearly it follows that the combined attractiveness of the outcomes of one course of action will tend to vary from the combined attractiveness of the outcomes of another course of action. Where this comparison is made, the stronger force will tend to explain the behaviour that it is feasible for the individual to engage in. This might be linked to Maslow's hierarchy of prepotency in the sense that the outcome of securing food when hungry might be considered to have a higher valence for the individual than an opportunity to learn to play the violin, for example.

The deliberate calculation of the relative attractiveness of different outcomes introduced into Vroom's theory, thus potentially carries the perception forward into the realms of rational decision-taking. Far from being 'driven' by inner needs which can only be satisfied by certain objects in the environment, the individual is now permitted in the theory to determine a course based upon individual perceptions and evaluations. It is this part of Vroom's conception which is then incorporated into what has come to be called expectancy theory, described by Landy and Trumbo as providing "a comprehensive framework for dealing with complex industrial behaviour" (Landy and Trumbo, 1976, p 309).

Expectancy theory
The most comprehensive theory of motivated behaviour is that which has been developed from the work of Tolman (1932), Lewin (1938), Vroom (1964) and Lawler (1968) by Porter and Lawler (1968), and sometimes known as 'expectancy-instrumentality-valence' theory (or 'expectancy theory', in short). Expectancies are defined as a special category of belief or theory about the nature and dynamics of the environment and in this sense are to be regarded as important to definition, judgement and decision-taking (or choice) by the individual. "Expectancies are simply the beliefs that individuals hold about what leads to what in the environment. . . . Expectancies specify the relationships between what a person does and what outcomes he obtains in the organizational environment. How expectancies influence the voluntary behaviour of individuals in organizations" forms the 'problem' to be explained by expectancy

theory (Porter, Lawler, Hackman, 1975, p 52). The use of the adjective 'voluntary' in this statement should be noted as suggesting a deliberate rejection of 'drive' theory from consideration, although as we shall see below, the concern of that set of theories with the content of motivation is still relevant to a part of expectancy theory.

The theory seeks to bring together a large number of separate factors which might be expected to influence the individual's expenditure of effort and his level of performance or achievement, these being the two related aspects of 'behaviour' to be explained. The factors thus identified as influential are the individual *perceptions* of these two factors and the link between them, and of the rewards and satisfactions available and likely to be allocated to him (together with the constraining factors upon performance, of skills and abilities and 'normative conceptions of that performance). The whole is encapsulated in a set of feedback loops which inform the perceptions of the individual, and which form a set of intervening and mediating variables between satisfaction-and-reward and effort-and-achievement. It is therefore essentially a decision-making model which seeks to link subjective factors and processes to environmental factors and processes (cf Simon, 1961; 1955) (see figure 7).

In its simplest form, the theory states that the individual's decision to expend effort will depend upon three perceptions or beliefs about the effort-receiving situation: first, that there are available rewards for *successful achievement* resulting from the effort to be expended and that these rewards have value or attractiveness for the individual; secondly, that the achievement of success as a result of expending the effort will in fact bring forth these rewards; and thirdly, that the expenditure of effort will result in successful achievement. It also states that successful performance (achievement) will depend not only upon this decision to expend effort but also upon the skills (or traits) and abilities of the individual (which set a boundary to potential achievement) and upon the role perceptions of the individual (which is essentially to be defined in terms of possession of appropriate standards or norms of 'success'). The theory allows that rewards associated with performance may be either 'intrinsic' (given by the individual to himself as a consequence of 'successful' performance) or 'extrinsic' (given to the individual by someone else in the same circumstances) but it admits also that whatever these rewards may be they do not stand alone in the sense that both must conform to the individual's perception of what is 'fair and equitable' in the way of reward for that performance, which is in turn likely to involve comparisons. Those rewards, when evaluated, are the source of satisfaction to the individual, and this 'satisfaction' in turn influences the value which the individual will subsequently place on any reward.

208

Figure 7
The structure of expectancies

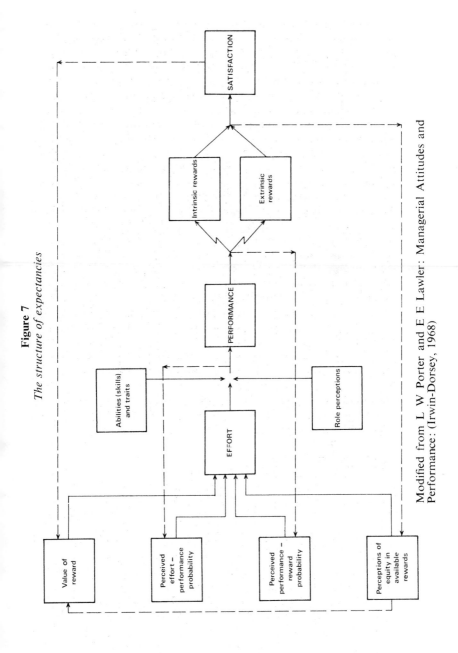

Modified from L W Porter and E E Lawler: Managerial Attitudes and Performance: (Irwin-Dorsey, 1968)

209

It appears to be worth changing the status of the factor 'perceived equitable rewards' in the Porter-Lawler model to permit this to be treated (along with the basic condition and the two types of expectancy) as a factor which will influence effort. In the original, it is seen to be derived from performance, since it is regarded as "determined by the individual's perception concerning how well he fits the role requirements of the job, and his perceptions of how well he actually performs on the job" (Landy and Trumbo, 1976, p 308). Mediated by the factor of 'satisfaction' it is then seen to feed back on the basic condition, the perceived value of rewards, and this is clearly likely to be so. But to see its 'effect' as occurring by this route disallows the possibility that conceptions of 'equity' in rewards, or of what is 'fair', might have a direct effect on effort in some distinction from the perception of rewards as valued objects in so far as they give satisfaction. This is discussed further on pp 217–23 below.

The number of influential factors incorporated into the theory makes it impossible to argue that in the normal case, either the payment of more money will produce more performance (cf Brown, 1954, p 186) or the happy worker is a high producing worker (cf Landy and Trumbo, 1976, p 309). With so many influencing variables, a positive effect of one might easily be cancelled out by the negative effect of another. Simple statements of what in the way of rewards or satisfactions will motivate individuals to higher performance are, the theory suggests, not realistic. The value of the theory therefore does not lie in reducing the theoretical propositions to a ·few simple rule-of-thumb statements.

Its value lies rather in the relationships on which attention is to be focused in seeking to explain high or low achievement and/or to initiate action to improve it.

Satisfaction and reward value
What might be referred to as the 'end' and 'beginning' variables in this chain of causality are 'satisfaction' and · 'value of reward'. Neither of them is explained or accounted for in the model, both being taken as facts which are related to one another in the sense that satisfaction experienced (or expected) is considered to have some influence upon the value of the reward (and therefore its valence or attractiveness) to the individual. "Satisfaction" according to Porter, Lawler and Hackman, "is determined by the difference between the amount of some valued outcome that a person receives and the amount of that outcome he feels he *should* receive. The larger the discrepancy the greater the dissatisfaction. Moreover, the amount a person feels he should receive has been found to be strongly influenced by what he perceives others like

himself are receiving (cf Lawler, 1971). People seem to balance what they are putting into a work situation against what they feel they are getting out of it and then compare their own balance with that of other people. If this comparison reveals that their outcomes are inequitable in comparison with those of others, then dissatisfaction results" (Porter, Lawler and Hackman, 1975, pp 53–54).

This concept is then seen in the model to have some influence on the value of the reward, or the valence or attractiveness which it has for the individual. The model does not concern itself with an explanation of how outcomes come to have valence, it implies that that which satisfies (positively) will come to have a higher attractiveness for the individual. But at the same time, this can only be so if the individual wishes to obtain that 'kind' of satisfaction: a person entering a café to enjoy a cup of coffee is unlikely to want or appreciate the satisfaction which, in other circumstances, a cup of tea might be expected to yield. The question of what satisfactions the individual might want is, however, not regarded as the concern of this model and for answers to that question it is necessary to look to the 'drive' theorists (Maslow, 1954; Herzberg, 1970).

The model therefore invites us to consider these questions of satisfaction, reward value and their interrelation with reference to three questions which are not dealt with in the expectancy theory itself. First, the question of what outcomes exist as potential objects of value or valence? Secondly, that of what comparisons the individual is likely to make in order to establish that value or valence? And thirdly, the question of why (ie in the nature of the individual) different objects associate with different satisfactions?

The primary condition
The first condition stipulated for the explanation of behaviour in accordance with expectancy theory is that there are attractive rewards or benefits available to the actor for the accomplishment of the action. This focuses attention on the individual's scale of preferences in terms of reward, and upon the belief or theory as to the availability of benefits for distribution.

Expectancy theory displays a strong affinity with the notion of theory as advanced by Stinchcombe "of how . . . activities can be organized to achieve the purpose of the organization" (Stinchcombe, 1967, p 156) where he defines theory as "any set of ideas that allows people to make predictions about what will happen if some specified variables are changed" (*ibid*, p 157) and suggests that the theory must include four sub-categories, technical-costs, market, benefit-distribution and personnel theories. The first and third of these link with the Type I and Type II Expectancies (see below, pp 223 and

211

227), but the second and fourth appear to have some relevance to this 'first condition' established in the theory.

The first part of this 'condition' is that people must believe that there are rewards available; that, in another set of concepts, there is a 'supply' of rewards available in the environment which may (by whatever process) be brought into juxtaposition with the individual's needs or 'demands'. This therefore compares with the concept of a sub-category of 'market theory' in the Stinchcombe analysis, in which the ideas which link supply and demand variables are identified.

The second part of this condition, which is implicit rather than explicit in the notion of 'expectancy' itself is that not only must the individual *believe* that the rewards exist, but also that they will be available to him. Unless this is made to rest upon the assumption of an impersonal agency working to make these available, the effect of this is to imply, first, that availability will be the resultant of human decision or action (cf Lewin, 1953 and pp 205–7 above), and secondly, that this human agency can be *trusted* to behave in a stable and predictable way—in accordance with the *expectation*, that is—in making the existing rewards available in appropriate circumstances (as described in the theory itself). It is this notion of 'trusting' other persons which lies at the root of Stinchcombe's third sub-theory: "the theory that, under specified conditions and arrangements, we can trust certain people or groups of people . . . is an essential component of all organizations" (Stinchcombe, 1967, p 159).

In expectancy theory, it is envisaged that any of a large number of objects might operate as rewards. Rewards then acquire attractiveness to the individual as a function of their ability to satisfy the person, and in this sense the question of whether any particular object has attractiveness as a reward will depend upon the nature of the individual and the cognitive and affective processes in which he or she subjectively engages. This therefore need not be inconsistent with the perspectives of the drive theorists. Valency and expectancy theorists do not regard it as necessary to the explanation of behaviour to impute any particular equilibrium-related theory as to how the individual deals with these processes. As in Vroom's theory, what is important is the preference which results from the calculation of relative valence.

Nevertheless, as Hackman makes clear in his development of Herzberg's views on the nature of the hygiene and motivator seekers, it is necessary to find some place in the theoretical construct for the psychologist's notion of 'individual differences' (Hackman, 1969). People are different in what they regard as attractive rewards—McClelland's identification of people with different drives

212

related to affect, achievement, and power provides an example of one kind of directly-relevant difference which would be expected to influence attractiveness (McClelland, 1951); they are different also in how they set up the criteria of judgement of attractiveness—Riesman's distinctions between tradition-, inner-, and other-directed personality types presents an example which also carries import for the outcomes of evaluation of different rewards which might be available (Riesman, 1950). Such differences are not denied in expectancy theory, which postulates merely that whatever rewards are found attractive by the individual will prove influential in directing his effort.

What rewards are attractive to the individual may therefore be ascertained. The individual may be able to indicate what in the way of satisfaction he seeks, and therefore which rewards (which acquire valence according to their capacity to satisfy that individual) are attractive to him. For any given individual, therefore, the opportunity to earn more money may be more attractive than the opportunity to develop satisfactory relationships with fellow workers, or vice versa, but only the individual can say which way the balance of value (on the Vroom-type calculation) falls for him. That the individual will be able to make, and will in fact make, this kind of comparative evaluation is what is necessary to the theory as stated. How he does it is not stated, except only in the sense that satisfaction and attractiveness or value of the reward are linked. That people can and do indicate, when asked, what it is they *want* out of their work-effort is testified by many early studies of 'job satisfaction' (see Brown, 1954, pp 190–1). But why these people should want what they say they want may be a mystery to the observer applying his own values to work in the environment of, for example, an abbattoir (*ibid*, pp 193–4).

The meaning of work
The question of whether this first condition is perceived to be met in work by workers of various grades and categories has exercised the minds of a number of researchers, although the question has most often been posed in terms of what work means for workers or what meaning workers attach to factors at work. This is not necessarily directed therefore towards answering the question about what rewards are perceived to be present, except in so far as 'meaning' allows inferences to be drawn as to the categories of reward (eg extrinsic and intrinsic) which workers perceive to be available. The manager considering means and methods of 'motivating' people to higher performances must, as does the exposition of expectancy theory itself, start with an assessment of perceptions of reward availability.

The one form of question which is asked in this context, which links directly to expectancy theory as an 'instrumentality' theory of motivation, is that which asks whether work is seen by those engaged in it *as an end* in itself or merely *as a means* to some other end(s). Do people working see their work simply as a means towards the end of earning a living, or does work for them serve other functions such as those considered as possibilities by Morse and Weiss (1955): "a feeling of being tied into the larger society, of having something to do, of having a purpose in life" (p 191). Their conclusions from a national sample survey were that workers could and did regard work as more than a means to an end and as sufficiently important to them for them to want to go on working even if they did not *have* to. Dubin asked a similar kind of question (1956) in seeking to establish the 'central life interests' of workers or what they saw as important to them in work. His conclusion was that his manual workers did not usually (ie in three out of every four) regard work and the workplace as central life interests: work was where they participated, and possibly found satisfaction, in organizational and technological concerns but it was not where they sought satisfaction in psychological and social terms: these satisfactions were sought and found outside work. Orzack replicated this Dubin study with nurses (1959) and found that they 'overwhelmingly' preferred work to non-work or community settings for the satisfaction of a wide range of interests. This 'class' distinction is also supported by the Morse and Weiss findings and by Lyman's conclusion from a review of a wide range of American studies: "They agree beyond doubt that persons at the lower end of the socio-economic scale are more likely than those at the upper end to emphasize the economic aspects of work, whereas those at the upper end more typically stress the satisfaction they find in the work itself" (Lyman, 1955, p 138). This conclusion needs to be borne in mind in considering the conclusions reached by Herzberg in his 1959 study of engineers and accountants, on the distinction between motivators and hygiene factors.

In Britain, Goldthorpe and a number of colleagues examined a closely related question in three factories in the Luton area, in order to discover "something of the way in which workers order their wants and expectations relative to their employment". They argue that "until one knows what *meaning* work has for them—one is not in a position to understand what overall assessment of their job satisfaction may most appropriately be made in their case" (1968, p 36). This notion of an orientation to work refers to the manner in which the individual orders his expectancies of work and the work situation and rests upon his perspective of what is desirable or possible for him to expect from them.

Thus it can be argued that all workers (or at least all employees) *must* sell their labour power, and have little choice in the matter.

214

Therefore, as Goldthorpe *et al* argue, "all work activity, in industrial society at least, tends to have a basically instrumental component" (1968, p 41) that it emphasizes that the work is a means (instrument) to some other end—like living—and can have chiefly "expressive functions . . . only exceptionally" (1968, p 38). Nevertheless, variations in emphasis are clearly discernible, in casual observation as in research studies and the dominant contrast which is most commonly offered to the senses is the one which appears in the American studies above, that between blue and white collar workers.

An alternative to this is provided by the distinctions in role occupied by the worker/family member/consumer in modern society, the multiplicity of such roles associated with the one person allowing behavioural orientations of a diverse sort according to which set of expectations are given salience. Goodrich (1921) highlights one such distinction when he poses four questions which might be of interest to the worker in his capacity as consumer (the first two) and as producer (the second two):

(a) how much the worker gets in the form of material resources to expend on consumption?
(b) what the production in which the worker engages is for, in the sense of whose ultimate benefit it most clearly serves?
(c) how is the worker treated in the system of production, in the sense of how free or dependent he is made in carrying out his work?
(d) what does the worker actually do in the work situation, in the sense of how inherently simple or complex the work assigned to him may be?

Goldthorpe *et al*, carrying out their studies at the time when the embourgement hypothesis was being widely discussed, could consider whether the worker's orientation was towards the consumer or the producer interest. Their conclusion on this question asked in relation to relatively affluent workers was that these workers were "particularly *motivated* to increase their power as consumers and their domestic standard of living, rather than their satisfaction as producers and the degree of their self-fulfilment in work", (1968, p 38) and that because of this peculiarity might be distinguished from other blue collar workers of a more "traditional kind" (1968, p 38).

The dominant orientation of these workers in relation to their work is therefore a largely 'instrumental' one, work having meaning for them as a means to ends external to the work and the work situation itself. In so far as the worker may place major emphasis on this orientation, he will experience his work as 'labour', in which he feels involved only to a very limited extent, tend to act as an economic

215

man in calculating whether it is worth his while in effort (cost)/reward(benefit) terms to remain in that job and, since he can find no great emotional involvement in his work because he does not see it as capable of yielding other kinds of satisfaction than the purely instrumentally-economic, he will tend to live a life which sharply dichotomizes between work and non-work (cf Anderson, 1961).

To recognize one such orientation in a particular case, and even if on the selling of labour power argument all worker orientations are likely to be instrumental to an extent, is to recognize that there might be other orientations applicable to workers. The producer-consumer distinction above offers the possibility that one such would be the producer, *homo faber*, orientation; but it is a part of the 'alienation' thesis that in capitalism and/or bureaucratic societies that man is denied, by the conditions under which work is organized, the opportunity to experience his work as providing intrinsic satisfaction. In so far as this appears, it is argued, it becomes associated with a 'social' orientation, in which work as a source of human relationships of some kind comes to be valued for its associations rather than for itself.

In Goldthorpe's recognition of this alternative, therefore, work is experienced as a group activity, the group being either the enterprise (in which case involvement may be of a moral and positive kind) (Etzioni, 1961) or the work group, the workers (as in a trade union branch) or the shop (in which cases involvement "is likely to be to some extent alienative; that is, workers are likely to be in some degree negatively oriented towards the organization and to see their group as a source of power against their employer") (Goldthorpe *et al*, 1968, p 41). Because the person can involve himself in the work and work-generated relationships, work has 'much more meaning' for the individual with a solidaristic orientation, and may represent a 'central life interest' for him, helping to structure his extra-work relationships and activities (one graphic example of this is to be found in Dennis, Henriques and Slaughter, 1956).

White collar workers might also be regarded as having something of the instrumentalist orientation but, in their case, as in the case of the solidaristic blue collar workers, there is likely to be a difference in emphasis. Goldthorpe *et al* acknowledge two possible variants, the bureaucratic and the professional orientations. In both, the meaning attached to work is that it is a service, either to an organization (bureaucratic) or to a client (professional) each of which will provide a steadily increasing income, social status and security (ie a career). The worker therefore involves himself morally in the affairs of the organization or the client-system, rendering either 'faithful administration' or 'selfless service to the client' as

216

the case may be 'in return for a relatively secure and privileged existence'. The worker's conception of himself must then become closely bound up with the work arrangement, amounting to a dependence of life-fate on the career, and ego-involvement is strong. In these circumstances, work and non-work may be extremely difficult to divide, the work providing the basis for a way of life, through which all relationships tend to be structured around the work processes. Whilst work is not quite an end in itself, its interdependence is such that it must become nearly so (cf Hughes, 1958).

These constructs thus help to summarize the categories of meaning which, from various studies, various groups of workers seem to attach to their work. They help to crystallize and systematize the general observation that some workers have no interest or involvement in their work whereas others live, eat and sleep their work, whilst the majority fall at some point in between these extremes. The implication of much of the work is that these differences in emphasis occur systematically, as between classes, occupations and even enterprises and parts of the country. The answer to the question 'What work means for people who work?' is that actuarially speaking it means different things to different workers. From this it follows that these different workers will seek or want different types of reward from their work in order to achieve the kind of satisfaction which their dominant orientation presupposes they regard as attainable. The meaning which workers attach to work therefore establishes the nature of the first condition postulated by expectancy theory.

The secondary condition
Whether, in the mind of the worker, the important relationship touching upon rewards is that between effort and reward or that between performance and reward, the evaluation of rewards as satisfiers needs to be considered not merely in relation to the 'inner' drives or feelings of the individual but also to their 'external' referents. An extrinsic material reward may, for example, be perceived to be available to satisfy a 'basic' need (in Maslow's conception) and an intrinsic reward may similarly be available to satisfy some higher order need such as 'recognition' (in Herzberg's schema); but whatever their potential for satisfaction of the individual in this 'direct' sense, they must also be evaluated against the rewards which others (taken as comparators) are perceived to receive for their efforts or performances. Thus a reward may be perceived to have a direct and individual value, and it may be conceived in the mind of the recipient to have an indirect and comparative value, which may be as significant in the chain of causality as the first perception.

This may then be thought of as concerned with the perceptions of the equity or fairness of the rewards available as distinct from the perceptions of the straightforward availability of rewards which may be expected to satisfy personal or inner needs. The recognition of this perception thus acknowledges that man's decisions about commitment of effort may not respond simply to inner drives, but may also respond to his perception of the comparative fairness which he detects in the way in which the distribution of benefits works in relation to him. It switches attention from the simple concept of a 'wage rate' to the more complex construct of a 'wage structure', or from rewards as affecting self-esteem to rewards affecting social esteem. Where the inexorable consequences of considering perceptions of reward availability lie in considerations of the 'incentive' opportunities and the manner of their perception, those of considering equity of reward allocation fall within the area of reward structure—with job evaluation rather than individual bonus practices.

The question now becomes, not which factor (effort or performance) does the worker consider to be rewarded but rather what he perceives as the foundation of equity as between his rate or reward with another. As Hyman and Brough (1975, p 1) argue, although "relations between managers and workers ... are commonly regarded as ... hard-headed and unsentimental ... the arguments of those involved in industrial relations are shot through with essentially *moral* terminology. In particular, appeals to the idea of fairness abound." It therefore appears to call for a 'place' in motivation theory other than as a possibly discreet 'need' in a hierarchy of needs.

The psychologists have sought to deal with this aspect via 'equity theory' (Adams, 1965; Pritchard, 1969). It entails a construction of a relationship between the individual's perception of two variables, the input and the output. The individual will see himself putting so much into 'work' and getting so much out of it and these can be expressed as a ratio. Both inputs and outputs are to be defined, in the individual's terms, very broadly. A similar calculation can be made, by the individual of the perceived inputs and outputs of any 'other' whom the individual regards as significant for purposes of this kind of comparison. The two ratios may then be compared, and the result of doing so is that either there is no difference or there is a difference, which may be differently directed, as between the self and the other. The theory suggests that where there is a difference, of either kind, the individual will be placed in a state of tension and will be motivated to take action to reduce it.

When tested in an experimental situation, instructions to subjects have been used to create four 'conditions'—under-payment or

218

over-payment on hourly rates, and under-payment or over-payment on piece rates—in each of which, the individual's attempts to reduce the tension are observed in terms of actions related to quantity and quality of performance. The findings of these studies have generally borne out the predictions that

(a) overpayment conditions will
    reduce the quantity of production on piece rate but increase the quality
    increase the quantity and the quality of production on time rates
whereas
(b) underpayment conditions will
    increase the quantity of production on piece rate but decrease the quality
    decrease the quantity and the quality of production on time rates

as the individual seeks to reduce the tension created by the instructions (cf Landy and Trumbo, 1976, pp 317–18).

This 'workshop' condition may be expected to produce such results but it would be expected, on the basis of reference group theory (Shibutani, 1962, p 168), that these directions of tension reduction would apply only where certain conditions of comparative reference obtained and where 'power' was such as to constrain other possible strategies in the withdrawal-aggression mould. The first of these is theoretically acknowledged in the expressions of equity theory, by the inclusion of the significant other, but in real life it would be expected that the 'level' at which individuals perceive such others would prove to be extremely important.

There are therefore two distinct features to this secondary condition which affect reward decisions. First, that any reward package or level must be capable of standing comparison with that of any other 'significant other' against whom the worker will compare himself. This comparison appears at different levels: the individual's satisfaction is likely to be affected by his comparisons with *his* comparators; the group's reactions to a given level of reward is likely to be based upon a comparison with another 'group' which may or may not include the individual's comparator; the bargaining agents may well introduce comparability arguments based on available data into negotiations and these may involve yet other comparators. Secondly, what constitutes appropriate comparators at any such level may well lose its direct relevance in the face of the sort of uncertainty generated by inflation or technological change; in such circumstances, the comparison may be made on the basis not of what the comparator is perceived to get in the way of reward, but rather of what the comparator is perceived as likely to secure within the period during which the individual's reward remains current. The condition of 'equitable' reward availability and distribution may thus be frustrated for either or both of these reasons.

The fact that such perceptions of fairness exist at different 'levels' of decision-taking with respect to rewards is widely attested in the literature. In the workshop, the actions taken in response to variations in work in association with incentive payments (see below, p 226) reflect beliefs that it is unfair for individuals to receive a dis- proportionate share of either 'good' jobs or 'bad' jobs and that therefore in such circumstances the men are justified in 'gold-bricking', banking etc in accordance with their own norms (of both performance-reward *and* status) (cf Roethlisberger and Dickson, 1939; Lupton, 1963, ch 10). At the level of the 'bargaining unit', it is suggested by Jaques, there exist conceptions of what is 'fair' in the matter of differentials rewards for those who are engaged in work whose character is understood by the respondents, this notion of fairness being characterized as having the quality of a continuing belief or value capable of being articulated and in fact used to determine what is equitable in the way of reward (Jaques, 1956, 1961, 1964).

Job evaluation methods in general rely upon similar notions, albeit at the more generalized level where they relate to cultural values: it is assumed that because such notions of 'proper' differentials exist in the culture, it is possible to discern them by these methods. Traditionally, people were thought to have assumptions on the relative worth or importance of different occupations, and that these could and would be associated with differentials in monetary reward. Caplow has provided one list of such assumptions:

(a) white collar work is superior to manual work
(b) self-employment is superior to employment by others
(c) clean occupations are superior to dirty ones
(d) the importance of business occupations depends upon the size of the business, but this is not true of agricultural occupations
(e) personal service is degrading, and it is better to be employed by an enterprise than to be employed in the same work by a person (Caplow, 1964, p 43).

To these might be added others; for example, that

(f) work which calls for higher skill, acquired by longer training, is superior to work which demands no or little training and skill
(g) work which requires the worker's intellectual competence to be

220

certified (as by a grading examination) is superior to that which does not require such certification.

Nevertheless, whilst these assumptions tend to hold in society, the fixing of the absolute level and the differentials of rewards will remain relatively easy: there is at least some firm ground for the administrative or the bargaining decision.

Although these assumptions have some continuing validity, they are less sufficient as explanatory variables than they may have been in the past. The differentials implicit in them are now disappearing or at least blurring by overlapping to such an extent that it may be questioned whether 'white collar work still attracts more reward than manual work' etc. Changes in the pattern of differentials in the post-war period have led to suggestion that certain other assumptions, whilst they still do not have universal validity, may nevertheless serve as explanatory variables. For example, in place of or to supplement the above assumptions, it might now be possible to assert that

(a) workers with bargaining power based on solidarity will be paid more than those with less power or lower occupational solidarity
(b) workers in large manufacturing establishments will be paid more than those in small or service organizations
(c) workers who make up a significant voting category will be paid more than those who do not obviously comprise such a category.

These are variations on a single 'power' theme and could serve as explanatory variables in relation to *some* emergent differentials. They also have the implication that some of the 'ordered' arrangements which were based on the alternative historical assumptions would now have little relevance or acceptability, and therefore that new 'ordered arrangements' might have to be devised to meet the emergent expectations.

If in the longer run assumptions of the first order were to be replaced almost completely by assumptions of the second, then the foundations on which wage and salary plans would need to be based would have to be revamped completely. The resultant plans would also be very different.

This shows itself in current bargaining strategies of unions where it is associated with an ability to pay type of argument: where once this was concerned with the simple question of whether an employer could pay the traditional, comparable 'going rate' for a given class of labour, it has now become more associated with challenges to the traditional division of the product of industry as between the main factors of capital and labour. Analysis of the data on distribution in the 1960s, for example, suggests that there was a secular shift in the relative amounts distributed to capital and labour (Glynn and Sutcliffe, 1972); a variety of policy changes in the 1970s at the level of government control of the economy also suggest that, at this level too, there is support for the proposition that 'ability to pay' exists whenever profit beyond a certain minimum level is made or distributed (eg see the White Paper, *The Attack on Inflation*, 11 July 1975). These changes, in effect, derive their theoretical justification from a very different set of assumptions from those given above.

Briefly, these assumptions are changed at least to the extent that the 'superior' work identified there is now increasingly seen to bring its own inherent rewards (because, for example, it is more interesting or more responsible or more contributive to social well-being, or cleaner etc) and therefore should not (as a value judgement) also attract higher pay. Therefore the economic distribution question can be resolved in totally other terms: everyone can be assured of a minimum amount of income (from whatever source) and the product necessary to maintain that minimum for the low paid or the pensioners can and should be taken from those who have previously had the biggest shares. In 1975, this emerged as the 'TUC-line' accepted by the Government as the foundation for its pay policy and only very few unions (the Electrical Power Engineers Association provides a significant exception in its paper to the Royal Commission on Income Distribution) are willing to express the contrary view that work ought to be rewarded according to its relative social value. In so far as this might then be taken as the new 'philosophy' of distribution in our society, it represents a distinctly different theory of 'benefit distribution' from the one which has served for the preceding century and a half.

The 'ability to pay' argument is therefore to be seen as one based on a particular conception of morality: it is not merely a matter of what 'can' occur but rather a question of what 'should' happen. At the simplest level, ability to pay may be determined by the answer to the question as to whether the firm has made a profit or not: if it has, then it 'can' find some money to pay more. This does not help in the determination of pay in the non-profit sector of the economy but there comparability can be adduced to maintain 'ordered progression'. At the next level of complexity, the argument becomes entwined with a social morality: even if a firm has not actually made a profit, there is still money to be found by narrowing the spread of differential payments to the staff, such that those at the top can give up some of their differential which can then be transferred to the lower paid. This is apparently where the present policies in pay determi-

nation are tending, with destabilizing consequences for conceptions
of equity in relation to reward-distribution.

Type I expectancy

The first relationship about which expectancies form is that between
effort and achievement, as this link is perceived by the individual.
This is equivalent at the level of the individual to that part of organization theory which Stinchcombe identifies as 'technical-costs
theory,' and which in his view must say, in effect, "it is possible to
achieve certain purposes by carrying out certain activities and in
order to carry out the activities, we must have such and such resources" (Stinchcombe, 1967, p 157). In this view, developed in relation to organizations but applicable here too, there are
components on 'know-how' (technical) and cost (effort or energy expenditure), both necessary to the achievement of successful performance.

It by no means follows that increased effort must produce
higher performance, and this is so even where the individual can be
assumed or observed to have adequate norms of success and sufficient ability and skill. The case of the worker who works hard but
ineffectively is well known. But in the context of British industry at
present, a number of reasons why the *perception* of this relationship
functions negatively might be hypothesized. One might be the perception of 'hard work' as a thing of the past in an age of 'automation'
in which the machine could perform more highly than the human,
with a much lower amount of human effort introduced into the equation. Another might be the comparative perception that, for whatever reason, no one else in a comparable position puts in the required
amount of effort to secure the norm of achievement. A third might be
that the effort expended at cost to the individual would be dissipated
by, say, an imperfectly-operating machine or by other less competent
persons which ruined the work. What all these have in common is
that the individual perceiving this relationship between effort and
performance is perceiving a relationship which is uncertain in its effects, because the worker is not in a position to control the consequences of his expenditure of effort.

It is a part of the theory that performance is also affected by
abilities and skills on the one hand and role perceptions on the other.
Given the perception of uncertainty, it is important to recognize that
ability can be interpreted in two different ways, and that the distinction itself offers one potential source of reducing the uncertainty.
Ability may refer to what an individual can do now, and what he can
demonstrate his ability to do if he tries. An individual may have the
actual ability (or the skill) to add 562 to 626, to lift a nine gallon firkin

223

of beer or to prune his rose bushes 'properly', and may be able to demonstrate these actual abilities by satisfactorily completing appropriate tests.

Alternatively, an individual may, at this moment, have no ability to carry out any of these operations but the explanation may lie in the fact that he has never been shown or learned how to do so. Yet if he were shown he might quite well be able to master the skills or the methods and, later on, be capable of demonstrating his 'ability' to carry through the operations.

These two aspects of ability are identified, usually, by the concepts of *achievement*—what the individual can do and can demonstrate his ability to do—and *capacity*—what the individual could do with appropriate experience or training even though he cannot do so now. Both of these are finite: achievement identifies a discrete set of abilities or skills, theoretically capable of being identified and measured; capacity identifies another and additional set of abilities and skills, which also has its limits and which ought in principle to be capable of identification and measurement.

The process of converting capacity into achievement is referred to as learning, or more generally as socialization. Although the opportunities offered to individuals may differ in form and quantity for a wide variety of reasons, it is through handling such opportunities as are offered that individuals acquire their skills or 'achieve'; but it does not follow that two people will learn as much from the same form and amount of opportunity, so that individual differences in achievement will persist even if such constancy in the offers of opportunities is achieved (see Jensen, 1960). For this kind of reason, it is asserted that capacities are both limited and affected by both innate and acquired ability to learn. It is in this sense, and for this reason, that abilities are regarded as setting finite limits to successful performance.

This is also true of the third factor which is seen as influential upon performance: role perception. Role is usually defined by reference to a status, which is conceived as a set of rights and duties which when they are put into effect form the role. The rights and duties may in turn be translated into a set of expectations of what the person in that status will do or be guided to do, and the role 'perceptions' in this theory merely allude to the extent to which the individual in the status in question perceives these surrounding expectations correctly or incorrectly. These expectations are sometimes spoken of in terms of norms, ideas "in the minds of the members of a group . . . that can be put in the form of a statement specifying what the members or other men should do, ought to do, are expected to do, under given circumstances" and which are associated with sanctions such that "any departure . . . from the norm is followed by some punishment" (Homans, 1951, p 123). Small groups may well have mechanisms of sanctions, as Homans demonstrates, which are partly designed to ensure that unwritten norms are nevertheless known and understood, but in many situations the norms or the expectations are likely to be only imperfectly understood by those who might in their various roles be expected to live by them. In particular, the individual may not understand clearly what 'successful performance' means and, if so, no amount of effort or ability by itself will effect successful performance except accidentally. Its achievement deliberately requires a clear appreciation of what is expected of the person performing the role in question, and in particular demands a perception of what is 'expected' performance.

It should not be inferred from this that there is necessarily only one set of expectations, if only it could be stated and appreciated. There may well be a number of conflicting expectations, and failure of an individual to act in accordance with one set of expectations may reflect only that he chooses to act in accordance with another. Nor should it be supposed that what might be termed 'official' norms will always be accepted when they are perceived and understood. A comment by Leyland Cars to the National Enterprise Board on the problems facing the Company in 1977 illustrates this kind of problem in British industry: "After a generation or more of people in manufacturing industry working gradually less hard, it is enormously difficult to reverse the trend. This is not purely a Leyland Cars problem" (see *Financial Times*, 3 November 1977, p 18). What may be postulated is that whatever may be taken to be the norm of performance will not be realized on the basis of effort allied to ability alone; it requires also appreciation of the norm itself.

Two studies of the role of manager-as-assessor in two different cultures may be used to illustrate this problem. In the first, Taft examined the conditions for successful performance appraisal by managers, and concluded that successful performance in judging others requires possession of appropriate judgement norms, ability to judge and motivation. Where a judge has a similar background to the subject, he is likely to have available for use appropriate norms for judging. Ability to judge seems to require both general intelligence and social intelligence, and possibly a factor of 'intuition'. "But", says Taft, "probably the most important area of all is that of motivation: if the judge is motivated to make accurate judgements about his subject and if he feels himself free to be objective, then he has a good chance of achieving his aim, provided that he has the ability and the appropriate judgemental norms. The act of judging one's self is a purposive piece of behaviour that involves not only conscious motivation but also ingrained attitudes towards social relationships, including the relationships inherent in the act of judging itself" (Taft, 1962, p 48). The three factors of expectancy theory appear in juxta-position.

In the second study, undertaken by Rowe of the same kind of process in a number of British companies, the main discovery was that it was carried out quite haphazardly, spasmodically and there-fore badly. Her explanation is similar in many ways to that advanced by Taft. There is some persuasive evidence in the study that apprai-sers are reluctant to appraise others, even when a set *pro forma* is given and an enjoinder imposed (ie when the norm is fairly clearly stated). The reasons for this reluctance might be put either in terms of the managers' inability or their unwillingness to judge. Rowe herself comes down in favour of unwillingness but this may make a too-easy assumption of managerial ability to judge, and a too-ready accept-ance that everyone knows what is the standard in relation to which judgement is required.

Some of the reasons might be connected with the sheer mechan-ics of the appraisal system: for example, that the system pays so little heed to the results that managers feel it pointless to work hard at the appraisal procedures. Some might be connected with meaning and comprehension: some of Rowe's managers alluded in interviews to difficulties of understanding just what the term meant (in spite of training) and perhaps even greater problems associated with ex-pressing oneself in appraisal in a way which would be understood correctly by a reader. Others are likely, in the light of this and other evidence on the skewness of these distributions, to be connected with standards or norms of judgement about many of the more vague con-cepts introduced, particularly on 'personal traits'. But behind all of these may lie a simple motivational reluctance which is often summed up in the moral imperative of our civilization: judge not that ye be not judged!

Whatever may be the actual relationship between effort and per-formance, the perception of that relationship as one set in uncer-tainty is likely to have a dampening effect on performance. Anything which reduces the uncertainty perceived to surround this re-lationship might be expected to have a positive effect upon perform-ance, other factors being assumed constant. This theoretical approach has provided one strand of justification for the movement towards job enlargement and job enrichment (or autonomous work groups) where one of the purposes to be served is to increase the amount of *control* which individuals (or the group) have over the re-lationship between effort and performance. It also, albeit more intui-tively, forms a part of the support for the shop steward's demand for more consultation ('letting people know where they stand' and 'improving the quality of the machine performance') at the immediate shop level. This might also be postulated as the kind of reasoning which has produced two broad patterns of constraint on management decision in recent years, those of training (intended to reduce uncertainty by improving skills or competence) under the Industrial Training Act, and of consultation/participation (intended to increase appreciation of role requirements and standards of performance) under the Trade Union and Labour Relations Act and the Employment Protection Acts.

Type II expectancy
The second expectancy in the theoretical model focuses upon the relationship between performance and rewards. If performance is seen to be the resultant of "the combined effects of effort expenditure, role perceptions, and ability and trait patterns" (Landy and Trumbo, 1976, p 307) rewards may be expected (or believed) to be the resultant of performance and *to that extent* draw forth the effort which gave rise to the performance. The expectancy necessary to the explanation, therefore, is that the successful achievement resulting from expenditure of effort will be inextricably associated with a benefit or advantage which will accrue to the individual. This is the equivalent of Stinchcombe's benefit-distribution theory, which might be paraphrased for present purposes from his original to state the idea that the rule governing distribution of benefits accruing from performance will operate in a way which is both predictable and beneficial to the one who has contributed the required effort (Stinchcombe, 1967, p 159).

The concept of 'reward' in this context has to be given its widest meaning—anything which the individual might draw from the successful performance to yield satisfaction is to be construed as a reward. In the latest formulation of the Porter-Lawler model, a broad distinction is made between intrinsic and extrinsic rewards. 'Extrinsic rewards are rewards administered by an external agent such as the individual's immediate supervisor. This line is wavy due to the sporadic nature of the relationship between successful performance and extrinsic rewards. External rewards are not always provided when a task is successfully completed; the supervisor may not be aware of the successess or may not have the time or inclination to administer the appropriate reward. Intrinsic rewards are rewards which satisfy higher order needs (in the Maslow sense) and are administered by the individual to herself rather than by some external agent. The wavy-line connection in figure 7 see p 209 above) implies that a direct relationship exists between performance and intrinsic rewards only when the job design is such that the worker believes that he felt challenged in the completion of job-related activities" (Landy and Trumbo, 1976, pp 307–308).

As we have already seen, work organizations may be perceived to be differentiated by their capacities to provide these rewards. Manufacturing industry which generates wealth may have wealth available to it to distribute but it may not have as many intrinsic rewards available to it to allocate because, it is usually asserted, of the degree of division of labour practised there. Organizations not producing wealth may have few material rewards to distribute but may make up for this dearth by providing greater security or prestige, or even opportunity for the acquisition of intrinsic rewards. But this by itself does not necessarily imply that the individual will not develop expectations of satisfying any category of need in either situation nor, to the extent that the deficiencies in each are stable, that the individual will necessarily experience dissatisfaction because of them, if he embarked upon his employment in the full knowledge of what he might expect (cf Dubin, 1956; Goldthorpe, 1968). The importance of the 'gap' between expectation and experience as a source of dissatisfaction or of motivation to withdraw from situations has frequently been remarked (cf Revans, 1954; Brown, 1954; Cyert and March, 1963; March and Simon, 1958).

From these same studies we might also expect that the class or occupational status positions of the workers in question will affect the expectancy that they hold on the relationship which ought to exist between performance and reward. The traditional manner of looking at this question in relation to manual workers has been one which sees the expected relationship to be between effort and reward (enshrined, for example, in the notion of a wage-effort bargain) not mediated by 'performance' as an intervening concept carrying its own expectancies (see Baldamus, 1961). The introduction of this 'extra' variable, logical though this may be, may still reflect a 'middle class bias' in the conception of the model. This is hinted at by Landy and Trumbo, for example, in their summary of the Schuster, Clark and Rogers (1971) test of that portion of the Lawler-Porter model which concerns the perception of the relationship of pay to performance, which meant gathering data from 575 professional employees in an industrial setting. "Their findings were generally supportive of the Porter-Lawler model, although . . . they found that the professionals perceived *performance* as a more important determinant of pay than effort" (Landy and Trumbo, 1976, pp 308–309). Whether manual workers regard performance as an important determinant of pay is likely to depend upon how they respond, perceptually, to the development of 'automation' in industry.

228

In recent years, it is just this intervening factor of technological change which has diverted some of the thinking amongst managements and management theorists as to the assumptions that might be made about the worker's expectancies of the relationship between effort and reward. Part of Baldamus's argument is that effort and wages become almost inextricably fused together in the minds of both workers and managers: "All judgements on effort values are a combination of effort and wage expectations: the evaluation of the right effort is inseparably fused into judgements on appropriate earnings" (Baldamus, 1961, p 99). The effect of this is, *inter alia*, that "effort standards become more precise than they otherwise could be" (*ibid*). In addition, both management and workers are more certain in recognizing the wrong relation of effort to wages than the correct one: "the various processes of adjustment (job-bargaining, job rotation, fiddling, rate-cutting, re-timing, quota restriction, goldbricking etc) are focused on effort values that are (from the worker's point of view) too high or too low. In other words, there is a margin within which job values may move up or down without provoking definite judgements and corrective adjustments" (Baldamus, 1961, p 99).

Because these two concepts are treated as one, at least in the sense of being assumed to move together, and because there is nevertheless a variable disparity between the two values (as is evidenced at the time of introducing new technologies), it remains possible to continue in the belief that wages are paid on the basis of effort but that the different interests of the worker and the employer are reflected in the tendency for both (in the view of the other) to get the relationship right. Behrend has therefore suggested that both managers and workers share (or collude in) a belief that if a worker works harder than is implied in the norm of a standard working day rewarded at a standard datal rate, he ought to be paid more for this. Bargaining about piece rates (and all the other adjustments listed by Baldamus) are then represented as explorations of the no-man's land to establish agreement on just how much extra effort should be drawn out by a given change in rewards (whether pay increases or bonus adjustments, or even 'self-financing productivity deals').

The traditional approach to incentives in industry, which has been carried over into measured day-work directly, has therefore been to conclude a "wage-effort bargain" in the form of a "financial incentive scheme" "whereby workers agree to raise their standards of effort in exchange for higher earnings" (NBPI, No 65 S, 1968, p 4). Similarly, in Baldamus's view, "the true purpose of time study is to guess these subjective effort standards as consistently as possible and then adjust the rates of pay to accord with them." (*ibid*, p 4). By

229

implication, there are subjective effort standards to be guessed at, and there is a relationship to pay which will be accepted as according with them. It is, however, this assumption which may, as the quotation from British Leyland (above p 225) suggests, be untenable at present. The course of its decline may be charted.

First, although in the late 1960s it was still possible to argue that the principle of more effort deserving more reward was still relevant, doubts were already being cast upon this (cf NBPI, 1968, p 5). Two factors, technological development and changing cultural values, threatened to spell its doom. Consistently with their 'contingency approach' to the selection of payment plans, Lupton and Bowey (1974, p 79) suggest that such changes in the situation help us to understand "the apparently conflicting prescriptions of people like R M Currie (1963) who advocated incentive bonus schemes of various kinds, and Wilfred Brown (1962) who recommends that piecework be abandoned. They had each been observing situations in which the particular system they were proposing had been successful, but were not aware that there was something peculiar about those circumstances which contributed to the success of the scheme." Thus, with Baldamus, they suggest that the production technology may correlate with type of plan.

Secondly, there is an increasing doubt being expressed about the underlying assumption because what people want out of work may be experiencing change. The Luton studies of Goldthorpe *et al* focus our attention on the instrumental orientation of the worker in which he is seen as willing, in Etzioni's term, to calculate the worth of a given reward against the required effort. But the Maslow and Herzberg perspectives of motivation suggest that either this is a special case or a passing phase (Maslow, 1954) or a highly dysfunctional conception because what is institutionalized as the manner of rewarding people is cosmetic (hygienic) and incapable of 'motivating' them (Herzberg, 1968). Although the empirical testing of this theory by Hinton (1968) particularly has cast some fundamental doubts upon it, it has produced offers of 'psychological' income instead of, or in addition to, money for increased contribution especially in high technology. (Robertson, 1969, Paul and Robertson, 1970). In general terms, therefore, this change has altered the theoretical base to incorporate the prediction that man will not work by money alone! and the package has therefore become much more complex as a result (see Schein, 1970; Mumford, 1972).

Thirdly, the definition by managers of the motivational problem has changed. Instead of seeking to explain motivation in relation to the wage-effort bargain itself, the problem is seen as one of

230

effecting overall commitment to the objectives of the enterprise. This, different authors suggest, may be brought about either by money mechanisms (the Scanlon Plan which provides a cash inducement on a plant-wide basis, offers one example) or by 'psychological' means (the emphasis on 'participation' in decision-taking in which the prime emphasis is not upon the monetary reward which such participation might secure but rather upon modifications of meaning associated with work, offers the example in this area). This view "is expressed by McKersie, who uses the concepts of participation, achievement and rewards to describe the essentials of an ideal incentive system. He sees participation as a mediating device for translating the primary goal of the employer—achievement—and the primary goal of the employee—rewards—into mutually shared goals. Advocates of this approach usually reject the beliefs and assumptions underlying direct incentive schemes" (NBPI, No 65, p 5).

The logical culmination of this set of developments as it affects *monetary* rewards is that to be found in the discussion of 'value-added' bases of pay and pay increases (see Wilson, 1977, p 101). Since value added is in no way correlated with effort, the assumption that value added will prove an acceptable foundation for reward policy, must reflect the belief that the accepting workers appreciate a distinct and separate relationship between effort and performance and between performance and pay. Although value added does depend to a varying extent upon the technology employed as well as upon the bought-in cost of the materials, (cf Wilson, 1977, p 102) as it affects the worker, it depends much more upon what he can achieve or upon his performance (with whatever capital assistance is appropriate) than it does upon his effort. The concepts of impairment and inurement, tedium and traction, weariness and contentment identified by Baldamus (1961, pp 51–80) as providing meaning to the concept of effort, remain relevant even if their form and incidents might change with technological development, but by managements pursuing value added concepts at least, the concept of performance as the direct link to pay is being substituted for effort. Whether the worker agrees is more problematical.

Expectancy-satisfaction audit
Expectancy theory thus provides a foundation for auditing demand-offer in the undertaking. The elements included in the model form the basis of questions which might be asked both about the employees' expectations and about the undertaking's offer. What do people want and what does the undertaking provide? and what changes may be made on either side in order to improve the general position?

Mumford, for example, has suggested that "if a firm can recruit and train employees whose need dispositions meet its role expectations, then there will be little conflict of interest and there should be a considerable overlap between the objectives of the company and the objectives of its staff. Similarly, if an individual can find an employer whose role expectations meet his need dispositions then the same degree of harmony should occur" (Mumford, 1972, p 77). This rests upon the initial pre-supposition that conflict of interest is not a necessary condition in the employment contract, but focuses management's attention upon the need to conceive of both personnel and job requirements in terms suggested by expectancy theory, ie in terms of expectancies and perceptions of conditions on the one hand, and organizational capacity to match these on the other.

Developing ideas about social and psychological contracts (cf Schein, 1970), Mumford was then led to offer a model to organize thought about the form and nature of these contracts which, harking back to chapter 1 above, might be regarded as concerned with filling in something of the 'implicit' terms of the formal contract. The five 'contracts' thus identified, the psychological, the knowledge, the ethical, the task structure and the efficiency contracts, also link across to the factors brought into the expectancy theory but focus

Table 12

The nature of the employer—employee contracts

	The firm	The employee
1 The *knowledge* contract	Needs a certain level of skill and knowledge in its employees if it is to function efficiently	Needs the skills and knowledge he brings with him to be used and developed
2 The *psychological* contract	Needs motivated employees	Needs factors which will motivate him, eg achievement, recognition, responsibility, status
3 The *efficiency* contract	Needs to achieve set output and quality standards	Needs an equitable effort-reward bargain; needs controls, including supervisory ones, which are seen as acceptable
4 The *ethical* (social value) contract	Needs employees who will accept the firm's ethos and values	Needs to work for an employer whose values do not contravene his own
5 The *task structure* contract	Needs employees who will accept any technical constraints associated with their jobs	Needs a set of tasks which meets his requirements for variety, interest, targets, feedback, task identity and autonomy

Source: taken from E Mumford, Job Satisfaction: A Method of Analysis, *Personnel Review,* 1 (3) Summer, 1972, p 51

thought upon the 'offers' of the enterprise or organization and the 'demands' or needs of the workers. The fact that they are separately articulated in this way serves to invite the enterprise/organization to carry out a careful analysis, not merely of the 'job' requirements in the mechanistic sense but of these separate factors, in the same way that in chapter 2 it was suggested that managers should carry out an audit of the work requirements, *in order to* guide those charged with selection of personnel on what kinds of persons (perceived in terms of needs and expectancies) are to be sought and on what kind of offer the enterprise/organization should make.

Figure 8
The relationships between employment contracts

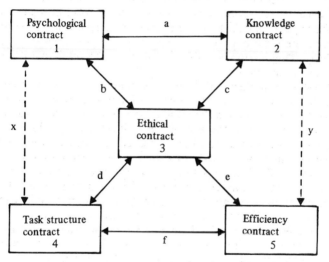

Source: taken from D Gowler, Values, Contracts and Job Satisfaction, *Personnel Review*, 3 (4) Autumn, 1974, p 5

The desirability of such an audit arises from the consequences of the offer position of the organization being deficient in terms of the expectancies of the individual(s) who comprise the contributor(s) to undertaking purposes. Expectancy theory focuses attention on the need for organizations either to provide opportunities for 'alternative' means of satisfaction-achievement on the part of the employee and on the likelihood of the converse of this leading to frustration. Whilst much will depend upon the worker's own individual orientation and expectancy, the organization which provides nothing in the way of satisfier other than money could expect either to frustrate those employees not oriented in this simple fashion, or to attract and retain only those who possessed the congruent orientation. A change of 'plan' (say from piece-work to measured day-work) might however be expected to increase the frustration of existing employees and only slowly effect a turnover of staff to bring in those with congruent atti-tudes—this is likely to be dependent upon the state of the local labour market.

The seriousness of this choice is reflected in the common ex-pression of the frustration-aggression hypothesis, that "aggression is always a consequence of frustration. More specifically the prop-osition is that the occurrence of aggressive behaviour always presup-poses the existence of frustration and, contrary-wise, that the existence of frustration always leads to some form of aggression" (Dollard *et al*, 1939, p 1). Later refinements suggest that frustration does not necessarily produce an aggressive response but that, alter-natively, if aggression is visible then it can be accepted that it is pro-duced by frustration.

As this is applied in the industrial context it is possible to ques-tion the extent to which the organizational arrangements of work present to the individual potential frustration-aggression situations. If one were to take the list of needs identified by Maslow, for example, one might consider whether the organization offers potential frustration to the individual in the attempt that he might make to satisfy his need for physiological, safety, love, esteem and self-actualization satisfactions. It would be possible, for example, for an organization to establish a kind of checklist to determine how far the situation presented to the worker is likely to result in frustration and, as a result, in some kind of typical response whether in the form of withdrawal, limitation, aggression or substitution responses to that frustration. Such an audit might then provide the basis for determining strategies for the 'motivation' of employees and thereby for defining the actions necessary to secure effort, performance and worker satisfaction.

Further reading
The major theme of this chapter is usefully covered in Landy and Trumbo (1976) and Porter, Lawler and Hackman (1975). Motivation in relation to rewards in the British context is dealt with in Bowey (1975) and Husband (1975); Baldamus (1961) remains a useful dis-cussion of the concept of effort in this context.

5 Strategies for performance

Introduction

The fact that personnel practitioners are engaged by undertakings faces them with the need to show concern not only to individuals and their goals and expectancies but to the undertaking and its purposes and objects. There has been a great deal of argument about just what the purposes and objects of modern undertakings are (Hughes, 1965; Brech, 1975; Walton, 1967; Silverman, 1970) but however they may be characterized they are certainly not identical with the goals of individual workers and in some views (Hyman, 1975; Allen, 1971) may be quite antithetical to them. Where they are conceived to be different but complementary, or different but mutable in the direction of greater mutual accommodation, they provide a rationale for the personnel management ideology which views its role as that of the man-in-the-middle or that of mediator. The question of how enterprise objectives are to be construed in distinction from those of the individual worker is thus an important one.

Of those undertakings in society which are primarily concerned with the discharge of an economic—wealth creating, distributing and exchanging—function, not all can be described as 'private enterprise' but, of those which are not, most are still oriented towards realization of similar ends. At the most generic level, those ends might be stated as the development of 'trade', to employ a phrase which has directed public policy in this country since the Middle Ages and which has tended to structure most of our institutions from the time of the Tudor monarchs onwards. More modern expressions to mean the same thing are to be found in Brech's reference to the aim of "making money" which can only be achieved "through the satisfaction of the market" (Brech, third edn 1975, p 6) and Cyriax's statement that "a company's objective should be to maximize its profitability . . . within the limits imposed by social obligations and the need to avoid a short-term viewpoint" (Cyriax, *Financial Times*, 23 February 1967). According to Beeching, responding to Cyriax's comment, nationalization merely makes

235

objectives "more numerous, more ambiguous and less distinguishable from qualifying conditions" (Beeching, *Financial Times*, 26 February 1967). There is however a view that such increase in number, ambiguity and indistinctiveness may also apply to the purely 'private enterprise' concern in the emergent situation (cf Winkler, 1975; Thomason, 1973).

If the responsibilities of 'the corporation' are being so extended as to create such a condition of ambiguity and imprecision (cf Walton, 1967) developments in the public service organizations suggest that there is a trend there towards subjecting those activities to more traditional management (Bains, 1972; Ogden, 1973; DHSS, 1972; Welsh Office, 1972; James, 1973). The fact that the various reports on 'reorganizations' in this field of service activity all look towards the development of corporate management via a 'team' concept should not be allowed to obscure the demand contained in them for 'management', nor blind us to the fact that a board of directors or an executive board or committee is a corporate team (Maurer, 1955). The rationale for this recommendation was the need for greater efficiency in the expenditure of society's wealth on services which it thought necessary or desirable. Such organizations may not be required to make a profit or a surplus, but there is a strong and frequently articulated demand that they should seek to establish the same standards of efficiency in the expenditure of wealth as are theoretically pursued in the wealth creating sector.

It is this concept of efficiency which is the key to understanding the objectives of *both* wealth creating enterprises and service organizations, and which relates to the twin concepts of 'satisfying' a market in the one case and 'satisfying' a clientele or a public in the other (Blau and Scott, 1963). The one may pursue profitability and the other not but both are expected to pursue efficiency: as a result the one may achieve its profit and the other an improved quality of service at lower cost, but neither end will be achievable without efficiency in performance.

This, however, places the emphasis upon one side of the distinction which Fox makes between what "work does *for* people" (as a consequence of its 'efficiency') and "what work does *to* people" (also as a consequence of the particular manner in which we realize that same efficiency by the use of people) (Fox, 1971, p 1). It also places the emphasis on the interest of the worker as consumer, not upon his interest as a producer, in the distinction made by Carter Goodrich (quoted above, p 215). It also explains a great deal of the difference between those who hold and express ideologies of liberal capitalism and those who hold and express ideologies developed from the Marxian view of man as essentially 'the producer' (*homo faber*) (cf

236

Banks, 1970; Hyman, 1975).

The major difference in this, from the standpoint of action, is whether 'efficiency' must necessarily be experienced as alienating or diminishing of the worker as a worker or whether changes can be made which will reduce or eliminate the problem without also destroying the economic benefit *for* people which has resulted from modern industrial organization. The categorical answer of the Marxian is that alienation and diminishment are necessary concomitants of capitalism (and in some variants of bureaucracy) and that they will therefore only be reduced when capitalism is replaced by another system entirely. The non-Marxian positions vary on this dimension, but most follow the Hegelian or Kantian philosophies to the extent that they acknowledge that improvements can be thought out and applied by man without necessarily supposing that revolution (in the Marxian sense) is a necessary condition for success. The development of this view by McGregor is one which has in recent years captured the imagination of the young manager and which has come to be regarded as offering greatest opportunity for improvement without fundamental system change. In oversimplified form, McGregor argues that the assumptions held by managers about the nature of man are crucial to the manner in which he will experience work, and that a change from 'Theory X' assumptions to 'Theory Y' assumptions will pre-condition a change of approach which will be experienced differently by the worker (McGregor, 1960).

This tends to challenge the older, paternalistic welfare assumptions of the employer and to offer a new equal-partners' perspective of industrial relationships. Instead of a model which emphasizes that workers will respond if the employer 'cares' for them adequately, a model is substituted which stresses that workers will contribute if they are trusted by and trusting of the employer. Both a number of the experiments with job enrichment, and some of the recent developments in legislative provision of rights are based upon this second model. The emphasis therefore is placed upon securing performance from workers by establishing a more adequate and acceptable framework or environment of trust between the employer and the employee, in place of a special kind of dependency relationship usually associated with paternalism. One 'strategy' for securing performance is, in this special sense, environmentally oriented—being concerned with getting the environment of work right in order to secure performance.

The other strategies which may be discerned, engaging supervision and reward, whilst they may have been with us for much longer than these experiments are then affected by this other, more fundamental change of framework for the productive relationship.

Supervision, for example, is shifted more deliberately in the direction of developing local leadership of a supportive and enabling kind, and 'incentives' become more subject to influence by the workers' expectancies (whether in formal negotiations or not), thus emphasizing more jointness or partnership in the creation of 'incentive' plans.

Employee welfare and welfare rights

One traditional strategy for securing performance (as well as loyal employees) in industry has been focused upon the concept of welfare. This had (and has) a number of distinguishable strands. One emphasized the individualistic nature of the relationship between the employer and the employee, and manifested itself in the employer determining to 'look after' the individual employee in various ways. In legal terminology, this is associated with the employer's duty of care: that the employer has a moral if not a legal duty to care about (a) what happens to his employees whilst they are in his employment (for example in terms of job security, reward for contribution or career development) and (b) what kinds of working environment the individual shall be provided with (which often reflected itself in the provision of various facilities which were seen to compensate the individual for harsh working conditions which could not be transmuted at the ruling levels of technological development). This gave rise therefore to two identifiable strands of the approach—one emphasizing the individual's security and the other his opportunity for re-creation. Thus welfare was not usually used as a term to indicate action taken on the main contractual dimensions of service and remuneration but rather to indicate action on peripheral or compensatory fringe benefits.

Traditionally, the conception of 'care' as a duty owed by the employer to his workers, was therefore translated into a mixed bag of provisions related to the environment of the work or the work contract. The contents were then associated with the welfare officer or the personnel manager, who often assumed direct line or executive responsibility for their provision. Included amongst the contents are usually:

1 Canteen facilities
2 Recreational facilities (including sports clubs and facilities, rest rooms and library facilities)
3 Information services (including certain forms of counselling, the provision of legal aid and advice, and help with holiday travel)
4 Welfare proper (including washrooms, cloakrooms, nurseries, housing, transport, sick clubs, benevolent funds, long-service grants, savings and pensions

238

5 Further education facilities
6 Medical services.

What distinguishes these is, perhaps, that they are none of them 'absolutely necessary' (in someone's view at least) to the normal functioning of the enterprise. Rather, to paraphrase a thought which can trace its ancestry back to Aristotle, one might say that the enterprise comes into existence equipped with methods of planning manpower, rewarding contributions, monitoring performance etc in order that it can function, but it then proliferates into a set of other activities and provisions in order that the members might live better within its context. If many of these provisions were made within a spirit of paternalism, they continue in existence because some people some of the time derive some advantage or satisfaction from them.

In the early years, welfare work in industry was not really to be distinguished from welfare work outside work. In both contexts, there was some tendency (a) to identify problems in the individual and to treat these by some psycho-therapeutic mode, and (b) to regard them as independent of the system of relationships and roles within which they occurred and thus to ignore system change. Personnel work in industry may have moved off this particular waveband as it was forced to come to terms with organized labour. Welfare work outside industry has been slower in making this transition, and broadly remains committed to case work. On this, "as a model" used to guide the social worker's actions, Perlman (1965) has commented that "it has validity" and that "for certain persons with certain problems this one-to-one model cannot be disposed of. . .". But he points out that "when case work moves into dealing with other sorts of problems (for example, those of crisis intervention) its clinical model may well need radical change" (p 177). But in the absence of a spontaneous growth of organization of citizens in relation to social welfare, "commitment to social action and social reform" remains to be advocated as a voluntary adjustment on the part of social workers and the social work profession. As Younghusband (1973) has argued, "the only hope for social work . . . is to realize that it is simply irrelevant to act as the "poor man's psychiatrist" when so much of the stress in people's lives is caused directly or indirectly by social circumstances, by poverty, bad housing, poor education, unemployment, being caught in the powerlessness to change one's lot."

Personnel work in industry may have avoided some of this problem by being caught up in 'system' concerns (such as manpower planning or payment administration) or in 'representational systems' (by which the worker's benefits might be established jointly) but the pendulum may in this case have swung too far the other way. The mechanisms for establishing 'welfare rights' of workers in employment have now become highly institutionalized, either through the formal collective bargaining machinery embracing the trade unions as powerful advocates, or through legislation and the institution of tribunals and arbitration boards under it and two dangers may be apprehended. First, that the individual worker becomes again confronted with a powerful bureaucracy against whose decisions and treatment he may still feel powerless, even if it is a machine established in his interest and with his support. Secondly, that those who, like the personnel specialists, developed roles which to some extent facilitate this development of a benign system for the establishment of rights, may now be reduced to a "servicing, amenable, or even resigned role" (as Morrison (1972, p 11) has suggested might be the outcome of increased statutory intervention in the provision of social welfare benefits outside work).

There is little doubt that some employers provided such welfare benefits as these in the past simply because they were genuinely convinced that it was part of the employer's moral duty to do so—one of the earliest examples of this approach is provided by Robert Owen. Nevertheless, to make such provisions (particularly when other employers were not doing so) did something to influence the perspectives taken of the employer by the employees and, no doubt, their recruitment and continued loyalty as well. There was, in these as in the development of the early personnel functions, a double element of ideology and enterprise self-interest and, if there was also a cost to be met in these provisions, that could be set against the moral imperative in the one case or the labour stability and motivation benefits in the other.

The older conception of welfare, and the benefits which it may have been expected to bring to the employer, may both be disappearing in the face of increasing standardization of such provision, whether as a result of the extension of collective bargaining or as a consequence of the creation of new (and standardized) statutory obligations upon the employer. Although some of the old 'welfare package' (on pp 238–89 above) may remain largely unaffected by legislation, much of it has been the subject of recent statutes, and has been transmuted from a privilege given as a consequence of the philanthropy of the employer to a right established in law. The personnel specialist's role has therefore come to take on more that of the administrator of statutorily-imposed welfare rights.

The Health and Safety at Work Act, for example, provides in part that the employer shall have a duty "to provide and maintain a working environment . . . that is, so far as is reasonably practicable, safe, without risk to health, and *adequate as regards facilities and arrangements for . . . welfare at work"* (italics added). The concept of welfare is nowhere defined in the Act, although one might presume, in advance of Court interpretation or definition in regulations or Codes of Practice under the Act, that it is to be defined in terms of provision of adequate air conditioning, lighting, fume eradication, facilities for rest pauses and meal breaks, and protection from inclement weather etc which affect the employee's physical well-being. If this is the kind of meaning intended, it does not admittedly go as far as the usual connotations of the term welfare as employed in the personnel management context, although it is (and this in itself may be significant) a traditional area of concern of the profession—after all, a lot of its current theoretical foundation originated in research work into the effects of just such physical variables in the work situation as these (see, for example, Brown, 1954).

If in other words this merely represents a 'catching up' by legislation with a historical position in the treatment of personnel at work, then, in this one respect of 'welfare' provision under the Act, there remains a great deal of scope for the development of more up to date (even fashionable) policies in this area. It *could* be interpreted more broadly than this and if so it might represent the harvesting of current 'good welfare practice' into a pattern of rights such as has already been happening with the 'rights' legislation of the 1960s and 1970s. For these, taking their cues from the 'good practice' in collective agreements, have brought within a new framework of law, a good deal of what could be described as policy or practice touching on the 'treatment' of employees—on notice of termination, information about conditions of the contract, compensation for peremptory dismissal or discrimination. What in general this legislation proposes is simply that an employee must in our society have certain basic rights in employment, and in particular must be treated without discrimination and with fairness and equity.

Such sentiments ought not to sound at all foreign to the welfare-minded personnel manager but, as he now pursues his tasks within organizations, the realization of fair treatment of employees becomes partly a matter of administering what is now established by law and partly a matter of building on that foundation treatment or welfare policies which are not mandatory under existing legislation. This is more likely to emphasize 'treatment' rather than traditional 'welfare' concerns and to be associated with conceptions of dignity and humanity—reflecting the subject-matter of the preceding chapter—as these are within the perspectives of the worker and his representative organizations. There may still be an 'environmental' component—dealing with conditions of bodily comfort in the old

241

industrial health and the more recent ergonomics senses—but there will also be more concern with mental conditions—the interest, challenge, and status of the job itself, as so far developed mainly in connection with job enrichment.

One effect of these changes, has been to standardize a good deal of what was previously idiosyncratic provision in the field of welfare. In the face of this, there may be scope for more individual creativity, and therefore for a new look at the old welfare function, as Kenny has suggested (1975).

A second element in the 'welfare' conception which begins to assume greater significance in this same context of change is that which relates to the environment of the working-life (as distinct from merely work). The physical and human environment in which an individual works is unlikely to be a matter of indifference to him, but he or she is also likely to have an interest in the continuity of that environment (or the 'security'—providing possibilities of the situation, in Maslow's terms). The exercise of care by the paternalistic employer did, to an extent, apply to 'looking after the labour' on a longer term basis; even if this aspect has been ousted by economic exigencies in the more clinical approach of recent years, the element cannot be ignored by personnel practitioners in the context of the welfare function.

We are in Britain a long way from the life-time employment concept of Japan, and the rejection of paternalism by organized labour in Britain is unlikely to allow such a concept to be similarly applied here. The donation of job property rights by legislation may help to bring the conception back into the game in another guise and, in so doing, force employers to consider the question of what kind of long-term 'career' they provide to their workers. If workers do have job property rights created by union agreements or legislation, they could well want to have more influence upon just what kind of situation they will be presented with in which they can enjoy those rights. If we use the term 'career' to indicate what it is that thinking should be focused upon, we should not assume that this must necessarily mean a 'career' in the middle-class, professional sense from whence it sprang (Hughes, 1958). Rather we should perhaps think of this in terms of 'employee development' by which improvements, as perceived by the individual, may be achieved without necessarily implying that these can only come via progress upwards through a hierarchy of status and authority such as is found in a bureaucratic system. Instead, the improvements might accrue from planned (and agreed) training and movement (job rotation) which, whilst preserving economic status, still permits those who so wish to broaden their experiences and develop their skill.

242

This calls for a view of the organizational environment as a strategic site on which individual employees of whatever rank and skill can find some opportunity either to stay put, if such is their wish, or to move for experience and challenge, if such is their wish, and in either case to achieve some benefit from their involvement by broadening of their experience, if they so wish, through specific tasks and projects. It is probably necessary to think out models of learning organizations in which this kind of environment is provided.

One such model has been put forward by Schein (1971) where he sees organizations as conical structures within which various types of career can be constructed. He defines career as "a set of attributes and experiences of the *individual* who joins, moves through, and finally leaves an organization . . . and as defined by the organization—a set of expectations held by individuals inside the organization which guide decisions about whom to move, when, how, and at what 'speed'" (Schein, 1971, pp 401–2). He depicts the organization for this purpose as a cone, in which rank or status is increased from bottom to top, centrality from the periphery to the centre (eg branch organization to headquarters), and separate divisions or functions are indicated by sections of the cone. Careers may therefore develop in one or a combination of three ways:

vertically, by increasing or decreasing rank within the undertaking
radially, by moving closer to the centre or further away from it
circumferentially, by changing from one function or division to another.

Combinations might allow change of function with movement towards or away from the centre, or with movement upwards; and movement upwards with movement between periphery and centre; and in a complete combination, some variation on the spiralling theme. Equally, the possibilities for segmentation by boundaries on any of these same dimensions might well function as barriers to career development as well as the more widely recognized barrier to communication.

If this kind of conception is married to recent developments in the field of motivational theory as applied in job enrichment, for example, the indicated solution is something more dynamic and wider-reaching than the mere provision of more challenging jobs (which are then equally as static as the ones they replace) or of 'autonomous work groups' (in which the individual members are made more subject to group pressures within the prison of the small working group). Now there is an indicated need to provide for movement, up, across or around, so that individuals can at least perceive some opportunity of escape (should they wish to) and therefore some

243

opportunity to plan their 'careers' within the organization. As yet this area is little affected directly by legislation, but some of the provisions relating to the offer of vacancies are tangentially relevant, and suggest some possible lines of future developments of policy on securing performance by more adequate structuring of the continuing environments of work.

Figure 9

The cone of organizational careers

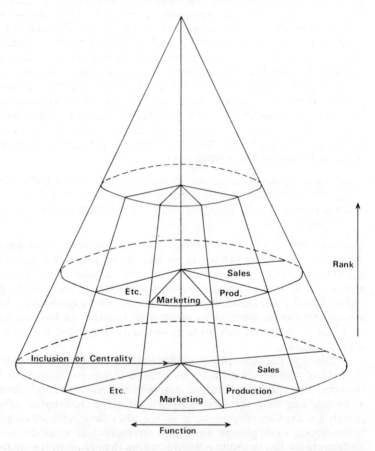

Based on: E H Schein: The Individual, the Organization and the Career, in *Journal of Applied Behavioural Sciences*, 7, 1971, pp 401–426. Figure 1: A Three-dimensional Model of an Organization, p 404.

Strategies involving direct supervision

One broad category of strategy for securing performance is that which relies upon direct supervision. In this conception, the performer's immediate supervisor (at whatever level in the hierarchy) is expected because of his role to secure desired levels of performance by direct control or leadership of his immediate work group. Usually this method will not be relied upon to the exclusion of other supports to the objective, but the opportunites for varying strategies may be expected to be contingent upon the situation to which they are to be applied and in some it may remain necessary to put considerable weight upon the strategy of direct supervision. Such situations may be characterized by low trust relations (Fox, 1974) on the personnel side, and important quality considerations related to non-routine activities on the technical side, but they do exist (cf Kahn and Katz, 1953; Likert, 1961; Sayles, 1958).

Direct supervision in this sense has a close affinity with classical conceptions of management. In this framework, the main task of management was seen to be that of securing a level of performance which met the undertaking's cost-benefit objectives. The emphasis was consequently placed upon 'control' and 'control of human performance' was normally focused upon three features of the organizational setting, those of selection, supervision and incentives (cf Tannenbaum, 1948). We have already looked at the 'selection' process in chapter 3. Once the required labour force is secured by selection, there remains the need to use other methods, namely supervision and/or incentives, to hold the selected employees to the appropriate courses and levels of action indicated by those objectives. This cannot be the task of the personnel manager solely for the reasons touched on at the beginning of the book but he has to advise on policy and practice.

Both supervision and incentives depend for their efficacy and fairness upon the ability of the enterprise to set performance norms relevant to the realization of the objectives set and to measure, assess, appraise or review the actual performance of the individual against them. The *setting* of work standards on the shop floor is usually the prerogative of the supervisor or line manager who may in appropriate cases of payment by results scheme or measured daywork operation be assisted by work study engineers. The *monitoring* of performance against these standards is a task similarly assigned, although with incentive schemes the closeness of the supervisor's checking role will usually be reduced, at least until such time as the scheme has been 'mastered' by the working group. This is a common arrangement in manufacturing industry, leaving little scope for the personnel manager to interfere directly, except where he is involved in the negotiation of the supporting agreements with the unions.

Strategies relating to supervision are increasingly coming to be seen as 'contingent' upon the situation to be 'supervised'. The main contrast can be illustrated by the 'bowler-hatted foreman' as the autocrat who carried his tough, no-nonsense approach to hiring and firing and discipline from one supervisory situation to another, compared with either local or cosmopolitan skills with which he can diagnose the most relevant 'style' to adopt with any given technological and human situation and apply it with effect and appropriateness. It is the second of these approaches that relies upon what has come to be referred to as the contingency approach: it predicates action upon a prior analysis or diagnosis of what is appropriate or relevant to the situation to which that action is to be applied.

The main ideas supporting this developing view of supervision have been developed within the framework of social psychology; in so far as there is a single adjective which identifies the studies which have contributed it is 'leadership'. For the most part, these leadership studies have tended to polarize 'leadership styles' between open, democratic, missioner, 'people-oriented' styles and closed, autocratic, bureaucratic, production-oriented styles. Within each of these sets there may well be subtle differences but the wide variety of terms used by researchers and consultants to present their ideas tends to be dysfunctional from the point of view of understanding the central message. It was in some reflection of this problem, that McGregor (1960) gave his two 'style' theories, the titles of X and Y, and thus also helped to avoid association with necessary concomitants of terms like democratic and autocratic. We should also note that, in the development of thinking about 'leadership' as a phenomenon, psychologists have moved through three quite distinct conceptions of what constitutes leadership and all three of these are relevant to consideration of supervisory strategies.

First, leadership was seen to be something to do with the leader himself or herself—there were traits or personal characteristics which distinguished the leader from others. (This proved difficult to sustain, although some fairly constant traits were discovered, and the basic conception remains of some relevance to the selection process.)

Secondly, leadership was seen to have something to do with the group of people who were being led or who accepted the leadership—there were universal group processes which would ensure that leadership would be conferred, even if not always on the person who looked as if he/she ought to be the official leader. (This also did not quite 'jell' with experience and study although the importance of the group in legitimating leaders is not to be discounted) (cf Homans,

246

1953, chs VI and VIII.)

Thirdly, leadership was seen to be something which emerged out of the task to be done, the work to be performed, or the problem to be solved, in the particular setting, and in particular out of the interaction of the task demands, the perceived needs or aspirations of the group, and the abilities and motivation of the leader to respond to these—which, in a sense, brings together some of the basic ideas of the first two approaches with the technical component of the group's task. (It is this perspective which underlies the grid training now widely used in management, Blake and Mouton, 1964; Reddin, 1964; Mangham, 1968.)

It is the third of these conceptions which is relevant to our present theme. Effective supervision, as a specific form of leadership, is perceived as having to do with

(a) the task set for the section or group supervised and its setting
(b) the orientations of the people in the section or group, and
(c) the skill and motivation of the supervisor.

In the usual polarization referred to above, it is assumed or demonstrated (in some cases) that the kind of technical task set for the group and the kinds of people involved in the doing of it are, by some process of self- and mutual-selection, congruent in the sense that the kinds of people demanded by the task will be 'supplied', and the demands made by the people doing the task upon that task will be met by it. We find something of this in Likert's characterization of situations in industry.

Likert detects in American industry one type of *situation* in which the technology of producing the product imposes upon the workers highly routine, short-cycle tasks which allow very little discretion to the worker, and in which the *control* environment emphasizes reward related to performance (which may also correlate closely with effort) and close supervision. An example is the large office carrying out standardized tasks on a mass basis, or the assembly and production line industries with similar characteristics. He contrasts this with the other kind of situation in which the technology offers opportunity for variety of tasks and discretion in carrying them out to the worker, and in which the control environment emphasizes self-control and high-trust relations (cf Fox, 1974) with the management and supervision. Examples are drawn from tool rooms and research and development departments.

In the one situation, because of the way in which the mutual selection process works out, the workers tend to display a low range of attitudes (they are, to put it over-simply, relatively alienated) and such attitudes do not matter from the production point of view be-

247

cause of the efficacy of control. In the other, however, the jobs and the workers also seek one another out; those who want to have high discretion jobs go for them and gatekeepers of the undertaking tend to select those whom they consider will cope successfully with such jobs and develop the right kinds of attitudes towards them. Here attitudes do matter (cf Herzberg, 1959) and those who enter the undertaking tend to be those who want attitudes to matter in work (cf Dubin, 1958; Orzack, 1959). In the two polar types of situation, therefore, there is a happy correlation between need and between the criteria of their satisfaction.

And so it comes about that the leadership strategy or style becomes 'contingent' upon the situation. Supervisors in the one situation will be expected by all concerned to approximate to the traditional bowler-hatted slave driver, and in the other to offer leadership in the sense of creating and expanding the opportunities for creativity and satisfaction (or motivation in Herzberg's terminology). (For a more detailed discussion, see Thomason, 1973, pp 61–80.)

Once the continuum between the two poles is implanted by this approach, it becomes possible to develop 'positions' along it, and thus to vary the mix of production and people emphasis which might be required to match the style of the supervisor to the variations on the two dimensions where they may be seen to be somewhat out of phase with each other because, for example, the manpower plan can no longer establish a match or, for example, technological or product changes have changed the requirement from a given labour force whose dismissal is no longer feasible. What this kind of approach does establish by way of contingent planning is that the strategy of supervision will be dependent upon, or reflective of, four elements in the 'situation':

(a) the task demands as these may vary with changes in the product, or in the technology of their manufacture, and with changes in the fundamental conditions affecting the offer of reward (by the employer) or of service (by the employee) (cf above pp 60–69)

(b) the personnel needs of those engaged in the tasks, as these may vary with the orientations developed in the person by their experience, some of which will be obtained within the undertaking itself

(c) the control setting within which these people carry out these (changing) tasks, which may be changing for reasons which may either be within or be without the control and discretion of those with authority in the undertaking:

   (i) the control in terms of strategies of supervision versus incentive, themselves responsive to other forces

(ii) the control in terms of public policy, legislative and general cultural changes outside the undertaking.

The identification of these influencing variables in the situation has already begun to influence strategies developed in relation to performance. The main illustrations of this are provided by:

1 The large-scale variation in the approaches made to the determination of rewards in work, where those rewards are still seen largely in material terms. The main recent development here has involved a movement away from payment by results systems to measured day work (and now possibly back again) as managers sought to respond responsibly to changes in production technology and to problems associated with quality of output (cf Brown, 1962). This development has also led to the development of 'contingency' theories of reward (cf Bowey and Lupton, 1973). (See also below, pp 263–67.)

2 The large-scale variation in the structuring of work tasks, particularly routine tasks, under identifying labels such as job enlargement, job enrichment or autonomous work groups. The response here was mainly to perceived changes in the attitudes and orientations of the workers which were considered to have led to deterioration in performance because those attitudes had got out of phase with the 'task-offer' of some modern industry (cf van Beek, 1964; Butteriss, 1971). The likely consequences of the development of higher discretion in work tasks for the roles of supervisor have not yet been faced in any very systematic fashion (cf Paul and Robertson, 1970; see also below, pp 394–99).

3 The increasing interest detectable currently (although it may as yet amount to little more than that) in those strategies and methods which might be calculated to help increase the loyalty of workers to the undertaking, such as the Scanlon plan or the Japanese life-time employment concepts. The interest here, although not necessarily the plans themselves, may be considered to respond to those general changes which have to do with (a) motivation as perceived internally and (b) constraint imposed from outside upon the employer's ability to treat his workforce as flexible with little consequential cost (see below, pp 257–63).

Taken together, these lines of development must throw considerable doubt upon the likelihood of strategies which involve high reliance upon traditional conceptions of supervision being developed in the future. In line with contingency theory, there will no doubt continue to be some situations (defined by work tasks and personnel) where such strategies will be relevant, in spite of the general changes associated with (c) above. But the general tendency will probably be for the supervisor as such to be replaced by a person whose role will be less associated with classical managerial control methods and more with open leadership or enabling functions.

Reward strategies

People work for some reward. How much work they will contribute for how much reward or what kinds of reward they seek for which kinds of work are subordinate questions which are important. But as the long-standing common law duty of the employer to pay wages indicates, some kind of benefit to the worker is a *sine qua non* of work. Whatever else may be said about work, it is important to consider how the employer may discharge his duty and, in so doing in a free society, secure an adequate work contribution from the worker.

Consideration of strategies on rewards must extend beyond answering the question how to attract labour from the market and retain such part of it as is contributory to the achievement of the goals of the undertaking (see above, pp 147–54). In addition, it must range over questions relating to efficiency or, in more individualistic terms, to 'contribution'. Generally, the aim in the development of wage and salary structures must be to optimize, but this can be expanded into a number of sub-objectives in relation to that contribution.

Although all who are employed are rewarded or paid for their labour contribution, it has been the convention that some persons' rewards were referred to as their wages whilst the rewards of others were referred to as salaries. 'Wage' and 'salary' are merely two terms which have gained common currency to describe that part of an employee's remuneration or reward which he received in the form of cash (or equivalent) at a regular interval of relatively short duration, such as a week or a month. Certain historical distinctions between wages and salaries can be discerned but the distinction is no longer clear cut (cf Lupton and Bowey, 1974, ch 4).

Traditionally, the payment of wages is associated with the reward of manual workers and that of salaries with the reward of white collar workers, although there is now increasing overlap between these two categories in the levels of remuneration. Also historically, the wage payment was linked with employment contracts which were terminable at relatively short notice, such as an hour, a day or a week, whilst the salary payment was more usually found with contracts which required notice at least as long or longer than this; but the increasing use of the device of staff status for wage earners blurs this distinction too. In the past it has been usual to determine wages by negotiation between trade unions and employers (or employers' associations) and salaries "individually—but the increase in unionization of white collar workers has now placed many salary earners in this same bracket" (Bain, 1967).

The aims of wage and salary systems have in the past often appeared very different from each other. Today, characterized by changing conceptions of the relationships (a) between white collar and blue collar rewards and (b) between effort (or contribution) and reward for it, this difference may be reducing and that which is common to all employees may assume greater significance. The greater flexibility which the method of *wage* calculation and payment offered to the employer may assume lesser significance as the proportion of direct production workers in the labour force decreases, but it becomes a less viable approach in the face of trade union pressure and legislative prescription. The need for such flexibility on *salary* payments with the corresponding growth in white collar employment, and the possibility of greater unionization amongst such staff leading to demands which are more class and less status oriented may, from the opposite standpoint, suggest some convergence.

There are sub-objectives in both categories which are concerned with efficiency, performance or contribution. In the statement on pp 149–50 above, on objectives in wage structures, this point is made. In the statements on objectives on salary structures put out by the National Board for Prices and Incomes, a comparable point is made in slightly more expanded form. A salary system "should facilitate the deployment of employees in such a way as will conduce to the maximum efficiency of the undertaking, be adequately related to the attainment and continuance of high performance by individuals, and seek to achieve all these aims at the least cost to the undertaking" (NBPI, 1969). Bowley's 'aims of salary policy' include comparable statements: "Salary policy should help to: encourage staff to make full use of their abilities and develop their potential; and to strive to achieve the objectives of their jobs and of the company, facilitate movement of staff across departmental, divisional or sectional boundaries, and achieve these aims at minimum cost—a drift into overpayment must be avoided" (Bowley, 1972)

The first consideration in the determination of policies of individual reward for work is concerned with what, in the terminology already employed about expectancy theory, exists in the way of rewards available from work in modern organizations. The main distinction to be drawn here is between material rewards (generally perceived to be available in wealth-producing organizations but possibly seen as more restrictedly available in the public services) and non-material rewards (regarded as less often available in modern

251

organizations, if the alienation thesis is to be believed).

The second is concerned with what, in the same terminology, the reward is to be related to. Even when the question is considered simply in relation to material rewards, the choices lie between reward of 'need' (expressed for example in terms of a 'family wage' (Fogarty, 1961) or in terms of the slogan 'from each according to his ability; to each according to his need'), reward of 'effort' (in the sense in which frequently discussions of what coal miners ought to be paid, are conceived), reward of performance (as might be illustrated by the director's share of the company profits which he helped to achieve) or reward of status (which tends to be associated with 'customary conceptions' of what named occupations or offices ought to be paid). The first of these figures relatively little in discussions of wage and salary determination, being met, in so far as it is met at all, within a system of social transfer payments administered by the state. The last tends to exert its influence upon all other conceptions, but the second and third are the foundations which are most regularly and systematically considered in wage and salary policy at the level of the undertaking.

The choices open to the undertaking on broad category solutions to these strategic questions may be characterized as follows:

job evaluation plans are essentially focused upon effort, in the particular sense of assessing the demands of the job upon the individual, but embrace related concepts of skills and role conformity

individual incentive or bonus schemes for the most part are linked to performance, or in a less direct sense to effort

certain group bonus plans and plans which involve some form of sharing in overall performance by the undertaking are associable with reward of performance and

negotiated systems of payment are likely to place appreciably more emphasis upon comparability and perceived customary relations, even when these are concerned with formal plans of the above types.

Plans for rewarding effort: job evaluation
The salary administrator faces the need to develop a structure of money rewards which can be justified in terms of some logic. It is frequently suggested that many existing wage and salary structures just grew up under the influence of eccentric pressures from the forces of the market, custom, power bargaining and even the boss's whim. To the extent that this is so, this in itself might suggest a need to search for a

more systematic foundation for what is generally regarded as a most important feature of modern societies. Coupled with an apparently increasing rate of economic and technological change in modern societies, one of whose effects is the greater fragmentation of existing jobs and work roles and consequently the creation of 'new jobs', this idiosyncratic system of determination of relativities in rewards seems even more strongly to be in need for revamping. Since job evaluation is the generic term which is applied to such attempts to produce new structures of differentials, it becomes associated with just this aim—that of creating a structure on a systematic base. That there are many plans of job evaluation does not deny this; they represent a number of different means by which this end might be achieved.

It is not intended here to discuss all the different plans of job evaluation which have been put forward, for which a whole book would in any case be needed (see Thomason, 1968; TUC, 1974; Paterson, 1972; Lupton and Bowey, 1974). Rather the purpose is to indicate how job evaluation plans in general are related to contribution by the worker, and in particular to argue that job evaluation is focused primarily upon the 'effort' or job demand element in the spectrum of factors brought into expectancy theory, and secondarily upon the factors of skills and abilities and role perceptions which are there associated closely with effort. In other words, it will be suggested that job evaluation is concerned to establish a structure of rewards on the basis of what the individual is expected by the organization to put into the job, and not on the basis of performance or need. However, the increasing tendency which has become apparent recently to involve representatives of the workforce being evaluated in the processes of evaluation offers some opportunity to them to pursue an objective of equitable comparison through their potential influence upon factor selection and assigned weights in these schemes.

It is universally asserted that the method of job evaluation concentrates entire attention on the *content* of the job, not upon the person doing it, and upon the inherent demands which the job makes upon the worker, not upon the particular worker who happens to be doing it. The 'content' of the job is thus assumed to have some close association with the worth of the job, and the task of the job evaluator is to rank all jobs in a job family (or an enterprise) in terms of this inherent nature, as a basis for associating them with comparably differentiated rewards for doing them. Just *how* this is done is what distinguishes one form of job evaluation plan from another. But because the job content or the job demands are concerned with the demand side of the effort performance equation, and the individual doing the job is what fills in the supply side, it may be suggested that *prima facie* job evaluation is more concerned with effort than with performance, and that it is the former rather than the latter which thus influence the reward fixed by this method.

Job evaluation plans vary in a number of ways. The most basic distinction in them is between the relatively simple 'whole job' ranking or classification plans and the relatively complex 'job factor' points rating and factor comparison plans. These are combined and permuted in various ways, particularly in order to give 'optimum fit' to different circumstances of their application, as in relation to white collar workers generally or managerial and professional staffs in particular. It is generally considered that the development of complexity reflects the decline in 'whole job' familiarity with technological change and the increase in 'new jobs' without as yet familiar conceptions, brought about by the same process. In effect, this development has tended to introduce into the essentially simpler plans some element of factor analysis, and it is these factors (which are thus becoming more universal in these plans) which indicate the association of job evaluation not only with effort—but also with the skills/abilities and role perceptions factors in expectancy theory.

In the two analytical schemes of job evaluation, points rating and factor comparison, the first step involves the determination of which factors will be taken into account in assessing relative worth of the jobs in the job family or enterprise. These are usually fewer in number than those identified by Lupton and Bowey in their procedure for making inter-organizational pay comparison (Lupton and Bowey, 1974, ch 2; and above, pp 152–24), but they are similar in many ways. The number of factors included in any particular points rating scheme may vary tremendously, although they may be cut down to about six: training; experience; mental application; physical application (or effort); responsibility; and working conditions. This list is usually varied in response to what are seen as local circumstances.

The factor comparison method of job evaluation is an extension of the points rating method, but one which takes into account the research finding that rating suffers from certain halo problems. For this reason factor comparison concentrates on five factors (usually): mental effort; skill; physical effort; responsibility; and working conditions. Concentrating on these, the problems of carry over and overlapping in the rating process are reduced. In both of these sets of plans, therefore, the element of effort or application, coupled with skill and ability, is obvious. In addition, the element of 'responsibility' appears and gives some inkling of the importance of the role prescription within which the job itself is done, just as the 'working conditions' factor acknowledges that the physical environment of the job may call for some compensation.

The two originally simpler methods of job evaluation gave more weight to the determination of relative money worth on the basis of general comparison. Both job ranking and job classification dealt with the job as a whole, but depended upon the raters having appreciable familiarity either with all the jobs (in job ranking) or with the bench-mark jobs (in job classification). The difference between these two methods lies in the order of proceeding but both of them *could* be concerned either with 'difficulty' (and therefore with 'effort') or with 'value to the firm' (and therefore with 'performance') although the practice in the determination of the criteria varies from scheme to scheme. Nevertheless, it cannot be argued that they are concerned even in the appropriate case, purely with performance criteria, as both depend for their success upon the possibility existing that ranking can be achieved on the basis of broad skill categories such as skilled, semi-skilled and unskilled (cf Stieber, 1959; Thomason, 1968).

As Raimon has argued (1953, p 181), this kind of broad categorization has become obsolete in many instances, and it is this that has led to the increase in the use of points evaluation and factor comparison plans, *and* also (and in association often with joint approaches to evaluation) led to the introduction of elements of points rating into these simpler methods. The two main categories of development from these simpler schemes are the direct consensus method and the job profile method both of which broaden the judgemental base and both of which bring these schemes more directly into line with plans which rest upon skill, effort and role prescriptions as the elements on which the differential reward will ultimately be based (cf Edwards and Paul, 1977).

In the white collar plans, a similar tendency is apparent. In the Institute of Administrative Management plan, which is basically one of the simpler non-analytical plans in its intention of avoiding 'factors', an attempt is nevertheless made to reconcile the type of work with the degree of difficulty, knowledge, skill and responsibility involved. For more skilled white collar grades, the tendency has been to employ points rating or factor comparison schemes, but where the former has been employed (NBPI, Report No 83, 1968) there has been a tendency to introduce more factors which either detail the skill requirements or amplify the role prescriptive elements (cf Cuthbert and Paterson, 1966). When a plan of job evaluation is to be applied to managerial, professional, technical and supervisory staff (either alone or in combination with manual and routine white collar workers) there is some tendency to attempt to cope with the 'differences' between grades of work by founding the plan on some theory

255

of information-exchange or decision-taking. A number of apparently very different tailor-made or consultant-branded plans could thus be linked together under this heading. The rationale of many such plans is roughly as follows: managers and others who do not necessarily have this title, take decisions; they also implement them; the work therefore calls for skills related to these; and it is this skill as much as anything which must therefore be brought into the plan. It is also true that this work is carried out in a context which might vary in the way in which working conditions vary for the manual worker; that it entails varying responsibilities; and that it calls for different levels of education and experience. These factors do not set the work apart from any other (except in the sense of having different relative values). But the skills applied and the 'raw material' to which they are applied do appear to be very different, and differentials ought therefore to reflect this. But what provides the 'bed' of the approach are the different role prescriptions which apply to these kinds of jobs. This may best be illustrated by the British Broadcasting Corporation plan introduced by Doulton and Hay (1962). Essentially a grading scheme, it also seeks to provide a basis for analysis of the complex sets of variables included in work tasks at the managerial and professional level. It specifies three steps in problem-solving, which is held to be the main characteristic distinguishing this broad class of jobs. The steps are:

(a) the selection of the best possible solution, which requires the collection of all relevant facts and information, the determination of possible courses of action and the assessment of their advantages and disadvantages
(b) the taking of a decision, involving the use of judgement
(c) the implementation of the decision.

In order to analyse "all the essential mental activities associated with solving problems of every type" they employ three factors related to step (a) and one related to each of the other two steps, together with a final additional difficulty factor:

(a) (i) application of specialized knowledge and experience
    (ii) exercise of powers of evaluation or reasoning (judgement)
    (iii) the production of new ideas in adapting or devising an unusual course of action (or creative thought)
(b) decisions—the extent to which the job holder commits the use of the organization's resources; by spending money, allocating facilities for activity, selecting staff for work tasks, undertaking new work programmes, and engaging in publicity
(c) man-management—the ability to handle other people in a

256

manner which enables the job holder to achieve his aim

(d) interpretative performance, a factor used where the different elements of the job are inextricably mingled and the physical qualities could not be assessed adequately by themselves.

Each of these factors is assessed in terms of five grades which are offered in the plan, and the final grading of the job is based upon the 'highest' grade achieved on any factor (ie, there is no attempt at summing or averaging the scores).

Enough examples have probably been given to support the contention that job evaluation plans seek to establish differential rates of payment on the basis—not merely of job content, as the textbooks have it—but of the effort or the demands which are made upon the individual by the job. Those aspects of the job demand which are constant for all work (or all work in the class or family under consideration) tend to be ignored as not contributing anything to the 'differentials', but for the rest it is what the job calls for in the individual which is assessed by one or other of these methods. Thus the performance of the individual—what he or she achieves in doing the job—is not in contention, since it is assumed that the job itself makes a necessary or minimum demand upon the person and it is this which is to be assessed to provide a foundation for a structure of differential basic rates.

Consequently that part of the effort of the individual which might be associated with what he or she puts into the job with some effect on performance, remains to be assessed by other methods than that of job evaluation. One aspect of this, consequently, falls to be assessed in terms of performance (eg the actual physical output) or perhaps in terms of cooperation (eg where the physical output is incapable of measurement and the 'effort' is assumed capable of equating in some way with the loyalty or industriousness displayed).

Rewards related to performance

Theories of both motivation and incentive have changed markedly since the war, and the emphasis which is given to different methods of structuring the wage incentive (using the term in its broadest sense) has tended to vary in consequence. There are many particular plans available for structuring the pay side of the wage-effort bargaining under the employment contract, but these fall into a small number of general categories:

1 Straight time payment systems: simply a matter of paying so much per hour worked, and seen as satisfactory only where you can trust the individual to work hard or give his best or where the level of supervision is such that the same result is achieved

2 Direct incentive payment systems: this category covers systems (whether piecework or standard hour systems) in which more payment is offered for more effort on the part of the worker, and where effort is supposed to correlate with output. Problems arise here when variations in effort are difficult to measure in this way and when employees discover how to fiddle the rates

3 Indirect incentive payment systems: these usually take the form of lieu bonuses, or bonuses for one category of worker determined by the performance of another; frequently they reflect the need to provide some incentive when it is not possible to use simple measures of output as a means of indicating variations in effort

4 Similar in many ways are the bonuses which are of a profit-sharing or the Scanlon plan type, in which the total contribution of everyone is pooled and shared on some agreed basis, so that again the incentive is a very indirect one. Here the problems which arise depend on how sensible it is to rely upon the assumption of a team spirit.

It may be said of any or all of them that the payment is related to the assumed effort involved but equally it may be suggested that what is actually paid for, as distinct from what is actually measured for the purpose, is the performance or the expected performance.

When the term incentive is used in its usual and narrow sense to apply to payment by results, (PBR) the plans which are subsumed tend to relate payment to performance. It is usual to measure what is being paid for in units of time, even in straightforward piecework payments, and this has the effect of focusing attention upon the assumption that time somehow measures effort, but particularly in the case of the piecework payment method, what is really being paid for are the 'pieces' or the performance. This is no less true of the schemes which work on the basis of payment (in some proportion) for time saved: the time saved correlates with pieces produced, even if it does encapsulate some assumptions about the relationship between time and effort (cf Lockyer, 1974, p 372).

These assumptions are dealt with in the application of time study, and in particular in the use of rating methods, (see below, pp 273–77) but the incentive payment methods themselves *then* link the performance of the individual to the reward. It is the use of the rating methods which seeks to accomplish the objectives of the guessing game which Baldamus (see above, p 229) suggests has to take place. Thereafter, what he refers to as the consequential adjustment is effected by the negotiation of rates and by the policy allowance, "the magnitude of which depends upon a managerial policy concerning the acceptable level of earnings of the grade of operator concerned" (Lockyer, 1974, p 165).

Once a time study standard has been set on the work in question, the one issue of how to set the ratio of bonus earnings to day-rate is dealt with by the policy allowance already mentioned, usually about 20–25 per cent. The other question of how to divide the element of time-saved is covered by the adoption of a payment by results plan (PBR) which permits the desired or negotiated division. Thus in a straight piecework scheme each piece is normally paid for at a constant 'piece' rate, although this could be varied. In the Halsey-Weir system, the division of the 'time-saved' is normally on a 50–50 basis between the worker and the company, but some other division could be substituted. In the Rowan scheme, the calculation of the division is more complicated but, essentially, this plan allows the split to increase in the employer's favour the higher the output achieved, a factor of importance, for example, where quality standards are important or work measurement difficult (cf Lockyer, *op cit*, pp 372–375).

Where a straight hourly, daily or weekly rate of pay is offered for 'work' whose amount and quality is notionally established in the employment contract, and supported by an implicit or explicit job description or statement of duties and responsibilities, it could be argued that the same principle of rewarding performance is involved. If the differential payments are worked out on the basis of job demands (as in the pay rate) there is at least a notional performance to be rewarded. This idea is carried forward more formally in the development of measured day work in which a datal rate is offered and paid for performance which is, again, established by the application of work measurement methods. Here the question of the standard of performance is neither notional nor implicit. In the variant, the premium pay plan (PPP) which is a stepped or graduated form of measured day work in which the individual can opt for whichever level of performance he wishes to work at in order to give him the particular rate of pay which he wants, the same idea is carried forward.

The tendency in all these plans to emphasize the linear relationship between effort and performance—by measuring through time-study at the level of effort whilst rewarding through various individual or group plans the performance given—has led to a considerable amount of friction and 'abuse'. The friction shows itself in disputed rates and disputed payments which have been held to keep the supervisors away from their main tasks of ensuring work flow and performance; the abuse usually takes the form of what is often referred to as fiddling, whereby the workers themselves vary the formal rules and procedures to suit ends which were not intended by the plan and which results in loss of control of its operation. Taken

together, these usually lead to management disenchantment and resolution to change the plan in order to re-establish control. This may
be achieved for a short time but the cycle does tend to repeat itself.
For this reason amongst others attempts have been made to devise
plans to reward performance on a much broader basis than that
which is implied in the notions of payment by results or measured
day work.

These plans are of two broad types, defined by reference to what
is taken as the source of any extra payment—either the value of extra
production or the profits which extra performance generate. In the
first category are the Priestman, Scanlon and Rucker plans, and in
the second the many profit-sharing and co-partnership schemes. It is
generally true that these plans conceive of performance in a much
wider frame than, say, conventional piecework. A better term might
be 'contribution' rather than performance, as they all tend to emphasize a general commitment to the ends of the enterprise, only part of
which is concerned with direct productive effort and some of which is
certainly concerned with acceptance of change and flexibility and
even avoidance of costly and time-wasting grievances over particular
payments for particular efforts or achievements.

In the first category, employees all receive a guaranteed basic
wage but in addition they are paid, as a group, an extra bonus based
upon the increase in production beyond the standard set (Priestman)
or upon the relative reduction in total labour cost (Scanlon). The
Priestman scheme has a complex method of fixing the standard or
base-line output where the undertaking is engaged in the making of
more than one product, although it is fairly easy in the latter case.
Even when by a points weighting process the base-line is arrived at,
the offer of an x per cent increase in bonus for an x per cent increase
in production above the base-line, the principle of a fixed relationship between reward for performance and the performance
itself is established. In the Scanlon and Rucker plans, the same fixed
relationship is established, usually by establishing as base-line the
ratio of labour cost to total sales value, variations from which then
affect the bonus paid. This bonus may involve a straightforward payment of the saving as bonus to the group or some division, such as 75
per cent/25 per cent.

In all these plans the effect sought is a greater commitment to
productivity, or at least to the reduction and solution of production
problems and it is this which, as much as anything else is rewarded,
and is claimed as the major advantage of the plan in question. They
thus involve 'a philosophy of how to run a factory', over and above
the actual method of calculating reward. They have had a limited acceptance on this side of the Atlantic and, as Lockyer says, "as yet

there is too little experience with [the Scanlon plan] outside the US to judge of its value in different employee/employer climates" (Lockyer, 1974, p 377; Butteriss, 1977, pp 34–35 and 60–64).

In the second category fall the profit-sharing schemes, and those for co-partnership or for extending share-ownership on favourable terms to employees as a bonus. There are many variations in the way of specific schemes upon these two general themes. Co-partnership and employee share-owning schemes generally aim to extend share-ownership to employees thus making the earners in industry the owners of industry (cf Copeman, 1975, p 148) by means of offers of shares on favourable terms for those who (usually) demonstrate their commitment to the undertaking by continuing faithfully to serve it as employees. Profit-sharing schemes, on the other hand, are usually to be compared with the Scanlon-type plans in so far as they declare a bonus payable to employees (usually in proportion to their earnings and usually at the financial year-end) after the final book-keeping exercises have been carried out to establish the overall profit and loss position for the year. The difference between the first and second category schemes is therefore centred upon whether the calculations of the distribution are made on intermediate measures (such as labour cost to sales value) or whether they are based on financial year-end calculations.

Both types of second category scheme have been used particularly to reward senior members of management, whose contributions may be regarded as most directly related to profits and to dividends (to which share-ownership gives title). More recently, as a matter of government policy, there has been some encouragement for the idea that such profit-sharing and share-distribution schemes might be extended to embrace all employees. (The Inland Revenue issued a consultative document on the subject on 2 February 1978.) If the project is to get off the ground in private industry a considerable modification of the present tax law is likely to prove necessary, as the present position is one in which both the offerers and the recipients regard the bonuses available as too insubstantial to allow them to proceed with such schemes. Part of the current interest links these schemes to participation in private enterprise (cf Balfour, 1973, pp 155–160; see also, current issues of *Co-partnership*). The TUC sees this proposition as an attempt to bolster private capitalism which does nothing for those outside the private sector of industry and diverts attention from industrial democracy.

In a related category but not necessarily involving any intention to secure or increase employment commitment, is the association of pay offers and settlements with added value. The main purpose served here is the determination of what are the limits to settlements of wage claims or what kitty exists from which to meet wage and salary costs. It is a truism that wage and other factor costs must be met out of what is left from sales revenue after material and consumables costs have been met. The formal use of added value as a measure in this context is new. The Engineering Employers' Federation provide a definition of added value which declares it to be the "value added to materials and other purchased items which provides, as a result of productive activities in the firm, the sum out of which wages, salaries and administrative overhead expenses are paid, leaving any surplus as profit" (1972/1976, p 18). The EEF seeks to demonstrate that the use of this concept allows both comparisons to be made of labour productivity, and the derivation of an index of the amount of any increase in added value which can be devoted to the payment of wages etc and still provide a minimum percentage return on capital (*ibid*, p 30). In the present context this use of the value added concept suggests that there is a growing predisposition to attempt to fix rewards for work on the basis of performance, rather than on the basis of job demand or effort.

It is only at this end of the spectrum of incentive and bonus schemes that there is any deliberate attempt to influence directly the 'contribution' element in the expectancy model (see above, p 208). Job evaluation schemes place their emphasis on the job demand or effort inherent in the job's content, ordinary 'incentive schemes' place theirs upon the output or contribution as assumedly related to effort and thus seek to establish rewards by guessing at the underlying relationships. But co-partnership and profit-sharing schemes, and indeed the Scanlon-type plans, may be seen to focus upon what, in the work context, constitutes contribution as this may be measured at the end of the day. They seek, in other words, to establish rewards on a basis other than the customary one.

Such plans tend to attract suspicion in the minds of many workers who see them as being in the same category as divisive merit rating plans, once used more frequently and energetically than at present. One of the main problems associated with them is the attempt to base reward on aspects of both effort and contribution, some at least of which are somewhat ethereal and difficult to define and recognize. Bittner (Dooher and Marquis, 1950, p 25) list a number of factors which supervisors are asked, in a number of schemes, to rate for each of their subordinates. The list shows a tendency to combine the objectively measurable (like quantity of output) with the unmeasurable and virtually unassessable versatility factor. His general list contains a number of variations on this continuum:

quantity of work

quality of work
planning ability / use of working time
ability to work with others / cooperativeness
ability to learn / knowledge of job
initiative / willingness to accept responsibility
dependability
safety consciousness
versatility and adaptability

These are usually accompanied by a requirement that the individual be assessed in overall terms, such as overall merit or promotability. Where such plans are retained after unionization, it is likely that they will embrace no more than (a) accuracy, (b) effective use of working time, (c) output, (d) application of job knowledge and (e) cooperation. It is usually assumed that the scores on each of these five scales can be totalled and that the total will give some correlative indication of the worker's total performance; it can therefore be used to determine the pay which he will receive in the next datum period.

Situational pressures on pay strategies
The choice of category of payment method adopted to reward performance may be expected to be constrained by certain internal factors. Broadly speaking, these pressures may be expected from

(a) the method production employed
(b) the demands or expectations of those employed
(c) the level of objective set by the management, ie as between an objective related to the wage-effort bargain *per se* and one related to overall commitment.

It has been suggested that both the objects of the organization and the goals of the workers will exert an influence upon just which kind of payment system will be adopted in particular circumstances. The effects of fashion (eg the abuse of incentive systems since the 1950s) and of mistaken decisions by managers, leading to inappropriate systems (given the objectives and goals) cannot be discounted. Managements might get it right or wrong, and for the right or wrong reasons. But there is some evidence, based upon the assumption that the mode is more indicative of what is right than any other case, that payment systems tend to associate with types of objective-technology and with worker or management goals.

Pressures for different forms of payment system
Since 1957 or thereabouts, there has been a growing volume of criticism of the usefulness of payment by results systems of a direct sort.

The evidence is certainly patchy and anecdotal but, if the number of words written is any indication, this particular type of payment system is becoming less popular. The upsurge which took place with the development of large scale mass production industry and flow-line techniques is now apparently to be reversed. But we should also note that what statistical evidence there is on the subject does not lead one unerringly to this conclusion.

The apparent reasons for both the growth and the decline might themselves be indicative of the sort of pressures which are generated by a given type of market and technological system, although what is often referred to as fashion cannot be discounted entirely.

It can be argued that the growth of the mass production firm was the factor which sustained the development of PBR systems. This does not mean that PBR is only applicable to these kinds of firm. But there is reason to suppose that, if you are producing a standardized item for a mass market by relatively standardized means, first, the profit margins in a competitive situation will be cut (Allen, 1961) and therefore, secondly, there will be pressure upon unit labour costs. Labour is the only factor of production which is capable of variation in increased efficiency per unit—in the sense that once the machine is designed and built into a flow-line, there is little more to be got out of it beyond its fixed speed, unless labour's contribution is somehow enhanced, eg work faster, harder, on shifts or with more constant application during the work period. PBR systems seemed to have this kind of advantage to offer to the firm faced with this kind of market-plus-technology prospect.

It has recently been argued in line with this discussion of the efficacy of PBR systems that, where the mass production technology is carried through to a higher stage, so that the worker's direct influence upon rate of production is much reduced, the justification for the incentive scheme in that form disappears. To abandon piecework and comparable systems under these circumstances is then just as appropriate as their embrace at the lower level of technology. Nor does this mean that all oil and chemical plants will immediately abandon these schemes, although many have, and some have carried productivity bargaining through to a higher level of sophistication than most engineering companies.

The small jobbing shop, or the small-batch producing unit usually avoids the simple, direct PBR system. Again, this is not clear cut but there is no reason why we should suppose that PBR systems are introduced merely for one reason in all cases. Similarly, and probably for similar reasons, the indirect element of a labour force, such as the maintenance crew or a yard gang, is often not subjected to PBR systems. But in these circumstances it is much less possible to measure that element in the situation which contributes to performance. Many different schemes have been tried, linking it to machine down-time or to time on a standardized maintenance job, but the kind of system which seems to be called for by the situation is different from that needed on the production line.

In fairly simple general terms therefore:

1 Unit and small batch producing units most commonly (ie modally) apply some type of straight time payment system
2 Manually-controlled line production of standardized products is usually linked with some form of PBR system
3 Automatically controlled line flow production systems (necessarily producing standard items) have commonly gone over to some newer system of payment, whether measured day work or more likely a productivity bargain type of payment system.

Fashion or whim can obviously affect the outcome, and so too can the element of panic or failure, in the sense that any firm which is failing by its existing methods of organizing effort could well seize upon a payments system straw to try to help itself. If there is a moral, it is perhaps that the market-plus-production system that the plant or company has seems to exert some pressure towards one pattern of payment rather than another (cf Lupton and Bowey, 1974).

Similarly, workers with different goals are likely to make different demands on the system which employs them. We are not so much concerned here with individual differences as with differences amongst identifiable categories of workers. There are a number of ways of identifying these differences, and there are a number of factors which have been singled out as associating with them (see chapter 4).

The instrumental group is more likely to demand a payment system which virtually guarantees high take home pay. The manner of its calculation is perhaps of secondary importance compared with its level relative to other pay packets, or with its constancy taking one period with another. These men are in it for the money and this is what they want out of work. Their manner of securing this may well vary according to the conditions of the labour market, and perhaps in particular of the local labour market. Where jobs are plentiful, the response to a low pay packet or to a fall in pay level will result in a tendency for the men to vote with their feet as they move into more lucrative jobs. Where jobs are not so easy to come by, or where there are no alternative jobs at anything like the same money, withdrawal is not a viable strategy but aggression towards the company to secure higher earnings becomes a stronger possibility.

The solidarist group is more likely to be concerned with the side-effects of the payment system. Although its members are also interested in money, they will seek their money rewards on more stringent conditions.

For example, a straight piecework or other direct incentive scheme, which will lead to differentiation within the worker group itself, is likely to be either discouraged or, more likely from the evidence, to be used as a means of increasing group solidarity through some fiddle or other. This is really a way of ensuring that the worker group can offer cooperation to management in the bonus scheme without appearing to themselves to be accepting the management's terms. Thus work will be "banked" when a lot is done and only a fairly constant amount will be booked for payment purposes, so that the 'bank' exists as a buffer against the 'off-day'. Or again, any minor variation in the methods or conditions of the work will be used as an excuse for attempting to renegotiate the rate. For workers who have this general type of orientation, it might be suggested that the payment system will become just another aspect of the situation over which the worker group will seek to secure increased *control*.

This sort of distinction does not merely affect incentive payment systems. Even with a straight day wage arrangement, the high-money-men will tend to seek such extras as overtime and week-end working, whilst the solidarist groups will be more concerned to ensure that there are arrangements within their control for sharing the available overtime working. Similarly, a solidaristically-oriented workforce is much more likely to organize and control arrangements for securing provisions at a discount (whether from the company from amongst its own materials or products, or by way of 'works' gardening, car maintenance, or photographic clubs) than is the more instrumentally-oriented one, and is likely to prevent fewer security or policing problems as a result.

There is also some suggestion that workers' reaction to methods of payment is partially determined by the sort of social system in which they have been brought up. One piece of research suggested, for example, that the rate busters on incentive are likely to have rural backgrounds, whilst the solidarist groups are more likely to have urban backgrounds (Whyte, 1955). The same research suggested that Catholics are more frequently found in the first category and Protestants in the second. In both cases, the standards of proper behaviour which are inculcated in the individual seem to make the difference.

There is also some suggestion that workers with different orientations will tend to select for themselves the sort of work and payment system which is most congenial to them; the rate busters will look for the system that will enable them to make big money and the solidarist groups will do the same, although in terms of their own orientation. If there are unlimited opportunities for employment, there could be a shake-out and a matching of expectation and experience.

It must be emphasized that such general propositions as those reviewed here are general or thought to be so. There is no reason to suppose that they must apply in particular situations, a point stressed by Lupton and Bowey in their reference to a contingency approach. This says, in essence, that no one payment scheme will meet *any* employer objectives or *any* worker objectives, and that the selection of a plan will demand close analysis of the given plan's properties in relation to the objectives and the situation in which it is to be applied. For this purpose, they offer the Lupton-Gowler profile method of assessment, designed to meet the proviso indicated at the beginning of this paragraph. Use of this method of assessment places the problem of determining which payment system to employ in a given situation on the same footing as any other management decision: it necessitates adequate diagnosis of situation and adequate analysis of the properties of alternative courses of action, before the final choice is made (or the decision taken).

Table 13

Pay and productivity in different situations

Type of work situation	Payment form	Productivity form	Worker orientation
Work situations with high discretion in the work role: problem solving			
1 Top management	High, secured by long contract	Creativity based on trust	Commitment to org objectives
2 R&D department	High, secured by professional career	Contribution to creativity	Commitment to creative tasks
3 Selling organization	High, secured by basic salary plus commission	Contributory to growth	Commitment to selling objectives
4 Supervision	Protected salary guaranteed by organization	Loyal execution of original directives	Loyalty to organization
Work situations with low discretion in work roles: execution			
5 Unit and small batch production	Day or piece rates guaranteed by the personal authority of boss	Flexible working on varied tasks	Expressive: work satisfies wide demands
6 Manually-controlled line production	Incentive payments secured by agreements	High and constant rates of production	Instrumental: work satisfies demand for money
7 Automatically-controlled line production	Pay and participation, secured by common commitment	Constant attention and intermittent action	Commitment to work tasks

Intrinsic rewards

A similar sequence or hierarchy of concerns is to be found in the attempts to develop plans of 'intrinsic reward' from work. If these remain necessarily intertwined with attempts to provide extrinsic rewards, there is appreciable evidence from the experience of recent years that greater concern is being shown with the former. Some of the main developments in this area have been:

1 The introduction of job enlargement, job enrichment, and autonomous work group schemes, whether under those names or in association with relaxation of demarcation restrictions in productivity deals, has sought—however successfully—to increase the worker's psychological 'income'
2 The introduction of various changes under the heading of staff status for manual workers, often associated with the levelling up of such fringe benefits as sickness and pension schemes through negotiation, has sought to enhance the status of manual workers (as well as his long term income)
3 Some conceptions of participation rest upon a belief that the worker in the enterprise has something to contribute to fairly high-level decisions and, where these rather idealized conceptions prove capable of realization, they contribute something to the prestige of the individual worker
4 The negotiation of such arrangements as the guaranteed week (or even the guaranteed year) and other income and employment security schemes (even before these were backed up by legislative provisions) promises to do something for the security of the individual worker as well as for his monetary reward, *per se*
5 In periods of strict incomes limitation, it is also not unusual to find enterprises allowing compensation in kind (for example in the form of generous discounts on commodities held by or produced by the firm) or treating employees (for example to end of year dinners or trips abroad) in order to supplement reward outside the wage packet.

All of these affect the compensation package in a way which does not depend simply upon adding to monetary reward: it is no accident that in the list of examples given there is some reflection of Maslow's hierarchy of need; nor is it surprising that both management and organized labour have found them to be acceptable.

However, even with a switch to this broader conception of reward, there is likely to remain the general problem of whether the level of remuneration in the individual case is likely to be seen as sufficient, regardless of its composition, to bring forth the level of contribution necessary. The incentive effect of money plus anything else may diminish in the midst of uncertainty, if only because people are likely to respond to a sense of being rewarded inadequately, first by diminishing their contribution and only secondly by quitting their employment. In the full employment conditions which have lasted for most of the post-war period, the gap between these two may have diminished because of the ease with which an individual could find another vacancy but, in less than full employment, even when this is temporary or confined to a local labour market, the distinction might widen. In conditions of full employment, both the employer and the employee are more likely to test the market rate than they are in those of less than full employment; in the latter, what is considered the market rate for a class of labour may therefore come to bear only an approximate relationship to the rate required for full contribution.

Only some of these developments, listed on the preceding page, could, however, be regarded as 'intrinsic' to the job itself. This would apply, for example, to job enlargement, job enrichment, and job rotations where they are developed within a framework of career (see the comments on Schein's model above p 243). These kinds of scheme might be regarded as having a good deal to say about the distinction made by Herzberg between intrinsic motivating factors and extrinsic hygiene factors in work. The changes in the jobs themselves and their grouping into rotational or career clusters might provide the individual with more interest, challenge, achievement potential, and bases for recognition by others and for esteem by the self, and thus 'motivate'.

There is a second conception of intrinsic which is worthy of consideration in reward strategies. This is concerned with what might be regarded as intrinsic to the work environment, defining that environment in terms of what is necessarily important to the individual carrying out a job of work. For example, in Dubin's study of central life interests, he discovered that manual workers tended to attach some interest to the technological and organizational elements of the environment of the work which they engaged in. Whatever might be the pay, or even the more generalized status of the worker in social and political arrangements at work, the technological and organizational constraints on that work are less escapable or less variable than they are. If the worker were then to be asked about his work, he might be expected to comment on the work itself and this immediate context within which he must necessarily carry it out. There may be some reason to suppose that motivation (through the work itself in Herzberg's conclusion) might well be negated by inattention to these aspects. In job enrichment schemes this is achieved, but it should not be assumed that merely to change the job content by itself will necessarily lead to motivation.

In a similar fashion, it might be acknowledged that the worker is bound up in his employment. It may be that many elements of this situation are hygiene factors but it may also be, without inconsistency in the suggestion, that some features of it are more fundamental to motivation than others. It may be that 'policies' and 'relations with supervisors or managers' are hygienic, whilst the extent to which the undertaking as employer conforms to expectancies of a 'good employer' or not, is not. The basic distinction which Herzberg makes between hygiene and motivator factors may in other words need some refinement to distinguish the cosmetic from the crucial even amongst the environmental factors in work. A good employer, in the sense of one who conforms to the expectancies of good employers, may be worth working for where a nonconforming bad one may not.

This brings the discussion round in a circle to where we started in this chapter. Although there may be a good deal in the old paternalistically welfare-oriented approach to be criticized, one feature of it (at least) was that it reflected a concern by the employer to be a good one, or to be thought to be a good one. Even if he did not achieve this in any objective sense or as measured by the gap between his workers' demands and his offer, he often attracted both work contribution and some loyalty or respect for trying. The suggestion that the welfare approach to personnel management ought to be resurrected (as is made for example by Kenny, 1975) may to some extent be necessary to focus attention on that which is intrinsic to the work or employment situation rather than merely intrinsic to the particular job itself. As a part of the strategy for improving performance, it may be necessary to think through the 'offer' position on all of these dimensions, and not merely on the one dimension of the job interest and challenge.

Further reading
In this chapter there are a number of interwoven themes.
On 'welfare', see Niven (1967), Hopkins (1955), Crichton (1967, chs 1 and 3), Young (1968), and Kenny (1975); Mitchell (1974), Howells and Barrett (1975)
On supervision and leadership, see Ross and Hendry (1957), Dunkerley (1975).
On pay and pay strategies, see Lockyer (1974), Lupton and Bowey (1974), Bowey (1975), Husband (1976), Paterson (1972), Currie (1977).

6 Evaluation, training and counselling

Implementing performance strategies

Whatever strategies for securing performance are adopted, it remains to put these into effect. To do so, it is necessary to engage in tactical activities which contribute to the evaluation of needs in relation to measured or assessed facts and trends, to the development of the individual's ability and skill to perform and to an increase in the individual's comprehension of the role requirements of that performance. These activities in turn call for skills, on the part of the executants, in mensuration and adjudication and in training and counselling—all in many specific manifestations.

One of the major constraints in this general area, is linked with the division of function between the personnel specialist and the line management/supervision. Its effect upon the personnel specialist's role is to affect the question of whether he is to apply his skills in these activities directly (ie as the executant) or whether he is to advise and train the line managers and supervisors to carry out these activities (thus leaving them within their responsibility).

We have already noted in discussing preparation of job descriptions that they must indicate just what the 'target' performance is. To describe the activities in the job without seeking to give some indication of the standard of performance required for satisfaction is to omit the opportunity to provide, from the outset, comprehensible criteria of that performance. This failure to take an opportunity results in both poor judgements of performance (because no one can grasp the appropriate judgemental norms) and dissatisfaction on the part of the person judged (because he or she must see the implicit norms employed as idiosyncratic). We noted it as incumbent on the personnel manager to ensure that such standards and such criteria are built into the job description, even if the services of the work study engineer or line manager have to be employed to secure this end (see above, pp 169–174).

In this area of 'measurement' it is usual for the operations involved to be carried out as part of the line management function, probably with the direct executive assistance of the rate-fixers and work-study engineers (in the 'management services' function and not—normally—in the personnel function). In 'appraisal', it is common for the line management superordinate to generate any judgemental norms and data, and in doing so he may receive assistance and advice from the personnel department, but rarely is he divested of the responsibility.

These data, from the various sources, may be made available to the personnel department for manpower planning and employee resourcing purposes but, in so far as this is done, it is a relatively recent development and reflects the historical attitude towards the personnel function that it was unconcerned with quantitative data. One development which has fostered this change has been the extent to which standards of performance and effort have become increasingly subject to negotiated solutions with the union representatives. The excursion into productivity bargaining in the later 1960s provided a major fillip (cf North and Buckingham, 1969; Flanders, 1964). It might be stated that the more the personnel department becomes involved in 'discovering' what the mutually acceptable notions of effort and reward are in the given sub-culture of the firm/occupation, the more will it become associated with these data in some fashion (cf Behrend, 1957; Baldamus, 1961).

It does not follow that, because the personnel specialist may require data of this kind for other purposes, he must also be engaged executively in generating them. The necessary 'control' can be established through data if:

either the line management and supervision makes its own assessment or measurement of subordinate's performance in the course of their carrying out their normal 'control' function

or the system of rewarding effort or contribution in money or other benefits is of such a nature that the contributors act 'independently' at a level of performance which is not only acceptable but is also linked to the level of reward.

In both of these conditions, the personnel manager *may* have no direct and certainly no executive role.

What he frequently does, is act as the repository of the organization's knowledge about assessment, which he must then impart to line management as required. This focuses upon

(a) knowledge of alternative methods of measuring and assessing performance
(b) knowledge of the difficulties and problems associated with these

(c) skills required to enable managers to measure, assess, interpret and counsel

(d) knowledge of system operation to permit the appraisal system to be monitored.

As the personnel function has evolved in most organizations, a tendency has developed of associating the personnel specialist with attempts to systematize the *assessment* (eg performance appraisal and merit rating) processes in organizations even when he is dissociated from attempts to measure performance on more objective criteria. This distinction is essentially one between those judgemental operations which are necessary to control, but which must depend upon relative scalar assessments, and those which are more readily supported by *measures* of time or quantity.

Setting performance standards
The setting of performance standards, or the 'discovery' of acceptable levels of effort or performance, is a necessary operation in any system of purposive activity, which is to achieve an equitable distribution of work and reward. But where a textbook on factory or production management will tend to discuss this operation mainly in relation to shop floor and routine clerical work (cf Lockyer, 1974) the personnel management textbook will tend to ignore this area of application in favour of discussion of managerial and professional standard setting (cf French, 1974). Possibly paradoxically, the tendency in the one is to treat the exercise as one of control by management (eg using work measurement methods) but in the other to emphasize the desirability of setting standards by 'participation' (eg employing management by objectives methods). On the other hand it is generally acknowledged that, where there is unionization, the standards set by the one method will form a constant topic for negotiation and re-negotiation, whilst in the managerial/professional area the standards once set will be more readily accepted as the basis for the subsequent review.

Whilst the application of the techniques of work measurement to routine shop floor work (cf Barnes, 1969; Randall, 1969; Fields, 1969) and to office work and indirect work (cf Cemach, 1969; Whitmore, 1971) is not the direct concern of the personnel specialist, the foundations of standards set and used and the method of applying the methods (with their consequent effects upon staff relations) are. These fall within the scope of the personnel specialist's authority, in his role as maker or validator of administrative policy or practice as it relates to personnel. He should therefore be familiar with the actual techniques employed—work study, work measurement, organization and methods (O and M)—but he should have a deeper appreciation of the standard-setting or normative processes involved.

Time study (or work measurement) is usually carried out in such a way that the 'work content' of a job is reduced to a single measurement unit—time. This on the face of it suggests that all that is necessary is to observe, and measure with a stop-watch, how long it takes a worker to carry out the job. But because there are individual and situational differences which might affect the time taken by the person who was actually observed and measured, some attempt has to be made to relate the observation to a 'norm'. It is this 'norm' rather than the final time standard which may be set for the job which falls within the purview of the personnel specialist.

The basic 'norm' here is that of the qualified operator (one who has the physical or mental skills and abilities to carry out the job) working at a normal pace in applying himself (ie without over-exertion) to the job over a normal working period. As Lockyer says, therefore, "an observer is thus required to have a very clear concept of the rate at which a worker who possesses the necessary physical and mental attributes, and the required skill, would satisfactorily carry out the task under observation, safely, accurately, at the correct speed and without undue strain" (Lockyer, 1974, p 162).

The 'basic' conceptions of what is 'normal' in these circumstances are conceptions of a person walking, without load, at a pace of three miles an hour (which is applied to body movement) and of a person dealing a deck of playing cards into four hands in 30 seconds, or half a deck in 15 seconds (applied to hand and eye movements). This standard rating point may then be expressed on a scale, and this on some scales is fixed at a 60 (the performance of the day-worker working without incentive) compared with an 80 (for a worker on incentive) and on others as 75 against 100 or as 100 against 133 (Lockyer, 1974, p 163). Practice in Britain is to rate this 'motivated' performance as a numerical value of 100 and to make no stipulation as to 'standard' unmotivated performance. Against this, actual performance can be related as a percentage (British Standards Institution, BS 3138, 1969).

These conceptions of the normal must then be translated into judgements of diverse patterns of body and arm-hand-eye motions. This can be done with practice under supervision of a trained rater. This is a special process which depends upon the expertise of the rater being accepted by the trainee as productive of 'correct' ratings—since there is no objective arbiter (like the standard imperial 'yard' in disputes about length of anything). It is now common to use film as a means of training, so that many more variations of movement in diverse patterns can be practice-rated in a similar context but the special nature of the influence process is not thereby removed.

Nor is it removed by the use of 'synthetic times'—work-factor system, methods time measurement, basic motion time-study or other similar variants. The earliest synthetics were developed by raters themselves, by the simple expedient of building up a data-bank of their own measurements, on which they could then draw for new jobs which included combinations of movements already timed and rated. The later, branded versions usually broke motions down into much smaller elements and used films in laboratory settings to amass data and derive standard times. This had the advantages of allowing motions too small or too quick for observations with the naked eye to be studied and measured, and of making possible the standardization of 'times' applied, provided that the trained analyst could break down any given job into its elemental motions and times. This has tended to standardize the rating or judgement factor, not eliminate it completely from the process of fixing standard times for work.

Essentially the same kind of problem falls to be tackled in job evaluation. In the simpler ranking and classification schemes, there is a dependence upon the rater's familiarity with the money value or comparative worth of the content of many or some jobs in the total population to be evaluated, which then enables ranking to be done (say, by the method of paired comparisons) or associations to be made between the more doubtful jobs and the benchmark jobs. Without such familiarity, raters would be more likely to produce unacceptable errors in ranking or classification, since they would have nothing to 'appeal to' as being the norm for the exercise of judgement. In the analytical schemes of job evaluation, as in rating for time study, it becomes necessary to train the raters to appreciate what 'qualities' of a defined factor (say of experience) are to be taken as the 'norm' for a given number of 'points' or a given sum of money. Differential familiarity amongst raters is therefore usually controlled by increasing the number and the 'familiarity spread' of the raters involved. The greater 'complexity' of the analytical schemes is usually held to justify the greater need for lengthy training or familiarization but part of that process, at least, is concerned with the implantation of standards of judgement or evaluation (cf Thomason, 1968, ch 3).

In both time-study and job evaluation, the need for a conception of what is normal—or the norm for judgemental purposes—is fairly easy to appreciate. Although it is difficult to perceive an 'objective' standard, there appears to be a presumption that there is a normal 'demand' upon or a normal 'pace' required of the qualified operator, working at normal pace without incentive etc, to be found. There may not actually be a standard foot ruler or pound weight but it is not difficult to appreciate that there should be one, if only we could dig it out.

Comparable problems of establishing norms as a basis for the exercise of judgement arise in both merit rating and staff appraisal. 'Merit rating' is a term applied to the process of making judgements about the loyalty, commitment or cooperation displayed by employees generally, but usually it is the manual or routine clerical worker to whom such plans are applied. 'Staff appraisal' may mean a similar kind of exercise but it is usually applied to more senior white collar personnel. Both tend to be treated with suspicion by both the raters and the rated. Merit rating is usually dismissed from unionized plants, if the unions are strong enough, and where it persists at all it is frequently little more than a way of assessing time-keeping and attendance as a basis for some kind of merit or bonus payment. Staff appraisal may still persist in white collar areas but there is a weight of evidence to suggest that the raters themselves are reluctant to rate or appraise in any very effective fashion, so that it too fails to hold to its original purposes and intentions. Here, however, the opportunity to link appraisal or rating norms to some apparently objective standard of performance is much less obvious.

The major problem likely to be encountered in merit rating plans is the problem of establishing what it is that is to be evaluated. Unlike job evaluation, which seeks to appraise the job content or job demand, merit rating concentrates on the qualities and individual conduct of the worker. Merit rating, and many staff appraisal plans, therefore invite the supervisor or manager to evaluate the individual on 'qualities' which are in some respects comparable to those developed in selection and promotion decisions. In effect, judgement is often called for on rather nebulous traits or qualities, about whose definition and *a fortiori* whose measurement psychologists would tend to disagree.

In merit rating plans, it is not unusual to find supervisors being expected to evaluate individual workers on traits as dubious as some of the following 12 drawn from one company's plan:

1	safety	7	industriousness
2	knowledge of job	8	initiative
3	versatility	9	judgement
4	accuracy	10	co-operation
5	productivity	11	personality
6	overall job performance	12	health

In one study, Bittner surveyed merit rating forms used in 18 companies. These showed that a "total of 35 supposedly different traits were being used. The greatest number on any one form was 19, the smallest number was four, and the average was 10" (Bittner, in Dooher and Marquis, 1950, p 25).

The production of a list of words which 'sound' as if they are sophisticated may, for this reason alone, seem to help in the reality of appraisal. Such words suggest that we have found a method of making articulate what was previously intuitive. This may, however, be far from the truth. We may merely produce a verbal sophistication which leaves the reality of judgement untouched.

First, we may be doing no more by this conceptualizing process than finding a number of different words to identify what *in reality* may prove to be one thing. This is closely linked to the notion of judgemental norms, and is frequently referred to in rating as the halo effect. Evidence of the halo effect of generalized status is provided by Levine and Butler (1952) in their experiment to test the relative effectiveness of a lecture and a group decision in changing rating behaviour. Their study involved 29 supervisors of 395 workers in a large manufacturing plant. The workers, who covered a wide range of skills, were paid an hourly rate according to the job class, in the spectrum of nine such classes determined by skill and training. Within each job grade three different hourly rates applied. The rate for a particular worker was determined by a performance rating carried out by the supervisor every six months. Rating scales were then established for five factors: accuracy, effective use of working time; output; application of job knowledge; and co-operation. The total score achieved by a worker on these five dimensions determined his rate for the following period.

The motivation for the study was that "the results of this rating system were not equal to expectations. The foremen . . . tended to overrate those working in the higher job grades and to underrate those in the lower grades. This positive and negative halo effect resulted in the workers in the lower grades of jobs receiving the lowest of their respective wage rates, while the more highly skilled workers consistently received the highest of their respective wage rates. Evidently the foremen were not rating performance of the individual worker, but the grade of the job as well." Using an arbitrary division of the nine labour grades into high (top five) and low (bottom five), the authors show the halo effect by the mean difference in ratings of the two categories. (The table illustrates this for the three groups used in the experimental procedure.)

277

Group	A	B	C
Foremen	9	9	11
Supervising	120	123	152
Mean rating (low)	1.7	1.7	1.8
Mean rating (high)	2.0	2.0	2.4
Mean difference	0.35	0.33	0.63
Significance*	0.01	0.07	0.01

* The probability that a difference of this size or greater could have arisen simply through errors of random sampling.

The halo effect might extend, not from job grade as in this case but from the actual work contribution. In any organization there may well be some norm, however well or ill-defined, relating to the work contribution of the individual, but no norm relating to other behavioural outputs or displays. It is therefore a distinct possibility that an individual will be able to make some assessment of this, but not of other outputs or attributes. If required by the system, he may still do so, by allowing the norms relevant to work performance to apply to the other factors as well.

Tiffin, alluding to this common halo effect, makes this point quite clearly. "Since", he says, "there is a marked tendency to rate men at about the same level on various traits—whatever these traits may be—a great deal of time and effort can be saved by having the ratings made on only one trait at the outset. Furthermore, most production men will agree that job performance is the basic factor in determining any employee's value to the company, and that the various other things such as cooperation, personality etc are worth considering only in so far as they contribute to the job performance. Rating on this basic characteristic is, therefore, made the foundation of this system" (Tiffin, 1950, p 14).

It is therefore likely that when plans such as these are implemented at this level, the factors to which judgement must be applied are often closely linked to performance and only loosely linked to personal qualities. The supervisor might well be required to judge or rate his subordinates at the shop floor level on (a) accuracy, (b) effective use of working time, (c) output, (d) application of job knowledge and (e) cooperation. It is then usually assumed that the scores on each of these five scales can be totalled and that the total will give some correlative indication of the worker's total 'contribution' and can therefore be used to determine the pay he will receive in the next data period. But in fact the halo effect may make such multiple ratings and their aggregations spurious and the common sense approach of the supervisor more intuitively correct.

If work contribution can serve as the main object of appraisal, it may, on the one hand, provide the real foundation for an overall judgement and, on the other, make it unnecessary to appraise on other factors. The use of a single factor in judgement would have the effect of eliminating double counting, but an organization may still require that both specific factor and overall judgements be undertaken simultaneously in order to make the latter more valid. The multiplication of factors may give the undertakings a spurious accuracy and may prove less accurate than rating on a single or overall factor, provided that the single factor was identified with the main purpose of activity for which norms are likely both to exist and be understood.

Staff performance appraisal

The phenomenon of employee rejection of appraisal methods *not* directly related to actual job performance is less visible, generally speaking, amongst white collar staff. With increasing unionization of routine white collar jobs this is beginning to change. At higher grade levels, however, the practice of direct and outright rejection of such plans is not widespread. One explanation is that a formal plan of performance appraisal will be accepted where the employees concerned perceive that there is some opportunity for them to progress upwards in terms of pay and status within the organization, and that an 'objective' assessment of their job performance might help to base this movement on this main indicator of current worth to the enterprise. Thus the man on the shop floor is unlikely to perceive his future as one including much upward movement, and any variation of his earnings around the norm for his category on the basis of some appraisal is likely to be viewed as just so much tinkering. As routine white collar personnel see their jobs being rewarded in a similar way, their predisposition to accept appraisal may also disappear. There remain, therefore, largely those whose jobs contain relatively high levels of discretion, and who see themselves as able to pursue an upward career path, who will consent to appraisal.

This pattern tends to place the personnel department in an interesting position. For manual workers, it is usually work study engineers, now probably identified wih management services, who provide standard data against which the performance of the individual can be assessed: it is usually the first or second line supervisors who make the assessment. The role of the personnel department will tend to be an indirect servicing one—providing general or specific supervisory training, for example. For more routine office work it is again the management services team which increasingly carries out the work necessary to derive standards and/or introduce incentive bonus schemes, such as CWIP, GCA or VFP* (see BIM Information Note No 67), and the role of the personnel department is again similar to that in manual worker assessment. In both instances, in the past when merit ratings schemes may have been more common than now, the specificity of the training given in rating or evaluation may have been high; now it is likely to be treated much more generally and simply as a part of the general process of exercising supervisory judgement of situations and people.

With professional and managerial white collar jobs this pattern does not generally apply. The determination of standards to apply to this kind of work tends to remain the prerogative of the manager who is accountable for the work in question, but this process may well involve the personnel manager if it involves anyone else at all. The personnel department will either advise the managers on how to determine appropriate standards for this kind of work (ie in a general way, possibly using information obtained by the personnel department from other organizations) or it may be charged specifically with the responsibility for introducing a formal plan such as management by objectives (MbO) and for giving this the servicing needed to assure successful implementation. The latter part of the exercise would naturally include a full-scale programme of training and counselling as well as administration. The personnel department's degree of participation could well, under these circumstances, be much greater than in the cases already discussed.

In addition to this, the personnel department's involvement is likely to be enhanced for a reason which is nothing to do with simple performance appraisal of the sort incorporated into, say, an MbO programme. Where MbO has been introduced it has usually applied only or mainly to those staff who see themselves, and are seen by others, to have career prospects and, in those circumstances, it is usually a part of the personnel department's role to deal with career planning and career development. Thus one might say that, even if there were no formal plans to facilitate the setting of performance standards and the appraisal of performance, many personnel departments would still be concerned with career planning etc which, in its nature, would require someone, somewhere to make appraisals of— if not performance—at least likely progress of staff. For this reason the personnel department frequently finds itself immersed in staff appraisal, and moreover engaged in a good deal of administrative and executive work in connection with it, if only because of its common concern with career planning and development.

* Clerical work improvement programme; group capacity assessment; variable factor programming.

Partly in consequence of this, the personnel department often finds itself attempting to devise a single appraisal programme to meet a multiplicity of objectives, some related to improvement of current performance, some related to career planning and development and some related to manpower planning at the level of the enterprise.

Ghiselli has put forward the following five purposes as relevant to assessment:

1 Informing the person who is being assessed as to how he is doing, at least in the eyes of senior management
2 Stimulating the person to better performance if this is seen to be warranted by the current level of performance
3 Indicating which skills need improvement if the performance is to be improved
4 Cataloguing the capabilities of the manpower on an organizational basis—a memory bank of information on capacity
5 Indicating the strengths and weaknesses of the organization's initial selection procedures.

In this case, the immediate purposes of the appraisal process (to identify and rectify deficiencies in performance) are supplemented by the equally important total organizational purposes of building up an inventory of usable control information and using it to check on the effectiveness of other administrative procedures.

In individual company plans, it is not unusual to find that the stated objectives of the assessment plan include:

1 Improvement of the current performance of the manager on the job through the recognition of current strengths and weaknesses in performance, and the elimination or reduction of the latter through counselling or training, inside or outside the company
2 Guidance of the individual manager or professional person on what his strengths and weaknesses are, what he might do to capitalize on the one and reduce the other and where his future career path might appropriately lie
3 Identification of more junior personnel with capacity and capability to move into more senior positions, usually with some development within the enterprise, so that the organization has some appreciation at any given time, of not only what stock of trained manpower it has available for its current needs but also of what potential stock it has to meet future requirements
4 Improvement of communications within the organization, particularly communications between the man and his manager (the son to father relationship) and frequently too between the man, his manager and his manager's manager (extending the relationship

to embrace the grandfather). This applies particularly with schemes like MbO.

Three very different things are being attempted in such plans. There is, first, the attempt to improve current performance (with the help of the man concerned); secondly, the aim to improve some aspects of organizational functioning, such as communications in the chain of command or manpower planning; and thirdly, the objective of producing data specifically for management succession planning. The first of these is a goal related to the short term, the second is one tied to the medium term, and the third is necessarily much longer term. Again, from a different standpoint, the objectives could be said to relate to the needs of the organization and also to the needs (or desires) of the individual—the distinction being between performance improvement and organizational planning on the one hand and career development for the individual on the other.

All managers must and do appraise, because it is an inherent part of their role to monitor performance of plant, people and system as a whole. Also, somebody somewhere must gather data about the organization as a whole for manpower planning and that role very often devolves upon the personnel department. Managers who must appraise might quite reasonably expect help (in the way of advice and guidance from the personnel department) on the modes and methods of carrying out assessments of the performance of subordinate staff. The dilemma into which many personnel departments seem to have got themselves is that by marrying their role as manpower planners (contributors to the corporate decision-taking) with their role as counsellors and trainers of the line management and supervision (as specialist 'staff' advisers) they have tended to speak with forked tongues: in the latter role they advise managers to stick to 'the job performance' as the surest basis (as far as research suggests it) for appraisal and to make it 'a mutual learning process' (as research into influence processes suggest it might be best accomplished); in the former role they often seek to have the manager appraise on unassessable dimensions of characteristics and carry out the whole exercise as essentially a central office one (see figures 4 and 5, pp 140 and 142).

Staff appraisal might therefore be said to provide a kind of acid test for the personnel department because of the need to resolve two different objectives. The difficulties of reconciliation in one plan may go some way towards explaining the four aberrant practices discovered by Rowe in her study of 1,440 completed appraisal forms in six companies (1964); namely that

(a) appraisers did not always complete appraisal forms when required to do so

(b) they did not always complete every section of the form when required to do so
(c) they did not always acknowledge their authorship
(d) the content of the entries was often evasive.

Rowe concludes that this reveals a very low motivation on the part of managers to appraise, to discuss appraisals with subordinates and to initiate any follow-up action on the appraisals. So strong is this tripartite conclusion that it must mean that something is disabling about the appraisal plans themselves (see above, p 226).

Mahler has also pointed to some of the practical difficulties which affect the raters *ability* to make accurate and consistent judgements:

1 The extent of his opportunities for observing the performance of the employee to be rated
2 His consciousness of the need to rate performance during the period of observation
3 His experience and training in translating observations into judgements
4 His personal characteristics as these might affect rating ability
5 The facility with which the rating form permits him to record his judgements

Mahler also identifies some of the practical difficulties in a rating situation which affect his *willingness* to rate:

1 His understanding of the entire rating programme
2 His acceptance of the stated purpose of the rating
3 His reflection of top management's attitude
4 His experience in applying the rating to employees under his jurisdiction and his assessment of how useful these are
(Mahler, 1950, pp 51–2).

Taking these various conclusions together, they suggest that:

(a) some people are better judges of other people and their attributes than others, and are so innately
(b) practice in exercising judgement may improve it, although whether because this affects the qualities which yield innate ability or not is not known.

It is, however, possible that practice influences two other factors which bear upon the quality of judgement:

(c) to the extent current and relevant norms for judgement are understood and accepted, the better the individual's judgement will be

(d) the more highly motivated the individual is to exercise judgement the better his judgement will be.

These may be expressed in a number of different ways, according to the situation to which the judgement is being related. It seems difficult to separate innate ability for emphasis in isolation from the other two factors of standards for use and motivation to use in assessment.

An individual performance audit
The conclusions from a consideration of common practice in appraisal in relation to research findings and theory might be summarized as follows:

1 An individual embarks upon employment in order to do a job and he expects to make some contribution to the achievement of the objectives of the organization
2 Where he has the power to determine how his contribution will be judged (eg with strong unionization) he will (a) tend to throw out assessments based on rather vague personal qualities or on equally vague categories of general behaviour, and (b) will seek his assessment on the basis of the job/work performance itself
3 Where an assessor is required to assess others, he too will tend to produce the same result as in 2, even if this is done less through organized power and more through a cautious approach to assessment which renders it worthless
4 Where appraisal of performance can be related directly to output this ought to be done. Where it cannot, acceptable criteria directly related to contribution or performance should be agreed upon and used in the assessment process to the exclusion of any others in the final stage even if some prior, and more detailed analysis is carried out. This is to increase validity and reliability of the single overall assessment of contribution
5 For a closely connected reason, appraisal schemes should have one objective; plans which seek to realize a number of different objectives should be avoided, especially those which seek to provide for succession and promotion in addition to assessment of current performance
6 It would then tend to follow that the assessment process would be one which would directly concern only the assessor and the assessed, and the central personnel office or the countersigning officer (the grandfather) would come into process, if at all, only to monitor the fact that the appraisal had been carried out, and not to engage in the appraisal process itself or to interfere with its outcome
7 The role of the personnel manager in this area would then focus on

the provision of adequate information and training for the three essential requirements of assessors: judgemental ability (an exercise in skill development), understanding of judgemental norms (an exercise in communication) and developed motivation to assess (an exercise in securing the enabling conditions—which might involve getting the 'system' right, as indicated in the above summary).

Such generalizations, about the plans and the response to them, must necessarily be related to the characteristics of the people and the situation to which they are to be applied. This is to suggest no more in effect than that any manager must apply diagnostic skills to situations and problems before applying general, off-the-peg solutions to them—the foundation of 'contingency' theories. In the field of managerial performance appraisal, this is not often done and a strong tendency remains towards application of a general plan as a means of pursuing greater central control.

Cummings and Schwab (1973, ch 9) have attempted to develop a systematic conception of appraisal which allows three different programmes of appraisal to be employed for three distinct purposes, but with links between them which allow management to switch individuals from one to another as the situation permits or requires.

In the first, the *development action programme*, the emphasis is placed upon planning work and the whole focuses upon setting goals in work, self-control of performance and feedback of data to the employee himself on performance. In the second, the *maintenance action programme*, the emphasis is placed upon the definition of acceptable goals and levels of performance, and the whole focuses upon the establishment of a means of identifying and correcting departures from standard acceptable performance by the employee. In the third, the *remedial action programme*, the emphasis is upon providing an alternative to dismissal (or deselection) and the focus is upon providing communications between a superordinate and subordinate to establish why performance is below what is expected, and what might be done to bring it up to an acceptable level (and thus avoid termination).

Clearly these three programmes would be more applicable to different types of performance, sometimes occasioned by motivational differences on the part of the employee, sometimes by technological and job definitional constraints on the individual. Equally clearly, when the cause is motivational, an individual employee might move from one type of performance to another and the 'programme' might therefore have to change to be consistent.

Categorization of programmes in this fashion seeks to establish

Figure 10 CONFIDENTIAL

Staff Assessment Form

Part I—Performance Report

Performance ratings in the same job		
Previous year	Last year	This year

Name:

Job title: Dept/Works:

Date: Group/Section:

Signature .... Section Head or Supervisor
Signature .... Group Head or Asst. Manager
Signature .... Department Head

CONFIDENTIAL

Part II — Personal Interview Record

A Views expressed by Interviewee (i) Present job: (ii) Future aspirations:
B Chief points made by Interviewer including any recommendations made for improving job performance:

Interviewer's signature.. Date..

Part III — Potential and Development

A   Fitness for Promotion (Please complete whichever one applies):

    1   Unable to assess yet ....

    2   Probably not promotable ....

    3   Probably promotable in .... year(s) and is considered
more likely to be suitable for:
(i) Promotion to a primarily (higher) supervisory position

        ....

        (ii) Advancement in a specialist or professional capacity................

        ....

    4   Promotable now to .... (suggested position)
and the highest level or job for which he might be fitted in about
five years' time is:

        ....

B   Development. Suggestions, if any, for courses of training and experience
        in other jobs:

C   Any other comments:

Department Head's signature..   Date...

287

distinct objectives for the appraisal system which can be related to the kind of employee and the kind of work role involved. Failure to make such distinction in the past may well help to account for the generally unsatisfactory state of performance appraisals in any situation to which they have been applied, for there are relatively few situations in which considerable reliability and validity has been reported.

Indicated decisions

The achievement of performance *control*, based on appraisal, must then depend upon a decision designed to improve system performance in some general or specific fashion. The initial stages of designing jobs and organizations, and the succeeding stages of defining the man (or woman) most likely to prove capable of doing them, and of appraising performance of personnel in them, must lead eventually to decisions about improvements in performance. The design and evaluation stages in this process of appraisal are, in other words, instituted in order to indicate the need for decisions about jobs and manpower, although they do not 'automatically' indicate the content of these decisions.

The *need* for decision in this area is given by observable disparity between that which is desired (indicated by the criteria built into the job description and man specifications) and that which is yielded (indicated by the results of performance measurement and appraisals). If, for example, performance criteria are given in terms of units produced and set at a level of 100 per day, and actual performance gives a constant 95 per day, the need to take decisions (or actions) to improve the latter or diminish the former is indicated. Alternatively, if a degree of cooperativeness is sought but is assessed not to be given, similar action may need to be determined upon in order to bring desired and actual into alignment.

The content of the resultant decision is, however, less easily specified. 'What ought to be done' is a more difficult question from that which asks merely 'Whether anything needs to be done'. It opens up a whole spectrum of possibilities from redesign of the work itself, to 're-equipment' of the individual performing it. Both of these broad areas of action are clearly in question under these circumstances, but in themselves may cover a wide variety of actions. Organizational redesign might involve a fundamental reappraisal of the organization and its procedures, or it might entail a change in supervisory or payment practice; individual re-equipment might give rise to more on-the-job training or a lengthy period of retraining in a totally different area of skill or knowledge.

If therefore, the question of whether a decision is called for depends upon judgement of reality, the question of what decision ought to be taken involves judgement of feasible actions to determine what is best or at least satisfactory.

In principle, the process of appraisal is usually not completed by making simple judgements of another's performance. As in many programmes, completion requires what is often referred to as 'counselling' from which will emerge agreed experience and training programmes for development of the individual in ways which will effect improvements. Counselling thus often serves as a preparation for the provision and acceptance of formal training and development. To the extent that performance appraisal indicates the nature of the 'problem' to be solved, its solution is likely to be found only if, by counselling, the individual can be persuaded that one course of action will both meet its organizational performance and its individual development aspects. Both the organization's representatives and the individual concerned are unlikely to be able to deal with it, if there is no systematic arrangement of possible and legitimated means to its solution.

Counselling
Early approaches to counselling tended to regard this kind of help or advice giving as something to be linked to individually pathological conditions. This was often defined by reference to actual physical health but it was first extended to mental conditions (eg worry) and then to those which were assumed to be pathological in the individual as a consequence of the equation of employee and employer interests: time-keeping, absenteeism, family problems, financial worries, alcoholism (see above, p 240). Very large companies now sometimes employ specialist counsellors (see French, 1974, pp 430–431) where smaller companies may feel it desirable to refer the employee with more obviously pathological conditions to external specialists and agencies. For the rest, it frequently falls to the personnel specialists to engage in counselling activities of all types, but increasingly in relation to the actual and potential 'threshold' situations encountered inside a work undertaking. These are chiefly career thresholds—at job change or promotion and at retirement—and the help may be supplemented by agencies such as career guidance counsellors outside organizations. It is this use which is now widely institutionalized.

Counselling is thus regarded as appropriate at each of the main stages of career development or career change, where the managerial decision-processes co-ordinate with the realization of the aspirations of the individual. Walker (1973) identifies these points of parallel decision and response which may be presented in tabular form.

Individual career planning decisions	Organizational resource planning decisions
1 Occupational and organizational choice	The recruitment of people into jobs and structure
2 Choice of job assignment	The matching of individual interests and talents with opportunities
3 Individual evaluations of progress and development	The provision of training and skill development programmes
4 Retirement	Pre-retirement programmes aimed at effective status transfer

Some of these where they occur *within* a work undertaking are con-strained in more obvious ways than are the others. In selection inter-views where, as Torrington says 'two people have to make a decision' one in terms of suitability of candidate for the job and the other in terms of suitability of the job for the applicant (Torrington, 1972, p 3) there are some important constraints which are systematically es-tablished, as we have seen in chapter 3. But in counselling sessions on career development or redundancy or retirement, important decisions have already been taken in each case and it is the 'client' whose criteria of judgement are important, whilst the counsellor can do little more than offer advice, suggestion or other such help. In the first kind of situation, the respective authorities are fairly well estab-lished and recognized, whilst in the other the authority for offering help has to be established in the mind of the client as a basis for effec-tive action. (Torrington, 1972, pp 56–57). Where career and occupa-tion guidance is being given outside the undertaking, the counselling offered by the career guidance staff falls into the same kind of frame-work as this second category.

Investigations have shown that the appraisal interview, usually seen as a form of counselling, has generally been undertaken with reluctance by the appraisers. Thus Rowe found that "in three of the six schemes an interview was an integral part of the procedure, although one of them provided space on the form for giving reasons for not holding an interview. In another scheme interviews were con-sidered highly desirable but were not insisted upon because of the newness of the scheme. In another, interviews were only considered desirable where written reports were required, depending on the per-formance grade given, but were not insisted upon and space was pro-vided for giving reasons for not holding an interview. In the sixth scheme interviews were not an integral part of the procedure and were only required if an unsatisfactory grade was given for perform-ance; no space was provided in the form for an interview report."

Randall *et al*, referring to Fisons, record that "many managers reported that they were uncomfortable in the interview situation and unsure of what was expected of them. This lack of skill had been confirmed by the training department, where managers attending a course on selection performance were asking for help and advice on how to conduct performance review interviews" (Randall *et al*, 1974, p 64). The authors found that managers were able to make assessments and identify areas of weakness, but usually stopped at this point, partly because they felt diffident about trying to assess motivation and 'the reasons why' a particular performance was given, and had difficulty in exploring areas like intelligence or individual goals in an interview (*ibid*).

Amidst the widespread recognition that appraisal processes frequently do not lead to remedial action, a number of undertakings have therefore sought to provide a checklist of possible lines of action, such as those provided in tables 14 and 15. These set out in systematic fashion what an individual might do and might be expected to do to improve his performance on the job and his career advancement prospects. In the particular case, the charts will also indicate precisely (eg by location) how the necessary help, information or training might be obtained and what policies and facilities exist within the undertaking to acquire them. The main merit of such checklists, is that they do offer to both the appraiser and the appraisee a range of possible aids to improvement which might form the bases of the counselling interview and the training programme. It follows that the checklist needs to be drawn up systematically and be comprehensive.

At the point of termination of contract, such help as can be given will tend to concentrate upon the counselling process. Particularly if the individual is being made redundant, but also if he is retiring or simply leaving voluntarily to obtain other employment, the changeover from one status to another may produce its own brand of problem. As that quite remarkable Personal Survival Kit produced by the Newport and Gwent Industrial Mission for those made redundant puts it, to be told that one is redundant is likely to set in train a sequence of reactions which can be described as shock, defensive retreat, acknowledgement and adaptation. Whether the individual moves rapidly through this from the negative to the positive reactions, and thus adjusts to the situation in which he finds himself, will in many cases depend upon the help and emotional support he can obtain. Although not all this is likely to come from a personnel officer, some of it appropriately can.

The personnel department ought to be able to give good advice on the alternatives open to the individual and to help him explore them as solutions to his problem. This is sometimes done in circumstances of redundancy, but whether the willingness of personnel officers to offer counsel is translated into real use of their services is likely to depend upon whether such counsel has been willingly and usefully made available during the person's period of employment. If, for example, counselling is offered as a part of normal career development during employment, and/or if it is offered as a normal pre-retirement service, it is likely to be used in other more traumatic circumstances such as redundancy.

Such counselling is not likely to be effective if it is provided on an *ad hoc* basis. Unless the organization has consciously sought to develop a programme of career development for its employees, there is likely to be little data available to permit counselling in conditions of redundancy or leaving for other reasons. Nor is it likely to be useful to the individual unless the personnel department also mobilizes other services such as the Employment Services Agency, and possibly recruiters from other organizations to support the counselling activity.

A broader conception of training and development
One of the main influences of the Industrial Training Act (1964) and its successor, the Employment and Training Act (1973), has been to lead many undertakings to take a more systematic look at training as a support for manpower planning and employee resourcing. In spite of some tendency to manipulate the grant and levy arrangements to the undertaking's advantage, the longer term effect has probably been to develop a more integrated approach to training, whether for shop floor, general white collar or managerial labour. Other legislation, particularly the Health and Safety etc at Work Act, has imposed the need for employers to look carefully at manual worker training outside the ordinary focus of skill training, and at training for other workers (white collar and managerial) to enable them to deal adequately with the discharge of the employer's various new obligations to his employees.

Legislation has probably had its biggest impact on managerial and supervisory training. The approach developed in this area has become more clinical and analytical, and has produced a more packaged conception of the skills and knowledge involved. Underneath this the conception of management training has come to place more emphasis upon the cosmopolitan values and less upon the local ones, a development helped by the growth of training in business schools. Application of this more cosmopolitan conception has emphasized the need for systematic on-the-job relationships, fostered for example through management by objectives (MbO), which in turn emphasizes the need for more on-the-job coaching and counselling (cf Mant, 1969; Humble, 1972).

This approach put together a number of different items in the manpower planning inventory of technique and method, with the promise that the whole would thus become an integrated systemic conception. First, the job description and the man specifications were improved as the starting point for any attempt to improve managerial performance. Secondly, this was supplemented by a systematic attempt (the function of MbO proper) to isolate what at any given time were the key results areas in which the manager would be expected to engage, and what should be the criteria by which success could be judged. Thirdly, this was followed up by a review of performance in these areas (also as a part of the MbO approach) in which superordinate and subordinate considered together what had and had not been achieved, and why: where under-achievement is in evidence, the manager has a basis for considering whether further training might help.

This conception puts together those elements which any *system* would identify: the *objectives* and criteria of success, the means to their attainment, the required action on the part of someone, the review and comparison, leading to the identification of any need for decision—in this case about training.

Fourthly, the sequence of stages moves to the decision phase of the process. On the basis of this *information* about performance, is there a problem of capacity, *ability* or *skill* on the part of the individual, or not? If there is, what form does it take and what training solutions might help to reduce it? Or, as the Industrial Society handbook on the *Design of Personnel Systems and Records* (1969) succinctly summarizes the business of training-needs analysis, "The first step in an analysis of training needs is a definition of what is required of each individual; a comparison can then be made with his current performance. Training will then concentrate on the areas or causes of weakness" (p 79). But for it to do so, a decision as to what kind of 'training' will meet the problem (or the objective of strengthening what is adjudged to be weak).

The influence of the 1964 and 1973 Acts has again been to encourage the development of an inventory of training opportunities which exist to meet just such weaknesses as this approach reveals. In a broad classification, we can identify three types or forms of training which might help with different types of problem.

(a) Informal development inside or outside the company, including performance appraisal, on the job training by experience, passing on advice from superiors (counselling), temporary replacement in more senior position, job rotation, and recommended reading of industry's journals or appropriate journals.

(b) Formal development, mainly within the company, including various types of formal course of instruction, possibly involving senior management, training staff or outsiders with relevant material to present. It should be noted that supervisors or managers cannot be expected to know how to carry out new policies or practices (eg performance appraisal), or to understand the workings of new plant, without some formal instruction.

(c) External formal development, making use of courses at universities, technical colleges or industry training institutions, on such subjects as management, public speaking, quick reading or processes within the particular industry. Membership of external organizations, likely to apply more particularly at senior levels, also comes into this category as a means of development.

These broad categories can be expanded into more specific instances of training, as is done in the following tabulation (p 296) which is based upon inventories from a small number of industrial and commercial companies. Whilst this does not claim to exhaust all possibilities, it does demonstrate the manner in which the personnel department, as advisor and custodian, might compile its own local inventory for distribution to managers who, in their supervisory capacity, might be called upon to decide upon training opportunities for subordinates. It is unlikely that this by itself will remove the problem identified by Rowe on the follow-up of appraisal, but it may prove to be a necessary if not a sufficient condition for its reduction.

The attempt illustrated in the *Development Activity Guide* to link the areas of weakness identified in the review and appraisal process, with possible means of overcoming them, may be more apposite to the personnel department's role. The left hand column lists what often appear in MbO as key result areas. Although some of these can be criticized for lack of definition (in the same sense that lists of personal qualities associated with selection processes or merit ratings can be questioned), they figure prominently and it is worth attempting to associate them (as training objectives) with the possible means to their achievement.

Approaches to training
The means of realizing training objectives are derived from the principles developed in the area of learning theory, which may be summarized under the three headings of pre-training conditions, objectives in training and the processes of training.

The first is primarily concerned with the question of the individual's motivation to undergo training, which may itself be influenced by counselling. Such 'motivation' is not a simple concept; it cannot be taken as axiomatic that everyone will necessarily want to undergo training in order to improve his or her skills or even 'himself'/'herself'. Just because a training opportunity is offered is not by itself sufficient reason for thinking that everyone will want to use it. The redundant employee, for example, may well resent being placed in a position where he needs training in order to go on earning a living, and this resentment may influence very strongly the motivation which he brings to his training. It is therefore important for the employer in general and the trainer in particular to pay some attention to the motivation of the potential trainees.

This is because the student who is reluctant to undergo training, or who is indifferent to the training offered, is unlikely to learn much from an instructor, however brilliant. It is necessary thus for the trainer to take time to ensure that the individual is at least aware of the benefit which might accrue to him from the training he is being offered. It may well be that the individual who resents the system for forcing him to undergo training could, by counselling, be led to recognize that the training might in the long run place him in a much better position than before. If this kind of change in attitude towards training can be brought about, the individual's motivation may well develop to a level where the instruction given will be worthwhile. There is a fine point of balance in motivation here which must be sought. A potential trainee who is over-motivated and who sees the whole of his future depending upon a notional success in the training process, may become so anxious about it that he will be prevented from learning: his own anxiety will introduce too much noise into the actual training process itself to permit him to work effectively. This often happens within the ordinary educational system, where passing examinations is given an excessively important significance in the life of the individual, so that he performs less well than he would had he attached less significance to examinations.

In training as in other activities, the motivation of the individual is likely to be affected by the rewards and penalties which are associated with performance in the training process. This is usually referred to here under the heading of reinforcement. It means simply that the individual must feel that there is some reward for him not only in the long but in the short run. It need not be a material reward and usually takes the form of encouragement by the trainer. The individual needs to develop some feeling that he is making progress through his training and the tutor's encouragement should be related

Table 14

Supervisory and managerial development
A build-up of training and development programme
for supervisors and managers

	Performance appraisal	On-the-job training	Counselling by superior	Temporary replacement for superior	Job rotation	Reading
Informal development	Annual review of performance and development needs	Under the guidance of trained instructor	Periodic discussions of progress	During vacations, illnesses, and other absences. Experience is gained for future promotion	Exposure to different jobs in department in order to gain broad technical knowledge	Supervisory and management journals

	Basic supervisory course	Personnel practices	Advanced counselling	Salary administration	Visitation programme
Formal development within company	To give an understanding of the scope of the supervisor's job, supervisory responsibilities, and training in supervisory skills. Methods of instruction—conferences, films	Understanding of supervisor's role in personnel policies of company. Visits to personnel department for orientation	Development of skill in obtaining facts, identifying the problem, reaching a satisfactory decision in personal and job problem situations through use of instruction and case method	Understanding company salary policies and procedures	Knowledge of other department functions

	Administrative practices	Seminars—company development	Developmental reading	Performance appraisal
	A series of case discussions involving policy formulation and administration	Periodic meetings with senior officers to become acquainted with latest developments in the company	Understanding of reading process and development of reading skills	Practice in rating procedure and counselling

	Membership in organizations attendance at conventions	Courses at universities	Special management schools	Effective speaking	Industry courses and conferences
Development outside company working hours	Examples are: BIM; IPM; IWM; JCC. Will add technical knowledge	To further self-development, evening or extension courses at universities or correspondence courses may be suggested. Eventually Henley or business schools	Seminars in: operations research, increasing productivity in office operations, managing punched-card systems, selection of office supervisors, etc	Preparing for public speaking engagements, sometimes representing company	To give broad knowledge of the industry

296

Table 15

Development activity guide

The purpose of this development activity guide is to assist supervision in the selection of activities to meet the needs of the individual as determined during the performance appraisal of management personnel

Performance characteristics	Development activities which may be recommended
1 Position knowledge	Coaching or counselling by supervision Special assignments in areas where knowledge is available Position rotation in areas where individual is weak Special courses in field of activity Technical societies Reading in fields related to work Field trips or plant tours
2 Analytical ability and judgement	Coaching or counselling by supervision Opportunity to use more analytical ability and judgement Special courses (problem solving) Special assignments requiring the use of analytical adapability and judgement Case studies
3 Planning	Coaching or counselling by supervision Opportunity to do more planning Special courses on subject Special assignment—where planning is required Special conferences on subject (BIM, IPM, IWM etc)
4 Initiative and acceptance of responsibility	Opportunity to accept responsibility and use initiative Special assignments—requiring use of initiative with responsibility for performance Chairman of committees or member, in and outside the company Officer of various organizations Coaching or counselling by supervisors
5 Dependability	Opportunity to perform with guidance, coaching and counselling Special assignments—difficult jobs stimulating and challenging—that will cause individual to extend himself—jobs that are important

continued

Table 15—continued

Performance characteristics	Development activities which may be recommended
6 Creative thinking	Opportunity to exercise this ability—encouraged and promoted by supervisor to do so Special assignments—where creative thinking is required—problem solving and development of new technique etc Institutional—special courses in creative thinking or other courses which require creative thinking Conference leadership Conferences—BIM, IPM, IWM etc Professional societies
7 Delegation of responsibility and authority	Special courses in management techniques Practice of principle by supervisor and upper echelons of management Encouragement by supervisor to delegate responsibilities and authority Courses—human relations (industrial psychology)—principles of supervision, conference leadership—oral communications Special assignments that require delegation of authority and responsibility

8 Personnel handling and leadership	On-the-job coaching and counselling, opportunity to perform in this type of activity
	Outside reading
	Special courses
	   Human relations (industrial psychology)
	   Job training techniques
	   Coaching—counselling—interviewing
	   Conference leadership
	   Oral communications
	Outside activities
	   Organizations
	   Management clubs
	   Conferences
	   Technical and professional societies

9 Relationship with others	Coaching and counselling by supervision
	Special courses
	   Oral communications
	   Conference leadership
	   Human relations (industrial psychology)

continued

Table 15—continued

Performance characteristics	Development activities which may be recommended
10 Attitude	Opportunity to make decisions that affect operations etc Coaching and counselling by supervision Supervisor—subordinate relationship Outside reading—selected Opportunity to participate in company-sponsored activities
11 Emotional stability	Coaching and counselling by supervision Special institutional course (industrial psychology) Special assignments requiring person to work under pressure and difficult situations
12 Health	Check-up with company doctor
13 Self expression	Communication courses Speeded reading Oral communications Written communications Conference leadership

to his performance and his progress in this way. Looked at from the trainer's viewpoint, this means that the training process has to be conceived in terms of some feedback system, whereby the performance of the individual is judged by the trainer and the results, with his reasons, must be communicated back to the individual trainee. Again, as in the general case, such encouragement is likely to have a much more functional value than administering punishment or penalties when mistakes are made. This is not to say that when the individual makes a mistake the trainer should ignore it. The trainer has a duty to show the individual where he is going wrong. But this can be placed in the context of the individual on what is going right and indicating what needs further improvement or development, as part of the training process. It is important that the individual undergoing training should be able to develop knowledge about the results of his learning; this may be achieved by the supervisor forming judgements and communicating them or, in certain cases of technical training, by building into the mechanical system itself some devices (dials etc) which can tell the individual immediately how he is progressing.

The objectives which are established for the training must clearly be communicated to the trainee to provide him with the first piece of knowledge he needs to carry out some self-evaluation. But it is not uncommon for the trainer himself to have certain objectives for the training process but not to communicate them to the trainee, assuming that the trainee has his own objectives which must coincide with those of the trainer. It has been one of the major contributions of the industrial training boards that trainers have been led to establish programmes of training in which not only have they worked out objectives clearly, but they have made them explicit in formulating the training programme and have explained them to the individual trainees. At one level the statement of objectives in training can and should be stated in general terms. For example, the object of a lathe operator's training ought to indicate just what capacity the individual ought to have to operate lathes at the end of his training. The steps aimed for during training must also be stated so that the individual has a hierarchy of sub-goals which he can seek to reach on the way to achieving the overall objective. In this context too there is a point of balance to be attained. If very limited goals are set they will probably frustrate the individual who is probably more highly motivated to develop his skills to a reasonably high level, in which he and his future employer could repose confidence. Setting goals which are too high for the individual to attain at the outset, or in the early stages of training, is also likely to cause frustration: the individual will then tend to give up because the goals seem so far out of his reach at that moment. Thus goals are important in training and have an important bearing on the likely state of motivation on the part of the trainee.

The mechanical aspects of the training process usually reflect certain principles which also arise from learning theory. First, and most closely connected with the previous set of propositions about objectives, is the principle of breaking down the total amount of knowledge or skill to be mastered into meaningful component parts which the individual can master in succession. The notion of a balance is obvious again in this context. To break down the total task into very small elements is likely to prove frustrating to the individual and therefore to detract from his motivation to learn. If he repetitively attempts to master very small parts of the job he will quickly begin to supply his own context to the small part, and inadvertently learn contextual elements which he will later have to unlearn. Instead of breaking the job down into small fragments, a conscious attempt in training is therefore usually made to develop sub-components of the total task, each of which has its own sub-objectives which enable the individual to take a number of fragments in a meaningful context even if that context is not the whole of the job.

Secondly, it is clear that the individual undergoing training needs to know not only what to do but also some of the reasons why he should do it. This relates to the question of whether the trainee should be exposed to the theory or background of the set of tasks or techniques he is learning. The training of an electrician, for example, may not call for knowledge of quantum physics but he should probably understand why certain techniques are used in preference to others; a certain amount of theory about electricity is therefore necessary if he is to understand why he has been taught to do the job in a particular way. Providing some theory in training has the advantage of helping the individual subsequently to transfer his skills without undergoing further training. If he is taught only a single technique, if the technology to which it is to be applied changes, he may have to be brought back for training in another technique. But if the individual has already been taught a certain amount of theory he may, on the basis of his own experience, be capable of transferring the technique originally learned into a new one more apposite to the new technology. This distinction is sometimes referred to as a distinction between logical training and rote training; although the latter may seem to involve less investment of time and money in actual training, it is likely that, with today's high rate of technological change, the other logical method of training may prove in the longer run to be the more economical approach.

Thirdly, it is also clear from a great deal of research that the individual does not learn a great deal about required behaviours or skills simply by being told in the form of, say, a lecture, what those skills are. Wherever training is related to behaviours, whether technical or managerial, the individual must be allowed to become involved in the practice. This gives rise to the notion of learning by doing rather than learning by listening. There are nevertheless problems about blending what above we have called theory and practice. Evidence supports the proposition that the individual who is undergoing training of one sort or another will learn more rapidly if he is allowed to practise the tasks or techniques in which he is being instructed. But to repeat a small part of practice *ad infinitum* is likely to prove less useful to the individual in learning than a spaced repetition of the task over a period. One of the advantages of traditional apprentice training was simply that it allowed the apprentice to develop his skills in a serial fashion and to repeat the particular skill in a spaced manner over a period. The actual involvement of the trainee in what he is learning can thus be made to contribute effectively to the learning process.

Finally, the approach to training tends to reflect the concept of a learning curve, which seeks to present diagrammatically the likely progress of a trainee from the moment at which he starts training to the point where he could be considered a fully trained operator. The curve ascends rapidly as time passes, showing increasing proficiency, but after some time begins to level out. This general form is less useful in guiding the approach to training than the particular form. In its particular form as presented for example by Sayles and Strauss (1960), the curve is relatively flat during what they call the discouraging first stage, when the individual can be somewhat frustrated by his lack of ability to cope with the new techniques which are being presented. This is then followed by a fairly rapid growth in proficiency, which they describe as a period of increasing returns where the individual makes his first breakthrough. But the individual is then less likely to 'plateau', in the sense of not increasing his proficiency through time as he develops practice in what he has learned, and as he prepares to carry his mastery to a new level in a fourth period which these authors describe as the period of peak proficiency. The latter may be described as the period during which the individual finally masters the basic skills or techniques presented so that he becomes a proficient operator.

The essence of learning curve theory is that learning does not end at this point. A period follows which may extend over quite a long time, during which the individual engages in what Sayles and Strauss refer to as overlearning but which may be described as a process of internalizing what has been learned through continued repetition; as a result of this continued involvement in practice, the individual ensures that he will not forget what it is that he has learned. The point is perhaps most easily understood in relation to learning to drive a car: during the actual training, the individual learns consciously and deliberately many patterns of motion which later on he will tend to discard; but if called upon to do so he could bring them back from memory and employ them as occasion demanded. But it is accepted that when the individual usually passes his driving test, he is not as good a driver as he might well be six months later after more practice.

What is implied in this concept of a learning curve must also be modified according to the nature of the potential trainee presented to the trainer. It is well established, for example on the basis of the study in the Harwood Manufacturing Corporation by Coch and French that, where the training involves operatives who are presented for retraining in techniques which are close to those they have already learned, there may be a period at the beginning of the training process where proficiency falls considerably. This is usually explained by the need for the individual to unlearn what he or she may already have learned and to replace that by new techniques. Since the unlearning process, or unfreezing process as Lewin would describe it, involves time and effort, this might then be enough to account for the falling off in proficiency. The second point to emerge from this study is that, in spite of what has been said about the individual undergoing training above, where a group of employees is subjected to training the group norms may themselves inhibit individuals from moving along the learning curve at the rate and according to the pattern described; the group norms appear to have the effect of halting the employees on the false plateau indicated by Sayles and Strauss. It was only after the investigators in that case had sought consciously to bring the group into the learning process, and thus attempted to ensure that the groups' norms became congruent with the objectives of the trainers, that the individual members of these groups were enabled to move on to the second plateau referred to as the over-learning period.

This feature of a training or retraining process at once permits the learning process to be managed but allows the individual to exercise some control over that management process. Training may be an exercise in the management or creation of learning opportunities for the people concerned, and may thus qualify as an opportunity for the organization through supervisors or training officers to manipulate (in Cartwright's sense) the individual; but the influence of the surrounding class, situational and group values and norms upon the individual will always help to ensure that he or she retains some control over the operation. The difficulties which present themselves to the trainer as motivational or capacity for learning problems may have their origins, as has been suggested here, in the learner's normative system, which in turn may be strong enough to prevent manipulation.

Evaluation
Training and development, like any other aspect of personnel management, may be evaluated in terms of its effects upon the individual worker or in terms of its consequences for the enterprise. In the first context, training consequences will link to the goals of the individual, whether these be immediate (as shown up in terms of greater job satisfaction, greater reward or greater job security) or distant (related, for example, to his expectations of career development and long-term job security or equally long-term considerations of his self-concept). In the second, training consequences will be assessed against the immediate contributions to improved job performance or immediate enhancement of the qualities of manpower required by the organization, and against the longer term opportunities which the training provides to avoid costly dismissal/recruitment exercises to effect adjustments between demand and supply. In both cases, there are costs incurred (by the individual who must take the trouble to unlearn some routine and acquire others; or by the enterprise which must expend money on the training and forego the individual's contribution whilst it is under way) and any benefits must therefore be calculated net of these.

It tends to follow from this that in a period of economic decline for the enterprise, the net benefit of training will tend to be small in the short run, since the main objective will then be retrenchment and the main constraint will be a shortage of revenue which will have the effect of making the cost relatively high and of discounting the longer term future benefits. Consequently, the enterprise will tend to cut its training activity in periods of recession.

Nor does it follow that the individual's conclusions from his calculation will be vastly different from this. Whilst the individual is employed in the enterprise, the main objective must be to secure his job-property rights, which tend to depend most closely on seniority in the job. In such circumstances, staying put and contributing at a level which is adjudged to be consistent with retention of employment, may prove a preferred strategy to undertaking training to improve some hypothetical future chances of employment or advancement. When the individual has no employment, this calculation may well produce a very different conclusion, as, indeed, it may do for those (such as apprentices and trainees) who are involved in a deliberate exercise of preparing for a future employment rather than in an established employment.

For such reasons, public policy has, in recent years, sought to meet the problem of preparing people for a changing employment pattern over the course of their careers by developing a programme of training for those in employment or recently out of it, in which the main initiatives are taken centrally, even if the cost of it remains partly borne by employers. In this respect the approach to training in public policy has something in common with the approach to the improvement of health and safety practices, although the training approach has not yet gone so far as to impose general or specific duties upon both employer and employee. But what has happened in this process is that training has become subject to more systematic planning and evaluation, with more attention paid to the setting of objectives, the establishment of relevant criteria, the development of technique and the evaluation of effects against the objectives set.

As Hamblin (1974) in particular has shown, however, the evaluation of a training process is fraught with difficulty because of the number of levels of effect which can be discerned. Objectives may be set, and effects may be measured, on the reaction of the individual trainee, the individual's learning of knowledge or application, the behaviour of the individual on the job, the performance of the organization as an entity, or the much longer term impact on individual or organizational performance or development. Measurement of success on these different levels may then be tackled by very different methods: reaction may be assessed in terms of trainees' opinions as to how interesting or relevant the training exercise was; learning by some form of test or examination; behaviour by before and after investigations at the behavioural level and so on.

Nevertheless, the further the evaluation moves away from the individual's reaction to the training exercise, the more difficult it is to establish that what is being measured is the consequence of the training exercise itself, rather than the consequence of some other variation whose occurrence cannot be controlled (eg a reorganization of the work or the department in which it occurs). In comparable fashion, the establishment of the objectives in training is fraught with similar difficulties, since any single objective which might be accomplished by a training exercise might also be brought about by other means (eg a reorganization of the work or the workers). Since even from the point of view of the enterprise it is difficult to carry out cost-benefit analysis (cf Thomas, et al, 1969) it is therefore difficult to establish that training is the only or the best way to bring about a desired objective.

At the level of the individual case it is somewhat easier to evaluate the effects of training. The individual's reaction can be sought and obtained, a test can be administered, and behaviour can be observed

305

before and after. Although, as Hamblin shows, there are problems of evaluation even at this level, some attempt can be made, and frequently is made by trainers. But the main evaluation problem, here as in many other aspects of personnel work, is that of aggregating the case data: from the point of view of the management of the training function, is it realistic to add the reactions of the individual trainees and draw a managerial inference from this? The answer to this question is that such a datum could only be one possibly quite small part of the total data which would have to be taken into account in taking decisions about training programmes. What the trainer may properly use as his yardstick of success in training, may therefore prove an inappropriate one for use by the manager of the training function.

The manager with ultimate responsibility for the training function must additionally take into account the effects of training upon productivity and efficiency. Such efficiency need not be measured only in relation to actual 'products' sent out of the despatch bay; it could also include the measures of safety or labour stability, where expenditure was being incurred on training for these purposes. But there is always a nice calculation to be made as to how much difference training will make to the actual production and productivity of the enterprise, because so many other factors can enter into the determination of these consequences other than training. The training expenditure is one which in the short run often seems to be avoidable, even if in the longer term the costs of achieving productivity and production are actually increased as a consequence. Here, 'saving' on training costs may be not very different from 'saving' on cheaper but inferior components or raw materials and the consequences may be similar in the longer-term. But only by including training as a part of the overall plan for performance, and regardless of what then the short-run decisions may be, can effective evaluations be made of its benefits in relation to its costs.

Thus what runs throughout this chapter is the conception of a standard to be employed in relation to performance, whether that is judged from the individual or the enterprise standpoint. The setting of standards expected in work—any work—is an important foundation for the tactical activities of securing performance by leadership, supervisory control, incentives, training or counselling, and selection and termination of labour. None of these activities is likely to produce the success necessary to continued viability, unless the standards are set, whether unilaterally or jointly, unless they are effectively communicated to those who must operate to them, and unless they can be incorporated into the normative structure of the individuals concerned by counselling or training as the case may be. Plans for performance must depend upon such standards, their clarity and their acceptability.

Further reading

On the general subject of standard-setting and the various forms of evaluation, see Barnes (1969) and Randall (1969). On motion and time study and work study, and Lockyer (1974) on its integration into production control

On merit rating and performance appraisal see Dooher and Marquis (1950), Whisler and Harper (1962) and Cummings and Schwab (1973)

On counselling see Torrington (1972)

On aspects of training see Gentles (1969), Ward and Bird (1968), Singer (1977), Thurley and Wirdenius (1973) and Thurley (1974).

7 Authority, power and influence

Challenges to managerial authority

In earlier chapters, it has been assumed that managers have an accepted and acceptable power and authority to carry out the employee resourcing and performance development activities which have been considered. As we have noted, important moral and legal constraints are now imposed upon the exercise of this managerial activity so that what might now be done with impunity or approbation is at least different from what might have been done when, say, Northcott was producing the last edition of his textbook. There have been many changes in jurisdicial principle and cultural value in recent years, and thinkers and theorists have sought to evolve usable models which might guide action. These changes may also portend something of importance not merely for the 'technical' theories which managers may find useful, but also for the conceptions and perspectives which surround the exercise of authority itself. Regardless of what the manager might do, questions about the power and the discretion he has or will be given to do it also arise. These will influence the structure within which, and the processes by which, managers will in future exercise their influence in undertakings, and at this point it is pertinent to examine some of the emergent ideas as a prelude to considering communications, influence and organizational activities performed by managers.

In conditions of change which we currently experience, people (managers or anyone else) necessarily face greater uncertainties, in so far as they just do not know what is likely to happen next, to which they must nevertheless make some response. In such circumstances they will seek ways of transmuting 'uncertainty' into 'risk', that is, into some set of propositions which can be associated with estimates of probability of occurrence of events in which they can repose a degree of confidence. This is one of the intentions behind the development of new and more relevant theories which purport to explain something of what is happening currently, such as the 'beyond contract' theory of Fox (1974), the 'expectancy' and 'equity' theories of

308

Lawler (1970) and Adams (1965) respectively, or the 'contingency' — theories which have been applied to wage systems (Lupton and Bowey, 1974) or 'organization' (Hickson *et al* 1971). To the extent that these enable us to retrieve a degree of confidence that we know what is happening or that we know where we are going (whether 'really' we do or not) they help us to appreciate the uncertain future as a risky one. In punter's terms, we think we can now bet on form rather than on the basis of the blind stab with a pin!

One manifestation of this uncertainty is the so-called de-motivated manager syndrome. This is supposed to portend that, in the midst of the many changes which both increase the hazards of managing and decrease the relative level of remuneration of the manager, he withdraws or, alternatively, on the withdrawal-aggression hypothesis, seeks the security of unionization (see Hartmann, 1974; Weir, 1976; Shackleton and Davies, 1976; Mant, 1977). In this case it may be that what is happening, or possibly about to happen, to that tender flower managerial authority offers some explanation of the syndrome, such as it is. The related concepts of authority, power and influence are so central to the exercise of the managerial role that changes in their nature are likely to produce serious consternation in managerial ranks because of the fundamental uncertainty which they must import into the basic relationships of current organizations. In his capacity as protector of the organizational system, and regardless of the effects of these changes upon him, the personnel manager is likely to be called upon to advise on policies and methods for reducing this uncertainty to the status of risk.

This calls initially for an understanding of the perspectives and models which are currently employed in debate about this subject. One way of indicating the change thought to be taking place is that which contrasts the paternalistic or autocratic models of organization with the constitutional (by analogy with constitutional democratic government) or the participative (implying a sharing of authority to decide between two or more equal partners) model. "A tradition of paternalism . . . stems from mediaeval society, from the network of obligatory and dependent relations established under the control of God. Many nineteenth century employers saw themselves as inheriting squirearchical authority and responsibility, exercising a religious obligation to control, reward and punish, to exercise care and responsibility and to expect dutiful obedience" (Anthony, 1977, pp 74-5). Participative systems are conceived as founded upon mutually shared control, possibly because the 'subordinate' workers in the system have sought to establish an 'equality' with the 'superordinate' management through independent organizations (the trade unions) but, whatever the means, the end sought is that in which Jack

309

is as good as his master and of equal status with him.

On the face of it, this way of characterizing the major difference seems to place the 'family' model over against a 'non-family' model, or a rural model against an urban one (cf Whyte, 1955). Stark, however, has argued that both such models are really derived from family experience, which has been used throughout the history of western thought to provide two distinct models of organization of authority and dependence, together with a possible, dynamic alternative which links them together (Stark, 1958).

He has suggested that "all social theory, however, complex and sophisticated the form in which it may at times appear, stems in the last analysis from a simple human experience: the experience of family life" (1958, p 1). On the one hand, the family perceived from the standpoint of the child born into it is a unity, an integral whole, which the child cannot escape even if the marriage partners still retain some of *their* independence of each other. The child's "very existence depends upon, and is derived from the existence of the group" (*ibid*). For the child, in the Aristotelean sense, the "whole is prior to the parts" (*ibid*). On the other hand, the family perceived by the marriage partners is seen to derive from an initial contract which involves two independent persons making mutual promises and who therefore, far from being compelled to approach this as a unity, approach it voluntarily and 'creatively' and seek to retain some of their independence. It might then be said that this family, thus created, "is to them no real entity in the ontological sense of the word; it is a fiction. Real are only the individuals whom we can see and hear and touch" (*ibid*, p 2). From this basic experience, argues Stark, organic and mechanistic perspectives of social reality have developed which "have between them dominated the history of sociological speculation throughout the centuries."

One perspective thus offers a conception of organic unity, in which all the members are perceived to be consequent to the entity, whose perceived interests must then take priority. This 'unitary' model was early given metaphysical significance and legitimacy in St Augustine's vision of the City of God in which all served and pursued the (prior) Divine will. The other perspective in contrast places more emphasis on the plurality of interests and wills, and therefore upon the achievement of a kind of unity as a consequence of pursuing individual or selfish interests based upon some desire for a maintained independence. This has its counterpart in St Augustine's City of Mammon in which each was seen to serve and pursue selfish interests. In more recent times, this same kind of distinction is to be found in the concepts of community and association (*Gemeinschaft and Gesellschaft* in Tonnies' book of this title, published in 1889) and of

310

unitary and pluralist frames of reference (as in Fox, 1966).

At the levels of both experience and abstract categorial theorizing, the existence of these two basic perceptions allows the possibility of a linking pathway between them to be seen. It may be recognized that marriage partners, in some circumstances at least, may achieve an organic unity by mutual accommodation and adjustment so that this state becomes consequent to the pursuit of separate interests. St Augustine also acknowledges that 'order' may *result* from the pursuit of selfish interests, so that the City of Man (or the Earth) may acquire some of the features of the City of God from this point of view. More recently, the view has been developed by systems theorists that complex organizations may achieve a unity by proper attention to communications and mutual influence (Boulding, 1956).

It was the first of these basic perceptions that helped to structure the mediaeval society. The family help or the servants were simply an extension of the family concept. "In a family, the master or *paterfamilias* who is a kind of petty monarch there, hath authority to prescribe to his children and servants . . ." (quoted in Hill, 1969, p 446). This basic idea was then translated, given the religious justification provided by St Augustine for this 'organic' form of organization, (cf Stark, 1958) into the rationale behind the mediaeval village, the corporate town and ultimately the corporate undertaking of any kind. By close association with the family as an organic entity therefore, in the words of Fox, "the relation of master and servant was diffuse and paternalistic" and "the positions of the master and servant were conceived in status terms" (Fox, 1974, p 185). In the translation the simple notion of affective relations between kin came to be metamorphosed into institutionalized relationships of a 'customary' or 'status' type which, whilst they may have assumed an underlying affect akin to that found in the family, nevertheless were conceived in metaphysical and religious terminology in order that they might transcend such simple family notions. The 'person' of the father was thus transmuted to the 'status' of *paterfamilias* or master.

It is the second of these perceptions which is now struggling to establish itself as the prime mover in decisions about the organization of authority. The doctrine of 'freedom of contract' in its most open form implies this same notion of partnership but, as we have already seen (pp 60–63 above), freedom of contract has been obfuscated by the legal fictions which developed within the common law to enable it to deal with the pathologies of what society wished to be the 'normal' situation, and that 'normal' did *not* include 'partnership' between really equal contractors (cf Kahn-Freund, 1977, ch 1). Nor has the development of thinking about modern organizations, which stems from Saint-Simon (1825; 1964 edn) and Weber (1921;

1947 edn), completely broken away from this familial and customary model, even though it did offer a means of breaking with the simple affect base in its acceptance of rationality as a foundation for the development of acceptable rules of conduct. In particular, Weber's treatment of 'bureaucracy' as founded upon rational-legal authority, whilst offering the possibility of the 'office' being treated as independent, nevertheless left it encapsulated in an institutional framework which had the effect of rendering the office a contractual one, embedded in inequality.

In reaction to this, the current 'ethnomethodological' approach to the understanding of organizational behaviour seeks to provide a foundation for the treatment of the place of the individual in complex organizations without the admission of this necessary dependency. Although this does not yet provide an adequate perspective of organizations, it does reflect the current predilection for challenging the existing perspectives of 'prior' organizational interests, and thus of 'authority'.

Managerial authority and power

It is because managers, associated with one structure of economic authority in our society, stand at the eye of the debate on the distribution of authority and power in the modern industrial state, that we need to consider the models which have been put forward to help explain these phenomena. Managers are seen to have 'authority' but to be in positions in which their authority is being challenged. It is often said that trade unions have acquired or been given too much power, so that managers are no longer able to exercise their authority in the interests of efficiency or productivity. There are further proposals for changing the structure of either authority or power in work organizations, in order to increase industrial democracy or participation of the workers in managerial decisions. Against this background of ferment, it is necessary to develop some perspective of authority and power, and also of the 'rules' which will apply to their exercise or use.

The concepts which are coming to be employed to analyse this structure and process are chiefly three—domination, rule and power—but in each case the meaning assigned to the concept tends to vary with the value position and intention of the user. The chief source of meaning is Max Weber's *Theory of Economic and Social Organization* (1947) and the works which have developed from or responded to this (eg Bendix, 1966; Dahrendorf, 1959; Clegg, 1975).

Domination is now more widely accepted as a translation of Weber's term *Herrschaft* which Henderson and Parsons originally translated as authority or imperative control. In Weber's original meaning, it indicated "the probability that a command with a given specific content will be obeyed by a given group of persons" (Weber, 1947, p 152), and was associated with the concept of discipline which was defined as "the probability that by virtue of habituation a command will receive prompt and automatic obedience in stereotyped form, on the part of a given group of persons" (*ibid*). Reflecting Weber's perspective which regards reality as immediately accessible to the human senses and as capable of being interpreted directly (without, that is, necessity for prior theoretical construction), domination is then recognizable in the reality of "one person successfully issuing orders to others" (*op cit*, p 153).

The term more commonly used hitherto, namely authority, is more properly employed, if a distinction has to be maintained, to indicate any particular form of domination which might be wholly or partly legitimated by custom, habits, rules or (merely as a special form of rule) laws. In Weber's words: "Legitimacy may be ascribed to any order by those acting subject to it, in the following ways:

(a) by tradition: a belief in the legitimacy of what has always existed
(b) by virtue of affectual attitudes, especially emotional, legitimizing the validity of what is newly revealed or a model to imitate
(c) by virtue of a rational belief in its absolute value, thus lending to it the validity of an absolute or final commitment and
(d) because it has been established in a manner which is recognized to be legal. This legality may be treated as legitimate in either of two ways:
   (i) on the one hand, it may derive from a voluntary agreement of the interested parties on the relevant terms
   (ii) on the other hand, it may be imposed on the basis of what is held to be a legitimate authority over the relevant persons and a corresponding claim to their obedience" (Weber, 1946, p 130).

Weber recognized three pure types of legitimate authority, but does not suggest that the whole of "concrete historical reality can be exhausted in the conceptual scheme ... developed" (Weber, 1947, pp 328–329). These three types, charismatic authority, traditional authority and legal authority, base "the validity of their claims to legitimacy ... on:

1 charismatic grounds—resting on devotion to the specific and exceptional sanctity, heroism or exemplary character of an individual person, and of the normative patterns of order revealed or ordained by him. ...
2 traditional grounds—resting on an established belief in the

sanctity of immemorial traditions and the legitimacy of the status of those exercising authority under them . . . or finally

3 rational grounds—resting on a belief in the legality of patterns of normative rules and the right of those elevated to authority under such rules to issue commands" (Weber, 1947, p 328).

Accepting Weber's disclaimer as to intention, it nevertheless appears useful to recognize that the third of these may have two main manifestations, which are in some ways comparable in their distinctiveness to that between the first two.

These two sub-categories, may be referred to as 'administrative' and 'professional' rationality and may be distinguished in terms of the 'dependency' inherent in the two concepts. In both of these "obedience is owed to the legally established impersonal order" but that order may manifest itself in two quite distinct ways. In both cases, it is possible to say that obedience "extends to the persons exercising the authority of office under it only by virtue of the formal legality of their commands, and only within the scope of authority of the office" (Weber, 1947, p 328). But it is the conception of office which may vary. In the administrative authority case, the statements of Weber may apply directly, and the foundation exists for discussing authority "with a bureaucratic administrative staff" (*ibid*, p 329 *et seq*) or in relation to collegiality (*ibid*, p 392 *et seq*). But in the professional authority case, whilst they apply, they do not necessarily carry the same implications for the notion of 'office', if by that there is necessarily imputed any connotations of 'bureaucratic administrative staff'; the concept of partnership appears to have more ('ideal-typical') association with this manner of organizing authority than does the concept of hierarchically or even collegially-defined 'office'. In the professional authority case, obedience extends to the person by virtue of an impersonally certified competence, which has formal legality, but the client has more opportunity to regulate the incidents of the terms of his obedience than has the client of the bureaucratic office-holder, just as the person himself has greater independency of the organization which seeks to define the scope of his authority. The distinction is not too dissimilar from that made between status and contract by such writers as Maine (1931) and Fox (1914).

Domination and discipline, defined and organized in the ways just alluded to, thus depend—in the sense of creating a foundation for the probability of obedience—upon legitimacy established through norm or rule *and* upon power in the shape of control over resources (in accordance with the norm or rule) to support the established pattern of domination. Thus a command will probably be obeyed, if that command and the obedience of it are both sanctioned in terms of some set of rules or norms, *and* if the commander can dispose resources in such a way that obedience is fostered and encouraged.

In Weber's categorial theory, rules *per se* are not given explicit recognition, the concept of 'order' often having this meaning, and what have been referred to as rules are included by him in the concept of 'convention'. Weber is interested in the 'social relationship', which he defines as the "behaviour of a plurality of actors in so far as, in its meaningful content, the action of each takes account of that of the others and is oriented in these terms". It exists only in the sense of a probability that there will be a discernible "course of social action'— can we, in other words, observe people orienting their actions to the actions of others? (Weber, 1947, p 118). If we can, then they may be doing so because of their subjective appreciation of what is the appropriate or 'right' mode of doing so; these appreciations may so coalesce as to form types, and it is in this development of a typology that rules and conventions find their place.

One mode of orientation to the actions of others may be seen to recur, and it may do so simply because it just happens that way— Weber regards this simply as 'usage'. "Usage will be called 'custom' (*Sitte*) if the actual performance rests on long familiarity" but it can arise out of a rational self-interest pursued by the individual (Weber, 1947, p 121). Both of these are seen as occurring without reference to "rules" which carry an "external sanction". There may however be rules according to which the individual acts, but he does so of his own free will and not because he knows of, or fears, some sanction which may be associated with them (*ibid*, pp 121–122).

Another mode of orientation may occur because the actors have a belief in what Weber refers to as "the existence of a 'legitimate order'" (*ibid*, p 124), and what distinguishes this is the existence of 'rules' which the individual will to an extent perceive as binding upon him or as a desirable model for him to imitate (*ibid*, p 124). "A system of order will be called convention so far as its validity is externally guaranteed by the probability that deviation from it within a given social group will result in a relatively general and practically significant reaction of disapproval. Such an order will be called law when conformity with it is upheld by the probability that deviant action will be met by physical or psychic sanctions aimed to compel conformity or to punish disobedience, and applied by a group of men especially empowered to carry out this function" (*ibid*, p 127). For the rest, convention subsumes 'norms' (where as by Homans (1954), these are defined to be sanction-carrying rules), rules themselves (where, as for example, in works rules, they act as maxims whose breach will call forth some penalty or punishment), and laws (as defined by Weber in this quotation).

The major distinction thus drawn here between custom and self-interest on the one hand and convention on the other is between the 'natural order' and the deliberately established rational order. Behaviour may respond to either set of modes of orientation to social action, but it is the second which relates to the notion of domination or authority by virtue of its deliberate establishment in the interests of establishing and maintaining particular 'social relationships'. Instead of using Weber's term 'convention' in this context, we will use that of 'rules' to mean the same thing since the modern meaning attached to convention is somewhat different from that implied by Weber, and the concept of 'rule' is now well established in the industrial relations context.

Rules may then be regarded (as by Clegg, 1975, p 63) as articulating the structures of domination or in simpler language as helping to ensure that the structure of authority relationships which exists will be maintained through their operation. This should also be cast as a statement of probability if only to allow for the possibility that, in the devising of such rules, people may have got them wrong. This is essentially what the current argument in industrial relations on collective bargaining (Hyman and Fryer, 1975) and participation, (Clegg, 1977) appears to be about: the procedural rules, or what is described below as the constitutions, being developed in this field, can be regarded as a development of rules to support whatever the pattern of domination is at the time of their development. According to the value position taken up by an evaluator, therefore, this process of rule-making can be regarded as 'bad' (eg, as 'corporating' the otherwise independent trade unions within an existing authority structure (Clegg, 1977; Hyman and Fryer, 1975) or as 'good' (eg as giving a new and preferable status to the trade unions by means of which they share authority under structural and procedural rules (cf Donovan Commission, 1968; Bullock Committee, 1977).

One way of relating the concepts of domination and power is to regard these rules as the mediating variable. This is argued by Clegg: "Power is about the outcome of issues enabled by the rule of a substantive rationality, which is temporarily and institutionally located. Underlying this rule is a specific form of domination. The progression is from domination→rules→power" (Clegg, 1975, pp 77–8). As this is translated and extended by Whitley (1977, p 57) "rules, therefore, objectify the structure of domination and are foci of orientation for individuals, thus providing the framework for everyday actions and the exercise of power", as Clegg attempts to demonstrate from his empirical study of social

316

relations on a building site. Thus power becomes "the visible exercise of constraint and coercion, while the form of domination is the 'deep structure' which provides the capacity to exercise that power" (Whitley, 1977, p 57). In this perspective, power is an attribute of the system or the organization and is exercisable by individuals (as persons or roles) only by virtue of the rules supporting the 'deep structure' of domination.

The alternative and older view of power is contrary to this in that it sees power as something possessed by an individual to the extent that he can compel others to respond obediently to decisions which those others might not wish to respond to in these ways. This is, *prima facie*, consistent with Weber's use of the term power (*Macht*) to indicate the "probability that one actor within a social relationship will be in a position to carry out his own will despite resistance, regardless of the basis on which this probability rests". (Weber, 1947, p 152). Although he expresses some 'suspicions' about the nature of power, Dahl (1957) has developed the idea that it is something to do with actors—whether individuals, groups, roles, offices, governments, nation-states or other human agencies—whose power over others is seen to rest on the possession of or control over valued resources. Virtually anything can in this sense serve as a valued resource, provided that other actors in the social relationship perceive it as having value. Dahl sees the base of such power as reposing in "all the resources—opportunities, acts, objects etc—that he can exploit in order to affect the behaviour of another" (1957, p 203). Bales suggests that the actor can dispose *more of* four categories of resource than those subject to his authority: (a) material resources, (b) 'political' authority (in the sense of power legitimately to give instructions), (c) status and prestige symbols and (d) a sense of self-indentification with the groups involved in social action (Bales, 1953).

The classical approach to authority has generally followed that of Dahl in regarding authority as made legitimate-domination by the perception of the 'right' of one person to orient the behaviour of another in a purposive fashion. The relationship of superordination and subordination found in the typical organization is then seen to involve individuals who are disparately possessed, as individuals, of the resources which form the basis of power and influence. This is clearly expressed by Simon (1953, p 11; following Barnard, 1938, p 163) in the form: "Authority may be defined as the power to make decisions which guide the actions of another. It is a relationship between two individuals, one 'superior', the other 'subordinate'. The superior frames and transmits decisions with the expectation that they will be accepted by the subordinate. The subordinate expects such decisions and his conduct is determined by them" . . . and "A subordinate is said to accept authority whenever he permits his behaviour to be guided by the decisions of a superior, without independently examining the merits of that decision. When exercising authority the superior does not seek to convince the subordinate, but only to obtain his acquiescence. In actual practice, of course, authority is usually liberally admixed with suggestion and persuasion" (p 11).

Simon himself recognizes a distinction between authority and 'influence', which already appears in the passage quoted. He goes on to make the distinction even more explicit: "The relation of authority by no means comprehends all situations where the verbalizations of one person influence the behaviour of another. The verbs 'persuade', 'suggest' etc, describe several kinds of influence which do not necessarily involve any relationship of authority . . . (As distinct from what happens in the authority relationship) . . . a person who receives a suggestion accepts it as only one of the evidential bases for making his choice—but the choice he will make depends upon conviction. Persuasion, too, centres around the reasons for or against a course of action. Persuasion and suggestion result in a change in the evidential environment of choice which may, but need not, lead to conviction. Obedience, on the other hand, is an abdication of choice" (pp 126–7).

It is also clear that not all of these relationships which imply authority and obedience can be expressed in simple superordination-subordination terms, and a more comprehensive review of the conditions of achieving order and coherence in the system on bases other than those simply of authority seems to be necessary. We will therefore examine the general processes of influence, primarily within the context of organization and management and treat 'authority' as only one special aspect of this general process.

This is not necessarily inconsistent with the Clegg perspective, if one were to ask the other question as to how does it come about that certain actors have possession or control over the resources involved: that may have something to do with the 'domination' question and, in so far as it does, the actor's power is given, but its exercise, as in attempts to influence others in their conduct, will vary with the skill or ability of the actor to deploy or manipulate the resources which the system places at his disposal as the foundation for his power (cf Lukes, 1974), as well as with the norms or truth which give it legitimacy.

This is consistent also with the observation often made that different kinds of organization possess differential amounts of resources of any given type with which to secure compliance of members with the objectives set and sought. Indeed, the *nature* of the organization may in some senses be said to reflect the distribution of such valued resources which it has available for these purposes. Etzioni, for example, typifies organizations on the basis of the power of the typical actor within the orgaization to "induce or influence another actor to carry out his directives or any other norms he supports" (Etzioni, 1961, p 4). He distinguishes three kinds: (a) "coercive power" which "rests on the application or threat of application, of physical sanctions such as the infliction of pain, deformity or death; generation of frustration through restriction of movement; or controlling through force the satisfaction of needs such as those for food, sex, comfort, and the like"; (b) "remunerative power" . . . based on control over material resources and rewards through allocation of salaries and wages, commissions and contributions, "fringe benefits, services and commodities"; and (c) "normative power" resting "on the allocation and manipulation of symbolic rewards and deprivations through employment of leaders, manipulation of mass media, allocation of esteem and prestige symbols, administration of ritual, and influence over the distribution of 'acceptance' and 'positive' response" (Etzioni, 1961, p 5).

In Etzioni's schema, these are congruently linked with three kinds of involvement or response, two of them with high emotional intensity and the other with low. 'Alienative involvement' associated with the first, tends to secure high alienation whereas 'moral involvement', associated with the third, tends to secure high commitment; but the 'calculative involvement' of the middle category tends to be low in intensity and either positive or negative in its consequence. The model he demonstrates is in the form of a matrix, as follows:

A typology of compliance relations

Kinds of power	Kinds of involvement		
	Alienative	*Calculative*	*Moral*
Coercive	1	2	3
Remunerative (utilitarian)	4	5	6
Normative	7	8	9

(*from* Etzioni, 1961, p. 12)

The positions 1, 5 and 9 are seen to be the most likely representations of developed relationships or, in Weber's terminology, the more likely positions which would be taken up in pure types of situation relying on these kinds of power. It is unlikely that such 'pure types' would be found in practice and the matrix should therefore be taken to indicate probabilities of social relations developing in the various ways under the various circumstances of the employment of power or power resources. If prisons offer the nearest illustration of the coercive organization and the religious sect that of the normative organization, most work organizations, whether of the mutual benefit, business, service or commonweal varieties (as distinguished by Blau and Scott, (1963, pp 45–57) on the basis of the prime beneficiary of cooperative activity), would tend to fall into the 'utilitarian' category. It is this which attracts much of the criticism directed at the 'unacceptable face of organizations' in modern society (cf Clegg, 1975).

Although the conceptual language employed to interpret the foundations of influence in organizations may have changed, this kind of categorization to be found in Etzioni has generally influenced the way in which managerial authority to influence others has been analysed. Where more recent writings emphasize domination, obedience to rules and power as derived from the deep structure, earlier writers spoke of authority, acceptance of authority and of power as a personal attribute. The major differences lie in the distinctions between domination as deep structure and authority as superficial process, and between power as institutionalized by the rules developing from the deep structure and power as a resource of influence which may be acquired by those with 'given' authority.

The test of these analyses, is whether they enable us to consider the manner in which changes are taking place in the choice and use of the methods of influence—the ability of one to secure the compliance of another with his wishes—which may theoretically be available to the person in a position of domination or authority. Because it is this dynamic process, indicated in Cartwright's assertion that "in choosing a means of influence an agent is guided by a theory of human nature and constrained by ethical and legal prescriptions deriving from the larger social environment" (Cartwright, 1965, pp 14–15) which must be the major interest of students of any brand of management.

The forms of influence
Partly because of these constraints upon choice, the actual forms taken by methods of influence in work organizations are often narrower and more specific than the broad concepts used by Etzioni imply. Thus physical coercion in the sense of confinement in a prison or the use of physical violence or its threat are not usually associated with work relationships, but confinement to a work bench or station and the subjection of the individual to threatening environmental conditions are not unknown. In addition some of the

320

more clandestine forms of the method may still be recognized, even in situations where some of the more blatant forms of manipulation would be regarded as quite abhorrent: the manipulation of rewards and penalties in unilateral or autocratic fashion may have given way to joint regulation of rewards, but the economic structure itself is taken as a fact of life and employed to limit the opportunities for the creation of alternative forms of incentive; persuasion may commonly exist in work organizations as a basis for developing compliance but the basic 'bargaining processes' are often conducted on the basis of the withholding of relevant information from the individual or the representatives of the trade union.

The methods of influence available within modern organizations may be categorized following the broad conception to be found in Etzioni, but relating the categories more directly to the normal (or more probable) situation to be found there.

Category of means	Open manifestation	Latent structure
Physical restriction	The 'discipline' of work	The underlying design of work tasks
Economic remuneration	The bargaining over rewards	The structure of the wage system
Normative recruitment	The work rules	The structure of authority

Thus work organizations do not make use of means of influence most typically associated with physical coercion in the general situation (such as imprisonment), but they do impose a discipline upon the worker in his performance of work. This discipline has both an open manifestation in the form of articulated and understood rules of work which are derived from the nature of the work task to be carried out, and a latent element which is associated with the particular manner in which the work tasks are constructed in the first place (eg on principle of division of labour within a framework of co-ordinated work activity). Thus even if all work rules were directed at no more than merely getting the work done in a co-ordinated fashion, they would still have some effect in *restricting* the worker physically in that interest. Where they also support the maintenance of existing status arrangements in organizations, they may also impose a greater physical restriction upon him.

The manager, as designer of the work tasks and the arrangements for co-ordination, thus has a 'power' to influence or compel compliance just because, like Lewin's 'gatekeeper', he can manipulate the physical (work) environment of the worker, and thus vary the nature of the restrictions imposed. In the work context, it is this capacity for controlling the physical environment which characterizes this method of influence, referred to as 'ecological control' in some treatments (eg Cartwright, 1965). Other methods of influence (eg persuasion and bartering) could similarly be treated as involving manipulation or modification of the environment—of the informational environment from which the individual might choose or of the reward and penalty environment within which he must make his calculative decisions—but in these two cases the aspects of the environment which change are essentially abstract (or more abstract) than in the case of influence by environmental restriction. Furthermore, the term restriction is used in this context because it is common for this method to be employed in a relatively secretive fashion, the object of manipulating the environment in a particular fashion not being disclosed to those who are likely to be affected (and hence the other element of the definition of manipulation that the subject is usually unaware of the influence attempt) (cf Gilman, 1962; Rosenberg and Pearlin, 1962).

This kind of manipulation or ecological control in the work context is currently subject to change, partly under the influence of new legislative prescriptions (eg for time off) and partly under the influence of the joint search for new structures of influence within this category (eg in the direction of job enrichment and autonomous work groups in line-flow work). To the extent that many more managerial decisions are being made subject to joint determination or agreement, the power of the manager to influence 'as a gatekeeper' in Lewin's sense is also being diminished, and consequently pressuring managements to discover a new set of acceptable rules which will allow the work to continue to be done at acceptable levels of performance. This is one way in which developments in the fields of job enrichment and productivity bargaining may be viewed, and it is also one explanation of the upsurge of interest on the part of managements in job design and methods of rule-making (see below, chs 8 and 9).

In contrast, work organizations do make significant use of the method of influence identified as economic remuneration. In such organizations, where the main objective is the production of material wealth, there is available to the owners or the controllers (if they are different) an amount of material resources which can be deployed in this way to secure compliance, ie to influence the behaviour of the employees, and largely for this reason such enterprises are essentially utilitarian in that they rely upon this kind of power to secure compliance with their rules, conventions and norms. In non-commercial enterprises, such resources are less readily to hand and compliance is less easy to secure by this means (see above, pp 257–67).

In its simplest and most open form, this method of influence is that of using the wage system and wage structure within the framework of the individual contract of employment, to effect 'compliance': it is the method of incentive in the broad sense of that term. The determination of the 'consideration' in the contract has over the years changed from being a matter of unilateral decision to being one of joint negotiation or bartering with the workers' representatives, and to that extent has become more open. But the wage determination processes take place within the framework of a wage system by which, social security and family income supplement payments apart, the distribution of wealth in our society is effected, and there is little pressure to change that part of the 'deep structure' of the system. Because of this greater 'openness' in the fixing of economic rewards, there are those who would regard this method of influence as the 'most democratic' because it is the most rational and the least associated with emotion.

In this method influence is attempted and effected by the offer of rewards and penalities associated with various behaviours and the autonomous decision of the other (the one to be influenced) as to which reward/penalty combination he will go for, and therefore which behaviour he will adopt in order to secure his most favoured position in the scale of material preferences. It is theoretically possible to conceive this notion in strictly non-material terms (eg by regarding say affection by a wife or information of a wise man as resources which could figure as 'rewards') but it is more useful to restrict the meaning to material resources which can be offered as a reward or removed as a penalty, for our present purposes, even if current theorizing in the social sciences promises to treat all human relationships as 'exchange' relationships (Berger, Zelditch and Anderson, 1972).

The main criticism levelled at this means of influence is that it subordinates all decisions to the power and the criteria of utility. The alternative viewpoint is that there are questions of right and wrong which have nothing to do with the utilities which may be generated by the choice presented.

These other questions—of right and wrong—form the focus of attention in the third means of influence identified above, that of normative recruitment, whereby one seeks to persuade another as to the rightness or wrongness of a course of action. There are therefore, those who would hold that this is a method of influence more consistent with democratic society than utilitarian methods. Persuasion may have the disadvantage that it takes time, but the advantage that it leads to commitment on a more moral and therefore more permanent basis. Much of the recent advocacy of methods of joint decision taking has rested upon just this supposition, that by such means people will be more likely to accept the decisions and act upon them (cf Bullock, 1977, p 25).

Like any other method of influence, persuasion can be employed openly as in debate or clandestinely as in the dissemination of propaganda and, like other methods, it can be directed by those who have ownership of or control over the information and the means of its transmission. Most discussions in the literature on this general subject have, for rather obvious reasons, concentrated on the mass media—newspapers, radio broadcasting, and telecasting—and have thus been concerned with issues of media monopoly, information distortion (as in brainwashing propaganda and advertising) and the inherent properties of messages in relation to influence. These studies have their direct relevance to the management process, but it is easy in discussing persuasion at this macro-level to fail to notice the functional equivalents of media monopoly and message construction at the level of the organization.

In the employment context, complete monopoly has probably never been possible in the period of the industrial revolution: it was never possible for the factory owner, however autocratic and powerful, to seal off completely the competing messages (favouring unions or any other alternative philosophy to that of despotism). Nevertheless, the structure of such employment organizations may be represented as attempts to (a) structure one-way communication from the top-down in pursuit of a monopoly of communication and (b) (when that patently fails) structure alternative channels of communication to supplement these, leading to a structure of multiple channelling, within which competition for control of men's minds or at least their loyalty takes place. Nevertheless, it is for this reason that the management textbook will spend a considerable number of words on the subjects of communications and channelling (see below, pp 344–61).

The choice of method
Which of the theoretically available methods of influence will be chosen in the particular case of intended influence will naturally finally depend on the situation in which the question is asked. Nevertheless the choice is by no means as open as a mere listing of the alternatives by itself would suggest. Although the choice will always be made by the individual influencer concerned, and therefore his predispositions and predilections will influence the choice, that choice will be constrained by factors other than his own reading of what would be correct or best in the situation. These are firstly, the cultural values which he has acquired through socialization; secondly, the

restrictions and opportunities created through the law; and thirdly, the restrictions and opportunities which are formed by convention. All of these are likely to play their part in choosing a method of influence.

The first of these cultural values is in essence a matter of acceptance on the part of the individual of that which is customary in usage. It is to be distinguished (in the present context) from that which is enforced through some agency (law) or that which is upheld by social and moral disapprobation but without formal agency (convention). What is customary in a given set of circumstances is not merely to be established by general cultural values (eg that people in our society generally eat breakfast in the morning) but also by the sub-cultural values of the enterprise or the occupational association or 'set' (or group) to which the individual may belong. Some authors have attempted to illuminate this aspect, and have done so in various ways and at different 'levels' of culture.

The identification of 'assumptions' held by managers about the nature of man and about human behaviour, by McGregor (1960) is an attempt to describe the most general determinants of the choice of means of influence in our society. This is to recognize that in our kind of society there are (at least) two broad sets of cultural values current which could lead managers or planners to adopt one set of means rather than another. He does not call forth any evidence of a specific relationship between assumption and choice of means, but his presentation is persuasive. By implication, he suggests that managerial style (the manner in which the manager addresses himself to his influencing task) reveals a conformity to one or other of these two sets of cultural value systems in so far as these allude to the nature of the human being.

The one set of assumptions which he associated with his Theory X style hold that:

(a) The average human being has an inherent dislike of work and will avoid it if he can
(b) Because of this human characteristic of dislike of work, most people must be coerced, controlled, directed, threatened with punishment to get them to put forth adequate effort toward the achievement of organizational objectives
(c) The average human being prefers to be directed, wishes to avoid responsibility, has relatively little ambition, wants security above all (pp 33–34).

In contrast, the assumptions behind the Theory Y style (which McGregor believes are more consistent with the findings of social science) are as follows:

325

(a) The expenditure of physical and mental effort in work is as natural as play or rest. The average human being does not inherently dislike work. Depending upon controllable conditions, work will be a source of satisfaction (and will be voluntarily performed) or a source of punishment (and will be avoided if possible)

(b) External control and the threat of punishment are not the only means of bringing about effort toward organizational objectives. Man will exercise self-direction and self-control in the service of objectives to which he is committed

(c) Commitment to objectives is a function of the rewards associated with their achievement. The most significant of such rewards, eg the satisfaction of ego and self-actualization needs, can be direct products of effort directed toward organizational objectives

(d) The average human being learns, under proper conditions, not only to accept but to seek responsibility. Avoidance of responsibility, lack of ambition and emphasis on security are generally consequences of experience, not inherent human characteristics

(e) The capacity to exercise a relatively high degree of imagination, ingenuity and creativity in the solutions of organizational problems is widely, not narrowly, distributed in the population

(f) Under the conditions of modern industrial life, the intellectual potentialities of the average human being are only partially used (1960, pp 47–48).

Clearly, from the terms used in these statements, the Theory X assumptions are likely to be held more congruently with a coercive and manipulative means of influence, and the Theory Y assumptions with a more persuasive and open means of influence. This is likely to be true only at high levels of generalization: there is no suggestion that there is a one-for-one relationship nor that there is any simple mutual exclusiveness involved.

Whilst examples can certainly be found of both managers and whole enterprises revealing congruent Theory X and Theory Y styles of management, it would not yet be possible to describe the Theory Y style (and its associated assumptions) as customary in our society. The Theory X style is more likely to attract this description. Interest must focus, however, on the way in which society may well be moving from the one mode of orientation to social action (Weber, 1947, p 120) to another, the one emphasizing the Theory X and the other the Theory Y style. Such movement, given the entrenched position of the one, supported as it is by both law and convention, must depend not merely upon the identification of alternatives as has been done through social scientific research and theorizing, but more importantly upon the importation of conventional sanction and legal enforcement to support the change, and/or the recognition by those in office that self-interest demands such a change.

Examples of all three can be quoted.

A consideration of very recent changes in the law on employment (ie without needing to take the broad sweep of legislative developments over the longer period of the industrial revolution), suggests that there is a movement away from coercive and clandestine means of influence. The greater security of employment enforced under various recent Acts can be regarded as an example of the use of law to remove at least some of the validation of coercive methods of influence. The requirements of the law on union recognition, disclosure of information, and 'participation' promise to make other means of influence more 'open' (see below, p 405 *et seq*).

What is merely fashionable in this area is difficult to distinguish from more permanent but new conventions. The new generation of managers, whose thinking and approach is influenced by the business schools from which they more often obtain their qualifications, may be expected to establish such new conventions by their actions. Informal sanctions to be found in this 'in-group' at least tend to uphold the value of a new rational approach to the managerial task, and this rationality includes that associated with the logics of the social sciences (see chapter 9 below). In more mundane terms, the emphasis is placed on better human relations, better communications, clearer definition of objectives, more carefully worked out methods and techniques etc, but it is considered that which makes things 'better' is a more fully developed 'rationality', based on the relevant policy and social sciences.

More directly apposite in this context of conventional approaches is the attempt to develop (in the 1960s) a kind of convention that payment of workers should be on a measured day-work basis. In industrial contexts, many brave attempts were made to abandon piecework and other forms of payment by results arrangements in favour of a system of flat rate payment for an 'incentive' level of performance (Brown, 1962). Although by no means everyone fell in with this new convention, it did assume a degree of sanction within the in-group (cf NBPI Report No 65). The particular interest of this development, which occurred at a time when the National Health Service and local government were moving in the opposite direction (see NBPI, Report No 169, 1971), lies in the restriction which management thereby placed upon itself in exerting influence on productivity behaviour. If coercion as a means was currently being reduced, and detailed manipulation of the economic gains and costs was to be denied to them, then influence would depend more upon persuasion in some form or upon the direct derivation of satisfaction from worker compliance with managerial authority.

Partly as a consequence of the application of this fresh element of rationality in managerial thinking, and partly as a continuation of an older-established pursuit of self-interest, managerial styles—particularly as they affect the treatment of labour—are changing. It is not yet universal, nor even customary, for managers to involve workers in decision taking but it is clearly becoming more so and, as has been suggested elsewhere (Thomason, 1971) the explanation for this change may lie in either or both of these two factors of convention and enlightened self-interest on the part of managers in a changing economic and social environment. The growth of job enrichment may, for example, reflect a more widespread managerial acquaintance with the work of Maslow (1954) and Herzberg (1959), but it also responds to the new climate of worker non-response to traditional means of influence; there was also some evidence in the development of productivity bargaining that some managements at least were able and willing to use this opportunity to create a new style in matters of mutual influence (see below, pp 399–403).

Thus, in summary, it may be that it is becoming 'more customary' to adopt methods of influence which are different in their underlying assumptions about man and different in their nature from those which have been habitually employed in work organizations. The direction of the movement appears to be no more significant than a reduction in reliance on coercion and on economic bartering and a greater emphasis on persuasion.

If "in choosing a means of influence an agent is guided by a theory of human nature and constrained by ethical and legal prescriptions deriving from the larger social environment", as Cartwright suggests (1965, pp 14-15) the manner in which this type of influence is brought to bear upon the agent's decision is likely to emphasize some much smaller membership group than 'the culture' or 'the society'. Whilst no doubt some at least of the values he holds will have been implanted in the family, the school and the various peer groups of which he has been a member, two organizations are likely to exert a more immediate and continuing influence upon him. The first will be the employing enterprise, within which he will be called upon to act; the second will be the occupational association in which he perceives himself to have meaningful membership.

The employing enterprise not only possesses purpose, objectives and 'policies', but some of those 'policies' are themselves prescriptive of standards to be applied in choosing means of influence to be employed. A commercial company which lays down what methods shall and what methods shall not be employed by salesmen in making a sale, or a service organization which prescribes and proscribes the methods of communication to be adopted in relation to clients, both provide examples of the way in which 'marketing' policies may set limits to the methods of influence which may be employed. Similarly, enterprises may restrict the means of influence to be employed in relation to employees—by 'abandoning piecework' or 'instituting a charter for the workpeople' (cf GKN-Shotton, 1970). Such policies then have the force of 'convention' within the more restricted context of the enterprise, and appropriate sanctions will be available and applied to effect compliance. In time they may acquire the stamp of custom.

How far managers are likely to respond to these kinds of constraint on their choice of means it is not possible to say except on the basis of empirical investigation of the kind conducted by Rosenberg and Pearlin (1962). Nevertheless, common observation suggests that these 'policies' and 'practices' have some impact, and that managers do allow their choices to be influenced by what is dominant in the standards laid down in this way. Possibly the commonest manner by which such changes in method are effected is that which follows from the adoption of new techniques which become fashionable and therefore acceptable to managements (or some members of the management group). Examples might be found in the spread of 'human relations', management by objectives, productivity bargaining (in some manifestations, see below, pp 388–402) or job enrichment. In each of these cases, some shift in the dominant means of seeking compliance can be discerned, even if (and there is empirical evidence to suggest this too) some managers caught up in these changes either refuse or are reluctant to go along with them, preferring instead and as far as they are able to continue with the old and known methods.

Power, rules and structure
Such developments may be treated as a managerial response to changes in cultural value and legislative requirement or, more simply, to what the managers perceive as the emerging motivational situation. But behind statements of this sort there lies a perspective which recognizes that the power itself, or the means of exercising that power, has been changed by these developments. Put simply, management does not have the means of influence available to it in the middle 1970s that it may have had in the middle 1920s or the middle 1870s. A manager does not have the power to dismiss an employee without sufficient reason or minimum notice for 'cause', and he has less power to maintain the worker's level of 'application' to his work by coercion or incentive than he had at some earlier date. A number

of experimental developments of the kind listed on the preceding page, may then be regarded as attempts to re-establish the power or the authority of the manager in the changed circumstances.

This is, in turn, attempted by rewriting both the substantive rules and the procedural rules of the manager's authority. On the one side of this coin, the rules about how work tasks shall be constructed are being rewritten under the headings of job design and job restructuring; the rules about how the consideration in the employment contract shall be determined are being rewritten in new conceptions of wage and salary determination and administration; the 'works rules' of discipline are being rewritten to conform to new legislative prescriptions and emergent cultural values. On the other side, the rules about how any of these kinds of substantive decision are to be taken—whether by 'the management' or by joint committees—are also being rewritten, usually by drawing the frontiers closer to the 'joint' end of the continuum than to the unilateral managerial end. Although this often does include the trade union representatives in the process, there are many examples where 'jointness' is perpetrated outside the strict framework of union participation, suggesting that this phenomenon is not solely the consequence of increases in 'trade union power'.

This development calls in question the whole conception of what constitutes the foundation of the manager's authority. In terms of strict bureaucratic organization theory, that foundation was provided by the appointment to 'office'; in terms of what seems to be emerging in the more open or organic type of organization, it may be founded upon what that manager (regardless, almost, of his formal 'office') can contribute to the resolution of the problems which people in that organizational situation face. That contribution in turn may not fall to be judged simply in terms of whether the manager can 'solve' the problem by unilateral decision but rather in terms of his help to others to create a solution in a way which they can appreciate and to an end which they can accept. Sapiential authority, rather than bureaucratic authority may be placed at a premium, and sapiential authority may in this context be conceived in terms of contribution to problem-solving or project-development rather than in terms of certified competence in a discipline (like accountancy or personnel management). If this is a correct interpretation of the present trend, the rewriting of the rules will mean a reconceptualization of managerial work (Burns and Stalker, 1961; see also chapter 9 below).

Taken in conjunction with the redefinition of worker and employer statuses in modern society, this trend may thus be expected to effect changes in the structure of work organization. The deep structure can be expected to have stronger tendencies to persistence, but the manifest structures of authority and influence may be expected to develop in the direction of the 'organic' organization based upon a more equitable kind of partnership (which may, but need not necessarily, reflect itself in comparative income levels). This can be expected, first, to be associated with considerable uncertainty—about the individual's place in the scheme of things organizational—and secondly, with increased communication intended to reduce it, which may in the longer term then produce new structures, supported by new rules, and different patterns of power and authority related to the securing of compliance with work tasks.

The challenge in this is to the pervasive pattern of bureaucratic organization to be found in modern society. 'Bureaucracy' in the conception advanced by Weber was an organizational vehicle for the application of rational-legal authority to the solution of work problems. He was little concerned with the precise or detailed manner in which modern undertakings were to be organized, and such questions were left to be tackled by the exponents of scientific management, like Taylor. Weber's interest was in the much more fundamental question of how it could be that people who were not related to one another (by kinship), who were not necessarily known to one another through neighbourly association (as in the traditional community) and who therefore might be thought of as strangers to one another, were nevertheless willing to allow themselves to be welded into a highly-efficient, cooperative activity, which was how he saw the modern bureaucracy. His description of the bureaucracy was therefore merely an attempt to answer this question, not to say in any detail how it actually worked.

What set the bureaucracy apart from other forms of organization for Weber (in addition to the distinction of its efficiency) were five characteristics of the new thing:

(a) the *division* of the total task into specific jobs or specialized offices which could then be defined with some precision
(b) the reliance upon a *hierarchy* of such offices to make co-ordination of the diverse tasks possible
(c) the animation of the office-holder's position in accordance with a well-developed set of abstract *rules and procedures*
(d) the avoidance of personal biases and favouritism by concentrating the office-holder's performance upon an *impersonal* approach to clients and problems
(e) the organization of the offices in such a way that an individual could be motivated to accept the conditions of employment in a bureaucracy by the creation of a legitimate expectation of a

'career' within it.

Together, as Weber saw them, these defined the individual member's role (both in tasks and in terms of dependency), offered him the incentive of personal progression in career terms and ensured that both aspects would be developed within a framework of equity (guaranteed by the formalistic impersonality of science or rationality).

Certain things inevitably followed from these characteristics:

First, that the bureaucracy must take care to ensure that the way in which work is divided up into official duties rests upon a kind of rationality which the individual himself could understand and appreciate (and not, for example, upon incomprehensible whim or fancy)—the care taken to describe jobs in modern organizations is one manifestation of this (see ch 3 above).

Secondly, that the bureaucracy must also take care to ensure that those who are given these 'offices' are competent to carry out the official duties, the competance in turn being treated in the same 'rational' way as the definition of duties so that the individual can determine it for himself (and so acquire it by education or experience): the emphasis on qualification and training in modern organizations is a manifestation of this (see ch 3 above).

Thirdly, that the bureaucracy must ensure that the necessary exercise of authority within the arrangement shall be subject to and limited by a set of rules, rationally-founded, and certainly not arbitrary (as has been indicated in the present chapter).

Fourthly, the organization would, in order to serve the interests of this same rationality, have to establish a coherent 'personality' of its own, so that it would have identity and integrity as a 'rational' entity. This manifests itself in structures which, *inter alia*, admit the possibility of adjudication of issues in terms of doctrines of rationality (cf Brown, 1951) and elaborated in processes of recording, reporting and storing information about the activities of the entity, so that no matter who happens to stay or leave, the undertaking has a 'memory' of its own which can be used and appealed to in the interests of consistency (cf Hahlo and Trebilcock, 1977, p 42 *et seq*; and above, pp 42–49).

These imperatives of organizations (cf Selznick, 1964) arise from the essential 'rationality' to which, in Weber's view, as it is expressed in rules, there is a probability that people (members) will orient their behaviour: it is therefore by virtue of this probability that the 'strangers' will allow themselves to be influenced by the rules which develop from this new rationality. This has many implications but two are particularly relevant to this discussion. First, that it is cast in terms of probability: there is no certainty, even in Weber's original characterization, that people *will* so orient their behaviours and indeed a large number of studies have been made of organizations which show just how limited may be the probability (cf March and Simon, 1958, ch 3, and in Pugh, 1971, ch 2). Secondly, that issue apart, there is nothing automatic about the orientation of the modern individual to the rationality of the modern organization: somebody, somewhere, has a task of effecting the kind of consequence which Weber is describing and analysing and thereby of increasing 'the probability'.

It was this latter aspect which attracted the attention of a number of men of experience of managing organizations, who felt it prudent to express in writing just what the role of management ought to be in these modern organizations, in order to make them in reality as efficient as Weber had suggested that, in theory, they were. Into this category fall a large number of writers, chief of whom are Taylor, Urwick and Fayol as the exponents of 'scientific management' (in which 'scientific' has similar connotations to the 'rationality' of Weber). Thus where Weber merely sought to answer the question 'what are the distinguishing characteristics of these modern organizations?', these other writers sought to indicate what it is that 'management' must do if it is to be efficient and 'rational'.

Taylor's main contribution to organization theory lay in his attempt to define competence in modern complex organizations. In his view, the main problem with large organizations was that management had not fully recognized what role was required of it and as a consequence was inefficient in managing modern enterprises. It was therefore necessary for managers to make systematic studies of the tasks that were required and, on the basis of such studies, to develop criteria and standards by which they could exercise their real functions of directing and controlling the activities of the workers. It was this which led him into his main preoccupation with work study and to develop his various theories of 'scientific management'. But these activities were essentially subservient to the general aim of defining not only the work which the individual worker would have to do but also that of the manager. Once these were known, it would be possible to define the required types and amounts of competence that both the managers and the workers needed. Where Weber had concerned himself with a simple description of how organizations achieved efficiency, Taylor set about prescribing the manner in which efficiency in modern organizations might be improved. The principles on which competence should be defined were virtually incidental to the realization of this particular objective.

In deriving these principles, like his co-founders of the scientific

333

management school and like Weber himself, Taylor tended to base his deductions upon a mechanical system analogy. An organization ought, if it was managed 'properly', to run like a machine. Urwick makes this quite clear in his argument that it is necessary to use an engineering design analogy in his prescription of organizational principles, simply because men are just not sophisticated enough to understand and develop organizations on the basis of an organic or chemical analogy. In his view, it is largely a matter of determining what the relationship shall be between line and staff or what the relationship shall be in a numerical sense between supervisors and supervised, and on the basis of this to put together the pieces of a jigsaw. If in the end the jigsaw is a rather loose one this must be accepted, so they argue, because although one can make the formal organizational definition fairly precise on these sorts of principles, one cannot equally machine the individuals who will have to carry out the formal duties which are thus defined.

The classical definition of management as it emerged therefore emphasizes that what distinguished managers was their use of authority to organize, direct and control the activities of non-managers (Tannenbaum, 1948). What emerged as the function of the non-manager was essentially to work at the behest of the manager who would automatically define the type and amount of work that the non-manager would be required to do. The possibility that this division of the task of co-ordinating activity in modern organizations might in itself lead to tension between the managers and the non-managers was not a matter to which Taylor gave a great deal of thought. For him it was self-evident that the efficient organization, run along these lines, would be as much in the interests of the workers as the managers or owners, and when once it had been explained to the workers it would be accepted by them in this spirit. The scientific management approach as this came to be called was therefore prone to condemn conflict whether verbal or behavioural as somehow being aberrational and, for Taylor, who was highly critical of what he called 'systematic soldiering', such reaction on the part of workers could be expected in those circumstances where management did not have proper control. This in turn for him meant that *management* was not competent and was not performing its 'official duties', as these might have been described by Weber.

In the work of these two men there is an implicit or explicit assumption that the adjustment of the individual to the role which he is given or acquires in organization will be effected through the mechanisms of the bureaucracy itself. That is, the individual will be enabled to adjust to his role according to the extent to which the organization defines the work role itself in a rational fashion, equally rationally defines the skill or competence that the individual requires for it and, thirdly, determines the system of rewards and punishments which will be applied to encourage the individual to behave in the required fashion. Whether this assumption would hold in practice was not questioned.

It was left to the psychologists to subject the assumption to testing. The early work in this field sought to determine the capability of the individual to exercise the roles which organizations were prone to assign to them. In Britain the work of the Industrial Fatigue Research Board (later the Industrial Health Research Board) followed in the mainstream of psychology at that time, which was mainly concerned with explaining and measuring the differences between individuals. They were not particularly concerned with organizational design. The kind of problems that were thrown up by the first world war, and which tended to structure the approach of British scientists to industrial problems, were essentially the sort which scientific management was quite ready to recognize. These were the problems of how long an individual worker could work without undue fatigue, of the effect various physical variables at work might have on work performance, and so on. This approach was also to be found in the United States and the earlier Hawthorne experiments conducted under the auspices of the Western Electric Company in the 1920s adopted a very similar approach even though ultimately the outcome of this research was to be significantly different. Although therefore the psychologists addressed themselves to rather different questions from those which interested Taylor and the other scientific management proponents, they were nevertheless concerned to supply answers to a similar kind of question, namely just what an organization could expect of an individual under definable conditions. The assumption here was that if the physical conditions of lighting, ventilation, heating and timespan were adequately controlled, improvements in productivity might be expected. It is true that some at least of this psychological experimentation was concerned to answer the question on what effect variation in the physical environment had upon the health or well-being of the workers, and not with the simple question of improved efficiency. Nevertheless, the sort of question being asked at this time was similar to the sort of question being asked by Taylor. The full development of scientific management therefore might be said to have depended not only on Taylor with his stopwatch but upon the psychologists with their attempt to relate efficiency to certain features of the physical environment.

Certain other writers on formal organizations, particularly Fayol and Urwick, tackled the related problem of how a person should be related to the work tasks of organizations. These writers were mainly men of experience who sought to use their experience to develop a set of principles governing the development of efficient organization. They tended to say, on this main question, that it was important for the organization to ensure that work activities were defined as precisely as possible (in this they simply followed in Taylor's footsteps) and then to attempt to select people as far as possible to fill these defined positions. Their view of human nature and human ability tended to be similar to or indeed under the influence of the early work of the psychologists, and they therefore concluded that there was no hope at all of securing individuals who would be as precisely defined in their competence and ability as the positions into which they would be put.

The burden of the argument of these authors is therefore that organizations must ensure, as far as is humanly possible to do so, that the purely formal (that is the non-human) aspects of organizations shall be as precisely defined as possible. Only in this way can the organization hope to move towards efficiency. Since it would rely on similarities between human beings to ensure the efficiency for the organization, then the organization must in turn seek to define roles within itself, so precisely as to ensure as much efficiency on this score as possible.

This led these writers to look in particular at two problems. First, that of finding a place for experts in organizations whose administration really called for people with *generalized* ability to supervise. They thus followed Taylor in making a distinction between the 'brainwork' and the 'supervision' of production. They also recognized that they could not have in the supervisors of production the same degree of expertise across the whole range that they might find if they hired specialists in each particular field. Therefore the problem became one of finding some organizational accommodation of both generalist supervisors and specialist experts. Their solution was the 'line and staff' organization.

The line part of this is made up of those who have authority over those who carry out the many specialist roles into which the production work tasks have been divided. The four people, the owner and the sales, financial and factory managers, together with their respective foremen and supervisors, are the examples in figure 11(a). Their authority and their responsibility for the co-ordination of these tasks therefore tends to be general. The staff part of the organization, on the other hand, will be made up of those who have expertness in particular areas. They appear in figure 11(b) as cost accountant, chief estimator, maintenance engineer and personnel manager. These people cannot be directly placed in the line management as the whole exercise would then tend to become confused. Therefore they are

336

given a less direct and specialist relationship to the line organization, whose roles they are supposed to supplement.

The second problem to which the writers on formal organizations addressed themselves is the problem of the span of control. Here again their view was that people are so variable in themselves and therefore so variable in the competence which they would have to supervise in other people, that the organization must give careful attention to the definition of the number of people they should be expected to control and co-ordinate. Examination of a large number of organizations suggested that a span of control of between six and 10 people seemed to be in the competence which they would possess to supervise other people. Certain other writers have suggested that the span of control can be worked out precisely on the basis of a mathematical formula. In order to do so, it is necessary to gather data on the features of organization explored by these writers. First, the precise definition of the work roles, supported by work study data and adequate competent instruction of the worker in his duties, which would indicate how much work there was and, from the supervisor's point of view, how varied it might be. Secondly, the precise delimitation of the extent of the co-ordination problem for the supervisor, the data on this being capable of presentation on the basis of line-of-balance charts, showing not only roles but also sequences and even the points at which other departments might become involved (see figure 12).

The suggestion in this is therefore at one with the idea that the organization's responsibility in these matters is to be precise in the definition of official duties (of which supervision is a part) and to leave the question of whether individuals can perfectly cope with this precise definition for consequential consideration. The effect of this with line and staff management is to suggest a principle on which the organizational designer might work. He now has an apparently precise relationship established which he can incorporate into organizational design decisions.

Between them, these various writers provided a basic justification of this manner of organizing authority and a fairly detailed blueprint for designing it. We are provided with both basic principles and formulae. From this, the bureaucracy could then be constructed and in principle it ought to have ensured efficient organization of authority, efficient co-ordination and control, efficient communications and influence (Belasco and Arlutton, 1969). Under some circumstances and in some situations all these consequences might indeed be expected to follow (Burns and Stalker, 1961) but in others not (Blau, 1955). Although there have been experiments with a large number of variants on this same general theme, for example, as in

337

matrix, project and professional organization (cf Thomason, 1973), there appears to remain unsolved the problem of designing organizations for flexibility and responsiveness to changes in the internal and external environments.

A growing body of research data on organizations is however available, which shows that quite different basic patterns of organization structure are to be discerned, usually as contingent upon novel market and technology situations (Woodward, 1958; Burns and Stalker, 1961). From these deliberately branded organizational structures have been developed which, after adequate diagnosis of the situation to which the structure has to be applied (ie contingency analysis), can be 'plugged in' to effect increased organizational efficiency or health.

Although most of these might appropriately be regarded as 'a series of footnotes to Weber' (as Katz (1964, p 431) regards all sociological theories of complex organizations) by virtue of their exclusive pursuit of rationality, they can also be regarded as attempts (perhaps even desperate ones) to find ways of decreasing the rigidity and increasing the flexibility of role prescriptions in changing environments. This is most clearly depicted in the continuum of 'organizational forms' provided by Rice and Bishoprick (1971, p 208), ranging from autocracy at the one extreme (of rigidity) to 'egalitarianism' at the other (of flexibility). In between, reading along this continuum, they recognize bureaucracy, systems, decentralization, collegism, and federation as providing identifiable points along it. Most of the current debate on this subject of structure tends to cluster around the middle of this range, stressing the differences between relatively closed or mechanistic organizations of essentially the bureaucratic/systems type, and the relatively open or organic organizations of the decentralized/collegist type. As the Burns and Stalker study in particular shows (see the descriptions of the mechanistic and organic structures offered on pp 119–122) there are very real and significant differences on the dimension of rigidity-flexibility over this relatively narrow range along the full continuum.

The main packages of 'alternative' organization structure, which are being placed before managers for consideration as solutions to the problems diagnosed by them, tend to emphasize the need to recognize and cater for both *change* over time (the notion of organic development) and difference in environmental demand or pressure (the notion of appropriate structures for different objectives and technologies).

Curiously, the principles which are in question were examined by Weber and Taylor in their respective works, although both tended to attach less real significance to them than they might well have

338

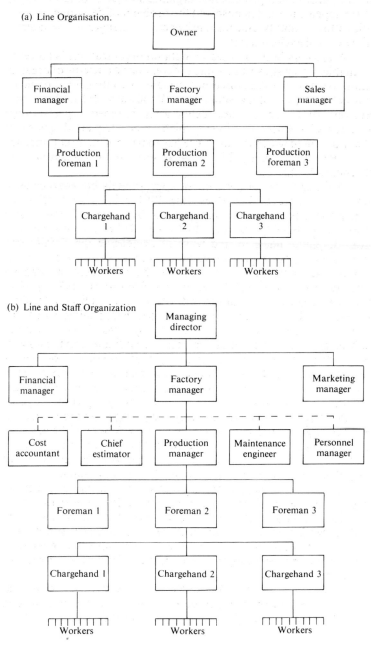

Figure 11

Basic patterns of organisation

(a) Line Organisation.

(b) Line and Staff Organization

Figure 12

A process chart, developed (A) in conventional form, and (B) to show movement between departments and division of work among operators

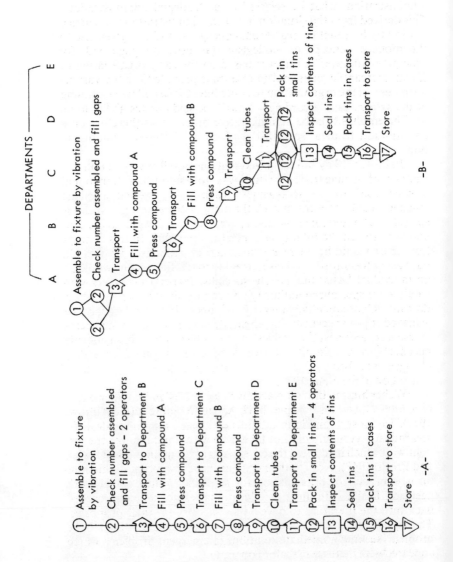

Source: H B Maynard, *Industrial Engineering Handbook*, McGraw Hill, 1967, p 2–60 (reproduced with permission by McGraw Hill)

340

done had they been able to observe the larger-scale service organizations of modern society.

Weber for example identified as one of the historical forms of administration, what he referred to as 'collegial administration'. This derived from the situation in which administration was carried out jointly by equal or near-equal colleagues, and has given rise to the modern concept of 'collegism' (as used on page 338, for example). Admittedly, this was based on the early organization of Italian mercantile cities, but in essence it provided for the various 'members' of the organization to contribute to the collective running of the system, each according—it might be said—to his ability to do so. The emphasis in the administrative process was therefore on a contribution from a 'specialist' base to a 'collective' administration.

In his turn, Taylor recognized that one possible way to take advantage of managerial expertise was to establish a 'functional organization'. In this arrangement, each highly trained specialist manager would concern himself throughout the enterprise with his special and limited function, contributing this, as it were, to the general need to run the totality as expertly as possible. In this conception, there would be no *general* manager or supervisor who would have general authority and responsibility for sections of the whole on an individual basis, but merely specialist (expert) managers who would have specialized authority and responsibility over the whole domain. Consequently, integrity of operation would only be achieved if the specialists saw themselves as required to achieve a 'consensus' amongst themselves—to use a term which has suddenly become currency in the service organizations following recent changes (see Brunel University, working papers on the Reorganization of the NHS, 1973).

Weber himself did not place much emphasis on his collegial administration, and his disciples have tended to ignore it (see Albrow, 1970). Taylor saw functional administration as a somewhat idealistic and industry certainly did not take it up with anything like the fervour with which it adopted the other parts of his main thesis (Urwick and Brech, 1947). Nor for the most part have the recent discussions on new models of organization for scientific bodies, social work agencies, health care units or educational establishments reached back into the literature to develop an ancestry for their proposals. They have instead tended to adopt a more pragmatic approach to the problem, seeking immediate solutions to emergent problems which appeared with increase in scale of operation.

It happens that much of the empirical work which provides the data for the construction of these new models has been undertaken in situations in which either the basic work roles were requisitely ones with high discretion (and low prescription), as with professionals in research and development departments (cf Orth, Bailey and Wolek, 1964; Thomason, 1970) or health and social work (Algie, 1970; Thomason, 1969) or the external and internal environments had changed or were different from the generality (Gouldner, 1955; Burns and Stalker, 1961). These factors appeared to force the organizational structures into more flexible moulds than the conventional 'autocracy-bureaucracy-system' appeared to permit in itself and thus suggested that (a) some problems cannot be solved within a monolithic structure, and therefore (b) some pluralistic coalition (Fox, 1966) or polyarchic stucture (Algie, 1970) which permits wider discretion at the lower (problem-solving) levels of the system, must be substituted for it.

It seems unnecessary to assume that this kind of development must respond only to the nature of the problems and/or the nature of the skill required to resolve them (eg as with the highly trained professional); where, for example, workers of any description have the power to refuse to accept bureaucratic authority, as do the professionals because of the nature of the work they do, a similar structural consequence might have to follow. In other words, changing socio-cultural values and attitudes in themselves may be admitted to the list of factors which might force a structural modification.

What in effect these variants permit is an incease in potential consensus as to objectives, standards, methods and techniques. The unitary and bureaucratic structures tend to rely upon and therefore encourage a degree of arbitrariness. This is tolerable when the centre roles are occupied by people who are themselves competent to take these decisions, but this is likely to happen mainly in relatively unchanging, static situations. Where either a process of change is taking place or where the situation is different from usual, the more 'contributions' in Burns's term which can be brought to bear upon decisions which have to be taken, the more likely is it that the necessary judgements (of reality, required action and optimal action) will be improved. Thus many of these 'alternative' models of structure may be seen as directed towards the encouragement of more normative sharing than is permitted in autocratic and other unitary systems.

Further reading
On the general themes of authority, power and influence, Clegg (1975); Cartwright, in March (1965); and Albrow (1970); or Etzioni (1961) are likely to prove most useful.

On the organizational theme, Blau (1956) and Schein (1970) are useful introductions, to be supplemented by Lupton (1966), Pugh (1971) and Burns and Stalker (1961).

8 Communication and consultation

A communications problem?

We are repeatedly told, usually by those who have some interest to pursue, that there is a communications problem in British industry. 'People', it is suggested, 'cannot work as effectively and as efficiently as they might, and as they might wish, simply because they are not given sufficient information about what is required of them, and are consequently not sufficiently "involved" in the business'. Whether that is true or not is a question which it would be impossible to answer because by dint of long-self-criticism, we have probably convinced everyone that it is so; rightly or wrongly, we therefore believe it to be a fact. By reason of long familiarity, it has, in Weber's language, become a part of the customary usage.

There are a number of reasons why we might regard communications in work organizations as *important*.

One is the reason already hinted at: namely that a large number of people believe it to be a 'problem' which we ought to do something about. In the 1950s, for example, the leaders of the 'human relations movement' became closely associated with a marketing campaign to 'improve communications' through a greater awareness of the role of the group in communication processes in complex organizations. In both world wars, and after the second one particularly, consultation with the generality of employees and goal-setting and review with individual ones developed with the same aim of increasing purposive involvement. For much of this later period, managers have been exhorted to take note of the greater success of first American and now Japanese industry in achieving results through just such involvement. The latest advocacy features the Japanese managing director of Sony who, in 1977, declared the 'English disease' to be a myth as far as Sony's operations in Wales were concerned. Productivity is high and the workers themselves express a considerable pride in their company, their work and their products, and the suggestion has been made that this develops from the regular morning meetings at which all staff discuss what production has been achieved and remains to be achieved in the factory, in the section and by the individual workers.

A second reason is deduced from 'systems theories' which we consider applicable to the work organization. The view taken is that in such systems "information exchange" is the life-blood of the system, just as "energy exchange" is vital to the operation of simpler electro-mechanical systems of action (cf Boulding, 1956; Buckley, 1967, pp 46–50).

This conception rests upon the assumption of an equilibrium condition being the prefered state; from this it follows that communication as the prime mover of complex organizational systems will necessarily occur whenever the equilibrium is upset as a part of the process of restoring it. As Jaques puts it: "Communication is an integral part of the process of change, and occurs whenever the social equilibrium is upset" (Jaques, 1951, p 301). Without efficient communication, therefore, it would follow that the 'system' would develop a pathological condition.

A third reason (which may be not unrelated to the other two) is that both the law, and the law supported by trade union sanctions, now compels an orientation to the development of communications within organizations. Legislation provides for the disclosure of certain types of information both to individual employees in some circumstances and to trade union representatives in others; supporting Codes of Practice, which still function in the Weberian sense as conventions, exhort improved communications through negotiative and consultative mechanisms; and possible future legislation on participation promises to sweep both of these into a new structure of communication in certain organizations, delimited by size. Even those managers who regard minimizing disclosure and consultation as the optimal reponse to this series of developments, are paradoxically, likely to find themselves caught up in increased communications activity in order to effect that response.

A model of communications

A useful starting point for any discussion of communication is provided by the simple closed loop model. At the root of communications lies the simple observation that communication involves one person passing a message of some kind to another who, in turn, is in some way affected by it at least to the extent of hearing or seeing it. Laswell (1969) has expressed this in the form of five questions: "who . . . says what . . . in what way . . . to whom . . . with what effect?". To answer these questions is to describe how communication takes place.

In this model there are therefore two processes which form the mirror image of each other. A *communicator* constructs a *form of message* which is *transmitted as the message* through some *medium* in order that it may be *interpreted* by another; that 'other', the *receiver*, in turn, constructs a *form of message* by reacting, and transmits this as the *return message* through some *medium* in order that it may be *interpreted* by the communicator. The one process is a process of feeding out a communication, and the other one of feeding back a reaction which is comparably 'a communication' which allows effect to be assessed. Following the approach adopted by Shannon and Weaver, (1949) and Schramm (1963), these descriptive statements can be depicted in the form typical of the closed loop or feedback model:

Figure 13
Elements in a communications process

FEEDOUT

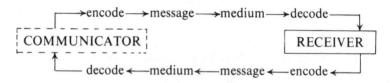

FEEDBACK

Something of the nature of each of these elements may be indicated in order to provide a foundation for consideration of more complex problems of communication in organizations.

1 *The communicator and receiver*   In our area of interest, the communicator and receiver are both *persons*; therefore anything which we might know about the nature of persons is relevant to our understanding of these two elements. But 'communicator' and 'receiver' are terms used to indicate two different roles in the communication process, and surrounding each there is a set of expectations about how the 'person' in question would act or behave in that role.

The communicator might be expected to engage in communication with certain intentions to influence another (or a number of them) and to do so in accordance with his job requirements. A manager, for example, giving instructions to subordinates might be expected to conceive his communication role as defined by the prescribed need to get the production out; in following this prescription he might well act differently from the way he would communicate if he were simply 'being himself'. To the extent that he acts in this way,

346

the way he frames his messages and the intentions behind doing this, will reflect his job prescription. But the formal job requirements are not the only role constraints to which he responds. His occupational group (eg personnel managers), his peer group (his 'generation' of friends) or his work group (the department in which he works) all tend to present role expectations to him, and he will tend to respond to a varying extent to these according to how he establishes *his* reference groups for purposes of comparing or guiding his communicative behaviours (Dalton, 1959; Shibutani, 1962). Such considerations suggest that we should not regard communicators in formal organizations simply as persons: the role constraints responded to will bear upon how they approach the tasks (cf Rose, 1962).

The receiver on the other hand may be regarded as similarly encapsulated in a structure of role expectations. What may be said about group identities in the one case may be applied to the other. But consideration of the receiver role raises another question: whether the receiver should be treated as independent in the receiving? The 'receiver' as the one who physically hears or sees the message may or may not receive it in any more meaningful sense: there may, in other words, be two categories of receiver to be distinguished. The most convincing material on this aspect is to be found in the study of mass media by Katz and Lazarsfeld (1955).

The problem to which these researchers addressed themselves was that of how a message from a newspaper, radio or television (about politics, product advertising or whatever) 'got through' to people. A person might see an advertisement for Brand X on television and this, in one hypothesis, might represent an effective communication in the sense that the individual heard, saw and acted upon it. But such a person is probably also exposed to an advertisement for Brand Y at roughly the same time; the question arises as to how the individual selects between competing messages of this sort, because patently he does not rush out and buy everything that he is urged to buy or vote for every candidate who might solicit his vote.

The answer to these questions is contained in a detailed examination of what emerged as a 'two-step' flow of communications of this sort: The seeing or hearing of the 'original' message is only step one; whether and how it gets translated into a verdict (which to buy or vote for) or an action (like buying or voting) depends on the other step, in which the content of such messages is mediated by a much more local and private group of friends or acquaintances. As Katz and Lazarsfeld uncovered these, they found them to consist of small networks of inter-personal relations within which there would probably be someone (whom they called an influential) who would play a major part in making up individual members minds and spurring them to some action or another. Thus there might be a fashion influential, a domestic chores influential, a political influential and so on, whose opinion on whatever the message was would be given more weight than others, but whose opinion, in turn, might well prove to be a necessary preliminary to any of the members of the network taking any notice whatever of the content of the message. Only when this second step in the communications process had been taken could response to the message really be expected in the case of most people (although of course not all).

In a number of situations which arise in work organizations, something similar to this might be seen to happen. A notice on the noticeboard is read but not acted upon until it has been chewed over in this little group or that; even then it is often possible to discern that not only do individuals go about it in various ways, but quite often little groups of them will respond positively and others negatively as the group influence makes its presence known. It is therefore a hypothesis which is likely to help us explain some of the phenomena which we might see around us in such organizations.

For this kind of varying response to be feasible, we have to recognize that these groups are really going through an evaluation process in relation to the message and that, in doing so, they are measuring possible meanings against their own templates, standards or norms. This must be so if some groups come out of the exercise saying 'Yes' and others 'No' to the same message. It is this feature of the group as a repository of standards of comparison and standards of meaning which is the important variable and not merely the fact of group existence *per se*. Because the group is so equipped, it can help to define reality for the members, as suggested above. It is the set of values which are inherent in such standards which serve to refract communications and which yield varying interpretations of the same message.

2 *Encoding and decoding* Encoding and decoding are relatively technical operations: "effectiveness is . . . dependent upon certain properties of the message transmitted. The possession of skill in constructing messages . . . is thus another base of influence", suggests Cartwright, (1965, p 19). Equally, the possession of a skill in decoding or unscrambling them is an important skill for the recipient, possession of which permits a 'correct' response, whatever the criteria of correctness are in his particular case. In these terms (ie of skill) the question of coding and decoding is likely to reflect upon 'individual differences'; the tasks of encoding or decoding call for attributes and

abilities in the population involved which may be expected to be randomly distributed (cf Miner and Miner, 1977, p 61 *et seq*). Since, as Cartwright reports, "much of the research on persuasion has been concerned with the problem of how to design effective messages" and has raised "issues both of logic and rhetoric in the Aristotelian sense", both the cognitive and affective attainments and dispositions of the individual (communicator or receiver) are likely to be involved (Cartwright, 1965, p 19).

It is widely accepted that categories of person who are widely distanced from each other in terms of life styles are likely to have developed modes of thinking about the reality and a language to support these, which are widely different from one another, and communication between such categories is likely to present major encoding and decoding problems. Whilst this can be done— managers write one 'kind' of report for the board and another for the shop floor in order to deal with this kind of problem—it is more usual to attempt to meet the problem by a chain of translation. In this, the communicator transmits an encoded message to a receiver not far distant, who then re-codes it with further translation for transmission to one not far distant from himself and so on, until the finally translated message reaches its 'final' destination. In effect this creates a potentially long chain of communication of the following form:

$$C \longrightarrow 1 \longrightarrow 2 \longrightarrow 3 \longrightarrow 4 \longrightarrow 5 \longrightarrow R$$

Hierarchical 'chains of command' are essentially of this nature, although they may not have been constructed solely to meet this problem of communication. They may have advantage of allowing suitable translation from one 'private language' to another but they are also likely to involve distortion: the first world war joke of the message being passed along the trenches from the young captain (C) to headquarters (R) illustrates this. C asked, 'Send me reinforcements, I'm going to advance', but R heard eventually 'Lend me three and fourpence, I'm going to a dance'.

Differing ability to encode and decode messages also has its consequences for the development of specialist translating and interpreting functions, which applies at both ends of the 'chain'. In management, for example, it is well established that some functionally specialist roles are created to develop the organization's communications ability and effectiveness (cf Renold 1950 for one example of this kind of response). This often places message construction in the hands of 'staff' specialists, and yet leaves message transmission in the hands of the 'line' managers and supervisors. As

Dalton's study of line and staff managers shows clearly, very real problems of 'communication' can develop between them which serve further to distort the messages which are transmitted (Dalton, 1959).

On the shop floor, the creation of formal positions of this kind may not be in evidence, but it is possible to interpret the findings of Katz and Lazarsfeld and some of the related small group studies in industrial organizations as revealing an informal 'staff' function surrounding the positions of the 'influentials' who mediate and monitor messages and meanings for their 'small groups'. These individuals are not necessarily and not always those who hold formal 'representative' roles within the workforce (Sayles, 1958). But quite often such representatives do carry out this function for their constituents, and with similar consequences for the communication of 'meaning' as were noted by Dalton. This has led some undertakings to take action to try to elevate the first line supervisors into the role of 'influential' in relation to their sections, but with varying success: one of the more recent general attempts to achieve this was made with productivity bargaining in the 1960s, where it was found necessary to extend the volume of communication about desired changes passing through the supervisors on a 'cascading' principle (cf Thomason, 1971, pp 13 and 44; Richbell, 1976, pp 13–19).

3 *The media* The would-be communicators and receivers may present and receive messages through a number of media, most of which are relevant to communications within formal organizations. They may be classified in three broad categories, those of oral, written and situational communications.

1 *Oral communication* The essence of this category is that a would-be communicator speaks to one or more other members of the organization. The recognizable sub-categories are distinguished in the nature of the relationship established between the communicator and those to whom he speaks:

(i) the direct face-to-face communication in which one individual speaks with another, thus allowing direct check by the communicator on the reception of the communication (eg by perception of the demeanour of the recipient or by return communication in the form of question or comment)

(ii) the direct communication in which one individual speaks with another, but via electro-mechanical means (eg a telephone) allowing some check by the communicator on the effectiveness of his message but through a narrower range of perceptions than is possible in the direct face-to-face communication

(iii) the direct communication with the communicator speaking with a small group of people, which has similar characteristics to the first sub-type, although with the added possibility of other influential communications being admitted to the process—whether functional or dysfunctional from the standpoint of the communicator's intentions

(iv) the direct communication with the communicator speaking to a large group of people (whether face-to-face as in a lecture, or on a no-face-to-face basis using one of the mass media) in which reverse communication from the audience is so limited (usually) as to be negligible, and in which therefore the construction of the first message is much more significant in terms of effective communication than in the other categories.

2 *Written communication* The essence of this category is that the message of the would-be communicator is committed to a visible and readable form (whether in words or symbols) and in this form acquires greater permanence and therefore offers a greater opportunity for reader check and interpretation. It would be possible to recognize sub-types on the same kind of dimensions as with oral communication, although this would probably result in a degree of artificiality; it is more useful to recognize sub-types on the basis of both the size of the readership and the intended degree of permanence associated with the communication:

(i)   the inter-personal communication, best exemplified by a letter or a memorandum from one person to a named other (or a few named others) which may serve the same intention as 1(i) or 1(ii) above, although without the same opportunity for communicator check on the efficiency of his communication (except by supplementary means) but with some greater opportunity to effect permanence in the communication

(ii) a more impersonal paper flow to those individuals on a distribution list, ranging all the way from circulation of a relevant journal carrying general information of assumed relevance to those on the list, to a work card which might pass through a whole sequence of operations (and therefore operators) informing each person through whose hands it passes of the decision/action required of him at the time when it does so

(iii) records and reports (to be distinguished only on the grounds of whether what is written remains stationary or is transmitted to others) which exist or are made available for reference purposes and therefore serve as a 'memory' function for the organization, capable of stimulating decisions or actions of a remedial or rectifying type; for this reason, these tend to have longish term

351

consequences as well as permanence simply because they are in written form

(iv) manuals, whether of 'practice' or 'policies', which serve mainly as sources of reference and are therefore designed to have long-term relevance and effects, supporting such other organizational processes as training or induction of personnel.

These forms of written communication tend to be generally more supportive of centralized decision-taking than the oral communications above and vary in their intended permanence of influence upon the action of others.

3 *Situational communication* The essence of this kind of communication is its existence largely independently of oral and written communications (although these may act as supplements or complements to it), communication taking place through example or contagion as the potential recipient perceives a message in the general behaviour of others or in the 'situation' in which he finds himself. The sub-types recognizable here are related to the extent to which the recipient of a message feels it is to be identifiable with a person or to be impersonally situational.

1 Communication by example is a process which has been noted frequently and is often referred to as 'behavioural contagion' or 'emulation' (Cartwright, 1965, p 12). This underlies a good deal of reference group theory, in which a person is regarded as copying (a) 'significant other(s)' in forming his own behaviours.

Rose has summarized this concept as referring "to the sources of values selected by an individual for the guidance of his behaviour, especially in cases where a choice has to be made. Reference groups may be groups of which an individual is a member, but sometimes they may not. In all cases they provide direction for the behaviour of the individual concerned, and so constitute important sources of social control." (Rose, 1962, p 128). This meaning attached to the term is to be distinguished, as it is by Shibutani, from that other meaning which is sometimes attached to it, where it "designates a group with which a person compares his fate" (or his wages!). For Shibutani, this is very different in import from the group "whose presumed perspective is used by an actor as the frame of reference in the organization of his perceptual field" (Rose, 1962, pp 232–233).

2 Communication through experience which is essentially situational and non-verbal is also well recognized. In the language of people on the shop floor, 'the way they treat you', 'the pittance they pay you for sweating all week', 'the conditions they expect us to work in', are expressions which, by the attribution of causality to an

unidentifiable 'they' (cf Hoggart, 1958, p 53) often serves to indicate the operation of these communications processes deriving simply from the situation. Important examples of these situational variables are the general expectations which exist as to standards of effort, contribution or performance, the apropriate levels and structures of reward, and the physical, social and psychological conditions within which people shall work. Another way of representing this aspect would be to associate it with the consequences for perception of the use of 'power' to effect behavioural compliance, independently of the visible forms which such exercises of power may take for the individual (cf Nichols and Beynon, 1977).

Because 'reality does not define itself' to individuals, situational communications of this sort are wide open to interpretation or definition by 'the group' as part of the group's usual function for the person. For the same reason, the necessity for explanation of 'the system' or the 'situation' by the custodians of it, is emphasized.

Barriers to communication
The notion of a 'barrier' to communication serves to indicate what in the nature of the individual component of the communication process serves potentially to prevent or reduce effective communication between one person and another. Some of these barriers may be associated with the nature of the person themselves, some to associate with the technical processes of encoding and decoding and some with the message (the data or information) itself. These cannot be treated in complete isolation from the others, and it could be argued that since the things and the actions are the product of human will they are all, really, to be associated with one or both of the persons involved. It is however useful for purposes of analysis to treat them in this way (cf Gibson, Ivancevich and Donelly, 1976).

The barriers natural to the persons concerned in communication are those associated with their *frames of reference*, composed as these are of affective and cognitive elements.

Generally, the individual's unique set of experiences will have helped shape how he perceives and evaluates the world about him, and therefore will, *inter alia*, help shape how he or she approaches the encoding and decoding operations of communication. Since no two experiences are exactly similar, two persons communicating can expect meaning to be expressed and perceived in more or less different ways according to the degree of variation between those experiences. Gibson *et al* develop this notion into two other linked concepts, of selective listening and value judgement: the first of these seems to be more usefully associated with cognitive processes in the sense that it involves an essentially cognitive response, whilst the second entails the assignment of worth to a message on the basis of the individual's pre-established preferences. Although these are treated by Gibson *et al* as three separately distinguishable barriers, they seem to 'belong together' as being three related conceptions of the individual's natural apparatus for communicating to or receiving meanings from his environment.

Secondly, the way in which each individual perceives and evaluates the other as communicator/recipient may be seen to serve as a potential influence upon the efficiency of the communication, in so far as it will affect both what is included in the message by the sender and what is abstracted from the message by the recipient. One side of this coin is represented by 'source credibility'—". . . the trust, confidence, and faith the receiver has in the words and actions of the communicator"—and the other by 'filtering' in which the perception of the other is allowed to produce deliberately biased messages. The bias may be motivated by a perception of 'what is good for the recipient' because of a view taken of that recipient, or of 'what is good for the communicator' given the related perception of what the recipient might do if he received a 'complete' message. These may then be related to the concept of *social distance* as an influencing factor upon messages, this usually taking the form of authority or status difference within industrial organizations.

Thirdly, these differences link closely with the technical question of the form of the message transmitted or received. Messages may be transmitted in the form of symbols of many different types, words, numbers, facial expressions and gestures, displayed behaviour etc. Since any of these may be 'captured' by groups or subcultures and made their own, with their own special meanings, communications effected through any of these forms may be subjected to distortion because of this. At the 'individual' level, this form of barrier is usually thought of in terms of *semantic* problems (the way in which I express meaning in words may not be the way in which you find that meaning in such words), but this usually carries forward to embrace group and sub-cultural differences in use of language, so that a member of one sub-cultural group will in using his in-group language convey to another in a different sub-cultural group a meaning different from that intended.

Finally, we may associate some problems with the operation of the communication system itself. Although these problems are within the control of the people concerned, there is a sense in which the problems are often seen to escape from this control. The main examples are the limitations of time in communication, which prevent the use of 'redundancy' (repetition in varied forms) as a means of conveying meaning more effectively, and the overloading of the communications process to the extent that adequate attention to communication or reception cannot be given. Both of these have opposites which may also be associated with communications problems: a plethora of time for communication is likely to lead to inefficient 'cycling' as the same messages go round and round with no added development of meaning, and an underloading of the channels is likely to result in atrophy and a suspicion (at least) that selective bias is being practised by the communicators.

Thus getting the balance right on all these dimensions is no simple task. Two modes (linked by a channel designed to carry a specific kind of message) maybe equal and opposite (or balanced with each other) so that the one is capable of conveying a meaning which is equally intelligible to the other, and the other is capable of receiving and interpreting it in the form in which it was intended by the one. The circumstances under which this kind of balance might be achieved in the context of inter-personal communication are likely to be few and far between, because node-capacities are likely to vary with all manner of factors like age, experience, education, class etc. In any one particular type of communication factors like differential status or authority distribution are also likely to produce an imbalance. In any purposive communication (ie one designed to influence in some way) it could be said that the fact that one person was the initiator and the other the intended recipient of the communication, might itself set up an element of imbalance because of the implicit dependency thereby introduced into the relationship (cf Kelley, 1951; Thibaut, 1950; Cartwright and Zander, 1953, pt IV).

In work organization there are two types of such 'dependency', one created by the flow of work through specialist jobs or 'stations', and the other by the structure of superordination-subordination developed for purposes of achieving co-ordination amongst such specialist activities. Given that specialization is unlikely to be eliminated, the twin needs of work-flow and co-ordination will remain, and might indeed be treated as 'permanent' features of the work system. It is this 'permanency' linked by some writers with the notions of domination and 'hegemony' (Clegg, 1976, Hyman, 1975) which may be associated with the communications problems usually identified. In the Kelley experiment, for example, the creation of 'permanently low status' and 'uncertain high status' positions in the 'game' used for the exercise appear to have been the main factors influencing the nature of the communications (ie influencing the choice of verbally- or behaviourally-critical responses) and the directions which they took (Kelley, 1951). If this allows the conclusion that permanent dependency or insecure independency must distort communications, and if these are necessary conditions of work organization, then the 'problem' of communications remains to be tackled in terms of both status and security.

This type of conclusion from experimental studies also suggests that it is not 'the group' *per se* which causes blocks or distortions to communication but rather the 'status' of that group or its members. Once the status is established the group merely serves its normal functions, which have been summarized as:

(a) to have some kind of instrumental value for the individual, to satisfy some need which he perceives himself as having and which he perceives identification with the group to be capable of helping him reduce

(b) to help the individual to assign meanings to things which do not have obvious meanings, and thus to help him to interpret various elements (like messages) in his environment in ways which may be special or peculiar to that group

(c) to support the individual socially and psychologically in conditions in which he might otherwise feel exposed and powerless, at the mercy of the cross-currents of life which bear upon him.

Other small group studies tend to confirm this search for independent status. They suggest that any factor which offers an opportunity for groups of people to differentiate themselves from others on some reasonable ground or excuse will probably be employed for this purpose. In formal organizational terms, groups under different charge-hands ' or supervisors, on different shifts, in different rooms or sections or buildings and groups associated with different plant or materials are all likely to coalesce around a perceived separate inden-tification and to develop a boundary with the remainder of the system which will serve to refract or distort communications across it. Any and all of these formal bases may be varied in their consequences by other factors which have little to do with the formal organization as, for example, variations of pattern are to be found in the bank wiring observation room in the Western Electric studies (Roethlisberger and Dickson, 1939). Some of these are to be found in Dalton's Milo study, differentiating the formally-educated from the experienced managers, and those who came up the hard way from those who walked in with a formal qualification well-documented (Dalton, 1959). Others are associated with different external experiences, such as a common area, town or country of origin in the case of mobile workers or common participation in leisure time activities (Lupton, 1963).

Such conclusions from studies may be grouped together to suggest that communications in organizations may be made difficult by individual identifications with formal or informal groups at different

356

'levels':

First, there are differences in class identification, which may provide a major distortion across these boundaries and produce problems of encoding and decoding.

Secondly, there are status differences, at least as perceived by the individuals concerned, which may serve to produce further fragmentation of group memberships on a wide variety of grounds, with similar consequences.

Thirdly, there are the inevitable individual differences, which may be masked by group memberships of one or both of these two types, but which nevertheless exist as problems of 'access'.

If therefore an assumption is made that the manner in which work is organized, formally, is relevant to effective communications necessary to both work-flow and co-ordination and control, the presence of these other distorting identifications must cause reflection upon possible alternatives or supplementations of the formal communications structures and processes with modern undertakings.

Formal channels

If we were to agree with Jaques (1951) that "communication is the sum total of directly or indirectly, consciously or unconsciously transmitted feelings, attitudes and wishes" and that being "an integral part of the process of change" it must occur "whenever the social equilibrium is upset" (Jaques, 1951, p 301), we would have to acknowledge that the communication referred to might flow from any node to any other node in the system. The managerial presumption on communication is different from this, and is more directly summarized in Simon's reference to the need for communication of value premises. "Communication", he says, "may be formally defined as any process whereby decisional premises are transmitted from one member of the organization to another" (Simon, 1953, ch VIII). This latter emphasis on authority and its acceptance via communications is more in tune with both managerial predispositions and the managerial structures which have been devised for the purpose. In any work organization, the intention to influence is markedly present, and a wide range of structural and processual devices have been adopted to allow these intentions to be carried into effect. Mostly they concern the 'usual' or 'formal' channels, some of which link the nodes (or roles) in the vertical dimensions of authority, and some those in the horizontal dimension of work flow dependency (see figures 11 and 12 above, pp 339–340).

Such organizations have an overriding purpose of converting something (such as raw materials or human skills) into something else (whether products or services) and much of the intention in communications in such organizations derives from this fact. These organizations must establish nodes and channels which will, it is to be hoped, allow the purpose to be achieved. *All* the nodes are linked by channels to all others but some are characterized as 'influencing' nodes and are normally identified as managerial or supervisory or similar roles. They are to be differentiated from those other nodes or roles which are primarily concerned with actually doing things (like making a product or rendering the service to the client) and which in the typical organization are so placed in the communications network that they will more frequently receive messages derived from the organization's purpose to transmit them (cf Burns, 1961).

The 'organization chart' represents one set of nodes and channels in the typical enterprise. The main meaning that this chart is intended to convey is the distribution of the nodes with authority to initiate and transmit such messages about the organization's requirements and the configuration of the 'usual channels' for carrying messages of this sort. In a very general sense, these messages might be described as by Simon—as conveying 'value-premises', established by those with authority and transmitted to the others in the organizational system in order to guide these others in their decisions and action. This is the manner in which the organization seeks to define the nodes and channels on the vertical dimension.

This same chart, in principle, seeks to define the horizontal channels and the nodes which feature in this other dimension. In this case, the channels are largely dictated not by personal authority considerations but by those of work flow. As a raw material is converted, it moves in a certain sequence and, as it does so, it passes through work stations which function also as nodes, and the work requirement at each needs to be stipulated. In its simplest form, the communications procedure here focuses upon something like the job card which moves with the work (or the patient's record in a hospital where the 'workers' visit the patient in one place). This seeks to ensure that the individual knows what has gone before, what is required of him and what action needs to be taken subsequently. The 'co-ordination' of this activity at a supervisory or managerial level also sets up a requirement of horizontal communication, and this is provided for (in channels) by the horizontial lines of the chart. The main distinction between the vertical and horizontal channels is that between the channels of authority in the usual managerial sense and those of work initiation in a work flow sense (see Klein, 1964).

In principle, these two sets of channels ought to be sufficient to carry all the communications necessary in the system. In practice, this is just not so. The view that communications occur in a simplistic fashion in the vertical and horizontal dimensions has been challenged by detailed studies of communications in managerial organization, such as those of Burns (1960) and Dalton (1959). Although these studies contain more ramified conclusions than these they respectively challenge, on grounds of the influence of authority difference and varied task demands, the traditional filter-amplifier conception of the node in the vertical channels and the simple mechanical conception of communication in the work flow channels between line managers and line and staff positions. Essentially, these conclusions are to the effect that communications do not (for whatever reason) conform to the pictorial image presented in the organization or work-flow charts.

One of the main 'reasons' why these channels are not sufficient in practice is the assumption that there are no barriers to communication in any structure of inter-personal relationships. People have distinct interests and aspirations, they have their own values and criteria of judgement and they are predisposed to take different courses of action. These may be gathered together by 'groups'—on the birds of a feather principle—and such groups may form around shared values, interests or places but the fact of the *difference* (however 'grouped') is what, in these and other studies of informal social structure, leads to perceptions of communications failure and to the design of more ramified communications systems and structures intended, not always successfully, to retrieve the failure.

Comprehensive communications structures
The apparent fact that there is a multiplicity of groups (or 'sub-units' in the Hickson et al (1971) formulation) within organizations and a multiplicity of communications channels between them (or their 'influentials') neither of which conform to the formal (chart) patterns of cooperation or communication, has created its own pressures to develop comprehensive structures of communication. These extant patterns may be regarded as essentially anarchist: they allow communications to take place outside the formal structure and, as many studies have shown, they could be supportive or destructive of the dissemination of meanings regarded as necessary to the pursuit of the undertaking's formal objectives. If therefore an informal group can from one point of view be regarded as source of refraction of meaning as messages cross the boundary, it can also be regarded as a set of constituencies whose influentials might be 'tapped' by drawing them into the formal communications network. From this point of view, the group structures of organizations can be 'incorporated' into the formal system (cf Clegg, 1975, ch 3).

This tends to stress the unitary conception of organization: the belief that all members of that organization are primarily or ultimately concerned with the pursuit of a single known and acceptable end. To act on such a belief is to endeavour to set up a number of separate channels of communication, all of them made 'official', in order to reach as many 'influentials' within these many groups as possible. This has been one of the traditional objects of 'joint consultation' in British industry and, from this point of view, it can therefore be regarded as an attempt to introduce multiple formal channelling of communications to supplement the formal hierarchial organization.

On the basis of the experience of the Glacier Metal Company, Jaques sums up the requirements of efficient communication in a way which amply illustrates this unitary conception:

1 A known and comprehensive communications *structure*. In Glacier this was attempted in the establishment of what came to be distinguished as "the executive, the consultative and the appeals channels" which were specified in the Company policy statement which represented an outcome of the long discussions in the Company undertaken with Jaques' assistance
2 *A code governing the relations* between people occupying various positions: in Glacier, this was attempted in the Company policy statement, the factory standing order on policy governing executive behaviour and by the largely unrecorded (informal) customs and procedures
3 *A quality of relationship* between people immediately connected with each other, such that "adaptive segregation may be mutually agreed, and stresses worked at so that rigid segmentation becomes unnecessary." In Glacier, the various discussions which were held with the various groups were either designed to produce this result or functioned to this end (Jaques, 1951, p 305).

These three propositions derive from the theoretical scheme for the analysis of organization which we noted above. The first emphasizes the 'relationships' between role incumbents; the second the beliefs of the role incumbent in the sense that if they can be made to subscribe to the code, this will tend to give communications on a basis of shared and accepted values about the system as a whole; when these two conditions are met, it is possible to recognize the probable consequence of this, which is what Jaques outlines in the third statement. The achievement of the consequence outlined in statement 3 thus becomes a statement about the condition of equilibrium in communications terms in an organization. Unless the structure and the accepted value system produce this "quality of relationship," equilibrium cannot be said to exist. The conditions of *striving* after equilibrium, which is imputed to industrial organizations, is little more than a striving after the achievement of this end; in the terms used by Simon (1956) and taken up by writers like Whyte (1956), this means that organizations will seek to achieve social order by influencing members in ways which will be supportive of themselves.

It is doubtful whether the result of lengthy discussions in Glacier was much more than the movement of the system a small step in the direction of a more efficient communications system. What was done there did however enable Jaques to advance certain conclusions about the conditions under which a movement of this sort can be affected:

1 the group of persons concerned must have a problem severe and painful enough for the members to wish to do something about it
2 there must be a sufficient cohesion of purpose (or morale) to render the group capable of tackling the problem and of seeking and tolerating any necessary changes.

The first condition, says Jaques, is usually accompanied by a sense of frustration and, because the group feels frustrated with its own efforts, it is likely that the outsider can help the group by working as a catalyst, precipitating action which might otherwise prove difficult to take by the group itself (see also below, pp 337–80).

Joint consultation
A number of models of joint consultation are now documented, in which guidance may be found on how to establish effective alternative channels of communication on subject areas which lend themselves to across the board communications. The more successful of these examples tend to acknowledge the third, trade union/collective bargaining channel of communications in organization and endeavour to demarcate the precise subjects for communication.

First, they acknowledge the fact of trade union existence and trade union attitudes, and seek deliberately to resolve the non-unionist issue either, as in the Glacier experiment by restricting representatives to trade union members or, as in the GKN-Shotton experiment by founding the whole exercise on the trade union representational and negotiating machinery (Jaques 1951; GKN-Shotton, 1973).
Secondly, they define the subjects with some precision and make them matters for decision by the consultative bodies

rather than simply for discussion. They do this by codifying the definitive policy and the conditional policy decisions required, allocating the latter to the consultative machinery for decision (albeit with a proviso that decisions must be unanimous in order to prevent inconsistency in the two sets of decisions), or by defining in advance certain areas of bilateral interest which may range from trade union bargaining subjects of a traditional sort through safety, welfare and discipline to forward manpower planning (Thomason, 1971).

These two features help to avoid the complication of discussion by introducing resentments and rivalries which increase the noise and the resistance in communications, and the usually almost insuperable difficulty of making the subject matter sufficiently real for people to want to discuss them and communicate them further amongst their constituents. Although they could be justified on these grounds alone, an additional rationale for their introduction asserts that it is desirable, even necessary for management to give away its traditional prerogatives to control in these areas in order to assure greater order in the work situation (see Thomason, 1971).

Recent successes in joint consultation have been associated with a deliberate prior allocation of subjects for discussion *and decision*; this is done so that a moral right to participate is created. Examples are (a) the Glacier experiment (b) a number of productivity bargaining arrangements and (c) the GKN-Shotton experiment.

(a) Part of the Glacier experiment in joint consultation, which began as a conventional joint production committee during world war two, entailed the evolution of a distinction between definitive policy decisions which must, under companies legislation, be reserved to the board of directors on which a statutory duty is imposed, and conditional policy decisions which need not be so reserved and which can therefore be allocated to the works council. This definition and allocation was itself worked out by the joint consultative machinery itself, although it should be noted that a number of company directors did sit on this at times during the working-out period. The fact that the distinction did evolve in this way may be of some significance in determining success; it is possible here only to indicate the outcome (Brown, 1960).

The final embodiment of it is contained in a company policy document (given in full as an appendix to Jaques, 1951). This makes a number of definitional points about policy; it provides for the establishment and running of a variety of joint consultative bodies in the works, but specifically reserves certain decisions (eg those about finance and financial control, and those concerning the appointment of directors and senior executives) to the board, whilst at the same time making other decisions (eg those about manning and terms and conditions of appointment of staff) open to discussion between the managing director (as the representative of the board) and the workers' representatives before resolution. On the face of it, the distinction is the one known to confederations: that matters not specifically reserved to the board by the Companies Acts and the Articles of Association etc are made the concern of the works council and the workers' representatives; the fact that the managing director must concur in any such conditional policy decision provides a safeguard against a total application of this confederal principle. With this proviso, the company policy document does create certain rights in matters of decision (of the binding in honour variety) which moves the frontier of control and responsibility forward from its usual position in work organizations.

(b) It is possible to draw a similar general conclusion from a number of exercises in productivity bargaining carried out during the late 1960s. In these situations, less attention was given in advance to drawing up a detailed constitutional arrangement, the focus of the exercise being almost exclusively upon the question of how the management and the workers' representatives could together work out methods of increasing productivity. This required companies engaging in this form of exercise to set up what were often *ad hoc* arrangements, such as joint productivity committees, but the discussions were unusually 'open' in the particular sense that management did not seek to use these arrangements to impose views which they themselves might have on how productivity could be improved. In some cases, although not all, the blank sheet of paper approach was total, in that management was willing to accept suggestions which might mean capital investment, but in other cases decisions were constrained by the imposition of a limit on the amount of capital investment which could be brought in contemplation of the committee (cf Oldfield, 1966; Thomason, 1971; NBPI Reports Nos 36 and 123).

Unlike the Glacier example, there was no attempt to spell out in advance the limits of participation in decision taking but such limits might be discerned to be present, and to take roughly the same form as in Glacier. Nevertheless, a productivity agreement arising out of this kind of discussion usually moved the control and responsibility frontier forward from its previous position, since productivity in this context often embraced matters normally identified as job enlargement, management by objectives, the status of employees (eg the acquisition of staff status by hourly paid personnel), the introduction of flexi-time, and changes in the methods and amounts of payment (annual wages, for example). The concept of a blank sheet of paper at the beginning of the discussions thus tended to yield a Glacier-type reallocation of authority to decide.

(c) The GKN-Shotton experiment, which was instituted following a period of unhappy industrial relations which culminated in a strike and a major lay off, could be said to institutionalize the kind of approach associated with some forms of productivity bargaining. A Charter for the Workpeople identifies a number of distinct areas of decision which will be reserved for resolution with a structure of five permanent committees. The main committee is charged with reviewing the operational performance of the company and the future need for research and development, manpower, training and rehabilitation, and with promoting and monitoring productivity agreements, as well as co-ordinating the work of the four sub-committees. They have separate functions; the first and major one identified is concerned with normal trade union bargaining matters, including all those related to manpower planning and employee resourcing. The other three committees deal with matters of safety, health and welfare; employee benefits, suggestions and leisure activities; and all aspects of discipline from the definition of works rules to the provision of an appeals channel for any employee who feels aggrieved at a disciplinary decision. Although this codification extends the control frontier little beyond the traditional one in bargaining, it does attempt to codify the distribution of authority.

In each of the situations described the structure of joint consultation is essentially similar. In all cases, there is a main generally representative committee, which is supported by other committees which maybe specialized by function or by geographical area. At Glacier, the main works council is composed of seven trade union-member representatives of the hourly paid grades of staff, three representatives of the junior white collar staff, two representatives of the foremen and middle management, and one representative of the senior management, together with the managing director who holds his position *ex officio* because of the crucial liaison role which he is called upon to carry out in the complex structure of policy making. In addition to this committtee, there are others similarly constituted on a departmental basis, in which more local policy and implementation issues can be discussed and from which suggestions for changes in conditional policy affecting all staff can be put forward; the shop stewards themselves also meet formally in a works committee which serves to co-ordinate approaches from the worker side.

In the typical productivity bargaining situation, there is usually some committee which co-ordinates activities. This may be the joint consultative committee or a special sub-committee of the main committee (see, for example, Thomason, 1971, p 44). This recognizes the potentially specialized nature of productivity bargaining and the likelihood that productivity bargaining is not the total area of concern of a joint consultative committee. However, the main co-ordinating committee is usually supplemented by a large number of other committees (the productivity teams) whose existence is necessary to ensure that communication is widespread and effective and can be effectively monitored.

In the GKN-Shotton case, there is a similar structure of a main committtee composed of eight management representatives and eight shop representatives elected from amongst the paid-up trade union members willing to stand for election, together with four sub-committees whose composition broadly reflects the distribution of staff in the enterprise. The Charter for the Workpeople in this company stops short of giving these representatives a clear constitutional obligation to communicate with their constituents; rather they are treated as shop stewards and, whilst they are assured of all facilities and protection of earnings whilst engaged on representative business, they are not specifically required to keep their constituents informed of matters discussed in the various committees.

Since in all these cases quoted success is claimed for the approach, it may be worth trying to find out what distinguishes them from the traditional approaches which have, rightly or wrongly, become closely associated with failure:

1 an attempt is made to identify the *subject areas* for discussion in joint consultation, and these are then introduced as matters which the participants have a moral right to discuss
2 an attempt is made to make these subjects issues on which the committee must *decide*, even if this has to be done within what is a normal pattern of constraint on any decision, and in some cases there is an implicit or explicit *status quo* provision in the absence of such decisions in these committees
3 an attempt is made to ensure that decision-taking processes are informed, either by the presentation of information by management and (usually and perhaps more importantly) by the

development of a working party structure by which matters for decision are worked through in more detail than a single committee meeting can normally aspire to

4 each situation acknowledges the actual distribution of loyalties amongst the people concerned: where the trade unions are well entrenched in the workplace, representatives must be trade unionists thus avoiding the tensions of trade unionists being required to sit alongside non-unionists from the same occupational category; also, foremen and middle managers are not left out or ignored

5 in each case, communications are seen to require a ramified structure of representation which is not satisfied by the creation of a single committee: in the more extreme forms of communications structuring a deliberate attempt may be made to take the communications processes through to the far ends of the organization

6 in all cases, representatives are given some form of executive role—they have something to do, which is more than merely sitting and listening and talking—and the danger of producing a talking shop in the joint consultative committee is at least recognized in the structures established

7 finally, it might also be inferred that, whatever may be the attitude of individual managers towards joint consultative arrangements, in these examples the creation of rights and the redistribution of authority places the manager in the position where he must participate in order to carry out his role successfully.

These precepts begin to divert the approach to communication in modern enterprises away from the inter-personal, towards a conception of communications as a process which must acknowledge the realities of differing values, differing objectives, different reference groups and different power/authority bases, and the consequential necessity for effective communications to be associated with (if not founded upon) a process of power bargaining rather than some effete form of consultation. This is the predictable direction of the solution to communications (and motivational) problems in the future and, if that solution is not yet much in evidence, the faltering steps taken since the late 1960s tend this way.

The first of these steps could be described as very hesitant indeed. It was associated with the exhortation to industry to institute joint consultation, to be found in the Code of Industrial Relations Practice promulgated with the Industrial Relations Act. This advocated all undertakings, and especially those with more than 250 employees, to set up consultative machinery, and to seek joint agreement with employees on the composition, structure and function of the committees and the range of subjects to be discussed in them.

(Code, 1972, p 17). This guidance started two hares running.

First, it generated some heat (at least as a result of linking the advice with the philosophy of the Industrial Relations Act) over the issue of non-unionists being given representative roles in joint consultation. The Code itself was, on the face of it, quite non-committal and certainly not novel, in what it had to say on this subject, but it did perhaps reveal a considerable lack of awarness of developments in theories (eg in the areas of conflict and reference group) and thus gave many the impression of being a bit old hat. By the time the non-unionist issue had been raised by the Industrial Relations Act itself, those omissions proved serious.

Secondly, it offered very little guidance on the problem of distinguishing consultation from negotiation, largely because it failed to grasp this nettle at all firmly. The Code merely referred to these as being closely related "but distinct processes" and suggested that "management and employee representatives should consider carefully how to link the two. It may often be advantageous for the same committee to cover both. Where there are separate bodies, systematic communication between those involved in the two processes is essential." In the light of what has been said above this is perhaps not a surprising set of recommendations.

The Consultative Document on the proposed Code, issued in the preceding June (1971), was much more explicit on the subject, setting out three distinct alternatives:

(i)   a unified system combining both functions (of consultation and negotiation)
(ii) separate processes for the two functions with the same representatives on both
(iii) separate processes with totally or partially different representatives.

The document did refer to the need to establish machinery appropriate to the local circumstances such that, for example, where "there is a substantial union membership the first or second of the above-procedures is likely to give better results". This advice was, however, watered down as a result of subsequent representations from industry.

It might be suggested that what was left out of account, and what might have helped to establish the Code as a more helpful document for industry, was the concept of redundancy in communications. The Consultative Document and the Code both treated consultation and negotiation as simple alternatives, as a kind of black and white dichotomy associated with the two major ideologies of management and trade unions. They might have suggested that effective communications (in both directions) required a multiplicity of communications channels, and perhaps a plurality of representatives (even if all of them were drawn from trade unions on the one hand and management on the other). The Code might then have provided industry with a greater opportunity to develop broad-based communications, through structures and procedures designed, jointly or separately as circumstances seemed to suggest, to cope with a wide range of matters (productivity, wages, welfare amenities, discipline, grievances, fringe benefits etc) some of which might traditionally have been associated with consultative machinery and some with negotiating machinery.

This black-white distinction has, subsequently, bedevilled discussion of participation, as this debate has developed in response to the proposals for harmonization of industrial practice within the EEC. The TUC has expressed itself as totally not in favour of the development of works councils on the Continental model, because of their association with non-unionists and their relatively passive role in monitoring application of agreements, and the employer and management organizations have therefore had to argue for a broader based participation (broader than that implied in the concept of worker directors or two-tier boards) from a somewhat false starting position. The restricting terms of reference given to the Bullock Committee of Inquiry, into the manner in which legislation might facilitate the growth of participation, are a further consequence of this earlier failure to deal informatively and imaginatively with the communications-consultation-negotiation problem in the early 1970s.

Generating the necessary information
Nevertheless, there is little doubt that in the future much more information will have to be given to employees (and to trade union representatives) than has generally been given in the past. Attention has focused mainly upon the requirements of legislation in requiring disclosure to trade union representatives for purposes of facilitating collective bargaining (which subject is discussed below, pp 430–35). But in addition the requirement of disclosure of information on the objectives and policies of the enterprise to employees in general, which originated in the Industrial Relations Act, still survives in the form of a recommendation in the Code Of Industrial Relations Practice and so continues to have some influence. It is also a recommendation that employees shall be informed of the present state of the company as indicated in the chairman's report, balance sheet and profit and loss statement. Although none of the legislation requires employers to produce information where it does not already exist, there remains a strong presumption that if good practice suggests

that forward plans ought to be disclosed where they exist, then they ought to exist: if they do not, employers may find themselves pressured to bring them into existence.

If there is a reasonable prediction as to future development, the personnel manager will be involved in producing such statements of objectives and policies in explicit form. Since many enterprises operate (not necessarily wrongly) without such explicit, forward looking statements, there will be pressure to proceed in this matter with formalistic rationality and the tendency towards increased bureaucracy will be accelerated.

Many enterprises will be forced to work out for themselves what their objectives and policies are or ought to be. They may well first adopt methods which are coming to be referred to by the generic term corporate planning. This is an approach still in its infancy and still relatively ill-supported by techniques in which full confidence might be reposed. It means that the enterprise must make explicit a sequence of underlying objectives, specific objectives, corporate strategy, long-range programmes and short-term programmes (or budgets) and must use diverse techniques as, for example, technological forecasting, capital and revenue budgeting, break-even charting and contribution analysis, and such new organizational arrangements as operational research departments or matrix organizations. Until this framework has produced results the pre-conditions for giving out the information required cannot be met.

Even then, if corporate planning is conceived in its common, narrow definition, it may remain impossible for the enterprise to communicate adequate information on its policies, particularly if it is to communicate to its employees the kinds of information which they are most likely to want. This is because corporate planning and its counterpart in the public service, national planning, are usually conceived in achievement terms. A commercial enterprise, for example, will usually plan in terms of its product(s) penetration of the market (ie in terms of growth) allied to profitability or asset growth: an agency of government will usually plan in terms of expansion of the number of houses built or jobs provided (ie in terms of growth of the service) allied to concepts of efficiency or cost-benefit. The need to consider human means only arises when the feasibility studies have suggested a line of *achievement* which might be postulated for the future.

This usually comes in terms of manpower planning, the main development in forward planning as it affects human means of production. In its separateness from other planning approaches, manpower planning has been developed to a reasonable degree of sophistication. Models and techniques do exist and are used. The

369

outcomes of this part of the exercise are likely to be of more interest and relevance to the employees than broader conceptions of what the enterprise aims to achieve in the future. But manpower planning, so far, rarely takes into account what might be termed the qualitative aspects of manpower as distinct from its quantitative features. Even when, for example, consideration is given to training, this is usually seen in terms of how much extra training will have to be given to how many people, if the enterprise is to have the number of adequately trained personnel it requires at a certain date; such questions as the quality of the employment offered or the needs of the employed labour are much less often taken into account in the manpower plan. The concept of employee resourcing, convoluted though it may be, does begin to suggest a broader qualitative conception of the treatment of means than manpower planning alone implies. In this wider meaning, it is likely to link on to the kinds of information which employees might well seek from the enterprise.

Objectives and policies may well have to be worked out in these kinds of terms before management can meet the spirit of the requirement.

Only when this has been done does it become possible to meet the other needs for information about individual and collective relationships with the enterprise. It is true that employers can meet the specific requirements of the Code by issuing a simple, mechanistic statement of the main terms and conditions of the individual employment contract, of the individual's rights to trade union membership and of the basic grievance procedure (Code, para 60). It might even be possible to meet the need for information about the matters listed above (Code, para 62)

Nevertheless, it might be equally possible for anyone so determined to run the proverbial coach and horses through certain items listed in the Code if they were to be constructed on a purely *ad hoc* or off-the-cuff basis. These are after all matters over which there is usually a conflict of rights or interest, or both, and ad hocery might well lead to festering disputes which might have to be resolved through invocation of some part of the statutory machinery. It may be insufficient to rely upon the observation that in the past these matters have not been prominent in disputes within the enterprise; their continuation in the Employment Protection Act and the new Code could well, by focusing attention on them, lead to a real change.

The remaining suggestions about communication contained in the original Code might further support this. In advising effective arrangements to facilitate a two-way flow of information, the Code details methods which might be employed. Feed-out of information from management will mean meetings for specific purposes, supplemented by written information on notice boards, house journals, handbooks, and induction and training sessions, more immediate face-to-face explanations by managers or supervisors, and arrangements for both consultation and negotiations. A parallel responsibility is imposed upon managements to secure feed-back of information through similar meetings. Since some attempt is made to identify what might be discussed, for example, in the bargaining and consultative meetings—including the performance and plans of the enterprise, and organizational and management changes which affect employees—managements will more often find or feel themselves pressed to work out their plans and policies more formally and systematically to meet the practices suggested in the Code (Code, para 57).

If such considerations apply in these areas, they are likely to apply *a fortiori* to those of manpower and payment policy and to the methods which are applied. Although the final version of the Code retracts the position of the original consultative document, it still retains certain requirements in Sections 24–50 which impose a similar difficulty upon managements. This part begins with the statement that clear and comprehensive employment policies are essential to good relations between management and employees; it goes on to suggest that, whilst management should initiate and accept responsibility for them, they should nevertheless be developed in consultation or negotiation with employee representatives. The policies identified are those relevant to manpower planning, recruitment and selection, training, payment systems, status and security and working conditions; the methods to be adopted by them—whilst not now so detailed or specific as before—are to be relevant to the work to be done and capable of being understood.

The problem which arises may be illustrated as follows: about recruitment and selection, it is stated that management should decide the qualifications and experience needed by the applicants, consider filling the vacancies from within the undertaking and obtain only as much information from applicants as is relevant to the selection process, avoiding enquiries which are "unnecessary for that purpose" and finally basing selection on suitability for the job. All these functions are clearly to remain management's responsibility but the earlier general statement does permit consultation or negotiation "as appropriate"; the question then arises as to who should determine whether consultation or negotiation are appropriate and how far expressions of opinion in that framework should be allowed to influence management's pursuit of its own policy in its own way. It is quite clear that, no matter how that question is resolved, management must be prepared to face challenges on its policies, procedures

371

and practices; it may well have to develop more sophisticated policies etc to meet these.

Further guidance on the kind of information which may have to be made available is provided by the requirements of the Industry Act (S 20). In this case, the disclosure is required essentially for national planning purposes, and anyone carrying on an undertaking in manufacturing industry which is of such a nature as to make a significant contribution to a sector of that industry (as the Minister may define this), may be required by the Minister to supply him or others with information about the undertaking. The Act provides in Section 30 for the provision of information on any of the following matters:

(a) the persons employed in the undertaking, or persons normally so employed
(b) the undertaking's capital expenditure
(c) fixed capital assets used in the undertaking
(d) any disposal or intended disposal of such assets
(e) any acquisition or intended acquisition of fixed capital assets for use in the undertaking
(f) the undertaking's output and productivity
(g) sales of the undertaking's products
(h) exports of those products
(i) sales of industrial property owned or used in connection with the undertaking, grants of rights in respect of such property, and contracts for any such sales or grants.
(j) expenditure on any research and/or development programme.

The Secretary of State for Industry is also given reserve powers on the disclosure of this information to trade unions or their representatives. First, he must allow employers a period of three months from the presentation of this information in which to disclose the information voluntarily to trade unions, but may then use his delegated powers to require the employer to disclose. Secondly, the Secretary of State may determine what information, if any, shall be disclosed, but the unions and the employers are given a right of appeal to a committee headed by a legally qualified chairman, whose other members will be drawn from management and worker representatives, although this committee is essentially advisory in its relation to the Minister. Thirdly, the Secretary of State may himself seek advice from the committee on what information, if any, should be disclosed to trade unions. If he chooses in any circumstances of referral to the committee to ignore its advice, disclosure can only be prevented by a negative resolution of Parliament. The duty imposed upon the employer by the Industry Act to disclose information to trade unions is therefore likely, in the short-term, to prove less onerous than the general duty imposed by the Employment Protection Act.

In both cases, certain immunities and exclusions are provided for. With the Industry Act, the duty to supply the information does not apply if its discharge would not, in the Minister's opinion, be in the national interest or would require the employer to contravene a prohibition imposed by or under an enactment. In the case of the supply of information for bargaining purposes, there are similar immunities Under S 154 of the original IR Act, and under S 14 of the Employment Protection Act, immunity may be granted where disclosure of the information would be against the interests of national security, would cause contravention of any enactment, would mean the employer breaking a confidence, would relate specifically to an individual who has not given his consent to disclosure, would be prejudicial to the interests of the employer's undertaking for reasons other than the effect of collective bargaining or had been obtained by the employer for the purpose of bringing, prosecuting or defending any legal proceedings.

In addition to these requirements further extensions of the duty are likely to arise in connection with any legislation on employee participation in decision-taking. Whatever these may prove to be, it is clear that employers must in future prepare to discharge a duty to disclose information to trade union representatives for collective bargaining purposes or to take an informed part in discussions of future company plans and practices. This kind of action has often been taken in recent years (and particularly in the nationalized undertakings where circumstances have combined to produce a cut-back problem). In these circumstances, giving information becomes a necessary part of the process of securing assent to change: examples are provided by British Airways, British Rail, British Steel and the National Coal Board amongst the nationalized concerns, and by British Leyland, Cadbury-Schweppes and GKN-Shotton amongst private firms.

The enjoinders to 'consult' independent recognized trade unions, and to disclose information both to their representatives and to the employees themselves, thus change the balance of power in the employer-employee relationship. Both knowledge and information have hitherto provided important foundations for the exercise of power under the rules in modern organizations; pressure to disclose more information, by itself and regardless of what might happen about 'knowledge', removes one such base and calls, as Varney has suggested in his discussion of group goal-setting (1976), for a new approach to the exercise of power under the new structure of rules. Thus, if information is reduced in significance as a base, it might be predicted that in exercises of influence involving the manipulation of symbols (as distinct from coercion and manipulation of utilities) the knowledge of the manager will have to assume greater importance. Sapiential authority based on knowledge, rather than administrative authority based on information, may thus become a more sought after foundation in this emerging situation.

Reading
On the general processes of communication, see Gibson, Ivancevich and Donnelly (1976); and Cartwright in March (1965).

On joint consultation, see Jaques (1951), Brown (1961) and the Code of Industrial Relations Practice (1972).

On the more theoretical approaches to these subjects, see Katz and Lazarsfeld (1955), Prohansky and Seidenberg (1969), Homans (1951); and Shibutani in Rose (1962).

9 Purposive interventions

Making things happen

In *Rise and Fall of the British Manager* (1977), Alistair Mant suggests that one of the major problems in British industry is the inability—for reasons which he discusses—of managers to make things happen within the productive system. He is not alone in this: not long before the publication of his book, *Der Spiegel* had had some unkind things to say about the British manager. The English disease, so well known to outside observers but usually not regarded as fatal by inside ones, is often attributed to similar deficiencies in management. These deficiencies may be expressed in the language of theories of class and status consciousness strongly reminiscent of Veblen's earlier strictures on the 'cultural survivals' and the dead hand of the 'business men' (who kept the engineers from solving the problems of the economic world). But they generally amount to the single charge of inability to make things happen—whether because of lack of motivation, lack of knowledge or lack of know-how (or 'technology' in its stricter sense).

Whether or not these views are warranted, the manager—or indeed anyone else caught up in work processes—is concerned with making things happen, getting out the production or providing the service and the *personnel* specialist or manager is not in any way absolved from this. In addition, by virtue of the claims which he tends to make for his occupation, he is also involved in helping other managers and specialists to make things happen for themselves. Consequently the personnel practitioner may be regarded as having a two-fold concern here, that of doing his own thing and of creating the wherewithal for others to do theirs.

There are many ways in which he might contribute to these—by carrying out appropriate activities in relation to 'employee resourcing', 'employee relations', 'employee motivating'—but whatever may be done in the light of requirement and the application of knowledge and theories of the sort considered in preceding chapters, at the end of the day the success or failure of the occupational role

375

will depend upon what it contributes to production, whether of goods or services, or to satisfaction. For this reason, all the other activities have to come together in the sense of creating a situation or set of circumstances in which not only the personnel specialist himself but the rest of the personnel have a maximum opportunity to contribute. Since it seems that we must always have a label to identify what we are talking about, this may be called OD, short for organizational development but embracing a lot of other 'development' than simply that of the 'organization'.

The term OD was originally coined to identify an interventionist activity initiated and supported by consultants, usually with an educational link. Bennis (1966), for example, defines it as:

(a) an educational strategy adopted to bring about planned organizational change, in which the change agent is always external to the organization and is a professional behavioural scientist who seeks to develop a collaborative relationship with the client system based on mutual trust; (for a discussion of the forms of collaborative relationship, see Mangham, 1968)

(b) an attempt to meet some current exigency faced by the organization, through which the educational and planned changed processes can be developed in the form of a strategy which relies heavily upon experience behaviour (as distinct from book learning) to generate publicly shared data via such methods as sensitivity training, data feedback and confrontation meetings

(c) the change agents share a social philosophy and normative goals which are consistent with the developing perspective of organizations which attributes to them certain analogous characteristics to those of the organism (see Thomason, 1973).

Two sets of theory come together to produce this OD approach. The first is the 'theory' that up to a point an organization may be treated as if it were a living organism, or at least an ecological system, with something that can be thought about as a life of its own. This system may then be thought of as having periods of growth and development or maturation between a succession of crisis points. In this view, therefore, there is a conception of successive maturation as crises are successfully surmounted, although in 'organizational life' terms it may be that failure to cope with a crisis results in a kind of regression which could not happen to a living thing (see Lippitt, 1969). The relevance of this theory to OD lies in the implication that the management of change must rest upon an awareness of the phase or crisis point in the life cycle, reached by the enterprise: management decisions, here as elsewhere, call for correct assessment of where we are and where we should be going.

376

The second is the socio-technical theory which lays down the process by which change occurs in organization, and by extension the process by which change can be brought about in organization. Strictly, there is no one theory in this area but several, each of which regards organizational change as initiated and progressed by modification of different sets of variables (see Smelser, 1967; ch 12).

OD approaches opt for that applied social theory in which organizational change is seen to be capable of being effected by external agency in some sort of partnership with the client system. The external roles, with different parts to play in the change, are linked together in a deliberate strategy to become powerful changers of organizations, whether of structures of relationships or of perspectives of role by those caught up in them. What limits there are to the power of the agency is usually only hinted at, but the perspective of Lippitt (1969) would seem to suggest that only some degrees and directions of change dictated by the phase of natural development reached are possible at any one moment.

There are in fact three crucial roles which are normally distinguished in this approach to planned organizational change, those of change agent, catalyst and pacemaker. These are defined by Jones (1969) in the following terms:

(a) a change agent may be a person, a group or an organization, but in any case "includes the property of professionalism", and adopts a role which involves "the stimulation, guidance, and stabilization of change in organizations" essentially as a 'helper', a 'mover' or a 'doer' (pp 19–20)

(b) a change catalyst is "any agent that causes, speeds up or slows down change (catalysis) in the organizational system" without undergoing any change itself, and may in the extreme case have no more complex role than that of simply bringing the change agent and the client system together, although it is a characteristic of this role that the effect of the role tends to be disproportionately great in relation to the input (pp 45–6)

(c) a pacemaker, like the change agent, may be an individual, a group or an organization but is seen as 'powered' by a source of energy which is external to the client system ('professional knowledge' would offer one illustration) and functions to stimulate and control the change process itself (pp 60–61).

In Jones's view, the change agent and the client system are to be regarded as the two principal 'actors' in planned change and the catalyst and the pacemaker as secondary ones. On the other hand, the client system and the catalyst are often regarded as 'internal' to the organization-as-client, and the change agent and the pacemaker

377

as 'external', at least in the sense of having external bases of power which enable them to exert influence. It is in this sense that there is a significant point in the conception of OD as a partnership between an external agency and the client system: when attempted entirely from within the client system, it is difficult to ensure that the necessary 'energy' or power required to stimulate and control change will be guaranteed to the internal actors for the period of time required (see Jaques, 1951, and above, p 361). Provided that the whole exercise remains conceived as a learning experience for all concerned in it, there seems to be no reason in principle why the initiative should not be taken from within the undertaking itself, and therefore why change agents should not be internal ones. This would presuppose that there was already sufficient flexibility in the organization to allow the necessary roles to be assumed (Burns and Stalker, 1961).

This general conception of OD allows a number of quite different role allocations from those associated with the common consultant-client-system model, although they are infrequently made and when they are they are often not acknowledged in these terms. There is for example a strong tendency to assume that the 'mutual trust' mentioned by Bennis (above, p 376) will only be present where the client system is a managerial system and the consultants are 'management' or 'business' consultants. It may well be, as Fox demonstrates in *Beyond Contract* (1973) that many client systems, defined to include the employees, are characterized by low-trust relationships but there are many situations where (at least) 'adequate-trust' relationships could be developed for the purposes of ensuring planned organizational change. A broader conception of the 'client-system' might thus admit to the discussion, the trade union representatives as change-agents, catalysts or pacemakers. (They have, after all, an external referent and external sources of power). What is problematical about this conception is the potential for sufficient 'mutual trust' in the exercise, but there are examples on record of planned change being carried through on this basis and with sufficient mutual trust, particularly in productivity bargaining.

This does rather suggest that what is important about the OD concept is not whether outside consultants are available and can be afforded, but the principles which animate the whole approach. These principles stem from an appreciation that change will tend to be resisted by anyone when they do not understand it, when their basic securities are threatened by it and when they have change imposed upon them. They emphasize the need for action by someone, alone or in partnership to remove the 'causes' of these resistances and to ensure that change occurs in a controlled fashion.

Consequently, OD emphasizes the need to conceive the approach as a comprehensive 'package' of actions (with their own technologies) which reflect the 'needs' of someone, somewhere in the undertaking for change. This has two important corrollaries: first, that it is necessary to start with 'needs' or, more usefully conceived, with human emotions (however well or badly these may be 'informed'); secondly, that it must accept that there are more 'rationalities' or 'philosophies' than one, relating to what is preferred change in the structure and operation of undertakings.

The 'professional' and 'normative' aspects of this OD approach belong very much within the mainstream of the 'human relations' challenge to scientific management. The social scientific professionalism and the normative prescriptions are both connected with that conception of man in organization which may be linked with McGregor's Theory Y assumptions and managerial style. Consequently, OD embraces a challenge to customary or conventional rationality within the context of work organization.

Identifying emotions

That particular rationality which has grown up around business and its management has tended to emphasize the exclusive relevance of cognitive knowledge in any decisions about proposed action. One of the major challenges of the Hawthorne experiments was, put simply, to demonstrate that there was an alternative rationality (or logic) to that of scientific management, (Roethlisberger and Dickson, 1939) and this has subsequently been demonstrated to be applicable to managerial systems themselves (Dalton, 1959; Burns and Stalker, 1961). The effect of the challenge was to suggest that emotions could not and should not be treated as aberrant or somehow outside the main stream of decision-taking in complex undertakings, but rather must and should be treated as an inherent part of that process. The development of concepts which might permit action adequately to respond to this insight has proved slow, and only begins to appear with the appearance of OD approaches.

The personnel specialist has for long displayed a concern with one side of this coin, particularly in his use of behavioural or attitudinal indices of 'morale'. Traditionally, this concept has been used in two different senses but with the one object of producing an audit of how satisfactory the general situation was from the standpoint of the employees. On the one hand, morale has been treated as a condition of contentment, satisfaction or happiness of the labour force as a whole (as distinct from the condition of any one individual member of it) and researchers have sought to develop various correlative indicators of that state. On the other, it has been defined in

379

terms of 'willingness to work', again at the level of the workforce as a whole and measured by indicators derived from similar data on timekeeping, absenteeism, labour turnover, aggression towards supervision and management, disputes and productivity levels, or by attitude survey. The link between these two concepts was effected by an assumption that a happy labour force would be a productive labour force, and that therefore a happy labour force could be regarded as one which might be described as willing to work (cf Beach, 1975, p 472; and Cuming, 1968, p 247).

The lack of hard evidence to support this assumption, and the disappointing results usually obtained from attitude surveys (Palmer, 1977, p 26), has led a number of undertakings into developing a more participative approach to both survey activities and consequential interpretation and decision taking. Useful though these developed methods may be, there remains the probability that, if people are asked about their attitude towards or evaluation of some phenomenon in their work environment, they will give an overwhelmingly favourable response (the '80 per cent' agreeing syndrome). This might allow us to infer that what is important about attitudes or opinions are the negative responses, where these are backed by strong feelings. Rather than a general survey of attitudes, what might be more useful is an opportunity for those who experience strong pro-change or anti-status quo feelings to express them and to feel that they might have some chance of influencing the situation.

Instead, therefore, of a concern with 'satisfaction' or the state of positive morale, it might be more useful to focus upon the dissatisfaction or 'distastes' (in the sense in which Pym (1967) employs this term) to identify the starting point, and consider subsequently the methods which might be employed to bring these into a relationship with objective setting. For it is not only by deliberately establishing a joint decision process that such relationships can be established. Just as there are a number of ways of killing a cat so there are many different methods of linking dissatisfactions (as indicators of emotional states) with objectives (as the ends to which organizations strive).

Whilst it is probably true that everyone is dissatisfied with his lot, position or circumstances to some extent, it is only in some circumstances that this can be employed to motivate. Sometimes it is a blind dissatisfaction, in the sense that the individual sees the cause of his dissatisfaction as inherent in the surrounding system: "It's the rich wot gets the pleasures: it's the poor wot gets the blame; it's the same the whole world over" etc. But there can be no reason why this should always be so, nor for that matter any reason why it should

380

only be capable of resolution by cataclysmic revolution. There are dissatisfactions whose source is seen to be quite capable of removal or reduction by 'ordinary' means. This may be so with a manager dissatisfied with the level of profit or of efficiency in his factory or department, with the worker who considers his current wage level too low or with the foreman who feels that the senior management no longer has his welfare very much at heart. In all these cases there are steps that can be taken, some short-term and some longer-term, to effect redress of the grievance against the system.

We should not blind ourselves to the fact that although in some cases power to change things (and therefore to tackle the source of dissatisfaction) is institutionalized, in others it is absent or minimal. In the three examples used in the previous paragraph, it might be said that (a) the manager's power is highly institutionalized from a long time ago; (b) the worker's trade union and negotiating power is now fairly well established in institutions of collective bargaining; but (c) the foreman's power is often extremely limited, if only because his position in one institutionalized system of power has been undermined whilst his position in the other has not yet been established. Many other examples of a similar type might be put forward but these are sufficient merely to establish this point.

The important point is that effective management must recognize that emotions will only work constructively in the general interest if they can be employed purposively in the particular interest. If the individual has a grievance which he wishes to reduce, it is necessary to allow this to be achieved within a framework of pursuing general interests. In simple terms, the reduction of a grievance about the relative wage level is to be reduced within a framework of securing greater overall efficiency. Putting this the other way round, it is unlikely that an individual will make his maximum (or even a large) contribution to overall efficiency if the system cannot or will not facilitate the reduction of his own particular wage grievance. In putting forward this idea, all that is being stated is the basic principle of incentive. All that is at all new about it is the extension of the idea to encompass any 'grievance' or source of dissatisfaction with the current operation of the system.

Whilst one does not wish to argue that all causes of dissatisfaction are reducible if the power to make changes is available, it is necessary to see that in a multiple goal system, a conscious attempt may need to be made to secure the reduction of as many of them as possible within the wider process of realizing the substantive objectives of the system. Nor is this a new idea. It is implicit in the model of industrial organization put forward by Barnard in 1938 and widely copied in other analyses since that date. In this model, the contributions (or burdens) of each category of participant (eg customers, workers or shareholders) must equate in the end with the rewards demanded by each category of participants in return for this contribution. What constitutes the 'right' return for each contribution is a matter of value judgement in each case and, in the definition of value for the individual, emotions as much as reason play their part. If it is usual to see Barnard's model in purely economic equilibrium terms, there seems to be no essential reason why it should be so restricted: burdens and rewards are terms which could well carry meanings beyond that of economics.

To get away from this limited conception, it is likely to be necessary to open up the perspective to admit that motivation processes are as complex as they are shown to be in the terms of expectancy theory (see above, chapter 4). This leads in turn to a realization that expectancies can be changed and that to change them it may be necessary to conceive organisations as, *inter alia*, concerned with the management of learning on a comprehensive scale. Since organizations cannot escape the consequences of people having feelings and perspectives of their own, they might acknowledge this and put it to effect to allow these people to develop their feelings and cognitions within a 'learning situation'. The volatility or changeability of real life situations, in other words, may require undertakings to develop styles of operation in which the different feelings and conceptions have an opportunity for development and influence.

This carries important implications for organizational or management style and for definition of managerial roles.

The rationale of the approach as it relates to these may be stated in the following observations and propositions:

(i)   all organizations have problems, some of them severe and some mild, some of them technical and some of them human or organizational: it is quite natural that they should if the enterprise is still alive

(ii)   all sections of the organization have a degree of awareness of these problems and, if they are severe enough in the way they affect the group in question, they will not be slow to identify them as problems; therefore any such group can identify the organization's problems in a rank order of severity or primacy *for them*

(iii)   an organization may not be able to solve all its problems (revealed in this way) either because it lacks people with the appropriate skills and abilities to do so, or because it erects some kind of barrier between those with the ability and skill and the action required on the problem

(iv) in either case, the company may seek to remedy its deficiencies by engaging someone (a consultant or permanent staff addition) with the skills required but, if it sets its face against this, it must tackle the other problem of developing the skills of its existing personnel or of developing the organization so that those with skills get access to the problem

(v) the reasons why it might sensibly set its face against the first solution in some cases are rather complicated, but there are many identifiable problems in an organization which require not merely individual expertize and skill but rather the application of a 'collected' or a 'concerted' expertize and skill amongst the whole group or large parts of it; (for example, a personnel manager can have a great effect on industrial relations or human relations but cannot himself restructure the system: he needs at least the help of line management and supervision)

(vi) a collected or a concerted approach does not mean that the show should be run by 'committees' in the usual pejorative sense of this term (camel—a horse designed by a 'committee'); it means rather that a group of people who have a common focus and influence in their work should consciously seek to develop a common philosophy or approach which is in line with the objectives sought overall by the enterprise

(vii) another way of covering this point is to describe it as an approach which is essentially systematic; the group must put itself in the position where it can question its own assumptions for decision and action without acrimony and recrimination but with 'skill' in organizing itself as a cohesive and effective team; this means developing not only an understanding of 'group dynamics' about itself, but also an appreciation of what approach lies at the root of 'order' in decision and action

(viii) on these last three points, it is clearly necessary to consider the allocation of roles, not simply in mechanistic terms (accountant, personnel officer, fitter or despatcher) but rather in terms of the concepts of change agent, catalyst, pacemaker and client-system defined above. This in turn calls for adequate formal training in the roles involved, whether through T-group, grid or any other brand of structured learning about roles in group structures

(ix) thus in summary, this approach means actively canvassing feelings about changes which might be to someone's benefit, providing opportunities for these to be explored in application, providing a framework of direction and control to ensure their ordered consideration and introduction and, in the process, providing more members of the organization with a chance to learn and to develop themselves along with the undertaking.

Structural and method changes

Some of these features are to be found in developments which have occurred in recent years where the object has been either to change methods of operation (practice) or to change social structures. It does not follow that a complete rationale lies behind all of these but significant features of it are incorporated in plans for organizational development, management by objectives and management style changes, some forms of productivity or efficiency bargaining, and in plans for the introduction of job enrichment and autonomous work groups. What may be said of these is that generally they are developed in a relatively *ad hoc* fashion, not as a package of changes designed to secure *general* development and *general* learning by all sections and categories of the undertaking. Thus MbO tends to be limited to a certain depth of management, productivity bargaining is often seen as concerned mainly with blue-collar work and organizational development is often evolved close to the corporate team. On the other hand, job enrichment is often thought of in isolation from developments in the area of representative systems and negotiations, although the latter kind of development could lead to some job enrichment.

To some extent, training to create greater awareness of alternatives in managerial style may be regarded as the more pervasive in its potential influence, but this too is often seen as a purely managerial kind of experience.

A changing balance between machines and people in the process of production effected by new technologies may be held to account for a comparable change in emphasis upon technical and personnel management. As suggested by the study of new technologies by Burns (1961), one effect of the change upon management in particular is to take the emphasis away from the mechanistically-defined 'office' or work role, and place it instead upon the organically-conceived contribution to the well-being or development of the undertaking: accountants and mechanical engineers turn into members of a developmental team who may happen to have certain types of basic knowledge. Generalizing this trend, it may be suggested that the new situations tend to call more frequently for skills in the area of inter-personal influence: impact upon existing structures and processes in existing organizations becomes of greater relative importance than before. Another way of expressing this is to suggest that the kinds of role identified above—of change agent, catalyst, pacemaker—become more in demand as those of cost accountant, progress chaser or even general foreman become less so.

This in turn has created a strong demand for training facilities to establish the ground rules of the new types of role and consultant organizations and academics have not been slow in offering them. There is a line of development in human relations training for managers, often expressed in group dynamics or T-group training sessions in the past but now increasingly linked with 'grid' training, in which similar exposures to perspectives are offered albeit within a structured 'forced-choice' framework of opportunity (see Blake and Mouton, 1964; Reddin, 1964). The rationale of this kind of exposure is, essentially, that managerial work activity is inter-personal or social in its manifestation, and that therefore the success or otherwise of managerial effort will depend in part at least upon the kind of impact that the managerial person makes upon the other person(s) with whom he must inevitably work; less obvious, but no less important for that, is the fact that the 'impact' will also depend upon the expectations which the other holds of behaviour emanating from the manager. This kind of training therefore seeks to hold up the mirror to the manager's own behaviour, so that he can the better appreciate its image and impact, and in grid training more explicitly demonstrates that there is a 'fashion' in expectations which has also to be borne in mind. The 'forced-choice' referred to, which poses this last issue for the manager, is that between a task orientation or a Theory X conception of the managerial role, and a people orientation or a Theory Y conception (cf McGregor, 1960). Although it is always emphasized that managerial 'style' (as the outcome of the training is called) does not *have to be* one which balances the alternatives, it is usually impossible to prevent managers in training from adopting some such perceived social value which it is thought will legitimate style.

Blake's grid is the creation of Robert R Blake whose writings on group dynamics, T-group and management training are prolific and figure as essential reading for those who go through the grid training exercise. He is currently a consultant, trading as Scientific Methods Inc of Austin, Texas, whose object is to sell the grid in the form of a six phase training package to any interested management group. An important part of the marketing exercise is that there are no 'part-packages': the package must be swallowed whole or not at all. Reddin's three-dimension grid is an extension from this. Reddin develops his concept from a criticism of both McGregor and Blake, centering largely on the place of 'effectiveness' in the scheme of things. His grid approach has been applied by him in a number of firms in Canada and abroad. In both cases, an aim is to develop a greater awareness of roles, both about the opportunities or choices open and the constraints imposed by the organizational purposes, at the level of the individual manager—a preparation for the adoption of those roles (like change agent or catalyst) which are requisite to organizational change.

The prime purpose of the grid approach is to secure managerial commitment to the aims and methods of the organization. In this it goes well beyond the group dynamics/T-group training approach, in which the object is to provide an unstructured problem-solving situation in which people can learn in interaction with others what their personal impact on others is like and, on the basis of this heightened knowledge, develop a greater awareness of both themselves and others and thus acquire a more positive foundation for understanding and communication. The grid uses these methods but in a more definitely structured situation, in which the structure is aligned to the prime object of recruiting commitment.

The starting point for this is the simple premise that an organization is both a production unit and a social organism. All organizations are seen to have two intertwined sets of objectives, one concerned with the development of a satisfactory relationship with the external environment (eg production for sale in a commercial company), and the other relating to the internal environment (eg the maintenance of a healthy, functioning production/selling organization). Much of the pre-seminar reading which participants in the exercise are required to do is related to this simple understanding.

Blake and Mouton have erected on this premise a simple chart on which managerial attitudes and performances can be measured. The two axes of the graph are identified as 'concern for production' (horizontal) and 'concern for people' (vertical). Each is scaled from 1–9, the numbers being merely gradations from low to high concern. The resultant matrix presents a theoretical 81 co-ordinates but for practical purposes only the four corner boxes and the middle of the graph box are employed. In effect, therefore, the grid employs the categories of 'low-low', 'low-high', 'high-low', intermediate and 'high-high' as the relevant and workable categories. A scale of 1–3 on each axis would therefore serve the practical purposes as well as the 1–9 scales now used, and it would still be possible to use the term 'grid' for it.

The grid itself is the basic device which provides the invitation to managers to move into the more acceptable and more desirable corner of the graph. As is illustrated in the chart below, the scale numbers become the shorthand jargon expressions for the identification of the 'position' of the manager. Since only the 9.9 or high-high position is perceived to be acceptable or desirable this is the obvious place for any manager worth his salt, hence the pressure to

386

Figure 14

Main dimensions of Blake's and Reddin's Grids
(for details see, Blake, R R and Mouton, J S, The Managerial Grid, Gulf
Publishing, 1964, p 10; and Reddin, W J, The Tri-dimensional Grid,
Training Directors' Journal, July, 1964, p 18)

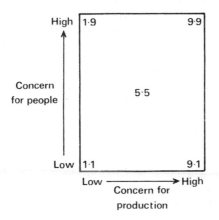

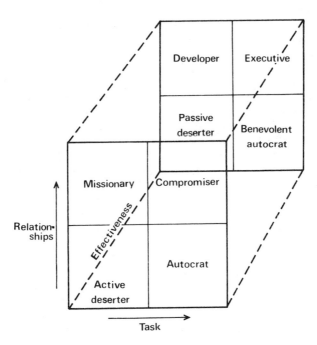

move towards it. In all the other (four) positions, the manager is found wanting on one or both scores to some degree (ie 1.1 means that he is completely wanting on both, 5.5. that he is partly wanting on both, and 1.9 and 9.1 that he is wanting on one or the other).

The social scientist will readily see the theoretical bases of this grid. First, it depends upon the achievement/maintenance distinction of the natural system theorist and of the recent understandings of leadership as a cluster of actions appropriate to system functioning. Secondly, it depicts in modified terminology the compliance relationships identified by Etzioni and locates Whyte's 'organization man' on the 5.5 management square; it attempts a modified synthesis of McGregor's Theory X and Theory Y approaches to management.

Reddin has criticized the ultra-simplicity of Blake's two-dimensional grid in terms similar to those which he levels against the basic McGregor dimensions. His main point is that where McGregor sees the pure relationship orientation as optimal, Blake brands this as ineffective because he sees effectiveness as possible only with a *combination* of the relationship and production concerns (ie the 9.9 management style). Reddin replaces the production concern by a task orientation; he puts forward a *three* dimensional grid which admits as a separate dimension the variable of effectiveness, and then assigns Blake's four 'ineffective' positions to the plane of ineffectiveness and his 9.9 style to that of effectiveness, which is then expanded to include other degrees of effectiveness but on *both* other planes.

He thus sees some possibility of retaining the underlying ideas of both McGregor and Blake in his new three dimensional grid but argues that the "assumptions" of the one and the "concerns" of the other must be recast as orientations and linked with a third dimension of effectiveness. Where Blake uses the terms 'concerns for production' and 'concerns for relationships' he substitutes "orientations" (as being more behavioural and less intellectual) first to "task" and secondly to "relationships" respectively and argues that either can be implemented effectively or ineffectively with 'effectiveness' defined in terms of "long-run production". Movement along the 'X' (task) and 'Y' (relationship) axes, he then refers to as indicating an increasing commitment to, or amount of, each oriented behaviour and that along the 'Z' (effectiveness) axis as "resulting eventually in optimum production" (Reddin, 1964, p 14).

Reddin depicts his grid in the form on p 387, in which four combinations of task- and relationships-orientations are indicated for each of the two planes of effectiveness and ineffectiveness. The terms used to indicate these are derived from current North American stereotypes of managerial style.

388

In spite of the distinction introduced by these two consultants between the descriptions of their various axes, there is a hint at least that both wish to draw a distinction between affective and cognitive concerns or orientations. Given the past tendency to emphasize the (cognitive) rationality of the work organization, the modification of this to take account of (affective) relationships in managerial style, can be viewed as no more than an attempt to redress the balance—and then to train a new cadre of managers to operate in this more balanced way. It is distinctly possible that the depicting of the choices in the form of a two- or three-dimensional grid is a useful way of communicating the essentials. But it is also possible that the maintenance of the cognitive/affective distinction helps to continue the belief that the two aspects must remain separate—that task orientations reflect the 'hard' or 'real' interest of the organization and its management, and that relationship orientations represent a 'soft' and somehow 'unreal' interest. The challenges to authority (or domination) which we have noted in chapter 7 may call for a new synthesis of such conceptions of real or proper interest in management: this may indeed prove to be the direction in which the new 'rules' which may be established on the changed power base may be leading.

Thus the training indicated by these grid approaches may prove advantageous in setting the limits of choice facing management which seeks to re-establish its authority in a changed environment of cultural value and changed allocation of power, but the *outcome* of that training may have to be a capacity to put together some answers to the real, cognitive and affective, problems facing work organizations at present. There are a number of categories of answer, in this sense, at which we may look because they are indicative of initiative to reformulate the approach to the resolution of real issues at various levels in organizations. Whilst the ones which are singled out here (managing by objectives, job enrichment and productivity bargaining) cannot be regarded as all-embracing solutions to the problem, they do in several ways and in relation to different elements of the organization's existence, offer an indication of the likely way ahead for the exercise of managerial authority.

Managing by objectives

These excursions into the development of greater awareness of managerial role processes and consequences are, it may be argued, unlikely to be proved successful (or effective in Reddin's sense) unless the undertaking itself is so structured normatively that it can admit effective style changes. A manager may be aware of what roles are necessary to achieve a given objective, but may see no way in which the objective itself is legitimated and therefore no basis on which he can adopt the requisite role. Furthermore, the legitimation required for this purpose may be of a type which passes beyond the 'authority of the boss'; it may need to have a minimal amount of legitimacy in the perceptions of 'non-bosses' if the role is to be sustained.

It is here that the developments which usually fall under the heading of management by objectives (MbO) assume relevance to the present discussion. As put forward by Drucker (1955) and pursued by many others since, this approach emphasizes the need for undertakings to find some method of so legitimating objectives that people will feel both able and willing to pursue them in the organizational context. This need is met by making objective-setting a deliberately joint exercise, between boss and subordinate, in which the latter is given the opportunity to indicate not only what he considers he could do but also what he thinks he should do. In this way, for example, the individual has some opportunity to secure legitimacy for his 'dissatisfactions' with what is current and for his 'theories' as to what ought to be done. It requires the 'boss' as the significant other in the exercise to adopt his co-ordinating role in relation to all subordinates, by urging the wider considerations which must constrain the one individual in his role but to do so within a framework of provision of opportunities.

This perspective is clear enough in Drucker's original outline of the approach. Management by objectives, he argues "requires each manager to develop and set the objectives of his unit himself" even if at the same time "higher management must reserve the power to approve or disapprove these objectives". "Their development" remains "part of a manager's responsibility" and furthermore "every manager should responsibly participate in the development of the objectives of the higher unit of which his is a part" (Drucker, 1961, p 111).

This not only gives the individual manager an opportunity to say his piece, under certain constraints, but also puts the more senior manager on the spot by exposing him to criticism (actual or potential) and by requiring of him the special efforts to ensure that not only are all his subordinate managers *au fait* with the overall objectives of the larger unit but that they are also freed from the encumbrances of misdirection (arising out of casual comments and suggestions or intermittent inspections).

The adoption of the goals and controls programme by the Purex Corporation, in 15 separate manufacturing departments in 1961–62 with the aim of improving managerial performance, gave Raia (1965) the experimental conditions necessary to make a study of the outcome of applying Drucker's proposals. His findings show how objectives and self-control of performance were both improved by an essentially participative approach. In the general management policy document about the use of goals and controls, the company stated that it was policy "to have every member of supervision work with his immediate superior to set goals for his area of operation and establish controls to assure their attainment". It also stated the purpose of establishing controls as that of supplying "information directly to the individual who is responsible for a definite area of operation so that he may on his own initiative act to correct any deficiencies and report the corrective action to his superior" (Raia, 1965, p 35).

The programme had, therefore, three main ingredients:

goal setting by the individual manager under the guidance of his immediate supervisor

control by the individual on his own initiative in response to control information supplied to him as well as superiors

periodic review in relation to established goals with an aim of removing identifiable obstacles to their attainment. (*Ibid*, pp 157).

Raia measured some aspects of performance—goal levels, goal attainment, productivity, introduction of new goals and removal of obstacles—and some aspects of attitude, motivation, authority and goal awareness. He produced a number of measures and indicators of the changes resulting from the introduction of this more participatory style and these may be summarized briefly.

Goal levels were measured for production goals, usually set in June, as a basis for the operating budget and adjusted quarterly. Although some adjustments were downward, particularly in the course of an operating year, four times as many were found to be upward adjustments over the whole period of the programme from 1962–4. Raia takes the goal level for the 1963 fiscal year as 100 and shows graphically that "the goal level increased from 95 per cent in the fourth quarter of 1962 to 100 per cent in the fiscal year 1963, and from 97.8 per cent in the fourth quarter of 1963 to 102 per cent for 1964," giving net increases of 3.0 and 2.7 per cent between the fiscal year targets.

Goal attainment was measured in terms of output expressed in terms of goal hours divided by labour hours actually expended, for the fiscal year 1963. On his evidence, Raia shows that "the average percentage of attainment of the original goals started at approximately 96 per cent, decreased to almost 93 per cent, and then rose to 98 per cent by the end of the period" and thus, at the end equalled the revised goal level.

In this company the use of standard work study data enabled Raia to measure productivity by dividing actual hours of work (ie including wash-up, maintenance etc time) by standard labour hours produced. For a number of technical reasons his time series was discontinuous but still permitted a before and after comparison, even though the vertical scale was omitted at the company's request from the published graphs. He found that where before average productivity for all plants was falling at a rate of more than 0.4 per cent per month, 13 improved their productivity levels and/or trends between the two periods, and after ran at an average level 18 per cent higher and was increasing at a rate of about 0.3 per cent per month.

Raia identified 'new goal areas' introduced as those making their first appearance in the written performance reviews, and improvements where such was reported subsequently or supported by statistics. He found that on this basis 14 of the 15 plants had introduced one or more new goals, amounting in total to 27 instances of measurable goals (14 subsequently reporting or showing improvements) and another 23 instances of new goals of a non-measurable variety (eg safety programme (9), plant cleanliness (4), training programme (3) etc).

Some attempt was also made in interviews with managers to assess opinions on the efficiency of the periodic performance review in helping to identify and remove obstacles to higher performance. Statistical data on this aspect are poor but a majority of those interviewed (eight out of 10) felt that the reviews were important from this point of view.

In the interview programme which Raia conducted with operating managers, he asked about certain perceptual and attitudinal reactions to the change. An attempt to measure both the "direction and intensity of the attitude of participants toward various aspects of their work led to the conclusion that there was a "relatively highly favourable attitude in all of the plants", all but two of the 112 interviewed scoring highly. Furthermore, "many . . . statements made during the interviews indicated that the periodic performance reviews provided participants with strong motivation to improve their performance" (p 43). Managers were also more aware of increased authority or scope as a result of the programme, and felt that the goals set provided a sounder, readier basis for the individual performance review as well as generally improving communications.

In similar vein, all participants in the programme were asked to indicate the relative importance they attached to each objective identified in a list supplied to them, by ranking them in order from one to 16. The production director was asked to do the same, and when the two were compared, the rank correlation coefficient was computed to be 0.9991, "indicating" says Raia, "a high degree of correlation between the two rankings (and) a high degree of awareness at the operating plant levels" although interview data suggested that this result might not be attributable simply to the goals and controls programme.

Thus the general effect is one of improvement from most of the points of view that managers or anyone else would regard as the relevant and important ones. Performance, productivity, organization and satisfaction seem to be higher in most cases, suggesting that everyone with an interest in the operation of the system might be getting something out of it. On the other hand, Raia is realistic in reporting snags which had not been ironed out. In particular he is able to show interview data on who participates in goal setting and who does not, and that whilst plant managers met their supervisors regularly, at the two lower levels of management "only a proportion reported that they attended regular scheduled meetings with their immediate superiors", suggesting that the programme was not being fully implemented at lower levels. He goes on to suggest that "there is considerable evidence that the company philosophy of growth for the individual has not yet permeated throughout the entire organization. There appears to be some distortion, particularly at the lower levels" and this may in turn account for the failure to achieve fuller implementation of participation.

It may be concluded from this study that this kind of more open approach to the solution of 'task' related problems in the organization, which simultaneously sought to allow more involvement of the individual's feelings and preferences, is that it produced some efficiency and some satisfaction benefits and some disadvantages on both scores. This might be expected on the *a priori* grounds that (a) people do differ in their perception of and reaction to any given environmental stimulus, and (b) people used to one kind of work environment will not necessarily 'take to' a change of this sort just because it has been introduced (even with their consent). But at the same time it is possible to detect in the replies of managers in the interviews some willingness to calculate the benefits and drawbacks of the new arrangement and, depending on the outcome, to give it a go if it promised some longer-term satisfaction—for task or maintenance reasons.

A number of organizations are now experimenting with changes of approach or style in which some of these same general features are to be found. Many of them are confined, as in the above case study, to relatively senior managerial personnel. We have already noted that managers (as a manifestation of white collar or professional workers as a class) are likely to attach particular meaning to their work; we would therefore expect this to colour their appreciation of such a change and to affect their willingness to go along with it. For the same reasons, we would not expect blue-collar workers to respond in just this same fashion; therefore any attempt to carry the principles or the lessons of this kind of managerial exercise forward into blue-collar activities would tend to generate expectations of a different kind of response from such workers. Nevertheless, if more open styles of organization and management are to have any future they will have to have implications and effects at this other level of organization. The question of just how comparable developments are to be effected there, in order to meet efficiency or satisfaction criteria or both, is by no means an easy one to answer but some experiments are discernible in this area too, which indicate a similar kind of OD approach.

Job enrichment

The various developments which go under the headings of job enlargement, job enrichment and autonomous work groups (although there are some differences between them) illustrate in some of their manifestations, first an interest in making some planned response to the *behavioural* messages of shop floor workers, usually in line- and machine-paced work, and secondly a concern to effect that response in a controlled and systematic fashion. By and large, many of these early schemes were developed on the foundation of an application of managerial knowledge and skill to the solution of a problem defined managerially; as they have developed, these more autocratic features have often given way to a more participative approach in which the people concerned, or their representatives, have been involved in the planning and evaluation exercises, so that the behaviour messages (absence, labour turnover, spasmodic application to work) came to be supplemented by oral expressions of concern.

Job enrichment attempts to augment the discretion which the individual has to determine his work pattern or pace or the manner in which he will order his decisions. It is therefore possible to give a salesman more discretion to negotiate prices and terms with customers, or an office worker to vary his routines to suit himself within wider constraints than he experienced before. In many situations, the variation thus allowed to the individual would necessarily affect others in the section or department, and one variant on this theme therefore seeks to place the increased discretion in the hands of 'the group' rather than the individual. In that context, the notion of the autonomous work group merges with that of job enrichment. Some of the more widely known examples of job enrichment fall into this category; the 'grouping' of assembly-line operations in Phillips,

Eindhoven, or in the Saab or Volvo plants in Sweden, for example. In these cases, the individual may benefit from the increased authority which is devolved to the work group but the group must itself 'take' the decisions for the sake of equity and co-ordination, so that the possibility exists that the group might be as constraining as the foreman might have been before. Consequently, in many of these experiments the attempt is made, via selection, to ensure that those who want to participate in this new arrangement are the ones who are given the opportunity whilst others who prefer to do so stay outside them: itself an attempt to allow increased discretion.

The changes in the structure of the work and the work groups which occur in these experiments indicate a reversal of a dominant trend in work fragmentation which has been with us over the whole of the period of the industrial revolution. For this reason if for no other, we should not expect that people will accept this change overnight. In fact, Walsh in his report on changes in the work of Electricity Board district offices (1969) indicates something of this where he points out (a) that *younger* people are more able to take this in their stride, whilst *older* people find it more difficult to adapt and to cope with the new situation, and (b) that supervisors experienced considerable *initial* difficulties in adopting the new role (revealed in anxiety) and that management in turn was within an ace of panicking in the *early stages* when performance fell off as people had to unlearn and relearn. By implication, the longer or the deeper involvement in or commitment to the existing system, the greater the difficulty of adjustment revealed. Although Walsh infers from this that the first step ought therefore to be the selling of job enrichment to senior management, the point might be extended to suggest that selling will be more necessary the longer or the deeper the involvement of the category of person/status concerned.

This is helped by the existence of long term benefits:

(a) more contentment in the enriched sections
(b) less supervision, and lower costs, without deterioration in standards of work
(c) the development of a better attitude to the job and much more recognition of the importance of good customer relations
(d) finally, staffs themselves say they have a better sense of participation in really worthwhile work. Their sense of achievement is greatly enhanced (*Ibid*, p 44)

The emphasis here upon 'the long-term' is important, although others report shorter-term advantages.

Van Beek reports one of the earlier experiments, that of the work on assembly lines in Phillips' Eindhoven TV receiver factory started in 1960. The basis of this experiment was the modification of the organization of the line and the work associated with it, and measurement of the consequences of these changes was attempted in terms of output, quality and morale.

A complaint about the amount of waiting time on the line led to the division of one line of 104 workers into five distinct groups (ranging in size from 14–29 workers) separated by (a) inspection points and (b) buffer stocks amounting to the equivalent of an hour's work. This change was reported as reducing waiting time due to lack of material to 55 per cent, increasing earnings, heightening morale and reducing absenteeism. Further evaluating studies suggested that "the shorter line with buffer stocks between adjacent workplaces offers the most favourable possibilities to achieve a good quality" (p 160).

Nevertheless, this is not achieved without cost and the investigators indicate some of these: "The small group . . . also presents disadvantages. Small groups will for example require more space and increase the intermediate stocks. In some respects the small group may also make more demands on supervision. Where in the long line a member of individuals had to be dealt with, the small group constitutes a nucleus of informal organization, "which will have to be guided into a positive direction" (*ibid*, p 171). Whilst one might still question, in line with modern systems theory, just what is meant by "a positive direction" this makes it quite clear that there are problems for management. It is not merely a matter of changing the spatial layout to improve productivity and morale. It is also a question of learning how to cope with the consequent organizational and leadership problems which are effected coincidentally.

One of the more encouraging features of the movement towards autonomous work groups etc, has been just this blending of an economic realism, represented by management's willingness to experiment if the cost-benefit position is demonstrated to be correct, and the more reliable findings of empirical social research.

The problem set for management is, as van Beek suggests, that rational methods ("job analysis permitting of dividing jobs into short cycle tasks which could be learned quickly and in which unskilled workers could reach a high level of proficiency, the assembly line promoting a regular flow of production and wage systems ensuring an equitable remuneration") may no longer provide an answer to some of the problems faced by managements. "Extensive specialization" renders the production system vulnerable, sophisticated wage systems prove ineffective, better education and changed attitudes work against rigorous division, so that "it is therefore highly necessary to study and reassess continually the organization of unskilled work" (van Beek, 1964, p 161).

396

Unless the concept of efficiency is comprehended in its broadest meaning, as defined, for example, by Barnard (1938) and those who followed him (particularly Simon, 1953), the managerial concern with and for efficiency is likely to lead him to seek changes only or mainly when the economic pay-off can be persuasively asserted or demonstrated to be higher than in the existing arrangements. The failure of the human relations school to achieve this end, through its empirical work and advocacy, accounts for some at least of the failure of the proponents to secure more widespread acceptance of their theories. The 'job enrichment' approach finds its academic ancestry in the work of Herzberg and his colleagues (1959) where 'motivators' were shown to be associated with work itself, and it seemed sensible to vary the actual work in order to increase the incentive effect. In the development of work organization over the years, attention seemed to fasten on the 'hygiene' (environmental) factors in work, as the principle of specialization remained inviolable and job enrichment promises to balance the two more evenly. As Paul and Robertson (1969) express this point of view: "At a time when there is a premium on individual effort, as labour becomes too costly to waste and concern about the underemployment of people in industry mounts, theory suggests that more attention to the motivators, a more critical look at the jobs themselves. . . . would pay dividends" (p 2). As managers have begun their own experiments in this field, and as more work has been done on costing what they yield, hard economic data is being produced to support the desirability of this kind of approach.

The work of van Beek, Paul and Robertson and the rest in this area of executive activity, ie at the level of shop floor workers, salesmen or draughtsmen, has something of a counterpart in management activity. In this case, reference is usually not made to 'job enrichment' as such, although the consequence might be comparable. At this level the emphasis is rather upon a kind of rediscovery of the relevance of the 'group' as a part of the decision-taking structure. Regardless of the extent to which employees on the shop floor have been regarded as individualists and individually responsible for their actions, at the managerial level the principle of individual responsibility and accountability has been almost invariably upheld. But there are exceptions: at the corporate level, custom and practice supported by the law regards decision-taking as something for the group—the board of directors; at the administrative level, a rather guilty custom and practice has developed of using the committee structure in decision-taking, although even then attempts are made to assuage the guilt by leaving the 'final decision' to some individual. These are however regarded as exceptions and few would hitherto

397

make much of the value of group decision (see Maurer, 1955).

The exceptions may shortly become the rule, even in business organizations. In 'normative organizations' there is stronger evidence that the change is already taking place: one could argue, as have Burns (1961), Ogden (1973) and Bains (1972), that the underlying model in such structures is one which depends upon group participation. What has happened more recently is that this use of the group has been formalized in local government, social work, hospitals and educational organizational decision taking. It specifically abjures the taking of decisions as a matter simply of individual initiative or responsibility and requires that a group, or more likely a 'team', shall accept the responsibility for taking necessary decisions. Most evidence for this degree of formalization is to be found in the proposals for management of the new and reorganized health services in the UK where the area teams and district teams of full-time personnel are expected to reach unanimity before administrative management decisions are taken at the level of the team's responsibility.

In high technology industries and in those parts of business which require highly trained staff (such as research bodies), there is some evidence to suggest that a similar 'team-decision' process occurs, even if such decisions remain to be agreed by the individual manager concerned. What seems to have brought about this state of affairs is the need to cope with highly specialized knowledge inside a decision structure which assumes omniscience at the top of a hierarchy, where such omniscience just cannot exist. The response has been to treat the 'group' as the fount of knowledge rather than the 'responsible individual'.

Even if this is done 'informally', and even if the individual concerned still ostensibly takes responsibility for the decision, both he and those who participate in the decision taking probably regard their jobs as 'enriched' as a result: he because he is freed from an impossible role constraint in practice if not in principle, and they because they are able to express their points of view in the face of the need to reach a decision. This is not necessarily all 'personal gain' or 'undiscounted psychological income': as Burns has commented about the organic type of management organization, it can be Hell for the participants, largely because for the subordinates in the system a good deal of the uncertainty previously absorbed by the monocratic decision-taking structure, is now left for absorption by the participants in the group decision taking process. Even if the people concerned are quite willing and capable of accepting this kind of challenge in the interests of self-development, there is a clear sense in which the changeover from one system to the other produces its share of 'shock' and 'frustration'. The evidence for this effect is to be found both at managerial and shop floor levels of participation (van Beek, 1964; Jaques, 1951)

These two types of development together call for the application of knowledge, know-how and skill on the part of someone to facilitate the changeover and to cope with the resulting problems faced by individuals and groups caught up in it. A rapidly growing literature on the general subject of OD attests to the existence of a demand for knowledge and know-how; the fact that many of these are written by freelance consultants further suggests that there is a dearth of sufficiently skilled manpower within organizations to deal with the problem. (see for example Bennis, 1966; Bennis, Benne and Chin 1969; Jones, 1968; Lippitt, 1969). More recently, experimental activity by organizations using their own manpower are more frequently being reported (Butteris, 1971 and 1975; Thomason, 1971) suggesting that some personnel departments have acquired and are willing and able to apply the skills required to effect such changes as these. Although the skills called for are in some cases ones which the personnel department has usually attracted in plenty—of advice and counselling, negotiation and training—in others they are relatively new since they demand an ability to analyse and change the directions and orientations of large groups of people, whether 'departmental' or 'occupational'.

Productivity bargaining

In some of the earlier approaches to productivity bargaining in the late 1960s, the possibility of using a general involvement method of securing agreement was adopted. Now that interest in the subject is being resurrected at the end of the pay policy period of the middle 1970s, (cf Jones, 1978) it may focus increasingly on the non-traditional bargaining stances taken up at that time in a number of (usually high technology) undertakings. The traditional position was generally one in which management, having engaged in analysis and planning before the negotiations, sought in those negotiations to secure agreement to the plan or something as near to it as the exigencies of the bargaining situation would permit. From the beginning, productivity bargaining began to open up the situation at the bargaining table by interposing novel stages. A plan might be arrived at but before it was put into negotiation soundings were taken and the plan modified in the light of them; only then was the bargaining process begun. This was the kind of approach associated with the Fawley agreement and also that in Alcan. Another variant of this was the production of a 'part plan' which was discussed in part, before the whole plan was formulated for introduction into bargaining, as happened with the ICI and Electricity Supply bargains in the middle 1960s (NBPI, Report No 36, 1968).

These might be regarded as tentative moves to open up the bargaining situation to a degree of problem-solving in advance of an actual bargaining process being undertaken. The problem foreseen, was that building sufficient trust to achieve this end might prove difficult. This is indicated in McKersie's statement that "one side needs to expose itself—it runs the risk of being victimized, but it also creates the possibility of having the trusting overture reinforced by a similar gesture" (McKersie, 1966, p vii).

The NBPI Report on Productivity Agreements suggested that the risk might be worth taking "in the light of this varied experience" and that "the advantage lies with joint discussion of principles with the unions before the presentation of formal proposals and with early discussions at workshop level. This view is supported by the contrast between the patchy reception of the ICI proposals and the reluctance of some of the men on the trial sites to go ahead; and, on the other hand, the ease with which British Oxygen's final agreement went through, was accepted and applied." (NBPI, 36, p 33).

Table 16

The evolution of productivity bargaining

Step	Stages in evolution			
	Traditional	*Esso Alcan*	*ICI Elect. Supply*	*British Oxygen Mobil Oil*
1	Plan	Plan	Part plan	Define problems
2	Imposition in bargain	Soundings	Discuss	Discuss and agree principles
3	—	Modification of plan	Full plan	Local consultation and agreement
4	—	Imposition in bargain	Imposition in bargain	Formal proposals
5	—	—	—	Agreement to joint solution

In the British Oxygen and Mobil Oil approaches to this problem, even more stages were introduced into the process in order to give more opportunity for discussion of general principles and criteria before plans were formulated and negotiated. On the basis of this and comparable experience in a number of other instances, a connected sequence of stages may be postulated as a means of reducing the risk already noted:

(a) a definition of the problems faced by the parties (not just one)
(b) a discussion and agreement on the principles which will be applied to the negotiation of their solution
(c) a spread of awareness, involvement and agreement throughout the departments or branches of the undertaking, so that all (management and workers) likely to be affected have a chance to express their views before a formal plan is made
(d) a gathering together of these views with the principles and the analyses of the problem, in the form of a plan which can be discussed and amended before the final negotiating sessions
(e) a formal negotiation on the 'equity' of the final solution as depicted in the plan.

The general import of this is that two major changes of principle are involved in the approach:

(a) the evolution of a new discussive—consultative—bargaining relationship out of the traditional bargaining framework
(b) the growth in the time-investment required to secure solution and acceptance before 'agreement'.

These changes do allow more emotional commitment on the part of the managers and the workers likely to be affected by any final agreement, and allow that criticisms which are often voiced after agreements have been arrived at to be put before the negotiation takes place. If there is a greater time commitment to communications and discussion in these approaches, this might be justified, as in a number of the undertakings mentioned above, on the ground that it is easier to modify plans whilst they are still being made than after they have been agreed between the parties.

Such deliberate attempts at total involvement in problem solving in relation to the wage-effort or reward-contribution bargain also changes the conception of learning and training in these undertakings. In effect communications and training become so interwoven that it is difficult to separate the two. On the one hand, there are frequent references to the 'place' of training in this bargaining process. The formal perspective is summarized by Harris (1968, p 18) in the following passage:

> The preparation and planning which must precede productivity bargaining cannot be done until management and all others involved have an adequate understanding of the basic economics of production and the means of measuring productivity: an appreciation of its financial implications is also needed ... The intensive consultation that must precede plant bargaining and the negotiation that ensues must involve many managers, supervisors,

employees and employee representatives. This communication will not be effective unless it is conducted with understanding, skill and conviction by all concerned. Training in the objectives and methods to be pursued may therefore be as important for effective communication and negotiation as for preliminary planning. This may mean training employee representatives as well as management and supervision in basic production economics. (Harris, 1968, p 18).

On the other hand the creation of a general awareness of productivity, and the problems and possibilities associated with it, in BP Plastics was accomplished by a complete cascade of discussions upon the issues throughout the organization, in which reliance was placed upon the line superordinate in every case running his own discussions and securing his own staff's contributions to the general debate. Initially, with the help of a consultant, the process was applied to the managerial staffs on the following basis:

First, the consultant briefed the top management in pairs. Then each pair of managers took the next level in pairs, and so on down the line. Discussions were held with pairs of managers so that they could provide support and help to each other. Shop stewards were attracted by what they were hearing of these discussions and asked if similar sessions could be arranged for them. To maintain the objectivity of these discussions, the consultant led a similar series of discussions with the shop stewards. The objective at this stage was to achieve a complete understanding of what obstacles lay in the way of improving productivity. Both sides were asked to list the obstacles involved and these were found to be virtually identical when compared. It is important to see this as a general orientation exercise concerned with problems and principles. It was put forward that there would be some sort of productivity deal, but the *content* was not considered at this stage.

This 'orientation' exercise, which preceded the drawing out and testing of productivity improvement ideas in teams under supervision, therefore had a great deal in common with what is often intended in training. Subsequently, the discussions between the supervisors and their section members to identify possible ideas and to test them out as feasible with the aid of staff specialists (accountants, work study personnel, etc), who acted as consultants on request, provided another kind of learning opportunity for those concerned. Thus even before the negotiations began with the union representatives on any formal basis, many people in the undertaking had already been provided with the opportunity to engage in a new experience, with learning potential built into it, from which they could derive (if they so wished) some of the advantages which are normally regarded as accruing from formal training. In this sense, the development of distinctly new approaches to negotiations in undertakings could prove as 'enriching' to those involved as formal plans of 'job enrichment'.

A conception of training

All four of these examples which have been used here involve different manifestations of an approach to the management of learning in the work situation. In grid training, the older conception of formalistic and mechanistic training is still employed. In the related process of management by objectives, this tends to be replaced by the notion of counselling in the review interviews, but still implies a degree of dependency in the relationship. In the experiments with job enrichment, this dependency is beginning to drop away as the discretion of the individual to order his own (or to share in the ordering of the group's) work is intentionally increased. In the categories of productivity bargaining which were examined briefly, a similar attempt to foster independency and initiative is discernible. But whether 'training' is formally involved or not, all acquire a structure by reference to the process of learning about the opportunities and the constraints involved in decision, as well as about the technical methods by which desired or desirable changes might be brought about.

This degree of 'structure' in the learning situation is unlikely to be escaped, and in so far as it is seen as the source of 'domination' it is also the source of realism in proposals for change in organizational systems. It is only in somewhat Utopian instances that one can conceive of occasions in which individuals or groups are perfectly free to choose; in real situations constraints will impose their own structure on the opportunities and to learn in them is to learn how to handle constraints in decision taking. This is no excuse, however, for maintaining a particular structure of domination which serves more faithfully the maintenance of a *status quo* than it does the solution of problems of the optimization of the general good (satisfaction). It is this feature which characterizes the more open training (or management of learning situation) propositions which are currently being advanced as a possible solution to some of the problems of productivity and performance associated with modern work organizations. In this way, 'training' comes to be subjected to the same kinds of consideration which have recently affected the more general employee relations practices of our society.

To say 'training' in this context is nevertheless to raise an important question about both its ends and purpose and its agents.

Many people, not only in the management group, will readily agree to try new ways of improving production or relations, provided they can be shown the *general* advantage that is likely to emerge; they will remain interested until they become convinced by experience or outcomes that the benefit is either not obtainable or likely to be retained by others. To secure the contributions of all in the organization to the establishment of viable enterprise in society, therefore, it will be necessary to make genuine attempts to create open systems of bargaining and benefit distribution. There must be an expected pay-off, but there must also be equity in its distribution and probably also a security for that distribution in the shape of agreed procedures for determining it.

Similarly, those who seek to act as agents of such change in organization structures and operations may be expected to convince others by their eloquence and their example, but increasingly they are likely to do so only if they can rest these upon adequate knowledge and understanding. Organizational development, in any of the manifestations which have been discussed, will call for more than mere book knowledge or specialized expertise in discerete subject areas: the 'more' is likely to be associated with application and ability to apply, and it is for this reason that such role conceptions as change agent, catalyst, pacemaker and the rest are likely to prove more indicative of what will be required of future managers than those of chief accountant or chief maintenance engineer or personnel manager. We may not be in a position in which we can create complete 'generalists' in management or supervision, and we may therefore have to rely upon such specialized expertise, but we may nevertheless require the specialists to make generally contributory interventions in organizational processes in order to achieve development. This is likely to apply to the personnel specialist as to any other, but his 'expertise' in organizational and psychological subjects must place him in the van of this kind of change.

Further reading
On the major theme of this chapter, OD, see Bennis (1966 and 1969); Lippitt (1969); Thomason (1973); Jones (1969)

On the particular examples used, see Blake and Mouton (1964); Reddin (1964); and Mangham (1968); Drucker (1961); Humble (1970 and 1973); Paul and Robertson (1970); Robertson (1969); and Butteriss (1971); Oldfield (1966); NBPI Report No 36 and No 123; Richbell (1976)

On conceptions of organizational training 'in the round', see Bass and Vaughan (1968); King (1968).

10   Industrial relations constraints: trade union and public policy

A changing scenario for decision taking

We noted in the introduction that one of the antecedents of the present personnel specialist was to be found in the 'industrial relations officer' whose position was created to deal with 'organized labour' or the threat that the employer's workforce would organize into trade unions. At present, there is not much doubt that personnel managers are deeply involved in 'industrial relations' activities (see Marsh, 1973, ch 6), if 'industrial relations' is to be defined with reference to the regulation both of terms and conditions of employment *and* of collective relationships through the agency of representatives of both the employer/management interest on the one side and the interest of organized labour on the other. Between those two dates at least one pattern of industrial relations, that which was almost exclusively associated with national, industry-wide bargaining, has come and if not gone at least waned in significance (Donovan Report, 1968). Furthermore, it has been suggested that the development of personnel management is both an effect *and* a cause of making industrial relations a more local and fragmental structure in the post-war period; in Marsh's survey in the engineering industry, there is some evidence to suggest that the more industrial relations matters are dealt with domestically within the undertaking, the more (proportionately) will the personnel specialist's influence be felt upon them (Marsh, 1973, p 153).

Against this background, it seems pertinent to look at current industrial relations, in the present context of personnel management, in terms of what the subject covers viewed from the standpoint of the undertaking. This is neither to deny nor to ignore the long history of industrial relations and the respective 'national' roles of employers' associations and trade unions. This will be referred to as necessary in the following pages. It is rather to take as a main point of reference what is entailed by objective setting, policy formation, strategy determination and executive activity at the level of the undertaking and in relation to what we call industrial relations.

It may be suggested at the outset that the most important policy issue which currently exists at that level in industrial relations focuses on the question of what kind of industrial relations structure is either to be preferred or feasible. This is to imply that the employer or management has discretion in the matter, and this is indeed where the big question-mark has recently been hung. Recent developments in economic policy and legislation, as we have already seen, have increased the 'status' of the worker (as a generalized category) and this has had its effect upon what the employer might 'expect' of him. Changes of a similar origin have also reduced the power or the discretion of management on

(a) recognition of independent trade unions
(b) unilateral determination of the shape of the bargaining unit
(c) capacity to limit the subjects to be negotiated about with trade unions and the 'levels' at which such subjects will be discussed
(d) ability to confine relevant information to themselves and to avoid disclosing it to trade union representatives.

The problem caused by these changes is therefore that of making adequate forecasts of the likely future. So much change appears to have been thrust upon the industrial relations system in Britain since the middle 1960s that the ensuing period looks like one of major discontinuity, and the normal extrapolative foundation for forecasts seems to be inappropriate to it. Nevertheless the new pattern, like it or not, seems to be emerging quite strongly, from the Trade Union and Labour Relations Acts, the Employment Protection Act and the Industry Act, on the one hand, and from the new-look in negotiation by government of financial and incomes policies on the other. Government policy changes in these matters have probably played a major part in shifting the power of managements and unions but, as recent government pronouncements assert, there is at present little inclination to dispose of the private economy in favour of an alternative form. What is beginning to emerge is a situation in which *joint* decision-taking on a wider range of matters is being both fostered by deliberate policy, and constrained by the government's own decisions as to how the economy should be managed.

There is some reason to suppose that the period of discontinuity in policy is now reaching its end, and that the shape of the likely future in this area is becoming more discernible. Forecasts which are likely to be broadly correct are therefore becoming more feasible.

Trade union objectives and trade union status

Trade unions have been defined in many different ways, although two are most frequently employed. First, the definition given by the Webbs, who saw trade unions as "a continuous association of wage earners for the purposes of maintaining or improving the conditions of their working lives" (S and B Webb, 1920, p 1). This is clearly rooted in the historical period in which they were writing, it emphasizes the 'class' relationship of the trade unions of the time and it implies a generalized political mission for the trade union, (a point to which we return below). Secondly, the definition of the law, as contained in S 28 of the Trade Union and Labour Relations Act:

> . . . 'trade union' means an organization (whether permanent or temporary) which either
> (a) consists wholly or mainly of workers of one or more descriptions and is an organization whose principal purposes include the regulation of relations between workers of that description or those descriptions and employers or employers' associations; or
> (b) consists wholly or mainly of
>   (i) constituent or affiliated organizations which fulfil the conditions specified in paragraph (a) above (or themselves consist wholly or mainly of constituent or affiliated organizations which fulfil those conditions), or
>   (ii) representatives of such constituent or affiliated organizations:
>   and in either case is an organization whose principal purposes include the regulation of relations between workers and employers or between workers and employers' associations, or include the regulation of relations between its constituent or affiliated organizations.

This has to be read in conjunction with the definition of worker in S 30 (quoted above, pp 57–60) which is defined to include anyone with employee status, except those in the armed and police services but not those with professional clients. Since 1977 this definition is employed by the Department of Employment for administrative, data-collection purposes, in which trade unions are defined as "organizations which appear to satisfy the statutory definition" whether registered, certified or not. This new definition excludes some organizations previously included in the figures (31 organizations with 167,000 in 1977—half in the police service) on the ground that they had negotiation as a central objective.

407

On this last definition, there were 462 separate trade unions and 46 federations of unions in the United Kingdom at the end of 1976. The total union membership was 12,376,000 (to the nearest thousand) but this includes some element of double counting for those who belong to more than one union, and includes membership outside the United Kingdom (mainly in Ireland). The figures are based mainly on the annual returns which all trade unions (and employers' associations) are required by S 11 of the TULR Act to render to the Certification Officer, who maintains (by authority of S 7 of the Employment Protection Act) a list of those bodies, whether or not they have applied to be placed on the list or not. Membership of the federations enumerated is included in the figures for the separate unions, not all of which are members of federations, and some of which are affiliated for some or all of their membership to more than one. The numbers of members has been increasing fairly steadily in recent years although the number of separate unions, and federations, has been falling (DE *Gazette*, November 1977, p 1203). The number of unions affiliated to the TUC at 31 December 1975 was 113 and total affiliated membership was 11,036,326. Generally speaking, the difference in numbers of unions in these two sets is composed of relatively small and often 'local' (ie town or district) unions, some of which would not support the general policy and ideological orientations of the TUC (TUC *Annual Report* 1976).

The number of unions having certificates as to their independence and competence to serve members was appreciably below these figures quoted in the DE *Gazette*, reflecting a prevalent view amongst TUC-affiliated unions that, since they are independent and competent, they need no certificate from the Certification Officer (Employment Protection Act 1975, S 7) to prove it. By October 1977, certificates had been issued to 270 trade unions of which 155 were affiliated to the TUC or were constituents of TUC affiliated unions; 29 applications from non-affiliates to the TUC had been refused by this date, another three having been withdrawn and one having lapsed (DE *Gazette*, October 1977, p 1131).

These data for the most part apply to the national organizations which are sovereign or autonomous in the sense of determining their own constitutions and rules. What they do not tell us is how many local and district organizations of trade unionists exist throughout the country. The vast majority of these associations have local branches (or lodges or chapels) and local workshop (undertaking) and combine (company) committees which organize the membership within these more restricted boundaries, and are specifically acknowledged in union membership agreements in the TULR Act 1974, S 30 and Sch 1 para 6 as amended by TULR Act 1976, S 3(3).

Of these definitions of trade unions, the difference which exists between that provided by Webbs and that found in legislation is quite often ignored in public and undertaking policy-formation. We tend to assume that trade unions are exclusively, or at least primarily, concerned with the objectives associated with collective bargaining which, in turn, guided by Flanders (1965) and Dunlop (1958), we have come to think of as 'job regulation' a process of converting the disagreements about the rules which should apply to work, in the workplace, into agreements. It is this assumed objective which is given prominence in the administrative and legal definitions of trade unions, although they do not exclude the possibility of others existing. It is also the characterization of trade union objectives which has recently been strongly derided by some writers on the subject of trade unions (see eg Hyman and Fryer, 1975, pp 170–82).

What is unintentionally or intentionally played down in these characterizations is the objective and activity which originally placed the trade unions outside the common and, for a time, the statute law, during the first three-quarters of last century. This was the aim of regulating competition amongst workers in the labour market, a purpose which was initially served by securing agreements amongst the workers themselves, to offer themselves on the labour market only in certain terms and conditions. It was this agreement, not the approach to the employer to negotiate terms and conditions with him (which up to a point was legal at the time), which made trade unions illegal conspiracies by virtue of their purposes—the necessary restraint of trade (or competition which was then equated with the older concept of 'trade'). It is not to be supposed that this was not concerned with the determination of the wage. It recognized that any action to restrict the free flow of labour to employers, whether in the shape of pestilence or trade union agreement to restrict offers, could be expected to increase the labour price. But for the early trade unions, this recognition led them into actions to restrict supply by agreement amongst themselves, and to 'impose the union rule book' as the embodiment of these agreed restrictions. (cf Fisher, 1971, pp 134–5).

When the employer refused to have anything to do with this, the trade union found itself in a negotiating posture and engaged in the logically-consequent process of 'bargaining' or, as the Webbs quite correctly put it, 'higgling' in the market. After 1824 (Repeal of the Combination Acts) when workers acquired the freedom to form unions, those unions could (and in the form of the new model unions did) engage in a very constitutional process of negotiation with employers over pay and other conditions of employment, but they remained vulnerable at common law because of their essentially criminal nature which sprang from their agreements *inter se*, not from those with employers. Thus, even after 1824 when the Combination Acts exerted no great influence on the situation, the Common Law doctrines could still be invoked against the trade unions when they acted 'blatantly' to impose their 'agreements' by striking and mounting a picket or by inducing another worker to break his contract of employment. This position was altered in three Parliamentary Acts, the Trade Union Act of 1871, the Conspiracy and Protection of Property Act of 1875, and the Trade Disputes Act, 1906, which between them gave the trade unions immunity under the Common Law from indictment for conspiracy and from actions arising from the pursuit of their restraint of trade purposes in conditions of a 'trade dispute'. These were, however, *immunities*, and in no sense rights which involved a reciprocal duty on anyone's part; without them the Common Law could still be invoked against them. This is why both in the now-repealed Industrial Relations Act of 1971 and in the Trade Union and Labour Relations Acts 1974–6, these same immunities are continued (see table 17) and therefore still apply to the actions of trade unions as defined on p 407 above. (TULRA 1974 S 28).

These immunities are important—both for trade unions and employers' associations which are treated in the same way in all this legislation: they permitted trade unions (and employers' associations) to grow and develop free of legal actions which could otherwise have been commenced against them because of their purposes and some of the means which they employed in pursuit of them. They also established the legally defined status of the trade unions for a century after 1871 (although there were some hiccups in 1901—6 after the Taff Vale case and before the Trade Disputes Act). Importantly, however, that status was defined largely in terms of 'immunities' from the rigour of the law which would in their absence have applied to them: they were tolerated, provided with some opportunity for development but not given a *carte blanche* or treated as fully paid up institutions of the society.

Nevertheless, they came to perform what Kahn-Freund has referred to as 'public functions' and thereby acquired a social status or acceptability which was not visible in the law. The first and in a sense the most important of these 'public functions' was their participation in bargaining on behalf of their members, a process which developed considerably over the first 70 years of this century. Had the trade unions not existed to engage in this process, it might have fallen to some other institution to carry out the role and, in some cases, where trade unions did not exist, the State had to step in in 1909 and set up joint bodies for the determination of wages (and

410

later other conditions of employment) in the wages council trades. Of course, the trade unions may in a sense have been pushed into these procedures by employers, as Clegg illustrates (1973, p 127) but however, they got into it, they came to be strongly associated with it.

Table 17
Trade Union and Labour Relations Act 1974
Restrictions on legal liability and legal proceedings

Section 13 Acts in contemplation or furtherance of trade disputes

(1) An Act done by a person in contemplation or furtherance of a trade dispute shall not be actionable in tort on the ground only—
   (a) that it induces another person to break a contract of employment; or
   (b) that it consists in his threatening that a contract of employment (whether one to which he is a party or not) will be broken or that he will induce another person to break a contract of employment to which that other person is a party
(2) For the avoidance of doubt it is hereby declared that an act done by a person in contemplation or furtherance of a trade dispute is not actionable in tort on the ground only that it is an interference with the trade, business or employment of another person, or with the right of another person to dispose of his capital or his labour as he wills
(3) For the avoidance of doubt it is hereby declared that—
   (a) an act which by reason of subsection (1) or (2) above is itself not actionable
   (b) a breach of contract in contemplation or furtherance of a trade dispute shall not be regarded as the doing of an unlawful act or as the use of unlawful means for the purpose of establishing liability in tort
(4) An agreement or combination by two or more persons to do or procure the doing of any act in contemplation or furtherance of a trade dispute shall not be actionable in tort if the act is one which, if done without any such agreement or combination, would not be actionable in tort

Section 14 Immunity of trade unions and employer's associations to actions in tort

(1) Subject to subsection (2) below, no action in tort shall lie in respect of any act—
   (a) alleged to have been done by or on behalf of a trade union which is not a special register body or by or on behalf of an unincorporated employers' association; or
   (b) alleged to have been done, in connection with the regulation of relations between employers or employers' associations and workers or trade unions, by or on behalf of a trade union which is a special register body or by or on behalf of an employers' association which is a body corporate; or

(c) alleged to be threatened or to be intended to be done as mentioned in
       paragraph (a) or (b) above
   against the union or association in its own name, or against the trustees of the
   union or association, or against any members or officials of the union or
   association on behalf of themselves and all other members of the union or
   association
(2) Subsection (1) above shall not affect the liability of a trade union or employers'
    association to be sued in respect of the following, if not arising from an act
    done in contemplation or furtherance of a trade dispute, that is to say—
    (a) any negligence, nuisance or breach of duty (whether imposed on them by
        any rule of law or by or under any enactment) resulting in personal injury
        to any person; or
    (b) without prejudice to paragraph (a) above, breach of any duty so imposed
        in connection with the ownership, occupation, possession, control or use
        of property (whether real or personal or, in Scotland, heritable or
        moveable)
(3) In this section, 'personal injury' includes any disease and any impairment of
    a person's physical or mental condition.

The trade unions were also 'guided' by another class of legislation
than that which we have already noted, namely the legislation which
sought to structure trade unions' (and employers' associations') performance in carrying out this public function. The chief illustrations
here are the Conciliation Act of 1896 and the Industrial Courts Act
of 1919, but in some ways the Trade Boards Act of 1909 had similar
import. These statutes open up certain avenues, which did not exist
previously, for the resolution of differences between the parties without recourse to strikes or lock-outs. (It is true that there were some
such private avenues before these Acts appeared but they were not,
as these Acts ensured, universally available). Another area to which
legislation for performance had been applied since 1871, but which
was also modified during the same period, was that of trade union
merger and amalgamation. The State paid little heed, and attached
little importance otherwise, to the internal procedures of trade
unions but, in this one area where members' 'property' interests
might be involved, there was legislation for performance (Trade
Union Act 1876, S 12); for the rest, the Courts had to be content with
'indirect enforcement' of some categories of union rule.
   The second public function was that of advising government
and other public agencies on many aspects of policies. The first world
war is generally seen to have given this 'function' a fillip, but it continued afterwards and led to trade unions being represented by their
'leaders' on many councils, committees and boards, and eventually
in the Government of the country. Regardless of the attitude of the

412

law towards them, they were now given a *de facto* status which might belie their *de jure* position to some extent. In a legalistic sense, what developed in this way was essentially a privilege (cf Barnard, 1946, p 207). It is, for example, of some marginal significance that when a Labour Government nationalized a number of industries between 1945 and 1950, it made no special provision in the legislation for the representation of trade unions on those boards, in spite of their awareness of the stated political objectives of a number of the TUC affiliated unions at that time (and indeed still). The privilege did not extend to a right supported by law!

By 1977, however, the trade unions had acquired a number of such 'rights' under law. Somewhat paradoxically perhaps, most of them have come about *after* the influence of the national structure (trade unions and employers' associations engaged in national bargaining) had waned in the post-war period and as a *result*, largely, of legislation which was intended to impose more restrictions and limitations on the trade unions (Donovan Commission Report, 1968, p 36).

In the relatively full employment conditions of post-war Britain the national system began to exert lesser control over the outcomes of bargaining and local domestic arrangements to exert more.

When the Donovan Commission looked at the position, it concluded that two parallel systems existed, the formal system and the informal system, between which there were, in its view, too few links. Because the informal system had grown in influence and importance, the arrangements for controlling performance (developed under the performance-related legislation mentioned above) were losing control. This had consequences for unofficial and unconstitutional action by local trade union representatives and led to both increased strike activity and wage drift, in the face of which the national system was powerless to control. Therefore, argued the Commissioners, more legislation to control performance, particularly now of the informal system, was required, to guide not only the unofficial groups *per se* but also the trade unions in their relations with local members, the employers in their handling of industrial relations questions, and the public agencies with a concern for this area.

From this various propositions developed such as *In Place of Strife*, from the Labour Party, and *Fair Deal at Work* from the Conservative Party, together with an actual statute which was to prove abortive as it stood but extremely influential even after its repeal. This statute, the Industrial Relations Act of 1971, was intended to structure performance in a number of relevant areas: the internal relationships of the trade unions, the organization of the employer for

413

industrial relations purposes, the processes and procedures of collective bargaining and job regulation, and the facilities provided to the parties by the State. It also continued the development of a 'more European' type of worker status with its provisions for protecting the worker from arbitrary dismissal *vis à vis* the employer and from trade union power exercised through closed shops. As it turned out it sought, in what proved to be the fatal mistake, to turn the 'old immunities' (as in Table 17, pp 411–12) into privileges for registered trade unions, and to make registration conditional upon the development of an externally-regulated contract between the now-incorporated trade union and the individual member (see Weekes *et al*, 1975).

The repeal of this Act by the Trade Union and Labour Relations Act 1974, as now extended in the Employment Protection Act 1975 and the TULR Act of 1976, changed the nature of the 'condition' attaching to the new rights granted to trade unions under all these Acts and the Health and Safety at Work Act 1975 but generally speaking carried forward the rights of the IR Act, where they related to performance, and removed some of that Act's restrictions on the achievement of higher degrees of union security (eg the closed shop).

The present position is therefore that the new 'rights' remain privileges accorded to independent trade unions but independence is now taken to be axiomatic for TUC affiliated unions and capable of being demonstrated by worker organizations which are not affiliated (in which case it will be necessary for legal purposes for the association in question to secure a certificate of independence and competence to serve the members from the Certification Officer). However, the old immunities remain available for any trade union or workers' association.

The rights which the independent trade union has now been accorded are:

(a) a right to be recognized by an employer and to present a claim to this effect through ACAS (S 11 EPA)

(b) a right to have information disclosed to it by the employer for the purposes of facilitating collective bargaining (S 11) and to be permitted to make a complaint to ACAS about an employer's failure to disclose (S 19 EPA)

(c) a right to appoint safety representatives with whom the employer must consult on health and safety matters, and who may request the establishment of a health and safety committee (Health and Safety at Work Act 1974, S 2 (4) and (7) and Health and Safety at Work Regulation, R 2(1) and Sch 1)

(d) a right to be consulted by the employer about redundancy (S 99) and to complain about an employer's failure to consult and secure a protective award (S 101 EPA)

(e) a right to join with the employer in seeking to have a dismissal agreement between them substituted by order for the unfair dismissal provisions of the Trade Union and Labour Relations Act (S 1(2) and Sch 1 Part II)

(f) a right to conclude an agreement with the employer abrogating the worker's right to strike which, under certain further conditions, would be accorded legality (TULRA, S 18)

(g) a right to apply to the CAC via ACAS for an extension of recognized, or general level of, terms and conditions of employment to an employer (under S 98 and Sch 11 of the EPA)

(h) a possible right to select representatives to sit on the reconstituted boards of companies with 2,000 employees or more, *if* the recommendations on this subject made by the Bullock Committee (1977) are ever established by enactment.

All these rights, together with the 'time off' and facilities rights which are accorded to trade unionists, affect the status of the trade union in modern society, but they relate to that status which is primarily concerned with the 'collective bargaining' function discharged by unions. In two respects, this is an incomplete statement: it is possible to regard the rights of recognition from the employer as concerned with the function of regulating competition in the labour market, and the oblique support given to the union membership agreement could be similarly related. But the point may be emphasized that the rights to recognition are *conceived* as relating chiefly to 'good industrial relations', and hence to performance.

That being accepted, these 'new' rights do not give, by way of status, a 'right' to restrict competition in the labour market. To achieve this would require a much more Draconic outlawing of new distinct and break-away trade unions not affiliated to the TUC. This would thus eliminate competition for membership and provide a basis for universal minimum union security for the 'independent' trade unions. These do not exist at present, although the stipulation that dismissals of non-members under a union membership agreement shall be 'fair' does support the principle of a closed shop without legislating one into existence (TULRA, Sch 1, S 6). This is in contrast to the USA where, in spite of the right to work laws, there is more legislative support for some degrees of union security.

Consequently the regulation of competition in the labour market element of the trade unionist's objective is still left to the unsupported and unfacilitated process of power bargaining. Since this problem is usually experienced at plant level rather than at that of the national trade union, the 'problem' of union security falls to be resolved at that lower level. The resolution will involve disputes over (a) recognition, focused on the application of the trade dispute and picketing provisions of the 1906 Act, together with the statutory powers of ACAS, and (b) union security or the closed shop, with problems arising from the attempts to harmonize British and European legislation and public policy on 'participation' (which places the nature of the 'constituency' in the forefront of any practicable plan) (cf Sullivan 1977).

External adjudication of union rights
The list of new rights for independent trade unions (see above, pp 414–15) are thus mostly directed towards the control or structuring of trade union 'performance' in industrial relations activities. They are, rights which are reciprocated, for the most part, by duties imposed on the employer and, for this reason and since disputes as to rights and duties and their proper assertion and discharge may be expected, it is necessary to establish machinery for their resolution. Before 1896, that machinery was 'private' where it existed at all; from that date public provision of such machinery was made, first through the Board of Trade and later through the Ministry of Labour/ Department of Employment (supplemented by the standing Industrial Court) and now (since 1974) the independent Advisory, Conciliation and Arbitration Service (supplemented by the newly named Central Arbitration Committee, the former Industrial Court). It might be said of ACAS and the CAC that their general functions are broadly the same as those of their predecessors, but that what is new is the adjudication of disputes over the rights given to independent trade unions in recent legislation.

During the period of new model unionism in the 30 years or so after 1850, many trade unions and employers voluntarily established neutral committees or conciliation boards to permit them resolve their differences in the event of failure to agree. This idea was copied by the State, following the Royal Commission report in 1894, through the Conciliation Act of 1896, which allowed the Board of Trade to establish facilities to conciliate, arbitrate, enquire and generally foster voluntary collective bargaining. The Whitley Committee, during the first world war, looked at this facility and gave it general approval but suggested that a "standing industrial Court" might be a useful addition to the provision. The Industrial Courts Act of 1919 implemented this recommendation. Although these arrangements were modified in 1940 by the Conditions of Employment and National Arbitration Order (1305) and although this modification was maintained in a slightly different form until 1958 under Order 1376 of 1951, these earlier provisions remained the essence of

416

the British system of bringing about disputes' settlement until the Advisory, Conciliation and Arbitration Service was established in 1974 to take over these duties from the Department of Employment.

Although ACAS had been formally established in 1974, the Employment Protection Act 1975 provided the statutory foundation for its activities and generally served to codify the arrangements. The 'independence' of ACAS of the Government was effected by making it a corporate body, with a chairman and up to three deputy chairmen, drawn from the ranks of the 'independents', and three council members appointed by the Secretary of State from nominees from each of the trade unions and the employers' associations. The general duty imposed upon the ACAS is that of promoting improvement in industrial relations, particularly through the encouragement of an extension of collective bargaining, and the development (and if necessary the reform) of collective bargaining machinery. The functions of the new body bring together those which had previously been developed in the Department of Employment or in various other recently established *ad hoc* bodies, like the Commission on Industrial Relations. Five functions can be identified.

1 The service is empowered to provide a conciliation service. Where a trade dispute is apprehended or in existence, the Service may either offer its assistance as a conciliator or provide such assistance at the request of one or more parties. The conciliators may be officers of the Service or independent persons: their role is to be to encourage the parties to reach a settlement by using any agreed procedures and, whether such procedures exist or not, to help them to come to a resolution of their differences "by conciliation or by any other means". In extension of this general conciliation role, the Service is empowered to designate some officers to perform the functions of conciliation officers in matters which are or could be the subject of proceedings before an industrial tribunal (S 2).
2 The Service is empowered to provide a service of arbitration. Where a trade dispute is apprehended or in existence, the Service may provide arbitration "at the request of one or more parties to the dispute and with the consent of all the parties" to it, either by reference to a single arbitrator or a board of arbitration (made up of persons who are not officers or servants of the Service) or by reference to the Central Arbitration Committee. This power is restricted to those circumstances in which procedures are ascertained to have been exhausted and in which conciliation is judged not to be capable of resulting in a settlement, provided only that there are no "special reasons" which justify arbitration even

417

though the procedures have not been exhausted. This section continues provisions of the earlier legislation but by S 3(4) provision is made for publication of awards of arbitrators or boards of arbitration "if the Service so decided and all the parties consent", and a firmer basis for establishing precedent in arbitration awards is thus established (S 3).

3 The Service is empowered if it thinks fit, "to enquire into any question relating to industrial relations generally or to industrial relations in any particular industry or in any particular undertaking or part of an undertaking". The Service is given powers to publish the findings of any such enquiry, together with its advice based on these findings, if the Service thinks that publication would help improve industrial relations, generally or specifically and after submitting a draft to, and taking note of the views of, the parties concerned with the inquiry. This Section continues the powers previously enjoyed by the Commission on Industrial Relations (S 5).

4 The Service is given powers to offer advice on industrial relations or employment policies, whether this is requested or not, to employers, employers' associations, workers and trade unions, and it may also publish general advice on these same matters. The Act offers a list of matters which are considered to be within the scope of this provision:

    (a) the organization of workers or employers for the purpose of collective bargaining
    (b) the recognition of trade unions by employers
    (c) machinery for the negotiation of terms and conditions of employment, and for joint consultation
    (d) procedures for avoiding and settling disputes and workers' grievances
    (e) questions relating to communications between employers and workers
    (f) facilities for officials of trade unions
    (g) procedures relating to the termination of employment
    (h) disciplinary matters
    (i) manpower planning, labour turnover and absenteeism
    (j) recruitment, retention, promotion and vocational training of workers
    (k) payment systems, including job evaluation and equal pay (S 4).

These provisions also continue the functions previously performed by the Advisory Service of the Department of Employment and the Commission on Industrial Relations.

5 The Service is given a permissive power to issue Codes of Practice

aimed at improving industrial relations. When it does draft a Code of Practice, it is required to publish the draft and consider any representation made to it about the draft and may then modify it in the light of such representations. The final draft must then be submitted to the Secretary of State who is required to lay it before both Houses of Parliament if he approves of it, or to publish details of his reasons for withholding approval if he does not. If, after the draft has been before both Houses for 40 days, no resolution to stay proceedings on the Code is forthcoming, the Code may be issued by the Service and will come into effect on such day as the Secretary of State may by order appoint. Revision of Codes is also permitted and this must take broadly the same course as in the original.

Special provision is made for Codes on two matters specifically provided for in the Act:

(a) disclosure of information by employers to trade unions for purposes of collective bargaining (Ss 17 and 18) (see below, pp 428–35).
(b) time off to be permitted by the employer to union officials or members (Ss 57 and 58) (see above, pp 93–95).

In these two cases, the powers of the ACAS are mandatory and the procedure to be followed, whilst generally the same as that above, is different in that approval by each House of Parliament is required before the Code may be issued and come into effect on a date to be specified by the Secretary of State, by order (Ss 6(2) and 6(5)).

These may be regarded as the general provisions of the new legislation for the development of improved performance by trade unions and employers in industrial relations matters and for the general support of the new rights accorded to trade unions. There are also specific provisions, which give the ACAS a role in relation to the specific rights mentioned, particularly those relating to recognition, information disclosure and consultation. The element of appeal in these cases, and in the Schedule 11 claims for extension of general or recognized terms and conditions, is provided for by continuing the former role of the Industrial Court (established 1919) but changing its name to Central Arbitration Committee (this is the second change: under the Industrial Relations Act it was referred to as the Industrial Arbitration Board). These two bodies, now independent of government, thus have two categories of role to perform, one general and related to the 'improvement of industrial relations in Britain' in a general way, and the other specific and related to the upholding of rights now accorded to independent trade unions. How they 'fit' in with these rights will be indicated in the following discussion of the manner in which these rights are established and intended to operate to yield improved industrial relations.

Recognition rights

Historically, recognition has been achieved by the trade unions by 'struggle', or by their own efforts after they had accumulated sufficient power to compel recognition from the employer. The early immunity-granting legislation imposed no reciprocal duty to recognize unions upon the employer. The effect of this process upon recognition has been to produce a highly fragmented bargaining situation in British industry. By and large, employers granted recognition and negotiating rights to employee organizations on the basis of existing membership, and then only when they showed themselves strong enough to claim it. In many plants, companies and industries, therefore, a multiplicity of unions have come to be recognized by the employers, at different times and for different sections of the workforce.

It cannot be disputed that the trade unions themselves have exerted a considerable influence upon this outcome but, as Clegg has asserted, "employers could, if they chose, exercise a good deal more influence over union structure in industries and services where membership is at present weak and recognition has not yet been granted." (1972, p 66). In the past, employer policy has been to keep the unions out except when it proved impossible to do so, and then to let in only those which had to be recognized and merely to represent limited classes of employees. Some open shop situations (where no unions are recognized) still exist, even amongst manual workers, but they are more often to be found (a) amongst white collar workers and (b) in some of the service industries.

By the late 1960s, this general approach to recognition had produced a situation in which different sections of the workforce were very differently treated. Bain's analysis of the position at that time suggested that the workforce could be divided into three broad recognition categories: first, those for whom there is no problem of recognition (eg workers in national and local government, nationalized industries and public services, manufacturing industry establishments with over 25 employees). Secondly, there are those who do have a problem of securing recognition (including workers in catering and similar services, manual workers in small manufacturing firms, workers in distribution, banking, finance and insurance and most white collar workers in manufacturing industry). Thirdly, Bain identifies certain other areas in which he considers that there would be a problem if the unions really did try to organize; he includes in this category, the professional and scientific services, the remaining areas of white collar employment in manufacturing industry, and a group of essentially personal services such as those concerned with motor repair or domestic service. He sees the unions having a partial recognition problem in the construction and agricultural industries (Bain, 1966, p 73).

Bain also expresses the firmly held view that employer recognition is an important influence on union membership: where the union is accorded recognition, membership will increase. The Commission on Industrial Relations' view, based on interviews with employees in non-union shop situations, was that many more would be prepared to join the union(s) if and when the employer gave it (them) recognition. (CIR Second General Report, 1971.) Bain further argues that what has been most potent in securing recognition has not been the strength of the unions but the influence of government policy, essentially in war-time (Bain, 1966, ch IV). Since that policy was generally not backed by specific legislation, subsequent changes in government policy which were supported by legislative change might be expected to have a real influence on (a) the recognition issue and through that on (b) union membership.

The situation described by Bain was that which developed in a period in which the State was essentially non-interventionist in its approach to the recognition question. Since that time, there has been a fundamental change.

This came about, first, because of the Donovan Commission's concern for the improvement of industrial relations, which it saw to depend partly upon a change in employer attitudes toward recognition. Then, secondly, the 1969 White Paper, *In Place of Strife*, made it clear that the new Commission on Industrial Relations (established under Royal Warrant at that time) was to be charged with examining and improving "the institutions and procedures for the conduct of industrial relations", and would be expected by the government "to favour recognition if the union is appropriate and can establish that it has a reasonable support". The CIR accepted this charge, and over the whole of its life (ie until it was abolished with the repeal of the Industrial Relations Act in 1974) it encouraged recognition by establishing certain principles governing it:

1 That support for a union was to be defined according to the circumstances of the case, and not simply on the basis of whether a majority of employees were members or voted in support of recognition, and in particular was to be defined to include minority support where recognition had not been accorded if there was reason to suppose that the support would increase if recognition were to

421

be accorded

2 That strong opposition to union recognition on the part of employees was to be given weight in recognition decisions, but a union should be encouraged so to disport itself as to "promote understanding and acceptance" amongst those opposed, whose rights were thought to be worthy of protection (at least in the Industrial Relations Act period, 1972–4)

3 That the question of whether a union was appropriate in the circumstances was regarded as dependent upon the political realities of the situation and whilst the CIR did not seek to favour one union or type of union over another, except where the competititon for recognition lay between an established TUC-affiliated union and a staff association or house union (in which case the first would be favoured), it did not particularly favour the continuation of multi-unionism (although it did little more in this matter than recommend rationalization of trade union organization to make recognition issues easier to resolve)

4 That these same principles were applicable to the white collar situations—where, indeed, they were very largely worked out during this period.

The third step along this road was taken in the Industrial Relations Act of 1971, which laid down a reference procedure for dealing with recognition issues, involving the CIR and the National Industrial Relations Court. The CIR followed broadly the policy indicated in the four principles above during this period in making its recommendations on recognition, and the Court added to these mainly in that it tended to deny recognition to house unions and staff associations (even though they might have secured registration) when they sought to challenge existing bargaining arrangements involving the TUC-affiliated unions, whilst at the same time upholding the rights of individuals and minorities both not to belong to a trade union and to have representation in pursuing grievances.

The fourth step involved the re-enactment of the major provisions of the Industrial Relations Act relating to recognition in the Employment Protection Act of 1975. S 11 provides that a recognition issue may be referred by an independent trade union (not others) in writing to ACAS which in turn is required to consult all interested parties on the question, to attempt to secure agreement on the issue through conciliation if thought appropriate and, finally, (if the request is not withdrawn in the meantime) to report on the issue and give any advice it thinks appropriate. (The provisions of the Industrial Relations Act which allowed initiation of this procedure by either the Secretary of State or the employer are not re-enacted.) The attempt to follow these provisions in the claim by the white-collar union APEX for recognition at the Grunwick Film Processing Laboratories, however, met with employer reluctance to make information available on the existing workforce. When ACAS based its recommendations for recognition on the views of the dismissed strikers and others, but not on those of the workers still employed, the recommendation was challenged through the Courts, and was eventually set aside on appeal (Grunwick Processing Laboratory *v* ACAS, (1977) *Times*, July 1977). One response to this was a private member's Bill, supported by the Government, which sought to protect the procedure laid down for the ACAS to follow in those circumstances where an employer withholds cooperation (at the time of writing, this Bill is not enacted).

Provision is also made in the EP Act for variation or revocation of an initial ACAS recommendation, either by the trade union or the employer or by the two jointly, (S 13) and ACAS is empowered to follow a similar procedure to that above in reaching its conclusions on the application. S 14 of the Employment Protection Act empowers ACAS, in pursuing its enquiries in response to either initial or subsequent application, to ascertain the opinions, by ballot or otherwise, of the workers to whom the issue relates, but it must inform the employer and any union which has members amongst the workers concerned of its intentions to hold a ballot, and consider any representations which might be made by any of them as a result. The same parties are to be informed of the questions(s) put and the results of any such ballot and the employer is charged with the duty of informing any and all workers invited to take part in the ballot of the outcome.

Where a recommendation for recognition of a union or unions is made, it will become operative 14 days after the ACAS report is received by the employer(s) concerned, or 14 days after any conditions in the report have been complied with, and remain in operation until either superseded by an agreement between the employer(s) and the union(s) or by another recommendation under the same Section of the Act, or until it is revoked after a request from the trade union and/or employer under S 13. After two months of operation, it is open to the trade union to complain to the ACAS (where this is relevant) that the employer is not complying (in whole or in part) with the recommendation and the ACAS is then charged with seeking to resolve the question by conciliation. If that fails, the trade union may complain to the Central Arbitration Committee which, after hearing the parties must determine whether and to what extent the claim is well founded, and if it does so find it, it may make an award requiring the employer to observe either the terms and conditions specified in the claim by the trade union or such other terms and conditions as the CAC considers appropriate. This award is to "have effect as part of the contract of employment of any . . . employee" covered by the award, and from the date of the award, unless superseded by a further award or more favourable agreement between a trade union and the employer. However, the basis for this kind of complaint is specified in the Act (S 15 (2)): that the employer "is not taking such action by way of or with a view to carrying on negotiations as might reasonably be expected to be taken by an employer ready and willing to carry on such negotiations as are envisaged by the recommendation". Recognition therefore constitutes a requirement to bargain in good faith (in the language of US industrial relations) and is not to be regarded as mere paper recognition.

As Kessler and Palmer conclude, "the fact that both Labour and Conservative Governments have now produced similar machinery to decide recognition issues, suggests that, in this area at least, the long quiescence of the State is ended . . . there is now general political agreement on the need for machinery to decide recognition disputes; for sanctions to back such decisions; and for some investigation to find the best solution in a recognition dispute" (see Kessler and Palmer, 1975, p 37).

ACAS is now charged with carrying on the function previously carried out by the CIR, and is likely to consider broadly the same policy, except in so far as the provisions of the Trade Union and Labour Relations Act and the Employment Protection Act combine to give rights only to those employee associations which can secure certification that they are (a) independent, and (b) competent, organizationally and financially, to represent their members. The CAC similarly takes over functions previously within the ambit of the NIRC and the Industrial Arbitration Board and, strengthened by the above-mentioned restrictions on recognition rights, is likely to continue the policy of favouring the existing bargaining agents in any inter-associational dispute over recognition.

On the face of it, the development of public policy through legislation in the 1970s appears to have pre-empted management's decisions in the matter of union recognition: where independent trade unions seek recognition and can show support of a type not likely to disrupt existing systems of collective bargaining, they are very likely to secure it.

As far as manual workers are concerned, this question is largely academic, except in small enterprises: most manual workers are already members of unions and their unions are recognized. However, for workers in service industries and white collar occupations the question is still very real: many of these, outside the public sector, remain non-union or only partially unionized and, as Bain has indicated, recognition is still only scantily given. In this area, therefore, the employer still faces some choice as to which unions he will consider most appropriate and recognize. Whilst it is true that the white collar unions already affiliated to the TUC consider that they have a prior claim on this area, a number of other staff and professional associations have recently either come into existence or actively sought certification as independent, and hope to press their claims in the same area. In this sense, there is potential for competing recognition claims to which the employer must respond. But there is also some scope for the exercise of discretion on the part of management, even though it may prove to be constrained by ACAS and CAC policies: it is axiomatic however that, if management has not considered its recognition policy in this area and decided its objectives and intentions, it is unlikely to exert any real influence on the outcome, and structures of bargaining units amongst white-collar workers may come to resemble the fragmented units associated with blue-collar unionization.

The development of systematically devised bargaining units has not proceeded very far in Britain except where, at national level, confederations of unions and, at local level, joint shop representative arrangements, have appeared. The Industrial Relations Act of 1971, sought to introduce the notion of a 'bargaining unit' to this country but with little impact. The proposal of the Bullock Committee for a Joint Union Meeting for Industrial Democracy to establish the representational pattern for that purpose, offers some opportunity for restructuring the bargaining, as well as the 'participation', units, but there is doubt as to whether that set of proposals will be accepted and translated into legislation. The only other major external influence upon this question at present is the development of union membership agreements, now permitted (as legal arrangements) under the Trade Union and Labour Relations Act 1976 (Sch 1, Cl 6 (5)); the effect of this provision is to reduce the opportunities for any spontaneous change in patterns of representation arising from the employees themselves and thus, potentially, to ossify the existing pattern of bargaining units.

Trade union 'security'
This question is closely linked with the tendency in current legislation to give 'positive' protection to trade unions (provided they are 'independent'). The much earlier legislation gave trade unions some protection, by rendering them immune from legal penalties or remedies which might otherwise have been visited upon them by virtue of

their purposes or their methods. Whilst these continue in current legislation (see above, p 411) this also provides some *indirect* support for the development of greater union 'security'. This concept of 'union security' derived from North America means some degree of protection of the union from attack or threat from 'outside', whether the outsiders be individual anti- or non-unionists or associations of workers seeking to poach members. The TUC itself has sought voluntarily to regulate union security amongst its own member associations, through the Bridlington rules governing transfer of membership from one affiliated union to another and the machinery established under them (see Lerner, 1958). The TULR and the EP Acts, however, have carried this notion of protection some way forward, although without going as far as the explicit sanctioning of closed shops.

One part of the new protection is focused upon the individual worker, and the actions which the employer may *not* take to influence his membership of or involvement in the activities of trade unions.

Under the EP Act, S 53, the individual is given four distinct rights ("as an individual" in the first three cases), in the form of a "right not to have action taken against him by the employer" for exercising them:

(i)   the right to join an independent trade union
(ii)   the right to be an active member of an independent trade union (provided that this is not restricted by a union membership agreement)
(iii)   the right not to have to join a trade union which is not independent (ie which cannot satisfy the conditions for certification by the Certification Officer)
(iv)   the right to refuse to join any trade union on the ground of religious objection to so doing.

As this affects the employer, it means that the employer must not victimize or otherwise discriminate against the individual seeking to exercise these rights: it is to be construed as including acts of both commission and omission, the imposition of a penalty and the witholding of a benefit to which the individual might otherwise have been entitled. The individual is offered the remedy of applying to a tribunal for a declaration of his rights and compensation as might be considered just and equitable in the circumstances. At the hearing it is for the employee to prove the act of alleged victimization but for the employer to show what its purpose was and that it was not an unlawful purpose. The employer is not allowed to argue that he sought to prevent a strike or other industrial action, but he can have

426

the case dismissed if he can show that the action was taken for reasons of national security.

In union security terms, the fourth of these rights is aimed at eliminating the 'free rider', except where the individual can pass the rigorous test to demonstrate genuinely held religious belief and an objection to joining any union whatsoever. The third is directed against the house union or 'staff association' of the type which was brought into prominence between 1971 and 1974 (during the Industrial Relations Act period) and which was usually thought to be employer dominated, controlled or influenced. The first in essence merely states a basic right. The second right is somewhat more complicated in its implications for the question of union security.

An employee is to be allowed to take part in the activities of an independent trade union 'at any appropriate time' (S 53 (1) (b). This must include any time when the individual is not required to be at work for the employer and, with the employer's agreement, any other time. It is likely that the individual can, with impunity, take part in activities on the employer's premises, before and after work, during tea breaks and meal breaks or whenever he is customarily on the employer's premises but not actually required to be working. The activities which are included (although not defined in the Act) are likely to be, at least, those included in the Code of Practice on 'time off' provisions—attendance at union meetings, taking part in ballots and other activities in which a union member might reasonably be expected to engage. A lay official of the union might also be covered for activities of collecting union dues, distributing literature or communicating orally with members and recruiting new members, since they are all customary duties of such official.

But this right is restricted where a union membership agreement is in force. A union membership agreement must (a) be made between the employer(s) and the independent union(s), (b) identify the 'class of employees' covered by the agreement, and (c) require those employees to join one of the unions which is a party to the agreement or which is specified in it (TULR Act s 30 (1) (or which is "accepted by the parties to the agreement as being the equivalent of a union so specified" (TULR Act, 1976, s 3 (3)). In addition a union will be regarded as specified if it has sought recognition through ACAS and the matter is still 'live' (EP Act s 53). Where such an agreement exists, the individual cannot exercise a right to be active in the interests of any 'other' union on the employer's premises, even if he happens to be a member of one and may be active in it in his own time and away from the employer's premises. This is aimed at preventing poaching by non-signatory and non-specified unions and at preventing those who may, under the agreement be exempted from joining

427

the or a union (by reasons of religious objection, age or because they were not union members at the time when the agreement was signed or implemented).

Trade union members and officials, provided the union is independent and recognized by the employer, may ask for time off to engage in trade union activities. The employer must give permission for this and, in deciding to refuse it, he would have to bear in mind that in the event of a complaint to a tribunal, he would have to show that the refusal was reasonable in the circumstances. But at the same time the employee-trade union member cannot simply take time off for this purpose. In order to avoid difficulties and disputes, the ACAS Code of Practice on this subject recommends that the employer and the trade union(s) representatives work out their own code of procedure for permitting time to be taken off for this purpose (see above, pp 93–5).

Although these 'rights' are established at the level of the individual, they have an obvious intent and effect of protecting the independent and recognized trade union(s) from both the indifferent free rider and the rival organization. But the legislation does not compel the parties, or either of them, to conclude a closed shop or union membership agreement. The closed shop type agreement is a matter for the parties themselves to determine through the ordinary processes of (power) bargaining: legislation neither prevents nor compels it. What the legislation does do is

(a) admit a dispute over a closed shop issue as a 'trade dispute', thus rendering industrial action in support of or against it lawful (TULRA s 29(1)(e))
(b) allow dismissal of an employee who refuses to become a union member or who is refused membership by a trade union (signatory or specified) to be regarded as fair, when the closed shop agreement qualifies as a 'union membership agreement' (essentially when it embraces independent trade unions) (TULRA Sch 1 para 6(a)) unless the individual establishes a religious objection.

These provisions represent a turn-about from the provisions of the 1971 Industrial Relations Act and, to an extent, reflect the TUC affiliated unions' anger at what was seen in the earlier Act as a deliberate attempt to remove the degree of union security which, to that date, the unions had themselves secured 'voluntarily' or by 'struggle' in negotiations with the employers.

Rights on disclosure of information
Both of these rights discussed in the two preceding sections have

something to do with the protection of the trade union as well as with trade union performance. On the trade union's right to have information disclosed to it and on possible rights to participation, the emphasis is almost exclusively upon trade union performance: the legislation seeks to facilitate the development of 'good industrial relations'.

Disclosure of information, as such, is not new. It has been required since the middle·of last century as a means of protecting investors and informing creditors (or potential creditors) although in 1967, a significant shift in public policy occurred with the requirement of some disclosure for purely 'public' (eg 'planning') purposes, and this has been extended by the Industry Act of 1975. Since then, a requirement of disclosure of information for purposes of collective bargaining has grown up and is now imposed, under various pieces of legislation, as a duty upon the employer to disclose some information to employees generally and some to independent trade unions having a collective bargaining interest particularly.

Disclosure to employees and their trade unions of information about the current state and future plans of an enterprise is something which trade unions have often sought in negotiations in the past: the view was taken that information was a basis for power and control, and that its retention by management provided the foundation for the exercise of a management prerogative. The TUC's 1974 Report of the General Council to Congress shows the direction of thinking: "The provision of information on the operations of the enterprise—whether public or private—to the employees and their representatives is an essential background against which extensions to industrial democracy can occur on a rational and informed basis." Already the 1970 TUC Report had given a shopping list of information to be sought for the facilitation of collective bargaining. This list included financial information, cost information and remuneration data, together with information on prospects and plans in the financial investment, marketing and manpower areas. What the trade union movement wants, and what it wants it for, is thus spelled out.

Disclosure of this general type of information entered the realms of public policy through the recommendations of the Donovan Commission for the development of orderly and effective industrial relations in British industry. The Commission argued that boards of companies would have to "collect systematic information on which to base action in [such matters as recruitment, promotion, training and retraining] and to make available to workers' representatives such information as they may reasonably require." This was taken up and extended by the

429

Labour Government's policy statement *In Place of Strife* and by its Industrial Relations Bill of 1970. It was also taken up by the Conservative Government, and promulgated in the Industrial Relations Act of 1971: by S 56 the employer was required to supply information to a trade union (or its representatives) where it could be shown that this information was necessary for the furtherance of collective bargaining at any and every stage, or that its non-disclosure would be detrimental to good industrial relations practice. This part of this Act was never implemented, but it did provide the basis for the CIR investigation into disclosure which appeared as a report, *Disclosure of Information,* in 1972.

The CIR placed main emphasis in its report on the desirability of securing an agreed policy on disclosure and then set out two categories of guideline, one on Types of Information and the other on Conditions and Methods. The report was conservative in its suggestions, arguing that it did no more than indicate what might be included in disclosed information where the circumstances were right and the parties agreed. It did not pretend to be exhaustive in either range or depth and did not suggest that in all undertakings information on all items should necessarily be given.

The Employment Protection Act 1975, S 17, reinstates the duty upon the employer to disclose information, originating in S 56 of the repealed Industrial Relations Act. The general duty is to disclose to recognized independent trade unions, on request by them (in writing if the employer so requires) "all such information relating to his undertaking as is in his possession, or that of any associated employer, and is both—

(a) information without which the trade union representatives would be to a material extent impeded in carrying on with him such collective bargaining, and
(b) information which it would be in accordance with good industrial relations practice that he should disclose to them for the purposes of collective bargaining"

and at the request of the union representatives this information may be required in writing.

The general duty is restricted by certain other provisions of the Act, in addition to the above restriction that both conditions (a) and (b) shall be present. Information against the interests of national security, which would contravene a legal prohibition, which is obtained in confidence or which relates to an individual, or which was obtained in connection with legal proceedings, need not be disclosed. Nor need information "the disclosure of which would cause substantial injury to the employer's undertaking for reasons other

430

than its effect on collective bargaining" (EP Act, S 18(1)). Nor is the employer under a duty to show or copy any document, other than that prepared by him to meet the request of the union representatives, or to compile or assemble information where to do so would mean an amount of work or expenditure out of reasonable proportion to the value of the information in the conduct of collective bargaining (S 18(2)).

Guidance to employers is offered in a Code of Practice, issued by ACAS under the provisions of EP Act S 6(2) and S 17(4) and operative from 22 August 1977. This five-page Code is in many ways comparable to the guidance offered by the CIR, both in its cautionary statements and its indications of appropriate information for disclosure. The Code by itself does not impose a legal obligation upon the employer, but the extent to which its guidance has been followed may be entered in proceedings under the EP Act in support of a claim or counterclaim. The Code therefore makes it clear that what is to be disclosed in the particular case shall depend upon local circumstances and requirements and shall reflect the general criteria of 'necessity' in those circumstances and 'good industrial relations' conducted voluntarily. It is also intended that the Code shall be read as stating a minimum standard of good practice which such collective bargaining could well extend.

The Code therefore lists some examples under broad category headings of the information which might in appropriate bargaining circumstances be disclosed, and points out that the main weight of responsibility for showing that any item of such information is necessary or desirable really falls upon the trade union representatives, who will have to identify their precise needs clearly and early in the proceedings. Similarly, the Code places the onus upon the trade unions to ensure that, by training or any other means, the representatives are in a position to define their need and to make use of the information when they have received it. Many companies have already developed policies on information disclosure which take their practice well beyond what is suggested in the Code itself, and the point of the Code's list of examples is therefore to offer broad and general guidance to those which still have to develop relevant policies (cf Smith, 1977, Management Survey Report No 31, BIM).

The Code lists

1 Pay and benefits: principles and structure of payment systems; job evaluation systems and grading criteria; earnings and hours analysed according to work group, grade, plant, sex, outworkers and homeworkers, department or division, giving where appropriate, distributions and make up of pay showing any additions to

basic rate or salary; total pay bill; details of fringe benefits and non-wage labour costs
2 Conditions of service: policies on recruitment, redeployment, redundancy, training, equal opportunity, and promotion; appraisal systems; health, welfare and safety matters
3 Manpower: numbers employed analysed according to grade, department, location, age and sex; labour turnover; absenteeism; overtime and short-time; manning standards; planned changes in work methods, materials, equipment or organization; available manpower plans; investment plans
4 Performance: productivity and efficiency data; savings from increased productivity and output; return on capital invested; sales and state of order book
5 Financial: cost structures; gross and net profits; sources of earnings; assets; liabilities; allocation of profits; details of government financial assistance; transfer prices; loans to parent or subsidiary companies and interest charged.

The Central Arbitration Committee is given a powerful role in requiring any employer to disclose information if, after receiving a complaint from an independent trade union, the CAC finds it well founded and in accordance with the 'good industrial relations' principles repeated in this Act that such information should be disclosed in order not to impede a trade union in its negotiations. Where an employer does not comply with this first request the CAC has power, if it receives a further complaint from a trade union and finds it well founded, to make a legally binding award of appropriate terms and conditions of employment, which would become part of the individual contract of employment.

The Code strongly urges employers and their recognized independent trade unions to work out and agree their general and longer-term information needs, as a foundation for the development of a systematic relationship in bargaining. Such an information agreement might conceivably develop from a review of what information is currently available or disclosed and what might be desirable if it could be made available. It would then seek to establish the form in which information might be presented, when and to whom this should be done, regularly or as required, generally to employees or specifically to bargainers. This would have to make some provision for the treatment of some information as confidential, particularly in the early stages of negotiation, for the protection of both 'sides' in the negotiating process. The agreement might also make provision for elucidation of information, after disclosure, a mechanism being agreed to allow this to happen, possibly outside the negotiating process itself. It would also be necessary to establish a similar mechanism for resolving disputes about what should be made available, or whether what had been agreed as capable of disclosure had in fact been disclosed as agreed.

Such information agreements might also form a part of the general disclosure or informing policy of the undertaking. This policy would need to take account not merely of the information to be disclosed for purposes of collective bargaining under S 17 of the Employment Protection Act, but also of the disclosure required by the Contracts of Employment Act 1972 to all (and particularly new) employees, by the Redundancy Procedures in Part IV of the Employment Protection Act and in some circumstances by the requirements of the Industry Act 1975. The 1972 Code of Practice, in so far as it relates to communication and consultation, also remains in operation as guidance on some of these aspects.

The first of these requirements (see above, pp 368–74, indicates the way ahead for the future in respect of disclosing information generally to employees, undertakings are already seeking to systematize their approach to this question, in some cases using the requirements of the Industry Act as a guide for the kind of information which might be made available generally. The procedures covering redundancies are somewhat different but they do also indicate that an era of more open decision-taking is upon us, and in any case relate to the more general question of manpower planning within the undertaking. But it is likely that such requirements on disclosure of information and consultation will soon be incorporated in more general provisions for participation or industrial democracy. If the proposals of the Bullock Committee on this subject were to be adopted, a much more open negotiation would be ushered in.

Industrial democracy
In order to form a view on what might be done in Britain to comply with the Fifth Draft Directive of the European Economic Community the Government set up the Bullock Committee in 1975, to consider how "a radical extension of industrial democracy" involving trade unions "can best be achieved" taking into account the proposals of the TUC, British experience and the EEC experience. The Committee reported in 1977 but the Government has shown no great wish to take up the proposal, although there is a general commitment to do something.

The Committee recommends that, initially in all companies in the UK with 2,000 or more full-time employees (including in this concept 'holding companies' as well as others), there should

433

be established by legislation an opportunity for the employees to vote on, and if the outcome is positive, for the independent trade unions to elect or appoint, representatives of the workforce to a single-tier board of directors for that company. The formula for the final composition of this 'unitary' board is that which is expressed as 2x + y, where x equals a number of shareholder or employee directors, and y equals a number of other directors who shall be an odd number greater than one and less than a third of the total number of directors. "We propose that in companies where all the conditions for the introduction of employee representation are met, the boards should be reconstituted to be composed of three elements—an equal number of employee and shareholder representatives, plus a third group of co-opted directors." These additional directors should be co-opted with the agreement of a majority of the other two groups of representatives, and will normally number three or five persons according to the size of the board which the parties would want to establish (ie one of 11 or 17 on the application of the formula).

The majority of the Committee think that in principle "all directors should have the same legal duties and liabilities. We propose that there should be some changes in the law regarding director's duties to ensure that the employee representatives are able to carry out their normal and reasonable functions as representatives of the workforce. We recommend that all directors should continue to be required to act in the best interests of the company, but that in doing so they should take into account the interests of the company's employees as well as its shareholders."

The majority of the Committee seek legislative division of the functions of the shareholders and the board to permit some matters to fall within the purview of the new board, even if others could be delegated to management. They draw a distinction between the attributed functions and the non-attributed. The first set, on which the board will have the exclusive right to submit a resolution for consideration at a shareholders' meeting, are:

(a) winding up of the company
(b) changes in the memorandum and articles of association
(c) recommendations to shareholders on payment of dividends
(d) changes in the capital structure of a company (eg on the relationship between the board and the shareholders, a reduction or increase in the authorized share capital; as regards the relationship between the board and the senior management, the issue of securities on a take-over or merger)
(e) disposal of a substantial part of the undertaking.

The objective in *attributing* these functions to the board is to ensure

434

that the body on which the trade union representatives sit shall have some kind of 'right' to determine these matters. But on the face of it their attribution takes away from the shareholders' meeting their existing right (whether they in fact exercise it or not in the particular case) to have the final say on these matters, where the existing Articles provide for their exercise of this right. It is not absolutely clear whether this 'ultimate' authority is to be removed. On the one hand, "it is for serious consideration whether our proposals should apply to all companies irrespective of board level representation, or only to those with employee representatives on their board" (Bullock 1977, p 77). On the other, they suggest that on the attributed functions, the "right to take a final decision would rest with the board of directors" *and* that "the shareholders' meeting would retain a right to approve or reject the board's proposals in certain specified circumstances" which are not indicated or specified (*ibid*). Later (p 81) the board is given "the exclusive right to convene a meeting (of shareholders) for the purpose of considering resolutions in these areas" and the shareholders' meeting "the right to decide whether to pass the resolutions or not", thus implying that the shareholders' meeting has power to refer back but not alter resolutions on the attributed functions with which it does not agree. How many times it may exercise this power before a terminus is reached will no doubt require a conscious decision by the legislators.

This attribution is, quite explicitly, recommended in order to allow the trade union representatives to act as representatives of their constituencies. The obligations of directors will be varied to allow other interests than those of the shareholders to be taken into account, but that said the trade union directors will then have the same obligations as other directors. But they will be answerable to their constituencies, not to the shareholders' meeting, a proposal clearly in accord with the 'democratic imperative'. However, the determination to clarify this 'representative' role, places the shareholder directors in the same 'representative' capacity. The shareholders' meeting, instead of retaining an authority role on decisions about the government and operation of the company, will itself become a constituency with powers of recall and re-appointment (or re-election) but not even such authority to influence directors' decisions as the interpretation of the dichotomy between Marshall's case and Scott *v* Scott ((1943) 1 All ER p 582) might permit. The problem for the trade union representatives may well prove to be the opposite of this.

If employee representatives are to be effective representatives and effective directors, they will require a range of rights beyond those directly associated with attending the board. In addition to

435

receiving board papers, employees will need to keep in close touch with their constituents. Accordingly they will need, with due notice to their immediate supervisors, to be able to take time off as of right. They will also need access to an office and a telephone, secretarial assistance of a confidential nature and perhaps other facilities.

The non-attributed functions are listed as:

(i) the allocation and disposition of resources to the extent not covered by (a) to (e) above, and to the extent to which they are not delegated to management

(ii) the appointment, removal, control and remuneration of senior management, whether members of the board or not in their capacity as executives or employees. Within these limits, no restrictions on delegation are envisaged, and existing rights and obligations in dealings with third parties, the shareholders' power to appoint auditors or to compel a Board of Trade investigation, or to appoint or recall the shareholder directors are not to be altered.

The majority of the Committee's proposals for the effecting of a degree of industrial democracy in the particular company which qualifies are that:

1 Once the enabling legislation has been passed, it will be open to any recognized and independent trade union (or group of them) which is recognized as 'covering' a fifth or more of the workforce employed in the company, to request a ballot on the question of industrial democracy. Bullock suggests that the question to be put ought to be "Do you want employee representation on the company board through trade unions recognized by your employer?"

2 Once this request has been properly made, the employer will then be obliged to conduct a ballot, at his expense, and in company time and on company premises as is convenient to allow all employees to vote in it. "All full-time employees, including any on short-time or laid off, but not part-timers will be eligible to vote in the ballot"

3 A positive result is defined in the majority report as a simple majority of those voting, providing that those in favour constituted a third of those eligible. "In addition to the requirement of a simple majority to vote in favour of the proposals, the majority should represent at least one third of the eligible employees"

4 If a ballot fails to produce the required majority in favour of representation on the unitary board, there is to be an embargo on further requests for a ballot on the question for two years; and when a reconstituted board is set up, there is to be an embargo on seeking a ballot to get rid of it for five years. (The mechanism is the same here as at inception)

436

5 After a vote in favour the onus of devising a method of selecting the representatives is placed on the trade unions recognized in the company, following the practice in Sweden. The Committee recommends that the law should not operate so as to close any of the options open to the trade unions to make their selection, but the Committee favours selection from the ranks of employees

6 The Committee recommends that, once a ballot has produced a verdict in favour, the shop stewards should set up a formal committee, called the Joint Union Meeting for Industrial Democracy (JUMID). This body would negotiate with the existing board on the size and structure of the new board to enable it to decide how the employee representatives on the board should be selected. All the independent unions recognized by the company would be eligible for membership of JUMID; if any such union was being excluded (and this could be demonstrated to the proposed Industrial Democracy Commission), the existing board would be freed from the requirement to meet with it or to accept employee nominations for the reconstituted board.

Once agreement has been reached on the size and structure of the reconstituted board, it will be up to the trade unions (through JUMID) and the existing board, to select respective representatives. *These* will then meet to determine the names of those to be co-opted to the (y) element of the new board, and once this has been done, the new board can assume office.

There are a number of important implications in this set of proposals. If the broad overall conception were to be accepted, the mechanisms proposed for bringing the unitary reconstituted board into existence, raises questions about the following:

(a) How many systems of both law and practice shall apply in Britain? Bullock suggests that the Committee is not in favour of having two different sets of law, for the large and the small enterprises or for the public and the private companies. But industrial democracy has usually been thought of in association with the scale of modern organizations, measured by numbers of employees—and the Bullock Committee's recommendations are cast in these terms. But the Fifth Draft Directive of the EEC is aimed at the 'public company' as this will come to be defined in Britain from the end of 1978 (see above, 43) and 'size' measured by subscribed capital will be a factor in this future distinction. Since 'size' by subscribed capital (£50,000 is suggested for Britain under the Second Directive) does not correlate with 'size' by numbers of employees engaged in the UK (Bullock's proposals relate initially to enterprises with 2,000 or more employees), which criterion ought to be used to determine opportunity for advance in industrial democracy, and ought size of labour force to be allowed to embrace private companies as well as public ones? In addition, it is not clear whether the 'attributed functions of the board' would apply to all public companies, or all public and private companies of a minimum size (measured by number of employees, regardless of whether the industrial democracy trigger is or is not pulled). Should this apply only to those companies where the employees vote for industrial democracy in the Bullock terms, there would be one pattern of authority in them and quite another in the non-democratized companies

(b) What is to be the authority of the shareholders' meeting in the new arrangements? The shareholders' meeting is, at present in Britain, arguably a part of the structure of authority in the government of industrial enterprise (see Sullivan, 1977, pp 569–80; Gower, 1969, p 474 *et seq*) although there is evidence to suggest that practice departs from the intentions of legal form (see Florence, 1953, Part V; Bullock, 1977, ch 7). The Bullock Committee's proposals (by the majority, pp 77–78) would reduce this authority, and convert the shareholders into a constituency for the election of the shareholder directors who, with the trade union directors and the 'y' element, would have power to initiate the actions listed above, for 'approval' by the shareholders in general meeting.

Bullock does not say how conflicts (ie where there is disapproval) might be resolved. The Confederation of British Industry and others have raised the spectre of failure to agree within the reconstituted board itself, but in addition it is clear that the question of resolving both the authority and the powers of the shareholders meeting, *vis à vis* the board, also calls for resolution in law as a guide for future practice

(c) The determination of directorships of executive managers where the numbers involved would require a reduction in the size of the shareholder representatives on the reconstituted board. The *Investors Chronicle* has estimated that about 1,000 such directors would lose their positions. The Committee suggests that rights under service contracts should not be abrogated, so that a director thus deprived of his position would be able to claim damages (up to two years remuneration), but transitional arrangements would allow existing directors to move into the 'y' component for a time

(d) The possible disenfranchisement of those employees and categories of employee who do not, at the moment, belong to a recognized trade union. This might include the non-unionists in any situation but it also includes, importantly, many managerial staffs outside the public sector industries who do not belong to trade unions, and who are in danger of being left unrepresented unless there is sufficient strength of will on the part of the existing board to require such representation in the longer term through the 'y' element of the board

(e) Since not all independent, TUC affiliated trade unions are necessarily in favour of the Bullock proposals (eg the AUEW or the EPTU, for different reasons) the JUMID proposal could lead to either difficulties or opportunities for a more unified structure of union representation. This degree of 'jointness' proposed for this purpose might have more positive outcomes in the form of trade union cooperation on other matters; in any event, the pressure to sort out a possibly small number of representatives in a multi-union situation might set up forces which might in the long run alter the existing trade union structure in the undertaking. This in itself is interesting as a possible long-term device for dealing with the 'bargaining unit' problem which has proved so difficult to handle over the years.

The coupling of industrial democracy arrangements with the local trade union representatives, to the virtual exclusion of full-time officials (they might appear in a small number of very special circumstances in the Bullock Committee majority's view), allows it to be argued that the Committee is really proposing to complete the process of bringing the shop stewards more effectively into the machinery of industrial relations which so exercised the minds of the Donovan Commission. The Bullock Committee argues:

> In practice, we think that the trade union machinery which most employees will wish to use is that which is internal to their company, the shop steward organization and its equivalents, rather than that which is external to it, the branch, the district committee and the national executive. We see considerable value in shop stewards being the key figures in a system of board level representation.

It is this which makes the proposal, arguably, a final stage of the incorporation of the trade unions, through the local representatives, into the 'performance' structure of industrial relations, thus emphasizing the need for considerable and careful local attention to the problems of local trade union security (ie closed shop and related arrangements) as the foundation for this performance. The change in the structure of authority or domination (see above, pp 308–20) which Bullock proposes may be regarded as too highly priced if it implies incorporation of the local union organization. Or the price in union security provisions may be considered too high a price for managements to pay for the benefits which some see as accruing from such incorporation.

Rationale of industrial relations policies
This particular approach to the solution of industrial relations problems is justified by the belief or assumption that the greater the involvement of workers in decisions about their working conditions or working lives, the greater their contribution to the enterprise may be expected to be. This belief replaces the older scientific management assumption that the more precisely and efficiently the work of the individual was organized for him, the greater his productivity. It is held by both sides of industry (except for the more extreme fringes) and it has been adopted by government to provide the foundation for intervention in this field since about 1960.

The catalyst for the change of approach on the part of government was provided by the increase in the number of strikes and the number of man-days lost through them, during the 1960s (for data see *Yearbook of British Labour Statistics;* for limitations see Turner, 1969). Strikes, as representations of breakdown in relationships, were, and still are, seen as more capable of being controlled by human action than other manifestations of withdrawal from work such as absenteeism or accidents, simply because the latter were not (at least until the Health and Safety at Work etc Act implied something different) regarded as a result of human will, whereas the former were considered to be brought about as a result of human volition.

It is this assumption which allows so much attention to be given to strikes or other industrial actions short of a strike, whilst the losses of production from absenteeism (for example) receive considerably less attention.

The industrial relations situation in Britain since 1960 might be best described as volatile. On the one hand, the amount of unofficial and unconstitutional action, which so exercised the minds of the begetters of the Donovan Commission and of the Commission itself, increased in the early part of this period at what was thought an alarming rate. (As Lord Watkinson said in the *Financial Times* (April 1974): "We all know that our nation cannot stand much more fratricidal strife in industry.") On the other, the number of suggestions for change in the authority structure under which people work has also burgeoned in this period, often responding to this same observed

440

strike rate and seeking to establish a new accommodation of human values in the industrial structure. The Secretary of State for Industry expressed something of this view: "What I am trying to do is to tackle the problems created by the inadequate or limited role given to people working in industry."

Putting these together, one can detect an answer to the question 'what causes strikes?' which will in turn tend to shape any plans made to avoid them. Thus the Donovan Commission examined the data on strikes and concluded that they occurred because the workers' local representatives (eg the shop-stewards) (a) had no adequate place or role in bargaining within enterprises because of lack of recognition, or because of ill-conceived structures and (b) were denied access to the real decision processes (and the information associated with them) for similar reasons. The varied plans of subsequent governments have reflected this analysis to the extent of at least seeking to formalize recognition, structures of bargaining, access to relevant information and access to real centres of decision, even if the various plans have sought to achieve these ends by marginally different means.

Public policy has, as the preceding pages reveal, accepted the premise that changes in the distribution of power in industry are needed if people are to contribute fully or to a necessary level, *and* that these changes are unlikely to occur (either at all, or sufficiently quickly) if they are left to be brought about at the discretion of the employer. Therefore two actions follow: first, the opportunities for organized labour to influence industrial decisions must be increased—via recognition and the development of new decision procedures, some extension of collective bargaining subjects, and some greater informing of the actual processes of joint decision-taking; secondly, the employer must be compelled to provide such opportunities when he shows himself reluctant to do so, via new legislation covering the matters referred to and allowing independent trade unions to bring reluctant employers to tribunal and CAC judgement.

Consequently, representative organizations should now be recognized for bargaining purposes and the bargaining itself should be in good faith (this should include subjects in which the workers have an interest); adequate bargaining structures ought to be developed, on the authority of a responsible board member, and supported by adequate procedures to contain differences of view; it should be the norm that decisions vitally affecting the workforce are the subject of consultation before they are actually taken by the management. Broadly, they are justified on the grounds that disruptive activities (such as strikes) may be expected to decrease if workers, by these means, are enabled to have a say, and a more informed say, in what the policies and practices of the enterprise ought to be.

These prescriptions now put constraints on employers' decisions in these areas and they have much less discretion than before. As a consequence, employers must take the necessary steps to develop appropriate and conforming policies on recognition, procedures, bargaining in good faith and disclosure. As a second consequence, employers must also develop policies and practices within this constraining framework to ensure that these changes will effect the consequences expected. It by no means follows, and this seems to be the burden of the argument in the CBI's submission to the Bullock Committee, that all workers want precisely the same thing by way of participation in decision-taking. To the extent that this is a correct assessment, the need for personnel managers to work out the actual demand pattern in their own circumstances is emphasized.

There is evidence to suggest that different situations have developed their own patterns of conflict which are supported by existing personnel. Political differences do exist, and will influence the kind of response made to any given proposition about power-sharing. The opportunities for discharging those who refuse to accept that any game, even a conflict game, must be played according to some rules, are fewer now than they were when some national companies discharged awkward shop stewards in order to put their industrial relations on a more even keel. That being so, the process of effecting a change in a locally volatile state is likely not only to be a long one, but also one in which some avenues of grievance bargaining are progressively closed and others opened to permit the emergence of a different set of representatives reflecting a different set of objectives in the workforce itself. A clean slate may be appealing but impossible; the progressive evolution of new structures and approaches will inevitably involve more time and a more sophisticated approach.

Thus, within this general approach, it remains for the employer alone or in concert with his fellows to develop policies and procedures appropriate to the particular circumstances. Many employers have already begun to do this, not simply as a response to changed statutory requirements, but as a managerial response to a changed situation and in accordance with theories which management itself holds as to the relationship between context and content of relationships on the one hand and avoidance of breakdown on the other. It would seem to follow that if changes are made for no other reason than that they are required by some external authority, or that they are fashionable, amongst other enterprises, there would seem to be no reason at all to suppose that they will produce the changes in commitment or contribution which provide the rationale for these changes in society at large.

442

It is also to be borne in mind that whatever the generality of the public policy and trade union attitude may be, the situation faced by any single employer will be unique. It is not therefore to be presumed that everything in this field must become standardized, even if that may prove to be the dominant trend. There will remain scope for initiative and creativity (possibly of the kind illustrated in chapter 9) and there will in any case be a need to 'apply' general precepts and principles to local situations. It is this aspect which we take up in the following chapter, where we explore the trend towards the development of constitutions at the local level against the background of public and trade union policies dealt with in this one.

Further reading
The most useful general background text on industrial relations is that of Clegg (1977 edn) and this may be supplemented on the public policy and law aspects by reference to Kahn-Freund (1977) and Hepple and O'Higgins (1976), and on the trade union policies and attitudes by McCarthy (1972) and Hyman and Fryer (1975) or Allen (1966).

On more specific elements, see also the Report of the Donovan Commission (1968), Eldridge (1968), Hyman (1972) and Lane and Roberts (1971) on strikes and the ACAS Codes of Practice on Industrial Relations (1972, as amended), Disciplinary Practice and Procedures in Employment (1977), Disclosure of Information to Trade Unions for Collective Bargaining Purposes (1977), Time Off for Trade Union Duties and Activities (1978) and Collective Bargaining Procedures (?1978) and the Report of the Bullock Committee (1977), on recommended procedures for their avoidance.

On the general approaches to industrial relations by the employer, see also Anthony (1977), Walton and McKersie (1965) and McCarthy (1973).

11 The structure of plant industrial relations

Introduction

Industrial relations in Britain is often spoken of as constituting a 'voluntary system' (eg Flanders, 1965). In essence what this seeks to indicate is that the main parties to industrial relationships employers, trade unions and the State agencies (Dunlop, 1958), follow their preferences for ordering their relations on a 'voluntary' principle which denies salience to State interference in the matter. The 'rules' governing conduct in this area therefore form the product of a kind of private law-making by the employers and the trade unions which is often regarded, even in legislation, as a substitute for public law (Kahn-Freund, 1977; and TULR Act, 1974, S 18). The theory which underpins this approach is that people will more readily accept laws or rules which they themselves have had a part in shaping, and that the better ordering of relationships in industry is to be achieved by leaving the law and rule-making activities to the autonomous decision of the parties.

Experience in Britain in the 1950s and 1960s has been held to cast doubt on this theory (Donovan Commission Report, 1968) as an adequate foundation for the 'voluntary system'. The first doubt centres on *who* is to be seen as participating in setting up the rules: the Donovan Commission's identification of a formal national system and an informal local (shop stewards with local (personnel) management) system served to focus attention on the possibility that *real* joint decisions were being taken at the plant and company levels in distinction from or in defiance of those still being taken at the national industry-wide level (Margerison, 1969). This led to a second doubt which focuses on what forms of procedural rules or conventions really do guide the conduct of the parties to the relationships: the 'procedural' rules developed in national negotiations to guide those negotiators in their conduct and approach to each other came to be seen as having little force and relevance to the relationships of the informal system. These are seen to be governed more by informal understandings, conventions and customs but potentially amenable to control by constitutions governing relations in the production system as distinct from the industrial relations system (Wood *et al*, 1975). The third doubt has then concentrated on the question of whether the (local) parties are capable of displaying sufficient creativity in devising constitutions to guide their relationships to satisfy the criteria of the wider society, related to considerations of efficiency, order and predictability in the production process itself (Goldthorpe, 1974).

It is the third of these which has guided the government's industrial relations policy for the past decade and a half, although with increasing confidence since the Donovan Commission reported. Although little has been said about Britain's emulation of continental European practices on bringing industrial relationships under constitutional control (except on 'co-determination') much of what has appeared in the way of legislation and government policy in the past 10 years bears a striking resemblance to those practices, albeit with some attempt to meet the different historical conditions in Britain. It is arguable that what has thus emerged so far in industrial relations practice in Britain in this more recent period, faltering and piecemeal though it may appear to have been, is a development of formal constitutions to govern industrial relationships within the factory, plant or company—in much the same fashion that government policies had established the essentials of the national system of procedural agreement control by about the first world war, and amounting to a pattern of constitutional control which is already comparable in its coverage to that provided by the German Betriebsrat (works council) under the Works Constitution Act of 1952 as amended in 1972 and 1976.

Whilst it may still be true that "Britain is the only Western European country where works councils are not mandatory either by statute or national agreement" (Appleyard, 1971, p 6) there may still be a sense in which the more pragmatic British approach to these questions has produced a very similar consequence. It does not perhaps matter that in Britain there is no particular body, the works council, which provides the focus for constitutional action; what is material is whether the arrangements at local level, shaped by legislation and State agencies in industrial relations, are producing a result that local, production-system relations are being increasingly subject to the same kind of constitutional control or containment. The fragmented nature of the local bargaining system will no doubt continue to complicate the process, although the potentiality of joint-shop stewards negotiating arrangements should not be discounted here. The continuing control and guidance of the national union leaders and negotiators should similarly not be written off, but the directions of their guidance on the matter are not yet singular and indeed may never be. The constitutions of the national trade unions may continue to prevent local unification movements but the finding of a more 'realistic' place for the shop stewards in union structures may also bring about movement in this direction (cf Goldthorpe, 1974).

It cannot be claimed, therefore, that Britain either has or will in the immediate future have, a works council and works constitution structure such as is found in, say, Germany now. But, it can be suggested that this image does provide the most apposite comparator for purposes of discerning where the British developments in this field in recent years are tending in the way of guiding philosophy and structure. By implication, this approach to the subject of industrial relations reduces the traditional emphasis upon the national trade unions, the employers' associations and the legislative support for national industrial relations systems. It redirects attention to the workers' local union associations, the company board responsibilities for industrial relations (as advocated by the Donovan Commission) and the legislatively established rights of 'trade unions' to recognition, negotiation, consultation, information and facilities, all focused on the individual undertaking and variously supported by the new machinery of the industrial tribunals and the Advisory Conciliation and Arbitration Service.

This is to justify the approach which is taken in this chapter to industrial relations. This does not deny the importance of a knowledge of national trade unions, employers' associations, the procedural and substantive agreements between them and the relevant state machinery. It does imply that industrial relations in the context of personnel management practice is more appositely considered in terms of the local system, and in particular within a framework which sees the nature of this 'system' as one of constitutionalization and control.

Agreements as constitutional rules

It may be represented that, in the local undertaking, there are at least two sets of relationships which fall to be ordered. Those in the 'production system' and those in the 'industrial relations system' may, from our point of view, be regarded as distinct for purposes of analysis. All that is intended by the use of the term 'production system' is that there are relationships established by and expressed in the contract of employment which call for regulation in some way: the concrete elements in this are the wages to be paid by the employer for service of a defined sort by the employee, the hours which will normally be worked and the holidays and other time off which will be allowed, the rules which will govern conduct whilst at work and so on. What is then intended by the use of the term 'industrial relations system' is that there are additional relationships which become established between those who acquire roles on the fixing of the terms and conditions of employment, and that these can be treated separately with advantage. In concrete manifestation, these latter relationships are usually regulated by 'procedural agreements' or rules, where the others are covered by 'substantive agreements' or rules.

In terms of this distinction, what will be explored in this present chapter are the agreements or rules which relate to the industrial relations system; the discussion of the other kind of agreement will remain for the following chapter. We must recognize that in practice the two are close together in how they are negotiated and what they portend for the relationships of the parties, and it is only for convenience that a major distinction is effected here. But this device of separating the two does enable us in the present chapter to consider the growth and development of the procedural agreement as a foundation for a 'works constitution' at the local level, on the assumption that the employer has already recognized the trade union (or a number of them) and that both are willing to enter into some kind of permanent regulation of their collective relations. This is not always so, of course: some employers still do not recognize trade unions and prefer to maintain their relationships in the production system in some other way (cf Myers, 1975) than through formal procedures agreed with trade union representatives; and some employees for various reasons prefer to avoid such relationships with the employer. New opportunities afforded to trade unions in recent legislation to extend 'negotiated' terms and conditions of employment to employers not party to the negotiated agreements (see below, pp 493–98) may, in the future and in some cases, foster a rethinking of non-recognition policies by employers.

The procedural agreement
Where the parties are willing to regard their collective relationships as having a degree of permanence, the need to develop a set of rules which will establish their respective rights and obligations and the manner in which they will conduct themselves towards each other becomes important. As with the substantive terms, the parties have a choice of working these out for themselves or having them evolved by, say, the State as a third party.

The doctrines of the common law and the terms of a collective agreement may be seen as alternative ways of regulating the 'procedures' of the parties. Generally, where the one applies the other is silent. The regulation of the 'collective relations' (Flanders, 1965, p 12) has depended largely upon procedural agreements or conventions adopted by the parties themselves. Until the 1970s at least the law, whether in the forms of common or statute law has had little to say one way or the other about the manner in which the parties to collective industrial relations affairs should *conduct themselves* in their dealings with one another. Where, therefore, the common law developed and applied a large number of procedural rules to, say, the contract of employment, the equivalent set of rules regulating the formation of a collective agreement has been largely built up from the interaction of the parties themselves. (Substantive 'rules' (Flanders, 1965, p 11) have in contrast been much affected by law and other expressions of public policy (see pp 491–8). The direction of causality in this relationship may be disputed. The fact that the law deliberately kept out of the process of regulating collective relationships may be considered, as Flanders implies, to have *caused* the parties themselves to enter into their own procedural arrangements. Alternatively, the probability that the parties are the only ones, or the main ones, who *can* regulate these relationships may, as Kahn-Freund implies, have *caused* the law to steer clear.

With the appearance of factory industry in the industrial revolution, the fixing of wages and other conditions of employment was specifically taken out of the hands of the magistrates (under the Elizabethan Statute of Artificers and comparable Acts) and ostensibly left to 'free individual bargaining' between the employer and the employee. Quite quickly and fairly inevitably, 'understandings' developed between the employer and his employees as to how the going wage was to be fixed, sometimes continuing old customs and sometimes creating new ones to meet the changed circumstances of the time. Certainly, not all of the customs thus established found a place for the emergent trade unions nor, even where they did, did they give much discretion to the union representatives to modify the procedures which the employer wished to follow in fixing terms. At this time, it was extremely rare for any of these understandings on procedures to be written down, and relations were largely governed by the employer's rules as to procedure. These often became the customary procedures or shared understandings.

In the development of industrial relations in Britain, it was initially the employer and the employers' association which pressed the adoption of such procedures upon the trade unions. This can be explained in terms of the employer's aim of ensuring that the relationship between himself and the trade union and/or his employees should develop in an orderly and therefore predictable fashion, even in circumstances where there might be considerable conflict and disagreement between them over the substantive terms. The renowned (but now abandoned) York Memorandum (see Marsh, 1973, ch 3) on procedure in the engineering industry represented an example of a procedure which was impressed upon the *unions* by the employers' association.

More recently, in the face of the switch of emphasis in negotiation from the national to the local (company or plant) arena, the national unions have appeared keener to develop procedural agreements than have the national employers. The individual employers, on the other hand, faced with a relatively novel situation as shop stewards (or their equivalents whatever title may be given to them in different industries) sought local negotiating rights and have been led into the exercise of attempting to control local collective relations by 'procedure'. This process has obviously been going on for longer in some industries than in others, and for this and other reasons it has been 'successful' in some and not in others. The 'unsuccess' of controlling collective relations by procedures locally developed and accepted became defined as a 'problem' in the 1960s.

From about that date, the State has become increasingly insistent upon the parties to industrial relations at any level reaching ententes of this kind, in order to control conduct locally and thus reduce the amount of unofficial and unconstitutional action by local worker groups led by the shop stewards. This concern was focused in the Report of the Donovan Commission, which argued that *all* employing units should have a range of procedures (listed in para 182), since they were conducive to the improvement of industrial relations. The Donovan Commission spoke for both employer and State in setting out what objectives it sought to serve by making its recommendations:

(a) to emphasize the responsibility of the board of directors for the conduct of industrial relations within a concern and for the framework of collective agreements within which those relations are conducted; and

(b) to highlight those aspects of industrial relations which the public interest required should be covered wherever possible by clear and firm company and factory agreements (Para 191–196, pp 47–48).

The Commission therefore recommended that boards should review industrial relations with the following objectives:

1 to develop, together with trade unions representative of their employees, comprehensive and authoritative collective bargaining

449

machinery to deal at company and/or factory level with the terms and conditions of employment which are settled at these levels

2 to develop, together with unions representative of their employees, joint procedures for the rapid and equitable settlement of grievances in a manner consistent with the relevant collective agreements

3 to conclude with unions representative of their employees, agreements regulating the postition of shop stewards in matters such as: facilities for holding elections; numbers and constituencies; recognition of credentials; facilities to consult and report back to their members; facilities to meet other stewards; the responsibilities of the chief shop steward (if any); pay while functioning as steward in working hours; day release with pay for training

4 to conclude agreements covering the handling of redundancy

5 to adopt effective rules and procedures governing disciplinary matters, including dismissal with provision for appeals

6 to ensure regular joint discussion of measures to promote safety at work.

Furthermore, the larger concerns should be subject to a certain element of policing: "Companies of a certain minimum size should be obliged to register their collective agreements with the Department of Employment and Productivity, or if they have none, to state why" (Para 1024, p 263). It was envisaged that initially only companies with 5,000 or more employees would be covered but the requirement was to be extended progressively. The Department of Employment had already advised larger companies that they should secure agreement from their recognized unions to the introduction of such procedural agreements if they did not already exist. In 1969, the Department took the first step in implementing the Donovan recommendation, inviting first 35 large companies and later 250 other large companies to register their agreements on a voluntary basis. This was generalized in the Industrial Relations Act of 1971, and the Code of Industrial Relations Practice gave more detailed advice on the nature of the procedural agreements sought. Ss 1–6 inclusive of Schedule 1 of the Trade Union and Labour Relations Act 1974 left the existing Code in operation and provided for its redrafting by the Secretary of State for Employment at his discretion, and Ss 1 and 6 of the Employment Protection Act 1975 provided for specific codes to be published on disclosure of information and time off for union officers and members and for more detailed codes on any subject which the Advisory, Conciliation and Arbitration Service considered likely to lead to 'the promotion of improvement of industrial relations'. The Employment Protection Act's other provisions on trade union

450

recognition and consultation on redundancies with recognized unions are likely to exert a pressure in the same direction of developing procedures to control relationships. The provision in the Health and Safety at Work etc Act 1975 for representatives is also likely to mean the setting up of other procedures.

The general pressure to develop more elaborate procedural agreements, stemming from public policy, and the requirements on recognition, negotiation and consultation contained in specific statutes together portend the development of elaborate written constitutions to govern 'collective relationships' at any and all levels at which they appear. Proposals for future extension of 'participation' under mandate or guidance from legislation must, whatever form this takes, lend weight to the argument for codifying the whole gamut of collective relations, if only to avoid confusion for everyone as to what relationships exist between whom for what main purposes. Under these circumstances, the procedural agreement is likely to look less like an entente arrived at between the parties themselves (a kind of private law making) and more like a set of statutory duties mandatory for the parties to establish in the interests of controlling industrial relations.

At present, the traditional voluntary system, together with the more abstract analysis of it, still tends to dominate thinking and conceptualization. It is therefore possible to discuss this matter either in terms of 'procedures' or 'procedural agreements' or in terms of 'constitutions' of the kind being nudged into existence by public policy. The terms 'procedure' and 'procedural agreement' can apply nationally and locally, but the concept of a 'constitution' is likely to be apposite only in the local situation of industrial relations. If we stay with the traditional terminology, therefore, we can conveniently discuss the main components of the developing constitutions in terms of four main areas of 'procedure' and 'procedural' agreement:

1 Procedures relating to the status of the parties who are willing to enter into a relationship with each other, these focusing particularly upon what steps each party will take to facilitate the other within the framework of rights established by the agreement itself
2 Procedures relating to matters of interest, indicating what matters shall fall to be decided within the relationship on a joint basis, touching on the objectives of the parties separately conceived—how negotiations shall be conducted
3 Procedures relating to matters of right, indicating how the parties will deal with problems of interpreting what is the intended 'consideration' to be shown or given by one party to the other under the agreements or understandings existing between them

4 Procedures relating to formal questions which fall outside the scope of the subjects considered to be within the framework of negotiation of interest issues, and usually referred to as procedures relating to consultation and the subjects traditionally associated therewith (see also above, ch 8).

Because of the piecemeal fashion in which these have either 'just grown' or been stipulated in legislation and government policy, there are a number of quite separate strands of influence upon the development of these procedures in recent times, and the nearest one comes to finding a coherent statement of the totality is the Code of Industrial Relations Practice, itself a bit out of date and tentative but nevertheless clearer in its general thrust than the collection of separate voluntary system and legislative provisions which form the alternative indicators. The ACAS is proposing to issue a consultative document on a more general Code on Collective Bargaining Procedures, including matters to be decided unilaterally by either trade union or management as well as those falling to be determined jointly, but at the time of writing this is not available.

1 Status agreements in collective bargaining

If we are to regard a procedural agreement simply as an agreement, a treaty or a truce (cf Allen, 1971) between two parties, locally or nationally established, the preamble will need to do little more than identify the parties and indicate the nature of their respective domains for purposes of applying the agreement. Thus the Code of Industrial Relations Practice suggests that such preamble should do just this. But if we are to regard this procedural agreement as a constitution governing industrial relationships in the undertaking, the preamble is likely to expand beyond this in order to give greater definition to the parties and how they themselves shall be constituted for purposes of approaching and dealing with the other party or parties. Further, if this extension of the conception of a procedural agreement is stimulated or dictated by legislative enactment, that enactment is likely to stipulate standard conditions which have to be met by the parties. Although therefore it is repeatedly asserted that what is made mandatory by statute or recommended by State agencies is nothing more than 'best practice' in British industry, the effect will be to create greater standardization of local constitutions than was present in the system previously.

In the simple act of identifying the parties to local procedural agreements, note must be taken not only of 'trade union power' but also of legislation. The statutory provisions on certification, independence and recognition are indirectly relevant to this, as are the stipulations on associated and successor employers, and in special circumstances the provisions of statutes relating to wages councils, statutory joint industrial councils and certain of the powers of the Central Arbitration Committee, in so far as these, taken together, either exclude or incorporate parties who might or might not otherwise be parties to the constitution. There remain questions to be decided not merely as to which unions shall be recognized, for example, but which unions can or cannot, will or will not, accept the embrace of a given procedural agreement. There is as yet nothing to compel a trade union or (except in the CAC's powers on recognition and recognized terms and conditions of employment) an employer to become party to a procedural agreement but, if the Bullock Committee recommendations on the Joint Union Meeting for Industrial Democracy were to be implemented in statute, this might be changed.

This part of the collective agreement may be said to be concerned "to establish rights and obligations, which together define status" (Flanders, 1965, p 11). To this end, it is necessary that the agreement should not only identify the parties, in the sense of merely recording the fact of who is to sign the agreement, but should also indicate something of who, in the language of the common law related to the employment contract, is *competent* to agree. It happens frequently that a company will recognize a particular trade union for a particular grade or category of staff and, having done so, will enter into an agreement with that union through the respective agents or representatives, with the possible consequence that where a number of different unions are recognized for different grades and categories, a number of quite separate and distinct agreements exist. It also happens that the company, as the one constant in these various agreements, will endeavour to have each agreement conform to a 'standard form' in respect of at least some of its terms. The next stage in this is likely to be an attempt to secure joint trade union acceptance of a single procedure agreement, even if separate negotiations are retained for reaching distinct substantive agreements. Once negotiations over the procedural agreement or constitution move into the area of 'joint' actions, the question of who is competent to agree takes on a new dimension.

The first part of this problem is concerned with the issue of which employee associations can be expected or persuaded to sit together. The traditional difficulty in the national and local arenas of negotiation has usually centred on the production worker–service worker distinction, with each group preferring to negotiate on its own, regardless of how many different unions might be involved in their representation. More recently, and as a result of tensions exacerbated by the Industrial Relations Act of 1971, separatism has been more frequently focused upon the TUC-affiliated union-non-affiliated association distinction and, although this has been found in both manual and white collar sectors, it now centres most stridently on the white collar sector, in which unionization has recently increased. In *this* general area, the preference of some professional and managerial associations for procedures which do not depend upon strike activity in defiance of professional norms of conduct tends to increase the predilections for separate statuses and separate agreements, and therefore the difficulties for the management in securing a generally applicable constitution. Such separatism depends upon a difference of view amongst the parties as to who is 'competent' to enter into such procedural agreements. The effect of legislative provisions relating to trade union certification and recognition tend to support the continuance of this kind of distinction but may well force the non-affiliated employee association out of the arena in due course.

Apart from its effect upon determining which representatives of which associations will sign a given agreement, this difficulty is also likely to be reflected in the manner in which the parties to the agreement indicate the *rights* which they are willing to accept as adhering to the other side.

These rights usually include a 'right to manage' in some form: the trade unions recognize the right of the company to manage its affairs, including its right to take steps to maintain or improve efficiency and to maintain order and discipline within the undertaking. In recent years, trade union pressure to have a *status quo* clause introduced into procedural agreements has tended to limit management's discretion here. It usually provides that where management seeks to change an existing practice and this is challenged, the *status quo* shall be maintained until the matter has been resolved in 'procedure'; this is frequently stated to imply the continuation of the practice in question and a continuation of 'normal working' by employees during the period (Incomes Data Service, *Status Quo*, April 1971).

The rights of the trade unions are also acknowledged in this section. Minimally, this entails recognizing the right of the named unions to represent their members' (or the relevant class of employees') interests. This may then be extended by a clause which names certain unions as appropriate for certain grades of employee, and states that the company will positively support the policy of encouraging all employees in these grades to become and remain members of the appropriate unions. This may be supported by the company agreeing to make possible the union's collection of union dues from members by the offer of a check-off arrangement; for example, the company will undertake to deduct union dues from wages or salaries on authorization in writing from employees (as required under the Truck Acts) provided that the trade union(s) distribute and collect authorization forms and pass these to the accounts office; but the company will not undertake to collect any arrears of dues or refund any dues returnable (see Ramsay and Hill, 1974, pp 9–13).

The outlawing of all but one special type of closed shop by the Industrial Relations Act of 1971 has resulted in focusing more positive demands upon companies for this degree of union security, now that the 1971 Act has been repealed and, in this matter at least, replaced by the Trade Union and Labour Relations Acts 1974–6. As a special case of rendering formal what was previously (pre 1971) an 'understanding' in many cases, the closed shop in one of its many manifestations.has now been written into a number of procedural agreements. This most commonly requires that not only will the company encourage membership of a union or unions but will require it as a condition of employment of new starters; in some cases this is applied to all employees without a religious objection (cf Sweeney and Gill, 1976; Trade Union and Labour Relations Act 1976, Ss 1A and 3 (3)).

Such developments, tending to increase the extent of 'union security' in the particular corporation, company or undertaking, thus restrict the discretion of managements to recognize other associations of employees not acceptable as participants in the development of local procedures or constitutions; and they may, where groups of employees refuse to affiliate with acceptable associations, lead to their disenfranchisement. The employer is usually in the position where, even if he were willing to accord status to such associations, he would have to risk the complete dismemberment of existing procedural agreements (and therefore of such constitutional arrangements as might already exist) in so doing. The right of management not merely to manage, but to select those representative bodies with which he is willing to negotiate, is thus increasingly denied as the trade union's pursuit of security into the local undertaking creates a new frontier of 'rights'.

In somewhat similar fashion, a new frontier line has been drawn in recent years between the facilities which the trade unions themselves will make available to shop representatives to enable them to do their industrial relations work, and those to be provided by the employer. Although there were a number of ante-dating exceptions, as a general rule this question has become a significant one since the Donovan Commission reported and the resultant legislation of the 1970s sought in various ways to respond to the

Donovan recommendation that shop stewards or comparable representatives should be more fully and constitutionally involved in both trade union affairs and industrial relations activities within their undertakings.

A first response to this and one for which there were a larger number of precedents, entails the recognition of shop stewards for bargaining purposes. In the procedural agreement, provision is usually made for a defined number of shop representatives to be recognized by management after election by the union members on a constituency basis which may also be agreed. The agreement is also likely to stipulate what duties such representatives will undertake during working periods, these duties reflecting partly what is contained in the union rule-book and partly what management in the local circumstances would expect such representatives to do as a *quid pro quo* for recognition by management. The procedure will often also make provision for the manner of electing these representatives, with constituencies indicated along with any service qualifications which management would expect a candidate to have as a condition of recognition if elected. In some cases, an increasing number under the stimulus of the Code of Practice issued by ACAS, the management will agree to make facilities available for voting to take place smoothly during working hours.

Once elected, the shop steward is commonly issued with credentials signed by duly authorized officers of the trade union and of management, thus formally establishing his status in industrial relations activities rather than merely as an officer of the trade union. It is also normal practice for unions with large numbers of members in particular companies or undertakings to appoint a convenor of shop stewards from amongst their numbers. Managements have often (and again increasingly often under the stimulus of the new Code) not only recognized such a convenor as the key representative of the union's members, but have given him freedom of access (within limits) to any part of the works and to the other shop stewards and to management and, in some cases, office and telephone facilities to enable him to carry out his role more effectively. One area which remains more contentious concerns the provision of training for shop stewards. Management is usually anxious that shop stewards receive training and, whilst management may be willing to provide it, the trade unions usually prefer that such training should be given by their own agencies (such as the TUC or the individual union college). The compromise most often adopted is that management gives the shop steward time off for training of defined types, and the unions arrange the actual training programme. (This too is now subject to the Code governing time off for union officers) (see, for an example of such agreements, Ramsay and Hill, 1974.)

Such developments may therefore be seen to change the old order in which shop stewards were often tolerated but scarcely helped in many organizations. Under the impact of the various Codes of Practice, including the most recent on time-off and other facilities for stewards, a more constitutionally founded status is developing for shop representatives. The emergent *de facto* practice in many large undertakings in the 1950s and 1960s has thus been made more standardized, and the uneasy relationship which developed between companies now has some opportunity to settle down to a pattern, whether good or,bad in its consequences, and there are of course different evaluations of the change on both sides of the bargaining fence.

The mutual recognition and facilitation thus built into the procedural agreement at local level is intended by both the parties themselves, and the State agencies charged with advising on industrial relations matters, to provide a foundation for cooperation between the parties to resolve differences between them over matters of interest or matters of right that might arise from their involvement in the working situation. This is also normally acknowledged in the preamble to the agreement, with statements recording that the parties agree that greater mutual benefit will be obtained through cooperation to ensure that differences are resolved 'through procedure' rather than through precipitate 'industrial action' by one party or the other.

2 Content agreements in collective bargaining

The problems of changing effectively from a 'national' industrial relations pattern to a local one are most clearly exemplified in the provisions in procedural agreements relating to bargaining over matters of 'interest' (in the usual American term). The distinction here is between those matters which the parties may wish to establish or resolve in some agreement, as it were for the first time, and those which might still arise as questions of interpretation once such matters of interest have been agreed in the form of 'rights'. Local procedures have quite often in the past provided for grievance or complaints or disputes procedures, where the emphasis is upon adjudication or policing of existing agreements or of custom and practice (which has not been codified in writing); until recently, procedural agreements have (less frequently) really made room for shop steward negotiations with management on matters of interest, but the continuing constraint of incomes policies has tended to give this aspect a boost even if rarely via a *written* procedural agreement.

Nevertheless, the Code of Industrial Relations Practice recommends that the procedural agreement should, as its first main area of substance after the preliminary status clauses have been agreed, deal with the question of what matters are to be bargained about at each and every level at which bargaining is allowed to occur. This brings together two quite different elements; what should be negotiated nationally, at company-level or within the individual undertaking, and what substantive terms and conditions in the employment contract shall at any or all of these levels be admitted as negotiable subjects. The two questions are clearly related, and one of the difficulties which arises in the attempt to develop adequate local constitutions occurs because national agreements frequently pre-empt negotiation of some issues at the local level. This is essentially what was intended in a situation which was highly supportive of national, industry-wide negotiations; but as full employment and changing cultural values appear to support more local autonomy in these matters, the continuation of these stipulations limit the range of opportunity available locally to effect changes.

Flanders' discussion of "the poverty of subject matter" in British collective bargaining indicates that this pre-existing pattern has had some responsibility for it but, writing in 1967, his comment that it left "considerable scope for further growth" is prophetic in view of what has developed in local bargaining since that time (Flanders, 1967, p 15). Much of what he saw as custom and practice, and as 'fringe benefits'—then still outside formal bargaining—has now been brought inside the range of subjects bargained over locally in a condition of constraint on formal movement of wages. But at that time certain broad distinctions, which still to some extent constrain local decisions, were properly drawn:

1 Usually not *all* the workers in a particular industry are covered by these negotiations: it is usual, for example, for manual and non-manual workers to be treated separately; and workers in particular occupational groups, like building or maintenance engineering, usually have their own distinct agreements if they work in other industries, like iron and steel, or the railway workshops
2 Negotiations on hours of work and holidays are often conducted on a wider scale than negotiations on wages. Both the Printing and Kindred Trades Federation and the United Textile Workers' Association had agreements with the employers on hours and holidays which covered the whole of the manual workers in the printing and cotton textile industries, although the affiliated unions had not reached the point where the federations have been entrusted with the wage negotiation on a similar scale. This stresses one of the main difficulties in the way of increasing the amount of industry wide bargaining, not only on wages but on

other issues as well. The existence of a large number of craft unions is not conducive to industry wide bargaining in this sense. This difficulty has been and is being partly overcome by the establishment of federations as in the two cases just quoted, but the federation is at best only a half-way house towards unified organization

3 The regulative influence of the resultant agreement, negotiated nationally, also varies quite considerably. Although the central agreement can be industry-wide and nationally negotiated, nevertheless the degree of control it lays down over the individual terms of employment varies considerably. In the railways, at one extreme, wages and conditions are centrally determined. In building, the national agreements permit regional and local variations, but approval of the national body must be obtained for proposed variation. In banking, certain basic minimum rates of wages are settled nationally, but member clearing banks negotiate actual pay rates and other conditions domestically. At the other extreme, in engineering and shipbuilding, only general wage changes are negotiated nationally, the whole range of local rates and practices remaining outside national control

4 The degree of national or central control is often correlated with the methods of wage payment prevalent in the particular industry. The regulation of time rates of wages throughout an industry by one collective agreement presents no great difficulty provided some form of job classification or evaluation is adopted to bring down the number of different jobs to a manageable size. Complications arise where there is a great deal of piece-work payment in the industry. It then becomes practically impossible to settle rates completely by negotiation. Three ways out of this difficulty have been adopted:

(i)   a standard piece-work price list can be negotiated for the industry as a whole or the main divisions of it

(ii) a level of earnings can be settled at national level, providing for a specific relationship to time rates, which then become the norm for fixing piece rates

(iii) a minimum time rate can be negotiated nationally and the amount of bonus earning can be left to negotiation in the particular establishment.

All these methods appear in one industry or another but none of them completely eliminate negotiation below the national level.

In the post-war period, with full employment aiding the growth of the shop stewards movement, local negotiations have come to push the nationally negotiated rates and conditions forward, along with the frontier between the negotiable and the non-negotiable. From this development has sprung the foundation for the two systems of industrial relations which the Donovan Commission remarked in 1968, and by virtue of the second, local system, the number of subjects negotiated has been markedly increased in recent years. This process has been given fillip by the succession of incomes policies which have sought to impose standard changes in payments and by legislation which has sought to impose minimum terms and conditions of employment upon the local bargaining activities (see above, ch 1). The necessary local flexibility and discretion in decision taking sought by managements, coupled with the need for local representatives to pursue a creative role as a basis for their status, have combined to uncover ways of getting round the standards thus imposed. This as much as anything else has helped to reduce the truth of Flanders' statement above: new subjects have locally been introduced into local (substantive) bargaining for this reason—ranging from claims for the provision of cars to all employees to reimbursement of the cost of colour TV licences—and new procedural rules have been developed to try to contain this emergent pattern of bargaining.

What is effected by the existence of these 'two systems' of bargaining is that in different industries there will be a different mix of rates and conditions determined by a mixture of national and local negotiations, each with its own procedures (see Munns, 1967). In highly centralized bargaining, many basic terms and conditions may be fixed and little discretion allowed to the local bargainers; in decentralized or looser arrangements, general guidelines might come from the national negotiators and the substance and range of coverage be left for local determination. Where the pattern of demand for negotiated terms and conditions is changing, employers face the need to decide which pattern they favour in all the circumstances of legislative constraint and shop floor volatility.

This problem has to be tackled by the independent (eg company) unit in relation to employers' associations. Should it at one extreme seek to retain all power to negotiate on all subjects with employees in the unit, or should it forego some of this discretion to a central employers' association to attempt to secure a common front in the face of union demands? The company's decision on this question is not necessarily unconstrained: the wishes of the employees have some part to play in determining the outcome. A number of other options are open to the individual employer: he might well decide not to join an employers' association or a national/district joint negotiating exercise, but nevertheless follow the terms and conditions of employment determined in this way in his trade or industry; alternatively, he might decide to join in such an exercise but

460

accept in advance only some part of the total package of outcomes, retaining to himself the opportunity to negotiate locally on others. Under the new provisions of the Employment Protection and Trade Union and Labour Relations Acts, these options are not so clear-cut as they were (see pp 493–98) but they do exist.

This is not a once and for all decision. As the pattern has developed, the two parallel systems of the Donovan analysis provide opportunities for determining one standardized set of conditions at the national or district level so maintaining a basic control over competitiveness, and another set of less standardized conditions at the company/plant level, giving·a more specific control and more flexibility for cooperation.

This presents a problem also to the multiplant company, whether the plants are factories, offices, shops or other service units. At present, a number of very different patterns of bargaining may be discerned within these:

1 The situation where all unit issues are decided domestically within the unit: this is a more common practice in the USA than in the UK, where the tradition of centralized bargaining has tended to militate against it, and where employers are more liable to fear the leap-frogging type of claim. On the other hand, the development of the fragmentation of bargaining in the post-war period has helped to bring this about even here

2 The situation where the unit has similar autonomy but where local discretion must be contained within an overall budget for the unit which may be laid down by a higher authority, but which refrains from interfering with the unit bargaining processes themselves. In recent years this kind of situation has often been subjected to pressures from the trade unions whose itinerant officers are often able to deploy a more universal knowledge of practice to good effect (cf Ramsay, 1971)

3 The situation in which unit negotiations are conducted within the unit's own structure of relationships but where negotiations from the employer's side are either conducted or directly supervised by managers from the centre. This is the obverse from the previous situation, in the sense that management seeks to deploy the more universal knowledge of practice to its advantage in the negotiations, and is likely to create pressures from the union side for a similar arrangement which might then turn the situation into one in which enterprise wide bargaining (as distinct from unit bargaining) was practised (cf McCarthy, 1971)

4 The situation, logically arising before company wide bargaining, where some subjects are negotiated at unit level and some at

461

company level. In effect this is likely to divide subjects in a manner similar to that practised in the Donovan Commission's two systems: wage rates, hours, and holidays may be centrally negotiated, whilst piecework prices, shiftwork arrangements and grievance procedures and grievances themselves are left for determination at the unit level (cf Hawkins, 1971)

5 The situation in which all bargaining is conducted at the centre by centre managers, so that local unit management has no discretion but to refer all such matters upwards. With the greater volume of controlling legislation present or expected in Britain, strong pressure may be expected upon managements in Britain to centralize their bargaining, at least for some time, as new standards and procedures are evolved to cope with the situation (cf Baker and France, 1954).

Similar considerations arise between the centre of public services, such as the Health Service or nationalized undertakings, and their local units (eg, hospitals or local airlines). It is broadly true that the power of the centre in bargaining here has remained much greater than in the generality of private industry in recent years. Although this reflects the structure of the respective enterprises, there remains some reason to suppose that the monolithic structures (such as that of the Whitley Council machinery in the National Health Service) may be under strong threat of change from the trade union side as they seek an alternative strategy to secure members' interests in a period of rapid inflation and of government economies.

Employers generally will be required to attend to this question in the future as they make some response to the various calls for 'an extension of collective bargaining', 'a participation agreement' or 'worker directors', all of which promise to bring other subjects within the ambit of some kind of negotiating framework. What is to be negotiated about, at what level, and involving what representatives of the parties may in some cases be constrained by promised legislation on participation, but the need for management to have some objective and some strategy in this area will remain in spite of that.

3 'Participation agreements' and the growth of subject matter
The concept of a 'participation agreement' is one which has been developed largely within management organizations. The CBI might claim main authorship, but a similar notion was advanced in evidence to the Bullock Committee by the Engineering Employers' Federation and the British Institute of Management. "The proposal for 'participation agreements' is the core of [the CBI] evidence.

462

Companies with more than 2,000 employees in the UK would be obliged to conclude such agreements with their employees within a four year period. These, to be valid, would require affirmation in a secret ballot by a majority of employees. The parties to an agreement would have maximum flexibility to determine the scope and contents of an agreement, provided it accorded with certain very general criteria which include safeguards for collective bargaining, for minority groups of employees, for profitability, confidentiality, and the executive functions of management" (Bullock Report, 1977, p 31). This is consistent with two principles which the CBI urged upon the Committee, that there should be flexibility to allow local conditions to be taken into account, and a gradual development of participation or industrial democracy from the job level upwards to the boardroom, rather than a sudden imposition of it by legislation at this top level alone.

The CBI evidence lists (paragraph 24) the kinds of structure which the Confederation thinks ought to be open to establishment within the compass of such agreements. These include "company councils; plant or subsidiary councils, with or without a company council, for multi-plant or groups of companies; non-executive directors to whom employee representatives have special access; trustee advisory 'boards'; direct employee representation on either unitary or supervisory boards, with a suitable representative structure beneath this level; and other variations and combinations." This list is then consistent with what the CBI sees as a major principle to be followed: namely, that the parties in the company itself should have maximum flexibility under the legislation to adopt whatever structure is most congenial to them. "A fundamental principle on which proposals for greater employee involvement in company affairs must be based, is that participative arrangements must be designed to fit a company structure, and not vice versa. Moreover, such participative arrangements must be sufficiently flexible to accommodate the various forms of participation already in operation successfully, and to the satisfaction of all the parties, in a number of companies" (paragraph 13) and "It is vital that employers and employees retain freedom of action to develop a form of participation which can reflect their wishes and the structure of their particular organization. A standard system applied to all companies, large or small, centralized or decentralized, could not possibly be suitable to meet the needs of employees and companies" (paragraph 9).

The demand for flexibility, for organic growth of participation or for freedom for the parties to do their own thing is, if conceded in that form, likely to prove a recipe for inaction. The problem here is comparable to that of redressing the balance of advantage between equality and freedom in respect of the employment contract (see above, ch 1). The 'will' of the employees to participate may indeed be low in some working situations but, whether as a matter of policy the State should accept this as a 'fact' and base a strategy upon it as if it were a fact, may be questioned (as indeed it has been by leading trade unionists in the course of this participation debate). It could lead to a perpetuation of a set of arrangements of the sort which the CBI evidence alludes to in another part of its evidence: "Many large and small companies already successfully operate formal, but voluntary consultative arrangements. The CBI favours this approach, and therefore proposes that the establishment of deliberative bodies representative of all employees, should be actively encouraged in all firms of a size where they would be practicable and where the need for increased participation is felt" (paragraph 19). It has to be asked, however, what is really being 'encouraged' here: encouragement of flexibility for itself may be one thing, but encouragement of the sham of 'consultation' in many situations is quite another.

There are, it is true, a number of variations of 'good practice' here, some of them old-established but many relatively new and responsive to the debate on participation itself. The CBI shows that it is mindful of this wide variation, in its recognition that some legal compulsion may be required to ensure that some large firms take some action. "In larger firms where, even over a reasonable span of time, it might not be possible, for whatever reason, for voluntary agreement on the form of participation to be reached, it would be necessary for there to be a requirement of law to provide compulsory arbitration by an independent party. This form of legislation would afford the maximum degree of flexibility possible, while providing considerable safeguards for the interests of industrial efficiency, as well as those of employees. The provision of an individual solution suited to the needs of the individual enterprise is essential" (paragraph 21).

This recognition is shared by the British Institute of Management and the Industrial Partnership Association. The BIM suggests that in the event of failure to agree on the form of participation, a procedure similar to that employed under the Employment Protection Act to compel recognition or disclosure of information could be adopted. The IPA favours a slightly different method of compulsion in situations where there is no agreement and the employees are dissatisfied with the *status quo*. In those circumstances, it suggests, the representatives sanctioned by a ballot of the workforce should be able to invoke a statutory fall back provision providing for a third membership of a supervisory board with limited mandate as suggested in the EEC Fifth Directive. This is argued to be more definite in that it makes certain what the alternative to no agreement would be, and less attractive to the parties than the probable outcome of agreement, so that it would not become an excuse for not agreeing.

But the CBI sees this tailoring of the form to the situation as growing organically "from the shop floor upwards" and argues that, in Bullock's paraphrase, "the willingness of employees to participate needs to be nurtured at lower levels [than that of the board], where their interest and attention can be captured by discussion of ideas of immediate, direct import" (Bullock Report, 1977, p 31). Bullock's response to this is that willingness to participate, and the destruction of apathy, would not be enhanced if "joint procedures stop short of major decisions, which are taken behind the closed doors of the boardroom" (Bullock Report, 1977, p 45).

This reflects a matter of faith, since there can be no proof of the proposition in advance of the scheme being put into operation. But it is equally a reflection of the CBI's view of the worker to suggest that his will to participate must be nurtured and cossetted further by already established mechanisms of consultation.

It is important to recognize that the Bullock Committee, in spite of its lengthy discussion of the effects of participation on motivation and productivity, really treats participation as a question posed in morality. In a democratic society, ought industry to be run autocratically or democratically? The clue to the answer lies in the quotation in approving fashion of the "democratic imperative" of the EEC Green Paper on *Employee Participation and Company Structure* which takes the form that "those who will be substantially affected by decisions made by social and political institutions must be involved in the making of those decisions" (Supplement 8/75, p 9). This 'imperative' is also acknowledged by those trade union leaders who have expressed themselves in support of industrial democracy on the TUC pattern of a two tier board with equal shareholder and worker representation on the supervisory board. Jack Jones, delivering the Birkbeck Foundation Lecture in December, 1975, outlined what he called a "new civilization" which would represent a "clean break from the authoritarian relationships" of the present society.

The opposition to the 'increased participation' proposals amongst the trade union leaders is also based upon a moral principle: that the worker should not sit with directors to exploit his fellow workers. This has been strongly argued by the Communist Party of Great Britain and by a number of trade union leaders who do not subscribe to its political doctrines. But some of the other opponents express their opposition in terms of what might be considered 'pure and simple unionism', by demanding as a preferable alternative the 'extension of collective bargaining'. Most articulate in this vein has been the EEPTU, whose evidence to the Bullock Committee pointed to a "fundamental and irreconcilable incompatibility between board representation and the [traditional] collective bargaining function of trade unions". This union's evidence described two interrelated aspects of the problem:

> First, there is the institutional impossibility of separating the boardroom consultation from the potential negotiating implications behind the issues under discussion. Second, there is the irreconcilable split loyalties of the worker directors themselves. They will find it immensely difficult to separate their boardroom responsibilities dictated by business priorities from their representative functions derived from their relationship with the workforce. The pursuit of trade union objectives will not then be helped by the disunity created in such an atmosphere. And this ignores the crude disagreements that must occur on occasion with worker directors, in possession of all the information, being party to a decision or policy that is opposed by the collective bargainers. Far better in the interests of those affected by a managerial decision that the responsibility for that decision is firmly laid at the management's door; then the collective bargaining machinery can oppose and moderate the impact of the decision when necessary (EEPTU Evidence, paragraphs 20 and 30; Bullock Report, pp 39–40).

The EEPTU, and its fellow union in the electricity supply industry, the EPEA, had had an earlier opportunity to express their views on this subject and had, in January 1976, secured recommendations from the Plowden Committee more in accord with their views. This Committee came out in favour of a single board for the generating and distribution arms of the industry, although it envisaged that six of the 12 positions would be full-time and six part-time (and therefore presumably open to the appointment of trade unionists if the Minister wished to make such appointments). In effect, this recommendation involved a rejection of the TUC view that the industry should be run by a supervisory board composed of equal numbers of trade unionists and government appointees, and an acceptance of the kind of argument advanced by management bodies on participation. In the Committee's view, a split board of the kind proposed by the TUC would not have a 'common purpose' unless it came about as a consequence of the development of a general desire within the industry for a board of this type. Worker representation at the board level, therefore, should result from a desire generated at the bottom, not imposed from the top. The two unions mentioned, and also the GMWU, nevertheless regarded the recommendations as sensible for the industry and sought to have the recommendations translated into legislation before the Bullock Report was produced in order that they might not be overturned thereby. In their view, the report and recommendations gave them an open field for 'extension of collective bargaining' as a preferred strategy.

This 'alternative' strategy, although seen in this light by some union leaders, was and is not necessarily a simple alternative. In fact, the TUC has also stressed the concurrent need for both industrial democracy and such extension. This is important and ought to be set against the tendency for management bodies to ignore or under-emphasize the issue of extension in considering participation, as for example in the evidence presented to the Bullock Committee. The problem arises because to tackle the problem of structure, as for example do the CBI and the BIM, is to divert attention from the subjects to be discussed within the structure. But the TUC was always clear that the idea of a supervisory board would bring "a wide range of fundamental managerial decisions" within the control of work people, but that the extension of this control locally would "require an extension of collective bargaining". It is therefore advocated that collective bargaining should be freed from the strait jacket of wage determination and extended to embrace a long list of subjects, including manning, training, recruitment, speed of work, work-sharing, discipline and dismissals. This in turn would require more information to be given to negotiators and improved procedures, but it would lead to greater "joint control over the immediate work situation" (TUC Congress, 1974).

Against such a background, it might therefore be anticipated that a 'participation agreement' would have to include three main areas of definition:

First, a definition of structure, of the kind advanced by the CBI in evidence to Bullock, but spelling out in more detail the nature of constituencies and the composition and relationships of committees and councils to be established

Secondly, a definition of subject matter for each 'part' of the system, which in effect would indicate what subjects (as for example, in the Bullock recommendations) would be for joint decision, and what subjects (as advocated in calls for extensions of collective bargaining) would be for management decision and union challenge

Thirdly, a definition of the procedure to be followed in *both* these areas, including the important voting procedures required in joint decision bodies but embracing procedures governing

467

challenge of those decisions which are to be taken by the joint board.

The effect of such agreements would be to bureaucratize the decision taking processes of the undertaking to an extent not yet common in Britain, and this alone might give the advocates pause. At the same time, none should be in any doubt that the 'democratic imperative' is an imperative, and the 'pause' could not be taken as an excuse for doing neither of the two things currently advocated.

4 Disciplinary and grievance procedures

In these last three sections, attention has been given to the development of procedures at different levels to govern those relations which are mainly established to deal with matters of 'interest'. The two following sections discuss the procedures which are advocated for the purpose of regulating relationships established to deal with matters of right, whether established in the one case by substantive agreements or in the other by statutory prescription.

In this category fall the disciplinary and dismissal, and grievance and disputes procedures, each pair linked together because in each case the one process and procedure tends to shade into the other at some stage. All of them, in their separate ways, are concerned with the policing of agreements already established. They also for the most part involve procedures for dealing with 'problems' or 'issues' which appear first as domestic matters within undertakings even if, in some cases, they eventually lead outside them if no internal solution is found. They are not particularly new, except in the sense that in recent years they have been subjected to more formal treatment because both public and trade union policy has been applied to them.

Disciplinary rules and procedures

The Employment Protection Act requires that a statement of the steps in a disciplinary procedure should be included within the particulars of the employment contract. All employers must therefore possess a disciplinary procedure. Guidance on the form such a procedure might take is given in the ACAS Code of Practice, No 1, on Disciplinary Practice and Procedures, effected 20 June 1977. The Code states that the object of establishing disciplinary rules and procedures is to ensure that standards of fairness can be set and applied fully, speedily and effectively. In addition, the legislative provisions on unfair dismissal may be more effectively met with a systematic procedure for drawing up, publicizing and applying the disciplinary rules.

468

Management's responsibility for maintaining discipline is underlined in the Code, but it is suggested that the drawing up of rules and procedures might be done by involving employees in the interests of securing readier acceptance. Although it is to be doubted whether rules can be drawn up to cover all circumstances and contingencies, it is recommended that rules should be specific enough to be meaningful to employees. They should be readily available to employees, usually in the form of a written statement or handbook, and opportunity should be taken to explain them orally. The Code suggests that particular attention should be given to indications of the consequences likely to lead to summary dismissal. These recommendations may appear to many companies to confirm what already exists: it is likely, however, that many sets of rules have grown like Topsy or simply been copied from other situations. In order to avoid rule-making at a time of crisis, it is usually worthwhile for the personnel specialist to run a critical eye over existing rules and penalties at intervals and in discussion with the line management who have to operate within them.

The Code also lists the 'essential features' of any disciplinary procedure. They should, says the Code, (i) be in writing, (ii) specify to whom they apply, (iii) offer a speedy sequence of steps, (iv) identify the disciplinary actions which may be taken, (v) specify which levels of management and supervision have what powers in relation to discipline, (vi) provide for individuals to be informed of complaints against them and to have an opportunity to state their case before a decision is taken, (vii) allow for the individual to be accompanied by a trade union representative or fellow worker as he or she might choose, (viii) reserve dismissal as a penalty for gross misconduct and then only after the complaint has been referred to higher management, (ix) provide for proper investigation of any complaint, (x) provide for explanation of the reasons for a penalty, and (xi) provide for an appeal and a procedure to be followed should the individual wish to avail himself of the right.

The now fairly standard procedure for dealing with misconduct is indicated on p 4 of the Code. It is acknowledged that certain categories of offence may warrant summary dismissal, although it is counselled that this penalty should not be applied to trade union officials until further steps and discussions have been held. In other cases than summary dismissal it is recommended that the procedure should follow the following broad principles:

(a) in the case of minor offences, the individual should be given a formal oral warning after the complaint has been investigated and he or she has been given a chance to explain his position; he or she should be told that this constitutes the first formal stage in the procedure

(b) in the case of repetition, or in more serious cases of misconduct, the individual might be issued with a formal written warning setting out the nature of the offence, and the likely consequences of further misconduct—again after investigation and hearing

(c) further misconduct might warrant a formal final written warning, which would contain a statement that any recurrence would lead to suspension or dismissal or some other penalty, as the case might be

(d) the final step might be disciplinary transfer, disciplinary suspension without pay (where these accord with the terms of the employment contract—whether express or implied) or dismissal, dependent on the nature of the misconduct. If the employee asks for a reason for his dismissal, he is entitled by law to receive one from the employer, and care should therefore be taken to ensure that a defensible reason can be given if this penalty is imposed.

Against each of these steps, some indication should be given of who is authorized to investigate and/or determine the penalty, and whom the individual can or should approach to obtain a written statement of the nature of the alleged offence. It is also now more necessary to keep records of any proven breaches of disciplinary rules and the action taken on them. These records should be regarded as confidential and provision might be made in agreements with the trade unions, or as an element of policy, that minor offences should be expunged from the record after a period.

One matter which often requires further attention in disciplinary procedures is the authority of different levels of supervisor or manager to handle disciplinary cases. The immediate supervisor is usually able to handle the first stages, although he or she is now more likely to be required to record his action.

It is not uncommon for penalties which are more severe than a warning to require bringing in more senior people, particularly on the management side but also sometimes on the worker's side. The principle seems to emerge that the more severe the penalty contemplated, the higher the status of those who can impose or accept it. Such movement up the status hierarchy is often made to serve as a sequence of appeals from lower decisions.

Grievance and disputes procedures
On the other side of the coin of discipline lies the grievance of the individual against his treatment within the employment. It is now common for procedures to be established, if only to meet the

requirements of the Contracts of Employment Act on information to be given to the employee. There are some points of similarity between this procedure and both the disciplinary and the disputes procedures, but the element of grievance can be and often is, treated separately. Essentially it provides a means whereby an individual who is aggrieved by his treatment may secure redress or at least a hearing. As an example, a man may feel that he has been given an undue amount of a particular category of undesirable work tasks. It is often held that, in such circumstances, the aggrieved employee should have some clearly defined opportunity to seek and perhaps secure redress of his grievance: this is usually provided through the grievance procedure. As in the other cases of procedures, this might exist at the discretion of management or it might constitute an agreed procedure; where trade unions are recognized, it is common for such a procedure to be agreed between the union and the management. Since the Donovan Commission Report there has been an increasing demand for such grievance procedures in employing organizations, if only to ensure that as far as possible individual grievances are not allowed to turn into collective disputes because of lack of opportunity for redress. This sentiment is quite explicit in the Code of Practice.

Because the grievance procedure is designed to meet possible requirements of the individual in employment, it is usually quite close in form to the disciplinary procedure, at least in that part of the latter which allows for appeal. But the desire to allow individuals the opportunity to secure redress before the grievance festers into a collective dispute tends to make the grievance procedure a process closely akin to a disputes procedure. In some cases, the two terms are used almost interchangeably.

In the narrower sense of the term, a grievance procedure usually spells out a number of steps by which the individual employee brings his grievance to the notice of management at ever higher levels accompanied, at his discretion, by representatives of his union who also vary in level with the seniority of the management. At the early end of the procedure the steps are usually identical with those built into a disciplinary procedure; at the later end, they become identical with the steps in the disputes and negotiating procedure. However, usually with greater precision than in those other two cases, time limits to the steps in the procedure are generally built into the grievance procedure. The extent to which this is true may well reflect the strength of the parties to a collective agreement and how long they have been negotiating together.

The Code recommends on this aspect that the grievance procedure should:

(i)   state the level at which an issue should first be raised
(ii)   lay down the time limits for each stage of the procedure and make provision for extension of these limits by agreement
(iii) preclude any form of industrial action until all stages have been exhausted and a failure to agree recorded.

The number of stages to be built into the procedure will vary with the type of establishment and the type of bargaining arrangements applicable. The procedure can state:

(i)   that the matter should first be raised by the employee representatives with the level of management directly responsible, or by the management with the level of employee representation most directly concerned according to union procedure
(ii)   what is the next stage of appeal in the procedure
(iii) what further stages will be involved, even to the extent of appeal to an industry-wide arrangement
(iv)   whether the appeals machinery should terminate within the establishment, at industry level or with a reference to the Advisory, Conciliation and Arbitration Service, and whether the parties agree to be bound, in advance, by any award made there.

Such procedures as these do little more than provide a constitution for the better ordering of relationships: whether they work or not must depend upon the willingness of both parties to abide by them. It can be, and often is, argued that trade unions will only do so when it suits them. But it should neither be assumed that management is always willing to follow procedure nor that what management sees as a conforming course of action on its part will necessarily be seen as such by a group of shop stewards—if, for example, they are faced with frequent adjournments of meetings to discuss grievances.

The time is probably coming when both negotiating and grievance or disputes procedures will need to stipulate some of the basic rules which the parties will agree in advance to abide by in the event of breakdown in negotiations over matters of interest or of right. The more bargaining on these aspects becomes a domestic matter, the more likely this is to be attempted and the more feasible it is to consider doing it. The more managements are led, as they have been in recent years, to considering payment to workers who have been on strike for the whole or the part of the period where it can be argued persuasively that the 'employer' played some causal part in the strike, the more the 'breakdown' itself becomes a negotiable matter which might be constrained by rules agreed in advance. It could well be that the legislators may wish in the future to reconsider the position of the law on this matter, particularly on picketing and, if that were to prove to be so, it is even more likely that some provision of locally agreed rules might be exhorted or recommended through the device of an associated code.

The first area for consideration in this context would be that relating to the giving of notice of strike or lock-out action. This is currently associated, usually, with the registration of one or more failures to agree and its consequences—whether it might then lead to conciliation or arbitration or to strike/lock-out action. The question of 'notice' of intention to strike or lock-out is normally covered in this context, but more attention may need to be given to the question of whether 'summary' striking or 'locking-out' is ever justified and, if so, under what circumstances. Given recognition of these possibilities, prior agreement might be sought on what 'procedures' for discussion of issues dividing the parties might be applied during the industrial action iself: the day when a simple refusal to negotiate or discuss until the action was terminated may well be past.

The second area which might benefit from prior discussion and agreement is that covering picketing in local and domestic disputes (picketing in mass and sympathy strikes are unlikely to be responsive to such agreements). What might be possible as a result of this kind of agreement is the establishment of a domestic code of conduct covering those areas which at present are inadequately dealt with by the law—in particular, the numerical size of the picket mounted on any given entrance to the works or office, and the manner in which vehicular traffic seeking to enter the premises shall be dealt with. At present, both of these issues fall to be determined by police officers acting under powers conferred upon them under legislation which has little or nothing to do with industrial relations affairs as such. Prior agreement to fix numbers of pickets for entrances and types of entrant, their authorization as pickets by the union, and their powers specifically on vehicular traffic, might help to minimize conflict on the picket lines for 'extraneous' reasons.

Such local agreements or codes would necessarily have to take cogniscance of the existing law, however unsatisfactory or inadequate that may be (cf Rideout, 1976, pp 292 *et seq*). The code cannot give 'rights' which the law would uphold, if the law denied those rights. But within the framework of the law, the local code could well make arrangements to govern conduct in the event of a strike and picketing. In some circumstances, such codes might help to 'cool' the situation which usually arises in the event of breakdown but it should not be assumed that, because a code exists, everyone will always be bound by it: in the nature of the case, emotions are aroused in disputes and such emotions may well rule the conduct of those caught up in the situation, however level-headed they may be otherwise.

4 Procedures for consultation

The fourth area which the 1972 Code suggests should be covered in a procedural agreement is that of consultation. 'Joint consultation' has developed a particular form in Britain, partly 'spontaneously' and partly under the thrust of government exhortation in war-time and, as the Code itself makes clear, there is considerable uncertainty and lack of clarity on what it ought to mean when associated with negotiations. Recent legislative requirements in this area have singled out two specific areas of consultation, those relating to proposed redundancies and to safety, health and welfare provision in employment. In association with both, there is a requirement for 'procedure' to be established under the legislation to enable this kind of consultation, at least, to be conducted. Although somewhat tangential to these consultative areas, the whole issue of provision of information, traditionally associated with the consultative process where it existed, is also within the scope of this constitutional prescription, and is likely to be made much more so if and when legislation is enacted on the subject of participation (and virtually regardless of the precise form which that takes).

In the Employment Protection Act 1975 and the Health and Safety etc at Work Act 1975 there are indications of a determination in public policy to structure consultation in terms of the parties to negotiations. In the one, by S 99(1), an employer "proposing to dismiss as redundant an employee of a description in respect of which an independent trade union is recognized by him shall consult representatives of that trade union about the dismissal".

The Employment Protection Act provides that trade unions shall be informed of *any* redundancy at the "earliest opportunity" and that consultation be initiated with the recognized independent trade unions at this time—on pain of a tribunal award of at least 28 days' pay to affected employees if this is not done.

Where an employer proposes to make 10 or more workers redundant he is required to consult representatives of recognized unions before implementing his proposals. (This applies regardless of whether the 10 or more work long or short hours, have long or short service (except the 12 weeks category) or are members or non-members of the recognized union.) If consultation is not so initiated by the employer, the *trade union* may seek and secure a protective award from a tribunal. This requires the employer to pay the employees whom it was proposed to make redundant for a stipulated period at the discretion of the tribunal, and up to a maximum of 90 days' pay where the redundancy involved 100 or more employees within a 90 day period, 60 days' pay where the redundancies involved

474

10 or more employees in a 30 day period, and 28 days' pay in any other case.

An individual covered by a protective award is entitled to the appropriate pay, and can bring a claim before an industrial tribunal to recover it, but such an award to an individual and any contractual payments or pay in lieu of notice falling within the protected period will go towards discharging the employer's obligations under the protective award.

It is required that consultations begin at "the earliest opportunity" with the recognized trade union, and time periods are laid down: 10 or more employees affected in one establishment must produce consultation at least 30 days before the first proposed redundancy, and the employer must therefore consider what to do about notice to individuals.

The sort of consultation which the legislators had in mind means that the employer has to give reasons for the redundancy and to indicate the methods of selecting and dismissing the employee(s) concerned, in writing. The employer must consider any representations made by the trade union representatives duly authorized and reply to them giving reasons for any rejection. This stipulation in effect defines 'consultation' in distinction from 'bargaining' in so far as it does not suggest that the employer can be compelled to accept the representations. Failure to comply with this requirement of timely consultation, where it would in the circumstances have been reasonable for the employer to do so, might lead to complaint by either the trade union or an affected individual to an industrial tribunal which is empowered to make a protective award, in the one case, and enforce payment of it in the other (see EPA, Ss 101–3). *This* kind of consultation is therefore made mandatory upon the employer.

In the Health and Safety etc at Work Act, by S 2(6) the employer has a statutory duty 'to consult any' representatives from amongst employees as may be elected or appointed by recognized trade unions under regulations which the Secretary of State is empowered to make (by S 2(4) & (5)) "with a view to the making and maintenance of arrangements which will enable him and his employees to cooperate effectively in promoting and developing measures to ensure the health and safety at work of the employees and in checking the effectiveness of such measures." The Health and Safety Commission have subsequently issued more detailed statements and regulations governing this aspect of the statutory requirement in which is amplified the general duty thus established on the employer. In so far as safety has in the past tended to be a matter for consideration within the framework of 'joint consultation' this duty thus transfers the matter from the purview of management's discretion, and requires more detailed procedural development as a matter of right and duty. As in the previous instance, the kind of consultation intended is that which requires the employer to listen to any representations made by safety representatives or members of safety committees (where these have been requested by independent trade unions) and to reach any decisions on health and safety in the light of what is thus communicated. Although it remains the employer's responsibility to take such decisions, it could happen that a decision which ignored representations for insufficient cause or on insufficient grounds might lead to the compounding of liability in the event of accident or disease. In both cases there is a sharpening up of the sanctions behind consultation, moving the process from the simpler kind already discussed in chapter 8.

The evolving constitution?

It is possible therefore to conclude from the discussion of these two chapters, that the regulation of relationships within the industrial relations system is now becoming increasingly 'constitutionalized'. On the one hand, Codes of Practice recommend that employers and their recognized and independent trade unions should make agreements covering such procedural facilities as information and time off etc and, on the other, they recommend the establishment of a host of staged procedures for negotiation, grievance bargaining, disciplinary action and dispute avoidance as well as consultation. Although large undertakings have often in the past developed such a range of agreements and procedures, the average and smaller undertakings are now being brought into the ambit of these recommendations. One possible consequence is that there will be a tendency for enterprises to standardize their provision at the minimum, but there is likely also to be some pressure to maintain the 'good employer' image in some cases by improving on these.

In so far as a considerable degree of standardization does result from the prescriptions of the legislation and the recommendations of the Codes, the regulation of the pattern of relationships in British industry and other undertakings is likely as a consequence to develop a strong similarity to the manner of controlling such relations in Continental undertakings, even if the actual conception of a works council does not materialize. However, to the extent that legislation compels the development of industrial democracy (or merely of two tier board arrangements to harmonize with partners in the EEC) the works council concept may appear in the guise of something like the Joint Union Meeting for Industrial Democracy. Since that will also need to follow acceptable standard procedures, the seeds of con-

476

stitutionality—at the formal procedural-rule level—may be well and truly sown.

Further reading
In addition to the general reading for the preceding chapter, students will find Flanders' last three books of use and relevance: Flanders, 1965, 1967, and 1969; and these may be supplemented by Chamberlain and Kuhn (1965) and Eldridge (1968).

To supplement the actual Codes of Practice mentioned in the reading list for the last chapter, a number of monographs produced by the IPM on union recognition, collective agreements and closed shop agreements provide useful discussion and illustrations.

Criticism of the pragmatism and reformism reflected in the Donovan and Bullock Commission/Committee Reports and in the trends towards constitutionalizing local industrial relations activities are to be found in Clegg, (1975), Hyman and Fryer (1975), Eldridge (1975) and Goldthorpe (1974).

12   Negotiation of substantive terms

Introduction
In the usual conception of an industrial relations system, three parties (hierarchies of workers and managements, together with State
agencies) are seen to interact in a behavioural arena in which their
actions are constrained by economic, technological and (power)
political pressures upon it, as a consequence of which they produce
two kinds of rule—those which guide their own relations in bargaining with each other and those which fix the terms and conditions
under which the members of the two main collectivities will work in
the 'production system' (cf Dunlop, 1958). This widely-accepted
view of industrial relations rests upon the assumption that the actual
members of the two hierarchies, the trade unionist-workers and the
employers-and-managers, attach a positive value to achieving order
in their relationships within the industrial relations *and* production
systems by these processes. If that assumption were not to hold in
some circumstances, then clearly the idea that there was an industrial
relations system capable of being described and analysed in this way
would prove to be a false one.

It has been a frequent criticism from the radical Left that this assumption is false, and that industrial relations behaviour is not
necessarily to be associated with predilections for ordered relationships and rationally-bargained terms and conditions. What
others have referred to as the 'English disease' (disordered industrial
relations at the plant level) is then quoted as evidence that industrial
relations is primarily to do with endemic conflict, which may nevertheless be punctuated by 'temporary truces' when the economic and
political circumstances limit the workers' power to challenge management (cf Hyman and Fryer, 1975; Allen, 1971). There is no way by
which the one view can be shown, scientifically, to be correct or more
correct than the other: which viewpoint is adopted is a matter for
choice on moral grounds not scientific ones.

What the challenge to the generally accepted view does, however, is suggest that we should not automatically assume that every

formal relationship between organized labour and management is to be regarded as the same as every other. The sub-cultural values held by employers are not homogeneous, nor are those held by trade unionists or their representatives. On both sides of the bargaining table, there is to be found a spectrum of value position ranging from complete acceptance of the central cultural values of the society to complete rejection of these values and a desire to set up a society based on quite other values. If therefore on the two sides of a bargaining table there were to be found representatives who both believed in the need to reject the central values and the bargaining objectives and methods usually associated with them, it is to be doubted whether the relationship developing therefrom could be described as a 'collective bargaining relationship' without doing great damage to the use of the English language. Even if such extreme juxtapositions of dominant value as between the two sides might be regarded as unusual, it should not be supposed either that they could not appear, at all or ever, or that mismatches of values albeit of a less extreme nature do not appear in the relationships between the parties to industrial relations. In the nature of industrial relationships, parties with different values and different derived objectives do face one another in the production or employment situation and, when this happens, the common characterization of collective bargaining may prove inapplicable or inept.

This idea is to be found in Walton and McKersie's attempt to identify a number of quite different relationship patterns in industrial relations, which they label: "conflict, containment-aggression, accommodation, cooperation and collusion" (Selekman, Selekman and Fuller, 1958, pp 4–8; quoted in Walton and McKersie, 1965, p 185). This categorization indicates that there might be five quite different sets of relationship, doubtless supported by five quite different perspectives and scales of preferences. But Walton and McKersie associated these with different situations of relationship, thus implying that the parties to the relationship share the objectives and values which these labels suggest. Equally possible is the conclusion that the separate parties might approach the relationship from any of the five positions so that, whilst there may be pressure to adopt consensual positions in any given relationship, there might still be a considerable possibility of mismatching.

Thus on either side of the bargaining table, there are at least five such salient value positions to be recognized. In table 18, these values are set against each other in a way which, reading along the horizontal lines, might yield the kinds of 'relationship pattern' identified by Walton and McKersie. In this table, I have suggested, in the central column, terms which might the more appropriately indicate the nature of the relationship which might be expected to develop over a rather wider spectrum of value (and associated philosophy or ideology) than that indicated in the Walton and McKersie statement. There are, for example, situations in which the employer attitude of completely unfettered individualism juxtaposed with an ideology which completely rejects existing forms of organization on the part of the workers or their organization, could yield little more than a revolutionary situation. In others, an employer attitude which emphasized his responsibilities to the workers or to workers-plus-other-groups, brought into association with a politically non-aligned workforce or unionism, might effect a high level of co-operation between the parties. In between these two situations, a number of intermediate positions can be distinguished, yielding relationships of rebellion, passive acceptance or constructive tolerance, or co-ordination. But the possibility must exist that in the

Table 18

Spectrum of salient values in industrial relationships with indications of types of guiding philosophy adopted by the parties

The corporate (employer) philosophy		The salient value of either party to the relationship	The trade union (worker) philosophy	
Individualism (unfettered by 'organization' of power)	F R E E	REVOLUTION	F A I R	Overthrow unionism in one of its many manifestations
Boulwarism* and similar abrasive employer philosophies		REBELLION		Unionism in the mould of a permanent and critical opposition
Demotivated abdication		a) ACCEPTANCE (passive)		Apathetic acceptance of what is
Pursuit of No change or *status quo*		b) CONSTRUCTIVE TOLERANCE		Preservation of what is thought to have been achieved
Constitutionalism: proceduralization of the relationship		CO-ORDINATION		Aggressive business unionism
Socially responsible	F A I R	COOPERATION	F R E E	Non-affiliated unionism (or 'non-political' unionism)

* For explanation see Walton and McKersie, 1965, p. 187 (Cf Walton and McKersie, 1975, p 189, from which this has been developed)

short-run (and therefore for shorter or longer periods within an ongoing relationship) the values and objectives of the parties must diverge, and so create situations in which one party (with one value-based objective) must react to the other party who is intent upon some other type of value-based objective. Conceived in this way, the assumptions that relationships are 'normally' to be found in the lower half of the spectrum and to be congruent with one another across the light are thrown into question. And, equally importantly, some of the 'extreme' relationships indicated on this chart may not qualify for the title of a 'collective bargaining' relationship at all.

Nevertheless, there is little doubt that in Britain and some other countries this relationship is predominantly one which can be characterized as one of 'collective bargaining'. There are some who think the term might be felicitously altered (for example to job regulation) and some who regard it as only one of a number of different types of relationship which might be established, even if it is the one to which most principals and representatives appear to orient themselves in these societies. In either context, the term might be considered to have shortcomings. But there is doubt as to whether collective bargaining in its purest and most apposite form is adequately described; alternatively, there may be reason to suppose that it is too often extended to cover patterns of relationship which might be better described as not being 'collective bargaining'.

We owe the term collective bargaining to the Webbs (1920). They saw it as one (and not necessarily the most desirable, even if at that time the most common) of three main methods through which trade unions sought to maintain and improve the conditions of the members' working lives. It was therefore in Flanders' summary "exactly what the words imply—a collective equivalent and alternative to individual bargaining" (Flanders, 1969, p 13). This conception is also to be found in the Donovan Commission's extension to cover "any negotiation in which employees do not negotiate individually, on their own behalf, but do so collectively through representatives" (Donovan Commission Report, 1968, p 8). Such substitution in fixing the terms and conditions under which individuals would be prepared to accept work was adjudged by the Webbs to be a sensible solution to the problem of unequal bargaining power in the free labour market, but as such it called for no other characterization than that applied to individual haggling in the market. Bargaining in this sense then becomes "the process by which the antithetical interests of supply and demand, of buyer and seller, are finally adjusted" culminating finally in an "act of exchange" (McIver and Page, 1953, p 474).

Implicit in this use of the term is the view that the total quantity of whatever is being bargained is fixed, and that what one party to the bargain gains forms the loss for the other. In this view of collective bargaining, the whole process becomes one of haggling, similar to that of the bazaar. The aspect of reality which the proponents usually have in mind is the process of haggling over the price of labour, the determination of which is then seen to take place in the same way that the price of an article is determined by a haggling process. By extension, this same idea is carried forward to meet other terms and conditions of employment: on hours of work or holidays, the extension seems reasonable but on 'the amount of say' workers shall have in certain decisions or on 'procedures' which might be agreed, the extensions seem awkward if not unreasonable. The determination of a set number of normal hours in the week can be costed or expressed in wage terms and so seem to accord with the haggling-in-the-market analogue; the determination of a procedure governing, say, discipline or dismissal does not seem to lend itself to such a computation based on the gain to one side being the loss to the other unless 'authority' or 'power' is seen in equivalent quantifiable terms.

Flanders considers collective bargaining to be better labelled 'joint regulation' because it is "itself essentially a rule-making process, and this is a feature which has no proper counterpart in individual bargaining" (Flanders, 1969, p 14). This admits that the employer might also have an interest in collective bargaining (a possibility which the Webbs did not consider particularly because of their prime concern with trade unions as 'modern' social institutions). In this view, collective bargaining (job regulation) establishes, in advance of the culmination of the act of exchange, the rules which will then be applied to determine the levels of contribution and reward and the form of the general conditions of employment which will be applied in that act of exchange. In their effect, such rules were and are not different from the terms fixed earlier by the magistrates under Elizabethan legislation, concurrently through the common law doctrines on the employment contract and more recently as a consequence of legislative enactment, in so far as they determine the 'conditions' in advance of the individual bargain being struck. The vital difference is the structure of dependence developed in each of the various forms of regulation, ranging from the complete dependence upon the magistrates as imposed arbiters to the complete independence of the small district union functioning on direct democratic lines, and with a number of variants in between.

These two views are combined by Chamberlain (1951) (later Chamberlain and Kuhn, 1965) with a third to provide a more generic definition of collective bargaining. He suggests that "collective bargaining is

1 a means of contracting for the sale of labour
2 a form of industrial government, and
3 a method of management" (1951, p 121).

These may then be labelled marketing, governmental and managerial theories of collective bargaining. The first is essentially the theory developed by the Webbs, but followed in essentials by Dunlop (1944) in his approach to wage determination and by Fischer (1971) who also sees the trade union in the position of a labour cartel. The second is comparable to Flanders' own theory of job regulation but the rule-making process is extended to embrace what Leiserson has called the setting up, definition and limitation of organs of government and the provision of "agencies for making, executing and interpreting laws for the industry and means for their enforcement" (Leiserson, 1922, p 61). In Chamberlain's own view of this conception of collective bargaining it involves both a sharing of industrial sovereignty (ie as between management and trade unions) *and* a joint defence by both parties of the autonomy of the two parties acting together (Chamberlain, 1951, p 128–9).

In the Leiserson conception, it is a little difficult to draw an adequate dividing line between collective bargaining as a means of industrial government and as a method of management, because of his incorporation of agencies for *executing* the laws jointly made. Chamberlain's own argument on this aspect is that because employers and unions combine "in reaching decisions on matters in which both have vital interests", the usual union disclaimer of any interest in usurping management's function can itself be discounted because "collective bargaining, by its very nature involves/them/in the managerial role" and they are "actually *de facto* managers" (Chamberlain, 1951, pp 137, 130 and 198). But this view is based upon the management function being seen as (simply) that of *deciding* on behalf of the enterprise, whereas in Chamberlain's own analysis of that function he also recognizes a three-level hierarchy of such decision taking which is variously attacked or influenced by union activity (Chamberlain, 1948, ch 2). If we are to distinguish the method of government as concerned with some aspect of industrial decision taking, it might be preferable to define the method of management in terms of subordinate decision functions of administration (deciding *how* the 'top-level' decisions are to be carried out) and execution (seeing to it that these decisions are implemented 'correctly' and 'appropriately'). This would remain consistent with the Chamberlain view that collective bargaining helps to make management more 'democratic' (as distinct from making the industrial government process so) (cf Flanders, 1969, p 33).

These two views of the objective of 'collective bargaining' may be associated with the two terms, bargaining and negotiation, which are usually employed interchangeably. Gottschalk (1973) suggests a different distinction but he does not appear to use it systematically. 'Bargaining' he suggests, may be used to "refer to the process of demand formation and revision which provides the basic mechanism whereby the parties seek to come towards an agreement", and 'negotiation' to "refer to the situation within which bargaining occurs (*ibid*, p 38). It seems more sensible to reflect the normal dictionary definitions of these two verbs, and to use the one to indicate a process of haggling or of establishing the terms of give and take in a zero-sum type of situation, and hence a process of determining a price or similar numerical quantity of something like amount of effort or hours, and to employ the other to indicate a conference with another or others with a view to reaching an acceptable compromise or agreement in the broader sense of a 'treaty' regulating a relationship for the future. In this view, the two meanings assigned do tend to associate with the perspectives of the two schools quoted above. The term collective bargaining is more properly employed by the Webbs and those like Dunlop (1944) and Fisher (1971) who follow them, and the term negotiation more appropriately employed to refer to job regulation processes as indicated by Flanders (1969) and by Dunlop (1958) in his other theoretical work.

In both a bargaining and a negotiating situation, there must necessarily be (a) two or more parties who are (b) separate from each other in their perceptions of the correct distribution of value or power but who are nevertheless (c) intending, if possible, to reach a settlement (whether a bargain or a treaty of rules) within a meaningful period as the parties define that, and which (d) the parties will then intend to abide by (at least for the time being). The adjective 'collective' indicates only that the parties now approach one another through representatives or agents rather than directly. The further qualification of voluntary, as this is often added in the British context, merely tells us something about the fact or the perception of the parties having autonomy to arrive at their own bargains or treaties, and may further import into the process a desire, shared by the parties, to defend that autonomy against any kind of third party encroachment—a fact which might influence the conduct of the parties towards each other in bargaining or negotiating (cf Flanders, 1965, ch 3).

The simple act of identifying the parties to industrial relations creates the probability that different relationships will be established between them. There are thereby shown to be not merely two 'monoliths' between which a relationship is to be discerned. Rather there are a number of principals and relationships between them and a number of agents or representatives who also develop relationships amongst themselves and with the principals. To contain these relationships it becomes desirable to establish a number of appropriate sub-processes of bargaining or negotiations. This, *inter alia*, is partially effected by Walton and McKersie (1965) who identify four distinct 'sub-processes' of formal labour negotiations, each regarded as "an instance of social negotiations" (*ibid*, p 4). They comprise "four systems of activity, each with its own function for the interacting parties, its own internal logics, and its own identifiable set of instrumental acts or tactics" (*ibid*, p 4). These four sub-processes are capable of being linked, on the ground of greater relevance, to the different conceptions of bargaining which emerge in other works.

The first sub-process distinguished, that of *distributive bargaining*, is said to be "central to labour negotiations and is usually regarded as the dominant activity in the union-management relationship" (*ibid*, p 11) and is seen to serve the function of resolving "pure conflicts of interest" (*ibid*, p 4). This would apply to the restricted perspective of collective bargaining, in which the conflict of interest lies in the distribution of the product.

The second sub-process, that of *integrative bargaining*, is not necessarily an alternative to distributive bargaining in a real negotiation, since "often, equally important objectives can be attained only through this process" (*ibid*, p 126). It serves to help "find common or complementary interests and solve problems confronting both parties" (*ibid*, p 4) and may be interleaved with distributive bargaining. It is seen to operate in two distinct areas, those of the substantive and the procedural issues. In the first of these, the most frequently quoted example is that of productivity bargaining in those cases where the bargaining was mutually accepted as looking towards the solution of work problems from which increases in both profit and wage might be expected, with the arguments over distribution as between them succeeding a prior agreement about increasing the size of the product. In the second, the area of establishing procedural rules autonomously to guide the bargaining conduct of the parties provides the main example. The notion of collective bargaining as a process of establishing guiding rules is thus capable of exploration within the logics and activities of this category of sub-process to an extent which might not otherwise be possible.

The third sub-process, *attitudinal structuring*, takes into account that bargaining does not only result in a division of the product and a solution of mutually recognized problems, but produces inter-party attitudes which are important to the collective relationships, both in

485

the treaty-formation and implementation stages. "The attitudes of each party towards the other, taken together, define the relationship between them," (*ibid*, p 184), and the sub-process is therefore designed to influence these defining attitudes in the interests of achieving more accommodating relationships. This process would appear to have considerable significance in relation to Chamberlain's third conception of the nature and purpose of collective bargaining, that concerned with management and its democratization (cf Chamberlain and Kuhn, 1965).

The fourth sub-process, *intra-organizational* bargaining, is of a somewhat different nature from the other three in so far as it is concerned with intra-party discipline, rather than with the relationships between the parties, although it could be expected to affect them. It is seen by these authors as having the "function of achieving consensus within each of the interacting groups", and therefore of significance for the other three processes of collective negotiations (*ibid*, p 4). It also "refers to the system of activities which brings the expectations of the principals into alignment with those of the chief negotiator" (*ibid*, p 5) and presumably also to the opposite process. Its relevance to all other sub-processes is readily apparent and therefore it is not necessary to link it separately to any of the definitions already advanced (cf Ross, 1948).

Although these are distinguished as 'separate' sub-processes, and although they therefore appear to be capable of characterization as different conceptions of bargaining, Walton and McKersie stress that they are inter-related and indeed may be discerned in any one single sequence of bargaining behaviour. They are concerned to demonstrate that each is associated with different motives, different objectives and therefore with different strategies, tactics and behaviours, which may place the actors in dilemmas during the bargaining process itself. What for the moment we wish to draw from this characterization, is merely that, as distinguishable sub-processes, these four help to extend the conception of collective bargaining to embrace a number of different patterns distinguished by objective, function and behaviour.

The collective agreement
There is little doubt that in Britain the most common outcome of interaction between the parties in the industrial relationship is the 'collective agreement'. This may be regarded as a generic term covering a variety of different agreements (see below) which takes its definition from the process of collective bargaining, which is seen to terminate in an agreement and hence in a collective agreement. It is a fairly recent pragmatic concept—post-dating 'collective

bargaining'—and it has to be seen in relation to other outcomes of the interaction—'understandings', 'continuing dispute or grievance', 'withdrawals of cooperation' and 'strikes and lock-outs'. It is often thought of as being the necessary outcome of the interaction, simply because it is now so prevalent, but really there is nothing 'necessary' about it unless the values and attitudes of the interacting parties make it so (cf Hyman and Fryer, 1975; Wood *et al*, 1975).

Where it can be assumed that such values and attitudes exist and predispose the parties to engage in collective bargaining and conclude this bargaining with an agreement, we might recognize that these values and attitudes and the orientation to action will themselves figure in a 'collective agreement'. This 'agreement' may be conceived separately from an agreement about the substantive terms and conditions of employment which will apply within the productive or work relationship itself as we noted in the preceding chapter. In the latter category, there may be one or a large number of agreements about the future content of the contract of employment, and in this chapter we are concerned with the processes of producing such agreements in the context of different interests and values on that relationship of employer and employee.

It is therefore possible to regard the collective agreement on the substantive terms which shall apply to the productive system as the object of collective bargaining: as a process of converting disagreements into agreements which will allow relationships in the productive system to continue. This is an important objective for the bargainers—like the personnel practitioners—and it underlines industrial relations activity as a service to production, not as an end in itself. Nevertheless it is easy for the negotiators themselves to become so involved in their own industrial relations processes and structures that the perfect 'industrial relations' solution to a problem becomes the displaced objective of this activity. What justifies the industrial relations activity is the service it can render or the contribution which it can make to productivity and efficiency objectives on the one hand, and to achievement and satisfaction objectives on the other, and it is against the criteria which can be derived from these that such activity must be assessed.

Once the collective parties agree to enter into negotiations they will seek to establish by agreement just what 'rules' will apply to the 'substantive' elements in the individual contract of employment. What will be the extent and amount of consideration involved for both parties or, more simply, how much remuneration for how much effort or contribution? Whilst in principle these matters could be determined in individual bargaining, they are now most commonly established collectively, and the substantive terms of the collective agreement are in this sense substitutes for those terms which would otherwise fall to be determined in individual bargains. It is important to note how this 'substitution' is effected because, in Britain (unlike some other countries), the collective agreement is not regarded as a legally-enforceable contract in law (Trade Union Act, 1871). Whilst enforcement of collective agreements is usually effected against the ultimate sanctions of strike and lock-out available to the parties, there is a generally-accepted legal position which sets some limits to that action.

The law tackles this general question of 'substitution' from two different standpoints, one relating to custom, and the other by extension to the collective agreement as a kind of 'successor' to custom. When the individual contract of employment is established by a minimal agreement between the parties (see above, pp 61–62), that which is customary for the trade or occupation or employer is often accepted by both parties as 'filling out' the simple terms. Early trade unions certainly took, and present day ones to an extent take, a very real interest in what is customary in the trade, and the *status quo* which has figured prominently in collective bargaining in recent years is in effect an attempt to maintain some customary way of proceeding or performing unless and until some new set of rules about it is agreed. In one sense, therefore, the collective agreement might be seen as either a 'successor' to unwritten custom or a 'codification' of it.

The common law has always been willing to take cognisance of 'custom' in imputing terms to an employment contract. But the law imposes its own conditions: it requires that custom must be reasonable, certain and notorious before it can be accepted as influencing decisions as to what is a term of the contract. 'Reasonable' customs must accord with the usual judicial views of what is reasonable: a custom of paying non-unionists less than unionists in a factory could be regarded as not productive of an implied term in the contract. To be 'certain' the custom must be precisely defined, so that none could establish that the custom could be interpreted in an alternative way to give a different conclusion, and since, almost by definition, customs are usually unwritten there is an obvious pitfall here. 'Notorious' means that the custom must be well-known to people in the trade or industry or factory concerned, and certainly not something concocted or invented by either trade unions or employers on the spur of the moment to support their case.

In addition, even customs which are reasonable, certain and notorious will be denied validity by the courts as sources of implied terms unless they are also reflective of an assumption of obligation on the part of the party. This is usually applied to the advantage of the employer, who may have followed certain policies for donkey's years because they are supportive of his business interests, but who does not see himself as *obliged* to anyone to pursue them. The *ex gratia* payment is an obvious attempt to permit money to be paid without creating any kind of customary precedent. But it can extend beyond this. The employer may pay gratuities or even bonuses over many years, and do so from a sense of philanthropy not of obligation. It would be pointless to seek to establish these as customary terms and conditions of employment in a court of law, although of course, in the process of collective bargaining such arguments might well be used and might succeed.

Over the years, what may have been customary has been progressively brought into formal understandings and agreements; increasingly these are now reduced to writing, so that a collective agreement in the middle 1970s can be an extensive document or set of them, covering many terms and conditions of employment which in an earlier period might well have been treated as customary. The 'subjects' covered have generally over time expanded from wage rates and ratios of apprentices to embrace hours, holidays, overtime and bonus payments, working arrangements, facilities (for washing etc) a range of 'fringe benefits' and even pensions. All these relate to the 'substantive terms' of the contract and the question arises as to how they are permitted to influence the terms of each individual contract.

First, a collective agreement is not in itself a contract which the Courts would enforce. This has been accepted to be the case since 1871, when the Trade Union Act ordered the Courts not to entertain actions to enforce agreements between trade unions. Even where a single employer negotiated an agreement with one or more trade unions, it was assumed that it would still remain unenforceable. In 1969, the Ford Motor Company Ltd sought to challenge this assumption in an action against the AUEFW (1 WLR 339; 2 All ER 481; 6 KIR 50) but the point was never determined for technical reasons and the outcome was taken to confirm what had been the accepted view. The position was changed, deliberately, by the Industrial Relations Act 1971 but has been re-established more explicitly in the Trade Union and Labour Relations Act 1974, S 18. This states that the whole or part of a collective agreement will be conclusively presumed not to have been intended to be a legally enforceable contract unless it is in writing and contains a provision which (however expressed) states that the parties intended that it or the part(s) shall be a legally enforceable contract. Any clause restricting a worker's right to take industrial action must meet additional conditions before it would be enforced, regardless of what may be said in such an agreement to the contrary.

But secondly, it has always been possible for the substantive terms of a collective agreement to be incorporated into the contract of employment and thus become enforceable in contract. This is not automatic. First, the agreements reached between the employer and the trade union cannot, by themselves, bind anyone other than the parties (ie the management representatives and the union representatives) and therefore what is agreed there can only bind others *if* the representatives are explicitly in an agency relationship to their members. Thus mere membership of a union does not place the worker in a position where the negotiators are his agents; individual union members must expressly authorize the representatives to act on their behalf or there must be an explicit union rule to this effect which will have the same force. Thus in the case of Rookes *v* Barnard (1964) (AC 1129) the judge held that "the representatives were authorized by their executive to bind the union as a whole and the members individually. The terms of the agreement thus became part of the terms of each individual contract of employment between (BOAC) and the members of (the Union)."

Thirdly there must be either express or implied incorporation of the collective agreement terms in the contract of employment itself. A term in that contract may specifically state that the contract incorporates the terms of the relevant collective agreement. (National Coal Board *v* Galley (1958) 1 All ER 91). Such terms must be capable of being translated into the individual's contract: procedural clauses obviously cannot be incorporated since they relate to the conduct of the bargaining parties, and others may apply only to union members or some other defined class or category of work so that they could not influence the contracts of those not in the category.

There must also be an absence of conflict as between different collective agreements which might conceivably be relevant: as O'Higgins summarizes this: "so far the (Court) decisions suggest that the Courts will only allow the worker to get the benefit of those terms in conflicting collective agreements which are least advantageous" (1976, p 35).

Implied incorporation may take one of two main forms. Either the parties may be assumed to have intended that the terms of the collective agreement were so vital as to necessitate their incorporation into the employment contract; or such incorporation may have been taking place in the trade or industry for so long that it could be regarded as established practice for this to happen, or the terms may have stood for so long that they have become part of the custom and practice of the trade or industry. Which brings us back round to the first point above that the collective agreement has some association with custom and practice.

The collective agreement may then be said to represent the realization of the purposes of the two parties or 'sides', at least for the time being: the agreement is the compromise which the parties reach after setting the power of the employer against the power of organized labour, and as such it represents the statement of the rules by which each will abide because in that power situation it must do so for as long as the situation continues. Seen in that light, there are reasons for regarding it as different in almost all respects from the individual contract of employment, as indeed it has been regarded for many years.

State intervention to fix substantive terms

The State has used legislation to impose amounts or levels of consideration in the employment contract in three main stages. First, to influence the *kind* of consideration involved (the Truck Acts of the first half of last century sought to prevent payment in kind or in vouchers redeemable at the company's 'tommy' shop, and to require payment in coin of the realm). Secondly, to influence the amount of wage offered and received in certain trades and industries where wages were considered to be 'too low' (the Trade Boards Act of 1909 established four trade boards to fix minimum wages and hours for four trades, and later legislation extended their number and scope). Thirdly, to influence certain other items, length of notice, compensation for redundancy and for 'unfair' dismissal, payment for layoffs, job security during periods of pregnancy etc, applied to workers (fairly) universally (the various Acts of the 1960s and 1970s, identified on pp 76–77 above). Government policies on incomes in the post world war two period have also influenced the amounts of pay received by workers, but only rarely have these policies depended upon legal enactment of the kind noted in the three categories above.

The same philosophies which lie behind the approach of the common law to this question of consideration have exerted their influence upon government action in this field. There is still evident in this country an acceptance of the principle that the government should not interfere directly in fixing remuneration of workers. According to Kahn-Freund, "it has never been possible for a government department to fix minimum wages without a proposal from an independent council or board. This, indeed, can be considered as another distinctive feature of British labour law. Outside agriculture, the ultimate decision whether or not wages should be fixed rests with the Minister (of Labour), but he cannot determine the substance of his decision. It is not he who settles remuneration and holidays. This is done by the wages council concerned and, although he does not have to act on proposals made by the council or board, (and may, if he disagrees, refer the matter back to them), he cannot in substance amend them" (Flanders and Clegg, 1954, pp 71–72).

There is thus no simple and direct statutory wage-fixing process in this country; it exists in certain cases as an indirect process which gives some scope to the 'representatives' of both employers and workers, even in the wages council trades, to participate in the determination of minimum remuneration and certain other conditions.

The State intervention which began in 1909 under the then new Trade Boards Act was confined to certain 'sweated trades' (revealed by the Sweated Industries Exhibition shortly before) in which it appeared clear that neither the forces of the market nor the activities of trade unions were capable of producing a minimum level of wages consistent with society's view of what an employee must receive from employment. As an experiment, boards were established to recommend minimum wages in four trades, ready-made tailoring, paper-box making, chain-making and machine-made lace and net finishing, and the Minister was empowered to give these rates statutory backing. The board adopted to make such recommendations brought together representatives of employers and workers in the trade, and three independent persons to provide expertise and continuity in the wage fixing process.

After examination by the Whitley Committee during the first world war, this experiment was broadened to admit trades where organization was poor, in addition to those in which wages were low for some reason. This was done by the Trade Boards Act of 1918 under which trade boards were established in a large number of small-scale and scattered industries. The same kind of approach was later applied to agricultural wages (in 1924 and 1937), wages in road haulage (in 1938) and to wages in catering (in 1943) under specific acts of Parliament. The Wages Councils Act of 1945 renamed the old trade boards and effectively brought wages in the retail trades under this same umbrella. By the 1960s, by which time all of these industries had been brought under wages council arrangements, it was estimated that about $3\frac{1}{2}$ million workers were covered by statutory minimum wages, hours, holidays and certain other conditions.

The Donovan Commission's examination of the success of the wages councils in improving pay levels and organization in the trades concerned suggested that the device left much to be desired on both counts (Donovan Report, 1968, p 59). It fell to the Commission on Industrial Relations to make detailed examinations of particular councils: it recommended retention of existing councils in only three of the cases examined, amalgamation of the separate councils in the retail trades into one, joining of Scottish and English and Welsh councils in two instances and outright abolition in no less than 10 cases. Although not all of these recommendations have been accepted (the retail trades are to be covered by two councils, one in food and the other in non-food retailing, for example), there have been abolitions and amalgamations in the 1970s which significantly reduce society's reliance upon this form of statutory intervention in the fixing of main terms and conditions of employment.

State support for collective bargaining

This process of change has been significantly hastened by two distinct provisions in the Employment Protection Act 1975: that which allows the wages council composed of representatives of workers and employers *and* three independent members, to be replaced under certain circumstances by a Statutory Joint Industrial Council composed of representatives of trade unions and employers in the trade or industry but without the independent members; and that which allows trade unions to bring claims to the Central Arbitration Committee to secure observance by individual employers either of "recognized terms and conditions" or, where such recognized terms and conditions do not exist, of the 'general level' of terms and conditions in the trade or industry in the district. Together these are calculated to bring more establishments (and employers) under the influence of the terms of collective agreements, especially in the small-scale and scattered trades and in white collar employments. The wages council experiment as such may therefore be at an end, but historically it was important as establishing the fact of the State's concern with consideration in the contract of employment which was until then usually regarded as something for private law making by collective bargaining.

Then in the 1960s legislation carried this idea further. In a number of areas (see ch 1 above) definite minima were established directly and universally by legal enactment rather than through some mediating body such as the wages council. As Rideout has said of some of the early legislation:

> The Redundancy Payments Act 1965 may fairly be regarded as the second of a series of Acts of Parliament importing statutory regulation directly into the contractual relationship between employer

and employee. There is . . . a considerable quantity of legislation affecting that relationship, from the Truck Act of 1831 to the Factories Act 1961. The Contracts of Employment Act 1963 and the Redundancy Payments Act stand apart since they affect what had hitherto been regarded, subject to certain protective statutory provisions, as the negotiable part of the contract. In the same sense they may be said to impinge on the field of voluntary collective bargaining (Rideout, 1969, p 7).

Since that time, various other legislative enactments (Industrial Relations, Trade Union and Labour Relations, and the Employment Protection Act) have continued this same interventionist approach, and thus made the present situation relatively replete (compared with 15 years ago) with statutory minima which "affect the negotiable part of the contract" and "impinge on the field of voluntary collective bargaining". Such developments must therefore be regarded as imposing constraints upon the decisions of those who set up the 'voluntary collective agreement' in our collective bargaining system. As yet, collective bargaining has failed to accommodate this change: agreements still tend to contain terms which are below the statutory minima, but which have been "negotiated" by the parties (see O'Higgins, 1976, pp 41–42), no doubt concerned to re-invent the wheel.

The second major change may be considered in three distinct parts: that relating to recognized terms and conditions, that relating to general terms and conditions and that relating to the situation in the former wages council trades specifically.

The Section (98) of the Employment Protection Act which deals with *recognized* terms and conditions, re-enacts S 8 of the Terms and Conditions of Employment Act of 1959, which is repealed by the EP Act but introduces some modifications. ACAS is given power to entertain a claim from a trade union or employers' association that, as respects any worker, an employer is not providing terms and conditions of employment as favourable as the 'recognized terms and conditions'. This concept is precisely defined:

the recognized terms and conditions means terms and conditions of workers in comparable employment in the trade or industry, or section of a trade or industry, in which the employer in question is engaged, either generally or in the district in which he is so engaged, which have been settled by an agreement or award, to which the parties are employers' associations and independent trade unions which represent (generally or in the district in question as the case may be) a substantial proportion of the employers

494

and of the workers of the description to which the agreement or award relates.

Thus recognized terms and conditions will normally be found in an industry-wide agreement. Either party may invite the CAC to raise the terms and conditions applicable, in the establishment of an employer who may well not be a member of the employers' association, to those in the national agreement. The Schedule clears up a doubt which has existed since the passage of the 1959 Act on 'minimum' terms and conditions in an agreement: henceforth where a national agreement lays down minimum terms and conditions, these will be regarded as the 'recognized' terms and conditions for this purpose, even though particular employers may be paying more.

Such a claim to the CAC may ask for a single term, some of the terms or the whole package of terms to be imposed upon the employer in question. In any of these cases the employer's only defence is to demonstrate that he is observing terms and conditions which, as a whole, are not less favourable to his employees, whatever may be the position on any one particular term. Thus by challenging one single term (eg the shift differential or the holiday entitlement) the trade union could virtually force the employer to reveal the whole gamut of the terms and conditions of employment in his establishment. The union could in this way find out what terms and conditions do apply in an establishment in which it is not recognized or in which it has no access to information.

The power of the CAC is to impose upon the employer observance of terms and conditions which are not less favourable and, once such an award is made, these become part of the individual contract of employment of each employee covered in the claim. Although this possibility has existed (in another form) since 1959, it was little used but recent incomes policies have led a number of unions to use this method of securing an increase in pay without infringing pay guidelines.

The provisions of the EP Act on *general* terms and conditions may prove more difficult for an employer to handle, when presented, even if they are possibly also more difficult for a trade union to substantiate. "General terms and conditions" is defined as meaning "the general level of terms and conditions observed for comparable workers by employers

(i) in the trade, industry or section in which the employer in question is engaged in the district in which he is so engaged; and
(ii) whose circumstances are similar to those of the employer in question.

Claims may be put forward by any trade union which has at least one member amongst the grade and category of workers concerned in the employer's establishment but, where the employer recognizes a trade union for collective bargaining purposes, only the recognized union can bring a claim under this heading. The powers of the CAC on these claims are comparable to those in relation to recognized terms and conditions, but there are problems for both parties in this instance.

The trade union may bring a claim in relation to one or more terms and conditions of employment, but the onus is upon it to establish that there is a general level (in the absence, by definition, of a national or district agreement with employers' associations). The problem arises because the 'general level' has to be established on five distinct criteria:

First, that there is a *modal* term or set of terms amongst a number of separate firms in the trade in the district—which presupposes that the union can accumulate sufficient data to establish this

Secondly, that the workers covered by the claim are *comparable* in the sense that they are doing similar (eg not less difficult) work than those elsewhere, even if they carry the same job title—which presupposes that the union can gather data on job descriptions coincidentally with the gathering of data to establish the mode

Thirdly, that the employers included are themselves '*similar*' in their circumstances to the employer in question, and this presumably relates mainly to questions of size and stage of the enterprise's development rather than to its economic circumstances at the time (eg whether it is profitable or not)

Fourthly, that the employers included for purposes of establishing the modal terms and conditions are involved in the *same service or productive process* as the employer in question—a matter which has given rise to considerable debate in the past before the Industrial Court and the Industrial Arbitration Board (about claims under the Fair Wages Resolution of the House of Commons, for example)

Fifthly, that the '*district*' can be appropriately defined for this purpose, since it is clearly not to be broadened to embrace 'national' but could otherwise vary according to the nature of the trade in question (eg shops in a city but aluminium smelting in a region); in the same vein, a multi-plant company need not on this score fear comparisons between different plants in different regions of the country as a basis for this kind of claim.

Quite obviously, a great deal will depend upon the extent to which the CAC is willing to interpret these five criteria in relation to such claims. For this reason, the extent to which this provision will make an impact upon industrial relations cannot be predicted, although it is likely to be potentially more important for those industries which do not have national agreements negotiated with an employers' association (including, that is, the wages council trades).

The third set of provisions (in Part II of Schedule 11) relates to those covered by wages councils, statutory joint industrial councils or the two agricultural wages boards, and generally allows claims comparable to those in respect of 'general terms and conditions' just discussed.

Independent unions with at least one member in those industries may put a similar claim to the CAC in respect of the level of pay in an employer's establishment, on the grounds that (a) the union is a party to one or more collective agreements which relate to establishments within scope of the council or board whose circumstances are similar, that (b) these agreements are either concerned with the trade as a whole (nationally) or in the same district as the employer in question, and that (c) the employer in question is paying less than the lowest current rate of remuneration to workers of the same description.

This is of potential importance, given the finding of the CIR investigations of the wages council trades that there were often agreements negotiated between trade unions and employers in scope which provided better rates of pay or better conditions than those laid down in the statutory minima. This procedure would then offer the independent unions in these trades some opportunity to generalize the pay terms of voluntary agreements through the rest of the trade or industry and thus raise the level of the lowest paid, possibly more effectively than the wages councils themselves have done. Clearly much will depend upon the interpretation which the CAC wished to place upon the phrase 'a significant number of establishments' in which the claimant union must have such agreements.

In all these cases, the employer has only one defence, which is to show that either singly (on single term claims) or generally the terms and conditions applicable in his establishment are not less favourable. This may be difficult for him to do in some circumstances but, where he relies upon the total package of terms and conditions being so much more favourable as to reduce the significance of any single item (which may be less favourable), he may be forced to reveal to non-recognized unions information which they would have no other method of acquiring.

The general effect of these provisions is likely to be, over a longer or shorter time, depending upon the alacrity with which the trade unions seek to make use of them, that employers in the under-organized trades and industries or sections thereof, will more readily embrace national association and national negotiation; for example, for white collar employees, in the distributive trades generally and in other public and private service industries where union density is low (cf Bain, 1970). In the wages council trades in particular these tendencies are likely to be equally marked, thus leading to a progressive diminution of the significance of this device and a progressive increase in the employment of ordinary collective bargaining processes.

As this happens, the influence of the State upon pay levels is likely to increase by way of incomes policies, whether imposed or negotiated with organized labour, so that the scope for old-style free collective bargaining may be curtailed, whilst the scope for applying a public policy on minimum terms and conditions of employment for all may be enhanced. Since the 1960s the State has, willy-nilly, taken a much more interventionist line in determining the actual, substantive terms of the individual's contract of employment (see Rideout, 1969, p 7) and the more recent legislative provisions provide no reason to suppose that in the future those who, like the union official and the personnel manager, have in the past sought to determine the actual terms and conditions of employment, will be any more free to determine them than they have become under various incomes policies and statutory controls since 1963. In spite of this, collective bargaining continues, even if constrained, and the activities associated with the process need to be examined.

Collective bargaining tasks
Those who engage in bargaining must perforce engage in certain tasks and those who engage, as representatives, *in collective* bargaining equally have discernible tasks to perform. These tasks may be thought or found to be differently structured and characterized according to which type of bargaining is being engaged in or which combination of value positions is involved. Thus, using the Walton and McKersie taxonomy, it might be predicted that these tasks will vary systematically according to whether the representatives are engaged in distributive, integrative or intra-organizational bargaining or attitudinal structuring; similarly, using the Chamberlain characterization, the tasks could be expected to vary according to the emphasis upon wage bargaining, industrial law-making or management democratization. Although the manner in which these tasks are defined in the particular case may also be influenced by the parameters of the bargaining exercise, and although the

representative's success in carrying out the task may reflect his knowledge, capacity and skill, it ought to be possible to describe the tasks involved in a way which would either allow testing of the hypothesis or reflect recorded experience.

An attempt to identify the tasks involved in the mainstream types of bargaining must be based upon two main pieces of work in this field, those of Walton and McKersie (1965) and Morley and Stephenson (1977). The one uses a method of retroduction and is based largely upon the American experience and the other that of induction founded largely upon experiment and simulation.

The assumption in all this is that collective bargaining can be regarded as a special (and specially structured) case of 'influence' (Cartwright in March, 1965, ch 1). It may therefore be deduced that certain types of task will be common to all bargaining. These tasks are derivable from general statements about the nature of the process of determining objectives, strategies and tactics, in the light of the situation in which the bargaining will take place, and of establishing adequate arrangements for control via feedback or information-gathering mechanisms. Such statements are thus based upon the generalized notion of decision taking as a process which relies upon open or closed-loop procedures (cf Buckley, 1967).

1 Situational evaluation

The first such task means an assessment of both the internal and the external environments of the matter to be resolved in bargaining, part of which entails a definition of 'the matter' to which attention must be addressed.

One part of this process involves a two-level assessment of the position of the 'other' characterized for this purpose as constituting the external position. The first 'level' is the 'immediate' one. Thus a shop steward may raise a matter for consideration jointly, and in so doing may define or describe the 'matter' in question; similarly, a foreman may initiate a discussion with the shop representative about a 'matter' which concerns him in his role and he too will give it some definition. Each receptor is immediately faced with the need to form a view on the nature of the issue or problem thus raised, and this may or may not mean acceptance of the definition presented by the initiator. This will therefore call for processes of comprehension of the message, and evaluation of its importance, leading to a definition of 'the problem' or 'the issue' and ultimately decision as to action required.

All three of these processes will be affected not merely by the 'matter' itself as a separate item conceived in a vacuum but will also be structured by a much wider comprehension, evaluation and

499

experience of action. This is alluded to by Parsons in his assertion that social action "does not consist only of *ad hoc* 'responses' to particular situational 'stimuli' but that the actor develops a system of 'expectations' relative to the various objects of the situation" (Parsons, 1951, p 5). It is consistent with Parsons' further amplification of this point to suggest that a party confronted with a particular stimulus will comprehend, evaluate and decide to act not merely in the light of that stimulus but in the light of experience or knowledge of the other party's objectives, values and likely action around the consideration of the issue. Thus this level of response may be differentiated from the 'immediate' level (cf Coddington, 1968, p 1).

Because these two 'levels' of appreciation interact and are likely to be interdependent, the 'definition' of the issue or problem cannot be considered in relation to the first communication alone. It takes the practical form: "X raised the matter of Y but what is really behind it?" The way in which this question is answered demands the development of an intelligence of the kind that is implicit in the value positions taken up by the sides.

Thus any one stimulus which can be identified may arise in the form of a problem or an issue. This rests on the distinction which Walton and McKersie make and, having made, associate with integrative and distributive bargaining respectively. "The agenda item appropriate for distributive bargaining is an *issue* . . . The fixed sum, variable share pay-off structure is our point of departure for defining an issue. It describes a situation in which there is some fixed value available to the parties, but in which they may influence shares which go to each. As such there is a fundamental and complete conflict of interests" (1965, p 13). The agenda items "appropriately handled by integrative bargaining are *problems* (p 13). . . . Problems are agenda items which contain possibilities for greater or lesser amounts of value which can be made available to the two parties" (1965, p 127). The first estimation required therefore is whether the motive of the raiser of the item is to define an issue or a problem.

In addition, it follows from this that what is behind the creation of the stimulus will tend to reflect the dominant value position of the raiser. To raise a matter as an issue is to imply a particular approach to the relationship, to emphasize the conflict of interests seen as inherent in the relationship, and thus to presume that the action and response will be held in a relationship which will link the parties in the upper half of the chart on p 480 above. To raise a matter as a problem similarly presupposes a particular kind of relationship, to be found in the lower part of the diagram, and emphasizes some possibility of cooperation between the parties.

It then also follows that a first consideration to be given to the stimulus is whether to respond in the 'same vein' as that implied in the raising, or whether to engage in a deliberate process of attitudinal structuring, before or during the course of the negotiations, in order to effect a change of expectations and a different relationship pattern as an intended consequence. This was what happened frequently in the 1960s as managements in particular began to respond to the criticism that they were too often merely reacting to trade union demands and on the trade union's own terms (Anthony and Crichton, 1969, p 107). To the extent that, as Walton and McKersie demonstrate, attitudinal structuring calls for different tasks from other forms of bargaining, the answer to this kind of question will call for more or less of the tasks associated by them with attitudinal structuring.

A second part of this process requires a comparable evaluation of the position of the 'self' (and the self's side, where the self can be regarded as having a representative position). This assessment can be thought of as involving two 'levels' of appreciation which are also inter-dependent. At the level of the self, the individual is faced with the necessity to consider what he is 'prepared' (ie willing and able) to do (ie to believe, to accept, to report, to act upon etc) in all the circumstances of the issue. This response may, as Parsons says in the same context as previously quoted, "be structured only relative to his own-need dispositions and the probabilities of gratification or deprivation contingent on the various alternatives of action which he may undertake" (Parsons, 1951, p 5). It may also respond to the expectations held of the 'other' as we saw above.

It will also tend to respond to the expectations of the reactions and responses of those others who constitute the self's-side, when the individual finds or feels himself to be in a representative position of some kind (which is normal for any and all who get involved in bargaining processes whether at a formal or informal level). The individual will therefore additionally tend to make his assessment of what he is prepared to do, in the light of his expectations of the consequences for him of his own side's reactions and responses. For him, this relates to the external environment, but to the extent that he is representative, it must be considered as a part of his 'internal environment' of assessment and response. This places the individual in the position of the 'involved' person in Donne's famous and much quoted passage (from his *Devotions* (1724), 17) but it is possible, as indeed is done by Coddington (1968, p 15) to represent this individual as if he were a non-involved entity treating the external environment as composed of *all* others regardless of the 'side' to which they belong.

The definition by the individual of what Barnard has called the 'occasion for decision' can thus be expected to respond to both of these kinds of perception of the internal situation. It takes the typical form: "What would I do in this case, *and* what would I be permitted to do (or 'get away with')?"

The objective sought and served by this part of the task is thus two-fold: On the one hand, it serves to define the nature of the 'problem' which the self may be called upon to resolve and, on the other, it serves to indicate the directions in which that self will have to look in order to find solutions to it, acceptable to both the self and those others in the situation whom he must treat as concerned referents. If the task were to be carried out systematically and in detail it would result in a schedule defining the 'problem' at different but interrelated levels of abstraction and it would yield a statement of the parameters to or constraints upon the possible lines of resolution.

In so far as the perception of the self and the expectations of others are different, there is scope for the initiation of intra-organizational bargaining. This depends upon taking a particular view of the representative role. It may be seen as that of a 'servant' of the side to which it relates, or it may be seen as that of a 'leader' of the side. In the one case, the assessment of the expectations held by the principals will lead to a conclusion on the expected action of the representative, in the determination of which he has little autonomy. In the other, the assessment may lead to a conclusion that, in all the circumstances, these expectations held by the principals are wrong or incorrect, and need to be changed by an exercise of influence initiated by the representatives. Thus whichever role conception is held there might or might not be scope for engagement in a deliberate exercise in what Walton and McKersie call intra-organizational bargaining.

Where the conception of the role does permit this, the assessment of the internal environment of the side may point the direction of action in intra-organizational bargaining required, in addition to any other considerations of objectives which may be sparked by it. Whether that bargaining is undertaken before or during the course of the development of a response to the stimulus in interaction with the other side is a matter of judgement and opportunity; but this part of the prior assessment process does throw up indications of the directions of this kind of action as may be required. The question is important for the company side in circumstances where specialist negotiators are engaged in preference to having such negotiations conducted by the top management; it has significance of a particular stamp for the trade union side in circumstances where full-time officials may be brought into negotiations.

2 Objective setting
The second task is directed towards the establishment of objectives in

bargaining: given the stimulus and the need to make some response, what ought to be the outcome of that response? In any bargaining situation, this 'outcome' is never likely to be singular; even a simple response like a pay increase is likely to have implications for other features of the relationship. Objectives are therefore likely to be cast in terms of achieving 'this settlement' plus a degree of maintenance of the relationship or a degree of attitudinal structuring. This aspect might therefore be extended to embrace not merely a simple, possibly quantifiable objective responding to the immediate level of definition of the issue, but also a bargaining character objective, in which a deliberate decision is made as to what kind of bargaining exercise will be sought or engaged in in order to resolve the issue as presented. For example, using the Walton and McKersie categories in an over simple fashion, one might think of the situation in which management decided to respond to a simple wage claim (conceived in distributive bargaining terms by the 'other') with an attempt at integrative bargaining (as indeed was often done in the productivity bargaining era of the late 1960s). (cf Oldfield, 1966).

Much has been written about objectives in bargaining, usually at a relatively high level of abstraction and in respect of distributive bargaining. (Dunlop, 1944 and 1966; Ross, 1948; Fisher, 1971; Flanders, 1969). For present purposes, we are interested less in objectives in this sense than in the process of objective-setting within the framework of any particular negotiation, and much less has been written about this (see Anthony, 1977). The first question to be dealt with, given some external stimulus, is what kind of bargaining character response is to be made to it. Here it is worthwhile considering the Walton and McKersie distinction between issues and problems as a first step. If it is chosen to treat the matter as an issue, when it is raised, it will follow that the bargaining exercise will be characterized in win-lose terms, and each side will therefore be concerned to keep its own end up and, eventually, win or secure enough to prevent loss of face. If it is chosen to regard any matter raised as a problem, there will be a presumption that the exercise will be one of problemsolving, jointly and that both parties will 'win' only if they can, together, reach a satisfactory resolution of the matter so presented, but will both 'lose' if this outcome proves to be impossible. A decision is thus required on whether the stimulus is to be taken as a cue for issue resolution or problem solving for distributive or integrative bargaining attempts.

In a related fashion, decisions are called for on the dimension of what effect is to be aimed for, either in respect of the relationship pattern between the parties itself (the attitudinal structuring process) or in relation to the solidarity of one's own side (the intra-organizational

503

bargaining process). Whatever the decision about how to treat the stimulus, these considerations of pattern maintenance must enter into the calculations about what to go for and how to go for it. Whether these considerations are treated as 'objectives' or as constraints upon objectives or the means to their attainment, they enter into the process of 'objective setting'.

It is not unusual to suggest, on the subject of distributive bargaining, that both parties do have objectives which have been set in advance. These are commonly regarded as having a target and a resistance point, and possibly a fall-back position. As Walton and McKersie argue, "negotiations involve a series of decisions interspersed with performance activities" and the negotiator needs something to aim at (a target) which is not a once-and-for-all or 'optimum bid' on which all negotiations would then turn, and a notion of a point below or above which it would prove preferable to lock-out or strike rather than settle. In distributive bargaining these will tend not to be disclosed, until in the judgement of the negotiator their disclosure would help his case, and therefore opening bids will tend to differ from either of these, allowing the negotiator to fall back to another position as his judgement suggests this might be appropriate to the case he is hoping to win. In Walton and McKersie's model, the target and resistance points which indicate complete or minimum success for the two parties, set limit to a range of 'settlements', which may be either positive (where those of the two parties overlap) or negative (where they fall outside each other's range) (Walton and McKersie, 1965, pp 41–45).

In Anthony and Crichton's (1969) discussion of distributive bargaining they include determination of objectives as part of the "preparation for bargaining (including the determination of negotiating objectives and the assembly of the agenda)" (p 106). But they go on to suggest that, although British industrial relations has been criticized because management allows the unions to take the initiative in establishing objectives, the same complaint is often heard from the union side that "the unions are entirely controlled by the strategies and initiatives of management" (p 107). They also contend that objective setting is probably carried out by the 'professional negotiators'—those who actually meet each other across the bargaining table—rather than by the 'sides' as entities (p 107). This is seen as happening in a non-conspiratorial fashion but nevertheless as responding to the professional role-self needs of the negotiators. The reluctance of management to specify its objectives ("targets and resistance points") on which these authors comment may then respond to this semi-covert process of fixing them and be aimed to avoid one's own side realizing just what they are as much as to prevent the other side from learning of them too quickly or clearly (*ibid*, p 108).

The serial process of objective setting on distributive bargaining is well authenticated in the literature. Objective setting on other types of bargaining is less well understood. There is some tendency to assume that integrative bargaining for example is simply concerned with problem-solving, and it is enough to say that the solution of the problem is a sufficient statement of the objective. The examples of objectives which might lend themselves to this kind of bargaining quoted by Walton and McKersie and others are job and union security, institutional security, including the control of various types of withdrawal behaviour (whether in the form of wild-cat strikes or absenteeism and labour turnover), payment structures, and health and safety measures, (cf Walton and McKersie, 1965, pp 127–37; Gouldner, 1955, pp 157–228). However, in a bargaining context, it has to be remembered that an objective of both parties must be to increase the size of the cake (whether that cake be an economic, a political or a social one, or any other variety). Thus ". . . the parties are exploring a problem in which it is *inherent* that some (low) amount of sacrifice by one will be associated with (considerable) gain on the part of the other . . . and there will be evident tendencies to disagree about problem definition, criteria for settlement, the alternatives to be considered, and the information to be divulged. There may well be differences in motivation to engage in integrative bargaining". (Walton and McKersie, 1965, p 140). Such differences may be what qualifies this as 'bargaining', but the fact of their existence does indicate that different objectives may be recognized in it, and that therefore decisions on objectives are as relevant here as in distributive bargaining.

The objectives in attitudinal structuring are open and articulated but are expressed in general terms. This may be because "the relationships and the attitudes which define them have implications for the parties and their joint dealings" no matter whether these joint dealings are cast as distributive or integrative (Walton and McKersie, 1965, p 190). Therefore "a party's preference for a particular relationship pattern may become an important objective of that party. Some . . . relationship patterns, such as accommodation, will presumably seem more appropriate as a goal than others, such as conflict, but sometimes a party will prefer a more conflictual pattern, perhaps for purposes of preserving internal cohesion" (*ibid*, p 190).

The objectives in intra-organizational bargaining may for similar reasons be summarized equally briefly: the objective is always to effect solidarity, consensus or the end to role-conflict arising out of different perceptions and/or expectations of the principals and their representatives. The targets are generalized—the bringing of "the expectations of his constituent group into alignment with his own" either "before the fact of settlement or afterward, or if perceived achievement is brought into alignment with expectations" (Walton and McKersie, 1965, p 303).

3 Deciding upon strategy

The development of strategies for the attainment of these objectives—the third stage in the process of preparation for collective bargaining—is also likely to produce discrete alternatives according to the objective chosen for attainment and the vehicle determined upon for this purpose. The resolution of a relative-shares issue by means of distributive bargaining will tend to call forth one range of strategies with subsidiaries linked to attitudinal structuring and intra-organizational bargaining; and the solving of a quantity-available problem via integrative bargaining will most likely call for very different strategies, albeit with its own distinct subsidiaries for attitudinal structuring and intra-organizational bargaining. In this area, a number of very different approaches have been developed to characterize the strategies possible, and these draw their philosophies and justifications from very different conceptions of competitive and co-operative interaction.

Thus distinct sets of theories attempt to explain and predict what forces are most influential upon the outcomes of bargaining, and these include the 'purely economic' theories such as that of Dunlop (1944) and the 'augmented economic' theories such as that of Levinson (1966), together with the psychiatric theories such as that of Douglas (1962). Other theories restrict themselves more to explaining what happens in the process, such as those based on game theories (Pen, 1952) or on problem-solving theories (Deutsch, 1973) or on straightforward social psychological theories (Cooper, 1975). Other researches are directed more to the determination of what skills appear to be influential in bargaining, and these tend to be based on simulation exercises (Morley and Stephenson, 1977). Generally speaking, although these may all prove relevant to the process, they do not complement one another since the questions asked by the students themselves are usually very different ones. But importantly each of these distinct sets of theories serves to throw up ideas as to strategies and tactics, which may be adopted in bargaining.

For reasons which are perhaps obvious (eg it relates to "the basic rationale for conducting labour negotiations" (Walton and McKersie, 1965, p 126)) distributive bargaining has attracted the greatest attention from the point of view of determining strategies (see Anthony, 1977, p 229 *et seq*). Building on the theories of the

506

economists, the institutionalists and the game theory exponents, Atkinson (1975) has distinguished "four broad categories of strategies which are most likely to be common to the majority of situations discussed" together with two others relating to the agenda and the bargaining situation itself. The basic four he identifies as strategies of

(a) the opening moves
(b) the zero movement position
(c) the sanction
(d) increasing bargaining power (Atkinson, 1975, pp 46–69).

The first of these rests upon the convention that the original demand and offer positions will be abandoned during the course of a negotiation, so that it becomes important initially to establish starting positions which can be departed from with least cost. Once the demand and offer are put into play, however, the basic shape of the negotiation becomes determinable; for example, whether the side making the demand seeks a high or a low settlement or a confrontation of some sort for other reasons. Where important matters of principle may be seen to be at stake, the opening move may be one which allows little subsequent movement, so that the plan may have to allow for the attracting of other demands or offers in order to give some opportunity for movement, and thus for working towards a settlement without compromise to the principle. Alternatively, it may be possible to change the relative bargaining power by delaying the negotiations (or speeding them up) or by bringing in other issues which have importance for the other side, but which give added power to one's own side or detract from that of the other's side. The question of whether sanctions will be threatened or used in the negotiation is also one which can be considered in advance, and particularly once the opening moves have been made known.

All such plans for developing the negotiation will inevitably be affected by two other aspects: first, the strength or weakness of the case itself, in the determination of which relative rather than absolute considerations are likely to prove important; secondly, the situation in which the negotiations occur, the crucial factors in this being the kind of relationship which the other party has come to expect of the first side. In the first of these, what is likely to be significant in influencing the ease of difficulty of the negotiation is the extent to which the other perceives the first side to be acting in conformity with common, normal or good practice— on both the offer or the demand and the manner of making, defending and modifying it. In the second, the history of the relationship as it has developed is likely to prove one indicator of the likely course of action, but a change of personalities (on either side) can upset this and lead to 'sudden' changes in the manner of address between the sides.

It would therefore tend to follow that, in preparing plans for negotiation, each side will have to consider in the circumstances of the matter arising what the relationship is likely to bear in the way of both conflict and agreement (or cooperation), what immediate and longer-term sub-goals are feasible and sensible, according to the strength of the respective cases, and in what sequence the moves will be made in response to the other side.

This strategic planning is likely to be guided by two con- siderations, however. There is the fact of possible gain or loss in a zero sum game to be considered: the employer might concede too much in the way of a wage increase if he does not plan ahead of the negotiation. There is also the equally important fact that whatever the outcome in these terms, the negotiation might disrupt the existing 'balance of power' between the parties in a way which will disrupt the relations, not only in the industrial relations system but also in the production system. (This kind of disruption is certainly not confined to the outbreak of industrial action, and indeed could arise without any such action occurring.) The likelihood of these *two* factors play- ing their part in determination of strategies is attested in the analyses of Walton and McKersie (1965) and Anthony (1977, ch 9), both of whom draw attention to the 'power' issue as a separate but equally important consideration in any plan for negotiations.

For this kind of reason, it is not sensible to consider the tactical moves of bargaining simply in terms of 'problem-solving' which can be analysed in terms of some instrument like interaction process analysis (Bales, 1951) and trained for in terms of inter-personal and communications skills. This problem is acknowledged both by those who have sought to apply social psychological methods of analysis to the negotiating situation as, for example, by Morley and Stephenson (1977). They developed the instrument of conference process analy- sis to try to overcome the "difficulty of recording and analysing the interaction between negotiators" (Gottschalk, 1973, p 52), but make modest claims only for it. It remains a major problem in the con- struction of training courses for negotiators on either side that our knowledge of what activities are to be woven into the skein of collec- tive negotiation is still rudimentary, (CIR, Report Nos 33 and 33A, 1973), although the categories used in conference process analysis are useful here. What can be hypothesized, however, is that the inter- personal or communications activities 'obviously visible' in nego- tiations only assume tactical (and therefore purposive) significance in association with the exercise of skilful judgement (a factor to which some reference has already been made in chapter 6). There are numerous references in the literature to the need to guess the other's next move, his resistance point or his fall back position, for example. All these allude in some fashion to the need for developed judgement in addition to a knowledge of 'the game' and its rules. The major problem for training in this area is therefore that associated with the development of judgement: a knowledge of strategic and tactical concepts (as in Atkinson, Walton and McKersie, or Gottschalk) may be necessary to the understanding of the negotiation processes, but it is not by itself likely to develop judgement in those who are caught up in them.

Judgement in negotiations
Judgement in negotiations may be treated as focused upon two quite distinct features of the situation: first, upon the dynamics external to the persons involved; and secondly upon the dynamics internal to them. This dual focus may contribute to the peculiarity of the nego- tiating process and contribute to the difficulties faced by those who seek to analyse it.

The making of judgements about the 'objective facts' of the situ- ation is not a process which distinguishes bargaining from any other kind of decisional activity. The assessment of the 'reality' (as Vickers, 1965, identifies it) is a common enough experience. It demands in this context an understanding of the movements or the trends or the de- velopments in the bargaining field: are differentials between blue- collar and white-collar workers increasing or decreasing, what are the new and fashionable subjects for negotiation, what is the level of settlement being reached or likely to be reached in this industry, what is happening to labour cost as a result? All such questions may be partly answered by information, but they require some assessment of the meaning of the facts for full answer. The assessment of what might be done in a given bargaining situation (the exercise of 'action' judgement) also calls for facts and evaluations: what objec- tives and strategies might be pursued in this context? The choice of a preferred alternative is then a matter of comparing each such an- swer against the appropriate scales of value.

The making of judgements about the human dynamics of the bargaining situation itself and of the constituencies behind it is an equally important and necessary part of bargaining. The reality is represented by the aims and strategies adopted or likely to be adopted, both by the representative and by his constituency, and there is no reason to suppose that these two must always be in accord. The questions of what the negotiators are really up to or what the men really want are frequently on the lips of managerial negotiators, because the discovery of answers to these questions about the negotiating reality is important to their approach. Since in the nature of the bargaining 'game' information is a resource to be manipulated, answers are not to be found simply in such data, but are to be inferred (judged) from impressions and understandings. The question of what action is to be taken in this inadequately revealed reality is then the more difficult to answer and the onus is more fully placed upon judgement. Choosing a best or optimum course of action must then become almost exclusively a matter of 'sheer' judgement.

Both processes are then complicated by the distinct probability that the scales of preferences or values adopted by the confronting parties will be very different from one another. This is almost a part of the definition of the collective bargaining process. Consequently, the understanding of the other side's objectives and conduct in the negotiation requires a suspension of one's own values and the assumption of his, whilst the determination of one's own objectives and strategies calls for a firm grasp and application of one's own values and the dismissal of his as being inappropriate or irrelevant. This kind of dilemma for the bargainers (regardless of which side he may be on) is indicated, although not perhaps fully described, in the use of such terms as bluff and double-bluff, threat and counter-threat etc. It is sometimes difficult in all this to appreciate what is true or correct and what is untrue and incorrect, and sorting out the two is one of the major skills which negotiators must develop. To this extent, therefore, negotiation calls for skills over and above 'mere' communications skills, and for an understanding of values and judgement criteria which belong to the production system as well as those of the negotiating or industrial relations system itself.

Further reading.
On the constraints upon the negotiating process as these have developed in recent years, see the various Government White Papers on the Social Contract and Incomes Policy; Glyn and Sutcliffe (1972); Balfour (1972)

On the processes of negotiation, see Anthony (1977); Walton and McKersie (1965); Morley and Stephenson (1977); and Atkinson (1975)

On aspects of training for negotiation, see Commission on Industrial Relations Reports Nos 33 and 33A (1972/3); National Economic Development Office (1973); Kettle (in Torrington, 1972); Kniveton (1974); and Sisson (1977).

13 Future conditional

A number of writers on the subject of personnel management have predicted a future for the occupation which emphasizes growth in numbers and significance, and an end to the trash-can/maid-of-all-work image. This is discernible in the assessment by Heller (see McFarland, 1971, pp 30–43) although the main burden of the argument is that such a future depends upon a greater use of theoretical knowledge and the assertion of greater independence of the professional group. It is more clearly spelled out by Fischer (*ibid* pp 21–29) in his four predictive propositions:

The personnel function will assume a more important role in the management of the business

The personnel function will become more creative, less mechanistic

The personnel function will be responsible for furthering the organization, not just maintaining it

Top management will become more directly involved in the deployment and development of human resources.

Although these propositions emerge mainly from American experience, where the history of the function is different, they have been accepted as having comparable relevance to Britain.

This came about because the occupation seemed to take off in the 1950s and 1960s. It freed itself from its case-work and paternalistic-welfare connotations, and became acceptable to enterprises as a part of the specialist management competence in *man*-management (as distinct from technical and product management). This seemed to suggest that what personnel managers were engaged to do was something that society wanted doing. The numbers involved were large enough to produce a strong occupational association, which came to give advice to society and to government on how the function should be developed. The coincidental growth in the output of the social sciences served to provide a more solid theoretical foundation for much of the personnel specialist's activities, and formal training increasingly embraced this kind of knowledge. Apparently assured of an economic future because of the demand for specialists, the occupation seemed to be poised to secure a charter from society as a profession—if only it could overcome the long-standing problem of securing independence (cf Kenny, 1976).

For those who would seek assurance about the future, therefore, there is much that would seem to supply it, although awkward questions do raise their heads from time to time.

The changes effected by public policy and legislation in the 1970s have, at one and the same time, increased the demand for people with this kind of competence, and have so altered the structure of power and authority associated with the role that further adjustments and accommodations appear to be called for. The occupational group itself and the enterprises which sustain it are therefore called upon to review once again the nature and future shape of the role of the personnel specialist.

The predictive statements which have been quoted above rest upon certain limited demographic and technological forecasts: the decline in the proportion of the producers in future society and the emergence of a new relationship between man and machine (usually subsumed in discussions of automation). But there are a number of other forecasts which can be made about work in the developing society, and it is upon these that a prediction of what will happen to the personnel function must rest. These merely provide the constraints upon the choices open to personnel specialists and their employers as to the kind of policies and practices which will be relevant to the emergent structure of work contributions and rewards. It is, however, worth outlining the future which can be reasonably foreseen, in order to provide some kind of foundation for discussion of the future shape of the personnel function.

1 What forecasts might be made?

What can be predicted as the future role of the personnel specialist depends primarily upon the view one takes of the situation in which it will be discharged. That situation will be composited of perspectives of the future performance and shape of the economy, of the directions of change in cultural value and their consequences for the institutions of British society, and of the attitudes which people develop in all these evolving circumstances. Nevertheless, some forecasts are likely to have a keener and more direct consequence for the personnel specialist role.

It might, for example, be predicted that the British economy must take some note of the changed terms of trade and of the loss of Commonwealth trading relationships, and that this adjustment will

be so influenced by changing demographic structure as to make productivity increases more necessary than may have been the case in the
past. Such a prediction would then offer a major constraint to
decisions about living standards and welfare benefits which the society and its constituent elements (such as firms or public service enterprises) might aim to provide. Nevertheless, changes in this area
are likely to affect the future role of the personnel specialist generally
rather than specifically.

It might similarly be predicted that the British society will
change the conditions under which it seeks to solve the economic
problem. After a short post-war honeymoon with a mixed economy
and a welfare state, we may be moving into a new situation in which
the private or individualistic element of the mixture is further diminished and the social or consensual element correspondingly increased. This might imply a development of corporatism (developing
the Galbraith/Winkler theses) or it might suggest little more than an
extension of the new cultural imperative that trade unions be more
fully integrated into the decision-structure, which will itself increasingly emphasize team-decisions and consultation (following the
Bains/Ogden/Brunel University propositions for public service
management). Whatever the particular outcome of these trends in
modern society, their general consequence will be such as to affect
directly the condition in which a personnel role will be carried out.

It might also be argued about this changing future that low
profitability, low investment and low confidence on the part of both
investors and workers, yield an unsatisfactory situation in which to
experiment with changes in institutions of the society: that, in a
word, we cannot afford participative management at the present
juncture. This argument cannot be ignored or completely discounted, because it is likely to affect human predispositions to accept or
reject the existing pattern or the future projection: unless people can
see some positive relationship between change and their own well-
being (whether they be investors or workers) they may well opt for
the *status quo* but, unless the current arrangements are seen to hold
sufficient promise of improvement in well-being, people may well
opt for change. How attitudes will develop on this dimension is extremely difficult to forecast: recent history seems to suggest a willingness to support the change-agents in many areas of life, and this may
provide a foundation for simple extrapolation. On the other hand, it
can be suggested that much more dialogue must take place on how
much of the idealism can be reduced to realism in terms of popular
support for radical programmes, and that therefore simple extrapolation is not a sensible ploy to adopt. Nevertheless, formation of a
view or a guess as to the way in which attitudes are likely to move is

513

material to any comment on what the personnel specialist will be called upon to do in the future.

Certain extrapolations can however be made with some confidence. Certain changes are discernible in social and cultural values which have already revealed an influence upon patterns of behaviour in society, and which are likely to continue without reversal even if at different rates:

(a) The output of the educational system will in future place greater emphasis upon the free abilities—to think, to create, to argue—than upon the rather mechanical abilities often spoken of as the three Rs, because of the approaches to the creation of learning opportunities in the educational institutions as much as because of the actual subjects taught: mechanical ability in reading, writing and arithmetic may well continue to fall away, but the capability to exploit the novel and the untried and traditional is likely to be much more in evidence amongst new workers

(b) The authority of the individual (whether in the form of a capitalist or of a manager or indeed of an influential leader of men) is likely to be undermined increasingly, and to produce the predictable consequence that those with responsibility will seek security in association with others in reaching decisions, or in consensus management

(c) The condition of dependency—of workers, or the poor or any other category—is likely to be further relieved both by transfer payments outside the strict employment context and by the donation of rights both outside and inside work, so that individuals will be better able to take an independent line than in the past

(d) The greater emphasis upon a kind of equality or fairness in social relationships is likely to support demands for a more formal and less personalized approach to their development; more concretely, relationships will be progressively subject to a kind of audit, which will emphasize the formally impersonalistic conception of the ideal type bureaucracy, and this will spawn a demand for more recording of inter-personal events occurring during the working period.

Some of these developments have almost direct counterparts in the predictable developments within the work context itself and related to the context in which work is to be carried out in the future. Thus the organizational context provided by the employer (eg (a) below) or by the workers (eg (b) below) at once reflects both cause and effect of change in cultural values; comparably, changes in societal norms of treatment of people ((c) below) or of distribution of rewards ((d) below) respond more directly to changed values in society generally but find their application more particularly in the industrial context:

(a) The scale of enterprise is unlikely to reduce, the tendencies towards oligopoly in private industry and commercial operations and towards larger scale public service organization, both supported by central government, being unlikely to reverse

(b) The extent to which society will rely upon organization of major categories of citizens (as in trade unions) to contribute to policy *and* to monitor its implementation is likely to increase dramatically and particularly for white collar employees, although this change is likely to exact its toll in the form of cooperation and conformity

(c) The imposition of minimum conditions of treatment of employees by legislation is likely to increase in volume, even if only marginally in the next few years, since no government is now likely to unravel the structure of welfare rights already in existence

(d) The material incentives available for managers and other supporting white-collar staff are likely to continue to decrease in comparison with those available to blue-collar workers, because the benefit-distribution system will itself continue to change in a direction which emphasizes the diminution of the significance of the wage system as the sole method of distributing title to material possessions amongst workers.

These predictive statements alone (and there are others which might be included) impute certain inevitable influences upon the personnel function.

Those changes which have already occurred in public policy require executive *action* to be taken. This might respond directly to the legislative prescriptions or it might be refined and extended through developed policies which seek to encompass them in a more forward reaching fashion.

Those changes which have occurred, or which will probably occur as a consequence of changing attitudes towards dependency and authority and towards distribution of rewards in society, will require some reformation of methods and techniques of assuring the appropriate levels of contribution. In this case there can be little question of a purely mechanistic reaction to requirements of the culture and a degree of creativity will be necessary to get the measures right.

The changes in the formal organizational or power structure will in turn call for a much more fundamental re-thinking of the nature of the decision process as it relates to man-management in modern large scale enterprises and as it responds to the organization of the members of the enterprise under the benevolent eye of the government. In this case it will be difficult to escape the need for developing new and more radical policies touching on the nature of the enterprise and the licence it enjoys to operate and make use of labour.

Indications of the likely changes in the role of the personnel manager, which may follow from these predictions, may thus be given under three headings which indicate three distinct levels of decision taking within organizations.

First, at the lowest or executive level, the future is likely to lie with the implementation of those policies and prescriptions as to rights and duties which are contained in both legislation and collective agreements. These can be set together, first because what has entered into social policy via legislation in recent years frequently (but not always—see the Health and Safety at Work etc Act) generalizes the best practice which has emerged from joint decision and which has formed the substance of collective agreements and, secondly, because legislation has also recently increased the legal standing of collective agreements as influencers of the individual contract of employment (although they still remain unenforceable in themselves).

Both therefore give rights to the individual employee, and impose duties which the employer must discharge, on pain of judicial sanction or industrial action by organized labour, or possibly both. Just as the shop stewards and other union officers can and do police this system in the interest of members whom they may advise and help, so too can and do the personnel officers advise and help the employer to discharge the duties imposed. This is not a matter which can be fully dealt with by personnel specialists, since anyone acting in the name of the enterprise in such a way as to manage labour must cooperate in the discharge of these duties. For this reason, therefore, the personnel specialist must also police the execution of policies of this sort.

The main point about this kind of activity is that it responds to a given set of policies, and in this sense involves executive action. The personnel specialist will therefore most probably function as

(a) a repository of knowledge as to the rules which must apply
(b) adviser or trainer of line management in the application of these rules
(c) monitor of the actual application of the rules, which must in turn emphasize careful record keeping.

At this level the personnel department of the future will be concerned, *inter alia*, with the constant up-dating of information, with its effective dissemination to other members of the organization and with continuous check on its implementation (see above chapter 1).

Secondly, at the intermediate or administrative level, the future is likely to call for the development of more sophisticated (or perhaps even just more complex) methods and techniques for ensuring the continued cooperation of the total workforce in the realization of the objectives of both the enterprise and its sectional members. It is possible to argue that the objectives of the enterprise ought to embrace both the economic goals of production and the goals of those brought into association with it, but the distinction is worth maintaining if only to signal that in future more attention may have to be given to the latter than has usually been true in the past. The conditions under which commitment to any of these objectives is to be secured are likely to be different in the future, and to that extent new methods and techniques for securing it may well be called for—from the personnel specialist.

Here, the personnel function will increasingly be called upon to create (or help in creating) new methods and techniques of handling three types of problem. First, the securing of abilities required, at all levels and in all functions. (This will focus upon the development of adequate stocks and flows of manpower through such recognizable processes as recruitment, development, and de-selection and discharge, all of which are now more narrowly constrained by cost-bearing limitations upon discretion than was true in the past.)

Secondly, the securing of the understanding or comprehension required to permit people to form adequate perspectives of their working environment. (This will demand attention to channels and methods of communication within the organization. Some new legislative requirements touch on the surface of this problem, but the main problem of effective communication is not tackled by 'idiots' guides' to the accounts or statements of contract particulars, and requires more detailed action of the type being developed in such organizations as BP Plastics, Smiths Industries or Reed Corrugated Cases.)

Thirdly, the development of commitment to the common tasks of the enterprise—usually discussed in terms of motivation in the management literature. (This will probably require the evolution of new conceptions of reward from work which, whilst they can scarcely seek to diminish the significance of material rewards in hard cash, will nevertheless seek to extend the notion of consideration in the formal contract in return for an extension of contribution as required in that contract: this will bring together what currently goes under the headings of pay and fringe benefits, and benefits which are currently thought of under the heading of psychological income

517

from work—including growth and development, training, job enrichment and the rest.)

It is mainly at this level of decision taking that the personnel specialist will be expected to base his contribution upon adequate theories. Theories in this context must be defined in similar terms to those used by Stinchcombe, to mean propositions which so explain a relationship between two variables as to permit the prediction of how the dependent variable will alter if and when a given change is made in the independent variable. These theories are the stock-in-trade of the manager, whether he recognizes this or not. For example, a statement that an increase in effort or contribution will follow from an increase in the pay offered, or a statement that the provision by a company of a sports and social club will increase the likelihood of employees staying in the employment of the firm, are essentially statements of a relationship between two variables which are used to make predictions and as a foundation for decisions.

There is some evidence to suggest that:

(a) personnel specialists require *more* and more sophisticated theories to sustain them in their emergent roles in administrative decision-taking. (These may be identified as theories about individual behaviour in groups or organizations) and

(b) personnel specialists need theories about different variables from those which have traditionally concerned them. (In particular, theories about clients-as-individuals now require extension into theories about the action or behaviour of human aggregates such as organizations, associations or power-groups) (cf Fox, 1971).

In one sense these differently focused theories come together in role theory, in which theories about the person meet those about the individual-in-organization but the separate sets of theory are necessary supports to comprehension of the synthesis. The concern with people and the concern with work organization, which we noted as part of the definition of the personnel function in the Introduction, might be replaced by a concern with roles, but understanding of persons and organizations is a pre-requisite of understanding roles (cf McKinlay, 1975).

Two further points might be made on this aspect of the personnel specialist's requirement in the future. First, the theories most appropriate to the function are so-called 'applied theories' (but cf Goldsmith and MacKay, 1966); the universalistic conception of human behaviour and relationships must be given a situational relevance, for example.

Secondly, the theories themselves are of little value or use to the specialist unless he also has sufficient facility in applying them, both at the individual level (the so-called social skills) and at the aggregate level (the so-called skills in numeracy).

At this level, therefore, the personnel department will be expected to be creative of new methods, approaches and techniques which, whilst they will be applied to the aggregate of the workforce, will nevertheless focus upon the individual member of it. New methods etc will require legitimation as policies, but their efficacy will remain assessable at the level of the individual, and for that reason a knowledge of the individual (and of individual differences) will be a prerequisite.

Thirdly, at the highest or corporate level, the future will tend to emphasize the need for a more fundamental re-thinking of what enterprise is all about. This debate has already begun, most commonly under the twin titles of the social responsibilities of industry and employee participation, but it has not yet either reached a realistic conclusion or even got its basic concepts sorted out (eg what is really the place and nature of profit in a large multi-plant or multi-national firm). There are, of course, positions to be defended and attitudes to be preserved, and the attempt to re-think is therefore likely to be long and hard. Nevertheless, a definition of the economic objectives of enterprise relevant to modern circumstances is clearly needed; without it the first and second levels of activity discussed above are likely to remain rudderless. This issue is much bigger than that which concerns the personnel specialist function alone, but it is one whose solution is a prerequisite for satisfactory personnel policy formation.

Importantly here, the responsibility of the personnel manager for the low productivity of British industry may be questioned. On the face of it, productivity is something which is achieved through the line management, not *by* the personnel specialist. The personnel manager may in the past have been seen to split the role of the foreman, into a generalist component left with the foreman and a specialist element which the personnel manager took to himself, but in so doing the latter did not remove the responsibility for getting the production out. Similarly, if the personnel specialist is to play a role at a more senior management level in developing policies, he may choose to see himself as taking the specialist advisory stance and as leaving the general line management with the responsibility for achieving objectives.

Comforting though such conceptions may be, they probably do nothing but decrease the likelihood that the personnel manager will ever play any very effective role at the corporate level. The Fawley productivity agreements, or the Devlin proposals for the modernization of the ports, or the more recent development of planning agreements in the motor car industry, all provide examples of situations in which somebody (whether personnel specialist or not, in the event) had to look again at the objectives of the enterprise, *and* to do so in terms of forecasts of likely productivity under varying conditions—eg doing nothing, investing capital in a particular direction, changing manning ratios etc. The 'hard' objectives of an enterprise may not be the prime concern of the personnel manager as such, but clearly corporate planning decisions depend upon the predictable labour response to varying conditions of change, and the personnel manager could be expected to assist with that kind of question. Since the stakes may be extremely high, and the runners are often ones with which the personnel manager is assumed to be familiar, the justification for his contribution seems established (see for example Killingsworth, 1962).

What more directly concerns the personnel function at this level involves him in personnel policy formation in terms of aggregates rather than individual cases. Such policies are required in two broad areas. First there is the reward-contribution area as a whole, which means in effect treating all types of reward and contribution together at a policy level. For example, a simple concern with pay structure, in which the basic criteria of evaluation are related to competitive or market rates for any given class of labour, is likely to be replaced, first with a concern for compensation programmes which are judged by the performance they elicit and, secondly, with a conception of reward for labour in conjunction with rewards to all other factors and contributors—something which, incidentally becomes more feasible with open disclosure of information to employees. In effect, this implies that the notion of profit as a residual benefit which 'automatically' accrues to shareholders of private industry as its prime beneficiaries, is one which has no useful place in compensation planning in a modern large-scale company where the contributions of capital from institutions are responsive to near-contractual arrangements for the treatment of dividends. It is unlikely that we shall have an adequate foundation for an acceptable policy on rewards for contributions to efficiency, if we continue to believe that big industry's profits go mainly to individual shareholders (cf Diamond Report, 1975) or that more efficiency must mean more profit to the capitalist, to that extent there is hardly likely to be a foundation for a satisfactory and acceptable policy governing rewards for greater contributions to efficiency.

Secondly there is the area which is essentially concerned with the determination and allocation of authority or discretion: this means essentially the development of some kind of concordat between the various interest groups in enterprise—workers, managers, shareholders, customers. Here too there have been major shifts in the situation to which the policies must relate. Some have been brought about through legislation on trade union recognition and bargaining structures and processes, and will be further developed in legislation on participation. Some have been brought about as a consequence of the greater involvement of governments in managing economies characterized by oligopolistic structures in major industries and by highly structured international competition—reflected in planning agreements and incomes policies. Some are brought about by simple—if still highly significant—changes in cultural values relating to work and by the greater capacity of society to articulate problems of power in modern society in the language of the social scientists. In effect, therefore, there have been sufficient significant changes in the circumstances of enterprise decision taking to make it extremely likely that new institutional forms to contain such decision taking will be required.

It can be reasonably foreseen that:

(a) disclosure of information must develop beyond its present superficial requirement, and
(b) new structures (whether in the form of structures to contain an extension of collective bargaining or those implicit in the notion of a participation agreement) will emerge over the next few years to embrace corporate decision taking.

It will not therefore require the exhortations of the Donovan Commission, the Industrial Relations Act or the Code of Industrial Relations Practice to make industrial relations a boardroom responsibility. In the emergent ball-game, the new rules dictate the need for new corporate policies on what might be termed the cost-benefit rules of the enterprise and on the kind of representational structure which will, in Brown's early phrase, sanction managerial authority (Brown, 1951). More to the point, in the present context, both these aspects will be ones on which the personnel specialist will be required to give advice and help, because they are both traditionally in his court—even if, as Fischer argues, he has in the past been more concerned with them as activities and must now become involved with them as policies (Fischer, 1964, quoted in McFarland, 1971).

Nevertheless it remains possible, as this discussion suggests, that the future personnel manager will still be concerned with activities—at the welfare rights, individual case level in the organisation. He will also continue in the role of developer of methods and techniques for various purposes—although, to use Fischer's commentary again, it is to be hoped that this aspect of the role becomes more animated by theory and conceptual understanding and less a response to the fashionable (*ibid*). The major change, although one which is already foreshadowed, will be that which places the personnel function more firmly and requisitely within the corporate planning team as contributor to policies on communication, involvement and commitment, and on structures designed to secure sanction of managerial authority.

The composition of the task

To distinguish the nature of the personnel function of the future in terms of different levels of decision taking does not by itself change the distribution of tasks within that function. A greater involvement in the making of policy on the treatment of personnel may give the personnel function standing within the management but it does nothing necessarily to produce an integrity at the level of the activities carried on under the umbrella title of the personnel department: the trash-can might be as much in evidence as ever it was, at least from the point of view of the diversity of task elements subsumed.

A first set of related tasks is concerned with manning. In this area, the concern is with securing involvement and commitment of people. It is expressed through a sequence of separately identifiable tasks, from recruitment through selection and placement, training and development, performance and personnel appraisal to termination, all of which can be swept together under the general heading of manning—or a concern to ensure that the enterprise has enough people of the right capability both now and in the foreseeable future to ensure that it will survive. The related questions of determining what work is required (a role often shared with the management services departments in large organizations), and of determining the level of reward necessary to ensure that the main manning objectives may be realized, are associated with this task sequence.

A second set of related tasks is concerned with mutual influence. In this area, the concern is to ensure that people know and accept what is expected of them at work. This is usually expressed in terms of induction, training, communications, counselling and the securing of commitment to the ends of the enterprise, where the emphasis is, in other words, upon getting across the organization's message to the workforce. This is never a completely one way flow of intended influence and, even if joint consultation may often be seen in this same framework, there is an increasing recognition of the need for organizations to secure two way communication, and for management to expose itself to possible influence from the other direction. The evolving relationships between enterprise managements and trade unions represent one part of this increasing acceptance of the need for organizations to equip themselves with

522

appropriate receptors and it tends to fall to the lot of the personnel function to carry out this role.

Both of these sets of tasks involve the personnel specialist in intervention in the on-going organizational process. On the one hand, he deals with the organization's need to make continual adjustments to its demography; and on the other, he deals with the enterprise's need to adjust to the conditions of loyalty and commitment presented by its working population. Intervention in the first case takes him into selection, promotion, transfer and deselection activitities, and in the second into informing, consulting and negotiating activities. But in addition to carrying out these activities *per se*, he must also therefore, thirdly, involve himself in interventionist activities in their own right; thus he finds himself having to establish interventionist relationships with managers and workers. Not only, for example, does the personnel specialist carry out selection activities but he does so by way of a service to some other manager or department in the enterprise, and the activities necessary to the making of that service available and availed of are separate and distinct from those indulged in in order to select a new employee.

This set of interventionist activities is not complete unless another aspect is recognized. Not only is a service (or advice) offered to the other, but that service (or advice) is founded upon certain standards (whether these be standards related to the quality of labour or standards related to inter-personal conduct or whatever). Interventionist activities are therefore to be seen as including not only those which effect some adjustment to changed circumstances, but also those which contribute to the determination of the standards which will make that adjustment a good or right one. In the past, it has often been the lot of the personnel specialist to accept standards which have been determined by the other in the service relationship (eg line management simply told him what they wanted). At present, there is much more of a partnership discernible in the establishment of standards and criteria of judgement. The link between the two was essentially the welfare officer role. Thus the third set of tasks on which the personnel specialist will find himself engaged will be tasks which are concerned with developing and maintaining standards through intervention in the on-going system, in much the same fashion that, in principle, the welfare officer intervened to maintain an enterprise conscience.

Finally, the fourth set of tasks which might be discerned is that which surrounds the act of objective setting or policy making. The tasks here are essentially those of collecting and collating data necessary to the reaching of decisions, usually on a collective or team basis. This tends to mean that the personnel manager must so organize that part of the intelligence system which is his special concern as to provide his fellow managers with readily assimilable information on personnel matters. Even if the team taking these decisions in future may compulsorily or voluntarily include representatives of the workforce itself, the tasks of providing the information will remain essentially the same.

There is a clear sense in which none of these categories of task is new: some of them are central to personnel management no matter where it is practised, and examples of the others are certainly to be found in modern enterprises even if they are not yet universal or central. The main argument being advanced here, however, is that because it is possible to make certain forecasts as to how the situation of the personnel function will continue to change, it is also possible to predict that the work of the personnel specialist will in future tend to focus mainly upon these four broad categories of task.

Nevertheless, such predictions will produce no automatic consequence. A personnel manager is no different from anyone else in the particular sense that he will only acquire a role in modern enterprise if he can bring to bear the skills which are necessary to the performance of that role. The identification of task areas is not therefore of itself of great importance, but it is particularly relevant to any attempt to define the kinds of skill which the personnel specialist will be expected to possess.

From what has already been said, for example, it is possible to predict that the future personnel specialist will be expected to possess two broad types of skill, one of which might be identified as the skills of the case worker and the other which might be labelled the skills of the manager. The case worker skills are traditionally associated with three areas:

First, the skills associated with the hiring and firing sequence (recruiting, interviewing, counselling, training and advising), coupled with consequential skills required to establish universal standards of fairness in the hiring to firing sequence, of decisions which the supervisor would be expected to implement.

Secondly, and not really as a separate category of skills, the personnel officer is then liable to be built into the appeals machinery in disciplinary matters and other grievance procedures, within which the individual worker is still to be seen as the focus: the skills called for remain essentially those associated with the manning sequence, interviewing, counselling etc, together with an ability to set and maintain fair standards and secure their successful implementation.

Thirdly, the personnel officer is usually given charge of that major element in the trash-can conception—the amenities (such as sports clubs) the canteens, the pension schemes, the sickness clubs and so on—which provides him with some resources which he can deploy to help in the solution of problems. In so doing, even if the justification is the interest of the enterprise or the employer, he is still operating (using skills) within the framework of the case worker role.

The case worker skills are essentially those which enable the specialist to help individuals to identify problems, explore solutions and make apposite choices in the circumstances. The conception of the welfare worker in industry rested upon just such a characterization of the skills required. However, in social welfare work generally, very real doubts have been expressed about the paternalistic overtones in this kind of role and in personnel work these same doubts must have similar validity. It is, for example, insufficient for the case worker to seek to help a client to solve his problems by his own efforts if the problem is system generated; the question of how far the case worker should go in helping to change the system in order to help the client solve his problems is as real in the industrial context as it is in the developing tension between the traditional social worker and the emerging exponents of community action approaches to social welfare.

This in itself indicates a change in the approach to welfare in industry, but it also says something both about the position of the personnel specialist in the scheme of things, and about the kinds of skill which a welfare role must command. He must both have the position and the skill to act as a change agent within the organization when the solution of personnel problems (at the 'case' level, as in disciplinary or grievance matters) requires the organization as well as the individual affected to change.

It also follows that the case worker will require two other broad types of skill, group work skills and negotiating skills.

The first category comprises skills which are by no means unknown to the personnel specialist at present; he uses them in committees or in training and he is used as a resource person for them by colleagues who need advice on these matters. It has been predicted above that in future much more communication is likely to take place in small group situations—work groups and working groups— and there is a likely demand for advice and assistance on how most effectively to communicate in such situations. Such relatively unstructured communication will tend to shade into consultation and negotiation, and comparable advice and help may well be required to facilitate these processes. In the general training field also, most communication is oriented towards small group structures, and advice will be required here even if the personnel specialist is not actually involved in the execution of the training activity. Such skills as are called in question in this context are those of the social psychologist or group dynamicist—by whatever brand name they may be known.

As a special sub-category of these skills, we might also distinguish the more structured or purposive application of communications and influence techniques. The distinction is between the group processes which might be applicable to the free group (on which much of the social psychological experimental work has been based) and those which are relevant in situations characterized by some variation on the negotiation theme, where what is sought is the intentional influence by one group (through representatives) of another group (through their representatives). In this context, the group ceases to be a free or spontaneous or natural group, and both sets of representatives must inevitably listen to their respective constituency drummers and march to their tunes, regardless of the extent to which as persons they may meet as a cohesive negotiating group. The skills involved in this constrained context may be comparable to those in the free group situation, but they acquire an added dimension of formality in the preparation and presentation of cases, and in the separation of personal predispositions from representative ones. The knowledge-support for this kind of skill is more likely to be found in role theory as developed by the sociologists.

It might also be suggested that the demands upon the personnel specialist will have both the personnel and situational connotations. The first are commonly considered in connection with leadership theories (and particularly those which focus upon action centred leadership: see Ross and Hendry, 1958) in which the skill of the person is linked to the requirement of action. The second are usually discussed in connection with structure, in which context the social, economic and technological features (ie external to the person involved) are seen to impose their own limits on what the person can do. Consequently, the personnel specialist may be expected to have identifiable social skills (perhaps even as a leader) and also such knowledge and skill as may enable him or her to effect restructuring of the situation in order to diminish the constraints upon action (ie to have knowledge and skills which, currently, are usually conceived of as adhering to interventionist strategies in OD (organizational development).

The fact that realization of standards of fair treatment is one of the ends to which personnel department skills must be devoted has led to a constant (and recently increasing) pressure to build on to the

526

function a role in personnel policy making, which will ultimately become a corporate function. Pressure from that starting point is also supported by the pressures which arise from the other task base of the personnel manager, the structuring of relationships with collectivities, and from the skills which associate with this—the manipulation of power and information in the negotiating situation. The need for policy here, developed through what have come to be referred to as processes of intraorganizational bargaining, is just as real as the need in the other area, and the increased power acquired by or given to the trade unions in recent years adds its own extra degree of urgency to its realization.

This development, which is already well in train in many organizations, imposes a new set of skill requirements upon the personnel function, associated with the collection, interpretation and use in decision taking data which, in this context, are not bounded by the parameters of the purely inter-personal relationship. These are the skills of the corporate planner as distinct from those of the professional who deals with individual client problems. In particular, they call for skills of judgement which must now be exercised in relation to data about persons and classes of persons, in circumstances where the opportunity to check that data against the human reality may be extremely limited. Movement of the role to this level within the enterprise increases the pressure on all organizations to develop a functional management organization, and to draw the fundamental distinction between hard and soft technologies (or between the knowledge of method applied to the physical resources and the knowledge of method applied to the human resources). As this kind of movement takes place, the personnel manager will be expected to advise on the structuring of the organization and will thus find the appropriate corporate role for his function.

By virtue of this expectation, therefore, the personnel specialist with the case worker/group dynamics orientation in his or her role, is provided with a linking bridge to that other conception of the personnel function which emphasizes the need for skills associated with management. In this second conception, the personnel manager is more concerned with the workforce as a whole and less with individual cases within it, and the major end of his endeavour is so to develop or manage the system as a whole as to reduce the number of problem cases which might be thrown up by its operation. The skills which permit successful planned intervention in organizational change will be different from those which are demanded for successful management of personnel, but both sets of skills are applied at the same level of organizational system.

The managerial skills required of the personnel specialist are those skills which the textbook is prone to associate with decision taking. However, everyone takes decisions about something or other, and it cannot therefore be decision taking *per se* which distinguishes the manager. The manner in which the textbook distinguishes management functions provides one clue to the distinction but, rather than using concepts like planning or controlling to define this process, it is probably more useful to see management as concerned with decision taking about wholes or aggregates (whether these are in fact sections, departments, firms or economies or alternatively the production, marketing or development functions). The specialist manager (such as the personnel manager) may well be concerned with the first type of whole (eg the firm as a whole) where a production manager may be concerned with the second (eg the production function). It is *then* possible to argue that managers are essentially involved in decisions about how these wholes should be organized, steered or controlled in order to achieve definable objectives.

Decision taking at this level (as distinct, say, from decisions about cases) calls for the kinds of skills which can be associated with the elements of that process: the defining of situational needs (or of recognizing problems), discovering possible or feasible solutions to the problems identified, and the making of appropriate selections from the range of alternatives given the circumstances in which the problem occurs. Just as the social skills mentioned above involve two differentiated orientations, so too in this case the skills identifiable can be linked to two main attributes of the person, knowledge and judgement, and to two features of the situation, information and normative standards. In other words, in order to participate successfully in this process of policy formation, the person must be knowledgeable about (what above we have called) theory and be able and willing to exercise judgement in relation to the situation, and feasible changes in it; but he must also be able to acquire (or be supplied with) information about the situation and conceptions of what normative standards are to be used in making evaluative judgements (cf Vickers, 1968).

It is this which creates the major form of tension discernable in the personnel manager's role, for it immediately provides for at least two sets of criteria of judgement, one of which emanates from the enterprise/employer objectives and the other of which springs from the goals of workers or the objectives of trade unions. Thereby the man-in-the-middle assumes the hot seat.

Criteria of evaluation

The diverse origins and orientations of the personnel management role have contributed to the confusions which have certainly in the past and may still at present surround the role. Given two potential clients, the employer and the employee, the personnel manager's contribution may be subjected to evaluation against two distinct sets of criteria which stem from their different objectives and goals. An employer who seeks an agent of his interest is likely to be distrustful if he finds himself with a case worker dedicated to serving the employee interest; the employee who seeks a mediator of his interest in his dealings with the employer is equally likely to be suspicious of the manager dedicated to the protection of the employer's interest. Either might then turn elsewhere, the employer to his association and the employee to his trade union.

The personnel specialist's criteria of self-evaluation might well reflect a similar divergence, but there is some reason to suppose that the personnel management profession, as a whole, now adopts criteria for self-evaluation which are derived chiefly from the employer's interest. Although up to the 1950s, it was not uncommon to hear personnel officers discussing their work in terms comparable to those used by social case workers (in whose training many of them had at that time shared) in the 1970s personnel managers are more likely to talk like managers.

This is perhaps not so surprising since the criteria associated with managerial roles have been more fully worked out in the industrial context. Work takes place within an economic context, and the criteria of success are efficiency oriented; personnel managers concerned with the workers but paid by the enterprise are therefore not unlikely to measure their success in terms of similar efficiency criteria. Indeed, greater sophistication—and as many would argue probably greater humanity—may be seen to lie in treating people at work in terms comparable to those used for the physical assets. As Giles and Robinson put it in the opening paragraph of *Human Asset Accounting*, which is chiefly concerned with training applications of the concept: "'Will it pay?'—the frequent cry of those concerned with the decision to do or not to do in management—usually means is it profit earning or will the end value be greater than the initial value plus the cost of our decision" (1972, p 9).

As they go on to suggest, it is only man amongst the range of resources available to management that has "so far completely eluded financial evaluation and expression in terms of asset/liability value" (*ibid*); and they suggest how, in training activities, this omission can be rectified.

Whilst it may be generally true as these authors suggest, that such evaluations as are discussed in the literature of personnel management tend to be expressed in behavioural terms—such as the assessment of length of stay of selected employees, of quiescence of the shop stewards following the introduction of a new set of procedures or the settlement of a wage claim—this approach should not obscure the fact that the length of stay or the quiescence are assumed or believed to correlate closely with cost-savings or asset improvement. The evaluation is therefore still linked to the same efficiency criteria.

Similarly, the function as a whole will tend to be evaluated by the employer in these terms: whether a firm introduces or continues with a personnel department is a question which will be answered in terms of whether it will pay, although the costs of discontinuation may still allow an established function to persist even when the immediate cost-benefit calculation is adverse. In the past, the welfare or training functions were more prone to be switched on or switched off according to the surrounding economic climate of the enterprise; if this is less so now, possibly because of the increase in the volume of specialized administration emanating from legislation, the basis of the assessment is likely to remain firm. The alternative criteria which might be applied to the work of the personnel department are certainly different from these but they are not necessarily diametrically opposed. Certainly they must link more closely and directly to the goals of those at work but whilst they could, theoretically, elevate these in significance to the exclusion of the objectives of enterprise, to do this would be both unrealistic and incapable of realizing the end because of the nature of the false choice involved in this approach. Just as a cost conscious enterprise cannot completely ignore the goals of workers, so a socially conscious enterprise could not completely ignore the economic objectives (cf Dubin, 1958).

These alternative criteria must therefore focus upon the development of an accounting procedure which places more direct emphasis on the social costs. The kind of question which arises is the extent to which, say, additional training costs should be assessed against private (eg enterprise) benefits or against social (eg the increase in the stock of trained manpower overall or the greater development of the individuals trained) benefits. It is this incorporation of social costs and benefits into the calculation which permits an alternative set of criteria to be established. These would then emphasize efficiency in the Barnard definition of the term, but calculated on a broader base than the single enterprise, and would be more supportive of the conception of personnel management as a professional concern.

One of the significant developments in British society over the past 15 years is the development of new conditions attached to what we referred to above as the licence of the enterprise. It is perhaps difficult to say where the beginning of this process lies, but manifestations of the change are at least heralded by the Terms and Conditions of Employment Act 1959 and formally announced with the Contracts of Employment Act 1963, and since then its presence has been increasingly felt. Some of the particular implications of this change have been discussed above: here we want to draw attention to the very real possibility that this imposition of standards from outside the enterprise (in the form of statutory duties) may create the conditions for a more independent role for the personnel manager. In effect, most of these changes effected via legislation make it more expensive for the employer to treat labour in traditional ways, which could be just another way of saying that more of what were previously social costs must now pass through the accountant's books within the enterprise.

Another way of representing these changes is to see them as redefining consideration within the context of the employment contract. In particular, some of those elements of the contract which were not readily reducible to, or compensated for, in money terms—such as dignity or security—have now been provided for in a set of rights capable of being upheld by the law and of being expressed as a cost to the employer, even if less significantly as a monetary gain to the employee. What is thus swept into the contract in this indirect fashion is the element of psychological income, which the human relations school have hitherto had much to say about but which has until relatively recently been treated as something over and above, or outside, the mainstream of what the contractual relationship was all about. Clearly, this process has not gone far and there is much more to the psychological contract than a few pieces of legislation have yet been able to underpin. But the significance of this change is perhaps that what was previously regarded as a bit of a luxury—the soft management approach—is now hardened through the device of a legally enforceable duty placed upon the employer. Given the historical association of the personnel management function with human relations or the soft management approach, these changes are likely to have their significance for the future development of the role but, more importantly in our present context, they serve to shift the balance of criteria of judgement of success.

Such influence as the personnel management profession has had upon the development of these social standards of interpersonal conduct, or of treatment of individuals and groups within modern organizations, ought to make it an ally of the trade union, on the face of things. Because it has sought to mitigate the harsher consequences of a pure economic rationality it is not possible to characterize the

531

role of personnel management as being completely within the ambit of profit optimization in private enterprise concerns, with no qualification to that statement. There is another strand of concern with treatment or fairness and justice, and this responsibility for the development of the corporate conscience should not be discounted too heavily. Just how much influence personnel officers have had upon shaping the way in which individual enterprises treat people at work would be difficult to assess precisely. But it can be said that in the past quarter century they have clearly brought a knowledge of method and technique in the behavioural science area into the management organization. This has helped shape the responses made to changing social values and motives, often channelled through the shop stewards' movements. If Donovan could cast doubts on the influence of the employer's associations, we can at least attribute some of the responsibility for ensuring that the employer influence was not completely amateur to the development of the personnel management function as one which had both a basis in human concern and a foundation of theory.

The problem which remains, however, is that which surrounds the response of organized labour to a personnel specialist role which is also managerial in its orientation: essentially, the problem is whether there is really anything at all in the suggestion that the personnel specialist is a man-in-the-middle. In his case worker role, there may well be something of this about it; in the managerial role, there may well be nothing. The differentiating factor is the perennial problem of independence in the role, usually spoken of in terms of professional independence.

If, however, there is anything in the prediction above about the continued diminution of respect for authority—whether sapiential or bureaucratic—it may be that the personnel specialist will be denied employee sanction of his authority along with everyone else. He will then have to win his own spurs either on the basis of his wisdom (sapiential foundations of authority) or on the basis of a freshly legitimated position (comparable to the position given to an auditor under legislation). This represents something of the nature of the choice before the profession—if the predictions above hold.

The kind of problem that, in practice, arises in this situation might be illustrated by comparing the personnel specialist not so much with the favourite comparison of yesteryear, the foreman, but rather with the union officer. The shop steward and the full-time official of the union undoubtedly have the sanction of their members in most situations and they are usually expected to carry out roles which, if they were to be expressed in personnel language, could be described as oriented towards securing the welfare of those who are represented. To that extent, the role of the personnel specialist and the union officer have a good deal in common. What skills might be needed by the one might also be predicted to be desirable in the other: the personnel specialist has often developed his on the basis of formal training and the union officer on the basis of native wit allied to experience. But what can or should the relationship between the two be?

What prospects are therefore for parallel development (with the personnel specialist and the union officer dealing with the same areas on behalf of two separate constituenies) and what prospects of complementary development (with the personnel specialist providing expertise to both sides of the relationship of trade union to employer/enterprise)? Clearly, if the personnel specialist is an active participant in a zero-sum, win-lose game of negotiation, the answer to the first of these questions is likely to be in the negative and the second does not then arise. But if the personnel specialist is able (permitted) to remain aloof from actual involvement in such processes or if zero-sum games are given up, then the first question can be answered in the affirmative and the second can be tackled by using the specialist as a resource person in the group dynamics sense. This is to state an ideal which is infrequently realized or even attempted in practice. But it does raise questions about the professional independence of the personnel specialist and therefore about the professional *role* which a personnel specialist will be enabled to take up in an employment situation.

To make these suggestions (or implicit predictions) is not inconsistent with the development of the role on a professional foundation. The evidence suggests that the development of a profession must rest upon a recognizable and distinguishable occupational role, *and* upon the opportunity to structure this role in some independence from others who may yet derive benefit from its exercise. To meet the first, the personnel management role must achieve its separate identity from other roles; to meet the second it must become at least as free and independent as, say, the role of the accountant in organizations. In the second of these, the recent development of constraining legislation assumes significance in providing at least a foundation for this kind of independence, and in allowing authoritative appeal to standards other than those set by the employer in the event of conflict. Whether this means that personnel management will develop a new professional standing, or whether it implies the demise of the profession as it now exists because the opportunity to decide policy is simply taken away from the enterprise itself, is not really the open question that it may seem. Whilst organizations continue to be given freedom to decide for themselves within any framework, they will, perhaps more often than in the past, have to decide their own policies about employees.

Bibliography

ADAMS A, Performance Appraisal and Counselling, in Torrington D P and Sutton D F (eds), *Handbook of Management Development*, Gower Press, 1973

ADAMS J S, Towards an Understanding of Inequity, *Journal of Abnormal and Social Psychology*, 1963

ADAMS J S, Inequity in Social Exchange, in Berkowitz L (ed), *Advances in Experimental Social Psychology*, 2, Acadamic Press, 1965, pp 267–300

AIKIN O, Damages After Dismissal, *Personnel Management*, January 1978, p 36

AIKIN O, A Question of Unfair Dismissal, *Personnel Management*, January 1974, pp 20–23 and 41

ALBRIGHT L E, Glennon J R and Smith W J, *The Use of Psychological Tests in Industry*, Muksgaard, Copenhagen, 1963

ALBROW M C, *Bureaucracy*, Macmillan, 1970

ALDERFER C P, *Existence, Relatedness and Growth: Human Needs in Organizational Settings*, Free Press, Glencoe, 1972

ALDERSON M R, Information Systems in the Unified Health Service, in McLachlan G (ed), *The Future: Present Indicatives*, Oxford University Press for Nuffield Provincial Hospitals Trust, 1973

ALGIE J, Management and Organization in the Social Services, *British Hospital Journal*, 26 June 1970

ALLEN G C, *The Structure of Industry in Britain*, Longman, 1961

ALLEN L A, *The Management Profession*, McGraw-Hill, 1964

ALLEN L A, *Improving Line and Staff Relationships*, National Industrial Conference Board, New York, Studies in Personnel Policy, No 153, 1956

ALLEN V L, *The Sociology of Industrial Relations*, Longmans, 1971

ALLEN V L, *Power in Trade Unions*, Longman, 1958

ALLEN V L, *Militant Trade Unionism*, Merlin Press, 1966

ALLPORT G W, VERNON P E and LINDZEY G, *Study of Values,* Houghton-Mifflin, Boston, 3rd edn 1960

American Management Association, *Rating Employee and Supervisory Performance*, AMA, 1950

ANASTASI A, *Psychological Testing*, Macmillan, New York, 1961

ANDERMAN S D, *Unfair Dismissals and the Law*, Institute of Personnel Management (IPM), 1973

535

ANDERMAN N, *Work and Leisure*, Routledge & Kegan Paul, 1961

ANDERMAN S D, *Trade Unions and Technological Change*, Allen and Unwin, 1967

ANSTEY E and MERCER E O, *Interviewing for Selection of Staff*, Allen and Unwin, 1956

ANTHONY P and CRICHTON A, *Industrial Relations and the Personnel Specialist*, Batsford, 1969

ANTHONY P D, Industrial Codes of Discipline, *Personnel*, 1964, pp 32–36

ANTHONY P D, *The Ideology of Work*, Tavistock, 1976

ANTHONY P D, *The Conduct of Industrial Relations*, IPM, 1977

APPLEYARD J, *Workers' Participation in Western Europe*, IPM, Information Report No 10, 1971

ARENSBERG C M and McGREGOR D, Determination of Morale in an Industrial Company, *Applied Anthropology*, 1, 1942, pp 12–34

ARGYLE M, The Concepts of Role and Status, *Sociological Review*, 44 (3) 1953

ARGYRIS C, *Executive Leadership*, Harper and Brothers, 1953

ARGYRIS C, Organizational Leadership in Participative Management, in Huneryager S G, and Heckman I L, 1967, q v

ARGYRIS C, *Integrating the Individual and the Organization*, Wiley, 1964

ARMSTRONG E, *Industrial Relations: an Introduction*, Harrap, 1969

ARMSTRONG E, Taking the Sweat out of Wages Councils, *Personnel Management*, December 1974, pp 20–24

ARMSTRONG T, *The Crowthers of Bankdam*, Collins, 1940

ARMSTRONG Sir W, *Personnel Management in the Civil Service*, HMSO, 1971

ARNFIELD R V (ed), *Technological Forecasting*, Edinburgh University Press, 1969

ARNISON J, *The Million Pound Strike*, Lawrence and Wishart, 1970

ASCH S E, *Social Psychology*, Prentice Hall, 1952

ASHTON D, Project Based Management Development, *Personnel Management*, July 1974, pp 26–28 and 36

ASHTON T S, *The Industrial Revolution*, 1760–1830, Oxford University Press, 1948

ATKINSON G G M, *The Effective Negotiator*, Quest, 1975

BACHRACH P and BARATZ M S, Poverty and Power, Oxford University Press, 1971

BACHRACH P and BARATZ M S, Two Faces of Power, in Castles F G *et al*, 1971, pp 376–88, qv

BAIN G S, *The Growth of White Collar Unionism*, Clarendon Press, 1970

BAIN, G S *et al, Social Stratification and the Trade Unions,* Crane-Russack, 1974

BAINS M A, *The New Local Authorities: Management and Structure*, HMSO, 1972

BAKER H and FRANCE K R, *Centralization and Decentralization in Industrial Relations*, Princeton University Press, 1954

BAKER J C, *Directors and their Functions*, Arnold 1945

BAKER R J S, *Administrative Theory and Public Administration*, Hutchinson, 1972

BAKKE E W, *People and Organizations*, Harper, 1950

536

BAKKE E W, *Bonds of Organizations*, Harper, 1950

BALDAMUS W, *Efficiency and Effort*, Tavistock, 1961

BALDAMUS W, Type of Work and Motivation, *British Journal of Sociology*, 2, 1952, pp 44–58

BALES R F, *Interaction Process Analysis*, Addison-Wesley Press, Cambridge, Mass, 1951

BALFOUR C, *Participation in Industry*, Croom Helm, 1973

BALFOUR C, *Unions and the Law*, Saxon House, 1973

BALFOUR C, *Incomes Policy and the Public Sector*, Routledge and Kegan Paul, 1972

BANKS J A, *Marxist Sociology in Action*, Faber and Faber, 1970

BARBER D, *The Practice of Personnel Management*, IPM, 1970

BARNARD C I, *The Functions of the Executive*, Harvard University Press, 1938

BARNARD C I, Functions and Pathologies of Status Systems in Formal Organizations, in Whyte W F (ed) *Industry and Society*, McGraw Hill, 1946, pp 207–43

BARNES R, *Motion and Time Study*, Wiley, 1969

BARNES L B, *Organizational Systems and Engineering Groups*, Harvard University Press, 1963

BARRETT B, RHODES E and BEISHON J, *Industrial Relations and the Wider Society*, Collier-MacMillan, 1975

BARRETT P F, *The Human Implications of Mergers and Takeovers*, IPM, 1973

BARRY A, Developing Tomorrow's Managers, *Personnel Magazine*, January 1966

BARTHOLOMEW D J (ed), *Manpower Planning: Selected Readings*, Penguin, 1976

BARTHOLOMEW D J and MORRIS B R (eds), *Aspects of Manpower Planning*, English Universities Press, 1971

BARTHOLOMEW D J and SMITH A R (eds), *Manpower and Management Science*, English Universities Press, 1971

BARTHOLOMEW D J, HOPES R F A and SMITH A R, Manpower Planning in the Face of Uncertainty, *Personnel Review*, 5 (3) Summer 1976, pp 5–17

BASS B M and VAUGHAN J A, *Training in Industry: The Management of Learning*, Tavistock, 1968

BASS B M, *Leadership, Psychology and Organizational Behaviour*, Harper, 1960

BATES J and PARKINSON J R, *Business and Economics*, Kelley, 1961, 2nd edn 1969

BATTEN J D, *Beyond Management by Objectives*, AMA, New York, 1966

BEACH D S, *Personnel Management of People at Work,* Macmillan, 1975, 3rd edn

BEISHON J and PETERS G, *Systems Behaviour*, Harper and Row, 1972

BELASCO J A and ARLUTTON J A, Line and Staff Conflicts: Some Empirical Insights, *Academy of Management Journal*, 12 December 1969, pp 469–77

BELL D J, *Planning Corporate Manpower*, Longman, 1974

BELBIN R M, *The Discovery Method in Training*, HMSO, 1969

BELL G D, *Organizations and Human Behaviour,* Prentice-Hall, 1967

BENDIX R, *Work and Authority in Industry*, Harper and Row, 1963
BENEMY W G, *Whitehall—Town Hall*, Harrap and Company, 1960
BENNIS W G *et al, The Planning of Change*, Holt, Rinehart and Winston, 2nd edn, 1970
BENNIS W G, *Changing Organizations*, McGraw-Hill, 1966
BENNIS W G, *Organization Development*, Addison Wesley, 1969
BERGER J, ZELDITCH M and ANDERSON B, *Sociological Theories in Progress*, Houghton Mifflin, 1972
BERLE A A and MEANS G C, *The Modern Corporation and Private Property*, Macmillan, 1932
BINDRA D and STEWART J, *Motivation*, Penguin, 1971
BIRNBAUM NORMAN, *The Crisis of Industrial Society*, Oxford University Press, 1970
BLAIR J, Three Studies in Improving Clerical Work, *Personnel Management*, February 1974, pp 34–37
BLAKE R R and MOUTON J S, *The Managerial Grid*, Gulf Publishing Company, 1964
BLAU P M, *Bureaucracy in Modern Society*, Random House, 1956
BLAU P M and SCOTT W R, *Formal Organizations*, Routledge, 1963
BLAUNER R, *Alienation and Freedom*, University of Chicago Press, 1964
BLOOD J W, *The Personnel Job and a Changing World*, AMA, 1964
BLOOMFIELD M and WILLITTS J H, *Personnel and Employment Problems in Industrial Management*, American Academy of Political and Social Science, 1916
BLUM F H, *Work and Community*, Routledge and Kegan Paul, 1968
BLUM M L and NAYLOR J C, *Industrial Psychology*, Harper and Row, 1968
BOARD OF Trade, *The Conduct of Company Directors*, HMSO, 1977
BOELLA M J, *Personnel Management in the Hotel and Catering Industry*, Barrie and Jenkins, 1974
BOSWORTH D and EVANS G, Manpower Forecasting Techniques, *Personnel Review*, 2 (4), Autumn 1973, pp 4–16
BOULDING K, General Systems Theory—the Skeleton of a Science, *Management Science*, 2, 1956, pp 197–208
BOWEN P, *Social Control in Industrial Organizations*, Routledge, 1976
BOWEY A, *Handbook of Salary and Wage Systems*, Gower, 1975
BOWEY A and LUPTON T, *Job and Pay Comparisons*, Gower Press, 1973
BOWLEY A, *Salary Structures for Management Careers*, IPM, 1971
BOYDELL T H, *A Guide to Job Analysis*, British Association for Commercial and Industrial Education (BACIE), 1970
BRAITHWAITE R and POLLOCK J, Analysing Response to Recruitment Advertising, *Personnel Management*, December 1974, pp 25–27
BRAMHAM J, *Practical Manpower Planning*, IPM, 1975
BRANNEN P, BATSTONE E V, FATCHETT D and WHITE P, *The Worker Directors*, Hutchinson, 1976
BRECH E F L, *The Principles and Practice of Management*, Longmans, London, 1975 edn
BRIDGE J and DODDS J C, *Managerial Decision Making*, Croom Helm, 1975
BRIGGS J H and MURRAY R, *Responsibilities of Industry in the Field of*

538

Health, Foundation for Business Responsibilities, 1975

BRECHER C, *Upgrading Blue Collar and Service Workers*, John Hopkins University Press, 1972

British Association for Commercial and Industrial Education, *Economic Growth and Manpower*, BACIE, 1963

British Institute of Management, *Merit Rating—A Practical Guide*, BIM, 1954

BIM, *The Cost of Labour Turnover*, Management Publications, 1959

BIM, *Absence from Work: Incidence and Cost Control*, BIM, 1961

BIM, *Absence from Work: Incidence Cost and Control*, Management Publications, 1961

BIM, *Job Evaluation*, BIM, 1961

BIM, *Academics in Industry*, BIM Notes 10 (4) August 1969

British Iron and Steel Trades Employers' Association, *Manning, Wages Structure and Security of Employment*, BISTEA, 1967

BROSS I D J, *Design for Decision*, Macmillan, 1953

BROWN A, LEICESTER C and PYATT F G, Output, Manpower and Industrial Skills in the U K, *The Residual Factor and Economic Growth*, OECD, Paris, 1964

BROWN J A C, *The Social Psychology of Industry*, Penguin, 1954

BROWN W, *Some Problems of a Factory*, IPM, 1951

BROWN W, *Piecework Abandoned*, Heinemann, 1962

BROWN W, *Piecework Bargaining*, Heinemann, 1973

BROWN W, *Exploration in Management,* Heinemann, 1960

BROWNING K W, Management Succession Planning, *Personnel Management* XLV (365), September 1963, pp 107–110

BRUNEL UNIVERSITY, *Working Papers on the Reorganization of the National Health Service*, Brunel University, 1973

BRYANT D J, Recent Developments in Manpower Research, *Personnel Review*, 1 (3), Summer 1972, pp 14–31

BRYANT D J, A Survey of the Development of Manpower Planning Policies, *British Journal of Industrial Relations*, November 1965

BUCKINGHAM G L, JEFFREY R G and THORNE B A, *Job Enrichment and Organizational Change*, Gower, 1975

BUCKLEY W, *Sociology and Modern Systems Theory*, Prentice-Hall, 1967

BULLOCK LORD, *Report of the Committee of Inquiry on Industrial Democracy* (Chairman: Lord Bullock), HMSO, 1977

BURGESS L L, *Top Executive Pay Package*, Free Press, 1963

BURNS T, Research Development and Production: Problems of Conflict and Cooperation, *IRE Transactions on Engineering Management*, March 1961

BURNS T, *Industrial Man*, Penguin, 1969

BURNS T, Management in Action, *Operations Research Quarterly*, 1957

BURNS T, Industry in a New Age, *New Society*, 31 January 1963

BURNS T, The Sociology of Industry, in Welford A T (ed) *Society*, Routledge and Kegan Paul, 1962

BURNS T and STALKER G M, *Management of Innovation*, Tavistock Publications, 1961

BUTTERISS M, *Job Enrichment and Employee Participation—a study,* IPM, 1971

539

BUTTERISS M, *Techniques and Developments in Management—a selection,* IPM, 1975

CAMPBELL J P, DUNNETTE M D, LAWLER E E and WEICK K E, *Managerial Behaviour, Performance and Effectiveness*, McGraw-Hill, 1970

CAPLOW T, *Principles of Organization*, Harcourt Brace, 1964

CAPLOW T, *The Sociology of Work*, McGraw-Hill, 1964

CARBY C, *Job Redesign in Practice*, IPM, 1976

CARSON D, Problem Schools of Management, *Management Today*, August 1967, pp 70–73 and 102–4

CARTWRIGHT D (ed), *Studies in Social Power*, Institute for Social Research, Ann Arbor, Michigan, 1959

CARTWRIGHT D, Influence, Leadership, Control in March J G, *Handbook of Organizations*, Rand McNally, 1965

CARROLL P, *Time Study for Cost Control*, McGraw-Hill, 1954

CARTWRIGHT D, and ZANDER A, *Group Dynamics*, Row Peterson, 1953

CARVALHO G E, Managing a Dynamic Compensation System, *Management of Personnel Quarterly*, 1965, Quoted in *Personnel Management* ed McFarland, 1971, qv

CASS T, *Statistical Methods in Management*, Cassell, 1973

CASTLES F G, MURRAY D J and POTTER D C, *Decisions, Organizations and Society*, Penguin, 1971

CATTELL R C, *Personality*, McGraw-Hill, 1950

CEMACH H P, *Work Study in the Office*, MacLaren, 1969

CENTERS R, Motivational Aspects of Occupational Stratification, *Journal of Social Psychology*, November 1948

Central Training Council, *Training of Training Officers: a Pattern for the Future*, HMSO, 1968

Central Training Council, *Training for Commerce and the Office*, HMSO, 1966

CHADWICK-JONES J K, *Automation and Behaviour*, Wiley, 1969

CHADWICK-JONES J K, BROWN C A and NICHOLSON N, Absence from Work: Its Meaning, Measurement and Control, *International Review of Applied Psychology*, 22 (2), 1973, pp 137–55

CHAMBERLAIN N W and KUHN J W, *Collective Bargaining*, McGraw-Hill, 1965

CHAMBERLAIN N W, *The Union Challenge to Management Control*, Harper, 1948

CHARLES R, *The Development of Industrial Relations in Britain* 1911–1939, Hutchinson, 1973

CHASE S, *The Proper Study of Mankind: an Inquiry into the Science of Human Relations*, Phoenix House, 1950

CHERRY C, *On Human Communication*, Chapman and Hall, 1957

CHILD J, *The Business Enterprise in Modern Industrial Society*, Collier-Macmillan, 1969

CHILD J, *British Management Thought*, Allen and Unwin, 1969

CHILD J, *Industrial Relations in the British Printing Industry: The Quest for Security*, Allen and Unwin, 1967

CHILD J (ed), *Man and Organization*, Allen and Unwin, 1973

540

CLARKE R O et al, *Workers' Participation in Management*, Heinemann, 1972

CLEGG H A, *A New Approach to Industrial Democracy*, Blackwell, 1960

CLEGG H A, *How to Run an Incomes Policy*, Heinemann, 1971

CLEGG H A, *Industrial Democracy and Nationalization*, Blackwell, 1951

CLEGG H A, *The System of Industrial Relations in Great Britain*, Blackwell, 1977

CLEGG H A, and CHESTER T, *Wage Policy and the Health Service*, Blackwell, 1957

CLEGG S, *Power, Rule and Domination*, Routledge and Kegan Paul, 1975

CLEGG S and DUNKERLEY D, *Critical Issues in Organizations*, Routledge and Kegan Paul, 1977

CLIFF T, *The Employers' Offensive*, Pluto Press, 1970

COATES K, *Can the Workers Run Industry?* Sphere Books, 1968

COATES K, and TOPHAM A, *Industrial Democracy*, Penguin, 1968

COCH L, and FRENCH J R P, Overcoming Resistance to Change, *Human Relations*, 1948, (1), pp 512–532

COCHRANE A L, *Effectiveness and Efficiency*, Nuffield Provincial Hospitals Trust, 1972

CODDINGTON A, *Theories of the Bargaining Process*, Allen and Unwin, 1968

COLLINGRIDGE J M and RITCHIE M, *Personnel Management: Problems of the Smaller Firm*, IPM, 1970

COLLINS R G and CRICHTON A, (1966), Quoted in Anthony P D and Crichton A, 1969, qv

Commission on Industrial Relations, *Second General Report*, HMSO, 1971

CIR, *Industrial Relations Training Reports*, Nos 33 and 33A, HMSO, 1972, 1973

CIR, *Report No 31: Disclosure of Information*, HMSO, 1972

COMMONS J R, *Legal Foundations of Capitalism*, Macmillan, 1924

Confederation of British Industries, *The Provision of Information to Employees: Guidelines for Action*, CBI, 1975

COOKE P J D, How to Learn from Curves, *Management Today*, November 1967, pp 72–5 and 148, 152

COOPER R, *Job Motivation and Job Design*, IPM, 1974

COOPER W W, *New Perspectives in Organizational Research*, Wiley, 1964

COPEMAN G, *Employee Share Ownership and Industrial Stability*, IPM, 1975

COPEMAN G H, *Leaders of British Industry*, Gee and Company, 1955

CORFIELD K G, *Business Responsibilities*, Foundation for Business Responsibilities, 1972

CORLETT E N, and MORCOMBE V J, Straightening out Learning Curves, *Personnel Management*, June 1970, pp 14–19

COSER L, *The Functions of Social Conflict*, Routledge and Kegan Paul, 1956

CRAIG R L and BITTEL L R, *Training and Development Handbook*, McGraw-Hill, 1967

CRICHTON A, *Personnel Management in Context*, Batsford, 1968

CRICHTON A, and COLLINS R G, Personnel Specialists—a Count by Employers, *British Journal of Industrial Relations*, July 1966

CRICHTON A and CRAWFORD M, *The Legacy of Nightingale*, Welsh Hospital Board, 1963

CRONBACH L J and GLESER G C, *Psychological Tests and Personnel Decisions*, University of Illinois, 1965

CROZIER M, *The Bureaucratic Phenomenon*, Tavistock, 1964

CRYSTALS G S, *Financial Motivation for Executives*, AMA, 1970

CUMING M W, *The Theory and Practice of Personnel Management*, Heinemann, 1975 edn

CUMING M W, *Hospital Staff Management*, Heinemann, 1971

CUMMINGS L L and SCHWAB D P, *Performance in Organizations: Determinants and Appraisal*, Scott Foresman, 1973

CUNNISON S, *Wages and Work Allocation*, Tavistock, 1966

CURRIE R M, *The Measurement of Work*, Pitman, 1972

CURRIE R M and FARADAY J E, *Financial Incentives Based on Work Measurement*, BIM, rev edn 1971

CUTHBERT N and PATERSON J M, Job Evaluation—Some Recent Thinking and its Place in an Investigation, *Personnel Management*, September 1966, pp 152–62

CUTHBERT N H and HAWKINS K, *Company Industrial Relations Policies*, Longman, 1974

CYERT R M and MARCH J G, *A Behavioural Theory of the Firm*, Prentice-Hall, New York, 1963

CYRIAX G, Setting Targets for Senior Management, *Financial Times*, 12 January 1967

DAHL R, The Concept of Power, *Behavioural Sciences*, 2, 1957

DAHL R, *Who Governs? Democracy and Power in an American City*, Yale University Press, 1961

DAHRENDORF R, *Class and Conflict in an Industrial Society*, Routledge and Kegan Paul, 1959

DALE E, *Planning and Developing the Company Organization Structure*, AMA, New York, 1952

DALTON G W, *Organizational Structure and Design*, Irwin, 1970

DALTON M, *Men Who Manage*, Wiley, New York, 1959

DANIEL W W, *Beyond the Wage-Work Bargain*, PEP, 1970

DANIEL W W and MCINTOSH N, *Incomes Policy and Collective Bargaining*, PEP, May 1973

DAVIES J L, MbO in LEAs and Educational Institutes, *Educational Administration Bulletin*, 1972 (1) pp 10–16, 2 (1) 1973, pp 38–54

DAVIES J L, *On the Contribution of Organizational Analysis to the Study of Educational Institutions*, BSA Conference Paper, 1970

DAVIES K, The Case for Participative Management, in Huneryager S G and Heckman I L, 1967, qv

DAVIS L E and CHERNS A B, *The Quality of Working Life*, Collier-Macmillan, 1975

DAWKINS R, *The Selfish Gene*, Oxford University Press, 1976

DEMPSEY P, Strategy and Tactics in Collective Bargaining, *Personnel Management*, April 1974, pp 22–25 and 43

DENNIS N, HENRIQUES F and SLAUGHTER C, *Coal is our Life*, Eyre and Spottiswoode, 1956

Dept of Employment, *Code of Industrial Relations Practice*, DE, 1972 (a)

Dept of Employment, *Company Manpower Planning*, HMSO, 1968

Dept of Employment, *Training for the Future*, DE, 1972 (b)

Dept of Health and Social Security, *Management Arrangements for the Reorganized NHS, HMSO, 1972*

DESSLER G, *Organization and Management: A Contingency Approach*, Prentice Hall, 1976

DEUTSCH M, *The Resolution of Conflict*, Yale University Press, 1973

DEVERELL C S, *Personnel Management: Human Relations in Industry*, Gee, 1968

DHSS, *NHS Reorganization: England*, HMSO, 1972

DIMMOCK S and FARNHAM D, Working with Whitley in Today's NHS, *Personnel Management*, January 1975, pp 35–7

DIX D K, *Contracts of Employment, including Redundancy Payments*, Butterworths, 1968

DODGE W, *Skilled Labour Supply Imbalances: the Canadian Experience*, British North American Committee, 1977

DOLLARD J, DOOB W, MILLER N E, MOWER O H and SHEARS R R, *Frustration and Aggression*, Yale University Press, 1939

DONALD B, *Manpower for Hospitals*, Institute of Hospital Administrators, 1966

DONOVAN LORD, Royal Commission on Trade Unions and Employers' Associations, HMSO, 1968

DOOHER M J and MARQUIS V, *Rating Employee and Supervisory Performance: a Manual of Merit Rating Techniques*, AMA, 1950

DOUGLAS A, *Industrial Peacemaking*, Columbia University Press, 1962

DOULTON J and HAY D, *Managerial and Professional Staff Grading*, Allen and Unwin, 1962

DRUCKER P F, *The Practice of Management*, Mercury Books, 1961

DRUCKER P F, *Managing for Results*, Heinemann, 1964

DUBIN R, Industrial Workers' Worlds, *Social Problems, III,* January 1956, pp 131–42

DUBIN R, *The World of Work*, Prentice-Hall, 1958

DUBIN R, *Human Relations in Administration*, Prentice-Hall, 1974, 4th edn

DUBIN S S, *Professional Obsolescence*, Hodder and Stoughton, 1971

DUMONT J P, Lip—a Lesson in Democracy, *Personnel Management*, August 1974, pp 32–9

DUNKERLEY D, *Occupations and Society*, Routledge and Kegan Paul, 1975

DUNKERLEY D, *The Foreman*, Routledge and Kegan Paul, 1975

DUNLOP J T, *Wage Determination under Trade Unions*, Kelley, 1944; revised edn 1950

DUNLOP J T and VASILU DIATCHENKO V, *Labour Productivity*, McGraw-Hill, 1964

DUNNETTE M D, *Personnel Selection and Placement*, Tavistock, 1966

DURKHEIM E, *Division of Labour in Society*, Free Press, 1947

EATON W H, Hypotheses related to Worker Frustration, *Journal of Social Psychology*, (35), 1952

EDWARDS R and PAUL S, *Job Evaluation*, Association of Professional,

543

Executive, Clerical and Computer Staff, 1977

ELBOURNE E T, *Fundamentals of Industrial Administration*, MacDonald and Evans, 1934

ELDRIDGE J E T, *Industrial Disputes*, Routledge and Kegan Paul, 1968

ELDRIDGE J E T, Panaceas and Pragmatism in Industrial Relations, *Industrial Relations Journal*, 6 (1), Spring 1975, pp 4–13

ELDRIDGE J E T, *Sociology and Industrial Life*, Nelson, 1971

ELLIOTT A G P, *Staff Grading*, BIM, 1960

ELLIOTT A G P, *Revising a Merit-Rating Scheme*, IPM, 1955

ELLIOTT D, *The Lucas Aerospace Workers' Campaign*, Fabian Society, 1977

ELLIOTT J, *Conflict or Cooperation*, Kogan Page, 1978

ELLIS G D, THOMPSON F F, PRATT S K and BARRACLOUGH T, Learning and the Human Resource Revolution, *Personnel*, September 1968

EMERY F E, *Systems Thinking*, Penguin, 1969

EMERY F E, *Characteristics of Socio-technical Systems*, Tavistock, 1959

EMERY F E and THORSRUD E, *Form and Content in Industrial Democracy*, Tavistock, 1969

EMERY F E and TRIST E L, Socio-Technical Systems, in *Management Sciences Models and Techniques*, Pergamon Press, 1960

Engineering Employers' Federation, *Business Performance and Industrial Relations*, E E F, 1972, reprinted 1976

Engineering Industry Training Board, *Training for Engineering Craftsmen: the Module System*, EITB, 1968

ESKIN F, The Reality of Health Care Planning Teams, *Health and Social Services Journal*, 9 November 1974

ETZIONI A, *Readings on Modern Organizations*, Prentice-Hall, 1969

ETZIONI A, *A Comparative Analysis of Complex Organizations*, Free Press, 1961

ETZIONI A, *Modern Organizations*, Prentice-Hall, 1964

EVANS G J and LINDLEY R M, *The Use of RAS and Related Models in Manpower Forecasting*, Research Paper No 22, Centre for Industrial Economic and Business Research, University of Warwick, 1972

EVELY R and LITTLE I M D, *Concentration in British Industry*, Cambridge University Press, 1960

EYKEN WILLEM VAN DER, A Mecca in the Midlands, *Financial Times*, 3 October 1968

FAGEN R E and HALL A D, Definition of Systems, *General Systems*, 1, 1956, pp 18–28

FAIRCHILD M, Skill and Specialization, *Personnel Journal*, ix, 1930

FALK R and CLARK I, Planning for Growth, *Management Today*, June 1966, pp 85–8 and 151

FARNHAM D and PEACOCK A, Raising IR on the Council Agenda, *Personnel Management*, December 1975, pp 25–9

FAYOL H, *General and Industrial Administration*, Durod, Paris, 1915

FESTINGER L, *A Theory of Cognitive Dissonance*, Row Peterson, 1957

FIELDS A, *Method Study*, Cassells, 1969

FINNIGAN J, *Industrial Training Management*, Business Books, 1970

FISCH G G, Line-Staff is Obsolete, in *Harvard Business Review*, 39 (5),

September—October 1961

FISCHER F E, Personnel Function in Tomorrow's Company, *Personnel*, 45, 1968, pp 64–71, and in McFarland D E, 1971, qv

FISHER M R, *The Economic Analysis of Labour*, Weidenfeld and Nicholson, 1971

FLANAGAN J C, Critical Requirements: a new Approach to Employee Evaluation, *Personnel Psychology*, 2, 1949

FLANAGAN R J and WEBER A R, *Bargaining Without Boundaries*, University of Chicago Press, 1974

FLANDERS A, *Trade Unions*, Hutchinson, 1952

FLANDERS A, *Industrial Relations: What is Wrong with the System?*, IPM, 1965

FLANDERS A, *Management and Unions: Theory and Reform of Industrial Relations*, Faber and Faber, 1970

FLANDERS A, *Collective Bargaining*, Penguin, 1969

FLANDERS A, *Collective Bargaining: Prescription for Change*, Faber and Faber, 1967

FLANDERS A, *The Fawley Productivity Agreements*, Faber and Faber, 1968

FLANDERS A, POMERANZ R and WOODWARD J, *Experiment in Industrial Democracy: a Study of the John Lewis Partnership*, Faber and Faber, 1964

FLETCHER E, The Road to Joint Control, *Management Today*, April 1970, pp 90–3 and 162

FLORENCE P S, *The Logic of British and American Industry*, Routledge and Kegan Paul, 2nd edn, 1961

FLORENCE P S, *Economics and Sociology of Industry*, Watts, 1964

FOGARTY M P, *Personality and Group Relations in Industry*, Longmans, 1956

FOGARTY M P, *The Just Wage*, Chapman, 1961

FOGARTY M P, *The Rules of Work*, Chapman, 1961

FOGARTY M P, *Company and Corporation—One Law?*, Chapman, 1965

FOGARTY M P, *Personality and Group Relations in Industry*, Longmans Green, 1956

FOGARTY M P, *Women in Top Jobs*, PEP, 1970

FOGARTY M P, *Sex, Career and Family*, Sage, 1971

FONDA N, Managing Maternity Leave, *Personnel Management*, January 1976, pp 25–29

FORBES A F, MORGAN R W and ROWNTREE J A, Manpower Planning Models in Use in the Civil Service Department, *Personnel Review*, 4 (3), Summer 1975, pp 23–35

FORDHAM H W, On Training Managers, *Personnel Management*, June 1963, pp 55–59

FORREST A, The Manager's Guide to Setting Targets, *Industrial Society*, 1966

FOSTER G, Executives on the Grid, *Management Today*, April 1966, pp 33–8

FOULKES D, *Law for Managers*, Butterworths, 1971

Foundation for Research on Human Behaviour, *Human Factors in Research Administration*, Graphic Services Inc, Ypsilanti, Michigan, 1956

FOWLER A, *Personnel Management in Local Government*, IPM, 1975

FOX A, *The Milton Plan*, IPM, 1965

Fox A, *Man Mismanagement*, Hutchinson, 1974

Fox A, *Industrial Sociology and Industrial Relations*, Research Paper No 3: Royal Commission on Trade Unions and Employers' Associations, HMSO, 1966

Fox A, Collective Bargaining, Flanders and the Webbs, *British Journal of Industrial Relations*, 13 July 1975

Fox A, Industrial Relations: A Critique of Pluralist Ideology, in Child J, 1973, qv

Fox A, *A Sociology of Work in Industry*, Collier-Macmillan, 1971

Fox A and FLANDERS A, The Reform of Collective Bargaining: From Donovan to Durkheim, *British Journal of Industrial Relations*, 7 July 1969

Fox A, *Beyond Contract*, Faber and Faber, 1974

FRASER J M, *A Handbook of Employment Interviewing*, Macdonald and Evans, 1950

FRASER J M, *Introduction to Personnel Management*, Nelson, 1971

FRASER J M, *Employment Interviewing*, Macdonald and Evans, 1966, 4th edn

FRASER W H, *Trade Unions and Society: the Struggle for Acceptance 1850–80*, Allen and Unwin, 1974

FREIDSON E, *The Professions and their Prospects*, Sage, 1974

FRENCH J R P and RAVEN B H, The Bases of Social Power, in Cartwright D, (ed) *Studies in Social Power*, Institute for Social Research, Ann Arbor, Michigan, 1959 qv

FRENCH W, *The Personnel Management Process*, Houghton-Miffin, 1974

FRENCH W, *Personnel Management and Organization Development*, Houghton-Mifflin, 1973

FULTON LORD, *The Civil Service*, Vol 1, Report of the Committee, HMSO, 1968, Cmnd 3638

GAGNE R M, *The Conditions of Learning*, Holt, Rinehart and Winston, 1970

GALBRAITH J K, *Economics and Public Purpose*, Deutsch, 1974 (a)

GALBRAITH J K, *The New Industrial State*, Hamish Hamilton, 1974, 2nd edn (b)

GARDINER G, *The Operating Executive and the Personnel Department*, AMA, Personnel Series, No 121, 1948

GARDNER W and TAYLOR P, *Health at Work*, Associated Business Programmes, 1975

GARNETT J, *The Work Challenge*, Industrial Society, 1973

GAYLER J L and PURVIS R L, *Industrial Law*, Harrap, 1972, 2nd edn

GENDERS J E and URWIN N J, *Wages and Salaries*, IPM, 1962

GENTLES E M, *Training the Operator—a Practical Guide*, IPM, 1969

GIBSON J L, IVANCEVICH J M and DONNELLY J H, *Organizations—Behaviour, Structure, Processes*, Irwin-Dorsey, 1976, 2nd edn

GILES W J and ROBINSON D F, *Human Asset Accounting*, IPM, 1972

GILL D, UNGERSON B and THAKUR M, *Performance Appraisal in Perspective: a Survey of Current Practice*, IPM, 1973

GILL H S, Handling Redundancy, *Personnel Management*, March 1975, pp 34–7

GILL J and MOLANDER C F, Beyond Management by Objectives, *Personnel Management*, August 1970

GILLING-SMITH D, *The Manager's Guide to Pensions*, IPM, 1974

GILMAN G, An Inquiry into the Nature and Use of Authority, in Haire M, (ed), *Organization Theory in Industrial Practice*, Wiley, 1962

GLUCKLICH P *et al*, Equal Pay Experience in 25 Firms, *Department of Employment Gazette*, December 1976, pp 1337–40

GLYNN A and SUTCLIFFE B, *British Capitalism, Workers and the Profits Squeeze*, Penguin, 1972

GOLDEN C S and RUTTENBERG H J, *The Dynamics of Industrial Bureaucracy*, Harper and Bros, 1924

GOLDSMITH M and MACKAY A, *The Science of Science*, Penguin, 1966

GOLDTHORPE J H, LOCKWOOD D, BECHHOFER F and PLATT J, *The Affluent Worker: Industrial Attitudes and Behaviour*, Cambridge University Press, 1968

GOLDTHORPE J H, Industrial Relations in Great Britain: A Critique of Reformism, *Politics and Society*, 1974, pp 419–52

GOODMAN J F B and WHITTINGHAM T G, *Shop Stewards in British Industry*, McGraw-Hill, 1969

GOODMAN J F B, ARMSTRONG E G A, DAVIS J and WAGNER A, *Rule Making and Industrial Peace*, Croom Helm, 1977

GOODRICH C L, *The Frontier of Control 1920*, Penguin, 1975

GORE W J (ed), *Administrative Decision-making: A Reader*, Free Press, Glencoe, 1962

GOTTSCHALK A W, A Behavioural Analysis of Bargaining, in Warner M (ed), *The Sociology of the Workplace*, Allen and Unwin, 1973, pp 36–81

GOWER L C B, *Company Law*, Sweet and Maxwell, 1969, 3rd edn

GOULDNER A W, *Patterns of Industrial Bureaucracy*, Routledge and Kegan Paul, 1955

GOULDNER A W, Organizational Analysis, in Merton R K, Broom L and Cottrell L S, *Sociology Today*, Basic Books, 1959, pp 400–28

GOWLER D, Determinants of the Supply of Labour to the Firm, *Journal of Management Studies*, 6 (1), February 1969

GOWLER D, Values, Contracts and Job Satisfaction, *Personnel Review*, 3 (4), Autumn 1974, pp 4–14

GOWLER D, and LEGGE K, *Managerial Stress*, Gower, 1975

GOYDER G, *The Responsible Worker*, Hutchinson, 1975

GRANGER C H, The Hierarchy of Objectives, *Harvard Business Review*, May/June 1964

GRANT J V and SMITH A, *Personnel Administration and Industrial Relations*, Longman, 1969

GRAY D H, *Manpower Planning: an Approach to the Problem*, IPM, 1966

GREENHALGH R M, *Industrial Tribunals—a Practical Guide*, IPM, 1973

GREENLAW P and SMITH R D, *Personnel Management: a Management Science Approach*, International Textbook Company, 1970

GRINOLD R C and MARSHALL K T, *Manpower Planning Models*, North Holland, 1977

GROSS N, MASON W S and MCEACHERN A W, *Explorations in Role Analysis*, Chapman and Hall, 1958

GRUNFELD C, *Law of Redundancy*, Sweet and Maxwell, 1971

547

GUEST D and FATCHETT D, *Worker Participation: Individual Control and Performance*, IPM, 1974

GUEST R H, *Organization Change—the Effect of Successful Leadership*, Tavistock Publications, 1962

GUEST R H, Managerial Succession in a Complex Organization, *American Journal of Sociology*, 68, 1962/3

GUION R M, *Personal Testing*, McGraw-Hill, New York, 1965

HABERSTROH C J, Organization and Design of Systems Analysis, in March J G, 1965, qv

HACKMAN R C, *The Motivated Working Adult*, AMA, 1969

HAGUE H, *Management Training for Real*, IPM, 1973

HAHLO H R and TREBILCOCK M J, *Casebook on Company Law*, Sweet and Maxwell, 1977, 2nd edn

HAINE M, *Organization Theory in Industrial Practice*, Wiley, 1962

HAIRE M, GHISELLI E E, and PORTER L W, *Managerial Thinking*, Wiley, 1966

HALEY SIR W, The Look of Management, *The Manager*, November 1964

HALL D T and NOUGAIN K E, An Examination of Maslow's Need Hierarchy in an Organizational Setting, *Organization Behaviour and Human Performance*, (3), 1968, pp 12–35

HALL J and JONES D C, Social Grading of Occupations, *British Journal of Sociology*, Vol 1, 1950

HALL M, The Death of the Career Company, *Management Today*, September 1963

HALL M, Productive Manpower Planning, *New Society*, July 1966

HALL M, Towards a Manpower Grid, *Personnel Management*, June 1965, pp 72–8

HAMBLIN A C, *Evaluation and Control of Training*, McGraw-Hill, 1974

HANIKA F DE P, *New Thinking in Management*, Hutchinson, 1965

HARRIS M (ed), *The Realities of Productivity Bargaining*, IPM, 1968

HARRISON R, *Redundancy in Western Europe*, IPM, 1975

HARSANYI J C, Measurement of Social Power, Opportunity Costs, and the Theory of Two-Person Bargaining Games, *Behavioural Science*, 1962

HARTMANN H, Managerial Employees—New Participants in Industrial Relations, *British Journal of Industrial Relations*, XII (2), July 1974, pp 268–81

HARVEY J, Elementary Economics, Macmillan, 1971 3rd edn

HARVEY B and MURRAY R, *Industrial Health Technology*, Butterworth, 1968

HAWKINS K, Company Bargaining Problems and Prospects, *BJIR*, July 1971

HAYWOOD S C, *Managing the Health Service*, Allen and Unwin, 1974

HEALD G (ed), *Approaches in the Study of Organizational Behaviour*, Tavistock Publications, 1970

HEINRICH H W, *Industrial Accident Prevention: A Scientific Approach*, McGraw-Hill, 1959, 4th edn

HEKEMIAN J S and JONES C H, Put People on Your Balance Sheet, *Harvard Business Review*, 1967

HELLER F, An Evaluation of the Personnel Management Function, in McFarland D E (ed), 1971, qv

HEMPHILL J K, *Dimensions of Executive Positions: a Study of the Basic Characteristics of the Positions of Ninety-three Business Executives*, Bureau of Business Research, Ohio State University, 1960

HENEMAN H G and SCHWAB D P, An evaluation of research on expectancy theory predictions of employee performance, *Psychological Bulletin*, 1972

HEPPLE B A and O'HIGGINS P, *Employment Law*, Sweet and Maxwell, 1976, 2nd edn

HERTZ D B and RUBENSTEIN A H, *Team Research*, Eastern Technical Publications, Cambridge, Mass, June 1953

HERZBERG F, *Work and the Nature of Man*, Staples, 1968

HESSELING DR P, *Strategy of Evaluation Research in the Field of Supervisory and Managerial Training*. Assen, Holland, 1966, Van Gorcum

HICKS J R, *The Theory of Wages*, Macmillan, 1932

HICKSON D J *et al*, A Strategic Contingencies Theory of Intra-Organizational Power, *Administrative Science Quarterly*, 16, 1971

HIGG M, The Training Package—What's in it For You?, *Personnel Management*, January 1976

HILL J M M, A Consideration of Labour Turnover as a Resultant of a Quasi-Stationary Process, *Human Relations*, 4 (3), August 1951, pp 255–64

HILL C, *Society and Puritanism in Pre-Revolutionary England*, Panther, 1969

HINTON B L, An Empirical Investigation of the Herzberg Methodology and Two-Factor Theory, *Organization Behaviour and Human Performance*, (3), 1968

HOGGART R, *The Uses of Literacy*, Penguin, 1958

HOLDING D H, *Principles of Training*, Pergamon, 1965

HOLLAND G, Training for the Nation, *Personnel Management*, October 1975, pp 33–6

HOLLOWELL P, *The Lorry Driver*, Routledge and Kegan Paul, 1968

HOMANS G C, *The Human Group*, Routledge and Kegan Paul, 1951

HONEY P, *Face to Face*, IPM, 1976

HOPKINS R R, *A Handbook of Industrial Welfare*, Pitman, 1955

HOPKINS T K, *The Exercise of Influence in Small Groups*, Bedminster Press, 1964

HOPPOCK R, *Job Satisfaction*, Harper Bros, 1935

HOWELLS G W, A Scientific Approach to Job Specification, *Scientific Business*, August 1964

HOWELLS R and BARRETT B, *The Manager's Guide to the Health and Safety at Work Act*, IPM, 1976

HUGHES C L, *Goal Setting: Key to Individual and Organizational Effectiveness*, AMA, 1965

HUGHES C L, Why Goal Oriented Performance Reviews Fail, *Personnel Journal*, June 1966

HUGHES E C, *Men and Their Work*, Free Press, 1958

HUGHES J and POLLINS J H, *Trade Unions in Great Britain*, David and Charles, 1973

HUGHES M G, *Secondary School Administration: A Management Approach*,

Pergamon, 1970

HULL C L, *Principles of Behaviour*, Appleton-Century-Crofts, 1943

HULL C L, *A Behaviour System*, Yale University Press, 1943

HUMBLE J W, *Improving Management Performance*, BIM, 1965

HUMBLE J W, Improving Management, *Personnel Management*, September 1965, pp 136–42

HUMBLE J W, *Management by Objectives*, Industrial Educational and Research Foundation, 1967

HUMBLE J W, Avoiding the Pitfalls of the MbO Trap, *European Business*, 27, Autumn 1970

HUMBLE J W, *Management by Objectives in Action*, McGraw-Hill, 1970

HUMBLE J W, *The Experienced Manager*, McGraw-Hill, 1973

HUNERYAGER S G and HECKMAN I L (eds), *Human Relations in Management*, Edward Arnold, 1967

HUNT R G and LICHTMAN G M, Counselling of Employees by Work Supervisors: Concepts, Attitudes and Practices in a White Collar Organization, *Journal of Counselling Psychology*, 16 (1), 1969, pp 81–6

HUNTER L C, *Labour Problems of Technological Change*, Allen and Unwin, 1970

HUNTER T D, Self-Run Hospitals, *New Society*, 14 September 1967

HUNTER T D, New View of the Hospital, in *The Lancet*, 11, (933), 1963

HUNTER T D, Hierarchy or Arena? The Administrative Implications of a Socio-Therapeutic Regime, in Farndale and Freeman, *New Aspects of the Mental Health Services*, Pergamon, 1967

HUSBAND R M, Payment Structures Made to Measure, *Personnel Management*, April 1975, pp 27–9 and 39

HUSBAND T M, *Work Analysis and Pay Structure*, McGraw-Hill, 1975

HUSSEY D E, *Corporate Planning*, Pergamon, 1974

HYMAN H H, The Value Systems of Different Classes: A Social-Psychological Contribution to the Analysis of Stratification, in Bendix R and Lipset S M (eds), *Class Status and Power*, Free Press, 1953

HYMAN R, *Disputes Procedure in Action*, Heinemann, 1972

HYMAN R, *Strikes*, Fontana, 1972

HYMAN R, *Industrial Relations: A Marxist Introduction*, Macmillan, 1976

HYMAN R and FRYER B, Trade Unions, in McKinlay J B (ed), *Processing People*, Holt, Rinehart and Winston, 1975

HYMAN R and BROUGH I, *Social Values and Industrial Relations*, Blackwell, 1975

Industrial Society, *Design of Personnel Systems and Research*, Goulet, 1969

Industrial Society, *Guide to the Health and Safety at Work Act*, Industrial Society, 1974

Industrial Society, *Practical Policies for Participation*, Industrial Society, 1974

INGHAM G K, *Strikes and Industrial Conflict*, Macmillan, 1974

IPM, *Membership Examination, Parts 1, 2, 3*, IPM, 1975

IPM, Statement on Personnel Management and Personnel Policies, *Personnel Management*, March 1963, pp 11–15

IPM, *Worker Participation in Western Europe*, IPM, 1976

IPM, *Perspectives in Manpower Planning*, IPM, 1967

IPM, *Personnel Management: a Bibliography*, IPM, 1968

IPM, *Personnel Management: a Bibliography*, IPM, 1973, 1974, 1975 (in six parts)

International Labour Organization, *Job Evaluation*, ILO, 1960

Irish National Productivity Committee, *Proceedings of Manpower Policies Seminar* INPC, Dublin, 1963

Iron and Steel Industry Training Board, *Levy Exemption and Levy Abatement,* ISITB, 1974

Iron and Steel Industry Training Board, *Identification of Training Needs,* ISITB, 1975

ISTED B, The de la Rue Comparison Index, *Personnel,* April 1968

JAAP T and WATSON J A, A Conceptual Approach to Training, *Personnel Management*, September 1970, pp 30–33

JACKSON J M, The Normative Regulation of Authoritative Behaviour, in *The University of Kansas, Comparative Studies of Mental Hospital Organization*, Kansas, 1962

JACKSON D, TURNER H A and WILKINSON F, *Do Trade Unions Cause Inflation?* Cambridge University Press, 1972

JAFFE A J and FROOMKIN J, *Technology and Jobs*, Praeger, 1968

JAFFE A J, and STEWARD C D, *Manpower Resources and Utilization*, Chapman Hall, 1951

JAMES R, Is there a case for Local Authority Policy Planning? *Public Administration*, 51, Summer 1973, pp 147–63

JAQUES E *Measurement of Responsibility*, Harvard University Press, 1956

JAQUES E, *Equitable Payment*, Heinemann, 1961

JAQUES E, *Time Span Handbook*, Heinemann, 1964

JAQUES E, *Progression Handbook*, Heinemann, 1968

JAQUES E, *The Changing Culture of a Factory*, Tavistock, 1951

JENKINS LORD, *Report of the Company Law Committee*, (Chairman; Lord Jenkins) HMSO, June 1962, Cmnd 1749

JENSEN G E, *Dynamics of Instructional Groups*, National Society for the Study of Education, Yearbook, 1960

JENKS E, *The State and the Nation*, Dent, 1919

JOHNSON D M, *The Psychology of Thought and Judgement*, Harper, 1955

JONES G N, *Planned Organizational Change*, Routledge and Kegan Paul, 1969

JONES G, BELL D, CENTER A, and COLEMAN D, *Perspectives in Manpower Planning*, IPM, 1967

JONES J K C, BROWN C A and NICHOLSON N, Absence from Work: Its meaning, measurement and control, *International Review of Applied Psychology*, 22 (2), 1973

JONES K, *The Human Face of Change—Social Responsibility and Rationalization at British Steel*, IPM, 1974

JONES P, Incomes Policy and the Public Sector, *Personnel Management*, 10 (2), February 1978

JONES R M, *Absenteeism*, Manpower Paper No 4, HMSO, 1971

KAHN-FREUND O, *Labour and the Law*, Stevens, 1972, revised edn 1977

KAHN R L and KATZ D, Leadership Practices in Relation to Productivity and Morale, in Cartwright D and Zander A, *Group Dynamics*, qv

KARN H W and GILMER B V H, *Readings in Industrial and Business Psychology*, McGraw-Hill, 1952

KAST F E and ROSENZWEIG J E, General Systems Theory: Applications for Organization and Management, *Academy of Management Journal*, December 1972, pp 447–65

KATZ E, The Diffusion of New Ideas and Practices, Schramm W L, 1963, pp 77–93, qv

KATZ E and LAZARSFELD P F, *Personal Influence*, Free Press, 1955

KAY H, DODD B and SIME M, *Teaching Machines and Programmed Instruction*, Penguin, 1968

KEENOY T, *Industrial Relations: Power and Conflict*, University of Oxford, D Phil Thesis, 1977

KELLEY E L and FISKE O W, *The Prediction of Performance in Clinical Psychology*, University of Michigan Press, 1951

KELLEY H H, Communication in Experimentally Created Hierarchies in *Human Relations*, 1951, 4, pp 39–56

KELLEY J, *Is Scientific Management Possible?* Faber, 1968

KELLY R W, *Hiring the Worker*, Engineering Magazine Company, New York, 1918

KENNY T P, Stating the Case for Welfare, *Personnel Management*, September 1975, pp 18–21 and 35

KENNY T P, The Asbestos Situation—Or Whose Safety First? *Personnel Management*, June 1976

KEPNER C H and TREGOE B B, *The rational Manager*, McGraw-Hill, 1965

KESSLER B S and PALMER G, Reconsidering Recognition, *Personnel Management*, July 1975, pp 18–21 and 37

KESSLER S and WEEKES B, *Conflict at Work—Re-shaping Industrial Relations*, BBC Publications, 1971

KILLINGSWORTH C C, The Modernization of West Coast Longshore Work Rules, *Industrial and Labour Relations Review*, April 1962

KING D, *Training Within the Organization*, Tavistock, 1968

KINGSLEY R and M, *An Industrial Day Nursery—the Personnel Manager's Guide*, IPM, 1969

KLEIN L, *Multi Products Ltd—a Case Study on the Social Effects of Rationalized Production*, HMSO, 1964

KNIGHT M W B, *Management by Objectives*, Smiths Industries Ltd, October 1966

KNIVETON B H, Negotiating: Some Training Implications, *Industrial Relations Journal*, V (3), Autumn 1974

KOONTZ H and O'DONNELL C, *Management: A Systems and Contingency Analysis of Managerial Functions*, McGraw Hill, 1976, 6th edn

KORNHAUSER W, *Scientists in Industry*, University of California Press, 1962

KORNHAUSER W, *Strains and Accommodations in Industrial Research Organizations in the United States*, University of California Institute of Industrial Relations, 1963

KRUISINGA H J (ed), *The Balance between Centralization and Decentralization in Managerial Control*, Stenfert Kroese NV, Leiden, 1954

LANDY F J and TRUMBO D A, *Psychology of Work Behaviour*, Dorsey Press, 1976

LANE T and ROBERTS K, *Strike at Pilkingtons*, Fontana, 1971

LANG D, Project Control Comes to Personnel, *Personnel Management*, May 1974, pp 27–30

LARKCOM J (ed), *Personnel Management Handbook*, Business Publications, 1967

LASSWELL H D et al, *Propaganda and Promotional Activities*, University of Chicago Press, 1969

LAWLER E E and SUTTLE J L, A Casual Correlational Test of the Need Hierarchy Concept, *Organizational Behaviour and Human Performance*, 7, 1972, pp 265–87

LAWLER E E, *Pay and Organizational Effectiveness*, McGraw Hill, 1971

LAWRENCE J (ed), *Company Manpower Planning in Perspective*, IPM/IMS, 1975

LAWRENCE J, Manpower and Personnel Models in Britain, *Personnel Review*, 2 (3) Summer 1973, pp 4–26

LAWRENCE P R, and LORSCH J W, *Organization and Environment*, Harvard University Press, 1967

LAWRENCE S, Productivity Bargaining: Resurrection or Reprieve, *Personnel Management*, January 1974, pp 29–31

LAWRENCE S, Industrial Relations Training: Oases in the Desert, *Personnel Management*, July 1973, pp 22– 29

LAWSHE C H, *Principles of Personnel Testing*, McGraw-Hill, 1948

LEAVITT H J, *Managerial Psychology*, Chicago, 1974

LE BRETON P P and JEMMOMG D A, *Planning Theory*, Prentice-Hall, 1961

LEE H C, Electronic Data Processing and Employee Perception of Changes in Work Skill Requirements and Work Characteristics, *Personnel Journal*, July/August 1965

LEGGE D E, *Skills*, Penguin, 1970

LEGGE K, *Power, Innovation and Problem-Solving in Personnel Management*, McGraw-Hill, 1978

LEICESTER C, *The National Environment for Manpower Planning* (Paper to Corporate Planning Seminar, School of Business Studies, University of Liverpool, 1968), in Bosworth D and Evans G, 1973, qv

LEISERSON M W, Three Studies, in Hugh-Jones EM, (ed), *Wage Structure in Theory and Practice*, North Holland, 1966

LERNER S W, *Breakaway Unions and the Small Trade Union*, Allen and Unwin, 1961

LESTER R A, *Manpower Planning in Free Society*, Princeton, 1966

LEVINE J and BUTLER J, Lecture versus Group Decision in Changing Behaviour, *Journal of Applied Psychology*, 36, 1952

LEVINE S, Occupation and Personality: Relationship Between the Social Factors of the Job and Human Orientation, *Personnel and Guidance Journal*, 41, 1963

LEVINGER G, The Development of Perceptions and Behaviour in Newly

Formed Social Power Relationships, in Cartwright D (ed), *Studies in Social Power*, University of Michigan, 1959

LEVITT T, The Dangers of Social Responsibility, *Harvard Business Review*, Sept–Oct 1956

LEVY A B, *Private Corporations and their Control*, Routledge and Kegan Paul, 1950

LEWIN K, *Field Theory in Social Science*, Harper, 1951

LEWIN K, *Principles of Topological Psychology*, McGraw-Hill, 1936

LEWIN K, Studies in Group Decision, in Cartwright D and Zander A, *Group Dynamics*, 1953, qv

LEWIS R and STEWART R, *The Boss*, Phoenix House, 1958

LIEPMANN K K, *The Journey to Work*, Kegan Paul, Trench and Trubner, 1944

LIKERT R, *New Patterns in Management*, McGraw-Hill, 1961

LIKERT R, *The Human Organization*, McGraw-Hill, 1967

LIKERT R, Measuring Organizational Performance, *Harvard Business Review*, March/April 1958

LILLEY S, *Automation and Social Progress*, Lawrence and Wishart, 1957

LINTON R, *The Study of Man*, Appleton-Century-Crofts, 1964

LIONBERGER H F, *Adoption of New Ideas and Practices*, Iowa State University Press, 1960

LIPPITT G L, *Organization Renewal*, Meredith Corporation, 1969

LIPPITT R, PORBANSKY N, REDL F and ROSEN S, The Dynamics of Power, *Human Relations*, 5, 1952

LIPPIT T R and WHITE R, Leader Behaviour and Member Reaction in Three Social Climates, in Cartwright D and Zander A, 1953, qv

LITTERER J A, *The Analysis of Organizations—Organization, Structure and Behaviour*, Wiley, 1967

LITWIN G H and STRINGER R A, *Motivation and Organizational Climate*, Harvard Business School, 1968

LIVY B, *Job Evaluation*, Allen and Unwin, 1975

LLEWELLYN W G, *Executive Compensation in Large Industrial Corporations*, National Bureau of Economic Research, 1968

LOCKYER K G, *Factory and Production Management*, Pitman, 1974

LOGAN H H, Line and Staff—An Obsolete Concept, *Personnel*, January–February 1966

LONG G, Dismissals in Europe, *Personnel Management*, February 1974, pp 38–39 and 43

LOVERIDGE R, *Collective Bargaining by National Employees in the UK*, Institute of Labour and Industrial Relations, University of Michigan, 1971

LUCIUS M J, *Personnel Management*, Irwin-Dorsey, 1975

LUKES S, *Power: a Radical View*, Macmillan, 1974

LUMLEY R, *White Collar Unionism in Britain*, Methuen, 1973

LUPTON T, The Practical Analysis of Change in Organizations, *Journal of Management Studies*, May 1965

LUPTON T, *Industrial Behaviour and Personnel Management*, IPM, 1964

LUPTON T, *Management and the Social Sciences*, Penguin, 1971

LUPTON T, *On the Shop Floor*, Pergamon, 1963

LUPTON T (ed), *Payment Systems*, Penguin, 1972

LUPTON T and BOWEY A M, *Wages and Salaries*, Penguin, 1974
LUPTON T and GOWLER D, *Selecting a Wage Payment System*, Kogan Page, 1969
LYMAN E L, Occupational Differences in the Values Attached to Work, *American Journal of Sociology*, 61, 1955
LYNCH J U, *Making Manpower Effective*, Pan Books, 1968
LYNCH P, Are Careers Obsolete?, *Personnel*, August 1968
LYNTON P R and PAREEK U, *Training for Development*, Dorsey, 1967
LYONS T P, *The Personnel Function in a Changing Environment*, Pitman, 1971
LYTLE C W, *Job Evaluation Methods*, Ronald Press, 1942
LYTLE C W, *Wage Incentive Methods*, Ronald Press
MACE M L, *Directors*, Harvard Business School, 1971
MACKENZIE DAVEY D et al, *Attitude Surveys in Industry*, IPM, 1970
MACKINNON D W, What do we mean by Talent and how do we test for it?, *College Admission, 7, The Search for Talent*, College Entrance Examination Board, New York, 1960
MADDEN J M, A Review of Some Literature on Judgement with Implications for Job Evaluation, in USAF WADD, *Technical Note*, 1960, No 60–212
MAGER R F, *Preparing Instructional Objectives*, Fearon, 1962
MAINE SIR H S, *Ancient Law*, Oxford University Press, 1861, 1931 edn
MAHLER W R, Let's get more Scientific in Rating Employees, in Dooher M J and Marquis V (eds), *Rating Employee and Supervisory Performance*, AMA, 1950
MALBERT D, *The Board Responsible to Whom?* Foundation for Business Responsibilities, 1973
Management Education, Training and Development Committee, *Management Training in Industrial Relations*, National Economic Development Office, 1975
MANGHAM I, Uncovering the Company Unconscious, *Management Today*, March 1968, pp 109–112
Manpower Services Commission, *Annual Report*, 1974–5, MPSC, 1975
MANSFIELD COOPER W and WOOD J C, *Outlines of Industrial Law*, Butterworth, 1974
MANT A, *The Experienced Manager*, BIM, 1969
MANT A, *The Rise and Fall of the British Manager*, Macmillan, 1977
MARCH J G (ed), *Handbook of Organizations*, Rand McNally, 1965
MARCH J G and SIMON H A, *Organizations*, Wiley, 1958
MARGERISON C J and ASHTON D, *Manpower Planning*, Longman, 1974
MARGERISON C J, What do we mean by Industrial Relations?, *British Journal of Industrial Relations*, VII (2), July 1969, pp 273–86
MARGERISON C J, *Managing Effective Work Groups*, McGraw-Hill, 1973
MARGUILES N and RAIA A P, *Organizational Development*, McGraw-Hill, 1972
MARKS W, *Induction—Acclimatizing People to Work*, IPM, 1974
MARKS W, *Preparing an Employee Handbook*, IPM, 1972, revised edn 1978
MARKWELL D S and ROBERTS T J, *Organization of Management Development Programmes*, Gower Press, 1969

MARPLES D, *The Decisions of Engineering Design*, Institute of Engineering Designers, 1961

MARRIOTT R, *Incentive Payments Systems*, Staples Press, 1968

MARSH A I, The Managerial Grid, *Industrial Welfare*, October 1965

MARSH A I, *Managers and Shop Stewards—Shop Floor Revolution?* IPM, 1973

MARTIN R and FRYER R H, *Redundancy and Paternalist Capitalism*, Allen and Unwin, 1973

MASLOW A H, A Theory of Human Motivation, *Psychological Review*, 50, 1943, pp 370–96

MASLOW A H, *Motivation and Personality*, Harper and Row, 1970

MAURER H, *Great Enterprise*, Macmillan, 1955

MAYMAN D, What Price People?, *Personnel Management*, December 1974, pp 35–37

MAYO E, *The Human Problems of an Industrial Civilization*, Macmillan, 1933

MAYO E, *The Social Problems of an Industrial Civilization*, Harvard Business School, 1949 (Routledge and Kegan Paul reprint, 1975)

MCBEATH G, *Organization and Manpower Planning*, Business Books, 1969

MCBEATH G, and RANDS D N, *Salary Administration*, Business Books, 1969

MCCAIG P A, Productivity Measurement of Staff, *Personnel Management*, June 1967, pp 61–65

MCCARTHY W E J, *Trade Unions*, Penguin, 1972

MCCARTHY W E J, Changing Bargaining Structures, in Kessler S and Weekes B (eds), *Conflict at Work*, qv

MCCARTHY W E J, O'BRIEN J F and DOWD V G, *Wage Inflation and Wage Leadership*, The Economic and Social Research Institute, Dublin, 1975

MCCARTHY W E J and COLLIER A S, *Coming to Terms with Trade Unions*, IPM, 1973

MCCARTHY W E J, *Making Whitley Work*, Dept of Health and Social Security, 1977

MCCLELLAND D C, *The Achieving Society*, Van Nostrand, 1961

MCCONKY D D, *How to Manage by Results*, AMA, New York, 1965

MCFARLAND D E, *Personnel Management Theory and Practice*, Macmillan, 1968

MCFARLAND D E, *Personnel Management*, Penguin, 1971

MCGLYNE J E, *Unfair Dismissal Cases*, Butterworths, 1976

MCGREGOR D, *The Human Side of Enterprise*, McGraw-Hill, New York, 1960

MCGREGOR D, *The Professional Manager*, McGraw-Hill, 1967

MCIVER R M and PAGE C H, *Society—An Introductory Analysis*, Macmillan, 1953

MCIVER R M, Professional Groups and Cultural Norms, in Vollmer H M and Mills D L, *Professionalization*, Prentice-Hall, 1966

MCKINLAY J B, *Processing People*, Holt Rinehart, Winston, 1974

MEAD SIR C, *Report re-appraising the Aims and Organization of the British Institute of Management*, BIM, 1968

MEADE J P DE C and GREIG F W, *Supervisory Training: a New Approach for Management*, HMSO, 1966

556

MEGGINSON L C, *Personnel—a Behavioural Approach to Administration*, Irwin, 1972

MELLISH M, *The Docks after Devlin*, Heinemann, 1972

MENZIES I E P, and ANSTEY E, *Staff Reporting*, Allen and Unwin, 1951

MEPHAM G J, *Equal Opportunity and Equal Pay*, IPM, 1974

MERRET A J, and WHITE M R M, *Incentive Payment Systems for Managers*, Gower Press, 1968

MERRIE A H, Evaluation of Manual and Non-manual Jobs, *Personnel Management*, July/August 1948

MERTON R, *Social Theory and Social Structure*, The Free Press, 1948

METCALF H C and URWICK L, *Dynamic Administration*, Pitman, 1941

MILLARD G, *Personnel Management in Hospitals*, IPM, 1972

MILLER E C, *Objectives and Standards—an Approach to Planning and Control*, AMA, New York, 1966

MILLER E J and RICE A K, *Systems of Organization: the Control of Task and Sentient Boundaries*, Tavistock, 1967

MILLER F B, *Personnel Research Contributions by US Universities*, New York State School of Industrial and Labour Relations, 1960

MILLER K, *Psychological Testing*, Gower, 1975

MILLER S, Relationships of Personality to Occupation Setting and Function, *Journal of Counselling Psychology*, 9, 1962

MILLER W, *Men in Business, Essays on the Historical Role of the Entrepreneur*, Harper, 1952

MILLERSON G, *The Qualifying Associations*, Routledge and Kegan Paul, 1964

MILLS H R, *Teaching and Training*, Macmillan, 1967

MILNE-BAILEY W, *Trade Union Documents*, Macmillan, 1929

MINER J B and MINER M G, *Personnel and Industrial Relations*, Macmillan, 1977, 3rd edn

Ministry of Education, *Technical Education*, HMSO, 1956

Ministry of Labour, *Dismissal Procedures*, HMSO, 1967

Ministry of Labour, *Glossary of Training Terms*, HMSO, 1967

Ministry of Labour, *Industrial Relations Handbook*, HMSO, 1961

Ministry of Labour, *Manpower Studies No 1: The Pattern of the Future*, HMSO, 1964

MITCHELL E, *The Employer's Guide to the Law on Health, Safety and Welfare at Work*, Business Books, 1974

MITCHELL W, *Employee Relations within the Factory*, Macmillan, 1973

MOORE W E, *Industrial Relations and the Social Order*, Macmillan, 1951

MORGAN J G, *European Approaches to Responsibility*, Foundation for Business Responsibilities, 1975

MORLEY I and STEPHENSON G, *The Social Psychology of Bargaining*, Allen and Unwin, 1977

MORRIS J W, *Principles and Practice of Job Evaluation*, Heinemann, 1973

MORRISON R F, OWENS W A, GLENNON J R and ALBRIGHT L E, Factored Life History Antecedents of Industrial Research Performance, *Journal of Applied Psychology*, 1962

MORRISON S, What is wrong with voluntary organizations, *Social Service*

557

Quarterly, July 1972

MORSE N C and WEISS R S, The Function and Meaning of Work and the Job, *American Sociological Review,* 1955

MORSE N, *Satisfactions of the White Collar Job*, Michigan, 1953

MOSER C A, *Survey Methods in Social Investigation*, Heinemann, 1971

MOSS A, A Company Approach to Industry Manpower Forecasting, *Personnel Review*, 3 (2) Spring 1974, pp 8–24

MOUZELIS N P, *Organization and Bureaucracy*, RKP, 1967

MOXON G R, *The Functions of a Personnel Department*, IPM, 1966

MUKHERJEE S, *Changing Manpower Needs*, PEP, 1970

MUMFORD A, *The Manager and Training*, Pitman, 1971

MUMFORD E, *Computers, Planning and Personnel Management*, IPM, 1969

MUMFORD E, Job Satisfaction: A Method of Analysis, *Personnel Review*, 1 (3), Summer 1972, pp 48–57

MUNNS V G, *Employers' Associations*, RCTUEA Research Paper No 7, 1967

MUSGROVE F, *Patterns of Power and Authority in English Education*, Methuen, 1971

MYERS C S, *Industrial Psychology in Great Britain*, Jonathan Cape, 1933

MYERS M S, *Managing Without Unions*, Addison-Wesley Press, 1976

National Advisory Council on Education for Industry and Commerce, *Committee on Technician Courses and Examinations Report* (Haslegrave), HMSO, 1969

National Board for Prices and Incomes, *Payment by Results Systems*, HMSO, 1968

NBPI, *Top Salaries in the Private Sector and Nationalized Industries*, HMSO, 1969

NBPI, *General Problems of Low Pay*, HMSO, 1971

NBPI, *Job Evaluation*, HMSO, 1968

NBPI, *Productivity Agreements*, HMSO, 1968

NBPI, *Salary Structures*, HMSO, 1969

National Economic Development Office (NEDO), *Productivity—a Handbook of Advisory Services*, NEDO, 1967

National Economic Development Office, *Management Training in Industrial Relations*, NEDO. 1975

NAYLOR R and TORRINGTON D, *Administration of Personnel Policies*, Gower, 1974

NEWCOMB T M, *Social Psychology*, Tavistock, 1952

NEWELL A and SIMON H A, Heuristic Problem Solving, *Operations Research*, 6, Jan/Feb 1958, and May/June, 1958

Newport and Gwent Industrial Mission, *Redundant? A Personal Survival Kit*, Newport and Gwent Industrial Mission, 24, Old Hill Crescent, Christchurch, Newport, 1975

NEWSHAM D B, *The Challenge of Change to the Adult Trainee*, HMSO, 1969

NEWSTRON J W *et al A Contingency Approach to Management: Readings*, McGraw-Hill, 1975

NICHOLS T H and BEYNON H, *Living With Capitalism*, Routledge and Kegan Paul, 1977

NICHOLS T, *Ownership, Control and Ideology*, Allen and Unwin, 1969

NIVEN M M, *Personnel Management, 1913-1963*, IPM, 1967

NORSTEDT J P and AGUREN S, *The Saab-Scania Report*, Swedish Employers' Confederation, Stockholm, 1973

NORTH D T B and BUCKINGHAM G L, *Productivity Agreements and Wage Systems*, Gower, 1969

NORTHCOTT C H, *Personnel Management, Principles and Practice*, Pitman, 1955

ODIORNE G S, *Management by Objectives*, Pitman, 1965

ODIORNE G S, *Personnel Administration by Objectives*, Irwin, 1971

ODIORNE G, *Management Decisions by Objectives*, Prentice-Hall, 1968

ODIORNE G, *Personnel Policy: Incomes and Practices*, Merrill, 1963

OECD, *Job Re-design and Occupational Training for Older Workers*, OECD, Paris, 1965

OGDEN, SIR G, *The New Water Industry: Management and Structure*, HMSO, 1973

O'HIGGINS P, *Workers' Rights*, Hutchinson, Arrow Books, 1976

OLDFIELD F E, *New Look Industrial Relations*, Mason Reed, 1966

OLDFIELD R C, *The Psychology of the Interview*, Methuen, 1941

OLSEN K, Suggestions Schemes Seventies Style, *Personnel Management*, April 1976, pp 36–39

OPSAHL R L and DUNNETT M D, The Role of Financial Compensation in Industrial Motivation, *Psychological Bulletin*, 66, 1966

Organization for Economic Cooperation and Development (OECD), *The Requirements of Automated Jobs*, OECD, Paris, 1965

ORTH C D et al, *Administering Research and Development*, Irwin, 1964

ORZACK L H, Work as a Central Life Interest of Professionals, *Social Problems*, 7, 1959

PADFIELD C F, *British Constitution Made Simple*, Allen and Unwin, 1972

PAHL R E and WINKLER J T, Corporatism in Britain: why protecting industry need not mean more bureaucracy, *The Times*, 26 March 1976

Palmers' Company Law, Stevens, 22nd edn

PALMER C J and McCORMICK E J, A Factor Analysis of Job Activities, *Journal of Applied Psychology*, 45, 1961

PALMER R, A Participative Approach to Attitude Surveys, *Personnel Management*, 9 (12) December 1977, pp 26–7 and 37

PARKINSON C N, *The Rise of Big Business*, Weidenfeld and Nicolson, 1977

PARKINSON H, *Ownership of Industry*, Eyre and Spottiswoode, 1951

PARSONS T, Suggestions for a Sociological Theory of Organization, *Administrative Science Quarterly*, 1, 1956

PARSONS T, a Sociological Approach to the Theory of Organizations in Etzioni A, *Complex Organizations: A Sociological Reader*, Holt Rinehart and Winston, 1964

PARSONS T, *Professional Groups and Social Structure*, Prentice-Hall, 1939

PATERSON T T, *Job Evaluation*, Business Books, 1972

PATTEN T H, *Manpower Planning and the Development of Human Resources*, Interscience, 1971

PAUL W J and ROBERTSON K B, *Learning from Job Enrichment*, Imperial

Chemical Industries, 1970

PEACH D A and LIVERNASH E R, *Grievance Challenge and Resolution*, Harvard Business School, 1974

PEACH L, Personnel Management by Objectives, *Personnel Management*, March 1975, pp 20–23 and 39

PEARSON H, How to Pay Salaries, *Management Today*, January 1967, pp 62–3

Pemberton Quarterly, How to Teach us our Business: Let's Cut Out the Confusion in Courses and Conferences, Pemberton Quarterly, No 15, Summer 1965

PEN J, A General Theory of Bargaining, *American Economic Review*, 42, 1952

PENROSE E T, *The Theory of the Growth of the Firm*, Blackwell, Oxford, 1959

PEPPERELL E M, Why and How we Introduced a Job-Evaluation System, *Personnel Management*, Jan/Feb 1948

PERLMAN H, Social Work Method: A Review of the Past Decade, *Social Work*, October 1975

Personnel Management, *Personnel Management Handbook*, Business Publications, 1971, see also Larkcom J

PETTMAN B O, Some Factors Influencing Labour Turnover: A Review of Research Literature, *Industrial Relations Journal*, 4 (3) Autumn, 1973, pp 43–61

PHANEUF M C, *The Nursing Audit*, Prentice-Hall, 1964

PHELPS-BROWN E H, *Collective Bargaining Reconsidered*, Athlone Press, 1971

PHELPS-BROWN E H, *Pay and Profits*, Manchester University Press, 1968

PHELPS-BROWN E H, *The Economics of Labour*, Yale University Press, 1962

PHILLIPS M H, Merit Rating for Skilled and Semi-skilled Workers, *Personnel Management*, June 1962

PIGORS P and MYERS C A, *Management of Human Resources*, McGraw-Hill, 1973

PIGORS P and MYERS C A, *Personnel Administration*, McGraw-Hill, 1977, 8th edn

PILDITCH J, *Communication by Design: a Study in Corporate Identity*, McGraw-Hill, 1970

PLATT J W, Education for Business, *Board of Trade Journal*, 27 August 1965

PLUMBLEY P R, *Recruitment and Selection*, IPM, 1968, revised 1976

POLLARD H R, *Developments in Management Thought*, Heinemann, 1973

POLLARD S, *The Genesis of Modern Management*, Edward Arnold, 1965

PORTER L W, Job Attitudes in Management: Perceived Deficiencies in Need Fulfilment as a Function of Job Level, *Journal of Applied Psychology*, (46), 1962

PORTER L W, A Study of Perceived Need Satisfactions in Bottom and Middle Management Jobs, *Journal of Applied Psychology*, (45), 1961

PORTER L W, Job Attitudes in Management: Perceived Importance of Needs as a Function of Job Level, *Journal of Applied Psychology*, (47), 1963 (a), pp 141–8

PORTER L W, Job Attitudes in Management: Perceived Deficiencies in Need

560

Fulfilment as a Function of Line Versus Staff Type of Jobs, *Journal of Applied Psychology*, 47(4), 1963 (b), pp 267–75

PORTER L W, Job Attitudes in Management: Perceived Deficiencies in Need Fulfilment as a Function of the Size of Company, *Journal of Applied Psychology* 47(6), 1963 (c), pp 386–97

PORTER L W, LAWLER E E and HACKMAN J R, *Behaviour in Organizations*, McGraw-Hill, 1975

PORTER L W and LAWLER E E, *Managerial Attitudes and Performance*, Irwin-Dorsey, 1968

PORTUS J H, *Australian Compulsory Arbitration*, 1900–1970, Hicks, Smith, Australia, 1972

POWELL L S, *Communication and Learning*, Pitman, 1969

PRANDY K, *Professional Employees*, Faber and Faber, 1965

PRENTICE G, Participation at Fry's, *Personnel Management*, May 1974

PRESTON R H, *Perspective on Strikes*, SCM Press, 1975

PRICE N, Personnel: Human Resources Management, in Brech E F L, 1975, qv

PRITCHARD R D, Equity Theory: A Review and Critique, *Organizational Behaviour and Human Performance*, 4, 1969, pp 176–211

PROHANSKY H and SEIDENBERG B, *Basic Studies in Social Psychology*, Holt, Rinehart and Winston, 1969

PUGH D S (ed), *Organization Theory*, Penguin, 1971

PURKISS C J, Manpower Planning Literature: Manpower Demand, *Department of Employment Gazette*, November 1976, pp 1–4

PYM D, Technical Change and the Misuse of Professional Manpower, *Occupational Psychology*, January 1967

PYM D, *Industrial Society: Social Sickness in Management*, Penguin, 1968

RAIA A P, Goal Setting and Self Control, *Journal of Management Studies*, February 1965

RAIMON R L, The Indeterminateness of Wages of Semi-Skilled Workers, *Industrial and Labour Relations Review*, 1953

RAIMON R L, Changes in Productivity and the Skill Mix, *International Labour Review*, October 1965

RAMSAY J C, Negotiating in Multi-Plant Company, *Industrial Relations Journal*, Summer 1971

RAMSAY J C and HILL J M, *Collective Agreements—a Guide to their Content and Drafting*, IPM, 1974

RANDALL P E, *Introduction to Work Study and Organization and Methods*, Butterworths, 1969

RANDELL G A *et al*, *Staff Appraisal*, IPM, 1972, revised 1974

RANDLE C W and WORTMAN M S, *Collective Bargaining*, Houghton-Mifflin, 1966

RAPOPORT A, Chapter 17 in *Toward a Unified Theory of Human Behaviour*, ed Grinker R, Basic Books, New York, 1956

RAY M E, *Practical Job Advertising*, IPM, 1971

READ A, *The Company Director*, Jordan and Sons, London, 1958

REDDIN W J, The Tri-dimensional Grid, *Training Directors' Journal*, July 1964

REDDIN W J, The Blake Approach and the Grid, *Training Directors' Journal*, December 1963

REDGRAVES, *Factories Acts*, Butterworths, 1966

REEVES J W and WILSON V W, *Studying Work*, National Institute for Industrial Psychology, NIIP, 1951

RENOLD G C, *Joint Consultation Over Thirty Years*, Allen and Unwin, 1950

RENOLD, SIR C, *The Organizational Structure of Large Undertakings—Management Problems*, BIM, 1950

REVANS R W, The Education of Managers: 1 The Theory of Practice, *Universities Quarterly*, September 1962

REVANS R, *Scale Factors in the Management of Coal Mines*, National Coal Board (internal paper), 1954

RHEINSTEIN M (ed), *Max Weber on Law in Economy and Society*, Simon and Schuster, 1954

RHENMAN E, *Industrial Democracy and Industrial Management*, Tavistock, 1968

RICE A K, *The Enterprise and its Environment*, Tavistock, 1963

RICE A K, *Productivity and Social Organization: the Ahmedabad Experiment*, Tavistock, 1958

RICE A K, An Examination of Part Institutions, *Human Relations*, 4 (4), 1951, pp 393–400

RICE A K and TRIST E L, Institutional and Sub-Institutional Determinants of Social Change in Labour Turnover, *Human Relations*, 5 (4), 1950, pp 347–71

RICE A K *et al*, The Representation of Labour Turnover as a Social Process, *Human Relations*, 3 (4), 1950, pp 349–72

RICHBELL S, Participation and Perceptions of Control, *Personnel Review*, 5 (2), Spring 1976, pp 13–19

RICE G H and BISHOPRICK D W, *Conceptual Models of Organizations*, Appleton-Century-Crofts, 1971

RICHTER I, *Political Purpose in Trade Unions*, Allen and Unwin, 1973

RIDEOUT R W, *Reforming the Redundancy Payments Act*, IPM, 1969

RIDEOUT R W, *Principles of Labour Law*, Sweet and Maxwell, 1976, 2nd edn

RIESMAN D, *The Lonely Crowd*, Doubleday, 1955

RITZER G and TRICE H M, *An Occupation in Conflict: A Study of the Personnel Manager*, Cornell, 1969

ROBERTS T J, *Developing Effective Managers*, IPM, 1967, revised 1974

ROBERTS B C and LOVERIDGE R, *Reluctant Militants*, Heinemann, 1972

ROBERTS B C and SMITH J H, *Manpower Policy and Employment Trends*, Bell and Sons, 1966

ROBERTSON K, Managing People and Jobs, *Personnel Management*, September 1969, pp 20–24

ROBINSON J and BARNES N, *New Media and Methods in Industrial Training*, BBC, 1968

ROBINSON O and WALLACE J, *Pay and Employment in Retailing*, Saxon House, 1976

RODGER A, *The Seven Point Plan*, NIIP, 1952

RODGER L W, *Marketing in a Competitive Economy*, Hutchinson, 1965

ROETHLISBERGER F J, *Man-in-Organization*, Harvard University Press, 1968

ROETHLISBERGER F J and DICKSON W J, *Management and the Worker*, Harvard University Press, 1939

ROFF H E and WATSON T E, *Job Analysis*, IPM, 1961

ROGERS R H A, What Price People?, *Personnel Management*, November 1974, pp 40–42

ROGERS T G P and WILLIAMS P, *The Recruitment and Training of Graduates*, IPM, 1970

RONISZOWSKI A J, *The Selection and Use of Teaching Aids*, International Text Book Company, 1968

RONKEN H O and LAWRENCE P R, *Administering Changes*, Harvard University Press, 1952

ROSE A M, *Human Behaviour and Social Processes*, Routledge and Kegan Paul, 1962

ROSE F A, Management by Objectives, *Works Management*, January 1967

ROSENBERG M and PEARLIN L I, Power Orientations in the Mental Hospital, *Human Relations*, 1962

ROSS A M, *Trade Union Wage Policy*, University of California Press, 1948

ROSS J, Predicting Practical Skill in Engineering Apprentices, *Occupational Psychology*, 36 (1 and 2), 1962

ROSS M G and HENDRY C E, *New Understandings of Leadership*, Association Press, 1957

ROWBOTTOM R, *Hospital Organization*, Heinemann, 1973

ROWE K H, An Appraisal of Appraisals, *Journal of Management Studies*, 1 (1) March 1964

ROWNTREE J A and STEWART P A, Estimating manpower needs—II: Statistical Methods, *Manpower planning in the Civil Service*, HMSO, 1976, pp 36–53

ROY A S, *Staff Grading*, BIM, 1960

RUBENSTEIN M, *A Practical Guide to the Employment Protection Act*, IPM, 1975

RUBENSTEIN A H and HABERSTROH C J (eds), *Some Theories of Organization*, Irwin-Dorsey, 1960

RUBENSTEIN M and FROST Y, Equal Pay Act—EAT to the Rescue, *Personnel Management*, February 1977

RUDDICK R, *Roles and Relationships*, Routledge and Kegan Paul, 1969

RUNCIMAN W G, *Relative Deprivation and Social Justice*, Routledge and Kegan Paul, 1966

SADLER P J and BARRY B A, *Organizational Development*, Longman, 1970

SADLER P, Personnel Policy in a Changing Society, *Personnel Management*, April 1974, pp 26–29

SAINT-SIMON H de, *Social Organization: The Science of Man, etc*, Harper, 1964

SALAMAN G and BRISTOW J, Why Appraisals Fail, *Management Today*, October 1970, pp 37–46

SAMPSON R C, *The Staff Role and Management: Its Creative Uses*, Harper, 1955

SAMUEL P J, *Labour Turnover: Towards a Solution*, IPM, 1971

SAMUELS H, *Industrial Law*, Pitmans, 1967

SANSBURY H, The Measurement of Productivity, *Management Accounting*, October 1966

SAVAGE I and SMALL J R, *Introduction to Managerial Economics*, Hutchinson, 1967

SAYLES L, *Behaviour in Industrial Work Groups*, Wiley, 1958

SAYLES L, *Managerial Behaviour*, McGraw-Hill, 1964

SAYLES L R and STRAUSS G, *Personnel: Human Problems of Management*, Prentice-Hall, 1967, 2nd edn

SAYLES L R and STRAUSS G, *Human Behaviour in Organizations*, Prentice-Hall, 1966

SCHAFFER R H, *Managing by Total Objectives*, AMA, 1964

SCHATZ H A, *Social Work—Administration*, Council on Social Work Education, 1970

SCHEIN E H, *Organizational Psychology*, Prentice-Hall, 1970

SCHEIN E H, The Individual, the Organization and the Career, *Journal of Applied Behavioural Sciences*, 7, 1971, pp 401–26

SCHLECH E C, *Managing for Results*, McGraw-Hill, 1961

SCHNEIDER A *et al*, *Organizational Communications*, McGraw-Hill, 1973

SCHRAMM W L (ed), *The Science of Human Communication*, Basic Books, 1963

SCHULTZ T, *Investment in Human Capital*, Free Press, Glencoe, 1971

SCHUSTER J R, CLARK B, ROGERS M, Testing Portions of the Porter Lawler model regarding the motivational role of pay, *Journal of Applied Psychology*, 55, 1971, pp 187–195

SCHWITTER J P, Computer Effect upon Managerial Jobs, *Academy of Management Journal*, September 1965

SCOTT J F and LYNTON R P, *Three Studies in Management*, Routledge and Kegan Paul, 1952

SCOTT W E and CUMMINGS L L, *Readings in Organizational Behaviour and Human Performance*, Irwin-Dorsey, 1973

SCOTT W E, Organization Theory: An Overview and Appraisal, in Greenwood W T, *Management and Organizational Behaviour Theories*, South Western, Cincinnati, 1965

SCOTT W H (ed), *Office Automation, Administrative and Human Problems*, OECD, 1965

SCOTT W H *et al*, *Technical Change and Industrial Relations*, Liverpool University Press, 1956

SEEAR N, Managers and National Planning, *New Society*, 14 July 1966

SEEAR N, *The Position of Women in Industry*, HMSO, 1968

SEEAR N, *The Re-entry of Women into Employment*, OECD, 1971

SEEAR N *et al*, *Married Women Working*, Allen and Unwin, 1962

SEEAR N, *A Career for Women in Industry*, Oliver and Boyd, 1964

SEEBOHM SIR F, *Report of the Committee on Local Authority and Allied Personal Social Services* (Chairman: Sir F Seebohm), HMSO, 1968

Selwyn's Law of Employment, Butterworth, 1976

SELZNICK P, Foundations of the Theory of Organization, *American Sociology Review*, 13, 1948

SELZNICK P, *Leadership in Administration*, Harper and Row, 1957

SELZNICK P, Towards a Theory of Bureaucracy, in Coser L and Rosenberg M (eds) *Sociological Theory—a Reader*, Collier Macmillan, 1969

SELZNICK P, *TVA and the Grass Roots*, Harper, 1966

SEMEONOFF B, *Personality Assessment*, Penguin, 1966

SEYMOUR W D, *Industrial Skills*, Pitmans, 1966

SEYMOUR W D, Recent Developments in Operative Training, *Personnel Management*, July–August 1949

SHACKLETON V and DAVIES J, The Unionized Manager, *Management Today*, June 1976

SHAFTO T A C, *Introducing Economics*, Nelson, 1971

SHALLENBERGER J B, Are European Managers Better Organized?, *The Manager*, November 1961, pp 855–58

SHANKS M, *The Stagnant Society*, Penguin Books, 1961

SHANNON C E and WEAVER W, *The Mathematical Theory of Communication*, University of Illinois Press, 1949

SHARP I G, *Industrial Conciliation and Arbitration in Great Britain*, Allen and Unwin, 1951

SHEPARD H A, The Duel Hierarchy in Research, in Orth C D *et al*, 1964, qv

SHIBUTANI T, Reference Groups and Social Control, in Rose A, 1962, pp 128–47, qv

SHIMMIN S, After the Assembly Line, *Personnel Management*, August 1974, pp 35–37

SHIMMIN S, Case Studies in Measured Daywork, *Personnel Magazine*, October 1966

SHONE K J and PATERSON R G, *Analysis of Controls and Design of Production Planning Control Systems*, Sawell Publications, 1963

SIDNEY E and BROWN M, *The Skills of Interviewing*, Tavistock, 1961

SILLS P A, *The Behavioural Sciences: Techniques of Application*, IPM, 1973

SILVERMAN D, *The Theory of Organizations*, Heinemann, 1970

SIMON H A, *Administrative Behaviour*, Macmillan, New York, 1953

SIMON H A, *The Shape of Automation*, Harper and Row, 1965

SIMON H A, Comments on the Theory of Organizations, *American Political Science Review*, December 1952, and in Rubenstein A H and Haberstroh C J, qv

SINGER E J, *Training in Industry and Commerce*, IPM, 1977

SINGER E J and MACDONALD I D, *Is Apprenticeship Outdated?* IPM, 1970

SINGER E J and RAMSDEN J, *Human Resources*, McGraw-Hill, 1972

SINGER E J and RAMSDEN J, *The Practical Approach to Skills Analysis*, McGraw-Hill, 1969

SISSON K, *Negotiating in Practice*, IPM, 1977

SMELSER N J, Social Change, in Smelser N J (ed), *Sociology: An Introduction*, Wiley, 1967

SMITH A R (ed), *Models of Manpower Systems*, English Universities Press, 1970

SMITH A R, Developments in Manpower Planning, *Personnel Review*, 1 (1) Autumn 1971, pp 44–54

SMITH A R (ed), *Manpower Planning in the Civil Service*, Civil Service Studies

No 3, HMSO, 1976

SMITH C G and TANNENBAUM A S, Organizational Control Structure, *Human Relations*, November 1963

SMITH I G, *The Measurement of Productivity*, Gower Press, 1973

SMITH M, *An Introduction to Industrial Psychology*, Cassell, 1943

SMITH W J, ALLBRIGHT L E and GLENNON J R, The Prediction of Research Competence and Creativity from Personal History, *Journal of Applied Psychology*, 45, 1961

SMYTH C S, The Industrial Training Act—its Scope and Significance, *Personnel Management*, June 1964, pp 55–9

SOMERS G G (ed), *The Next Twenty-Five Years of Industrial Relations*, IR Research Association, Madison, 1973

SPALTON L M, Is Management Wasting People?, *The Manager*, November 1965

SPENCER P and SOFAR C, Organizational Change and Its Management, *Journal of Management Studies*, March 1964

STAINER G, *Manpower Planning*, Heinemann, 1971

STARK W, *Social Theory and Christian Thought*, Routledge and Kegan Paul, 1958

STEERS C E B, *Clarifying Objectives in Supervisory Training*, BACIE, 1966

STEPHENS L, Personnel Advice from Government, *New Society*, 23 June 1966

STEWART J D, *Management in Local Government: a Viewpoint*, Charles Knight and Company, 1974

STINCHCOMBE A L, Bureaucratic and Craft Administration of Production, *Administrative Science Quarterly*, September 1959

STINCHCOMBE A L, Formal Organizations, in Smelser N T, *Sociology*, Wiley, 1967

STOCKDALE G and BUTTERWORTH J, To See Ourselves as Others See Us, *Personnel Management*, August 1970, pp 26–28

STOKES R S, Management Training—the Fashion Persists, *Personnel Management*, September 1967, pp 137–80

STONE C H and KENDALL W E, *Effective Personnel Selection Procedures*, Staples Press, 1957

STOUFFER S A et al, *The American Soldier*, Princeton University, 1949

SULLIVAN G R, The Relationship Between the Board of Directors and the General Meeting in Limited Companies, *Law Quarterly Review*, 93, October 1977, pp 569–40

SUMNER G and SMITH R, *Planning Local Authority Services for the Elderly*, Allen and Unwin, 1970

SUPER D S and CRITES J O, *Appraising Vocational Fitness*, Harper, 1962

SWANNACK A R and SAMUEL P J, The Added Value of Men and Materials, *Personnel Management*, February 1974, pp 26–29 and 41

SWANNACK A R, Small Firm Salary Structures, *Personnel Management*, January 1975, pp 31–34

Swedish Employers' Confederation, *Job Reform in Sweden*, SEF, 1975

TAFT R, The Ability to Judge People, in Whisler T L and Harper S F, 1962, qv

TAGIURI R, Value Orientations of Managers and Scientists, in Orth C D *et al*, 1964, qv

TALBOT J R and ELLIS C D, *Analysis and Costing of Company Training*, Gower Press, 1969

TANNENBAUM A S, *Control in Organizations*, McGraw-Hill, 1968

TANNENBAUM R, The Manager Concept: A Rational Synthesis, *Journal of Business*, 1948

TAVERNER G, *Design of Personnel Systems and Records*, Industrial Society, 1973

TAYLOR F W, *Scientific Management*, Harper and Brothers, 1947

TAYLOR J, *Unemployment and Wage Inflation*, Longman, 1974

TAYLOR P, Absenteeism—the English Sickness, *Industrial Society*, July 1970

TAYLOR P J, *Absenteeism—Causes and Control*, Industrial Society, Notes for Managers, No 15, 1973

TAYLOR G W, SMITH W R, GHISELIN B and ELLISON R, *Explorations in the Measurement and Prediction of Contributions of One Sample of Scientists*, Report No ASD-TR-61-96, Personnel Laboratory, ASD, Lackland, AFB, Texas, 1961

THAKUR M, *OD: the Search for Identity*, IPM, 1974

THIBAUT J, An Experiment Study of the Cohesiveness of Under-privileged Groups, *Human Relations*, 3, 1950

THOMAS K, *Attitudes and Behaviour*, Penguin, 1971

THOMAS J, Group Capacity Assessment, *DATA Journal*, May 1967

THOMAS J L and ROBERTSON M, *Trade Unions and Industrial Relations*, Business Books, 1976

THOMAS B, MOXAM J and JONES J A G, A Cost-Benefit Analysis of Industrial Training, *British Journal of Industrial Relations*, VII (2), 1969

THOMASON G F, *Job Evaluation*, IPM, 1968

THOMASON G F, *The Professional Approach to Community Work*, Sands, London, 1969

THOMASON G F, *The Management of Research and Development*, Batsford, 1970

THOMASON G F, *Experiments in Participation*, IPM, 1971

THOMASON G F, *Improving the Quality of Organization*, IPM, 1973

THOMASON G F, DOUGHTY G H and SPEAR H C, *Industrial Relations in the London Fire Service*, ACAS, 1977

THOMASON G F, *The Individual, The Trade Union and the State: Some Contemporary Issues*, Irish Association for Industrial Relations, 1978

THOMPSON J and ROGERS H R, *Redgrave's Factories, Truck and Shops Acts*, Butterworth, 1956, 19th edn

THOMPSON J D (ed), *Approaches to Organizational Design*, University of Pittsburgh Press, Pittsburgh, 1966

THORNDIKE R L, *Personnel Selection: Test and Measurement Techniques*, Wiley, 1949

THURLEY K E and HAMBLIN A C, *The Supervisor and His Job*, HMSO, 1963

THURLEY K and WIRDENIUS H, *Approaches to Supervisory Development*, IPM, 1973

THURLEY K and WIRDENIUS H, *Supervision: a Re-appraisal*, Heinemann, 1973

TIFFIN J and MCCORMICK E J, *Industrial Psychology*, Prentice-Hall, 1965

TITMUS R M, *Commitment to Welfare*, Allen and Unwin, 1968

TOLMAN E C, *Purposive Behaviour in Animals and Man*, Century, 1932

TOMLINSON R C, Operational Research in the Coal Industry: 2, Study of Manpower Problems, *Colliery Guardian*, December 1964, pp 789–92

TORGERSON P E, *A Concept of Organization*, American Book Company, 1969

TORRINGTON D, *Encyclopaedia of Personnel Management*, Gower Press, 1977

TORRINGTON D, *Handbook of Industrial Relations*, Gower Press, 1972

TORRINGTON D, *Face to Face*, Gower Press, 1972

TOSI H L and CARROLL S, Some Factors Affecting the Success of Management by Objectives, *Journal of Management Studies*, 7, (2), May 1970

TOWERS B, WHITTINGHAM T G and GOTTSCHALK A W (eds), *Bargaining for Change*, Allen and Unwin, 1972

TOWNSEND P and BOSANQUET N (eds), *Labour and Inequality*, Fabian Society, 1972

Trades Union Congress, *Automation and Technological Change*, TUC, 1965

TUC, *Costs and Profits: Financial Information for Trade Unionists*, TUC, 1970

TUC, *In the Automated Office*, TUC, 1964

TUC, *Collective Bargaining and the Social Contract*, TUC, 1974

TUC, *Job Evaluation and Merit Rating*, TUC, 1974

Training Services Agency, *A Five Year Plan*, HMSO, 1974

TREITEL G H, *The Law of Contract*, Stevens, 1975 edn

TRIANDIS H C, *Attitudes and Attitude Change*, Wiley, 1971

TRIST E L, HIGGIN G W, MURRAY H and POLLOCK A B, *Organizational Choice*, Tavistock Publications, 1963

TURNER H A et al, *Is Britain Really Strike Prone?*, Cambridge University Press, 1969

UNGERSON B (ed), *Recruitment Handbook*, Gower Press, 1970

URWICK L, *Problems of Growth in Industrial Undertakings*, BIM, 1949

URWICK L and BRECH E F L, *The Making of Scientific Management, Volumes I, II, III*, Management Publications, 1945–1948

URWICK L, *The Elements of Administration*, Harper and Brothers, 1943

VALLENTINE R S, *Performance Objectives for Managers*, AMA, 1966

VAN BEEK H G, The Influence of Assembly Line Organization on Output, Quality and Morale, *Occupational Psychology*, 38, 1964, pp 161–72

VARNEY G H, Group Goal-Setting in MbO, *Management by Objectives*, 5 (3), 1976

VEBLEN T, *Imperial Germany and the Industrial Revolution*, University of Michigan Press, 1966

VEBLEN T, *The Theory of Business Enterprise* (1904), Mentor Books, 1958

VEBLEN T, *The Theory of the Leisure Class* (1899), Mentor Books, 1953

VERNON P E, *Personality Assessment: a Critical Survey*, Methuen, 1964

VETTER E W, *Manpower Planning for High Talent Personnel*, University of Michigan, 1967

VICKERS SIR G, *Towards a Sociology of Management*, Chapman and Hall, 1967

VICKERS SIR G, *The Art of Judgement*, Chapman and Hall, 1965
VICKERS SIR G, *Value Systems and Social Process*, Tavistock, 1968
VITELES M S, *Industrial Psychology*, Norton, 1932
VOLLMER H M and MILLS D L (eds), *Professionalization*, Prentice Hall, 1966
VROOM V H, *Work and Motivation*, Wiley, 1964
VROOM V H and DECI E L, *Management and Motivation*, Penguin, 1970
WAINWRIGHT D, *Race and Employment*, IPM, 1970
WALKER J W, Individual Career Planning: Managerial Help for Subordinates, *Business Horizons*, February 1973
WALKER K F, *Personnel and Social Planning on the Plant Level*, International Institute for Labour Studies, Geneva, 1970
WALLINGTON P, Discrimination, Equal Pay, and the Living Changing Law, *Personnel Management*, January 1978, pp 28–31
WALSH W, Enrichment in the Office, *Personnel Management*, 1 (6), October 1969, pp 42–4
WALTON C B, *Corporate Social Responsibilities*, Wadsworth, 1967
WALTON R E and MCKERSIE R B, *A Behavioural Theory of Labour Negotiations*, McGraw-Hill, 1965
WARD P B and BIRD M W, *Identifying Supervisory Training Needs*, HMSO, 1968
WARREN N and JAHODA M, *Attitudes*, Penguin, 1969
WATSON T J, *The Personnel Managers*, Routledge and Kegan Paul, 1977
WEBB S and B, *History of Trade Unionism*, Longman, 1894
WEBB S and B, *Industrial Democracy*, Longman Green and Company, 1920
WEBER M, *The Theory of Social and Economic Organization*, Free Press, Glencoe, 1947
WEBSTER B, Participation—Power Shift or Power Sharing, *Personnel Management*, November 1975, pp 20–22 and 34
WEDDERBURN A, Waking Up To Shiftwork, *Personnel Management*, February 1975, pp 32–35 and 47
WEDDERBURN K, *The Worker and Law*, Penguin, 1971
WEEKES B, MELLISH M, DICKENS L and LLOYD J, *Industrial Relations and the Limits of Law*, Blackwell, 1975
WEIR D, Radical Managerialism: Middle Managers' Perceptions of Collective Bargaining, *British Journal of Industrial Relations*, XIV (3), November 1976, pp 324–338
WELLMAN G, Practical Obstacles to Effective Manpower Planning, *Personnel Review*, 1 (3), Summer 1972, pp 32–47
Welsh Office, *National Health Service Re-Organization in Wales*, HMSO, 1972
Welsh Office, *Management Arrangements for the Re-organized NHS in Wales*, HMSO, 1972
Welsh Office, *Guidance Manual on the Health Service Planning System in Wales*, HMSO
WEXLEY K N and YUKL G A (eds), *Organizational Behaviour and Industrial Psychology*, OUP, 1975
WHISLER T L and HARPER S F, *Performance Appraisal*, Holt, Rinehart and Winston, 1962

WHITE M, *Motivating Managers Financially*, IPM, 1973

WHITEHEAD R, Communications and Control, in Wells G and Yearsley R (eds), *Handbook of Management Technology*, Heinemann, 1967

WHITELAW M, *The Evaluation of Management Training*, IPM, 1972

WHITLEY R D, Concepts of Organization and Power in the Study of Organizations, *Personnel Review*, 6 (1), Winter 1977, pp 54–9

WHITMORE D A, *Measurement and Control of Indirect Work*, Heinemann, 1971

WHITTINGHAM T G and GOTTSCHALK A W, *Bargaining for Change*, Allen and Unwin, 1972

WHYTE W F et al, *Money and Motivation*, Harper, 1955

WHYTE W H, *The Organization Man*, Penguin, 1960

WILD R and HILL A B, *Women in the Factory: a Study of Job Satisfaction and Labour Turnover*, IPM, 1971

WILD R, *Work Organization*, Wiley, 1975

WILENSKY H L, The Dynamics of Professionalism, *Hospital Administration*, Spring 1972

WILLIAMS SIR B R, Pyramids of Disillusion, *Management Decision*, Winter 1967

WILLIAMS D J, *Capitalist Combination in the Coal Industry*, Labour Publishing Company, London 1924

WILLIAMS R H, *The Theory of Action in Operations Research and in Social Sciences*, John Hopkins University, 1950

WILLIAMS W M, *Occupational Choice*, Allen and Unwin, 1974

WILLE E, *The Computer in Personnel Work*, IPM, 1966

WILLS G, *Technological Forecasting*, Penguin, 1972

WILSON B, The Added Value of Pay, *Management Today*, November 1977, pp 101–4

WILSON N A B (ed), *Manpower Research*, English Universities Press, 1969

WINKLER J T, Law, State and Economy: The Industry Act, *British Journal of Law and Society*, Winter 1975

WOOD D A, *Test Construction*, Merrill, 1960

WOOD S J et al, The Industrial Relations System Concept, *British Journal of Industrial Relations*, XIII (3) November 1975, pp 291–308

WOODWARD J, *Industrial Organization: Theory and Practice*, Oxford University Press, 1965

WOODWARD J, *Industrial Organization: Behaviour and Control*, Oxford University Press, 1970

WOODWARD J, *Management and Technology*, HMSO, 1958

WORTMAN M S, JR, *Creative Personnel Management*, Allwyn, 1967

WORTMAN M S and RANDLE C W, *Collective Bargaining: Principles ad Practices*, Houghton Mifflin, 1966

YODER D, *Personnel Management and Industrial Relations*, Prentice Hall, 1970, 6th edn

YODER D, Personnel Administration, in Somers G G, 1973, pp 141–56, qv

YORK D and DOOLEY C, Checking the Manpower Costs, *Personnel Management*, June 1970

YOUNG A, Models for Planning Recruitment and Promotion of Staff, *British*

Journal of Industrial Relations, III, 1965

YOUNG A and ALMOND G, Predicting Distributions of Staff, *Computer Journal*, 3, 1961

YOUNG A F, *Social Services in British Industry*, Routledge and Kegan Paul, 1968

YOUNG S, *Management: a Systems Analysis*, Scott, Foresman, 1966

YOUNGHUSBAND E, The Future of Social Work, *Social Work Today*, March 1973

YUKL G A and WEXLEY K N, *Readings in Organizational and Industrial Psychology*, Oxford University Press, 1971

ZEIST N L and LIEVEGOED B J, *Developing Organizations*, Nederlands Pedagogise Institute, 1972

ZELDITCH M and ANDERSON T R, *Basic Course in Statistics*, Holt, Rinehart and Winston, 1972

ZERGA J E, Job Analysis: A Résumé and Bibliography, *Journal of Applied Psychology*, 27, 1943

ZIS G, The 1969–70 Wage Explosion in the UK, *National Westminster Bank Quarterly Review*, February 1974, pp 55–68

Zuckerman Committee Report, *Report of the Committee on Hospital Scientific and Technical Staff*, HMSO, 1968

Author Index

582

583

Index

Ability, abilities, 25, 29, 30, 141, 174, 208, 223–4, 225, 226, 227, 247, 251, 252, 253, 254, 256, 263, 271, 274, 283, 285, 293, 297, 302, 318, 320, 336, 341, 349, 382, 399, 404, 517, 524
Ability to pay, 147, 221–2
Absence, absenteeism, 128, 289, 380, 394, 396, 418, 432, 440, 505
Accidents, 189, 440, 476
Advertising, 85, 177–81, 324, 347
Advisory, Conciliation and Arbitration Service, 92, 93, 95, 414, 415, 416–20, 422–3, 424, 425, 427, 428, 431, 446, 452, 456, 468, 472, 494
Advisory role of personnel specialist, 6, 120, 245, 272, 280, 282, 399, 516, 521, 523, 524, 525, 527
Agent, concept of, 20, 46–9, 62, 64, 162, 186, 320, 328, 403–4, 452, 484, 485, 490, 529
Agreement, collective, 62, 163, 164, 177, 179, 241, 242, 246, 322, 409, 423, 424, 429–33, 447–8, 449, 452–76, 484, 486–91, 493, 494–9, 516
    participation, 462–8, 521
    procedural, 446–52, 452–77, 485, 487
    (*see also* procedures)
    substantive, 446–7, 453, 460, 468, 485, 487
    (*see also* participation)
Agreement, individual, (*see* contracts, employment; and bargaining, individual)
Appraisal, performance, 112–3, 139, 166, 190, 226–7, 245, 272–3, 276–88, 289, 294, 522
    person, 139, 173–86, 225–6, 276–88, 432, 522
    (*see also* selection)

Apprentices, 156, 158, 185, 305, 429
    training of, 155, 158, 302
Arbitration, 83, 86, 116, 240, 415–9, 421, 423–4, 425, 432, 441, 453, 464, 473, 482, 494–9
    (*see also* Central Arbitration Committee; Advisory Conciliation and Arbitration Service)
Attitudes, 16, 247–8, 249, 283, 295, 357, 361, 380, 391, 392, 396, 443, 486, 487, 512, 513, 515, 519
Audit, 231–4, 379, 514
Authority, managerial, 1, 6, 7, 8, 17, 24, 66, 242, 248, 273, 298, 308–43, 354, 355, 357–9, 364, 366, 374, 389–92, 435, 438, 440, 441, 461, 470, 481, 512, 514, 515, 520, 522, 532
    (*see also* power)
Automation, 223, 228, 512
    (*see also* technology)

Bargaining, collective,
    agent, 219, 424
    general, 20, 21, 24, 62, 93–4, 151, 193, 240, 361, 362, 364, 368, 373, 381, 404, 409, 410, 414, 415, 416–8, 429, 452–77, 477–86, 488–9, 494, 497–8, 521
    procedures, Code, 452
    processes, 149, 321, 400–1, 414, 415, 428, 441, 442, 452–77, 486
    structure, national, 405, 413, 444–6, 449, 451, 457–62, 495, 497, 498
    subjects, 457–62
    tasks, 498–510
    types,
        attitudinal structuring, 485–6, 498, 501, 503, 505, 506
        distributive, 485, 498, 500, 503,

590